STANDARD LOAN

UNLESS RECALLED BY ANOTHER READ fore
THIS ITEM MAY BE BORROWED

THE MARIAN EXILES
1553–1559

The Clarakloster (23), Klein Basel: home of John Foxe and the
English Exiles, 1557–9

After the map of Matthaeus Merian, 1615 (Staatsarchiv, Basel)

THE MARIAN EXILES

A Study in the Origins of Elizabethan Puritanism

BY

CHRISTINA HALLOWELL GARRETT
M.A.

CAMBRIDGE
AT THE UNIVERSITY PRESS
1938
REPRINTED
1966

PUBLISHED BY
THE SYNDICS OF THE CAMBRIDGE UNIVERSITY PRESS
Bentley House, 200 Euston Road, London, N.W.1.
American Branch: 32 East 57th Street, New York, N. Y. 10022
West African Office: P.M.B. 5181, Ibadan, Nigeria

Publisher's Note
Cambridge University Press Library Editions are reissues of out-of-print
standard works from the Cambridge catalogue. The texts are unrevised
and, apart from minor corrections, reproduce the latest published edition.

First published 1938
Reprinted 1966

First printed in Great Britain at the University Press, Cambridge
Reprinted in the United States of America
Library of Congress Catalogue Card Number: 38-25099

CONTENTS

AUTHOR'S PREFACE

At the very outset I should like to make it clear that my approach to the Marian Exile has been entirely from the political side. When I crossed the Channel in pursuit of new material for its interpretation, I went not as a student of theology, nor as a religious partisan, but as an historical detective bent upon discovering the origin of the cabal against the queen which certainly existed in Elizabeth's first parliament and was the element that obstructed the passage of the Supremacy Bill. All the obscurities, all the contradictions of that enigmatic struggle can be traced to its sinister influence. But what did the existence of this cabal mean? Why, in a protestant House of Commons, did a protestant faction oppose a protestant measure against the will of a supposedly protestant sovereign? We can hardly doubt that the House itself knew the answer to the riddle, but if so, both protagonists in the parliamentary duel were at equal pains to conceal the facts: the cabal, because it was temporarily defeated; the queen, because it would have been disastrous to her at the moment to reveal to the world that her chief enemies were those of her own household. After patiently searching for a clue to the mystery among English archives, I became convinced that if an answer still survived it would be found, not in England but on the Continent. For in the years from 1553 to 1559 it was true in a sense more actual even than to-day, that the 'frontiers of England lay upon the Rhine'. There a 'little England' had established itself, whose influence upon Elizabethan politics—indeed, upon England's future— has been, perhaps, too sedulously ignored. In the following *Introduction* and *Census of Exiles*, I am presenting my own attempt to solve a problem that lies at the very root of the Anglican Settlement. Yet the *Introduction* is but the summary of an answer provided by the biographies of the 472 self-exiled Englishmen who were later to constitute the protestant 'opposition' to Elizabeth. In other words, my conclusions rest upon the evidence of the Census, which is a 'Who's Who', very nearly comprehensive, of the early Puritan party.

Without the information that has come to light in the compilation of it, and in the effort to identify what in many cases were mere names, I doubt whether the truth regarding the genesis of that party would ever have become manifest. Inaccuracies in the Census there may be: I can hardly hope to have avoided them, so difficult has been my task, single-handed. But even so, two clear facts emerge from the sum of probabilities: the migration was that of the defeated faction of Northumberland, lay and clerical; and the movement, in essence, was revolutionary. If its full operation was deferred for nearly a century, the delay was owing to the unsuspected wisdom of the new queen on the one hand; and, on the other, to the possibilities of adventure that opened in the two Americas. Mary's (or Gardiner's) willingness to permit England's unruly elements to leave the kingdom in 1554 was astute politics not lost upon Mary's sister in 1559. But unfortunately the Channel had proved too narrow a barrier. It could be bridged by the printed page. The Atlantic, however, was wide: wide enough for safety during several generations to come. Thus Elizabeth was destined to draw profit to the kingdom and to her own stability from the very elements among Englishmen that destroyed Mary and condemned her pitiful reign to obloquy.

The whole book is in the nature of an historical mosaic where every small piece is essential to the completed picture of a migration, premeditated and 'directed'. It is true that the book offers little more than the materials of history, but I hope at a later date to complete a full narrative, linking the Exile to the first year of Elizabeth's reign.

My indebtedness for help received during my researches is greater than I can pay. In the course of them I have learned one thing at least of intimate knowledge, that the world to the wandering student is a very kind place indeed. For six years the Bodleian Library has offered me a home and all the assistance in its power. So has the Cambridge University Library. Abroad, if I have had the rare good fortune to dis-cover certain material believed to have been destroyed, and certain other, whose existence was not suspected in England, my success has been due only to the generosity of the Archivists of Strasbourg, Aarau and Basle; and to the patient helpfulness, both then and since, of Monsieur Vaucher, assistant Director of Archives at Geneva, of Professor Nabholz of the University of Zurich and of Professor Dr Bing of Basle. Some of my grateful acknowledgements have been made to them by name in the *Introduction*, but by no means all. For sympathy in my undertaking, for valuable advice and criticism in the course of it, for the reading of much of my manuscript in its early stages, my warmest thanks are due to Dr W. H. Frere, till lately bishop of Truro, and to Professor Powicke of Oxford. But since they have not yet seen the final results they must be held in no way responsible for my deductions. I can only hope that those deductions will meet with their approval. To Professor McIlwain of Harvard, *fons et origo* of the enthusiasm that has carried me through six years of labour, the work owes its inspiration and its inception. Two generous awards from The Social Science Research Council of New York have made it possible for me to complete the book, and I stand deeply indebted to them for their invaluable help.

Finally to those friends, E. F. M. and J. A. M., whose patient sympathy and support have known no limits, I must give the book itself in payment—for it is theirs.

C. H. G.

OXFORD
January 1938

THE MARIAN EXILE
IN THE LIGHT OF NEW DOCUMENTS

I

'MIGRATION' OR 'FLIGHT'?

Nearly four hundred years have passed since the English refugees to Germany in the reign of Mary first told the story of their exile (1554-9) in their own way. In all that time the accuracy of their version of it has never once been seriously questioned: they were protestants, forced solely for the sake of their religion to take refuge abroad from the persecution of a bigoted and cruel queen. So the record has stood.

As a mine of information for the life of John Knox, the period has been well exploited. But as an episode having dramatic unity in itself, and an historic significance out of all proportion to its duration in time, the Marian Exile has had no historian. Not since 1574, when William Whittingham[1] first published at Zurich his polemical pamphlet under the suggestive title of *The Troubles begun at Frankfort*,[2] has anyone cared to penetrate below the surface of the ingenious legend with which the fugitives cloaked the real purpose of their enterprise. For if the facts, after being arranged in their chronological sequence, are then impartially examined, there can be little doubt that the so-called 'flight' of 1554 was not a flight but a migration, and, as such, one of the most astute manœuvres that has ever carried a defeated political party to ultimate power.

[1] For the ascription now generally accepted, see Dr McCrie's argument incorporated in the Introduction (pp. v–ix) to Petheram's reprint (1846) of the 1575 edition of the *Troubles*. See also Prof. Pollard's article on Whittingham in the *D.N.B.* But we venture to think that it was not Whitehead, as McCrie suggests, but Thomas Cole, "late deane off Sarum", who continued the narrative after Whittingham's departure from Frankfort (*Troubles*, p. 59 and 'Thomas Cole', Census).

[2] *Short Title Catalogue*, no. 25442.

When the body of Edwardian clergy and 'students', who formed a majority of the first migration, left England, they had suffered no persecution.[1] Their party had gone out of office; and they were being called upon, in their turn, to accept changes in administrative personnel, for which Edward's reign had established a precedent having less canonical justification than Mary's. A few, certainly, had been imprisoned, but for flagrant acts of sedition, not for heresy. And with unexampled clemency, the greater number of even these political offenders were soon released. Perhaps no words more aptly describe the nature of the protestant exodus at its inception, than those used by Laurence Humphrey to describe the flight of his friends from Magdalen: it was a 'voluntarium in Germania exilium'.[2]

Mary was proclaimed queen in London on 19 July 1553. If certain occurrences during the first months of her reign are carefully correlated[3] and placed in sequence, they show that a general emigration of protestants was being preached as early as August 1553; that definite steps to carry the plan into execution were taken during September; and that the movement was actually in progress during January before any coercive religious measures, even of deprivation, had been enforced by the Marian government. Mindful of Calvin's fervid exhortation, 'Sorts hors du païs de ta nativité, quant nous sommes là contraincts de faire contre nostre conscience...',[4] those reformers whom Simon Renard wisely distinguished from their fellows as 'the hardened followers of that sect',[5]

[1] Of the five Edwardian bishops who took refuge abroad (1553-4), Bale of Ossory seems to have 'shoke the dust' of his diocese 'of [his] fete' almost as soon as the news of Mary's accession reached Kilkenny on 25 July. By about the middle of September 1553 he was gone (R. L. Poole's Preface to Bale's *Index*, p. xix). Coverdale of Exeter, Ponet of Winchester and Scory of Chichester had to surrender their sees to those whom they themselves had dispossessed, that is, John Voysey, Stephen Gardiner and George Day. Scory had also been an open adherent of Lady Jane, and was always a firebrand. Barlow 'resigned' his bishopric of Bath and Wells in 1553, but no licence to fill the vacancy was issued until 13 March 1554 (Le Neve, I, 144; for his 'resignation' vs. 'deprivation' see W. H. Frere, *The Marian Reaction, etc.* (1896), pp. 21-2 and p. 21, n. 4; cf. also Dixon, *History of the Church of England*, IV, 46-7 and notes). [2] *Vita Juelli*, p. 73.
[3] Cf. below, pp. 45-6. [4] J. Bonnet, *Lettres de Jean Calvin*, I, 97.
[5] *Span. Cal.* 1553, p. 217.

determined, as a party, and at the outset of the reign, to make no accommodation with idolatry. *There were too few of them.*

Accordingly, it was in January 1554 that the great movement to Germany began.[1] In February it had reached floodtide. It was not till March[2] and the close of Wyatt's rebellion, that Stephen Gardiner, 'nowe sumwhat hette with thiese treasons',[3] instituted the first proceedings against married priests.[4]

It is true that in the previous December, at the close of the parliamentary session in which the Edwardian statutes permitting clerical marriage had been repealed,[5] a proclamation[6] was issued (15 December 1553) to the effect that after 20 December 'no prest that has a wyff shall not menyster nor saye masse...'.[7] But nearly three months were allowed to elapse between that decree and any concerted effort to enforce obedience to it. For this delay the explanation usually given, or implied, is that the government's hands were too fully occupied with Wyatt's insurrection[8] to issue the necessary injunctions. Yet, even so, six weeks had passed between 15 December and the outbreak of that rebellion on 25 January.[9] And during that time, though individual cases

[1] See below, pp. 8–10.

[2] On this question Dixon (IV, 155–6 and note; cf. Frere, *op. cit.* pp. 46, 63–4) gives without citation two contradictory statements of Foxe. That one which assigns the first deprivations in London to the week of 25 February I have so far been unable to find, while the second (Foxe, VI, 426) gives the date of Bonner's commission correctly as 4 March. Wriothesley asserts (II, 113) that 'The first daye of Marche, the parsons and curates of the Cittie of London that were wedded were cited to appeare in the Consistorie in Paules afore the Bishop of Londons Commissioners, and there deprived from their benefices.' Was Foxe, in his zeal, perhaps confusing Bonner's 'Monition' to his clergy *re* confession, dated 24 February (Foxe, VI, 426), with his proceedings against the married clergy?

[3] Gardiner to Petre, 28 January 1554, J. A. Muller, *Letters of Gardiner* (1933), p. 459; *Chron. of Q. Jane*, p. 184. The latter gives the date as 27 January, which Muller corrects.

[4] Burnet, *History of the Reformation*, vol. V (ed. Pocock), Collections, pp. 381 ff., nos. X, XI, XII. Nos. XI–XII, dated 13 and 15 March; no. X, only March, but Foxe (VI, 426) supplies the date as 4 March.

[5] *Journals H. of C.* I, 29; passed 7 November 1553.

[6] Steele, *Tudor and Stuart Proclamations*, I, nos. 434, 435.

[7] Machyn's *Diary*, p. 50; Strype, *Mem.* III, i, 79; Foxe, VI, 542.

[8] Burnet, II, ii, 439; Dixon, IV, 132.

[9] The date of Wyatt's manifesto at Maidstone.

of sedition and unlicensed preaching had been punished, those married clergy who had not already fled continued apparently without molestation to hold their livings and exercise their functions.[1]

Fanciful as it may at first seem, we believe that another and truer explanation of that respite is to be found in the policy of tact and clemency which Gardiner adopted in dealing with the protestant problem. For this we have his own words,[2] to be quoted later; and in support of his words, a multitude of corroborative instances of their application which cannot be ignored.[3]

Upon such a theory, the proclamation of 15 December would have been in the nature of a warning of the queen's intention to re-establish ecclesiastical discipline.[4] Ample time was then allowed to such of the clergy as preferred withdrawal from England to the surrender of their wives to profit by it. And many of them did profit by it, but far fewer for the cause of marriage alone than has generally been supposed.[5]

---

[1] Strype, *Cranmer*, pp. 471–2.

[2] See below, p. 11 and note. [3] *Ibid.*

[4] That the measures were intended to be disciplinary rather than punitive (even though the word 'punish' is once used) is made clear by the moderation of the articles themselves. More clemency, for example, was to be used with those 'whose wives be dead' (Burnet, v, 383–4). Those who would put away their wives and do penance were under certain conditions to be admitted 'again to their former administration' (*ibid.*; cf. Bonner's certificate in regard to Scory, *ibid.* 389, no. XIII, and Mr Geoffrey Baskerville's conclusion in his 'Married Clergy and Pensioned Religious in Norwich Diocese, 1555', *E.H.R.* XLVIII, 45, 'that nearly all the clergy whose names are in the "Deprivation Book" were almost immediately instituted to other livings...'); while those who had been ordained 'after the new sort and fashion' were to be retained in the ministry at the bishop's discretion, after 'that thing which wanted in them before' was supplied (*ibid.* 385; for the interpretation of these words, see Dixon, IV, 134 n. and Frere, *op. cit.* pp. 117–26). It is odd to reflect that had Mary wished to justify far severer courses than these, she could have done no better than appeal to Théodore de Bèze's work *De haereticis a civili magistratu puniendis*, published in this same year (1554), in justification of the burning of Servetus. Bèze's definition of a heretic as one who 'rompt la paix et consentement de l'Église, en ayant une fausse doctrine et en persistant à la propager' could hardly have been better worded to fit her needs (French translation of 1559), cf. Lavisse, *Histoire de France* (ed. 1911), v, pt II, p. 207.

[5] Cf. Gairdner's statement (*History of the English Church*, IV, 391), that 'Hosts of married clergy also migrated to the Continent...', with the evidence from Norwich (below, p. 5).

The chancellor's apparent absorption in other matters than the enforcement of clerical celibacy came only as an unexpected and persuasive stimulus to a movement already begun. In the majority of cases it will be found that resignation and flight preceded official deprivation, often by weeks, sometimes by months. And though it is probably true that the actual enforcement of the order did determine a few to take refuge abroad,[1] it is also clear that flight was by no means an invariable, or even a usual sequel to deprivation. On this point the episcopal registers, when compared with my list of exiles, speak plainly. From the diocese of Norwich, for example, where 'the total deprivations for marriage' have been estimated at the surprising figure of 'something over 360',[2] only four of those deprived can be said with certainty to have fled to the continent, while at most the number was but seven.[3] Again, in the diocese of Bath and Wells not one of the twenty whom Bishop Bourne dispossessed in April and May (1554) is to be found on the roll of exile.[4] Apparently they all remained in England, and it is worthy of note that only one of them suffered martyrdom[5] for his temerity.[6] Altogether sixty-nine deprivations (or 'resignations') are recorded in the same register between 30 April of that year and 31 March 1556, but among them all Theodore Newton, rector of 'Bagworth',[7] appears to have

[1] As for example the archbishop's brother, Edmund Cranmer (see Census).

[2] Baskerville, *op. cit.* pp. 45, 49–64. I can, however, count only 339 names in Mr Baskerville's list, of which seven at least are repetitions. Even if we add to these the fifteen deprived whose names do not appear in the Deprivation Book (p. 45, notes 1 and 3) that total is but 347.

[3] These four were Gilbert Bartley (or Berkeley), William Johnson, John Matchett (or Machet), and Henry Raynold (or Reynold). The three doubtful ones are John Fisher, possibly brother to Fisher, parson of Amersham, John Browne, and Richard Davies. See Census.

[4] Bourne's Register, Harl. MS. 6967. Printed Dixon, IV, 148 n.–155.

[5] John Tayler, alias Cardmaker, late chancellor of Wells, burnt at Smithfield 30 May 1555. He had twice attempted to escape, under suspicious circumstances, with Bishop Barlow (*P.C.A.* 1554–6, p. 20: 10 May 1554 and Machyn, p. 75: between 14 and 18 November 1554).

[6] Cf. with the above list S. R. Maitland's list of martyrs, *Essays* (1899), pp. 449–55.

[7] Badgeworth in Surrey, see Census. It is interesting to find that this same Newton was refused a canonry of Canterbury in 1560 because he was not a priest (Strype's *Parker*, I, 144).

been the only fugitive. Of him it is recorded that he 'resigned';[1] and as we know that he was first ordained deacon
by Bishop Grindal in 1560,[2] his misdemeanour was obviously
not that of marriage (or marriage alone) but of having 'under
colour of priestly orders...unlawfully mingled [himself] in
ecclesiastical rights'.[3] Among the refugees will be found
many of those self-constituted clerics who passed henceforth
under the name of 'students'.

Much the same situation is revealed in the case of the 110
priests and deacons ordained under the new English ordinal.[4]
So far as we have record, only 19 of them in all went abroad;
and of these, 8 alone were priests,[5] while the other 11 had
been admitted deacons only.[6] Of the priests, a certain Richard
Grason (or Gresham) is the single instance of one, who apparently being deprived solely on the score of marriage, fled
in consequence. Yet of the remaining 92 all but three[7]
would seem to have lived on in England unmolested.[8] It
comes very much as a surprise to find how few of those who
received orders according to the new English rite found their
way to Germany. Even if the Marian Acts of March 1554 be
regarded in the light of persecution, they can hardly upon
such evidence as this be held responsible for the inception of
the withdrawal to the Continent.

That emigration, whatever the springs which fed it later,
was inaugurated, we believe, as a voluntary movement, and
directed to the fulfilment of a clearly conceived purpose.
Yet, as a policy, it so happily met the needs of the Marian

[1] Bourne's Register, Dixon, IV, 153 n.

[2] Strype's *Grindal*, p. 54: 25 January 1559–60.

[3] Bourne's commission to his vicar-general, Strype, *Mem.* III, i, 352.

[4] Frere, *op. cit.* p. 105. The full list is given *ibid.* Append. XII, pp. 181–219.
Including bishops, there had been 116. Of the bishops Hooper alone was
burned. The other five, who fled, are accounted for above, p. 2, n. 1.

[5] These were Thomas Lever, Robert Crowley, John Fynch, Richard Grason,
John Pullain, Edmund Thompson, William Turner, and Thomas Warter (or
Walter). See Census. John Veron, being French and thus omitted from the
list of exiles, is also omitted from this list. He was ordained deacon and
priest, August 1551, and fled to the Continent.

[6] By comparison of the Census with Frere, *op. cit.* pp. 181–219.

[7] *Ibid.* p. 110.

[8] That is, remaining of the total of 116 Edwardine bishops and clergy combined, of whom 24 fled.

government, that in its early stages (to the late autumn, probably, of 1554) William Cecil and Stephen Gardiner actually appear as collaborators in the same religious enterprise. A fortuitous but fateful partnership. Were they aware of each other's immediate purposes? For to both alike a protestant withdrawal to the continent at this juncture seemed to offer the only practical solution of the religious problem: to Cecil it meant the survival of protestantism; to Gardiner, the survival of England. Gardiner we suspect of having been cognizant of what was afoot from the beginning, and of welcoming Cecil's design as a godsend. It cannot have been Renard alone who knew in September that there were 'plottings, discontent, and secret communings between the hardened followers of that sect;....'[1] But whether or not he successfully deceived Cecil by his subsequent violence of manner and show of obstruction, who can say? Perhaps not even Cecil to himself. Yet in this Gardiner was only the opportunist looking to rid the realm of a seditious element which threatened its stability; and in a few months' time the exodus he facilitated was to become a boomerang destructive of his purpose. Cecil, on the other hand, shows himself the statesman, building by the same means for a greater future. His project was in effect the movement of a potential commonwealth, whose machinery of transit was by mid-January already set in motion.

The very word 'machinery' used in connection with the Marian Exile would seem to be an anachronism. Still more unexpected is the modern part played by London bankers in its operation. From the beginning the project was heavily backed by English merchants,[2] men no doubt honest in their protestantism, but probably not uninfluenced by hopes of a secular future in which trade would be untrammelled. Possibly as early as December 1553 a committee of Ways and Means had been organized in London, consisting of twenty-six persons of wealth and influence, both men and women, who were known as the 'Sustainers'.[3] Five of them were merchants

---

[1] *Span. Cal.* 1553, p. 217: Renard etc. to the Emperor, 9 September 1553.
[2] Forty went into exile themselves. See Census.
[3] Strype, *Mem.* III, i, 224

who already had commercial affiliations with the cities of the Empire, especially with Strasbourg. These five,[1] together with a certain Richard Chambers, possibly a gentleman of Northamptonshire and certainly a man of wealth, agreed to finance one of the cardinal purposes of the exodus—the education abroad, in an atmosphere unpolluted by idolatry, of a body of students of divinity who, it was intended, should one day become the clergy of a reformed Anglican Communion. On 24 February 1554[2] Peter Martyr wrote from Strasbourg to Bullinger,[3] 'English youths have come over to us in great numbers within these few days, partly from Oxford, and partly from Cambridge; whom many godly merchants are bringing up to learning, that, should it please God to restore religion to its former state in that kingdom, they may be of some benefit to the church of England.'

Under what condition these youths crossed the Channel, whether singly or in groups, we have no trustworthy evidence to say, but we do know that, once abroad, they are found organized into companies which show every evidence of preliminary planning. Each company travels, for example, under a leader and is inevitably preceded by a courier sent ahead to make provision for it at its destination. A case in point is that of the English colony at Zurich. Whether this was the first settlement to be thus organized we cannot say. Possibly Emden preceded it. But it is certainly the first for which we have an authentic date. On 5 April (1554) Henry Bullinger notes in his diary[4] that a party of ten Englishmen, 'exules studiosi Angli',[5] made their appearance in the city and,

---

[1] Richard Springham, John Abell, Richard Hilles, Thomas and George Heton—all later refugees but Hilles.

[2] This date is of particular importance in relation to the deprivations.

[3] *Orig. Let.* II, 514.   [4] *Diarium*, p. 46.

[5] Though Bullinger says ten he gives a list of thirteen names: Richard Chambers, Robert Horne, Lever [*sic*; can this have been Ralph or John? for Thomas Lever had already left Zurich for Geneva, see *Orig. Let.* I, 153–7], James Pilkington, Michael Renniger, John Mullins, Thomas Spencer, Henry Cockcroft, Thomas Bentham, Robert Beaumont, Laurence Humphrey, William Cole, and Nicholas Carvell. The official letter, addressed by the exiles to the magistrates of Zurich, gives only 11 (*Orig. Let.* II, 751–2). But the discrepancy is probably explained by Bullinger himself in a letter to Hooper (Coverdale, *Letters of the Martyrs*, p. 169) where he says that 'Tenne of them

immediately as it would seem, established themselves in a house belonging to Froschauer the printer,[1] where they lived henceforth as if 'in collegio'.[2] Their coming had not been un-expected. On the previous 10 March,[3] Thomas Lever, late Master of St John's College, Cambridge,[4] had arrived with a letter of introduction to Bullinger from John Burcher, an English merchant then living at Strasbourg.[5] And having in his two weeks' stay secured for them a house and a servant,[6] Lever then went on to Geneva.[7] The precise dates given by Bullinger are extremely valuable as an indication of the time when the party must have left England. Ordinarily the journey to Switzerland was a matter of a month to six weeks according to the time of year and the number of travellers. A man alone might do it in a month;[8] a group seldom if ever accomplished the trip in less than six weeks.[9] Thus to arrive on 5 April the 'students' can hardly have left London later than the first of March, while Lever, even granting his ability to travel faster, must have started by the first week in Feb-ruary, or even more probably, upon the evidence of Peter Martyr's letter quoted above,[10] as early as January. In either case it is obvious that the movement to Germany had begun not only before the deprivations of March, but even well

dwell together [i.e. in Froschauer's house], the reast remaine here and there with good men'. Neither Beaumont nor Carvell appears in the official list (*Orig. Let.* II, 752).

[1] This was situated 'zu der hinderen Linden, hinder der Trüw und vorderen Linden' (*Diarium*, p. 46). It is now Stüssihofstatt 13 (Th. Vetter, *Relations between England and Zurich, etc.* (1904), p. 54).

[2] *Diarium*, p. 46. [3] *Ibid.*

[4] In November 1551: Strype, *Mem.* II, ii, 267.

[5] Dated 3 March 1554, *Orig. Let.* II, 685.

[6] The exiles' consideration for this housekeeper of theirs, who was the widow of a preacher, is one of the pleasanter episodes of the exile; cf. *Orig. Let.* I, 126 and *Zur. Let.* I, 136; II, 108-9.

[7] Cf. Bullinger to Calvin, dated 26 March, *Orig. Let.* II, 744 and Lever to Bullinger, *ibid.* I, 153-4. [8] Cf. *ibid.* p. 154.

[9] Peter Martyr's journey, alone, London to Strasbourg—41 days—*Orig. Let.* I, 372; and cf. Gorham, *Gleanings*, p. 306 with *Orig. Let.* II, 505. John Abell and Peter Martyr, Basle to London—46 days—*Archaeologia*, xxi, 469–73. John Jewel and his party, Zurich to London—57 days—*Zur. Let.* I, 9.

[10] Lever had certainly reached Strasbourg before 3 March (see above), and he was very likely leader of the party of students from Cambridge whose arrival Martyr notes on 24 February.

before the proclamation against foreigners of 17 February. And this fact lends additional confirmation to the belief that the withdrawal took place in accordance with some definite plan of action adopted earlier still. The character of the group itself supports the conjecture. For it was no heterogeneous company that came to Zurich, such as the accidents of flight might have brought together, but one which had manifestly been carefully selected. All of them were men of learning, representing the two Universities.[1] And at their head was a leader of some eminence, Robert Horne, late dean of Durham, to whom Bullinger gives the title of 'senior'.[2] Associated with Horne, not only now but throughout the entire period òf exile, we find the wealthy layman, Richard Chambers, called by Bullinger 'oeconomus et pater'.[3] It was Chambers, always in company with Horne, who 'bore the bag', that is, acted as treasurer of the common funds for all the English communities until their return to England. And such was the authority evidently attached to his office, that at Frankfort it was feared that he and Horne, 'they 2 together [might come to] exercise...a moste vnworthie lordshipp ouer the poore, and by them all other...',[4] a dictatorial power most detrimental to the autonomy enjoyed by each separate colony.[5]

So much for the English community at Zurich. Full six months before the first martyr suffered at the stake,[6] five other colonies established in much the same manner,[7] and further organized as religious congregations upon the Genevan model, had come into existence in Germany. The presumption is strong that they were not isolated settlements due to chance, but units in one carefully devised system.

Thus the character of the exodus would in itself seem to

[1] Thomas Lever, as we have said, had been Master of St John's College, Cambridge; James Pilkington, a Fellow of the same College. Thomas Bentham, Laurence Humphrey, John Mullins, Michael Renniger and Thomas Spencer, were all ex-Fellows of Magdalen College, Oxford; while William Cole, a former Fellow of Corpus Christi College, Oxford, was later to become its first married president. For further details see the Census.

[2] *Diarium*, p. 46.   [3] *Ibid.*   [4] *Troubles*, p. 167.

[5] At the close of formal letters from the English 'Students' to the magistrates of Zurich the signatures of Horne and Chambers usually appear together and alone.

[6] John Rogers, on 4 February 1555.   [7] See below, pp. 47–9.

preclude any possibility that flight had been either haphazard or precipitate. And as the 'students' travelled in companies, so the gentry travelled by households, carrying with them their wealth in the form of letters of credit.[1] Naïve stories of their hairbreadth escapes from England carry no conviction with them. It is not easy to believe in the desperate plight of the Duchess of Suffolk,[2] who found it possible to flee for her life with a major-domo, 'a gentlewoman' and six servants—a joiner, a brewer, a kitchen-maid, a laundress, a 'Greek rider of horses', and a fool.[3] This unique flying squadron took five weeks to get from London to Gravesend (1 January—5 February), resting awhile in Kent, and all this, we are asked to believe, was accomplished without Gardiner's knowledge, though 'the fame of her departure reached to Leigh, a town at the land's end, before her approaching thither'.[4] Rather it would suggest that Gardiner had considerately turned a blind eye in the direction of the fugitives, for Katharine, the half-Spanish fourth wife of Charles Brandon, Duke of Suffolk, was a dangerous woman who later became as much of a trial to Elizabeth as she was to him, and what his methods were in such cases, Gardiner has himself explained. For he confided to Renard, that he had 'hit upon a good device for getting the Lutherans out of the country, without publishing any order or edict. When he hears', says Renard, 'of any preacher or leader of the sect, he summons him to appear at his house, and the preacher, fearing he may be put in the Tower, does not appear, but on the contrary absents himself;...'.[5]

[1] Cf. the Ratsbeschluss of the Frankfort Council, 23 March 1559, given in Jung, p. 7.

[2] Her husband, Richard Bertie, had already obtained from Gardiner in a personal interview an official safe-conduct which permitted him 'to pass and repass the seas' as often as he chose. The narrative given in Foxe, viii, 569–76, is supposed to be his own story (see 'Bertie', Census).

[3] Foxe, viii, 571. Cf. the imposing departure into exile of Francis, Earl of Bedford, with 'his bags, baggages, utensiles and other necessaries', his eight men and his eight geldings (Miss G. Scott Thomson, *Two Centuries of Family History*, p. 206). See also 'Francis Russell', Census.

[4] Foxe, viii, 572.

[5] *Span. Cal.* 1553, p. 217, of date 9 September 1553. Dr J. A. Muller, in his *Stephen Gardiner and the Tudor Reaction* (London, 1926), has quoted this indirectly (p. 232), but would seem to limit its application to the foreigners then in England. There are, however, so many instances of Gardiner's

Whether the reformers themselves were aware of Gardiner's
purpose to leave them free to depart,[1] one would doubt, but
his clemency placed them in a very awkward dilemma. Only
as martyrs for religion's sake could they hope to find an
asylum among their fellow-protestants abroad. On this point
the cities of the Empire were particularly explicit. When John
Burcher,[2] the English merchant, wished to obtain the freedom
of the Canton of Zurich in 1545, his friend Richard Hilles
wrote on his behalf to Henry Bullinger, explaining that he
understood that 'according to the laudable custom and law
of your city, he [Burcher] is prevented from obtaining [this]
until he can produce a testimonial signed by some persons
worthy of credit, to shew that he was born in lawful wedlock,
and that he has not fled *from his country by reason of any*

employing just this method of suggestion in the case of English protestants, and always with entire success, that we are inclined to believe that
he adopted 'the artifice' as an habitual policy. By this means he hastened
the departure of the duchess herself (Foxe, VIII, 571), while the case
of John Foxe is another admirably in point. Though the circumstances of the
story differ somewhat in the various versions, the central fact of Gardiner's
warning remains the same. We are paraphrasing the account given in the
earliest life of Foxe (unpaged) prefaced to vol. II of the 1641 edition of the
Acts and Monuments. Foxe was tutor to the grandsons of the Duke of Norfolk,
but seeing 'all sorts of men troubled for their Religion's sake, some imprisoned
and others burnt [it may here be remarked that by 3 December 1554, well
before any burnings had taken place, Foxe was safely in Frankfort, *Troubles*,
p. 26]; in brief nothing on all sides, but flight, slaughter, and gibbets', Foxe
began to consider leaving England. Coming suddenly one day into the Duke's
[i.e. the future Duke's] room, Foxe found him closeted with Gardiner, and
hastily closed the door. But Gardiner, who had seen him, asked who he was.
'My Physitian', was the reply, 'who is somewhat uncourtly, as being new come
from the University.' 'I like his countenance...', said Gardiner, 'and when
occasion shall be will make use of him.' This was enough. Foxe fled, relent-
lessly pursued by Gardiner's warrant so carefully timed as to arrive always a
day too late.

[1] Burnet says, quite to the contrary (II, 403), that the Council took pains to
see that no Englishman should escape out of their hands. In support of this
statement he has misconstrued and misapplied a special order of search
issued by the Council, which refers only to the Glastonbury Weavers (*P.C.A.*
1552–4, p. 349; 16 September 1553), into a general order concerning all
would-be protestant refugees, and applicable to the whole period from 1553
to 1558. Its real purport, however, is made clear by a previous letter of the
Council dated 5 September (*ibid.* p. 341). The departing Walloons were to be
searched to make sure that they had made 'no spoile of thier howses before
thier departures'.   [2] See 'Burcher', Census.

crime against the state;[1] but rather for having embraced the pure and christian doctrine, and freely made a profession of it'.[2]

From the Strasbourg protocols we know that the same provision against political offenders was in force there, and most strictly interpreted. Nor was Frankfort more lax. But as nearly every English exile had recently been involved either in active treason or in seditious preaching, the finding of an asylum became a difficult matter, and the more so in that his unlawful activities had been directed against the prospective daughter-in-law of the Emperor. Events show that the exiles' problem was not a hypothetical one. They had to assert roundly that they were persecuted or go homeless. Immediate banishment was to be the price paid by Knox at Frankfort, in 1555, for his seditious utterances against Queen Mary.[3] At Geneva, Calvin took particular care to dissociate himself from Knox the politician and his doctrines of tyrannicide.[4] When in 1556 the town of Wesel suspected that certain members of the English congregation had been implicated in conspiracy,[5] it requested their departure.[6] Strasbourg seems to have been particularly vigilant in regard to prospective citizens. Seeking refuge there in 1555, Sir Anthony Cooke, Sir Richard Morison, and Edwin Sandys, late Vice-Chancellor of Cambridge University, all three of them gentlemen whose political record was by no means clear, earnestly assured the magistrates that they had been 'banished by Queen Mary because they could not accept the religion of the Papacy'.[7] But while Morison and Cooke were admitted to temporary residence, Edwin Sandys's request for permanent citizenship was refused.[8] The fact that he had been publicly

[1] Author's italics. [2] *Orig. Let.* I, 246, Strasbourg, 15 April 1545.
[3] *Troubles*, p. 44. [4] *Zur. Let.* II, 34–6, Calvin to Cecil.
[5] See below, pp. 50–51.

[6] *Orig. Let.* I, 163–164, Lever to Gualter; and *ibid.* p. 168. Cf. also Strype, *Cranmer*, pp. 507–8 and Fuller, *Church History of Britain* (ed. 1845), IV, 205–206.

[7] Strasbourg protocols, 7 September 1555, Append. p. 366.

[8] Sandys was one of the very few who were willing to take such oaths of allegiance as would prevent their return to England. Though the protocol does not indicate the Council's final decision in regard to him, his name does not appear upon the list kept at the 'Archives' of those who obtained full citizenship.

involved in the 'business of Queen Jane' and imprisoned for treason[1] was no doubt the cause. Later Hugh Singleton, the printer, was denied the 'Bürgerrecht' on the same grounds.[2] And Thomas Baxter, the London 'book-binder' who could not give a satisfactory account of himself, was politely 'bidden to go whithersoever it [might] please God to take him'[3]—so that were away from Strasbourg. Yet all alike, whatever their past, agree in asserting that they are men persecuted for religion's sake and for no other reason. Even John Hales, when he believed that a warrant for his arrest had been served upon him by Queen Mary's commissioner John Brett, protested before the 'Consul' at Frankfort that the thing had been unlawfully done 'to vexe hym and others that for theyr refuge and concyens sake were commed thyther to flye persecucion in Englande...'.[4] Yet this is the same John Hales of Coventry[5] who supported the Suffolk claim to the throne well into the reign of Elizabeth, and for his treasonable pamphlet on the succession was put by her into the Tower.[6]

Between religion and politics in the mentality of the Marian Exiles the difference was but a hair's breadth. Yet France, who would gladly have received them as political refugees, would have been far less tolerant of their religious principles than England.[7]

[1] Strype, *Mem.* III, i, 17, 24.
[2] Protocols, August 1557, Append. p. 370.
[3] *Ibid.* February 1558, Append. p. 371.
[4] Brett's 'Narrative' (*Royal Hist. Soc. Trans.* n.s. XI, 120).
[5] For the question of the identification of John Hales of Coventry with John Hales, Clerk of the Hanaper to Edward VI, see *Bulletin of the Institute of Historical Research*, vol. I, no. 2, pp. 63–4, vs. I. S. Leadam, *R.H.S. Trans.* n.s. XI, 116–18, n. 6.
[6] Harl. MS. 1555 (not '1550' as in *D.N.B.*). Published by Nath. Boothe, London, 1723.
[7] The Chambre Ardente had been reconstituted by Henry II for the extirpation of heresy on 8 October 1547 (Lavisse, *Histoire de France* (ed. 1911), v, pt II, p. 202). That English protestants were fully aware of its efficiency may be gathered from a lively passage at arms between Sir Robert Stafford and Calvin. Calvin wished to detain Sir Robert's sister-in-law, Lady Dorothy Stafford, in Geneva after her husband's death. Sir Robert, protesting vigorously, expressed himself as 'bien esbahy que des ministres [meaning Calvin] qui sont ainsi zélateurs ne vont en France là où il y a du troupeau qu'ils laissent brusler' (C. Martin, *Les Protestants Anglais, etc.* 1915, p. 57).

It was out of this predicament (to which many other aspects of the protestant problem, as that of a political minority, contributed) that the need arose for a legend of persecution and banishment. Hence it was that in all their supplications for shelter, these voluntary exiles became in their own phrase 'die armen vertrybnen Engellender',[1] and 'poor banished Englishmen' they have remained in the sympathy of the world to the present day.

This must not be understood as said wholly in condemnation. These were fanatical pioneers in a new movement, and, granting their premises, were men under compulsion. Suddenly confronted with the alternative of flight or reabsorption into the catholic majority, they contrived a 'working fiction' to meet their needs, as every dynamic minority has done either before or since. Very soon they came, as all others have done, to believe ardently in their own fiction. Only in deference to truth it should at last be recognized that it *was* a fiction and that by their seditious action abroad they very probably induced for others the persecution which in their own case was imaginary.[2] 'This we can assure you,' wrote Whitehead from Frankfort in the autumn of 1555, 'that that outrageous pamphlet of Knox's added much oil to the flame of persecution in England. For before the publication of that book, not one of our brethren had suffered death: but as soon as it came forth, we doubt not but that you are well aware of the number of excellent men who have perished in the flames;....'[3] Now that the dust of controversy has somewhat cleared away, the Protestant Exodus of 1554 may be seen in its true light, as an experiment, though as events proved, no more than a temporary one, in religious colonization: the first to be undertaken by Tudor Englishmen, and the training school for all their later undertakings.

---

[1] The exiles at Basle to the magistrates, 10 April 1555. See Append. pp. 358–9.

[2] See below, pp. 43 and 47.

[3] *Orig. Let.* II, 761, Whitehead to Calvin, 20 September 1555. But this arraignment of Knox as an agent of persecution would have applied almost equally well to Becon, Ponet and many others—authors of seditious pamphlets abroad. Nor can it be urged in extenuation that they were ignorant of the consequences of their press campaign, for Bullinger himself had warned them of its probable effect (see Census, 'Haddon' and 'Banks').

Cecil we hold to have been originally responsible for the idea of migration. With the execution of Northumberland in 1553 and the Duke of Suffolk in 1554, leadership of the Suffolk faction of the protestant minority had fallen to four men: Suffolk's younger brother, Lord John Grey,[1] later called 'of Pyrgo'; Francis Russell, soon to be second Earl of Bedford (1555); William Parr, Marquis of Northampton; and Cecil himself. These four now seem to have formed themselves into a kind of executive council for protestant affairs,[2] and it is significant that it was these same four men who later constituted that 'secret cabinet' in the first year of Elizabeth, to which was delegated (though not by the queen) the alteration of religion. In 1554 Cecil would have held in relation to it a position somewhat analogous to that of a permanent under-secretary to-day. For years now he had been familiar, intimately so, with the handling of executive machinery. It was he, moreover, who, as Somerset's agent, had been closely associated with the settlement in England of groups of foreign religious refugees, organized as congregations under their own pastors.[3] What more likely than that he should seize upon this idea as the solution for the protestant problem? That which he had done for foreigners in England he would now do for Englishmen abroad—colonize them in regions sympathetic with their particular shade of protestantism, there to await a favourable moment to return and to prevail.

In this scheme Cranmer seems to have collaborated earnestly, embodying in the movement a further purpose of his own. Both together guided its initial stages. But after the death of Cranmer the influence of Cecil, and of the executive committee acting with him, is distinctly felt through various channels—one of them being Richard Chambers,[4] treasurer of the exiles, the other, Cecil's father-in-law, Sir Anthony Cooke, at Strasbourg, with whom he was in constant communication.[5]

---

[1] See 'John Graie', Census.   [2] *Mem.* III, i, 223–4.
[3] Schickler, I, 11–12.   [4] See 'Richard Chambers', Census.
[5] Apparently Cecil had even entertained the thought of directing the migration in person, from which he was dissuaded by Sir John Cheke. In his submission to Queen Mary he writes, 'I did fully set me to flee the realm', though he claimed that his purpose in this was to avoid being implicated in

Although only two aspects of this colonial experiment can be considered here, these two are fundamental, both to an understanding of the episode itself, and to a just appreciation of the magnitude and complexity of the religious problem which confronted Elizabeth at her accession. First, what was its size? Secondly, what its essential nature? Was it, like its Walloon and Dutch predecessors in England, no more than a religious protest of humble artisans? or was it something which in composition and in intent differed from any other protestant movement that had gone before it? one which had in it the elements of political revolution? one which even carried in its train the settlement of the new world? It is no mere flight of fancy to suggest that Cecil's policy was responsible in the very next year, 1555, for a similar but more ambitious French project to which Admiral Coligny lent his moral support[1] and three ships—we mean Villegagnon's attempt to plant the first colony of French Calvinists in America.[2]

Hitherto answers to these questions have not been forthcoming. Information has been too meagre and preconceived ideas too strong. Now, however, by the recent discovery of documents abroad,[3] it has at last become possible to compile a comprehensive list of exiles and for the most part to establish their identity. The cumulative evidence which this Census provides in favour of the theory of a 'directed migration' should go far to establish its truth.

At the outset it must be remembered as the cardinal fact in

the proclamation of Lady Jane Grey (Tytler, II, 194, Item 21. Endorsed by Cecil himself as of 1553).

[1] Coligny had not yet given in his allegiance to protestantism, nor is he considered to have done so until his letter of acceptance to Calvin, 4 September 1558 (A. W. Whitehead's *Coligny*, p. 69).

[2] His colonists were largely drawn from the French protestants, almost entirely artisans, who had already taken refuge in Geneva. Though the settlement which was made in Brazil proved to be a failure, it would seem to have inspired all the later Huguenot attempts (Lavisse, V, pt II, p. 242). This Villegagnon is the same who, in 1548, was employed by the French to convey the Queen of Scots from Dumbarton to Lorraine (*Orig. Let.* II, 643, n. 3). For an account of his reasons for founding the colony in Brazil, see Jean de Léry's *Histoire d'un Voyage faict en la Terre du Brésil* (ed. Paris, 1880), p. 40. De Léry was himself one of these Huguenot refugees who on their way to embark at Honfleur passed by Châtillon to obtain Coligny's blessing (*ibid.* p. 44).

[3] See below, pp. 353–372.

the lives of these 472 English refugees, that for five years, or the greater part of that time, they were men living in a foreign land *outside the limits of any effective jurisdiction.*[1] In this fact lies the supreme significance of their experience. For by the crossing of the Channel these subjects of Queen Mary had passed beyond the reach of her coercive arm, while at the same time they stubbornly refused,[2] as the Strasbourg protocols reveal, to bind themselves by oaths of allegiance to the cities of their adoption, for fear that such oaths would endanger their right to return to England.[3] What civic responsibilities they assumed were voluntarily undertaken and could be resigned at will. They made it clear that such services implied no recognition of the city's sovereignty in relation to themselves. Beyond being amenable to police and guild regulations,[4] they were politically free men, free to come and go as they chose,[5] to bear arms or not as they chose, and above all free to order the internal affairs of their own little communities as they chose. When, as at Frankfort, they were given a separate church to worship in, exile rapidly developed into a school of self-government.

Unfortunately this same voluntary relation also carried with it serious disadvantages. If the exiles were not bound by it, neither were the town magistrates. What the English asked for in return for taxes paid, and military service rendered, was protection, yet it was just protection that the town, in view of the informal nature of their association, felt free to give or to withhold as it saw fit.[6] No foreign power was to be offended for the sake of a few wandering Englishmen. John Brett's effort to deliver Queen Mary's warrants at Frankfort[7] strikingly illustrates the precarious situation in

[1] Brett's 'Narrative', pp. 120, 125–6.
[2] The exceptions to this rule are so few as to be negligible and will all be noted in passing.
[3] Cf. the cases of Thomas Heton, John Abell, etc., Append. pp. 362, 364, 365.
[4] That these were rigidly enforced is clear from the instance of John Carus in 1556 (Append. p. 369) and the particularly interesting case of Thomas Gibson, the physician (*ibid.* pp. 364, 366, 367, 371).
[5] If a man had 'bought' the 'Grossbürgerrecht' he apparently had to obtain the magistrates' official permission to leave, but this seems to have been little more than a formality (cf. Thomas Gibson, Append. p. 371).
[6] Brett's 'Narrative', pp. 120–1.   [7] *Ibid.* pp. 119–21.

which these expatriated men actually lived their daily lives. If they had been surrounded by a wilderness of nature instead of a wilderness of foreign tongues they could hardly have been more isolated from their fellows or more dependent upon their own resources. Isolated and segregated, they found themselves in the midst of an organized society of which they formed no integral part. In this respect their spiritual descendants in New England were better off than they.

Otherwise the experience of 1554 bears a prophetic likeness to that of the Puritan Migration of 1630. For the Marian fugitives were the first to break through the barriers of insularity which England, 'this scarce discerned Ile, Thrust from the World',[1] had been gradually raising between herself and Europe since the close of the Hundred Years' War. The crossing of the Channel was, no doubt, a necessary prelude to the crossing of the western seas, and those who took the decisive step were, in a true sense, pioneers. They did not come to *traverse* but to *live* in a foreign land though, as they trusted, their exile was to be for a short time only. And like pioneers they suffered hardships. Even the richest of them (and contrary to general belief many were rich, the aggregate of their taxable property at Frankfort alone amounting to 42,860 gulden)[2] could not buy adequate accommodation in the crowded walled cities of the Rhine valley.[3] They had literally to be herded together, sometimes five families to a house,[4]

[1] Cf. Samuel Daniel's *Musophilus*, lines 426–9, quoted Miss Yates, *John Florio*, p. 33.

[2] Jung, pp. 29–30. Fynes Moryson, in his guide book to the Continent called *An Itinerary* (London, 1617), gives the value of the silver gulden in 1559 as 'three shillings foure pence English' (pt I, p. 285). The silver gulden formed the common basis of reckoning, but as Moryson complained 'yet is there no such coyne in the Empire' (*ibid.*). 'Fifty or sixty pounds sterling yeerley', says Moryson, 'were sufficient...when I was beyond sea [1589], to beare the charge of a Trauellers diet, necessary apparell, and two journeys yeerley... and also to serue him for moderate expenses of pleasure...' (*ibid.* pt 3, p. 13).

[3] After the influx of Italian refugees into Basle in 1555 that city had to close its gates against any more aliens (*Orig. Let.* I, 148, Sir Richard Morison to Bullinger, 23 August 1555).

[4] This was the case in John Kelke's house at Frankfort, where the five families living together numbered twenty-two persons (*H.S.P.* IV, 89). In the case of Thomas Sandes (or Saunders) one roof sheltered only three families but twenty-eight persons (*ibid.*).

in quarters far too small for them. And they experienced all the evils of overcrowding, from exacerbated tempers to the plague.[1]

No doubt such uncomfortable conditions contributed very largely to the restlessness which Bullinger complained of as characteristic of most Englishmen who, as he said, 'cannot be at rest, who can never be satisfied, and who have always something or other to complain about'.[2] They became incessant travellers, so much so that Whittingham exclaimed bitterly that exile had become to many 'a pleasant progresse or recreation'.[3]

Yet it was through travel that the mental vision of these islanders was to be widened to comprehend new horizons; and their ears to become accustomed to the *sound*, at least, of alien tongues, even though they rarely understood, and more rarely still learned to speak any language but their own.[4] Latin was used for communicating with magistrates[5] and, of course, between scholars. But the gentry's ignorance of French, besides contributing to English isolation, sometimes created serio-comic situations. One of these, which occurred at Strasbourg, provides a humorous commentary upon the protestant demand for religious services in the vernacular. Pierre Alexandre, but lately prebendary of Canterbury as Peter Alexander, was in 1555 minister of the French congregation at Strasbourg with whom the English worshipped.[6]

---

[1] In 1555 Richard Vanville, pastor of the French Church, died of the pest at Frankfort (Bonnet, *Lettres de Calvin*, II, 82 n.); and it is not unlikely that the plague was also responsible in 1556 for the death at Strasbourg of John Ponet, then only forty-two, as well as of Sir Richard Morison and James Haddon.

[2] *Zur. Let.* II, 152, Bullinger to Beza, 15 March 1567.

[3] *Troubles*, p. 59.   [4] *Ibid.* p. 5.

[5] It has been generally supposed that the English congregation was allowed to worship in the famous Lutheran church of St Thomas, whose pastor was Conrad Hubert. But I am assured by Monsieur Jean Adam, pastor of Dorlisheim, and the learned author of the *Evangelische Kirchengeschichte der Stadt Strassburg* (1922), that this is an error. He tells me that, though baptisms had to be performed according to the Lutheran rite and at St Thomas's, the English themselves were members of the French refugee congregation which, until 1561, was allowed the church of St André (situated on the Place Gutenberg but no longer existing) for the celebration of their cult. This unsuspected identification of the English with Calvinism, at Strasbourg, is a fact of the highest importance.

[6] Of Brussels. 'He had been condemned by the Inquisition in 1545, at which time he probably went to England' (*Span. Cal.* 1553, p. 217, note).

It came to Calvin's ears that Alexander was beginning to mingle Latin phrases with his French in the liturgy, and a sharp reprimand came from Geneva. Alexander promptly defended himself. It was not 'from any attachment to popery' that he introduced his Latin periods, but because he numbered among his flock so many English lords who could not understand French that without these interpolations they would have been unable to follow the prayers.[1]

Thus the peculiar segregation of the English, due in part to a native distaste for foreigners, in part to a fixed idea that their exile would be short, was in even greater part the result of sheer inability to hold speech with their neighbours, or their neighbours with them.[2] English on the Continent was as yet a tongue unknown. 'It is a language that wyl do you good in England,' says John Florio contemptuously, 'but passe Douer, it is woorth nothing.'[3] Now the consequences of this segregation were important and twofold: one, incessant quarrels among themselves; the other, a breaking down of social barriers. Gentlemen, merchants, and craftsmen were sometimes obliged to live under the same roof. And to all three alike normal activities were denied: the 'gentleman' was divorced from his land, the merchant and the craftsman were both prevented from following their callings by the jealousy of the local guilds.[4] A daily life so circumscribed would have been intolerably aimless without animosities and plots. Also it was natural, in such conditions, that the

[1] Pierre Alexandre to Calvin, 12 October 1555. *Calvini Opera*, vol. xv, no. 2321, cols. 817–18. Cf. also R. Reuss, *Église Française de Strasbourg* (1880), chap. ii, p. 45.

[2] Jung (p. 7) would explain the separation of the English from all the other communities of religious refugees at Frankfort entirely on social grounds. This was, of course, one factor in the situation, but would have been of less significance at Strasbourg, Basle and Aarau, where English isolation was equally marked. A curious and interesting survival of such isolation into modern times is to be found in the English College at Douai which the Abbé Dimnet (*My Old World*, p. 156) attributes very largely to difference of language.

[3] Florio's *First Fruits*, p. 50, quoted Miss Yates, *John Florio*, p. 32.

[4] Jung, p. 17; also Strasbourg protocols, below, pp. 364, 366, where the case of the English physician, Thomas Gibson, presents several aspects of this prohibition. Only at Aarau (possibly also at Geneva, though that situation has yet to be investigated) were English artisans permitted to practise their trade (see below, p. 51).

artisan and the servant should become aware of their en-
hanced value as individuals. Often a single vote was a matter
of supreme importance in party strife, when the whole male
community, as at Frankfort, numbered but sixty-two.[1] And
after the rejection of episcopacy there by the English divines
in March 1555,[2] the rapid evolution of that congregation
towards ecclesiastical democracy must be attributed in part
to some such awakened sense of equality as well as to the
highly significant fact that no English ecclesiastic of rank was
a member of the community. Less than two years later, in the
face of ministerial opposition, the Frankfort 'church' declared itself a self-governing body-politic.[3] Having already
rejected the jurisdiction of king and bishop it now chose to
repudiate even the domination of its minister, declaring that
the congregation was the source of law. That was in February.
The following April two servants, significantly enough those
of John Hales, were permitted to vote upon the adoption of
the new democratic Discipline.[4] And since nearly every
county in England was represented among the fugitives, and
every class, including the yeoman, it may be said that England
itself shared vicariously in this experience of exile.

Who were these men who in the space of five years contrived to set forward the political clock by decades, and went
home determined to force the pace of their countrymen in
religion and politics?

Bare lists of them have been left us by Whittingham in the
Troubles at Frankfort; by John Bale in his *Scriptores*; and by
the editors of the Emden edition of Cranmer's *Defensio*.[5]
But none of these catalogues tells us much of their condition
and still less of their antecedents,[6] though it is only in the

---

[1] *Troubles*, p. 96. This was in 1557. The number fluctuated slightly.

[2] *Ibid.* p. 47, marginal note; and for the reason of this rejection cf. the
explanation of Fuller, *History*, IV, 218.   [3] *Troubles*, p. 72.

[4] *Ibid.* pp. 133–4. Richard Mason and Peter Sade. Further light is thrown
upon the social situation by the casual words used in that clause of the
Discipline which concerns 'The manner of receauing *all sortes off persons*'
into the congregation. 'The same' are to submit to the Discipline and to
testify 'by subscribing therto *yf they can wryte*' (*Troubles*, p. 128).

[5] Cranmer, *Works* (ed. Parker Soc.), I, 9 (close of the volume).

[6] For these Strype, who used Foxe's manuscripts, has served as the chief
source of information.

light of their antecedents *and* their social status that the true character of the Marian Exile stands revealed.

⌄ Perhaps the over-emphasis placed heretofore upon the controversial aspects of the interlude is responsible for the fact that historians have left it practically undiscovered country. Not till the opening of the nineteenth century did it become known that valuable material, as yet untouched, existed in the archives of Switzerland. Then, in 1831, the Livre des Anglois, a register of John Knox's English congregation at Geneva, was discovered and given to the world in a not very accurate transcript published by J. S. Burn.[1] Then followed, in the decade of the 'forties, a rich find at Zurich of the letters which had passed between English and Swiss reformers from 1537 to the opening of the seventeenth century. This intimate correspondence of Edwardian and Elizabethan clergy with Henry Bullinger and his Zwinglian circle[2] may have been collected with some idea of re-asserting the early protestant affiliations of the English Church, at a time when the Oxford Movement was laying stress upon its catholic continuity.[3] Still, their publication did not arouse sufficient interest in England to induce any further explorations abroad. Except for the apparently sporadic discovery in 1894 of the register of the English Church at Frankfort, transcribed by M. de Neufville for the Huguenot Society,[4] curiosity appeared to be satisfied.

After the middle of the nineteenth century, however, and probably as a direct consequence of English researches, there came a sudden awakening of Swiss interest in the connection between England and Geneva, England and Zurich. First there appeared at Geneva in 1855 M. Théophile Heyer's *Notice sur la Colonie Anglaise...de* 1555 *à* 1560, in which he

---

[1] The only facsimile of the Livre des Anglois in existence has recently been acquired (1935) by the Bodleian Library.

[2] The *Original Letters* and the *Zurich Letters* were published between 1842 and 1847.

[3] Compare with this the issue in 1846 of a reprint of the 1575 edition of the *Troubles at Frankfort*, and also the article published anonymously in the *Edinburgh Review* in 1847 (vol. LXXXV) under the running title of 'The Marian Exiles'. The authorship of this has been ascribed by Dr Lorimer to J. A. Froude.

[4] See 'Sources', p. 65.

analysed the Livre des Anglois and added to its list of English names certain others found in the Registre des Habitants.[1] Then, between 1891 and 1893, Theodor Vetter, in two valuable studies, dealt with the origin and development of the English affiliations with Zurich from 1531 to 1554.[2]

Four years later at Basle came Dr August Hubert's[3] all too brief account of the part played by that city as an asylum for religious refugees.[4] His tantalizing references to certain important Marian fugitives among the rest, fugitives not mentioned by John Bale in his list,[5] were largely responsible for my conviction that on that subject much still remained to be found and said.

It was left, however, to Dr Rudolf Jung, of the archives at Frankfort, to appreciate the immense historic importance of the prosaic lists of English burghers, residents and taxpayers that he found preserved in the city's records. His article on 'Die englische Flüchtlings-Gemeinde in Frankfort-am-Main' (1910),[6] in which he collected and printed, with an admirable running commentary, all the material that survives concerning the English community of 1554–9, is the first completely dispassionate account of that episode which has yet appeared. His unselected and consequently unbiased information serves to throw an entirely new light upon the conditions of exile and

[1] Vol. IX, pp. 337–90 of *Mémoires et Documents*, published by the Société d'Histoire et d'Archéologie de Genève. Unfortunately M. Heyer's unfamiliarity with English surnames made for frequent errors of transcription, which were later perpetuated in an English transcript of the Livre des Anglois printed at Geneva, to which Dr Ferrier Mitchell wrote a preface. As far as possible I have corrected these errors by collation with the original Register, finding that several of the twenty-six names (cf. Heyer, Tableaux no. II, and also Martin, p. 47) were duplicates of those in the Livre des Anglois. These corrections I have indicated in my Census.

[2] Briefly: *John Hooper, Bischof von Gloucester, etc.* (Zurich, 1891), and *Die Englische Flüchtlinge in Zürich während der ersten Hälfte des 16. Jahrhunderts* (1893). The substance of this second study was later published in English under the title of *Relations between England and Zürich during the Reformation* (Address to the 23rd Anglican Church Congress, 1904).

[3] Dr Hubert was then Director of the Staatsarchiv. His article entitled 'Die Refugianten in Basel' appeared in the *Neujahrsblatt* of 1897.

[4] Basle, I am told, is still in the twentieth century playing this same humanitarian rôle.

[5] *Scriptores*, p. 742.

[6] Heft 3, *Frankfurter Historische Forschungen*, ed. by Prof. Küntzel.

the circumstances of the exiles. Yet, except for the inclusion of its title in Dr Conyers Read's recent *Bibliography of British History*,[1] the monograph has aroused no interest. The copy at the British Museum had never been handled until it was used for the compilation of the present Census. And since its publication, no other studies of the Marian Exile based on these manuscript materials have, so far as I know, been forthcoming.[2]

Up to this point we have been speaking only of books or of articles in which foreign records have been incorporated. We must now turn to the records themselves.

Long before 1910, certain of the Swiss archives relating to the exiles had been made available in print. At Aarau in 1880 a list of the members of the little English colony that had arrived there from Wesel in 1557 was published in the preface to the *Urkundenbuch der Stadt Aarau*. The list had been compiled by a citizen named Hans Dür (or Thür),[3] with whom Thomas Lever the preacher, and his brother John, 'lodged for 40 weeks'.[4] Hence the specific information it contains must have been given to Hans Dür by Lever himself, who was both the minister and the leader of the English congregation. Not only does it give the name of each member of the fugitive community, but his class or occupation, the county from which he came, and often his town.[5] In short, the document is unique in the annals of exile, being even more precise and illuminating than the Livre des Anglois at Geneva; yet no word of it, to my know-

---

[1] *Bibliog. Brit. Hist.* (Clar. Press, 1933), p. 142.

[2] This statement does not except Mr H. J. Cowell's papers on the Frankfort and Strasbourg colonies, published in 1929 and 1934 (vols. xiv, xv of the Huguenot Society's *Proceedings*), nor Mr Alexander Clay's article on 'Reformation Contacts with Zurich' (see the *Modern Churchman* for June 1933).

[3] I was told by Dr Amann, Director of the Archives of the Canton of Aargau, that the original copy of the list has now disappeared, and that no information survives regarding the identity of Hans Dür.

[4] *Argovia*, xi, *Urkundenbuch, etc.*, chap. i, Introduction, pp. lxiii–lxv. Cf. Sources, p. 65.

[5] Or, in the words of Hans Dür himself, 'Hienach volgent die namen, geburt, stet, gebiet und herrschaften aller deren umb des evangelions willen vertriebnen Engellenderen...uffgenommen und beherbärget sind worden mentag nach Jacobi anno 1557' (*Argovia*, xi, p. lxiii).

ledge, has ever been quoted, nor has it been included in any English bibliography. Aarau itself had nearly forgotten its existence.

Twenty years later, and still at Aarau, this list, which, though undated, probably belongs to the year 1557, was followed by the publication of a second, or 'official', list drawn up, apparently, after 19 January 1559,[1] when the exiles were on the point of returning to England.[2] Though the two contain the same names with one exception,[3] there are certain slight differences between the two documents, which add peculiar interest to them because they seem to mark the passage of time. A few children have been born in the interim; some young men, who were single when they arrived, have married. Otherwise the two show most accurate correspondence in details, though Hans Dür supplies more information in regard to the fugitives' English origin, and the official list more facts concerning their life in Aarau.[4]

My knowledge of these two invaluable registers is due to the kindness of Dr Walther Merz, the present archivist of the town archives. While to Dr Binz, then librarian of the University Library of Basle, I owe an introduction to another list of Englishmen, almost equally important yet known heretofore only in an abbreviated form, to be found in the Matrikel, or register of the graduates of the University from 1460 to 1568.[5] Between the years 1554 and 1559, this register records the presence of no fewer than thirty-eight English students,

[1] See Append. pp. 353–6.
[2] See the passport issued to them by the authorities of Berne, 2 January 1559, Append. pp. 359–60.
[3] That of Robert Harlestone (or Harlesdon) (*q.v.*), probably Archbishop Parker's brother-in-law or nephew, who is mentioned by Hans Dür but not in the official list.
[4] Certain differences in the spelling of proper names led the editor, Dr Diebold Merz, to consider the official list the more accurate of the two, but these differences are of no real importance since they prove to be merely two phonetic renderings of the same name.
[5] Universitätsbibliothek Mnscr. AN. II, 3, f. 191. Cf. Bodleian MS. Facs. D. 49. The University of Basle has published an incomplete list of their names in a handbook entitled *General Information for Foreign Students*. Further abbreviated, this appears on p. 135 of Scott Pearson's *Thomas Cartwright* (Camb. Univ. Press, 1925). The first complete list for the years 1554 to 1559 will now be found in the Appendix, pp. 357–8.

all of them protestant refugees, most of them men of future eminence.

Quite unexpectedly, however, the richest harvest of new material was gathered at Strasbourg where, by general belief, the city's records had all been destroyed in the fire of 1870.[1] Fortunately this has proved to be untrue. Much has gone,[2] but the minutes of the imperial city's governing council—the 'Council and 21'—survive, and of these there is an unbroken series for the years 1553 to 1559.[3] As the volumes have never been indexed, and as the German spelling of the English surnames makes these difficult to recognize as English, it had not been realized that these 'protocols' are a veritable store-house of information regarding the English exiles[4]— their civic status, their privileges and limitations, their comings and goings, the attitude of 'authority' towards them, and their own mischances. Not the least valuable contribution of the almost daily records is the accurate chronology they provide for English activities, even to the days of the week.

Mystery has always surrounded the group of important English gentry and clergy who gathered at Strasbourg, among whom were Sir John Cheke, Sir Peter Carew, Sir Thomas Wrothe, Sir Anthony Cooke, Sir Richard Morison; John Ponet, late bishop of Winchester, Edwin Sandys, future archbishop of York, Thomas Becon, and Thomas Sampson, called the late dean of Chichester;[5] together with the bankers Thomas Heton and John Abell. The list is a catalogue of notabilities in Edward's reign; of conspirators in Mary's. The suspicion that the colony served as a centre for political propaganda; that it was in constant touch with London on the one hand, with Paris and Rouen on the other, is strongly confirmed by the undercurrent of wariness in dealing with English refugees that pervades the protocols. Nowhere else was the same care

---

[1] Cf. the statement, pp. 77–8, of the *Hug. Soc. Proc.* vol. xv (1934): 'No original records can be traced to-day in Strasbourg itself as to the company of influential English refugees who were so hospitably treated...during the years 1553 to 1558.'

[2] For what still exists at Strasbourg in the way of parish registers, etc. see Sources, p. 66.

[3] Vols. 32–6 incl. [4] See Append. pp. 362–72.

[5] Cf. Frere, *op. cit.* p. 189, n. 2.

taken to inquire into the antecedents of those who wished to become burghers or residents of the city. But at Strasbourg a certain John Carus was actually deported.[1] Sir Thomas Fracht [Frogget?], whoever he may have been, was threatened with the same fate[2] if he did not observe his obligations to the magistrates. Hugh Singleton, refused burgher rights as we have seen, because of his past record,[3] was later at Basle not only admitted to citizenship but also to membership in a printers' guild known as the Safranzunft.[4] Double guarantees were demanded of Sir Richard Morison and Sir Anthony Cooke[5] before they were admitted even to 'residence'. Sandys's request to be made a permanent citizen seems to have been refused altogether. The council's open distrust of Thomas Baxter,[6] who from being a humble craftsman suddenly acquired wealth enough to buy the 'Grossbürgerrecht' and later a large house and garden,[7] strongly suggests that the man was a spy—he had until recently been Sir Anthony Cooke's 'servant'.[8] During the time that Sir Thomas Wrothe, who had been an accomplice in Suffolk's second rising,[9] was at Strasbourg, his younger brother Oliver was at Paris[10] in close touch with the Dudley conspirators. From John Brett's allusion to the agent of Calvin, 'Archeheretik of Geneva',[11] whom he saw entering Sir Anthony Cooke's house, we have little doubt that there was the head-quarters of intrigue, from which emanated many of the mischievous pamphlets of Ponet and Becon, which, by way of Emden,[12] were carried into England. Here the special reference is to an almost unnoticed tract, entitled *The humble and unfained confession of the belefe of certain poore banished men*,[13] published in 1554, and prob-

---

[1] Append. pp. 368–9.   [2] *Ibid.*
[3] Cf. above, p. 14.
[4] Basle: Safranzunft-Archiv 25, p. 221. See Append. p. 361.
[5] Cf. above, pp. 13–14.   [6] *Ibid.*
[7] Append. p. 371 and Frankfort, Jung, pp. 39–40.
[8] See Census.   [9] *Chron. of Q. Jane*, p. 184.
[10] *For. Cal.* 1553–8, p. 278, O. Wrothe to Wotton, 22 November 1556.
[11] Brett, 'Narrative', p. 130.   [12] See below, pp. 48 and 49.
[13] See *Short Title Cat.* no. 5630 and the biographies of Becon and Ponet. Its running title is 'The Confession of the Banished Ministers'. First noticed by Nicholas Pococke in 1895 (*E.H.R.* x, 417–44), but left unidentified by him, this mysterious pamphlet of which only three copies are known to exist

ably the combined work of Becon, Sampson and Ponet; and to Ponet's own justification of tyrannicide known as *A shorte treatise of politike power*,[1] which, appearing in the spring of 1556, we believe to have been written as a broadside in support of the Dudley conspiracy.[2]

Of course no startling revelations of such treasonable activities are to be found in the Council minutes. Nevertheless their general tenor goes far to justify the inference that Strasbourg was the foreign centre of Cecil's plans for the future.

All the information which these hitherto unused documents of Aarau, Basle and Strasbourg have supplied are now incorporated in my Census of Exiles, which, as far as it concerns the Marian exodus to Germany, is believed to be comprehensive. Yet inevitably a margin of error must exist in a task so complicated. The main purpose of these fugitives was to escape notice. Foreign tongues often deformed their proper names into things unrecognizable, while the vagaries of sixteenth-century English spelling and the habit of Latinizing surnames have also added immensely to the difficulties of identification.[3] Nevertheless, so wide a net has been spread to catch them, that the number of exiles who have escaped it, we dare to hope, will be found very few indeed.

(two at the Bodleian and one in the Cambridge University Library) next attracted the attention of Mr Champlin Burrage (*Early English Dissenters* (Cambridge, 1912), I, 76–8), but apart from an interesting controversial analysis of the text, he made no attempt to 'place' it historically or to discover its authorship, merely inferring from the colophon (quite fictitious, as I believe) that it was the work of an unknown colony of English refugees at Wittenberg.

[1] [Strasbourg?] 1556. *Short Title Cat.* nos. 20178, 20179.

[2] For a discussion of the historical significance of these two pamphlets see the biographies of Ponet, Becon and Sampson in the Census.

[3] A case in point is that of John Pretio, who at Geneva appears as John Pretty; at Aarau, as John Pretie; on Bale's list, as John Praty; and at Zurich, as John Pretio. This Latinized form, if translated, becomes Price. Was he then John Pretty? or was he the John Price, member of convocation in 1562 (Strype, *Annals*, I, i, 490), or the John Prat, friend of Foxe, also mentioned by Strype (*ibid.* pp. 354, 491, etc.)?

II

THE EXODUS TO FRANCE

Since lists are in themselves dull things, the Census may need a persuasive word of justification. Yet it is obvious that without knowing, more accurately than we have done, what percentage of the population of Tudor England was represented in the exodus, what proportion of the Edwardian reformation was represented, or what sections of English society shared in the experience, its influence cannot well be traced, nor its importance gauged in relation to the future. Theories may not safely rest upon ambiguities. Zeal and imagination have both played too large a part in earlier computations.

Of course it is upon the word of John Foxe, himself an exile, that all later estimates of numbers have been based, and Foxe says that 'many Englishmen fled...well near to the number of 800 persons, students and others together'.[1] Perhaps the vagueness of this statement will not be immediately apparent, but—who were these 'others'? Men or women? Does Foxe intend his '800' to be a comprehensive figure, including *all* those who fled throughout the five years, or does it cover the number of men only? He leaves us to guess. Fuller evades the question altogether. Heylyn makes two statements which, though they appear to be contradictory, may have been intended to remove one of Foxe's ambiguities. Three hundred 'or thereabouts', he says, fled under cover of the foreigners[2] (that is on 17 February 1554)[3] and 800 'had forsook the kingdom',[4] which we take to mean 'in all'. He still does not explain whether this number comprises women and children. Burnet, leaving all conservative estimates behind, says roundly that 'above a thousand' fled,[5] and in this wholly unsupported assertion he has been followed by such scholars

---

[1] Foxe, vi, 430.   [2] *Eccles. Restaur.* ii, 103.

[3] Steele, *Tudor and Stuart Proclamations*, i, no. 445.

[4] Heylyn, ii, 171, 175.

[5] Burnet (ed. Pococke), ii, 403. Burnet's paragraph on the subject is an outstanding example of what mischievous history can be written when the little matter of dates is ignored.

as Baron Schickler in his *Églises du refuge en Angleterre*.[1]
More irresponsible persons still have even improved upon
Burnet by placing the number of laity alone at about 1000,
exclusive of the clergy.[2] Yet on the whole Foxe's statement
has been accepted as authoritative[3] and the dilemma in which
he leaves us seems to have troubled no one. 'What', it may
be asked, 'does it matter?'

Confidently it may be answered, 'Much'. For the questions
really being left unanswered are these:

How many Englishmen, accustomed for some five years to
practical immunity from the control of the Crown, returned
to England in 1559 to take part in the Elizabethan Settlement
of Church and State?

How many children did these Englishmen possess, who
having been educated in the centres of foreign protestantism,
were likely to perpetuate their experience of nonconformity
and self-government into the next generation?

Finally, were the exiles men of sufficient eminence, lay and
clerical, to exert any influence after their return upon the
decisions of parliament?

It was for the purpose of determining just these points, that
the present Census was undertaken. In the list that follows it
has been intended to include no one whose title to the name
of refugee for the sake of religion or politics is doubtful. On
the other hand, some few have been included who, fleeing
from the persecution of Henry VIII's last years, remained
abroad, and who, because of their abhorrence of 'popery',
were unwilling to return to England in the reign of Mary.
Others again, whose presence on the Continent as exiles has
been conjectured but cannot be proved, have been omitted.[4]

---

[1] F. Schickler (Strasbourg, 1892), I, 73, n. 1.

[2] J. B. Marsden, *History of the Early Puritans* (1850), p. 17.

[3] By Strype (*Cranmer*, ed. Eccles. Hist. Soc. III, 38); by Neal (*Puritans*, I, 74);
and by Canon Dixon (*History of the Church of England*, IV, 684).

[4] As, for example, the twenty-nine English and Scottish followers of Sir
Thomas Stafford who were taken at Scarborough in April 1557 (Strype, *Mem.*
III, ii, 518–19). It is impossible to establish the fact that they had all come with
him from France. There is also danger that some of them who bear the same
surnames as those of known exiles may already have been counted as their
unnamed sons. Nevertheless, for safety's sake the list of names will be found
appended to the Census.

Calculating upon this basis, the total number of adult males whose names have been recovered is 472; the total number of individuals, named and unnamed, men, women, children and servants, is 788. This computation does not include the foreign women who became the wives of exiles abroad, nor the children born abroad, of whom many died, but only those English persons[1] who are known to have crossed the Channel. Of these the analysis stands as follows:

Men, named	472
Wives	100
Women unaccompanied by men	25
Children and adolescents ..	146 (approximate)
Servants, unnamed	45
Total	788

It will be seen that this total tallies almost exactly with Foxe's 'well near to the number of 800 persons'.[2] His general accuracy has thus been vindicated at the same time that his ambiguities have been removed. We possess at last a figure sufficiently scientific to warrant, we think, the drawing of certain new distinctions and conclusions in regard to the nature of the Protestant Exodus.

The first and essential distinction must be that between the two main streams of refugees—one, the earlier, which went to Germany; the other, following Wyatt's rebellion and Dudley's conspiracy, which mainly went to France. The fact that these separate currents have generally been treated as one is no doubt responsible for many of the misconceptions which have arisen in regard to Marian religious policy. In reality the two movements differ from each other at so many

[1] Or Scots who had either held preferment in England or come into close association with the English reformation movement.

[2] It would be above this figure if we could include in it all of Stafford's English and Scottish adventurers, and be sure that all the fellows of St John's College, Cambridge, who resigned with Lever—Lancelot Thexton, Richard Fletcher, John Bee, Henry May, Thomas Kechyn and William Taylor—did actually migrate to the continent. There is however no trace of the latter to be found, in spite of Dr Frere's surmise that they did go (Frere, *op. cit.* pp. 183, 184, 203, 204); while of the former, only those have been admitted to the list who are recorded in the *Foreign Calendar* of 1553.

points that it is very doubtful whether that to France found any place in Cecil's original project. For whereas the first must be considered a genuinely religious movement, even though one in which an undercurrent of politics ran so strongly as ultimately to dominate its activities; the other was frankly political, openly anti-Spanish, and only 'protestant' in so far as that term covered hostility to the Spanish match. One, again, was in character patriarchal, a migration of families; the other, a precipitate scramble for safety on the part of single individuals but lately conspirators. Finally, one was the trek of a religious society in which every class was represented; the other a 'class' demonstration, in which practically none but gentry took part. But to say that the two manifestations of protest differed is not to say that they did not co-operate abroad to the realization of a single purpose—the overthrow of the Marian régime. Since the story of the French adventure has already been told in some detail[1] we shall lay stress only on one aspect of it, as perhaps representing the genesis of a persistent type of later colonial enterprise.

The rebels of 1554, fixing their head-quarters at Rouen and at Caen, seemed as by prescriptive right to be repossessing themselves of Normandy. Yet in 1554 Mary's ambassador at Paris, Dr Nicholas Wotton, gave the estimate that their number 'was never above 150, among whom [were] some Scots and French'.[2] And his figure probably remained a fairly constant one throughout the whole period, since of those who ceaselessly came and went among them, the names of only forty-four in all have been recovered.[3]

The majority of those in France would seem to have been younger sons out for adventure. Some had been henchmen of Northumberland; others were refugees from Wyatt's rebellion and the rising of the west in 1554. Among the latter

---

[1] By A. B. Hinds in his *Making of the England of Elizabeth* (London, 1895). Though his book adds nothing to our knowledge of the exiles in Germany, his account of those in France is based on original material drawn from the French archives, which he discusses in a preface. The book has no bibliography.

[2] *For. Cal.* 1553–8, p. 108.

[3] Barring, as has been said, Stafford's thirty-one associates, of whom only the six, including Stafford himself, that are named in the *Foreign Calendar* have been recorded in the Census.

were the Carews and the Killigrews,[1] men of Cornwall and of Devon, who had turned pirate in the last reign. And though what had been piracy under Edward was held to be laudable patriotism under Mary, still they were merely typical of those lawless elements in an age of transition, which any government would be obliged to repress.

In the present case, however, the pleasures of conspiracy would seem frequently to have palled after a few months. Many, even Sir Peter Carew himself,[2] sued for pardon from the queen (which she generally granted) and the right to return to England (which she generally refused). Instead, the late rebel was often given the privilege of turning spy upon his recent confederates. And this metamorphosis from a state of sin to a state of grace was often so rapid as to make it almost impossible to distinguish between the continuing rebel and the queen's agent.

Two plots, both abortive so far as their immediate purposes were concerned, were fomented by the fugitives with the discreet assistance of the French king. The last of them, Sir Thomas Stafford's attempt to make a landing at Scarborough in 1557,[3] was so childish an affair that fiasco was a foregone conclusion. But the other, Sir Henry Dudley's conspiracy to kill the queen and seize the exchequer, though it was discovered in its initial stages early in the spring of 1556,[4] transferred itself to France, where it had far-reaching consequences. Ultimately it must be held responsible for the loss of Calais;[5] immediately, its effect upon the policy of Mary was as decisive as that of the rebellion of the Northern Lords in 1569 upon the policy of Elizabeth. In both cases conspiracy

---

[1] Strype, *Mem.* II, ii, 31.

[2] *For. Cal.* 1553–8, p. 109, 11 July 1554; Wotton to the Queen, p. 108; and Mason to Petre, 3 July 1555, p. 177.

[3] *For. Cal.* 1553–8, pp. 305–6: Wotton to Bourne, etc. 11 May 1557. Stafford was called by Dudley, in derision, the 'King of Scarborough' (*For. Cal.* p. 306). The manifesto with which Stafford hoped to rouse the country affords an excellent summary of the position of the anti-Spanish party (Strype, *Mem.* III, ii, 515–18).

[4] *Dom. Cal.* 1547–80, pp. 76–84:16 March–31 May. A short table of the events in that conspiracy will be found below, pp. 305–6.

[5] *For. Cal.* 1553–8, pp. 275, 276, Wotton to Queen, Letters of 12 and 30 November 1556.

frustrated what had been a genuine effort at clemency.[1] Not until after Dudley's outbreak did Mary seem to feel herself relieved of all further responsibility in regard to the protestant minority among her subjects, and the commission for Pole's visitation of the diocese of Lincoln, in reality an effort to search out the agents of sedition, followed promptly;[2] 'nor is it expected', wrote the Venetian ambassador, 'that they, or the others who from time to time may be convicted, will by any means obtain either pardon or remission, it being said that the Queen has thus determined, by reason of the small fruit derived from her past indulgence and clemency.' Thereafter those who fled to the Continent no longer did so voluntarily but as men proscribed. A third exodus ensued, in which the political and religious elements are so mixed as to be practically indistinguishable. Many of the fugitives of 1556 can be identified by means of the Frankfort tax-lists of October and January 1556–7,[3] with the sums of money that they had been able to carry out of the realm. Thomas Carell was one. He is probably the Thomas Carwell who with Edmund Beauper[4] had been in command of Wisbech Castle,[5] and a Margaretha Beauper, wife of Dominic,[6] is mentioned for the first time at Frankfort, in the spring of 1557.[7] Cuthbert Warcup was another, the son of that Mistress Warcup who had befriended Jewel in his flight from Oxford;[8] and Jane Wilkinson, the Mistress Wilkinson of the 'Sustainers',[9] who now brought with her to Germany the very considerable sum of 6100 florins.[10] At her death soon after, a generous proportion of this fortune was bequeathed to the support of the exiles.[11]

[1] Cf. *Ven. Cal.* 1555–6, no 37 with *ibid.* no. 482, p. 447: 12 May 1556.

[2] Lambeth Register of Card. Pole, f. 17: 25 April 1556. The preamble to this document, not very accurately transcribed by Strype (*Mem.* III, i, 476–7), is very illuminating. The region covered was that in which Trudgeover, agent of the exiles, had been most active (*Mem.* III, ii, 43 and *P.C.A.* 1556–8, pp. 18, 129–30, 142).

[3] Jung, p. 30.

[4] Of Wel (Wells), Norfolk (Harl. Soc. XII, 381).

[5] *P.C.A.* 1552–4, pp. 302–3: 24 July 1553.

[6] See p. 103, note 2.   [7] Jung, p. 32 and *Hug. Soc. Proc.* IV, 89.

[8] Humphrey's *Jewel*, p. 82.   [9] Strype, *Mem.* III, i, 224, 226–7.

[10] Jung, p. 29.   [11] *Troubles*, p. 178.

It was also in the summer of 1556 that the Marian government first took steps to deal directly with the Englishmen gone over-seas. Efforts to reach them through parliament had failed.[1] Extradition was still a matter of polite agreement between two governments, and uncertain in its operation.[2] If a man was wanted quickly the surest method was to kidnap him. And so Sir John Cheke and Sir Peter Carew[3] were kidnapped near Antwerp on 15 May.[4] A month later, however, an attempt was made to improve upon this drastic method of procedure by issuing a commission[5] for the delivery of 'certeyne letters and commaundementes under their Maiestyes pryvy seale'[6] to those of their subjects who were residing in Germany without permission. A certain John Brett was the bearer of it. But we shall never know whether the letters he carried were warrants for their arrest or merely exhortations from the queen to return home on promise of forgiveness, as Brett would have had the recipients believe.[7] For when the unfortunate messenger attempted to present them he was met by John Hale's claim, made 'Minatory and with threates that the Quenes Maiesty had no power to sende proces into those parties...'.[8] The same claim of no-jurisdiction was made by the Duchess of Suffolk at Weinheim: 'in case they were proces', she said, 'they wolde not receave them sithen they were within an other Prynces domynyons.'[9]

Poor Brett barely escaped with his life from this futile expedition. But his report of it made to the Council on 18 October[10] remains one of the most illuminating documents of the Exile. From it we learn that even as late as 1556 the

---

[1] *Journals H. of C., Parliament of* 1555, pp. 45–6: 26 November–6 December.

[2] *Span. Cal.* 1553, p. 217, Renard, etc. quoting Gardiner, 9 September; cf. also Mary's request for the apprehension of Dudley and Assheton, ignored by the French government, *For. Cal.* 1553–8, p. 221 and *Ven. Cal.* 1555–6, p. 424.

[3] What is probably the first printed account of the affair is to be found in Ponet's *Politike Power*, Sig. I, 6ᵛᵒ–7, but we believe that Sir John Cheke was betrayed on this occasion by his friend Sir Peter Carew. See Census, 'Carew' and 'Cheke'.

[4] *Orig. Let.* I, 132–3, and Fuller, *History*, IV, bk VIII, pp. 232–3.

[5] Brett, 'Narrative', p. 113.   [6] *Ibid.* p. 118.

[7] *Ibid.* pp. 125–6.   [8] *Ibid.* pp. 119–20.

[9] *Ibid.* pp. 125–6.   [10] *Ibid.* p. 131.

English government was proceeding against the fugitives not as heretics but as authors of sedition. All the eleven persons named in the commission were laymen and gentry.[1] The very existence of the 'gospellers' is officially ignored, and casual mention made of only three—Barlow, lately bishop, because he acted as spokesman for the Duchess of Suffolk;[2] Arthur Saule,[3] because he attempted to suborn Brett's servant; and Thomas Becon, who remarked, as he watched Brett ride away from Strasbourg, 'that he wolde not haue bene in [his, Brett's] cote for a Thowsand poundes to haue commed to deliver any letteres in those parties'.[4]

Had the exiles refrained from conspiracy, there can be little doubt that they would have been left abroad in peace to practise what manner of religion they pleased.

But to return for a moment to France: not to the kaleidoscopic plots of Dudley on land, in spite of their tragic outcome, but to the freebooting activities in the Channel which were openly directed against the Spaniards. In March 1554 we hear of 'three ships of Englishmen' who 'have already gone to the sea with Killegrew... to intercept the king of Spain,...'.[5] In 1556 'of the design of Sir Thomas Carden [Cawarden], and others, to stay any treasure going over to King Philip'.[6] There is, in fact, a constant succession of such piratical cruises[7] in which Carews, Killigrews and Horseys figure as the prototypes of that long line of pirates for the propagation of the Gospel who were so soon to transform Elizabeth's insular kingdom into a colonial power. And in all these operations on the sea we are conscious of a spontaneity and abandon quite lacking to Dudley's plodding efforts to rouse the French king. Had the touch with Normandy awakened sleeping instincts? It is as if Englishmen, before they left the old world

[1] Those named were: the Duchess of Suffolk and Richard Bertie, Sir Thomas Wrothe, Sir Henry Nevill, Sir William Stafford, knights; Anthony Mieres, Edward Isaac, William Fyeneux, Roger Whetnall, John Hales, Esquires; and Jane Wilkinson, widow (see Brett, 'Narrative', pp. 114–17, and Census).

[2] Brett, 'Narrative', pp. 125–7.

[3] *Ibid.* p. 129.   [4] *Ibid.* p. 131.

[5] *For. Cal.* 1553–8, p. 66, Thomas Crayer to Lord Grey, 24 March.

[6] *Dom. Cal.* 1547–80, p. 79, Examination of Dethick, 18 April 1556.

[7] See Index to the *Foreign Calendar* for 1553–8.

for the new, needed to renew their strength by contact with those racial elements, Norman and Germanic, from which their peculiar genius derived. Even they themselves were aware of some compelling call of kinship. 'Are not we allianced with Normandy?' said Sir Peter Carew. 'In what ancient house is either there or in France, but we claim by them, and they by us? Why then should we not rather embrace their love, than submit ourselves to the servitude of Spain?'[1]

But if the English sea-dog had his appropriate re-birth in Normandy, the English colonist of the seventeenth century with his persistent bias towards political and religious freedom, was no less a product of exile in Germany. During the next four years (1554–9) this distinction between 'colonist' and 'adventurer' was to be sharply accentuated by experience. And eventually it was to reappear in America in the two essentially different types of colonization which were to carry men of English race across a continent—one, the 'irregular' advance of the individual Southern pioneer, the adventurer; the other, the 'ordered' progress of the 'New England congregation', the corporate colonist.

III

THE MIGRATION TO GERMANY

We must turn now to a more careful analysis of the situation in the Rhine valley as it is revealed in the subjoined list of exiles and in the foreign archives. This was the true 'directed migration', composed of men whose sincere religious convictions were inextricably compounded with politics. Their aims, clear from the beginning, became clearer still as expatriation gave them time to brood upon their condition, and as the pens that defined their political philosophy were further sharpened by their injuries.

When the 75 who were rebels in France and Italy are subtracted from the whole number of 472 fugitives, there are left 397 whose claim to the title of exile for conscience' sake is

[1] *For. Cal.* 1553–8, p. 67; Edgar Hornyold to Bourne, 28 March 1554.

probably genuine. Not all of them, however, went to Germany. Two at least, Thomas Wilson[1] and George Acworth,[2] found their way to Rome. Thomas Bickley of Magdalen, who had been chaplain to Edward VI and was to become bishop of Chichester, is believed to have hidden himself in France.[3] Two, Hamby and Soccus, remained throughout students at Padua; while of 31 others the place of refuge is unknown. This leaves about 361 who may be definitely assigned to one or other of the English colonies in Germany, and to whom belonged the 100 wives and 146 children who left England with them. Calvin's injunction to let their departure be 'tel comme d'Egypte, troussant vos hardes avec vous',[4] had been literally obeyed. Often, as we have said, entire households, like that of Sir William Stafford at Geneva, moved into exile in feudal state, and possibly with feudal self-sufficiency, for though all are not enumerated in the Livre des Anglois, it seems not unlikely that several of the 'rubantiers', 'cordonniers' and 'couturiers', even 'laboureurs' who are registered as Englishmen in the list of Genevan 'residents', were servants of his or of William Fuller's.[5] In lesser degree the same thing was true of the gentry at Strasbourg and at Frankfort; while Brett's account of his first view of the castle at Weinheim leaves the impression that the Duchess of Suffolk's original retinue of eight had been heavily augmented in transit.[6]

If such were the conditions in which flight was undertaken, it seems more than ever improbable that escape could have been achieved without the connivance of the English government.

Nevertheless, all told, the 'gospellers' with their families and servants amounted to no more than 678 souls[7]—a number

[1] Lawyer for Chetwood in his papal suit (see Census).

[2] *For. Cal.* 1558-9, p. 18, no. 58, Acworth to Cardinal Pole, 1 December 1558; cf. Acworth to Elizabeth, *ibid.* p. 31.

[3] Humphrey's *Jewel*, p. 73.

[4] Bonnet, I, 259, Calvin to 'un Seigneur français'.

[5] Cf. Registre des Habitants, Geneva, f. 196.

[6] Brett, 'Narrative', pp. 122-3. Bishop Barlow, for example, had become attached to her household, whether with his wife and children or not we are not told.

[7] These figures take on a new significance in the light of the recent emigration from the Saar. It is estimated that 4830 Saarlanders entered France

so small in relation to the population of England that with-drawal must have seemed to them imperative if they were not to be lost in the overwhelming catholic majority. 'God is not to be tempted,' exhorted Knox, 'but is to be hard [*sic*], feared, and obeied, whan thus earnestlye he calleth and threteneth not without cause, passe from the middes of her O my people (...) that you bee not partakers of her plages.'[1] Fear of persecution may have lurked in the consciousness of many protestants as it did in Cranmer's,[2] many had already experienced it under Henry, but the dominant note in all the letters and pamphlets of the period from August 1553 onward is 'to flie the infection of the antechristian [*sic*] doctryne by departure oute of the realme', for fear of absorption.[3]

But those who preferred banishment to conformity were, even so, only the extreme left wing of the Edwardian reforma-tion—a minority of a minority. We have seen already how small a proportion of those receiving priest's orders between 1548 and 1553 went to the Continent—only eight.[4] For the whole number of exiles the proportion of fully ordained clergy to 'students' was probably not more than 67 to 119. In 1559 it was from the ranks of these students, educated abroad, that a large number of the first Elizabethan ordinands were to be drawn.[5] Flight had separated them from the

between 13 January and 20 February 1935 (cf. *The Times*, 1 February and *The Daily Telegraph*, 20 February) out of a population of just under 800,000 (*Statesman's Year Book*). Yet this minority is held to be 'numerically in-significant', in relation to the whole. The population of England in the six-teenth century is roughly estimated at four million. Thus the proportion for the English religious exodus stands at 678 to 4,000,000.

[1] Knox's *Admonition to the Faithful* (ed. Dorcaster), Sig. E4; cf. also Ridley to the Brethren, Coverdale, *Letters of the Martyrs*, f. 28; P. Martyr's 'Epistle touching the Flying awaie etc.', *Commonplaces* (ed. 1583), pp. 65–81 (close of the volume).

[2] Cranmer's Letter to Mrs Wilkinson, Strype, *Cranmer* (Eccles. Hist. ed.), III, 460–1.

[3] Ridley, *Piteous Lamentation*, Sig. C 5vo.

[4] Only 63 are given in the List in the *Defensio*, Cranmer's *Works* (Parker Soc.), which, with Strype's eight additions, becomes 71 (*Cranmer*, III, 38–9).

[5] Cf. Grindal's ordinations for 1560 (Strype, *Grindal*, pp. 58–60) and Parker's significant admonition to him 'to forbear ordaining any more arti-ficers and others that had been of secular occupations, that were unlearned; which they, the Bishops, had been forced to do at first...for the supply of the vacant churches:...' (*ibid.* pp. 59–60).

English Church; accident alone, that is the dearth of clergy to fill the vacancies,[1] seems to have been responsible for ever re-uniting them to it, but for many the connection was not long to endure. Nearly all remained in high disfavour during the reign and most of them, as their biographies will show, were sequestered for nonconformity before its close. For we are dealing with the embryo of the Puritan party both clerical and lay.

The Census has revealed that the predominant character of the exodus was aristocratic. In the following table I have attempted to give an approximate estimate of the distribution of the exiles according to classes. It must be understood, however, to be *only* approximate. Accurate ascription in very many cases has been impossible. Several of the clergy, for example, might equally well be numbered among the gentry, while several of the 'preachers' were of very humble origin. The social status of the 'printers' is indefinable. It has therefore been thought wiser to make the analysis upon the basis of function and occupation rather than of birth. Even so, 19 men have eluded classification altogether. But of the remaining 453, there were probably of

Gentry	166
Clergy, in priest's orders ..	67
Theological 'students' ..	119
Merchants	40
Artisans	32
Printers..	7
Total	431

To these must be added 3 lawyers, 3 physicians, 3 yeoman and 13 servants (named), making the total of 472: 453 classified, 19 unclassified.

That only three would appear to have had any connection with the common law serves to corroborate the conservative tendencies of the profession under Elizabeth. But of the

---

[1] Citations are too numerous to be given here. The absence of 'shepherds' is the burden of the correspondence of returned exiles. See *Zurich Letters*, etc.

other figures, the revelations run counter to tradition. Compare, for example, the relatively small number of priests with the large body of 'students', comprising Edwardian deacons,[1] theological students in the making, self-constituted 'preachers' and ex-religious not in orders. It will be seen that already the anti-sacerdotal trend of this ministerial migration was assuming significant proportions. Of those again who were actually priests, it will appear upon analysis[2] that by far the greater number, in fact 59 to 8, had been ordained under Henry, not under Edward. In other words, they were men who had already experienced persecution in an earlier reign. At least six of them had once before trodden the path to Zurich.[3] If then persecution must still be accounted one of the original impulses to flight, let the adjective Henrican be substituted for that of Marian before it.

The next illuminating comparison is that between the artisans and the gentry. The country gentlemen are revealed as the largest single group in the total migration; the artisans nearly the smallest. This fact alone goes far to prove how fundamentally the character of the English Protestant Exodus differed from its Italian and Flemish predecessors, as well as from the contemporary movement of French protestants to Geneva. The dominant influence in it was aristocratic and political at a time when in France even the Colignys had not yet openly espoused the protestant cause.[4] The aloofness of the French upper classes was in fact a matter of considerable mortification to Calvin.[5] And the Registre des Habitants at

---

[1] The status of the deacon abroad was peculiar, altered significantly by the fact of his exile. At home he was a cleric who would normally have proceeded to priest's orders—in short an embryo priest. But abroad this was not so. No provision for further ordination existed in the revised liturgies of either Frankfort or Geneva. Canonically, then, the deacon was never to be more than a deacon, and as such could not administer the Sacrament. Functionally, then, he remained a layman.

[2] Cf. above, p. 6.

[3] Bale, Coverdale, Traheron, William Turner, Edmund Allen, and John Finch.

[4] Lavisse, v, pt ii, p. 242. See also above, p. 17, note 1.

[5] Bonnet, ii, 163, Calvin to Antoine de Bourbon, 14 December 1557, or *Calvini Opera*, xv, no. 2774, p. 731. Lavisse (v, pt ii, p. 238) quotes a letter of Calvin to d'Andelot Coligny, written in 1558, in which Calvin says that

Geneva show scarcely a gentle or even a professional name among the countless artisans who took refuge there. Some years yet were to elapse before the protestant cause in France was to enter the political field as the Huguenot party.[1] But from 1554 to 1558 the protestant gentry of England were using the opportunity of exile to organize themselves into a formidable 'opposition'. Through misfortune they had gained solidarity as a party; and in the comparative security of Germany they soon developed a political technique which employed every device known to later campaigning from the party 'slogan' to the party 'press'. At Dantzig in 1554 a certain Englishman named Hotson (q.v.) had had printed a libel against Queen Mary of which some hundred copies were sent back to London there to be strewn in the streets.[2] The pamphlet literature of the period is enormous, and though theological in form is political by implication.[3] All of it was to be disseminated in England for purposes of propaganda. English printers were thus suddenly thrust into a rôle of importance hitherto unknown to them. Three who became ardent servants of the Elizabethan reformation were probably among the exiles either at Strasbourg, Basle, or Geneva,[4] and of these John Day,[5] who, in the words of his epitaph, first 'set a Fox

'Jusques icy ceulx qui ont esté appelez au martyre ont esté contemptibles [méprisables] au monde, tant pour la qualité de leurs personnes que pour ce que le nombre n'a pas esté si grand pour un coup', but so far I have not been able to trace this particular letter either in the *Calvini Opera* or in Bonnet's *Lettres Françaises de Calvin*.

[1] The birth of the 'party' is assigned to the autumn of 1559. It did not come into being officially until 1560. Cf. Mariéjol, *Catherine de Médicis* (Paris, 1922), p. 71.

[2] *For. Cal.* 1553–8, nos. 238, 239, p. 105: 17 April 1554.

[3] Cf. John Bradforth's objections in his *Letter to the Earls of Arundel, Derby, etc.* that its real political import was too much obscured by religious propaganda (cf. pp. 340–1 of Strype's version, *Mem.* III, ii, pp. 340–54), but the inaccuracy of Strype's transcript of this most interesting letter should be noted by comparison with the original edition in the Brit. Mus. (C 8. b 8). See 'Bradforth', Census.

[4] Rowland Hall at Geneva and Robert Crowley at Frankfort must also be included.

[5] John Gough Nicholls is my authority for this statement in his article on Day in the *Gentleman's Magazine* quoted above, but the conversation between Day and Rogers in prison (Fox, VI, 610) makes it almost certain that Day did go abroad.

to wright how Martyrs runne';[1] Richard Jugge, who became Elizabeth's official printer;[2] and probably Edward Whitchurch,[3] who with Richard Grafton had published both the first and second Prayer Books of Edward VI, are to be reckoned the most important. And now Hugh Singleton, printer of seditious pamphlets and book-binder,[4] can at last be numbered with certainty among the refugees;[5] while the asylum of Thomas Gibson, printer and physician, is found to have been Strasbourg, the political centre of exile, and not Geneva.[6]

No doubt it was this early association with the reformers in exile which confirmed the strong bias towards puritanism and away from humanism which distinguished the English from the French printer of the sixteenth century—a bias deplored by the late Sir Sidney Lee.[7] But this formidable alliance between the protestant party and the press[8] is one of the secrets of its rapid triumph over the catholic majority. By June 1559 the English reformers had gained possession of the fabric of the churches (as they never did in France),[9] of the official pulpit, and of the press.[10] The combination proved irresistible.

[1] Facsimile printed in the *Gent. Mag.* November 1832, opp. p. 417.

[2] This identification of the 'Jugge' of the Emden list with the printer has been made by others, but is not absolutely proven.

[3] It is believed that he fled, and married abroad Cranmer's widow (*D.N.B.*), but no trace of him has been found there.

[4] *The Library*, xiv, 134.

[5] Strasbourg protocols, Saturday, August 21, 1557, Append. p. 370. Basle, Öffnungsbuch, viii, f. 179, Append. p. 361. For previous speculation on the problem of Singleton's whereabouts between 1553 and 1558, see Gordon Duff's *Century of the English Book Trade* (p. 148), which says merely that what he was doing 'is not known'; H. R. Plomer's article in *The Library*, i, 3rd ser. pp. 54–72, which suggests that he may have been in Dublin; and that by H. J. Byrom, *ibid.* xiv, 121–56, which inclines to the belief (pp. 125–8) that he remained in London.

[6] Append. pp. 366–7, and cf. J. S. Burn, *Livre des Anglois*, p. 11, n. 29.

[7] *The French Renaissance in England* (1910), pp. 88–9.

[8] For the same alliance in France, cf. Battifol, *Century of the Renaissance* (London, 1927), p. 179.

[9] Cf. Lavisse, v, pt ii, p. 219.

[10] It is quite likely that the association of *Mary's* official printer, John Cawood, with Richard Jugge, as *Elizabeth's* official printers, was due to the queen's direct intervention. Even in the printing trade a just religious balance was to be preserved.

'Students' trained under Calvin at Geneva, or in the hastily improvised 'universities' established by Peter Martyr at Strasbourg,[1] and by the English divines themselves at Frankfort,[2] were ready to fill the places of the clergy who had defected from the protestant ranks. A set plan and an undeviating purpose seem to be apparent in nearly every aspect of the Marian Exile, and it may be as well at this point to review the evidence which has led to this conclusion.

First let it be remembered that the English protestants already possessed what might be called 'working models' for the very type of religious colony which they afterwards created in Germany. These were the foreign congregations that between 1550 and 1553 had established themselves in London and Glastonbury[3] under the direct patronage of Somerset, William Cecil, his secretary, Sir John Cheke, and Archbishop Cranmer.[4] Each congregation was presided over by a minister who acted both as its preacher and executive head.

Again, the actual order of events between 6 August and 15 September[5]—between, that is, John Roger's 'vehement' sermon preached against 'pestilent popery'[6] only three days after Mary's entry into London, and the voluntary withdrawal to Denmark of John à Lasco's congregation[7]—admits but one plausible interpretation: the protestants were choosing to break the religious truce. In those six weeks by a series of provocative acts, among which Cranmer's forced declaration

[1] Fuller, *History*, IV, bk VII, p. 230.

[2] *Troubles*, p. 60.

[3] In London: the Dutch congregation under John à Lasco and Peter Deloenus, which by patent was granted the church of the Austin Friars for a 'Temple' (*Cal. of. Pat. Rolls*, Edward VI, III, 317); the French congregation, under François Peruçel; and the Italian, under Michael Angelo Florio, father of John Florio. At Glastonbury: the community of Walloon weavers under Valerand Poullain, which was later to be closely associated, liturgically, with the evolution of the English Prayer Book at Frankfort. Mr H. J. Cowell has brought together the recorded facts in regard to it in an article in the *Hug. Soc. Proc.* XIII (pp. 483–515) and in a brochure printed at Glastonbury (1928) under the title of *The Church of the Strangers*.

[4] Schickler, I, 11 and Strype's *Cranmer*, pp. 336, 346.

[5] Cf. above, p. 2.   [6] Foxe, VI, 592.

[7] It will be remembered that the proclamation against foreigners was not issued until February 1554.

against the mass on 5 September had peculiar significance,[1] the extremists of the faction seized the initiative and deliberately forced the protestant issue upon a government that would gladly have held it in abeyance. Having secured by these shrewd tactics a much needed light on the true state of public opinion, which they declared had become 'vox populi, vox Diaboli',[2] they also secured cover for their projected withdrawal and gave to that withdrawal its show of justification.

Further, the sudden departure of Sir Francis Knollys to the Continent at this early date would be inexplicable except upon the hypothesis that he was being sent on a journey of reconnaissance to review the European ground and to discuss with Calvin the practicability of an English exodus.[3] Then, after a lapse of time just sufficient to cover his survey of the situation and a report upon it, that exodus took place, and did so in orderly fashion—gentry by households, students by groups under a leader. And with the single exception of Zurich, where Englishmen needed no introduction, the cities chosen for refuge were those and only those where the fugitives had been preceded by one or other of the foreign congregations so recently their guests.

Indications then follow abroad of continued control from England. A messenger service was established between London and the colonies which functioned without apparent interruption; traces survive, though not easy to interpret, of two attempts to bring the separate colonies into some closer form of association,[4] while it is clear from the significant words used by 'Maister purse bearer Chambers',[5] that he was but a subordinate acting for superiors and that financial control of the whole experiment was retained elsewhere, presumably by the committee of four in London whose guiding intelligence was William Cecil.

Finally, as in itself an indication of a considerable degree of effective organization among the colonies themselves, and

[1] See 'Scory', Census.   [2] *Span. Cal.* 1553, p. 217.
[3] See 'Sir Francis Knollys', Census.
[4] An attempted explanation is given under 'Ponet' and 'Whittingham' in the Census.
[5] See 'Richard Chambers', Census.

between those colonies and the protestant party in England, there is the grimly efficient working of the exiles' press campaign against the queen—a ceaseless, pitiless pamphlet warfare which the Council was powerless to stay. 'Wherever they go,' wrote the Venetian ambassador,[1] 'whether to Italy, Germany, or France, they licentiously disseminate many things against the English government and the present religion. . . .' If this was not the first, it was certainly one of the earliest instances of the power of the press to make and unmake governments.

In all, eight communities were organized during the five years of exile. But three of them, Basle, Geneva and Aarau, were later offshoots from the original five—Emden, Wesel, Zurich, Strasbourg and Frankfort. And just as we have seen at Zurich, that the way was prepared by an advance agent,[2] so at Emden, Wesel, Strasbourg and Frankfort arrangements for the coming of the English were made by the fugitive groups of Dutch and Walloons who had opportunely left England in the previous September (1553).

At Wesel, François Peruçel,[3] *alias* de la Rivière, late pastor of the French Church in London,[4] had established his congregation before 13 March 1554.[5] It was to Peruçel, who had received kindness from the Duchess of Suffolk in London,[6] that her husband, Richard Bertie, wrote in February 1555, asking him to obtain permission from the magistrates for their settlement in the town. Peruçel's door was not 'casually discovered'[7] by the fugitives on the stormy night of their arrival, as has been related.

At Frankfort, the Glastonbury Weavers under their

---

[1] *Ven. Cal.* 1555–6, no. 274, pp. 243–4: 11 November 1555.

[2] See above, pp. 8–9.

[3] This name is variously spelt, Perrussel, Perusell, etc. He was a French shoemaker who had been 'Instructor of Novices' in a Paris convent and who became later minister of the French refugee churches of London, Wesel and Frankfort, and chaplain to the Prince de Condé (Schickler, I, 9, and Beza, *Hist. Eccles.* I, p. 47 and note).

[4] Founded about November 1548, Utenhovius to Fagius, 20 November 1548 (quoted by Schickler, *ibid.*).

[5] See Calvin's Letter, 'Aux Frères de Wesel', of that date, Bonnet, I, 418–22: 13 March 1554.

[6] Lady Bertie's *Five Generations*, p. 25 and Foxe, VIII, 573.

[7] *D.N.B.*

minister, Valerand Poullain,[1] obtained an authorization from the city's council on 18 March 1554 to organize their cult.[2] It was on 19 April that their first service was held in the church of the White Ladies[3] which the English afterwards shared, yet William Whittingham and his company of three Englishmen did not make their appearance until 27 June.[4] That same night Valerand Poullain came to Whittingham's lodgings to report on the arrangements he had succeeded in making for their reception.[5] Only upon the supposition of some previous and even quite recent communication between the two men can Whittingham's peculiarly off-hand manner on this occasion be accounted for. Otherwise his way of acknowledging the Frenchman's good offices must appear quite gratuitously discourteous.

At Emden, a portion of John à Lasco's London congregation held their first public service on 20 May 1554.[6] John Scory, who was to become minister of the English refugees there, could not have arrived until after 14 July,[7] on which date he had made a recantation and been absolved by Bonner.

At Strasbourg the exiles were preceded by Peter Martyr and by Pierre Alexandre,[8] of whose French congregation they were to be members. The latter probably left London with à Lasco on 15 September 1553. The former, after receiving his passport from the Council,[9] took ship about the same time, and reached Strasbourg on 29 or 30 October[10] (1553). The first Englishmen did not arrive there until the spring of 1554. Thomas Heton's request for burgher rights on 4 April is the

---

[1] Again the name is variously spelled. He was the son of a bourgeois of Lille who graduated at Louvain and became a priest in 1540. He had already been pastor at Strasbourg from 1547 to 1548, then became tutor to the son of Lord Derby in 1551 (Schickler, I, 59 ff.).

[2] Schickler, I, 72, n. 1; Bonnet, II, 81–2, note.

[3] E. Doumergue, *Calvin* (1899–1927), II, 530; Anne Hooper to Bullinger, *Orig. Let.* I, 111.

[4] *Troubles*, p. 5.   [5] *Ibid.*

[6] Utenhovius, *Narratio*, p. 233.   [7] Burnet, V, no. XIII, 389.

[8] Late prebendary of Canterbury deprived in March 1554, but already fled (Strype, *Cranmer*, p. 472). He had been a guest in Cranmer's house (*ibid.* p. 279).

[9] *Orig. Let.* I, 372.

[10] Cf. Martyr to Calvin, 3 November 1554; Gorham, *Gleanings*, p. 306; and Martyr to Bullinger, *Orig. Let.* II, 505.

first official intimation we have of their presence in the city, but from Peter Martyr it is learned that a considerable body of students had already made their appearance there in February.[1]

Each one of these colonies had a special character of its own. Possibly each one had also its special function in the general scheme, though in comparison with the prominent parts played by the others the rôles of Wesel and of Emden have heretofore been somewhat obscure.[2] Fuller's statement that Emden was the financial clearing-house for the exiles—'there the merchants which bear the bag'[3]—has so far not been borne out by the evidence. In fact Strasbourg, with its group of resident English merchants, would seem to have had a better claim to play that part than Emden. But what is becoming increasingly clear is that Emden was the exiles' headquarters of propaganda. As a port it was admirably situated for the purpose, being in easy touch both with London and the Rhine valley. There, too, was the press of Egidius van der Erve, alias Gellius Ctematius, the Dutch printer who had lately been a deacon in John à Lasco's London congregation. Recent researches on the part of Colonel Isaac have now established the very strong presumption that it was van der Erve's press which was responsible for printing, not only the Emden edition of Cranmer's *Defensio* (1557),[4] but many of the English pamphlets designed by Knox and Scory and William Turner for the torment of Queen Mary.[5] Dr Turner had been the Duke of Somerset's physician, Scory was the pastor of the 'not very frequent' Emden congregation. These men had no doubt been van der Erve's friends in London, and with them at Emden was Sir John Cheke, 'also for some time', says Strype, 'in this place'.[6] We make bold to suggest that Cheke was no other than the 'director of propaganda', which, if so, would go far to explain why he of all the refugees was

---

[1] Protocols, vol. 32, f. 113, see Append. p. 362 and *Orig. Let.* ii, 514; cf. above, pp. 8–9.

[2] Cf. Fuller's well-known summary, *History*, iv, bk viii, pp. 205–6.

[3] *Ibid.* p. 208.   [4] Strype, *Cranmer*, p. 374.

[5] See Col. F. S. Isaac's *Egidius van der Erve and his English Printed Books*, Bibliographical Society, London, 1931.

[6] Strype, *Cranmer*, p. 374.

singled out by the Marian government for capture.[1] In these pamphlets a lively trade was carried on across the Channel by means of the 'messengers'[2] already spoken of, who were regularly employed for their dissemination in London and Kent.[3] And from the ports, they were carried through East Anglia by Trudgeover, whose activities were also directed by the exiles.[4]

Wesel, again, was a short-lived colony, but eventually experienced a re-incarnation at Aarau. Originally about 100 English, men and women,[5] had gathered there around the 'Lady Suffolk', whose 'goodly wit', complained Sir Richard Morison, was waited upon by 'too froward a will'.[6] Perhaps the most important member of this group was John Bodley, father of Sir Thomas, who may be suspected of having largely financed the anti-Spanish rebellion in the West.[7] The exiles are peculiarly reticent in regard to this community, whose eviction from the town was due, they claimed, to Lutheran animosity. Animosity on the part of the citizens there certainly had been. Before Lutheran Wesel would receive them at all in 1554, Melanchthon's intervention had to be sought.[8] The guilds, too, may have been hostile, since a large proportion of the English were weavers. Nevertheless the fact remains that their departure was not demanded by the magistrates until the significant year 1556,[9] when there is good reason to believe that the colony had become involved in Sir Henry Dudley's designs on Calais.[10] Not only do we now know from Hans Dür's list that at least five members of the Wesel congregation

[1] Cf. above, p. 36, note 3.

[2] Among these was Elizabeth Young, a woman working alone; Thomas Bryce, 'that brought books from Wesel'; John Ledley (Foxe, VIII, 384; *Mem.* III, ii, pp. 63, 148, 415); Thomas Horton (Census); William Porrege (Census); Thomas Sprat (Census). Only those who are believed to have had their headquarters abroad are included in the list of exiles.

[3] Strype, *Cranmer*, p. 511, and cf. Pollard, *Pol. Hist. Eng.* VI, 162.

[4] See above p. 35, note 2, and especially *Ven. Cal.* 1555–6, p. 578.

[5] *Mem.* III, i, 233.

[6] Cf. Morison to Throckmorton, *For. Cal.* 1547–53, p. 101.

[7] *Autobiography of Sir Thomas Bodley*, pp. 1–2; see also Census.

[8] *Cranmer*, pp. 507–8.   [9] Lever to Bullinger, etc., *Orig. Let.* I, 168.

[10] *For. Cal.* 1553, pp. 144, 157, 158, and cf. H. F. Chittle's article on Calais, *E.H.R.* 1935, p. 500. He places the disappearance of the protestant minority from Calais in 1554, which tallies with the arrival of the English at Wesel.

had been townsmen of Calais (some of them, like the Turpins, important townsmen), but we also know that another member, Lord John Audley, was, in all probability, the father-in-law of Dudley himself.[1] Where, too, John Bodley and the Berties were, there we may be sure was also active opposition to the Marian régime. It thus became most undesirable for Wesel to harbour the colony any longer at a point so near to the borders of the Netherlands.[2]

Accordingly, in the spring of 1557, the fugitives went a second time into exile. John Bodley finally settled at Geneva;[3] a few joined the Frankfort colony; the Berties went first to Weinheim, then to Poland; but the majority, 93 persons in all, at last found shelter at Aarau on 11 August 1557.[4] Until now little has been known of this congregation, born late in time, beyond the rather confused account of its wanderings given by Thomas Lever.[5] The site of Aarau on a hill-top over-looking the river Aar between Basle and Zurich is one peculiarly remote, an excellent hiding-place, and the group of fugitives who came to it differed in character from any of the other English communities. It is the only one where the majority were of humble origin, the only one which was pre-dominantly industrial; and the only one, we believe, which was officially permitted to pursue a gainful calling while abroad.[6] Twelve, perhaps even seventeen,[7] of its thirty men,

---

[1] *P.C.A.* 1554–6, p. 101: Lady Audeley from the Council, February 1554–5.

[2] Fuller gives their proximity to the Netherlands as the reason for their withdrawal but inverts, we believe, cause and effect (IV, 205–6). Cf. with this *For. Cal.* 1553–8, p. 275, Wotton to Mary, 12 November 1556; also Strype, *Mem.* III, i, 566–70.

[3] *Autobiography*, pp. 2–3, and Livre des Anglois, Martin, p. 333: 8 May 1557.

[4] For the date see the Official Record, Append. p. 353; Lever's letter to Gualter (*Orig. Let.* I, 166–8) was thus written on the very day of their arrival.

[5] His letters, with two important ones of John Young, alias Johannes Jung (*q.v.*) (*Orig. Let.* I, 164, 167, and notes), a Swiss, who acted as advance agent for the English, are printed in *Orig. Let.* I, nos. LXXXII–VII, pp. 160–70. From the evidence of the official record the dates of nos. LXXXII–V should be 1557 and not 1556.

[6] For Frankfort, Jung, p. 17. For Strasbourg, see Append. Gibson, p. 365, and Singleton, p. 370. Johannes Jung (see Census, under 'John Young') obtained for them a 'license to engage in the manufacture of wool, in spite of the opposition of the more wealthy of the inhabitants' (*Orig. Let.* I, 167, n. 2).

[7] Including five for whom no calling is given.

and several of its women, were weavers. Five only were
gentlemen, but with the single exception of 'Lord John of
Audeley', none was a man of rank. Yet among the eight
students and preachers is to be found no less a person than
Miles Coverdale.[1] His two years spent in the absolute seclu-
sion of Aarau with his wife and children form an episode
hitherto unknown in his life. Leisure for study must have
been his object, for apparently no pastoral duties devolved
upon him. Those were performed by Thomas Lever, who had
shepherded his flock all the way from Wesel. On Sundays
'nebend denen Stünden, als wir [the Argovians] unsere
Predginen habend',[2] Lever was permitted to preach in the
Stadtskirche to his congregation of ninety-three souls, representing no fewer than twelve English counties ranging from
York in the north to Devon in the west, and Kent in the
east, and thus presenting a curious geographical epitome of
England.[3] Four of its humble members had belonged to
Rowland Taylor's[4] parish of Hadleigh in Suffolk; three were
weavers from Lancashire; five, as we have seen, came from
Calais. Largely, no doubt because its members had work to
do, Aarau has the enviable distinction of being the least
quarrelsome of the English colonies. 'For we have been
truthfully informed', reads their passport, 'that each and
every one of them has...conducted himself there as an honest
and peaceful Christian.'[5]

It was also the most stable of the communities. What
changes in personnel occurred between its arrival on 11
August 1557[6] and its departure about 2 January 1559[7] were

---

[1] Official List, Append. p. 355, and Hans Dür's list, *Urkundenbuch*, pp.
lxiii–v.

[2] Append. p. 354.

[3] Devon, Dorset, Essex, Hertford, Kent, Lancashire, Lincoln, Somerset,
Suffolk, Sussex, Worcester and York.

[4] Martyred at Hadleigh, 9 February 1555.

[5] Basle, Kirchenakten, A. 3, f. 198, see Append. p. 359.

[6] Cf. Append. p. 353. There seems to be a slight discrepancy between
Hans Dür's list and the official one in regard to the date of the English arrival.
Hans Dür says that it was on the 'mentag nach Jacobi' (see above, p. 25).
Now St James's day is 25 July, and in 1557 'the Monday after James' would
have fallen on 26 July.

[7] Append. p. 354.

caused by birth and death,[1] not by the restless coming and going of its members. Yet neither its stability nor its good temper gives Aarau its special claim to remembrance, but rather the fact that in its movement from Wesel *as a congregation under the leadership of a pastor*,[2] it provided after 1630 a model for the development of a new type of corporate colonization in New England[3]—which thereafter became distinctively characteristic of the whole Puritan movement westward to the Pacific from Massachusetts Bay.

Twice already we have hinted at the usually unstable nature of these English congregations whose normal condition seems to have been one of permanent impermanence. Throughout the term of exile, each colony, though it continued to exist after its own special pattern, to legislate for itself according to its own peculiar religious and political persuasion, to quarrel uninterruptedly within its own confines as well as with its English neighbours, yet continued to change its membership so constantly that the component parts of any one community are found, in different combinations, to have formed the component parts of nearly every other community at some time during its existence.

On the 'permanent' side of the ledger, however, we find considerable buying of property on the part of the refugees. Most unfortunately no records survive at Strasbourg which make it possible to identify the houses bought or rented there by Englishmen, though no doubt many of these are still standing. As also at Frankfort, four hundred years seem to have obliterated even the memory of the English sojourn,[4] but the streets of the old town in the quarter known as Little France, or in the neighbourhood of the Hospital, must wear much the same aspect to-day, with their timbered and carved

[1] Eight died (Append. p. 356), most of whom were children. There is no official record of births, but some evidently took place.

[2] Curiously reminiscent of the Greek method of colonizing by potential city-groups carrying the sacred fire, and under the leadership of an official oekist.

[3] E. Channing, *History of the United States*, I, 399–411; H. L. Osgood, *American Colonies in the Seventeenth Century*, vol. I, chap. VII; and cf. above, p. 38.

[4] Upon the authority of Monsieur le Pasteur Adam, whose knowledge of old Strasbourg is exhaustive.

houses, as they did to the eyes of Sir Anthony Cooke and Sir Thomas Wrothe in the sixteenth century. That Sir Anthony Cooke *had* a house there we know from John Brett's rather sinister reference to it. The 'Riter kneght' who was hired by the English to dog his footsteps, perhaps to kill him, was procured, he says, by 'a frencheman that came with the Archeheretik of Geneva [Calvin] which frencheman was well acquaynted in Sir Anthony Cookes howse in Strawsebourg'.[1] Whether Sir Richard Morison eventually decided 'not to decline the house voluntarily offered here, and which by reason of the garden adjoining is very convenient',[2] we do not know, but as he remained in Strasbourg till his death in March 1556, he very likely did. John Ponet, we find from the Protocols, leased a house in the Winemarket. Unfortunately it was burned to the ground before the transaction was actually completed and with it the fugitive bishop of Winchester lost 4000 crowns worth of silver, jewels and cash, acquired we know not how, for which he asked and apparently received compensation from the city.[3]

At Frankfort our knowledge is more specific. The various lists of strangers, compiled for and by the authorities, yield an abundance of explicit information in regard to their dwelling-places. Thomas Becon, we are told, dwelt 'uff dem Rossmarck';[4] Richard Davies, who in 1561 was to become bishop of St David's, lived 'bey dem Prediger closter';[5] Sir John Hales's house, into which Brett actually penetrated with his letters, stood 'bey der cronn [probably an inn] in der fahrstatt [vorstadt?]'.[6]

Sometimes these transactions serve to throw a little light on the private lives of the exiles while abroad, of which otherwise we know so little. In May 1556, for instance, we find that David Whitehead, who was to be a member of the committee of Prayer Book revision in 1559, bought a 'Haus und Hof' with a garden, at the corner of 'the Breiten Gasse',[7] for 500

---

[1] Brett, 'Narrative', p. 130.
[2] To Henry Bullinger 23 August 1555, *Orig. Let.* I, 148.
[3] See 'Ponet', Census.   [4] Jung, p. 41.
[5] *Ibid.* p. 48.   [6] *Ibid.* p. 51.
[7] *Ibid.* p. 63.

gulden. Evidently this was a considerable piece of property.[1] Yet in October of the same year he sold it again to Thomas Wattes,[2] a fellow-exile, and we find that in those six months Whitehead had lost his wife Anna. Without a 'Hausfrau' to oversee it, evidently he found his establishment too heavy a burden for him, and abandoned it to live with his two children under the same roof with Richard Luddington.[3]

Generally speaking, however, the traces left by 'die Engellender' in the cities of their adoption are very few indeed.[4] In spite of the numbers and worldly importance of those who lived in Basle, minute search has discovered but two private houses occupied by them. One was that of the merchant, John Bartholomew, on the Petersplatz,[5] and the other the 'kleine hüslin',[6] formerly 'inhabited by Sister Ursula',[7] which we suspect was hired for the use of Lady Dorothy Stafford when she fled from Geneva after her husband's death.[8] Where Sir Francis Walsingham lived when he was a student at the university in 1555;[9] or the three sons of Sir Anthony Denny; or Elizabeth's councillor Sir Francis Knollys, that we do not know, unless they lodged with the community of English 'students' who later dwelt together in the Clarakloster across the river. The records of this building, once a convent attached to the church of St Clara, reveal that in 1557 it was leased to 'die Engellender' for a yearly sum of £24.[10] Fortunately there also survives a practically contemporary map of the Claraplatz,[11] showing the size of the Clarakloster and its

---

[1] Belonging originally to Adolf von Glauburg, nephew of John Glauburg, who was 'one off the chiefest Senators' and especial friend of the English refugees. 'Adulphus Glauburge' was a Doctor of Law and became a supporter of Cox's party (*Troubles*, p. 45).

[2] Jung, p. 63. [3] *Hug. Soc. Proc.* IV, 89.

[4] Cf. Jung, p. 3 and p. 6, n. 1.

[5] Staatsarchiv, Gen. Reg. der Personen, 1551–60.

[6] Possibly this is the little house which in the plan stands at right angles to the cloister. See Frontispiece.

[7] Staatsarchiv, St Clara R. Corpus, 1557, f. 23. For £4 yearly.

[8] Martin, *Protestants Anglais*, pp. 57–8. See also her reception as a burgher, Append. p. 360.

[9] Matrikel, I, f. 193. See Append. p. 358.

[10] St Clara R. Corpus, 1557, f. 17vo, Append. p. 361. A fact not known before even in Basle.

[11] See Frontispiece.

situation in relation to the church. And from this again it may be plausibly argued that a house,[1] of the same proportions and of the same general lines, which stands in exactly the same position to-day was built upon the old foundations, and is, therefore, a fairly satisfactory reproduction of the building in which John Foxe wrote his *Book of Martyrs*.

The discovery answers many questions in regard to the daily life of the community of English 'students' at Basle. Evidently they lived here 'in collegio', as they did at Zurich in the house belonging to Froschauver. Built originally for a dormitory, the Clarakloster was probably large enough to accommodate a considerable number of persons in an age not too fastidious about its sleeping-quarters. Hence it may also have been used as a general students' hostel in case of need; and possessing, as it must have, a refectory, this very likely served them as a church on Sundays. If so, it would account for the fact that only at Basle and at Zurich the problem of a building for the exiles to worship in apparently never arose.[2] Their services, according to the Prayer Book of 1552, must have been held within their own four walls, though not, alas, in peace or in singleness of mind. In a letter to Thomas Ashley at Frankfort, who had asked 'to know the state of [their] Church' at Basle, John Bale gives vent to his exasperation: 'to be plain in a few words,' he says, 'it is troublous at this present. I find the admonishment of S. Paul to Timothy, and of S. Peter to the dispersed brethren, most true, and in full force in this miserable age. They said, that in the latter times should come mockers, liars, blasphemers, and fierce dispisers. We have them, we have them, Master Ashley; we have them even from among ourselves: yea, they be at this present our elders, and their factious affinity.'[3]

Bale's mention of 'elders' leads to the belief that a congre-

---

[1] This, I am told, actually dates from the eighteenth century. It is at present numbered from 1 to 5.

[2] At Strasbourg the English worshipped with the French in the church of St André (see above, p. 20, n. 5); at Frankfort, first in the church of the White Ladies, alternating their services with those of the French, then in the All Saints' Chapel granted for their exclusive use (see Jung, p. 6, no. 2, and p. 16 for the Council Acts); at Aarau, in the Stadtskirche (see above, p. 52).

[3] Strype, *Mem.* III, ii, 313, from Petyt MSS., Library of the Inner Temple.

gation had actually been organized, but that, though the walls of the Clarakloster may have helped to preserve its outward decorum, its inner life showed no more evidence of Christian charity than its sister church at Frankfort, or than the French churches there[1] and at Strasbourg. Quarrels would seem to have been the inevitable concomitant of exile, and are not only an indication of its abnormal conditions, but an index of the intellectual and physical restlessness of the decades which immediately preceded Europe's expansion into the West. Apart from the parochial records[2] of deaths and marriages, there exists (or did exist)[3] at Basle only one other public trace of the English fugitives. That is the tablet erected in the church of St Theodor to the memory of John Bartholomew, 'a merchant of London', who, we are told, was 'Relig. pius, consil. prudens / vitae integritatae laudabil. / propter Christi Evangelium / exul / conditus sub hoc saxo / obiit / Anno Dn. M. D. LVIII. V. Kl. Aug.'[4]

Bartholomew was one of the nineteen who are known to have died in exile. Eight more died in England before Elizabeth's accession. Three are doubtful. If we may believe Il Schifanoya's report to the Mantuan[5] ambassador,[6] sixty others met their death as they were returning to England, going, as he irreverently says, 'to fish in the realms of Neptune...'.[7] This would leave about 382 who came back to play their part in the Elizabethan Settlement. Two of them, Sir Edward Rogers and Sir Francis Knollys, were to be members of the Queen's Privy Council. Sir Francis Knollys

[1] For Foxe on the 'troubles' at Frankfort, see his letter to Peter Martyr (Strype, *Mem.* III, i, 405) in which he 'lamented the hatreds, the envies, the defamations, the evil-speakings, the suspicions and jealousies that were among them;...'.

[2] In the Registers of the churches of St Alban and St Theodor (see Sources, p. 65).

[3] Whether it still exists in the interior or not I cannot say, for I failed, after repeated efforts, to get inside the church. The interior has been remodelled and it is thought that the monument has disappeared. At least it is not among those now fastened to the building's exterior walls.

[4] Johannes Tonjola, *Basilea Sepulta*, 1661, p. 299.

[5] Italian observer in London and correspondent of the Mantuan ambassador at Brussels.

[6] *Ven. Cal.* 1558-80, p. 53: 21 March 1558-9.

[7] *Ibid.*

with Sir Anthony Cooke was to lead the attack upon the
Royal Supremacy in Elizabeth's first House of Commons,
where several of his fellow-exiles were also to sit as members.
Of the committee of eight appointed for the revision of the
Prayer Book in 1559, four were exiles; and three of the four
had also been members of the committee which sat for the
same purpose at Frankfort in 1555 and drafted the Liturgy
of Frankfort.[1] There is good reason to believe that this same
Liturgy of Frankfort, with slight alterations, was the book
attached by Sir Anthony Cooke as a rider to the Supremacy
Bill in February 1559.[2] Had it not been for its rejection in
committee of the House of Lords in March,[3] the Book of
Frankfort would, in all probability, have become the 'book
of England'. Nearly all the exiled clergy are to be found in
opposition to the Crown in the Vestiarian Controversy of
1562 onwards. Some of those probably responsible for the
Confession of the Banished Ministers in 1554 collaborated on
the so-called 'first' Puritan Petition to Parliament in 1572.[4]
These are but a few of the threads which attach the years of
exile to the era of Elizabeth. But its influence was to pass
much farther afield. Edwin Sandys, late of Strasbourg, became in time archbishop of York, and father[5] of Sir Edwin

---

[1] Brit. Mus. Egerton MS. 2836, printed in H. J. Wotherspoon's *Second
Prayer Book of Edward VI and the Liturgy of Compromise* (1905), pp. 230–56.
This liturgy, hitherto ascribed to the authorship of Knox and Whittingham,
and believed by Lorimer to be identical with the Frankfort 'Liturgy of Compromise', adopted on 6 February (*Troubles*, p. 37; Wotherspoon, pp. 226–7,
but note the doubts of Dr Sprott; *Cat. of Egerton MSS.* p. 388; and Hist.
MSS. Comm. Append. to 2nd Rep. pp. 76–7), is rather, I believe, upon the
strength of internal evidence collated with Jung's documents, no other than
the result of that revision of the Prayer Book accomplished under the inspiration of Richard Cox and accepted by the congregation as the 'Liturgy
of Frankfort' on 28 March 1555 (*Troubles*, pp. 46–7), *plus*, however, the
additions of a Discipline and Catechism made during that summer (see
'Cox', Census).

[2] MS. Jour. H. of C., 1 Eliz., Feb. 15, f. 189a, and D'Ewes, *Parliaments
of Elizabeth*, p. 47.

[3] MS. Jour. H. of L. ff. 34–42, or *Lords Journals*, 1 Eliz., 13–18 March
1558/9, pp. 562–3; D'Ewes, p. 23; *Ven. Cal.* no. 45, p. 52: 21 March 1558/9;
and cf. *Span. Cal.* 1558–67, p. 37, de Feria to Philip, 19 March.

[4] W. H. Frere, *Puritan Manifestoes to Parliament* (1907); cf. Abp. Bancroft's *Pretended Holy Discipline*, p. 42.

[5] By his second wife Cicely, sister of Thomas Wilford, another exile.

Sandys of the Council for Virginia (1607). Sir Thomas Wrothe, also of Strasbourg, had a grandson, another Sir Thomas Wrothe, who in 1609 was a subscriber to the Virginia Company, in 1620 a member of the Council for New England, and in 1648 the mover in the House of Commons of the resolution of impeachment of King Charles the First.

Yet these personal links binding the Tudor exiles to the England of the Stuarts might be fortuitous, whereas the political significance of the Marian experiment is intrinsic: within it lies the genesis of that peculiarly English phenomenon, *party*—party that is, in anything like the sense in which the word is used to-day. As a political *faction*, a group of disaffected country gentlemen, for the most part closely related, left England in 1554: as a political *party* they returned to it again in 1558, augmented in numbers; allied for party ends with a body of protestant ministers; experienced in self-government untrammelled of bishops; trained in effective methods of propaganda; and actuated by a political philosophy that looked askance at the prerogative of kings. In 1559 these country gentlemen organized a secret cabal in Elizabeth's first House of Commons to fight the passage of the Supremacy Bill. In 1642 their descendants, in spirit and in the flesh, openly opposed the Crown in the Long Parliament, using as campaign documents the political pamphlets of the Marian Exile. The *Troubles begun at Frankfort*[1] were to close in civil war.

[1] Republished in 1642 for the use of the Long Parliament. In 1639 Ponet's *Treatise of Politike Power* was also reprinted and again in 1642 (see 'Ponet', Census).

THE CENSUS OF EXILES

A Social Portrait of a Transitional Decade

1. EXPLANATORY NOTE

The sketches of the Marian exiles which follow may need a word of explanation. They are intended to be *identifications*, not biographies; and they aim to be complete only in what concerns the life of the man while abroad. Nevertheless they are frequently something more than *mere* identifications, for into many of them, especially into the accounts of Ponet and Sampson; of Sir Francis Knollys, John Gray and Richard Chambers; of Sir Peter Carew and Sir John Cheke, there has been woven not only much new material but also a good deal of the theory to which that material has given form and substance. Need I say that the facts assembled are without prejudice? In the case of the younger exiles, they are usually the only facts that I have been able to discover in that impersonal and inarticulate pre-Elizabethan decade. Conspiracy, it has to be remembered, was the order of the day—the only channel of expression open to hot blood and minority opinion. While if we come to the Marian episode in sentimental mood, looking to these refugees for modern standards of personal conduct in matters of honour, private honesty and self-control, we shall be disappointed—they are not to be found even among the clergy. Tudor gentlemen conducted their lives tumultuously. Many of their younger sons, with little to lose, found in the protestant movement the only legitimate outlet then existing for that restlessness of theirs to which the new world owes its being. Pioneers have seldom been exponents of the gentler virtues, and were these men to pass in the flesh before our eyes, few of them, even at twenty, would be found possessed of whole bodies. I choose the following at random from the register of the English 'students' at Padua between 1592 and 1600:'Richard Sands, Englishman, with a small scar on the face; Henry Neville, Englishman, with a scar on the middle finger of the left hand; John Gray, English nobleman, with a scar on the left thumb; Edward Cecil, English nobleman, with a scar between the eyes;...' and so on through the monotonous list of over four pages, where, out of seventy-three names, but thirteen are those of men unscarred—as yet. (Andrich, pp. 133–7.)

However, the refugees were by no means all young men. In fact the Marian Exile may be likened to a bridge between two epochs upon which Henrican old age met and made common cause with Elizabethan youth. In that intercourse, monks and friars, once the pioneers of a world now dying, provided a new theology for those soon to be pioneers in a world just at the birth. It is chiefly in this aspect of my census as a social portrait of a transitional and prophetic decade that its value and, I dare to hope, its interest lies.

In several instances it has been possible to correct cases of mistaken identity. Three men, masquerading as Englishmen, have been restored to their proper nationality—Michael Cope,[1] in reality Michael Cop, a French Swiss of some importance; John Young, properly Johannes Jung, again a Swiss; George Black, otherwise Georgius Niger (or Negri), an Italian from the Valtelline. But in those cases where persistent effort has failed to establish certain identity, clues have been provided which others, more fortunate, may follow to success.

The heading of each paragraph is intended to provide the chief facts necessary for rapid identification, such honours as the man had achieved before exile, and whether or not his wife went with him into exile. The numbers concluding each paragraph refer to the sections in the list of sources which follows, and from which the names of the refugees have been drawn: thus Nicholas Abbott, Geneva, A IV a & B V a, shows that his name is recorded, as an exile, in the Livre des Anglois at Geneva, and, also as an exile, in Cardinal Pole's Visitation of the diocese of Lincoln in 1556. A list of abbreviations for all other sources of information used will be found on pp. 373–8.

In regard to the spelling of proper names the problem has proved nearly insoluble. No standard adopted can really be followed consistently. Therefore, for the sake of ease in identification, I have in the Introduction spelled the names of persons as they appear in the *D.N.B.* or in the Index to Strype's *Works* (Oxford, 1828). Whereas in the Census I have generally chosen as the first form of the name that in which it most frequently appears abroad, particularly in the *Troubles at Frankfort.* For place names, on the other hand, modern spelling has been used throughout, except in direct citations.

Certain indications which have come to light since the manuscript was in type, make it probable, though still not proven, that the Griffin Jones who appears on p. 200 was the same person as Galfri Jones. But since this identification in no way affects my conclusions, yet would necessitate altering every figure in the Introduction as well as the paging of the Census, it has been thought better to leave the text as it stands.

[1] See the *Dictionary of National Biography.*

2. TABLE OF SOURCES

A. FOREIGN ARCHIVES

I. AARAU (published)
 (a) Hans Dür's List, 1557 [?]: *Urkundenbuch der Stadt Aarau, Argovia*, vol. XI, pp. lxiii–lxv.
 (b) Official List, 1559 [?]: *Kirchliches Jahrbuch, etc.* VI; see Append. pp. 353–6.

II. BASLE (still in MS.)
 (a) Matrikel [University of Basle], vol. I, 1460–1568; and cf. Append. pp. 357–8.
 (b) Burgher List: Öffnungsbuch, vol. VIII, 1557–9.
 (c) Property List: Historisches Grundbuch, 1557 and 1559.
 (d) Parish Registers:
  St Alban: Kirchen Archiv, X. 8. 1.
  St Theodor: Orig. in Brit. Mus., MS. Egerton 1927.
 (e) Rector's Account Book: 'Rationes rectoratus', 1533–69 (St A. Univ. Arch. K. 8).

III. FRANKFORT (published)
 (a) R. Jung's *Englische Flüchtlings-Gemeinde, etc.*
  1. Burgher List: Bürgerliste, 1554–8.
  2. Church List: Standesliste, *ca.* 15 November 1555.
  3. Tax Lists: Steuerlisten, October 1556 and January 1557.
  4. Dwelling List (alphabetical): Wohnungsliste, 10 June 1557.
 (b) *Huguenot Soc. Proc.* vol. IV, from Archives of the French Church:
  1. List of Church Members with 'Preamble', cf. Jung, 'Standesliste'.
  2. Dwelling List (by families), 10 June 1557, cf. Jung, 'Wohnungsliste'.

IV. GENEVA
 (a) Livre des Anglois: facsimile, Bodleian, MS. Facs. d. 49;[1] transcript,[2] C. Martin's *Protestants Anglais etc.*
 (b) Registre des Habitants, Habitation A I, 1549–60 (still in MS. Archives d'État de Genève).

V. HEIDELBERG (published)
 Die Matrikel der Universität, ed. Gustav Toepke (1866).

---

[1] Only existing facsimile.
[2] All references to the Livre des Anglois are to this transcript.

VI. PADUA (published)
De Natione Anglica et Scota...Universitatis Patavinae, ed.
A. Andrich (1892).

VII. STRASBOURG (still in MS.)
(a) Protocols of the 'Council and 21', vols. 32–36, 1554–59,
cf. Append. pp. 362–72.
(b) Parish Registers:
St Thomas (baptisms), Ser. A vol. no. 259.
(c) List of English exiles sent to the Duke of Württemberg,[1]
Württ. Staatsarchiv, Stuttgart.

VIII. ZURICH (published)
(a) Original lett rs, vols. I and II.
(b) Zurich Letters, vols. I and II.
(c) Diarium of Heinrich Bullinger.

B. ENGLISH SOURCES (PUBLISHED)

I. Catalogue of Divines, from Emden ed. (1557) of Cranmer's
Defensio.
(a) In Latin—Cranmer's Works (ed. Parker Soc.), I, 9
(end of volume).
(b) In English with additions: Strype's Cranmer (ed.
Eccles. Hist. Soc.), III, 38–9.

II. BALE'S LIST, 1557–9, from his Scriptores etc. p. 742.

III. 'TROUBLES BEGUN AT FRANKFORT'
(a) Signatories to letters.
(b) Signatories to Discipline, April [?] and December 1557.

IV. CONTEMPORARY NARRATIVES
(a) John Brett's, 1556, R.H.S. Trans. n.s. vol. XI.
(b) Sir Thomas Hoby's Diary, 1554–5, Cam. Misc. X.
(c) Machyn's Diary, Cam. Soc. 42.
(d) Chronicle of Queen Jane and Queen Mary, Cam. Soc. 48.

V. MISCELLANEOUS
(a) Pole's Visitation of Lincoln, 1556, Strype, Mem. III, ii,
no. LI; or Lambeth MSS., Register of Cardinal Pole, f. 17.
(b) Calendars of State Papers.
1. Foreign, 1553–8.
2. Domestic, 1547–80 and Addenda 1547–65.
3. Venetian, for the years 1554–8.
(c) Baga de Secretis, 4th Report, Deputy Keeper of the
Public Records, Append. II, pp. 250–6.

[1] Facsimiles now in the Bodleian. Shelfmarks, Autographs I. R. Pal. fol.
180 and MS. German C. 10.

CENSUS OF EXILES

(An asterisk marks those in the list who were not exiles.)

1. ABBOTT, NICHOLAS: *Priest*(?).

Mis-transcribed as 'Arbott' by Burn (*L. des A.* (1831), p. 11). He had been rector of 'Branfelde' (?) Brantfield, Herts., but was cited for non-residence in Cardinal Pole's Visitation of the diocese of Lincoln, at Easter 1556 (*Mem.* III, ii, 392). On 29 March 1558 he was received into the English congregation at Geneva.

Geneva, A IV a; B V a.

2. ABELL, JOHN: *Merchant-banker.* Of London. Wife. d. *ca.* 1569.

Possibly of the family of the Abels of Herring Hill, Kent, of which a John Abel was Baron of the Exchequer, temp. Edw. II (Hasted, I, 198). In August 1547 Abell accompanied Sir Thomas Hoby on a journey from London to Strasbourg, where they were the guests of Martin Bucer (Cam. Misc. X, 3). His errand at Strasbourg seems to have been official, for when he returned to England in November he took back with him the scholars Peter Martyr and Bernardinus Ochinus. From the fact that he presented his bill of £126 for expenses to the Privy Council (*Archaeologia*, XXI, 471–3) it would seem as if Martyr and Ochinus had come at the invitation of the Council as well as at that of Archbishop Cranmer. In 1548 Abell was again in Strasbourg with Sir Thomas Hoby, this time also in association with Richard Hilles and John Burcher (*q.v.*), who were already living in the city (Cam. Misc. X, 6). Immediately after King Edward's death, he helped to organize, with Hilles, Richard Springham, and Thomas Heton, all bankers, a committee of twenty-six persons, known as the 'sustainers' (*Mem.* III, i, 224), for the purpose of financing a group of young protestant students of theology abroad (*ibid.* and *O.L.* II, 514). Soon afterwards John Abell himself was a fugitive at Strasbourg. On Saturday 14 April 1554, he appears before the city's 'Council and 21' as spokesman for Sir Richard Morison, Sir John Cheke, and Sir Anthony Cooke, who were then on their way to Italy (Protocols, vol. 32, f. 131 vo). From that time on he frequently acts as intermediary between the Council and the English fugitives, and his functions as master of ceremonies were various. On a Sunday in Advent, 1554, he stood godfather to Bishop Ponet's son Elias (Archives of St Thomas, Series A, N. 245, f. 61 vo). During the summer of 1555 he was Miles Coverdale's companion on a journey from Wesel to Frankfort, which he probably financed himself (Coverdale, *Remains*, p. 528). In May 1557 the magistrates of Basle suggest that he be made in his proper person a bureau of passport information for his countrymen (Protocols, vol. 35, f. 205). And on 29 September 1557 his signature is found with that of Sir Thomas Wrothe, Sir Francis Knollys, and others, appended to a letter of attempted reconciliation between the warring religious factions of the English Church at Frankfort (*T.* p. 174). Abell's protestantism seems to have been a matter of deep religious conviction, as the tone of his correspondence shows (*Z.L.* I and II, see Index), but upon Elizabeth's accession he did not hurry back to England. In January 1559 he acted as temporary guardian to Thomas Cranmer, son of the archbishop (*ibid.* I, 8). It is not till 1563 that he is found re-established in London (*ibid.* II, 108), where henceforth he becomes an indispensable channel of communication between the restored clergy and their friends abroad. It was through him that letters and parcels were transmitted and books bought (*ibid.* I, 25, 211; II, 22, 24, etc.). He himself corresponded on terms of friendship with Bullinger at Zurich (*ibid.* II, 108, 117), and the references to him in the letters of Horne and Grindal are constant and affectionate. On 13 August 1569 Grindal announces to Bullinger that 'our brother John Abel' has 'exchanged this life for a better some months since' (*ibid.* I, 211), but it is not till 1571 that regretful references to him cease. A Robert Abell settled in Weymouth, Mass., in 1642 (*New Eng. Reg.* IX, 171).

Frankfort, B III a; Strasbourg, A VII a & b; Zurich, A VIII a & b; B IV b.

3. ACWORTH, GEORGE: *Student.* Of London. d. 1580–2 (Venn).

Matriculated from Peterhouse, Cambridge, 1548. Fellow, 1553–62. Perhaps the son of Thomas Acworth, Merchant Taylor (Clode, *Mems.* pp. 117, 127). Though in 1555 he had subscribed to the Catholic articles, he still felt it necessary to go abroad, and he tells Cardinal Pole that he studied at Louvain, Paris, and in Italy (*For. Cal.* 1558–9, p. 18). In 1558–9 he was student and Consiliarius at the University of Padua (Andrich, pp. 33, 131), and on his return to England received his LL.D., 1560–1. In 1573 he answered the *De Visibili Monarchia* of Nicholas Sanders by the order, Strype thinks, of Archbishop Parker (*Parker,* II, 181). Later he fell into disgrace because of his dissolute habits and, losing his preferments, was relegated to Ireland, where he was made Judge of the Prerogative Court, 1577.

Louvain; Paris; Padua, A VI; *D.N.B.*

4. ACWORTH, THOMAS: *Student.* Of London (?). d. 1576 (?).

B.A. Trinity College, Cambridge, 1553–4. One of those educated abroad for the protestant ministry. Probably a younger brother of

George Acworth. His name appears once only, at Frankfort in 1557, when he signed the 'new discipline'. He was ordained deacon by Bishop Grindal, 26 January 1560 (*Grindal*, p. 73), and one of his name became vicar of Wandsworth, Surrey, 1560, and prebendary of Lichfield, 1561–6.
Frankfort, B III b; Venn.

5. ADAMS, JOHN: *Gent.*(?). Of Sussex(?). d. 1557.

Cannot be identified with certainty. Evidently a soldier of fortune in France, recommended by Sir Peter Carew and Sir William Pickering to a place in Captain Crayer's English company in March 1554 (*For. Cal.* 1553–8, p. 67) and apparently ending his life in Stafford's abortive attempt on Scarborough in 1557 (*Mem.* III, ii, 518).
France, B v b 1.

6. ADE, JOHN: *Merchant*. Of London(?).

He was one of the wealthy exiles who financed their poorer brethren. He first appears at Frankfort on the Standesliste of 1555(?). In 1557 he was living in the house of Robert Horne, and on the tax-list of 16 October 1556 his property is rated at 1000 florins (Jung, p. 29). John Brett mentions him as one of the exiles whom he saw when he was in Frankfort on 8 July 1556 (p. 119). In the quarrels of the Frankfort congregation, Ade appears to have belonged to the more conservative faction which supported Horne as pastor. On this account he refused to serve as an officer, probably deacon, of the church when he was nominated to that office on 25 March 1557 (*T.* p. 97). Nevertheless, in the following December he finally subscribed to the 'new discipline'. Upon Elizabeth's accession he did not return to England immediately, for on 23 August 1559 he is found appearing as a witness with John Binks (*q.v.*) in a hearing that involved the French Church at Frankfort (Jung, p. 39).
Frankfort, A III a 2, 3, 4 & b 1, 2; B III a, b; B IV a.

7. ADISHE (ADIS? ADICE?), PHILIP: *Gent.*(?).

Appears at Frankfort as the signer of the 'new discipline' in April. Nothing further is known about him.
Frankfort, B III b.

8. AGAR, THOMAS: *Artisan*. Of Suffolk(?).

Son of Alice Agar, a widow of Colchester (Martin, p. 333), who came to Geneva in June 1557, and there married Thomas Spenser (*q.v.*) of Wroghton (*ibid.* p. 337). On 14 October 1557 her son, Thomas, was admitted as a 'resident' of Geneva and called 'rubantier'.
Geneva, A IV a & b.

9. ALCOCSON (ALCOCKSON), HUMPHRY: *Student*. d. 1560.

B.A. Oxford, 1552; chaplain of Magdalen Hall, 1553. He then migrated to Strasbourg, probably as one of the subsidized body of students, and there was signatory to the colony's reply to Frankfort on 23 November 1554, in regard to the Prayer Book dispute (*T*. pp. 22–3). The following December he was one of those who profited by the Duke of Württemberg's bounty, receiving, as his share, 8 gulden. After that we know no more of him until his return to England in 1560 when, on 7 July, Grindal made him a prebendary of St Paul's (Le Neve, II, 390). He died, however, in the same year.

Strasbourg, A VII c; B III a.

10. ALFORD, HUGH. *Gent.*(?). Of 'Wysskomme in Devonia' (Wiscomb in Devon, near Honiton).

He was the only member of the English colony who married a Frankfort woman, the widow of a burgher (Jung, pp. 19, 39). His name first appears as signatory to the letter of invitation written by the Frankfort congregation to John Knox (*T*. p. 20). On 24 May 1555 he became a citizen of Frankfort, paying '8 s. 6 h. Bürgergeld' (Jung, p. 24). Henceforth he is never mentioned on any other of the lists of Englishmen abroad; and it may be inferred that he left Frankfort, possibly to return home.

A John Alford of Devon matriculated at Exeter College, Oxford, in 1596 (Foster, I, 14). A John Alford in New England petitioned against imposts in 1668 (*New Eng. Reg.* IX, 85).

Frankfort, A III a 1; B III a.

11. ALLEN, EDMUND: *Deacon*. Of Norfolk. d. 30 August 1559.

Fellow of Corpus Christi College, Cambridge, 1536; M.A. 1537; and one of the Henrican refugees to the Continent. He was probably ordained deacon in 1536 (Venn) but after 1539 went abroad, where he may have received his degree of B.D. By 1543, however, he had returned to England, for he was then chosen by Queen Catherine Parr and Nicholas Udall, head master of Eton, as one of a group of scholars set to translate the Paraphrases of Erasmus (P. S. Allen, *Erasmus etc.* (1904), p. 71). In 1549 he became chaplain to the Princess Elizabeth. His place of second exile, under Mary, is unknown, though his name appears both on the Emden list and on Bale's. But it may be inferred that he was among the first to return to England, for in June 1559 he was being sent by Cecil to the Continent again on some diplomatic mission (*For. Cal.* 1558–9, p. 337). Already he had been cited for the bishopric of Rochester, for he fears in his letter that during his absence abroad he may incur danger for not compounding for his firstfruits (*ibid.*). But he was to die before his consecration (*Machyn*, p. 208).

n.p.; B I a; B II; *D.N.B.*

12. ALLEN (ALEN, ALYN), Thomas: *Student*. Of Kent. Wife.

This was perhaps the Thomas Allen who in July 1553 received his M.A. from Lincoln College, Oxford, but not the Thomas Allen of Pembroke Hall, Cambridge, who was a friend of Bilney, the exile being a much younger man. He was born at Canterbury, lived at Dover, and became a member of the colony at Aarau, where he lodged with his wife, two children and a sister in the house of Mauritz Meggers. As Thomas 'Attyn' he was one of those who signed Thomas Lever's letter to Bullinger, written on 5 October 1557, to announce the safe arrival of the colony at its destination and to thank him for having addressed to them his 'midnight studies and lucubrations' (*O.L.* I, 169–70). Possibly this was the 'Thomas Alline' whom Grindal made vicar of Saling Magna, Middlesex, in August 1567 (Newcourt, II, 514); possibly also, the 'Allen' who had been deprived in 1564 with Percival Wiburne (*Grindal*, p. 145) and who with him then 'took to husbandry' (*ibid.* p. 146). An 'Allen —' was associated with the Classical Movement and signed its 'Discipline', 1585–6 (Usher, p. xxv).

Wesel (?); Aarau, A I a & b; Foster.

13. ALVEY (ALVEI), John: *Preacher*(?).

Appears only in the Emden list and cannot be identified. His place of exile unknown. A John Alvey, perhaps his son, matriculated from Cambridge at Easter 1578 (Venn).

n.p.; B I a & b.

14. ALVEY (ALVAIE), Richard ('Father Alvey'): *Priest*. Wife. d. 1584.

Fellow of St John's College, Cambridge, 1537; rector of Thorington, Essex, 1539, and canon of Westminster, 1552. By 5 April 1555 he had reached Frankfort with his wife; and on 10 June 1557 we find them both inmates of the house of Richard Luddington (*q.v.*). As a member of the committee for the revision of the Prayer Book in the spring of 1555, he signed both Cox's letter of explanation to Calvin and Whitehead's protest of the following September (*O.L.* II, 753–5, 755–63). His taxable property was rated at 70 florins on the Steuerliste of October 1556, and in the spring of 1557 he subscribed to the 'new discipline' without having played any conspicuous part in the Frankfort quarrels. On his return to

England he was not only restored to his living of Thorington and to Westminster (1558) but in 1560 was also made Master of the Temple (Venn).

Frankfort, A iii a 2, 3, 4 & b 1, 2; B ii; *D.N.B.*

15. AMONDESHAM (AGMONDISHAM or ANSAM), RICHARD: *Gent.* Of Heston, Middlesex. d. 1558.

Arrived in Geneva before October 1555 (Martin, p. 332). Became a 'resident' 14 October 1557 (f. 196) and also a burgher of the city (Rose-Troup, *Sir Thomas Bodley's Father etc.* p. 16). On 30 January 1558 he married Elenor of Totnes in Devon (Martin, p. 337), who was perhaps the same person as Elenor, servant to John Bodley (*ibid.* p. 333). On 20 September of that year he died (*ibid.* p. 338), so that he cannot be the 'Parson of Craynford' as suggested by Burn (p. 7, n. 13), since the latter lived till 1612. Possibly he belonged to the same family as John Agmondesham of Surrey, who sat for Reigate in the parliament of 1571 (Browne Willis, p. 84 and Harl. Soc. XLIII, 53–4).

Geneva, A iv a & b.

16. AMONDESHAM, WILLIAM: *Gent. and Student.* Of Middlesex (?).

Probably a younger brother, possibly a son, of Richard Amondesham, since he also arrived in Geneva before October 1555. Between 1556 and 1557 he was a student at Basle (Matrikel, f. 195ᵛᵒ, and below, p. 357) and in 1564–5 he matriculated fellow-commoner from Pembroke Hall, Cambridge (Venn).

Geneva, A iv a; Basle, A ii a.

17. APPLEBY, JOHN: *Preacher* (?). Of London (?).

Except that he appears in the Emden list and in Bale's, nothing is known of him, even his whereabouts on the Continent. A Walter Appleby was martyred at Maidstone 18 June 1557 (Maitland's list, *Essays*, ed. 1899, p. 453). Possibly both men were related to the Nicholas Appleby, rector of Gateby, who was deprived for marriage at Norwich in 1554 (Baskerville, *E.H.R.* 1935, p. 50).

n.p.; B i a & b; B ii.

18. ARGALL, LAURENCE: *Gent.* Of London and Essex.

Appears to have been the second son of Thomas Argall, Esq. (Harl. Soc. XIII, 137), who was one of the notaries at the trial of Gardiner in December 1550 (Foxe, VI, 94, 95, etc.). Laurence had very probably been implicated in the Dudley conspiracy since he arrived in Geneva, 5 November 1556 (Martin, p. 332), with Francis Withers (*q.v.*). His function in later life would seem to

have been that of a 'mourner' at funerals. He is twice so mentioned by Machyn (pp. 237, 311) and with 'Mr Withers' was one
of the 'gentlemen mourners in gowns' at Archbishop Parker's
funeral (*Parker* II, 432). He married the daughter of 'one Master
Berre' of Oxfordshire.

Geneva, A IV a.

19. ASHLEY (ASTLEY, ASTELEY), JOHN: *Gent.* Of Norfolk.
    d. 1595.

A cousin of Queen Elizabeth and husband of her dear friend and
woman of the bed-chamber, Mistress Katherine Astley (Ashley),
daughter of Sir Philip Champernowne of Devon. According to
the Astley pedigree (Harl. Soc. XIII, pt I, 138–9), Sir Thomas
Astley of Hilmorton and Melton Constable, Norfolk, had two
sons named John, the elder, who died in 1558 (cf. Lord Hastings's
article in *Eastern Daily Press*, 15 August 1936), by his first wife
Ann Cruse, the younger by his second wife Anne Wood, sister of
Anne Boleyn's mother (*ibid.* and Harl. Soc. *ibid.*). It was this second
John Astley, first cousin to Queen Anne Boleyn, who was the
future Master of the Jewel House. He came to court on the
occasion of Anne's marriage, and later introduced his friend, Roger
Ascham, as a tutor for the Princess Elizabeth. He must therefore
be identical with the John 'Ashley' whose letter to Ascham is
printed in the latter's *Report on the state of Germany* published by
John Day. In 1554, probably because of some connection with
Wyatt's rebellion, he fled to Padua, where Sir Thomas Hoby met
him in August (Cam. Misc. X, 116). But Cooper notwithstanding
(cf. II, 182 and *D.N.B.*), it was not John but *Thomas* Astley (see
below) who went to Frankfort. John, nevertheless, remained
abroad till after the death of Mary.[1] Upon his return he was made
Master of the Jewel House, an office which he held for more than
thirty years, and was also given by the queen a house called the
Palace of Maidstone, which had been forfeit to the Crown after
Wyatt's rebellion. It is at Maidstone that he is buried with his
son, John. As his second wife he married Margaret, daughter of
Lord John Grey of Pyrgo.

Padua, B IV b; *D.N.B.* under 'Astley'.

20. ASHLEY (ASTLEY, etc.), THOMAS: *Gent.* Of London and
    Writtle, Essex.

Son of Thomas Astley of Melton Constable in Norfolk, by his first
wife, and so elder half-brother of John Ashley (above) (Harl. Soc.
XIII, pt I, 138–9). He himself married Mary, the daughter of Sir

---

[1] I am deeply indebted to Lord Hastings himself for supplying me with most
of the evidence contained in this brief account of a member of his family.

Anthony Denny of Hertfordshire. Under Henry VIII he was a
Privy Councillor and in 1551 a member of the Marquis of Northampton's embassy to France (Cam. Misc. x, 67). Probably he was
also the Thomas Asteley who in 1550 was ordered by the Privy
Council 'to joyne with ij or iij honest gentlemen in London for the
observacion of the usage of the Communyon in Powles, whereof
informacion was given that it was used as a verie masse' (*P.C.A.*
1550–2, p. 138). Under Mary he fled to Frankfort, where he was
seen by Sir Thomas Hoby in September 1555 (Cam. Misc. x, 123).
It was the obscure quarrel between Ashley and Horne beginning
in January 1557 (*T.* pp. 62ff.) that led to the transformation of
the Frankfort congregation into a church commonwealth, and
eventually to the adoption of the more democratic frame of Church
government, known as the 'new discipline' (*ibid.*). At Frankfort
Ashley shared the house of John Hales. On the tax-list of January
1557 his property was rated at 1000 florins. On 19 October 1558
he became a citizen of Frankfort (Jung, p. 24) paying 8 fl. 12 s.
Bürgergeld (*ibid.* p. 39). For his correspondence with John Bale,
see *Mem.* III, ii, no. XXXIX, 313.

Frankfort, A III a 1, 2, 3, 4 & b.

21. ASHTON (ASCHTON, ASTON), Roger. Of Kent and Calais.

We only know from the Aarau lists that he was an old man, who,
though born in Kent, lived at Calais, and lodged at Aarau in the
house of Melchior Zenders. He thus proves not to have been the
'Ro. Ashton', rector of Moccleston and vicar of Sondon, who was
deprived for being married (*Mem.* III, i, 169; cf. Cam. Misc. IX, 47).

Aarau, A I a & b.

22. ASSHETON, Christopher, Esq. ('the elder'). Of Fyfield, Berkshire.

One of the ringleaders in Sir Henry Dudley's conspiracy, and
proclaimed a traitor in April 1556 (*Machyn*, p. 103). He was
indicted with the other conspirators (Baga, p. 254) but had already
fled to France, where he became the centre of plots against Mary,
and was characterized by Wotton as a 'craftier fox than Thomas
Stafford' (*For. Cal.* 1553–8, pp. 305–6). He fitted up ships to prey
upon the Spanish treasure galleons bound for the Low Countries
(*ibid.* pp. 264–5, 282, etc.). In May 1557 he planned a descent upon
the English coast at Weymouth, of which Wotton informed the
Council (*ibid.* pp. 305–6).

France, B v b 1 & c.

23. ASSHETON, Christopher ('the younger'): Gent.

Was also proclaimed a traitor, 4 April 1556. But in their exploits
abroad it is difficult to distinguish father from son. One of them,

the younger apparently, was caught and imprisoned and appears to have been present when Rosey confessed the objects of the conspiracy (*Dom. Cal.* 1547–80, p. 81) and later at the interrogation of Peter Killigrew (*ibid.* p. 86, no. 26) in August 1556, in regard to the piracies in the Channel, Killigrew was forced to admit that 'young Aston was at the sacking of the Spaniard' (S.P. Dom. 11, IX, no. 26).

France.

24. AUDLEY (ANCLEY, ANDLAEUS, AUDELEY), Lord JOHN. Of Somerset. Wife.

Probably the Lord John of Audley, of the family of the Touchets, who was a friend of Cecil and upon a time undertook his cure by sending him a recipe for 'a sow-pig boiled with cinnamon and raisins' (Tytler, II, 169). Through his wife, Mary, daughter of John Griffin of Northamptonshire, he was connected with the town of Calais, and seems to have had early associations with it (G.E.C. I, 200 and *Chron. Calais*, pp. 11, 22). Possibly he was the father-in-law of Sir Henry Dudley (*P.C.A.* 1554–6, p. 101). He fled to Basle in 1556, where he appears as a student at the university, paying 'VI sol' for his matriculation (Matrikel, f. 196).[1] The following year he is found at Aarau, where he lived with his wife and three children in the house of Jacob Mürer, a shoemaker. In Hans Dür's list he is described as an 'Edelman' born in Somerset, who had 'served at the king's court' (*Argovia*, XI, p. lxiii).

Wesel (?); Basle, A II a; Aarau, A I a & b.

25. AUGUSTINE (AUSTIN), WALTER: *Student.* Of Essex.

A Walter Thomas 'sometyme of Croghowell in Wales, Gentleman' came to 'Writtell' in Essex during the reign of Henry VIII (Harl. Soc. XIII, pt I, 310). It was very possibly a younger son of his who as Augustine (or Austin) Water (or Walter), reversing his name in the Welsh fashion, was ordained priest in 1532 as an ex-Franciscan of Norwich (Baskerville, *E.H.R.* 1933, p. 52). In 1554 he was deprived of his living of Haynford for marriage; and it was probably his son, again reversing the names, who as Walter Austen matriculated from Christ's College, Cambridge, in 1551 (Venn, I, 58), and who, in 1555, appears as Walter Augustine among the 'students' on the Standesliste of Frankfort. He may well have been a protégé of Thomas Astley, also of Writtell in Essex, who arrived at Frankfort in the same year, but nothing further is known of Augustine abroad.

Frankfort, A III a 2 & b; Venn.

[1] This may have been John Audley the printer, but we believe not.

26. AYLMER (AELMER, ELMER), JOHN: *Archdeacon.* Of
Aylmer Hall, Norfolk. 1521–94.

M.A., Queens' College, Cambridge. Friend of Roger Ascham.
Became tutor to the children of Lord Grey, and especially to Lady
Jane, who was devoted to him in spite of his letter to Bullinger,
asking that divine to instruct his pupil 'as to what embellishment
and adornment of person [was] becoming in young women pro-
fessing godliness' (*O.L.* I, 278). In 1553 he was appointed to the
archdeaconry of Stow (Lincs.), of which he was deprived (Le Neve,
II, 80) within a year. He was one of the six Edwardian divines to
hold a seat in the first convocation of Mary (*Mem.* III, i, 73 and
C. 461), but soon afterwards left England, making one of those
miraculous escapes so dear to the heart of the protestant chronicler
(Fuller, *Worthies*, II, 447–8). It is supposed[1] that he went to
Strasbourg and there published, in English, Lady Jane Grey's
letter to the 'apostate Harding' (Aylmer, p. 7). From Strasbourg,
Strype believes that he went to Zurich (1557), where Foxe consulted him in regard to the *Book of Martyrs* (*ibid.* pp. 7–8); but
there is no evidence other than Strype's for Aylmer's wanderings
abroad. He is mentioned as a fugitive only in the Emden list and
in Bale's. His name never appears in the correspondence between
Frankfort and either Strasbourg or Zurich. Nor is he found among
the English who studied at the University of Basle. Probably his
close connection with Lady Jane made him think it advisable to
remain hidden. For a time he was at Jena (*ibid.* pp. 10–11), and
somewhere in his travels he acquired as a pupil Thomas Dannet
(*q.v.*), a cousin of Cecil's and the 'Onesimus' (*ibid.* p. 7) of Aylmer's
letters, who was later instrumental in securing for his tutor the
archdeaconry of Lincoln (*D.N.B.*, and cf. Maitland, *Essays*, no. x,
p. 172). Strype also says that Aylmer was at Basle in 1558 and
present at the prophetic sermon of encouragement preached there
by John Foxe the day before Queen Mary's death (*Mem.* III, ii,
162). While still abroad he wrote *An Harborowe for Faithfull and
Trewe Subjects...*, which was published (probably in London by
John Day) in April 1559 (*S.T.C.* no. 1005) and purported to be
an answer to Knox's *First Blast of the Trumpet*. In it he attempted
to dissociate himself from those exiles who were opponents of the
Royal Supremacy, but he still took the occasion to admonish
Elizabeth,—'a woman weake in nature, feable in bodie, softe in
courage, vnskilfull in practise, [and] not terrible to the enemy,...'
(Harborowe, Sig. B 2ᵛᵒ) in regard to the type of church and
religious behaviour that the exiles expected of her. On his return
he was chosen one of the disputants on the protestant side in the

---

[1] But cf. 'Haddon' below.

Conference of Westminster (1559) and eventually became bishop of London in succession to Sandys.

Strasbourg (?); Zurich (?); Jena (?); Basle (?); B I a & b; B II; *D.N.B.*

27. BAGNAL (BAGENAL), Sir RALPH, Knt. Of Dieulacres Abbey, Staffordshire.

Son of a merchant of Newcastle-under-Lyme (*E.H.R.* XXIII, 656); brother of Sir Nicholas Bagnal and a relative of William Whittingham. Is described by Strype as 'lusty young Rafe Bagnal' among the dicers 'infamous in King Edward's days' (*Mem.* II, i, 180). Was the friend and 'loose' companion of Edward Underhill, whom Bagnal later, in derision, dubbed 'the hot Gospeller' (*ibid.*). He has been amusingly apostrophized by the editor of Foxe (VI, 776) as 'this noble-minded individual' who alone, of Mary's parliament, refused to submit to the pope (cf. *Mem.* III, i, 324). He fled to Calais and there played an obscure part in the Dudley plots (*ibid.* p. 568 and *Dom. Cal.* 1547-80, p. 80). In October 1557 he seems to have been in the Tower in connection with Stafford's invasion (*P.C.A.* 1556-8, p. 181; but cf. *ibid.* p. 229). But he sat for Staffordshire in the first parliament of Elizabeth (*E.H.R.* XXIII, 656) and in 1564 appears in the Bishops' Census of that year (Cam. Misc. IX, 41-2) as one 'miet to be called' to the office of Justice of the Peace.

Calais; *D.N.B.* Suppl. I, p. 96.

28. BAKER, JOHN: *Cordwainer*(?). Of London(?).

Among those who arrived at Geneva, 5 June 1557 (Martin, p. 333). There is no indication given of his status either there or in the Registre des Habitants, but in the Acts of the Privy Council we find mention on 22 January 1553/4 of a 'Johannes Baker, de London, Cordyner', who is summoned before the Council with Anthony Uvedale, as owing the queen certain moneys (*P.C.A.* 1552-4, p. 390). This is possibly the same man.

Geneva, A IV a.

29. BAKER, REIGNOLDE (REGINALD)(?).

Except that he signed the Frankfort 'discipline' in December 1557 we can find no other trace of this person.

Frankfort, B III b.

30. BALE, JOHN (alias 'Henry Harryson' or 'Henry Stalbrydge'): *Bishop and ex-religious.* Of Cove, Suffolk. 1495-1563.

Of Jesus College, Cambridge. An ex-Carmelite of Norwich. Married Dorothy (?). In 1534 held the living of Thornden,

Suffolk. A protégé of Thomas Cromwell, Bale fled from England on the latter's fall (1540) and spent eight years of exile 'in inferiore Germania'. He was probably at Zurich in 1543, at Basle in 1544 and at Geneva in 1545 (Vetter, *Eng. Flücht.* pp. 116–17). On 2 February 1552/3 he was consecrated bishop of Ossory at Dublin, but fled from his diocese the following September (Poole's Preface to Bale's *Index*, p. xix), though according to his own account he had not concurred in the proclamation of Queen Jane (*Vocacyon*, f. 23). In his *Vocacyon* (ff. 32vo–42vo) he gives a lively, if disingenuous, account of his frequently interrupted flight to Zeeland. Maitland suspects him (*Essays*, pp. 73–4) of having been 'not far off' when John Ponet, whose former chaplain he was, took part in Wyatt's rebellion. We know, in fact, very little of what Bale was doing between September 1553 and the first appearance of his name at Frankfort on 24 September 1554, when he signed that congregation's invitation to Knox (*T.* p. 20). He says of himself that he was landed somewhere near Antwerp (*Vocacyon*, f. 41) and kept a prisoner there for three weeks, apparently on suspicion of treason (*ibid.* no date). After which he may have gone first to Emden or to Wesel before settling at Frankfort, where he allied himself with the Knoxian party in the Prayer Book controversy (*T.* p. 26). Yet he seems nevertheless to have been a member of the Coxian committee for Prayer Book revision in April 1555 (*O.L.* II, 753–5) and was still living in Frankfort, 'hinder dem Juden', as late as November 1555 (Jung, p. 40), though soon afterwards he must have left for Basle, where his name appears among those matriculating at the university in 1555/6 (Matrikel, f. 193). It was, no doubt, in the Clarakloster (see frontispiece) that Bale worked upon the edition of the *Scriptores Illustrium Catalogus* published at Basle, 1557–9. Almost, we might say, he finished it between the quarrels that rent the peace of that establishment (*Mem.* III, ii, no. XXXIX). On his return to England he was made prebendary of Canterbury, and died there in 1563.

Frankfort, B I a & b; B III a; Basle, A II a; D.N.B.

31. BANKS, JOHN: *Student.*

Matriculated from Michael House, Cambridge, 1544. Fellow of Trinity College, 1548. Probably a son of Richard Bankes, the London printer, whose 'long shop' was in the Poultry (Gordon Duff, pp. 7–8). He was a friend of James Haddon, late tutor to Lady Jane Grey, and the two men appear to have made their way to Strasbourg together, arriving about 9 July 1554 (*O.L.* I, 291). Thence, on 9 December, Haddon wrote a letter of introduction for Banks to Bullinger, hoping that the latter might find for him 'a situation with some respectable and pious printer' (*ibid.* p. 296). Already in March 1554 Banks had himself written to Bullinger, enclosing his own translations of Lady Jane Grey's letters to her sister Lady Catherine Grey (Foxe, VI, 422) and to Thomas Harding (*ibid.* p. 418), with her statement made before execution, and the summary (*ibid.* pp. 415–17) of her conference with Feckenham (*O.L.* I, 303–5). As he disclaims any personal acquaintance with Lady Jane, it is possible that Haddon had sent the documents to John Banks's father for publication, but the project appearing too hazardous, the two men carried them to Strasbourg, where Michael Angelo Florio was allowed to use them for his *Historia de la vita e de la morte de l'Illustriss. Signora Giovanna Graia* (Florio's *Apologia*, p. 58, quoted by Yates, *Florio*, pp. 9, 14). A place was secured for Banks in January 1555 with a printer at Basle (*O.L.* I, 297). It may therefore be inferred that the 'Jacobus Bantus, Anglus', inscribed in the Matrikel (f. 193) of the university for the winter of 1555–6 is Banks himself. If so, it must have been at this time that he allowed Foxe to insert his documents of Lady Jane in the *Acts and Monuments.* He may also be the 'Banks' whose name appears in 1559 on a list of Cecil's of 'spiritual men without promotion at this present' (*Annals,* I, i, 228), but there is no indication that he ever received preferment.

Strasbourg, A VII a; Basle, A II a; Cooper.

32. BARCHER (BARKER), EDMUND ('alias Chapman'): *Student.* Of Sussex. Wife. 1538(?)–1602.

Born in Hastings (*Argovia,* XI, p. lxiv). Not the Barker who was 'parson of Prittlewell in Essex' (Davids, p. 116; cf. Venn, I, 85) but very likely the Edmund Chapman, 'alias Barker', who matriculated from Gonville Hall in 1554 and was later to receive his B.A. (1558–9) and a fellowship (1560) from Trinity College, Cambridge (Venn, I, 85, 321). In exile he lived at Aarau with his wife and one child. He may also be the 'Edward' Barker who in 1560 was appointed by Parker one of the six preachers of Canterbury (*Parker,* I, 144; II, 25), but if so he was not in orders at the time, for as 'Chapman alias Barker' he was not ordained deacon till 8 June 1566 (Venn). From 1569 to 1576, as 'Chapman', he was a prebendary of Norwich (Le Neve, II, 497), but was then deprived for his zealous puritanism. In 1582 we find him as an organizer of the Dedham Classis, for he is, I believe, the 'Chapman' mentioned by Usher (p. xxxvii) and not the Edmund Barker also mentioned by him (p. xxxv) who was matriculated from St John's College, Cambridge, 1559 (Venn).

Aarau, A I a & b; Venn and Foster.

33. BARLOW, WILLIAM ('alias Finch'): *Bishop and ex-religious.*
Of Essex or Lancashire(?) (cf. Venn). d. 1568.
A man, says Fuller (*Worthies*, II, 389), 'of much Motion and
Promotion'. Austin canon. Canon of St Osyth's (*Scriptores*,
p. 715), then prior of five religious houses in succession, of which
he owed the last to the favour of Anne Boleyn. After 1548 became
a protégé of Somerset, to whom he owed his translation to the see
of Bath and Wells (1547/8, Le Neve, I, 300). Married Agatha
Wellesbourne (1550?). 'Voluntarily resigned' his see in 1553
(*Cranmer*, p. 443; cf. *Mar. Reac.* p. 21, n. 4).

As early as 1536 he had become a reformer and a prolific
pamphleteer. He had shared in the composition of the *Institution
of a Christian Man* and been made a member of the commission
for the Reform of Ecclesiastical Laws, but he was not trusted by
Cranmer. According to the *Greyfriars Chronicle* (p. 84) he was
committed to the Tower, 15 September 1553. His attempt in April
1554 (*P.C.A.* 1554–6, p. 13) to escape to the Continent with John
Cardmaker ('alias Tayler') suggests strongly that he had not been
entirely inactive in the Western rising. He was captured, but
released on 10 May 1554 (*ibid.* p. 20). The omission of his signature
from the 'declaration' of the bishops in prison on 8 May 1554
(Foxe, VI, 553) may have been due to a desire not to compromise
his chances of release. However, he seems to have made a second
unsuccessful attempt in November of that year to get abroad with
Cardmaker, for Machyn says (p. 75) that the two were re-arrested
as 'thay wher gohyng over see lyke marchands' and put in the
Fleet. On 22 January 1554/5 he recanted before Gardiner in
writing (*Mem.* III, i, 241; Sampson to Calvin, *O.L.* I, 171), then,
'afterward, being delivered[?]' from prison (Foxe, VII, 78), he fled,
perhaps to Emden, where Fuller (*Worthies*, II, 389) says he was
minister. From there he probably went to Wesel, for when we next
meet him he is a member of the Duchess of Suffolk's household
at Weinheim (Brett, pp. 125–7), presumably her chaplain. In the
parley with Brett over the nature of the queen's letters (1556)
Barlow acted as her spokesman (*ibid.*) and, still in the service of
the Berties, he preceded them to Poland in 1557 with 'letters of
great thanks to the king [of Poland] and palatine', who, at the
instance of John à Lasco, had offered the Berties an asylum (Foxe,
VIII, 574). On this journey he travelled in the company of John
Burcher (*O.L.* II, 687, 692). As nothing further is heard of him
till Mary's death we presume that he remained with the duchess
at 'Crossen', in Poland. On his return to England he assisted at
the consecration of Archbishop Parker, and on 18 December 1559
was himself made bishop of Chichester (Le Neve, I, 249).

Emden (?); Wesel (?); Weinheim; Poland; B I; B IV a & c; *D.N.B.*

34. BARON, JOHN: *Student and printer*(?). Of Edinburgh. Wife.

A son of Andrew Baron (Knox, VI, 534, n. 1) of Edinburgh. Married Anne Goodacre, an Englishwoman (*Parker*, I, 297). His name first appears at Basle in the register of the church of St Theodore (Egerton MS. 1927, p. 14) when his son John was baptized there on 8 January 1554. He is next found in Geneva, where on 14 October 1557 he was made a 'resident' (f. 196) and later on 21 June 1558 a burgher (Martin, pp. 70, 331). In August 1557 a daughter, Susan, was born to him, who died the following October (*ibid*. pp. 336, 338). He seems to have been among those called to collaborate on the Genevan Bible, possibly as a printer (Hayer, p. 360), and in November 1559, he, with William Whittingham, was held answerable to the Council for the orthodoxy of Knox's *Treatise on Predestination* (Martin, p. 142). In March 1560 he was still in the city (*ibid*. p. 260), but on his return to Scotland he became in 1563 minister of Galston in Ayrshire (Knox, VI, 534, n. 1) and not long afterwards appears in Parker's correspondence (I, 297-8) as the principal in a 'cause célèbre' which, but for Parker's wisdom, might have become an international affair. For Baron's English wife ran away from him and took refuge in York. To get her back, her husband invoked the aid of the General Assembly of Scotland, which, in turn, appealed to the two archbishops of England in a letter of which Knox himself was part author. But Parker, moved perhaps as much by sympathy for the wife as by prudence, 'doubted how agreeable it were for him to satisfy such requests'. He feared that assent might establish a precedent upon which other nations might act, and we hear no more of the affair. In February 1566-7 Baron was translated to Whitehorn in Galloway (Knox, *ibid*.).

Basle, A II d; Geneva, A IV a & b.

35. BARTHOLOMEW, JOHN: *Merchant*. Of London. Wife.
    d. 5 August 1558.

Nothing has yet been discovered about this man beyond what is to be found in the records of Basle. His name may possibly appear somewhere disguised in one of the many abbreviated forms used for the name, Bartholomew, but not easy to identify. Evidently he was a person of consequence, as well as a merchant. In 1556 he was a student at the University of Basle (Matrikel, f. 195); and from the *General Register of Persons* (vol. VI, 1551-1600)[1] we know that he had a house in the Petersplatz, though any further particulars about his occupation of it seem to have disappeared. In August 1558 he died and was buried in the church of St Theodore, where

[1] In the Staatsarchiv, an alphabetical index to other documents.

a monument with an inscription (see above, p. 57) was placed to his memory (Tonjola, p. 299). The following January his wife gave birth to a posthumous son, Gerson, to whom Lady Dorothy Stafford and Thomas Steward (*q.v.*) stood godparents when he was baptized in the church of St Albans.

Basle, A II a & d.

36. BATEMAN (BATMAN), JOHN: *Gent. or Merchant*(?).

His name does not appear as a member of John Knox's congregation, but he was admitted a 'resident' of Geneva (f. 264) on Monday, 24 October 1558. He may well be the John Bateman who sat for Nottingham Borough in the parliaments of 1555 and 1559 (Browne Willis, pp. 50, 65).[1] Since no indication of his calling follows Bateman's name in the Geneva Register, there is more likelihood of his having been a gentleman than a merchant or an artisan.

Geneva, A IV b.

37. BATES (BATUS), THOMAS: *Merchant*.

He was a member of the English congregation at Frankfort in 1555, but was not one of the subscribers to the 'new discipline' in 1557. His house stood 'bey dem mellwogenn' (Jung, p. 40). It is not impossible that this is the same Thomas Bates who transmitted money to the Earl and Countess of Northumberland 'during or since the rebellion' [of 1569], for which transaction he was examined 'on the interrogatories' by Sir Francis Jobson and Sir Henry Nevill (*Dom. Cal.* 1547–80, pp. 366, 368).

Frankfort, A III a 2 & b 1.

38. BAXTER (BAGSTER), THOMAS: *Book-binder*. Of London. Wife.

This is one of the obscure names which excites speculation. He has the distinction of being the only artisan at Frankfort, if his claim to being a book-binder is an honest one. In December 1557, when first mentioned, he was one of the subscribers to the 'new discipline', but in February 1558 he is found in Strasbourg with Robert Wisdom (Protocols, vol. 36, f. 65[vo]), claiming that he came there in the service of Sir Anthony Cooke, and that, his worldly circumstances having changed, evidently for the better, he would like to become a burgher. This request entailed an inquiry into the reasons for his having left Frankfort, the results of which not redounding to his credit, he was asked to leave Strasbourg (*ibid.* f. 124[vo]). He returned to Frankfort, where on 6 January 1559 he

---

[1] This is corroborated by the *Return of Members*, pt I, p. 394, where Bateman is given as 'generosus'. Bayne (*E.H.R.* XXIII, 669) thinks he was a citizen, since the name often occurs in the Borough Records.

bought from Jacob Bierss a house and garden on the Klapperfeld for 450 gulden (Jung, pp. 39–40). There he lived until 29 March 1559, when he commissioned the schoolmaster John Knippius to sell it for him on the occasion, as we suppose, of his return to England. His sudden acquisition of wealth and his association with Sir Anthony Cooke both suggest that the man was a spy. His name does not appear in Gordon Duff's list of printers (*A Century of the English Book Trade*) nor in the *Dictionary of English Printers* edited by McKerrow, nor in the Stationers' Register (Arber).

Frankfort, B III b; Strasbourg, A VII a.

39. BEAUMONT (BEAMONT, BEMONDE), ROBERT: *Student.* Of Leicestershire. d. 1567.

Peterhouse, Cambridge, M.A. 1550. He was admitted to Gray's Inn, 1541 (Venn, I, 119). He was not among the first group of English to reach Zurich but had arrived by 13 October 1554, when he appears as a signatory (Beamont) to the letter sent by that colony in answer to Whittingham's invitation to remove themselves to Frankfort (*T.* p. 16). By November 1556 he had gone with James Pilkington to Geneva, where they became members of Knox's congregation. On 14 October 1557 he was received as a 'resident' of the city (f. 196). There exists in the Bodleian Library (Rawl. D. 857, f. 222 and D. 923, f. 189) a curious MS. letter (in two parts) unsigned, but having on the back of one leaf a list of books on theology with the heading 'libri Roberti Beaumont'. The date is of 6 March 1557, and it appears to be an early appeal from Geneva to Frankfort for peace between the two English congregations. It is not included in Cooper's bibliography of Beaumont nor in that given in the *D.N.B.* On his return to England, Beaumont was ordained priest at Ely on 7 July 1560 (Venn). At Cambridge, where he first became Master of Trinity (1561), then Vice-Chancellor of the University (1564–5), he was one of the leaders of the Calvinist party. He was also one of those who voted for the adoption of a 'discipline' in 1562 (*Annals*, I, i, 512) and in 1565 appealed to Parker against the queen's order to wear the surplice (*Parker*, I, 386).

Zurich, A VIII c; B I b; B II; Geneva, IV a & b; *D.N.B.*

40. BEAUVOYS (BEVOYES, BEAUVOIR), WILLIAM: *Merchant.* Of Guernsey.

For the identification of the name with Beauvoir see Foster, I, 98. He had arrived at Geneva before 13 October 1555. On 27 July 1556 he was received as a 'resident' (f. 151) and there denominated as a merchant of Guernsey. On 15 December 1558 he was among those who signed Geneva's appeal to Frankfort for peace and co-operation in an anti-ceremonial crusade (*T.* p. 188).

Geneva, A iv a & b; B iii a.

41. BECON (BEACON), THOMAS ('alias Theodore Basill'), B.D.(?)[1]: *Priest.* Of Norfolk. *ca.* 1511–67.

Probably of St John's College, Cambridge. Ordained 1538. Vicar of Brenzet, Kent, and of St Stephen's, Walbrook, 1548–54. Twice made to recant in the reign of Henry VIII (Foxe, v, 448). Lived for some time in Staffordshire with his friends Robert Wisdom and John Old, who later were both exiles with him. Became chaplain to Cranmer (*Cranmer*, p. 417) and also to Protector Somerset (*D.N.B.*). On 16 August 1553 he was committed to the Tower (*P.C.A.* 1552–4, p. 322) for his association with Bradford and Veron in the riot at Paul's Cross on 13 August. On 24 March 1554 he was released (*Works*, ed. Parker Soc. p. x), 'because', says Foxe, 'providence blinded Winchester's eyes, in mistaking his name!' (Foxe, v, 696), and fled with Bishop Ponet to Strasbourg, where he became one of the earliest adversaries of the 'regiment of women'. Both his *Con*[sic]*fortable Epistle too* [sic] *Goddes faythfull people in Englande...* (*S.T.C.* no. 1716), and his *An humble supplicacion vnto God for...the churche of Englande* (*S.T.C.* no. 1730) were read aloud to the secret protestant gatherings in London, and because of a similarity of style, Becon may well have been the author of the virulent 'Prayer for King Philippe and Queen Marie', which was attached to the Liturgy of Frankfort (Wotherspoon, pp. 255–6) for use in the exiled congregations. In addition, we believe that he collaborated with Ponet in writing the pamphlet called the *Confession of the banished Ministers* (above, p. 28, n. 13 and p. 59) which was addressed to the lords and commons of Mary's third parliament, evidently as a protest against the reconciliation with Rome. Internal evidence shows that it was compiled, not in May as the colophon states, but about September 1554 (see also Ponet). It is therefore not surprising to find Becon's name on the list of those whose books were proscribed on 13 June 1555 (Steele, I, no. 461). During the spring of 1555 he appears to have taken part in the revision at Frankfort of the second Prayer Book of Edward VI, probably as a member of the committee, since his name appears among the signatories of the letter written to Calvin in explanation of the work (*O.L.* II, 755). He also endorsed Whitehead's later justification of the revision (*ibid.* p. 763) against

---

[1] 'Said to have been B.D.' (Venn, I, 114); 'commenced D.D. at Oxford' (Cooper, I, 247), but not listed as a D.D. in the Emden catalogue.

Calvin's criticism. After which date (20 September 1555) Becon seems to have remained for a time in Frankfort, where he appears among the 'students' on the Standesliste and is said (Jung, p. 41) to have lived in the Horsemarket (wohnhaft uff dem Rossmarck). But in 1556 it was he who dismissed Brett from the city of Strasbourg with the ominous words that he would not be in Brett's coat for 1000 pounds (above, p. 37). And as his name is not on the 'dwelling-list' of 1557 he may have thought it safer after this to retreat to Marburg, where Bale says he was living towards the close of the exile (*Scriptores*, IX, 756). In 1558 he returned to England, was restored to his benefice, and made a canon of Canterbury, 1559.

Strasbourg, B IV a; Frankfort, A III a 2 & b 1; A VIII a; Marburg, B I a & b; *D.N.B.*

42. BEDELL (BYDDYL, BIDELL, etc.), JOHN: *Student.*

M.A. Oxford, 28 May 1543 (Foster). This man has been identified by Jung (p. 41) as the John Bendall (*q.v.*) who signed the Liturgia Sacra at Frankfort in July 1554, but as the names of both John Bedell and John Bendall appear together in the Emden catalogue, this is manifestly an error. Apparently John Bedell, who first appears as a 'student' on the Standesliste of November 1555, remained at Frankfort throughout the period of exile, living in the house of William Master (*q.v.*). In the tax-list of 1556 his property is rated at 80 florins. In April 1557 he was a subscriber to the 'new discipline'. But unless he was the 'Mr Bedell' who was one of the pall-bearers at Parker's funeral in 1575 (*Parker*, II, 433), we know nothing of him after 1557.

Frankfort, A III a 2, 3, 4 & b 1, 2; B I & B II.

BEDFORD, FRANCIS, second Earl. *See* Russell.

43. BEESLEY (BESLEY, BISLEYE, BYSELEY), RICHARD, B.D. *Priest.* Wife.

Fellow of All Souls College, Oxford (Foster, I, 117). An old chaplain of Henry VIII (*Dom. Cal.* 1547–80, p. 287) and a favourite of Thomas Cromwell, who declared 'I owe him all'.[1] Rector of Cumnor, Berks. (1541) and of Staplehurst, Kent. One of the six preachers at Canterbury in 1547 (*Cranmer*, p. 229), but was 'pronounced contumacious' under Mary (*ibid.* p. 472). He lived at Frankfort with his wife and two children in a house in the 'Mentzer gassen' (Jung, p. 41). In the tax-list of 1557 the words 'hat nichts an narung' appear after his name (Jung, p. 30). He

---

[1] Quoted from a record in the church at Wootton, Berks.

subscribed to the 'new discipline' in April, and was still in
Frankfort in January 1559, since he signed that congregation's
reply to Geneva (*T*. p. 190). Upon his return to England he was
again made one of the preachers at Canterbury (*Parker*, I, 144).
In 1562 he signed the articles altering rites and ceremonies (*Annals*,
I, i, 504) and also the petition for a discipline (*ibid*. I, i, 512). He
was restored to the living of Cumnor after 1559.

Frankfort, A III a 2, 3, 4 & b 1, 2; B II; B III a & b.

44. BENDALL, JOHN: *Student*(?).

Nothing whatever is known of this man except that his name
appears in the Emden catalogue, and that he was one of the
English subscribers on 29 July 1554 to the liturgy of the French
Church at Frankfort, known as the Liturgia Sacra. He may have
been a Scot.

Frankfort, *Liturgia Sacra* (ed. 1554), p. 92; B I.

45. BENTHAM (BENTAM, BENTON), THOMAS: *Student*. Of Sherburn, Yorkshire. 1513–78.

Fellow of Magdalen College, Oxford, 1546. Made Dean of Arts
in 1552 (Wilson, *Magd*. p. 99). According to Humphrey's obscure
account (*Jewel*, p. 73) he was deprived for an act of sacrilege
committed during Gardiner's Visitation (1553), but actually
occurring at the same time as Bickley's (*q.v.*) disturbance in 1548
(Wilson, *Magd*. p. 88). It appears that in September, before the
Visitation began, Bentham, with five others, four of whom became
exiles, 'had sought for and obtained leave of absence for various
periods' (*ibid*. p. 101). He seems to have been one of the nine
actual Fellows, removed at the Visitation, to whom a special grant
of money was made 'ex voluntate inquisitorum' (*ibid*. p. 103). This
sum he may have used for his journey to Zurich, where he appeared
in April 1554 with the first group of students (*O.L*. II, 751–2). He
was still there on 13 October, when he signed the admonitory reply
to Frankfort's invitation to join them (*T*. pp. 13–16) but not long
afterwards he left for Basle, where he is registered as a student for
the year 1555–6 (f. 194). While at Basle he was made preacher to
the exiles there, and Bale includes him in the list of those 'in
nostro collegio' (*Scriptores*, p. 741), that is, in the Clarakloster.
In January 1557, however, he was in Frankfort again (*T*. p. 65),
where he seems to have supported Horne in the quarrel with
Ashley (*ibid*. p. 97) and on that account refused to become an
officer in the church. Previously he had been made a member of
the committee of eight arbiters in the quarrel (*ibid*. p. 77), and
Whittingham commends him for showing himself 'indifferent and
equall to bothe sides'. In November he went to Geneva where,

probably because of his knowledge of Hebrew, they wished for his collaboration on the Genevan Bible. There on 20 November he was received as a member of Knox's congregation and on Monday, 29 November (1557), as a 'resident' of Geneva (f. 226). Sometime before January he married 'Mawde Fawcon of Hadley in the county of Suffolk' (Martin, p. 337), who had probably been one of Roland Taylor's congregation. Before the close of Mary's reign Bentham returned to England to become preacher to the hidden congregation in London (*Mem.* iii, ii, 132–3). His letter to Thomas Lever written from there on 17 July 1558 describes some of the martyrdoms at which he himself was present (*ibid.* pp. 133–5). Upon the accession of Elizabeth he was consecrated bishop of Coventry and Lichfield, 24 March 1559/60 (Le Neve, i, 556).

Zurich, A viii a, b, c; Basle, A ii a; Frankfort, B iii a; Geneva, A iv a & b; London, July; *D.N.B.*

46. BERKELEY (BARKLEY, BARTLEY), GILBERT, B.D.: *Ex-religious and priest.* Of Lincolnshire or Norfolk. 1501[7]–1581.

A Franciscan of Northampton and York successively, who was ordained priest in 1535 (Baskerville, *E.H.R.* 1933, pp. 56, 201) and received a B.D. from Oxford in 1538 (Foster, i, 113). From 1547, until his deprivation under Mary, he was rector of Attleborough, Norfolk. Then he took refuge at Frankfort, where Strype says that he encouraged Traheron to publish his lectures on Revelations (*Mem.* iii, i, 544), but where he is officially mentioned but once—on the Steuerliste of 1556, when his property is rated àt 80 florins. On Berkeley's return to England he was consecrated bishop of Bath and Wells, in place of Bourne, on 24 March 1560 (Le Neve, i, 144); but Strype's praise of him as a man of 'singular integrity of life' is hardly borne out by his lax and venal administration of his diocese.

Frankfort, A iii a 3; *D.N.B.*

47. BERTIE (BARTEWE, BARTUE), RICHARD: *Gent.* Of Bersted, Kent. Wife. 1517–82.

B.A. Magdalen College, Oxford, 1537 (Macray, *Reg. Magd. Coll.* ii, 75–6). Husband of Katherine, Duchess Dowager of Suffolk. Summoned before Gardiner on 23 March 1554 (Foxe, viii, 569). Left England by the queen's licence in June 1554, with permission 'to pass and repass [the seas] so often as to him seemed good' (*ibid.* p. 571). He then went to Venice and Padua, where he is mentioned by Sir Thomas Hoby as among the English gentlemen of doubtful loyalty, gathered in that city in August[1] 1554 (Cam. Misc. x, 116). In January 1554/5, either he returned to London for his wife or sent for her to join him in Germany; and on 1 January 1554/5 there followed the extraordinary flight of the duchess and her household to the coast (above, p. 11). So much has been written on the Berties abroad that we shall do little more than present their itinerary as given, probably, by Richard Bertie himself (Foxe, VIII, 569–76).

They embarked from Gravesend, 5 February 1554/5, and going to Santon, in Cleves, took a house. From there, Bertie 'practised' to obtain 'a protection from the magistrates for his abode' in Wesel (Foxe, VIII, 573) through the instrumentality of François Peruçel, lately of London, now minister of the French Church at Wesel. There they hired a house under an assumed name and there a son, Peregrine (Lord Willoughby de Eresby), was born to them. (For the legend of his birth in the porch of the church of St Willi-brod, see *Notes and Queries*, 5th ser. I, 366, 474; and for a refutation of it from the Town Records of Wesel, cf. Rev. J. Anderson's *Ladies of the Reformation*, pp. 352–3.) It would seem that the gathering of the English at Wesel was in direct consequence of the Berties' presence there. For we learn that 'the brute theroff was the cause that moo Englishe people in shorte time resorted thither' (*T*. pp. 184–5). Many seem to have come from Calais (cf. Records of Aarau) and also from Emden, which would explain the am-biguity of Strype's paragraph (*Mem*. III, i, 233), which makes no clear distinction between the colonies of Emden and Wesel. But when in April 1556 the Berties were obliged to leave, they went by way of Strasbourg (Lady Bertie, *Five Generations*, p. 29, n. 2) to the castle of Weinheim, offered to them as a refuge by the Duke of Deux Ponts (Bypont) at the intercession of Coverdale (*T*. pp. 184–5). There Brett sought them (on 10 July 1556) with his warrants from Queen Mary. The story of his hostile reception and his parley with Bishop Barlow are graphically told in the 'Narrative' (pp. 121–2). A year later, in April 1557, Bertie was asked by the magistrates of Frankfort to become a member with Cox and Sandys of a committee to arbitrate the dispute over the 'new discipline' (*T*. pp. 99, 101). The family was then probably on its way to Poland, where they had been offered a second refuge by

---

[1] But on 31 August Richard Bertie was still in Venice, for on that date the Council of 10 granted him a permit to see the jewels of the Sanctuary (*Ven. Cal*. 1555–6, p. 122 and note). As the permit is issued to 'Mr Richard Bertie, husband of the Duchess of Suffolk *of England*', a title given to his wife in right of her first husband, the editor of the *Venetian Calendar* infers that she was then with her husband in Venice. If true, this would complicate still further the problem of her flight from London in January 1555.

King Sigismond Augustus (*T*. p. 185). Barlow (*q.v.*) went ahead with John Burcher (*O.L.* II, 687ff.) at the instigation of John à Lasco to prepare the way, and there in the earldom of Kroze, called by them 'Crossen', they remained until after 4 March 1559 (S.P. Dom. Eliz. III, 9). Eventually the Berties passed into legend, and the ballad of 'The Most Rare and Excellent History of the Dutchess of Suffolk and her husband Richard Bertie's Calamities', sung 'to the tune of Queen Dido' (T. Evans, *Old Ballads* (ed. 1784), II, 92), no doubt played its part with Foxe's *Book of Martyrs* in popularizing the miseries of the Marian Exile. Before she left 'Crossen', the duchess, in a letter to Cecil (S.P. Dom. Eliz. III, 9), spoke her mind sharply on the evils of 'halting between two opinions' in matters of religion, and exhorted him 'to forward the true faith'. Cecil can have found her no more agreeable as a coadjutor than Gardiner had found her as an adversary. Sir Richard Morison complains bitterly to Sir Nicholas Throckmorton of the 'Lady Suffolk's heats', which have 'oft cumbered him'. 'It is a pity', he concludes patiently, 'that so goodly a wit waiteth upon so froward a will' (*For. Cal.* 1547–53, p. 101).

Santon; Wesel; Padua, B IV b; Weinheim, B III; B IV a; Frankfort, B III;
Poland, A VIII a; *D.N.B.*

48. BEST (BEAST), ROBERT: *Weaver*(?) *and student*. Of St Botolph, Colchester. Wife.

A Robert Beast is in the list of those 'forced to abjure in King Henry's days' (Foxe, IV, 585). Strype calls one of this name a weaver of Colchester, and says that he was 'a reader and teacher of the new opinions' who was examined before Tunstall (*Mem.* I, i, 117, 121, 125–6) and was accused of knowing the Epistle of St James by heart and of being one of those known as 'brethren in Christ'. He is found at Frankfort on the list of 'students' in 1555 and is rated in 1556 as worth 20 florins (Jung, p. 29). In 1557 he was living with his wife and child in a house with Robert Crowley. He was of Whitehead's party in the congregation (*T*. p. 174) and subscribed to the 'new discipline'. If he returned to England, nothing more is known of him.

Frankfort, A III a 2, 3, 4 & b 1, 2; B II.

49. BETTS, WILLIAM: *Weaver*. Of Suffolk. Wife.

Had lived at Hadleigh (Hadelea) and was probably a member of Rowland Taylor's congregation. On the Continent he was one of the colony at Aarau, where he and his wife lodged in the house of one Joachim Schmutzingers.

Aarau, A I a & b.

50. BICKLEY, Thomas, B.D. (1552): *Deacon*. Of Stowe in Buckinghamshire. 1518–96.

Fellow of Magdalen College, Oxford, 1540–54. Ordained deacon, 29 March 1551, but did not receive priest's orders under Edward (*Mar. Reac.* p. 213, cf. Macray, *Reg. Magd.* II, 81). In 1553 he became vice-president of the college, following Walter Haddon's election to the presidency (October 1552). His biographer (*D.N.B.*) questions the truth of the story that he had thrown down and trampled on the Host in Magdalen Chapel (1548). But not only does Laurence Humphrey (*Vita Juelli*) record his act with approbation, but H. A. Wilson, in his *Magdalen College* (pp. 87–8 and note), finds it substantiated in the college records, though not mentioned in the vice-president's Register. Bickley was then a man of thirty and already a Fellow of long standing. At the time of Gardiner's Visitation (1553) he was expelled; and according to both Humphrey (*op. cit.* p. 73) and Wood (*Ath. Oxon.* II, 840) retired to France, where he studied at Paris and Orleans. No trace of him has been discovered in any of the English colonies in Germany. On his return to England he became chaplain to Archbishop Parker (*Parker*, I, 344) and was a subscriber to the Articles of 1562. Later he was elected warden of Merton (1569–85) and eventually (1585/6) bishop of Chichester (Le Neve, I, 250). He seems always to have conformed and to have been much trusted by Parker and Cecil.

Paris; Orleans; *D.N.B.*

51. BINKS, John: *Merchant*.

Appears as 'Joannes Binckus' in the Frankfort Standesliste, and as 'Byntzss' in the Steuerliste of 1556, where his property is valued at 1000 florins (Jung, p. 42). On 25 March 1557 he refused to serve the Frankfort congregation (probably in the capacity of deacon, since these had the distribution of the funds) and must therefore be considered a member of Robert Horne's party in the quarrels that rent the Church (*T.* p. 97). He was also one of those who signed a protest to the Frankfort council against the use of the 'new discipline' (*T.* pp. 168–9). In the dwelling-list of June 1557 he is found to have been an inmate of Horne's house (*H.S.P.* IV, 89). He remained at Frankfort for some time after Elizabeth's accession and between April and August 1559 served as a witness in the quarrels of the French Church which were heard before a commission of the Senate (Jung, p. 42). No trace of the man has been discovered in England either before or after his exile.

Frankfort, A III a 2, 3, 4 & b 1, 2; B III a.

52. BIRCH (BIRSCH), James (cf. Jung) or William(?): *Student.*
Of Manchester(?). d. 1575(?).

If this was William Birch, he was the second son of George
Birch, Esq., of Birch, Lancs. The name appears but once in any
foreign list—that of Frankfort's tax-list of 1556, where he is rated
as worth 20 florins, followed by the words 'wird nur hier genannt'.
He may possibly be the John Birch, parson of St Botolph's Lane,
imprisoned at the same time as Thomas Becon in connection with
the Six Articles (*Mem.* I, i, 567), but we are more inclined to
believe that he was the William Birch (Byrche) of 'Benett College
in Univ. Cant.' who was ordained deacon (but not priest) by
Ridley in 1552 (*Mar. Reac.* p. 202), was ejected from Corpus
Christi College in 1553 (Venn, I, 154) and is supposed by Cooper
(I, 562) to have gone abroad. If so, he probably went in company
with Thomas Lever. When he returned to England in 1559 he
received preferment, and was finally made prebendary of Durham
in 1562, but in 1567 was deprived for nonconformity, though he
retained the living of Stanhope till his death. No *James* Birch has
been discovered for that date either in Foster or in Venn.

Frankfort, A III a 3; Cooper.

53. BIRCKBECK (BRICKBEKE, BIRCKBATE, BRICK-
BATE), Christopher: *Merchant.* Of Kendall (Jung,
p. 43), Westmoreland. Wife.

We suspect this man to have been one Christopher Simpson, who
assumed his wife's maiden name of Birkbeck. In the genealogy of
the *Birkbecks of Westmoreland* (1900) there is no 'Christopher'
recorded until the eighteenth century (p. 6); nor does the name
occur in Foster's *Westmoreland Pedigrees*, 1615. But 'sometime
before 1550' Henry Birkbeck's daughter, Elizabeth, had married
a Christopher Symson (*Birkbecks, etc.* p. 15), and probably this is
the man who, as Christopher Brikbeke, was received a burgher of
Frankfort on 18 April 1555 and paid 2 florins 8 albus Bürgergeld.
In the autumn of 1555 he was dwelling in a house of his own 'by
the great fountain' ('wohnend bey dem gross born', Jung, p. 43)
with his wife, three children, and a maid (*H.S.P.* IV, 88). In 1556
his property was assessed at 800 florins. In 1557 he was included
by John Hales among those 'that semed desirous off the peace off
the churche' and was therefore invited by Hales to co-operate with
him in finding 'the beste waie to quiete this styrre' (*T.* pp. 64–5).
On 25 March, with other adherents of Horne the pastor (cf.
'Binks' above), Birkbeck refused office in the church. He remained
in Frankfort after Elizabeth's accession and on 3 January was one

of the subscribers to Pilkington's refusal to take part with Geneva in a crusade against ceremonies (*T*. p. 190).

Frankfort, A III 1, 2, 3, 4 & b 1, 2.

*BLACK, George.

This is one of two cases (see 'John Young') in the *Original Letters of the Reformation* where the name of a foreigner has been most misleadingly translated into English. The 'George Black', 'son of Francis Black', mentioned by Burcher to Bullinger as one of the company travelling with him to Poland in December 1557, was no Englishman, but 'Georgius Niger', son of Franciscus Niger (or Negri), an Italian from the Valtelline, who became a protestant and a teacher of the classics at Chiavenna.[1] An interesting account of him will be found in F. C. Church's *Italian Reformers*.

54. BLACKMAN, Robert.

This man, whoever he may have been, became a member of the English congregation at Geneva on the same day as did Laurence Humphrey, 28 April 1558. On 24 October 1558 he was received as a 'resident' of the town (f. 264). Possibly he was a relative of the William Blackman of Colchester who had been forced to abjure in King Henry's time (Foxe, IV, 586). An Adam Blackman later migrated to New England (*New Eng. Reg.* I, 287).

Geneva, A IV a & b.

55. BLAKE, John: *Student*.

A certain 'Johannes Blochus, Anglus', for whose name we hazard the English equivalent of Blake, matriculated from the University of Basle on 12 May 1558. On 25 January 1560 Grindal ordained as priest a 'John Blake' who is probably the same man (*Grindal*, p. 55), and also one with the 'Blake' mentioned in the *Annals* (I, i, 228), who in the same year is found on a list presented to Cecil of 'Spiritual men without promotion at this present'. His name is not to be found among either Oxford or Cambridge alumni.

Basle, A II a.

56. BODLEY (BODLEIGH, BUDLEIGH), John: *Merchant*. Of Exeter, Devon. Wife.

Of the family of Bodleigh of Dunscombe-by-Crediton, and father of Sir Thomas Bodley, founder of the Bodleian Library. He is called by Fuller 'a princely merchant'. In 1549 he had financed the suppression of the rebellion in Devon against the introduction

[1] I owe this identification to the great kindness of Professor Hans Nabholz of the University of Zurich.

of the first Prayer Book of Edward VI (Rose-Troup, *The Western Rebellion of* 1549, pp. 239–40; Fuller, *History*, IV, 45–6). Though it is said that he sought safety abroad 'on account of his known Protestantism' (*D.N.B.* on Sir Thomas Bodley), there is likelihood that his money had proved useful to Sir Peter Carew and others in the rising in the West of 1554 (Rose-Troup, *Sir Thomas Bodley's Father etc.* p. 9).[1] His son, in his *Autobiography* (p. 1), speaks of his father's having been 'cruelly threatened' and 'narrowly observed, by those that maliced his religion', though at the time no official persecution was in force.

They went first to Wesel, where Bodley was evidently one of the circle that gathered round the Duchess of Suffolk. He was obliged to leave Wesel at the same time as the Berties, and from there went with his family for a short time to Frankfort, then to Geneva (*Autobiography*, pp. 1–2), where on 8 May 1557 he was received with his wife, his three sons, his daughter, and three 'servants', as members of John Knox's church. On 7 June he became a 'resident' of Geneva (f. 180) and on 31 May 1558 was received as a burgher (see Preamble to the Livre des Anglois and Rose-Troup, *op. cit.* p. 17). In the same year he and William Kethe assisted the congregation of Wesel to find a new home, travelling, as it is said, over a great part of Savoy and Switzerland before a suitable sanctuary was found for them at Aarau (*T.* p. 185). In December 1558 he helped to establish, with William Williams, a printing office at Geneva (Reg. du Cons. vol. 61, ff. 87vo, 88vo; cf. Martin, p. 70 and note) and gave to Rowland Hall (*q.v.*) the direction of printing the Geneva Bible. On 16 December 1557 he was made a senior of the English congregation, and the following year was re-elected to the position with Miles Coverdale (Martin, p. 335). Though his son Thomas, then twelve years old, was lodged in the house of a physician, Philibertus Saracenus, and became an auditor of the lectures of Chevalerius in Hebrew, Berealdus in Greek, and of Calvin and Beza in Divinity (*Autobiography*, pp. 1–2), yet, even without him, the character of John Bodley's household was patriarchal. Not only did it shelter his immediate family, now increased by the birth of two sons abroad, Miles (*vide* entry Livre des Bourgeois, cited Rose-Troup, *op. cit.* p. 17) and Zachary (Martin, p. 336), but also his servants, his brother Nicholas, and his two 'merchant apprentices', Boggens (*q.v.*) and Vivian (*q.v.*). And with this household he left Geneva on 5 September 1559 (Reg. du Cons. vol. 55, f. 91; cf. Martin, p. 260) to return to England. There he established himself in London. There too, about

---

[1] In the Bodleian Library (shelfmark, 2182 B. a. 12). Other MS. material used by Mrs Rose-Troup is also deposited there.

1560, he was granted a patent for seven years for the exclusive printing of the Genevan Bible (*Dom. Cal.* 1547–80, p. 166). Nor did his personal connection with Geneva cease. Some five autograph letters of his, written in 1583–4, are still preserved in the Archives of Geneva (Rose-Troup, *op. cit.* p. 22).

Wesel; Frankfort, B III; Geneva, A IV a & b.

57. BODLEY, NICHOLAS: *Merchant*(?). Of Exeter, Devon.

Brother of John Bodley, and received with him into the church at Geneva on 8 May 1557. There is no evidence that he became a 'resident' of the town. Possibly, like Henry Withers (*q.v.*), he was a student in Calvin's new university.

Wesel (?); Geneva, A IV a.

BODLEY, THOMAS, later Sir Thomas Bodley, founder of the Bodleian Library (see 'John Bodley' above).

He has been counted among the children.

58. BOGGENS, JOHN: *Merchant apprentice.*

Though spoken of in the Livre des Anglois as 'servant' to John Bodley, this appellation is carefully corrected in the Registre des Habitants, where the word 'servant' is crossed out (f. 197) and the words 'compagnon marchant' substituted. He was admitted to residence 14 October 1557.

Geneva, A IV a & b.

59. BOLTON, JOHN: *Weaver.* Of Reading, Berkshire.

Imprisoned, either for speaking against the mass in Lent 1554 (Foxe, VI, 575–7) or for railing upon Queen Mary while feigning madness (Thackham's story, *Narr. of Ref.* p. 96). Bolton's own account of his imprisonment has been preserved by Foxe, but two other versions of it, Thackham's and Moyer's, are to be found in Nichols's *Narratives of the Reformation*. Thackham claims that he went bail for Bolton, upon which Bolton fled from Reading leaving him to pay the forfeit (*ibid.* p. 97). Moyer intimates (1564, *ibid.* note b) that the price of Bolton's release had been a recantation, he being then 'bereft of his senses' (see also *Mem.* III, ii, 427–30). Finally in the 'Information gathered at Reading in 1571' (*Narr. of Ref.* p. 96, note b) it is asserted that he 'was set at lybertie by Sir Fraunces Inglefield, without any suerties'.[1] The only incontrovertible fact in Bolton's story seems to be that he fled to Geneva,

[1] And Gardiner, it seems, when passing through Reading in 1554, had himself tried to release Bolton; but since the latter 'most boldly reproved the said Bishop to his face', he had to be sent back to prison (J. A. Muller, *Life of Gardiner* (1926), p. 258).

whether because he was 'burdened in conscience' for his recantation (cf. Moyer) or no, and that there on 5 November 1556
he was received into the English Church, while on 14 October 1557
he became a resident of the town, as 'John Bolton tisserant'.
After Mary's death he returned to London, thereafter following
his trade in 'Long's lane by Smythfield' (*Narr. of Ref.* p. 96, note b).
And he was probably the same John Bolton who was a member
of the dissenting 'Plumber's Hall' congregation in 1567 (C. Burrage,
Early English Dissenters, I, 88).

Geneva, A IV a & b.

BORTHWICK, Sir JOHN. *See* Burtwick.

60. BOYES (BOYS), EDWARD: *Gent.* Of Kent. Wife. d. *ca.* 1596.
Almost unquestionably the Edward Boyes of Fredwell in Nonington,
who was sheriff of Kent in 1577 (Hasted, I, p. xcii; Berry, *Kent, etc.*
p. 441). His marriage relations are peculiarly significant and
typical, for his first wife was Clare, daughter of Sir Nicholas
Wentworth of 'Lyllingstone Lovell, Oxon' (now Bucks.), 'Knighte
Porter' of Calais, and father of Peter Wentworth (Harl. Soc. LXXV,
123–4). A daughter by her, Gersona, evidently born in Frankfort,
was buried there (*ibid.* p. 124); but his surviving son Edward
eventually married his cousin, Mary Wentworth, the daughter of
Peter Wentworth by his second wife, Elizabeth Walsingham, a
sister of Sir Francis Walsingham. Thus Edward Boys of Frankfort
was both the brother-in-law of Peter Wentworth (cf. J. E. Neale's
'Peter Wentworth', *E.H.R.* XXXIX, 36, 175) and the uncle and
father-in-law of Sir Francis Walsingham's niece. In 1557 he was
an exile in Frankfort, living in the house of Thomas Sandes (or
Saunders (?); cf. Jung, p. 42 and *H.S.P.* IV, 89), with his wife, three
children, and four servants. He signed the 'new discipline' in
December, and in the same year went to Geneva with Thomas
Lever and four others (*T.* p. 185) to aid in establishing the former
congregation of Wesel, at Aarau in the jurisdiction of Berne. But
the Aarau lists prove that he was never, as Fuller asserts (*History*, IV,
206), a member of that colony (see also John Bodley). On Boyes's
return to England he seems to have been for a time out of favour.
Parker, in 1563, lamented that one 'whom he took to be an honest
gentleman' was not a Justice of the Peace (*Parker*, I, 290). In 1558,
when a serious case of image-breaking occurred at Dover, an
'Edward Boyes, esq.' was admonished by the Council to examine
into it diligently (*P.C.A.* 1558–70, p. 67) and henceforth his connection with Dover was to be continuous. In 1580 he served on
a commission with Lord Cobham for the repair of Dover Harbour
(*Dom. Cal.* 1547–80, p. 671, no. 26) and by April 1585 he had been

made treasurer of the works (*ibid.* 1581–90, p. 236, no. 14). But we must suppose, for lack of further mention, that he died about 1590 (*ibid.* 1581–90, p. 647).

Frankfort, A iii a 4 & b 2; B iii a & b.

61. BRADBRIDGE (BRODBRIGE, BRODEBRICHE), AU-
GUSTINE (AUSTIN): *Student.* Of Chichester. d. 1567.

Fellow of New College, Oxford, 1546–53 (O.H.S. i, 242) and probably brother of William Bradbridge (below). In November 1554 he was at Strasbourg and took part in the Prayer Book controversy with Frankfort (*T.* p. 23). That same winter he appears as a student at the University of Basle, where he is designated as of 'dioc. Cicestren.' In December 1554 he received 12 gulden as his share of the Duke of Württemberg's bounty (Württ. Staats-archiv). As Augustin Brodebriche he became a member of Knox's congregation at Geneva on 8 May 1557, and a 'resident' of the town, styling himself 'estudiant', on 14 October 1557. In 1559 he was made a canon of Chichester, and chancellor in 1560 (Foster, i, 165).

Strasbourg, A vii c; B iii a; Basle, A ii a; Geneva, A iv a & b.

*BRADBRIDGE, WILLIAM.

Probably not an exile. In the Emden list (B i) the name Bradbridge does not appear at all. But in Strype's additions to this list (*Cranmer*, p. 450) the surname is given without a Christian name. In the notice of William Bradbridge in the *D.N.B.* he is said to have fled from England with Barlow and Coverdale in 1553 (in any case an error for 1554), but since there is no record of a *William* Bradbridge abroad, and as Wood states (ii, 816) that in March 1554 William was made prebendary of Salisbury, and Foster (i, 165) that in the same year he was appointed 'custos of St Mary Hospital, Chichester'; and as both William and his brother(?) Augustine Bradbridge were eventually chancellors of Chichester, William succeeding Augustine in 1562, it is not unlikely that, in the point of exile, the two men have been confused. Strype, indeed, says that he fled. But neither Wood nor Foster records the fact.

D.N.B.

62. BRADFORD (BRADFORTH), JOHN: *Spy*; *Gent.* Of
Nantwich, Cheshire. d. 1557.

An extremely interesting person, who must be sharply distinguished from the martyr (cf. Pollard, *Pol. Hist.* vi, 147 and note). He was the author of one, perhaps two, lively pamphlets, but says of himself in *The copye of a lettre sent by J. Bradforth to the earles of*

Arundel, Darbie, etc. (Brit. Mus. C. 8, b. 8 and *S.T.C.* no. 3480) that he had been 'serving-man' to Sir Thomas Skipwith [father-in-law of Sir Peter Carew] and was 'without all knowledge, or learnyng' (Sig. A 4ᵛᵒ). Nevertheless he was insinuated, probably by Sir Peter himself (cf. *For. Cal.* 1553–8, p. 79) into the household of the Duke of Medina-Coele (Sig. B 1), and there for two years, as 'Chamberlain' (Sig. D 5), played the spy upon him. This must have been between 1554–6 (cf. *For. Cal.* above) for he was apprehended in the Dudley plot in 1556 and in his examination is described as a 'gentleman' of Nantwich, Cheshire (Baga, p. 258). However, he must have escaped again to France, for he is doubtless the same 'John Bradforde' who as a member of Thomas Stafford's expedition of 1557 was caught at Scarborough and executed at Tyburn (Baga, p. 258). As given by Strype from the Foxii MS. (*Mem.* III, ii, 339–54), *The copye of a lettre, etc.* differs materially from the original pamphlet. Whether it was transcribed from another draft, or whether Strype, not penetrating its catholic disguise, was tempted to modify its violent anti-protestantism, must remain a question. Maitland suggests (*Essays,* p. 86) that since Bradford mentions (Sig. A 7–A 7ᵛᵒ) *A supplicacyon to the Quenes Maiestie* (Herbert's Ames, III, 1582 and Brit. Mus. C. 37, b. 26) he may also have been its author; but differences of style (though not of purpose) suggest, rather, that though it emanated from the same circle, it was not by the same hand.

France, B v c.

63. BROKE (BROOKE), JOHN ('alias Sigismund'): *Gent.* Of Kent. 1534–94.

That the John Broke, licensed to bear arms at Venice in July 1555 (*Ven. Cal.* 1555–6, p. 145), and the Sigismund Broke, for a short time inmate of Thomas Crawley's house at Frankfort in 1557, were one and the same person would seem to be indicated by the initial 'J' which appears before his name when listed among the members of Crawley's household (Jung, p. 47). Otherwise this 'J. Brokus' is known at Frankfort as 'Sigismund' (*ibid.* pp. 33, 43; cf. also *H.S.P.* IV, 88). And this John Broke or Brook, 'alias Sigismund', was very likely John, third son of George Brooke, seventh Lord Cobham (d. 1558), once deputy of Calais (1544), who numbered among his forebears both Courtenays and de la Poles (*Somerset Arch. and Hist. Soc. Proc.* XLV, 13). If so, John was also first cousin to Sir Thomas Wyatt the younger,[1] which may well account both for the presence in Padua of a 'Mr Brooke', encountered there by Sir Thomas Hoby in August 1554 (Cam. Misc.

---

[1] His aunt, Elizabeth Brooke, having married about 1520 Sir Thomas Wyatt of Allington (*Somerset Arch. and Nat. Hist. Soc. Proc.* XLV, 10 and *D.N.B.*).

x, 117), and for the absence of John Brooke's name among those of his brothers, William, George and Thomas, in Dudley's conspiracy of 1556 (Baga, p. 241), he being still abroad. From Padua he seems to have gone to Venice in 1555 (cf. *Ven. Cal.* above) either to meet the Earl of Bedford or merely as a stage in his journey to Frankfort, where he is found in June 1557. Possibly he was even then on his way to England, for he appears but once at Frankfort (Jung, p. 33), and on 16 August 1557 a Sigismund Brooke was appointed one of the executors of the will of 'Barnard Sandiford of Paddington, Middlesex, clerk', together with Richard Kendlemarsh and Laurence Nowell (*Dom. Cal.* Addend. 1547–65, p. 458, no. 35). Later 'he fought bravely and successfully' in the Netherlands and ended 'his pious life' in 1594. His monument is in the church of Newington, Kent, where his wife, Alice Cobbe, Lady Norton, is also buried (*Somerset Arch. and Nat. Hist. Soc. Proc.* XLV, 13, 15).

Padua, B IV b; Venice, B v b 2; Frankfort, A III a 4 & b 2.

64. BROME (BROMUS, BRUNE, BROWNE?), JOHN: *Student*.

Registered among the English 'students' at Padua during 1555–6, when he was chosen as their Consiliarius (Andrich, pp. 31, 131). He is very possibly the John Brome or Browne who studied at Christchurch, Oxford 'in and before 1564' and received his M.A. in 1566 (Foster). Foster's mention of the alternative surname 'Browne' (cf. also O.H.S. I, 253) makes it not unlikely that the student of Padua and that of Christchurch are identical with the John Browne who signed the Frankfort 'discipline' on 21 December 1557. This person seems at the time to have been living at Strasbourg, since in the previous September he had been a signatory of that colony's effort to reconcile the warring factions in the Frankfort Church (*T.* pp. 173–4). By 1559, however, he had removed to Frankfort, where he subscribed to Pilkington's letter to Geneva, 3 January 1559, and was still living there on 10 March (Jung, p. 43). He is probably the 'Mr Brome' who was Archbishop Parker's commissary in 1571 (*Annals*, II, i, 182).

Padua, A VI a; Strasbourg, B III; Frankfort, B III.

65. BROWNE (BRUNE?), JOHN: *Gent.* Of Dorset(?). d. 1557.

A John Browne, one of Thomas Stafford's expedition to Scarborough in 1557, was executed at Hull in the autumn of that year (*Mem.* III, ii, 68). Very possibly he was the John Brune, son of John Brune of Dorset, who we are told in the family pedigree was 'iunior miles temp. Reginae Mariae' (Harl. Soc. XX, 22), and whose widow Jane, daughter of Bamfeild, married Charles Wingfeild (*ibid.*).

France (?).

66. BULLINGHAM (BOLINGHAM), Nicholas, D.C.L.:
    Archdeacon. Of Worcester (city). 1512(?)–76.

Probably a son of Thomas Bullingham, a bailiff of Worcester. Fellow of All Souls College, Oxford (1536); chaplain to Cranmer; archdeacon of Lincoln (1549) and rector of Thimbleby, Lincs. (1552). But as in the table of those bishops consecrated in the province of Canterbury 1559–62, he is designated as a 'secular minister' (*Annals*, I, i, 230), it is possible that his deprivation in 1554 was due to insufficient orders (cf. *Mar. Reac.* p. 77 n. and *Parker*, I, 127). For a while, after Mary's accession, he remained in England, but seems eventually to have fled to Emden about 5 December 1554 (Cooper, I, 350), where he may have collaborated in the edition of Cranmer's *Defensio*, published in 1557. On his return to England he became, successively, bishop of Lincoln (1560) and of Worcester (1571).

Emden, B I a & b; *D.N.B.*

67. BUNNY (BUNY, BONNY), Richard: *Gent.* Of Wakefield, Yorkshire. d. 1584.

Admitted to Gray's Inn in 1539 (Gray's Inn Reg. col. 13). Paymaster in the North and Treasurer of Berwick under Henry VIII and Edward VI (*P.C.A.* 1552–4, p. 5 and Index). He was also the father of Edmund Bunney, who has been called 'the most fluent preacher in the reign of Queen Elizabeth' (Macray, *Reg. Magd.* II, 150–3). Though it has been said of Richard that 'he suffered as a protestant under Mary' (*D.N.B.*), his offence seems rather to have been a 'mysdemeanour in his office', no less, in fact, than the forging of a note for £95 in the hand of Northumberland (*P.C.A.* 1554–6, pp. 3, 43–4), for which he was sent to the Fleet on 26 March 1554. When his case came before the Council in June, Bunny confessed to the forgery and surrendered his office, but when summoned again on 29 September he had either managed, or been permitted, to escape abroad. During the winter of 1554–5 he was registered as a student at the University of Basle under the name of Richard 'Bunnus' (below, p. 357). From Basle in 1555 he went to Paris, where he wrote a tearful letter to Nicholas Wotton (*For. Cal.* 1553–8, p. 191) bewailing 'his sadly reduced circumstances'. He is sure that 'the finishing of his days draws nigh', and explains that he 'only left England after his strait imprisonment...for fear of being further punished and troubled, as he was led to believe he should'. After thanking God for the lesson he has learned from 'the holy man St Job', he professes his loyalty and begs to be allowed to return to England. No record of pardon, however, has been found, yet he survived his exile and is said to have received compensation from Elizabeth for the impounding of his estates (*D.N.B.* without citation).

Basle, A II a; Paris, B v b 1; *D.N.B.* under 'Edmund Bunny'.

68.   BURCHER (BOURCHER, BOURCHIER, BURCK-HARDT), JOHN ('alias Anglo-Tigurinus'): *Merchant.* Of Calais(?). Wife.

Probably the illegitimate son of John Bourchier, Baron Berners, Lieutenant of Calais and translator of Froissart (Wood, *Ath. Oxon.* I, 72–3), who died in 1532/3 's.p.m. legit.' (G.E.C. I, 344–5).[1] This son, one of the most interesting among the English exiles, seems to have been brought up in England (*O.L.* I, 248), but to have retired to the Continent before 1540. There until 1542 he lived at Basle, 'seeking to maintain himself by manual labour' (*ibid.* p. 247). Probably he worked as a type-setter, first with Oporinus, then with Myconius (*O.L.* II, 638). His first dealings as a merchant were in a special kind of wood growing near Zurich, which was excellent for making bows (*ibid.* p. 632) and in this venture Bullinger's 'active exertions' on Burcher's behalf evidently brought him success and Bullinger's friendship. Thus Richard Hilles's letter of 1545, which introduces Burcher to Bullinger as 'a man of spotless character, and suffering...for the sake of the gospel...' (*O.L.* I, 247–8), would seem to have been a pure formality required of those seeking 'the freedom of the canton' of Zurich. But sometime in 1546 Burcher entered into partnership with Hilles as a cloth-merchant and thereafter appears to have lived chiefly at Strasbourg (Cam. Misc. x, 6). Separated from Bullinger, the two men carried on for twelve years an intimate correspondence which affords a running commentary upon religious changes in England between 1546 and 1558 (*O.L.* II, 638–701). Later Bullinger's sons became inmates of Burcher's house (Vetter, *Relations*, p. 21). And after 1553 this same house became an asylum for English refugees when, with John Abel, Burcher acted as their sponsor to the Strasbourg magistrates. In 1554 Sir Anthony Cooke lodged with him, and when on his way to Italy, in September, received from Burcher an introduction to Bullinger (*O.L.* II, 686). By this time his enterprises were on such a scale that his sudden departure from the city in 1556 created a financial panic (Protocols, vol. 34, ff. 309–10vo). Nor were his transactions purely commercial. In November 1557 he went to Poland on what seems to have been a half-political, half-evangelical mission which cloaked itself as an effort to intro-

[1] Burcher showed reluctance to send for testimonials from England to prove 'that he was born in lawful wedlock' (*O.L.* I, 246).

duce English methods of brewing at Cracow (*O.L.* II, 689). But the presence of William Barlow in his company as the agent of the Duchess of Suffolk to the King of Poland, as well as Calvin's interest in the journey, seem to indicate that other matters than brewing were afoot (*ibid.* pp. 687, 693). Unlike Hilles, Burcher never conformed under Mary, and so commands respect. Also he was evidently a man of education with wide connections and many and warm friendships, though his marriage was not a happy one. His return to England in 1560 was delayed by divorce proceedings which his friends thought amply justified (*Z.L.* I, 90, 98) but he soon married again and by 1563, according to John Abell, had closed his varied career by becoming 'a clergyman not far from London' (*ibid.* II, 109).

Basle, A VIII a; Zurich, A VIII a; Strasbourg, A VII a; Poland, A VIII a & b.

69. BURTWICK (BORTHWICK), Sir JOHN, Knt. A Scot. d. *ca.* 1570.

Younger son of William, third Lord Borthwick, slain at Flodden in 1513. In 1539 he appears to have been in the French king's service (Laing, I, Append. p. 533), but in 1540, having been cited before Cardinal Beaton on a charge of heresy (*vide* his own Narrative, Foxe, v, 606–21), he escaped to England, where he was henceforth employed as a diplomatic agent. On a mission to Sweden in 1549 we find him making complaint of poverty in the heavily jocular vein of Sir Richard Morison (*q.v.*), 'For', he writes, 'I have one quotidian fever which is clepit in French tongue faut d'argent, and remains (*sic*) in my living as testudo in concha, in prayers calling to our Master Christ, Da nobis, Domine, infunde nobis, Domine' (*For. Cal.* 1547–53, p. 36). In 1552 he was sent to 'induce the Dane, to come to a stricter amitie with England, for the better Defence of the Reformation against all opposers. And by the by to talk of a Marriage of the Prince of Denmarke, with one of the Kings sisters, especially with the Lady Elizabeth who is also a Protestant' (*Cat. Harl. MSS.* I, 204, no. 353 (6); cf. *Salisbury*, I, 100). Even on the accession of Mary, however, he remained in favour, for in 1554 Sir Edmund Peckham was ordered to pay him £40 'as the Quenes Heighnes' rewarde' (*P.C.A.* 1554–6, p. 48) for some service unknown. But in 1556, significant year, he fled to Geneva, where he was received with 'John Kellye his page' as a member of Knox's congregation before 12 July. Already on 24 February he had married at Geneva Jane Bonespoir of Brittany (Martin, p. 337). Strype considers him (cf. Index) to have been the 'Borthic' who was Mary Queen of Scots' messenger to Elizabeth in 1569 (*Annals*, I, ii, 559).

Geneva, A IV a.

70. BURY, EDMOND (EDWARD): *Gent.* Of Warwickshire.

This is probably the Edmond Bury of Barton-on-the-Heath (Warwick), who married Elizabeth, daughter of Edward Underhill, the 'Hot Gospeller' (Harl. Soc. XII, 265). In 1558 he arrived at Geneva and on 24 October was, with Robert Blackman (*q.v.*), admitted to residence (f. 264). There is no record that he became a member of Knox's congregation. He may also be the same person as the Edward Bury of Raighlye Park who apprehended Anthony Tyrrell in 1574 and sent his papers to Lord Rich (*Dom. Cal.* 1547–80, p. 487).

Geneva, A IV b.

71. BUTLER, JOHN: *Gent.* Of Wardington, Oxfordshire(?). d. *ca.* 1553.

It seems probable that this man, whom Strype describes as of a noble family (*Mem.* I, i, 545), was the second son of John Butler of Aston-in-the-Wall (Northants.), who married Margaret, daughter and heir of John Sutton de Dudley, uncle of John, 'Lord Quondam' (Harl. Soc. V, 141 and Staffs. Hist. Colls. IX, *The Barons of Dudley*, p. 11). If so, he was not only allied to the House of Dudley, but was brother-in-law to William Fuller, exile at Geneva (*q.v.*), whose wife Jocosa, or Joice, was sister to this same John Butler (Harl. Soc. V, 141) who himself married Elizabeth Gray, daughter of a London merchant and widow of Andrew Guarsi of London, an Italian surgeon (cf. John Marston, *D.N.B.*) and probably a protestant. Butler's dates also make it possible that he was the John Butler admitted to Gray's Inn in 1533 (Register, col. 10). Strype implies that he fled to Germany as a result of the Act of the Six Articles in 1539, but Conrad Pellican records in his 'hauschronik' (quoted Vetter, *Eng. Flücht.* p. 3) that Butler with a certain William Udroff (Woodruff?) first arrived in Zurich on 18 August 1536. In the autumn of 1539, the same diary (*ibid.* p. 4, n. 6) says that Butler returned there fleeing from the pest at Basle, but he had meanwhile been again in London, whence he wrote to Pellican on 8 March 1539 describing himself 'as yet unmarried', and adding that he 'might have an honourable post about the king' were he not 'smitten with the love of the muses' (*O.L.* II, 626). In 1540 he was back in Basle (*ibid.* p. 627), where he evidently formed a close friendship with Amerbach the printer. A few letters of his written to the latter and referring to a recent visit to Constance (preserved there in the University Library, MSS. G. II, 15, ff. 480–2), do not appear among Butler's correspondence printed by Hastings Robinson (*O.L.* II, 621–36). Whether he lived to see the Marian Exile is doubtful. The last discoverable date in connection with him is that of 9 July 1553, when Richard Hilles mentions him to

Bullinger as alive at Zurich (*O.L.* i, 274). He is said to have travelled widely abroad, and to have lived in Switzerland in considerable state (*Mem.* i, i, 545). He was also both friend and patron to Wolphius the printer, who in 1552 dedicated to Butler the second edition of Peter Martyr's treatise on the Sacrament (*ibid.* p. 546).

Basle, A viii a; Zurich, A viii a.

72. CALTHAM (CALTON?), JOHN: *Merchant.* Of London(?).

Probably the John Calton, 'late of London, goldsmith', who was indicted in the Dudley conspiracy (Baga, p. 254; cf. Visitation of Huntingdon, Cam. Soc. XLIII, 40) and fled with Henry Dudley to France (*Machyn*, p. 103). There he was to be employed to counterfeit English coin out of the bars of Spanish silver to be stolen from the exchequer (*Verney Papers*, pp. 70–1 and note), the money to be used to employ 'a great power of armed men' drawn 'from amongst the Queen's rebels and traitors, then being in parts beyond the seas' (Baga, p. 254; and cf. Wotton to Queen Mary 4 August 1556, *For. Cal.* 1553–8, pp. 243–5). The King of France obligingly provided a castle near Rouen for the enterprise (*Ven. Cal.* 1555–6, p. 423). A George Calton seems to have been imprisoned for forgery under Elizabeth (*Dom. Cal.* Addenda, 1547–65, pp. 526–7, 530).

Rouen.

73. CARELL (CARYL, CARWELL?), THOMAS, Esq.: *Gent.* Of Sussex(?).

We believe this to have been the same person as the Thomas Carwell who, on 24 July 1553, was put in command of Wisbech Castle with Edmund Beauper (*P.C.A.* 1552–4, pp. 302–3, 415). In January 1557 a Thomas Carell is found in exile at Frankfort in possession of taxable property to the amount of 1950 florins, on which sum, however, he was made to pay only half the tax, because he had been in the city but half a year (Jung, p. 30). This fact would place his arrival in the previous July (1556) and suggest strongly that he had been involved with Henry Dudley, and had very possibly betrayed his trust at Wisbech;[1] a conjecture which is strengthened by the presence in Frankfort, also, of Margareta Beauper, wife of 'Dominic' Beauper. 'Dominic' is probably, here, an error for 'Edmund',[2] since the wife of Edmund Beauper

---

[1] Evidently the exiles' conscience was not altogether clear in regard to the morality of such betrayals. See Goodman's third question to Bullinger, below, p. 164.

[2] I can find no Dominic in the family of Beauper (Beaupre) (cf. Blomefield, VII, 460 and Visitation of Norfolk, Harl. Soc. XXXII, 33–4). Edmund was evidently a henchman of Northumberland (Blomefield, VII, 269).

of Wells in Norfolk was a Margery, daughter of Sir John Wiseman (Harl. Soc. xxxii, 34). As to Thomas Carell himself, it is not unlikely that he was a son of John Carell of Warnham in Sussex, Sergeant-at-Law to Henry VIII, by his marriage (whether first or second is not clear) with Elizabeth, daughter of Robert Palmer of Sussex (Harl. Soc. liii, 25). This would have made Carell a cousin of the Sir Thomas Palmer executed in August 1553 as an accomplice of Northumberland (*Chron. Q. Jane*, pp. 22–4). At Frankfort, Carell was among the moderates in the Ashley-Horne quarrel (*T*. p. 65) and did not sign the 'new discipline' (March-April) though he was in Frankfort in June, lodging in the house of Erckenwald Rawlins (*q.v.*).

Frankfort, A iii a 3 & b 2; B iii b.

74. CAREW, Matthew: *Gent.* Of Anthony, Cornwall. d. 1618.

He was the tenth of the nineteen children born to Sir Wymond Carew and his wife Martha Denny, sister of Sir Anthony Denny (Harl. Soc. ix, 33, n. 1 and *D.N.B.*). He was educated at Westminster School under Alexander Nowell and became a Fellow of Trinity College, Cambridge, in 1551, where, according to the *D.N.B.* he remained in residence for ten years. Yet in August 1554 Sir Thomas Hoby found him with his brother Roger (*q.v.*) at Padua among the English exiles (Cam. Misc. x, 116–17), which suggests that he had taken part in the Western Rising with other members of his family. If, as Blomefield asserts (iii, 644), he was but twenty-one when made archdeacon of Norwich, he could then have been no more than twelve years old. Venn (i, 291) apparently accepts the statement that he was ordained 'exorcist acolyte and sub-deacon at Norwich' in August 1558. If this was indeed the Matthew Carew of Cornwall, then he must have returned to England under Mary and conformed. But if he also became archdeacon of Norwich in 1563, his conscience was more than usually accommodating. At least there can be no doubt that eventually he devoted himself to the law, studied at Louvain for twelve years and in 1583 was made a Master in Chancery. The memorial tablet to him in St Dunstan's-in-the-West[1] made no mention of his compromising sojourn at Padua (*Collect. Topog. et Geneal.* v, 206).

Padua, A vi b; *D.N.B.*

75. CAREW, Sir Peter: *Gent.* Of Mohun's Ottery, Devon. 1514–75.

Perhaps of all the exiles the most significant and prophetic figure 'whose chief desire was to travel countries, and to see strange

---

[1] Still there in 1873 (*Her. and Geneal.* vii, 575).

fashions' (Vowell, p. 16). Younger son of Sir William Carew of Mohun's Ottery, Devon, by his wife Joan, daughter of Sir William Courtenay of Powderham. Through his grandmother, Catherine Huddersfield, he was also related to the Raleighs and Champernownes (Harl. Soc. vi, 45 and ix, 32), while the Carews had intermarried with the Bodleys (*q.v.*) of Dunscomb. He himself married Margaret, Lady Talboys, daughter of Sir William Skipwith (cf. 'Bradforth', above). His stormy youth was spent as a soldier of fortune in France and Italy, but later he grew into the favour of Henry VIII and was M.P. for Tavistock in 1545. The part he played in suppressing the Prayer Book troubles in Devon, however, was too zealous a one to commend him to Queen Mary, and though he proclaimed her in the West, her marriage with Philip sent him into opposition. In 1554 he was one of the leaders of the Western Rising, but more fortunate than his uncle, Sir Gawen Carew, he managed to escape from Weymouth to France on 25 January (Vowell, Append. E, no. 9, p. 180; cf. Steele, i, 46) and there established his headquarters at Rouen with intent to 'practise with France' against Spain (*For. Cal.* 1553–8, p. 67 and cf. above, p. 38). Hiring for the purpose 'sundry English mariners with their vessels' (*ibid.* p. 61) his plan was to land his 'rebels and others at Lee in Essex and the Isle of Wight' (*ibid.* p. 79). But by 11 July 1554 (*ibid.* no. 243, p. 109) he was humbly suing for pardon and protesting to the queen his 'unfeigned repentance', in proof of which he proposed to forsake France for Italy. Leaving, then, the French king to curse 'the inconstancy of Englishmen' (*ibid.* p. 107) Sir Peter then withdrew to Venice where, in spite of Mary's tentative forgiveness (*ibid.* p. 89), he narrowly escaped death at the hands of her ambassador, Peter Vannes (Vowell, pp. 61–2). Yet in September the queen herself was permitting supplies to reach him through the agency of his wife (*P.C.A.* 1554–6, p. 75). Perhaps it was this act of clemency that tempted him to return to England in the spring of 1555, though Vowell gives the impression that on leaving Venice he went directly to Strasbourg (Vowell, pp. 61–2). From the records of the Privy Council it is obvious that during April he was with his father-in-law, surreptitiously 'lodged in the said Sir William Skipwith's howse...' (*P.C.A.* 1554–6, p. 119). If his purpose was to obtain his recall, it failed. In the following October he was at Antwerp where Courtenay, Earl of Devon (*q.v.*), seeing him, reported to Petre that he found him 'well disposed towards the service of the King and Queen' but with a conscience still 'influenced by his religion' (*Dom. Cal.* 1547–80, p. 72) and, we may add, by his determination to get home. To this end he now employed his wife. Lady Talboys, faithful and obedient as ever, crossed the Channel to intercede for her husband with King

Philip at Brussels. The plea impudently preferred was that he, Sir Peter, had not lost the queen's favour 'from any fault of his own', and that 'should he know his case to be hopeless' he would 'be compelled to enter the service of the King of France' (*Ven. Cal.* 1555–6, p. 227). Philip, remembering that the suppliant was 'the chief gentleman of Cornwall' who might be very useful to him in the future, did as he was bidden, and the queen answered, though reluctantly, 'that for his great gratification she [would] pardon Sir Peter Carew' (*ibid.* p. 258). When reporting the incident to the Doge on 24 November, Badoer, the ambassador, dryly explains that the king 'confers any favour he can on any Englishman, however ill-disposed he may be, with a view to obtaining their services in the affairs of that kingdom', an opinion of Philip's policy in which Michiel, Venetian ambassador in England, heartily concurred (*ibid.* and *Ven. Cal.* 1556–7, p. 1066).

Ostensibly, then, it was to thank Philip for his good offices that Sir Peter made a trip to Brussels in December 1555 from Strasbourg, where he had been living during November in close association with John Ponet and Sir John Cheke (*ibid.* 1555–6, pp. 258, 282). The plan first agreed upon was that Carew should return to England with Sir Philip Hoby and Sir John Mason in February—not sooner, because the queen had yet to send him 'a written release' (*ibid.* p. 282). Actually it was not until 16 March that Philip was able to acknowledge to the queen the receipt of 'the two[1] pardons for Peter Carew' (*Dom. Cal.* 1547–80, p. 75). What may seem a matter of trivial importance—this question of the pardon—has been dealt with in detail because we believe that Carew finally purchased it only at a price, and that price the betrayal of his friend Sir John Cheke into Philip's hands. To catch Cheke; to stop by any means in their power the ceaseless flow of incendiary pamphlets into England for which Cheke, we have no doubt, was chiefly responsible, had become the government's first necessity (see 'Cheke' below). Thus we take the famous kidnapping that took place near Brussels on 15 May 1556 to have been contrived by Sir Peter Carew himself, who had already betrayed his associates in the Dudley conspiracy to the king (*Ven. Cal.* 1555–6, p. 447). But it will be objected that Carew was also captured on that occasion and, like Cheke, lodged in the Tower when he got to London. True enough, but Sir Peter had a reputation to maintain among his protestant countrymen. To have deserted them under cover of a pardon from the enemy would, in itself, not have endeared him to his fellow-exiles. But the selling

---

[1] That is, we suppose, a *general pardon* and also a *special permit* to return to England.

of Sir John Cheke could never have been forgiven. Hence the
necessity for being captured with his victim. Possessed of his
pardon, Carew seemed now to have no fear for his own ultimate
safety. If, for appearances, he had to be imprisoned, he evidently
relied upon the magnitude of his recent service to obtain a quick
release. Michiel's circumstantial account of the affair, sent to
Venice, leaves no other interpretation of it possible. On 2 June
he wrote to the Doge, 'One of the chief members of the Privy
Council, who busied himself with this arrest, and was perhaps the
author of it [can this be Paget?], has said that Carew is arrested
because being in the company of Cheke, *against whom alone the
warrant was given*,[1] he, together with his servants, chose to resist
the provost, which is but slightly verified, he himself not being
subsequently released, as his servants were; and indeed this same
lord has repeated that as Carew is taken it would be desirable on
several accounts *to find him guilty of something...his presence here
being of no profit*'[1] (*Ven. Cal.* 1555–6, p. 475). Paget's naïve
conclusion must have been awkward for Sir Peter, then in the
Tower—a miscalculation on his part. But in July Michiel observes
that 'Carew will adjust his affairs by payment of a fine, some
persons telling me that he has already done so, by agreeing to
disburse 2000 l. sterling' (*ibid.* p. 526).

Now it must be remembered that this private report of Michiel's
never appeared in print in England until the Venetian Calendar
of State Papers was published in the nineteenth century. The first
account of his kidnapping to see the light was that of John Ponet,
incorporated in his *Treatise of Politike Power* (ed. 1556, Sig. I, 6ᵛᵒ)
and it is this involved story of Ponet's repeated by Vowell in his
Life of Sir Peter Carew (pp. 62–7), which has ever since remained
the standard version. Excellent as a press notice in Sir Peter's
favour, it served its purpose. Yet not perhaps with Queen
Elizabeth, who, with her usual dexterity in such cases, later found
a safe outlet for Carew's hot energies in Ireland.

But there is another and less sinister aspect of Sir Peter Carew
that must not pass unnoticed. Had he been a younger man at
Elizabeth's accession he might now have held an honourable place
among sixteenth-century English pioneers in the Western seas, for
it is almost certain that during his years abroad his mind was
preoccupied with the thought of Spain's wealth in the Indies and
a desire to intercept its flow at the source. Carew hated Spain.
His harangue to his retinue at Rouen in 1554 shows the turn that
that hatred was taking (cf. above, p. 38). One is not often privileged
to intercept the actual train of thought of a man long dead. Yet

---

[1] Author's italics.

such an experience as this has lately come to me with my discovery at the Bodleian of a book which, in all probability, was once Carew's own. This is a copy of Peter Martyr of Angleria's[1] *Decades of the New World*, first published in English in 1555 (Bodley: 4to, L 84 Art.). In it is twice scribbled his full name, 'Peter Carewe', once in writing at the beginning of the 'Epistle', once in 'fancy' printing on the last page; while on the title-page appear the printed initials 'P. C.' Unfortunately the handwriting, though of the sixteenth century, is not Carew's own, but may well be that of his secretary (cf. P.R.O., S.P. 69, vol. III, 170 and vol. IV, 243). And there are certain other facts in connection with this work of Peter Martyr's which strongly support the belief that some copy of his book, and very possibly this particular copy, was in the possession of John Ponet at Strasbourg. Carew and Ponet were, as we know, together there during the autumn of 1555 when *The Decades* had but just appeared in English. We also know that Ponet made special reference to *The Decades* in his own *Treatise* (see 'Ponet', below), and there are in this very copy bearing Carew's name a series of marginal notes made in a hand strikingly like Ponet's.[2] Nothing more possible than that Carew lent his book to Ponet when he himself left for Brussels. And it is an interesting fact that the chapters most carefully annotated are those which treat 'of the ordinary navygation from Spayne to the Weste Indies' (p. 175) and of the wealth to be found there. In fact, by means of these notes, *The Decades* has been made into a simplified handbook for all those, like Carew, 'whose chief desire was to travel countries'. Dead men's deeds we know and such of their thoughts as they have chosen to reveal; but seldom their secret plannings, their dreams of deeds never, in the event, to be performed.

France, B IV b 1.

76. CAREW, ROGER: *Gent.* Of Antony, Cornwall.

Elder brother of Matthew Carew (*q.v.*) and an exile with him at Padua (Cam. Misc. X, 116–17). One of the original Fellows of Trinity College, Cambridge, in 1546 and B.A., Oxford, in the same year (Venn and Foster). In 1551 he was admitted to Gray's Inn (Reg. col. 21) and from 1563 to 1567 he was M.P. for St Albans.

Padua, B IV b,

---

[1] This Peter Martyr (not Vermigli) was of Milan, Councillor to the King of Spain and Protonotary Apostolical (*Decades*, p. 1).

[2] Mr Hilary Jenkinson at the Record Office, to whose expert knowledge I submitted some photographs of these notes with examples of Ponet's handwriting, was not willing to assert that they were the same, though he does admit that between the two there are certainly points of resemblance, and tha there is nothing to preclude the possibility that the marginalia are Ponet's.

77. CARIAR (CARRIER, CHARIOR (*vide* Strype) and CARYER), ANTHONY: *Student.* Of Kent(?). d. 1582(?).

First appears at Frankfort on 24 September 1554, when he signed that congregation's invitation to John Knox (*T.* p. 20). He was one of the party of Whittingham; was signatory to its declaration of secession on 27 August (*ibid.* p. 55); and followed Whittingham to Geneva, where he joined Knox's congregation on 2 December. After his return to England he was preferred in 1576 to the living of Little Chart in Kent (Hasted, II, 227), which he apparently held till 1582 (*ibid.*). His son, Benjamin Carrier of Corpus Christi College (Camb.) was more notable than he, for after serving as chaplain successively to Archbishop Whitgift and James I, he eventually went over to Rome and became a noted controversialist (Foster). Frankfort, B III a; Geneva, A IV a.

*CAROWE (CAREY?), HENRY.

This man, who appears but once abroad and that in Frankfort, *after* the accession of Elizabeth (*T.* p. 190), was never, we believe, an exile at all but an emissary from Cecil to discuss with the remnant of the Frankfort colony the English government's plans for an alteration of religion. He with 'John Graye' is one of the signatories to Frankfort's refusal on 3 January 1559 (*ibid.*) of Geneva's recent invitation to join them in an anti-ceremonial crusade (*ibid.* p. 186). Never before, I think, has attention been called to the accurate foreknowledge of religious events which that letter displays—a foreknowledge difficult to account for except upon the hypothesis that this 'Henry Carowe' was, in reality, Elizabeth's cousin, Henry Carey, soon to be created Lord Hunsdon, for the support of the protestant party in the House of Lords; and 'John Graye', no other than Lord John Grey of Pyrgo, a member of that 'secret committee' of four (Camden, *Annals*, ed. 1625, p. 10) to which was entrusted the task of a return to protestantism (cf. above, p. 16).

78. CARUS, JOHN: *Gent.* Of Lancashire or Westmoreland(?).

Probably an unchronicled brother or younger son of Sir Thomas Carus of Kirkby Landesdale, Westmoreland (Chetham Soc. no. 81, p. 60) and of Haltan, Lancs(?), a justice of the King's Bench and M.P. for Lancaster Borough in 1553 and 1555 (*Journals H. of C.* I, 43; *Return of Members*, I, 382, 393), whose sister Margaret married Christopher Sandys, younger brother of Edwin Sandys, the archbishop (Harl. Soc. XL, 6 and Tyldesley, *Diary*, p. 72 note). In the Bishops' Visitation of 1564, Sir Thomas was pronounced 'favorable' to religion (Cam. Misc. IX, 77), but John Carus at Strasbourg, the 'comrade' of Sir Thomas Fracht (Frogget, *q.v.*), was no credit to the reformed party. Evidently he was of that unruly type of young Englishman then so frequent on the continent, and the Strasbourg magistrates, finding him too disturbing to be tolerated, sent him back to England sometime in the summer of 1556 (below, p. 369). His case provides an interesting example of effective extradition in the sixteenth century.

Strasbourg, A VII a.

79. CARVELL (CARVILE, KARVYLE, etc.), NICHOLAS: *Student*. Of Dorset. d. 1566.

M.A. King's College, Cambridge, 1553. In October 1554 he was one of the group of 'Students' at Zurich (*T.* p. 16). But in 1555 he went to Frankfort, where in the tax-list of 1556 he is said to have been without property. In 1557 he was still at Frankfort living in the house of Robert Harrington. His return to England may have been in 1558 (*D.N.B.*) and in 1560 Horne proposed the name of a 'Mr Carvill' to Cecil, as candidate for a prebendal stall at Durham (*Dom. Cal.* 1547–80, p. 149). The authorship of a poem in the *Mirror for Magistrates*, which bears the signature of 'Maister Cauille' (ed. 1578, ff. 166–74), has been attributed to him (*D.N.B.*).

Zurich, A VIII a, b, c; B II; B III a; Frankfort, A III a 2, 3, 4 & b 2; *D.N.B.*

80. CAUNT (CANT, GAUNT(?)), EDWARD: *Gent.*(?). Of Kent(?). Wife.

A family of Gaunts seems to have been connected with Rochester (Hasted, IV, 454) and a John Caunt was given a 'B.Can.L.' at Cambridge 1496–7 (Venn) but no certain identification of this Edward Caunt can be made. In June 1557 he was living at Frankfort with his wife and one child in the house of Thomas Sandes (or Saunders). On 29 November 1557, as Edward 'Cant', he is found as a 'resident' of Geneva (f. 226).

Frankfort, A III a 4 & b 2; Geneva, A IV b.

81. CAWBORN,[1] JOHN: *Labourer*.

Received as a 'resident' of Geneva on 14 October 1557, with the designation of 'laboureur' (f. 196).

Geneva, A IV b.

---

[1] One of the names mistranscribed by Heyer, who gives it as 'Datoborn' (see above, pp. 23–24 and note 1).

82. CHAMBERS, RICHARD: *Gent.* (?). Of Northamptonshire (?).
d. 1566.

Though Richard Chambers, treasurer of the refugees, probably holds in his identity the key to the Marian Exile, that identity cannot be fixed. Even the most persistent search[1] has failed to reveal either the family, or the class, or the county, from which he came. All that can be said of his origin is negative: he did not, for example, belong to any of the county families of Chambers either in Shropshire, Leicestershire, or Middlesex. If he had, as we suspect, some kinship with the Chambers of Hertfordshire, it must have been by the left hand. And to this solution of the problem one is inevitably driven. It seems impossible to reconcile the facts of his quasi-public activities, his wealth, his scholarly sympathies, his relations with the earls of Bedford, and the complete mystery surrounding his birth, upon any other hypothesis than that of illegitimacy. Very possibly he was the natural son of John Chambers, last abbot and first bishop of Peterborough, who owed both his episcopal dignity and the immunity of his property from confiscation to the intervention of his close friend, Sir John Russell, with Cromwell (Wright, *Monasteries*, pp. 259–60). This John Chambers, abbot and bishop, died in 1556. It is not unlikely (for the *D.N.B.* is silent as to *his* parentage) that he too had been illegitimate—the son of Laurence Chamber (or Chambers), fourth son of Thomas Chamber of Wolsted Castill, Cumberland, in the reign of Henry VII, and himself Lord Abbot of Peterborough (Harl. Soc. VII, 6). This Laurence Chambers's eldest brother, a Richard Chambers,[2] migrated to Royston in Hertfordshire, a town noted for its militant protestantism: the only one to oppose Queen Mary's triumphal progress to London in August 1553 (*P.C.A.* 1552–4, pp. 310, 313; 1555–6, p. 217) and the birthplace of Thomas Cartwright (Urwick, p. 800). So much for conjecture: we pass now to the few facts actually known of the exiled Chambers's early life. Laurence Humphrey, who calls him

---

[1] This has included every available source of information, printed and manuscript, known to me—county histories, county historical collections, parish records, wills, Heralds' Visitations, Proceedings in Chancery, the Calendars of the Patent Rolls and, of course, the State Papers. The number of 'Richard Chambers' in Tudor days proves to be legion, yet none fills all the necessary conditions of Chambers the exile. I have pursued him from the College of Arms and Somerset House to Birmingham (where are now many of the Rutland and Northamptonshire wills); I have invoked the kindly aid of many friends and strangers, but Richard Chambers eludes me still.

[2] It was hoped to identify this man's grandson, Richard Chambers of Barkway, with the exile, but, inconveniently, he died in 1549 (Harl. Soc. VII, 6; XXII, 137; *Vict. Co. Hist., Herts.* III, 251).

the Maecenas of protestant scholars, tells us that he generously befriended John Jewel, giving him a yearly allowance of £6 with which to buy books (*Vita Juelli*, p. 32). Strype says that he expended 'great sums of money' in behalf of university students and of the 'godly poor'. Upon the basis of a letter written in 1537 by a Richard Chambers whose signature is singularly like that of the exile,[1] it would appear that he began his semi-official career in connection with the appointment as dean of Exeter of a certain Dr Heynes, possibly a candidate of Sir John Russell (*L. and P.* XII, pt II, no. 182, p. 60). In the course of this letter, Chambers is at some pains to tell Heynes that he can speak no Latin, which would tally with the fact that, so far as is known, Chambers the exile had not been a student at either university. And this ignorance of Latin would also explain why (as recorded by Strype) he always 'took a preacher with him' when dispensing his charities. Strype says that it was to 'instruct' the 'receivers of his bounty', but it was rather, perhaps, to 'test' the quality of their scholarship, as Chambers himself could not (*Mem.* III, i, 225). In 1549 we know that he acted with Sir John Cheke and John Joseph (*q.v.*) as a witness against Bonner at the latter's trial (Foxe, v, 770). At Mary's accession he at once became one of the committee of 'sustainers'. Then, apparently in an official capacity, he followed into exile the protestant students he was subsidizing (Lever to Bullinger, *O.L.* I, 155). In the spring of 1554, Chambers arrived at Zurich (*Diarium*, p. 46) and thereafter, jointly with Robert Horne, distributed from the common purse to the needs of the various colonies. But in so doing, he himself explicitly states that he was not a principal but a subordinate, acting only under the authority of certain persons whose names were to remain unknown. The secret of those whom he served has been jealously guarded; but it is my conviction, already expressed (above, p. 16), that they were the four leaders of the protestant party in England— Lord John Grey, now head of the family of Suffolk; the Marquis of Northampton, Lord Russell and Sir William Cecil. Francis Russell, soon to be second Earl of Bedford, was perhaps chiefly responsible for financing the experiment (cf. his efforts at relief recounted by Underhill, *Narr. of Ref.* pp. 145–7). If Chambers were indeed the son of his father's old friend, the bishop of Peterborough, and if he had already been in the Russells' employ, the choice of him as treasurer of the exiles would be fully explained. When in 1557 the colony of Frankfort accused Chambers of

---

[1] I have compared this letter at the Public Record Office with one almost undoubtedly written by the exile (*Dom. Cal.* 1547–80, p. 186) and am persuaded that the two are by the same hand.

peculation and angrily demanded an accounting of him, he refused point blank to give one, except as he said, 'vnto them whiche haue authoritie to demaunde it off me' (*T*. p. 183); and he swore that he would keep both 'names and summes secret' as he was 'bownde' till by 'them whiche haue iuste authoritie to louse me I be otherwise appointed' (*ibid*.). Such language as this points unmistakably to centralized financial control of the whole migration. And it should be remembered that Chambers was a member of the earliest colony to be established, that at Zurich, in relation to which Bullinger designates him as 'oeconomus et pater' (*Diarium*, p. 46). Yet Chambers disclaims all responsibility for the colony's establishment, referring to the Englishmen at Zurich as 'the Students whom I neuer placed there' (*T*. p. 183). Twice during the liturgical quarrels at Frankfort, he came in the capacity of diplomatic agent to compose the strife—first from Zurich on 4 November 1554 (*T*. p. 17), then from Strasbourg on the 28th—showing that his official connection was not with Zurich alone, but with the English colonies as a whole. When in 1556, Horne was chosen pastor of the Frankfort congregation, Chambers came with him, thenceforth making Frankfort his headquarters (*T*. p. 62). From there, on 3 February, the two men wrote a letter of thanks to the Senate of Zurich for the hospitality they had received (*O.L.* I, 126–9). But on 8 July it was Chambers alone who was a witness of John Brett's presentation of Queen Mary's letters to Mistress Wilkinson (Brett, p. 119). In the following October (1556) his property was rated on the Frankfort tax-list at 500 florins (Jung, p. 29). Senior of the congregation during February and March 1557, he acted as Horne's staunch ally throughout the latter's stormy pastorate, and is therefore not to be found among the subscribers to the 'new discipline' (*T*. pp. 73, 76, 133–4). Nor does his name appear in the dwelling-list of June, when he may have been absent on official business. Whether he acquitted himself well or ill in the Horne-Ashley quarrel, it is impossible to say at this distance of time and upon evidence supplied only by Chambers's enemies. As treasurer he was in the delicate position of one acting for superiors many miles away, and we must simply echo Master Sutton's charitable hope that 'for so much as Maister Chambers in this controuersie [was] very sore charged amonge the reste: who yet, was thought off manie wise and godly men, to be verye godly, vpright, and honest...so no dowte he tooke his leaue of this lyffe:...' (*T*. p. 181). But he did not die until 1566 (*Z.L.* I, 148). It is odd, therefore, that but one hint survives regarding his activities after his return to England. In 1561 we find him writing to Francis, Earl of Bedford, in the matter of the deprivation of Coveney, then President of Magdalen. Chambers says that he has proposed, as

Coveney's successor, Dr Laurence Humphrey, a fellow-exile, who, as we know, was eventually installed. He is here openly acting as the agent of the Earl of Bedford in the matter of an appointment and the situation is strongly reminiscent of the earlier action in 1537 of a Richard Chambers in regard to the appointment of a dean of Exeter. In that case, too, the man was very likely acting for the Russells. It is hard to believe that two men of the same name, whose activities were the same, whose signatures are almost identical, who are both shy about disclosing the place from which they write, and who both were agents—one surely, the other probably—of the Earls of Bedford, were not one and the same man. Whether this man was also the son of Sir John Russell's old friend, John Chambers of Peterborough, must remain conjecture. Still another Richard Chambers, said to be the exile's son, matriculated from Christ's College, Cambridge, in 1560 (Venn, I, 318). This assertion of kinship, adopted both by Venn and by Urwick (p. 635), appears to rest solely upon the authority of Strype, who further says of the son that he became the non-subscribing vicar of Hitchin, Herts., who in 1570 drew up a testimonial in favour of Cartwright, whose lectures he had attended (*Annals*, II, i, 2, and cf. the Chambers family and Royston, above).

Zurich, A VIII a & c; Frankfort, A III a 3; B III; B IV a; Strasbourg, B III.

83. CHEKE, Sir JOHN: *Gent*. Of Cambridgeshire, 1514–57.

The story of Sir John Cheke, first Regius Professor of Greek at Cambridge; tutor to Edward VI; close friend of the foreign reformers in England, especially of John à Lasco; associated intimately with the revision of the Prayer Book in 1552; and faithful secretary to 'Queen Jane', is too familiar to bear repetition. Instead I mean to dwell upon certain aspects of his exile, which offer a plausible, and, I believe, novel explanation of his mysterious kidnapping near Brussels on 15 May 1556 (Ponet's *Politike Power*, ed. 1556, Sig. I, 6vo–7). That he was betrayed to Philip by his friend Sir Peter Carew in return for the latter's pardon is a fact which, on the strength of the narrative of two Venetian ambassadors, admits of little doubt (see 'Carew', above). But why Cheke's capture was of sufficient importance to the English government to be exacted at the price of Carew's pardon is a question not yet answered.

First, however, as having some bearing on the matter, and as a typical instance of the interlocking relationships which bound the protestant party together almost as a clan, Cheke's own family connections require a word. He was first the brother-in-law of his pupil, Sir William Cecil, who married Cheke's sister Mary; then through his own marriage with Margaret,[1] daughter of Richard Hill (or Hillis), a wine-merchant of London, he became the son-in-law of Sir John Mason, whose wife, daughter of Sir Thomas Isley of Kent, was Richard Hillis's widow and Lady Cheke's mother. Thus Sir John was also brother-in-law of Richard Hilles (or Hillis) the younger, who from 1541 to 1548 had been an exile in Strasbourg (see his correspondence, *O.L.* I, 196–274).[2]

Because of his close connection with Northumberland, Cheke was very naturally imprisoned on Mary's accession (28 July 1553, *P.C.A.* 1552–4, p. 421), but being released, he obtained a licence to travel and in the spring of 1554 set out for the Continent. Thanks to the Strasbourg protocols, we can follow him stage by stage on his way to Italy, for he reached that city on 14 April and there procured guides for himself and Sir Richard Morison to take them as far as Basle (vol. 32, ff. 131vo, 167). Sir Anthony Cooke, who had arrived with them, was left behind (see below), but Cheke, perhaps Morison also, spent May and June in Basle, gaining proselytes there for his new method of Greek pronunciation. When at last he reached Padua on 10 July (*For. Cal.* 1553–8, p. 112) his companion was no longer Morison but Sir Thomas Wrothe (*ibid.*). His purpose there, as he wrote Sir William Petre, was 'to learn not only the Italian tongue... but also philosophically to course over the civil law', and he trusted that he should not 'mislike this part' of his exile, though his mind was in great distress over the 'travail and misery' of his wife and children left in England (*ibid.*). Nevertheless a plan to remain abroad beyond the expiration of his licence was already maturing (*ibid.*). Meanwhile he lectured on Demosthenes to Thomas Wilson (*q.v.*) and other young Englishmen then in Padua (Strype's *Cheke*, p. 96), and there on 23 August Sir Thomas Hoby rejoiced to find him (Cam. Misc. x, 116). Two months later the two Hobys carried Cheke off on a pleasure trip to Mantua with Sir Anthony Cooke, who had now joined them (*ibid.* pp. 117–19). But in the spring of 1555, after a serious illness (*For. Cal.* 1553–8, p. 174 and Strype's *Cheke*, p. 98), Cheke determined to go northward, and joining the Hobys at Caldero, made his way to Germany with them, till on 20 October we find him in Strasbourg again (Cheke to Calvin, *O.L.* I, 142) and intending to pass the winter there. Whether he kept to this plan or not is an important question.

[1] So given in Prof. Pollard's article on Sir John Mason (*D.N.B.*), and not her sister, Mary, as stated by Cooper in his account of Sir John Cheke (*D.N.B.*), who married Sir Francis Spelman.

[2] This Richard Hilles remained in England under Mary and conformed. His apostasy made a breach in his long friendship with Bullinger which was never really healed (see *Zurich Letters*).

He was certainly there on 18 February 1556 (Strype's *Cheke*, pp. 99–101) and on the following 12 March (*O.L.* i, 145–7), but in the intervening three months he may well have been in Emden, where Strype assures us that he spent some time superintending the publication of Cranmer's *Defensio* (*Cranmer*, p. 374). And this is the more likely, since a man of Cheke's importance could hardly have remained in Strasbourg without obtaining rights of residence, yet the protocols are silent in regard to him. We also have it on Strype's authority that Emden was the centre of protestant propaganda (*Cranmer*, p. 511) and Col. F. S. Isaac has now established a strong presumption that it was the press of Egidius van der Erve at Emden which published not merely this new edition of the *Defensio* but many of the pamphlets[1] which were circulated in London and the eastern counties by such agents of sedition as Trudgeover.[2] To call Cheke the 'director' of this campaign of propaganda is perhaps giving too modern a cast of precision to his relation to it, but there can be little doubt from the reports of the Venetian ambassadors that he was regarded by the English government both as the author and disseminator of incendiary literature. It is also significant that, during November and December 1555, coincident that is with the only time in Cheke's life abroad when he could have been in Emden, the press campaign against Queen Mary became peculiarly virulent and was almost certainly connected with a plot against her life, antedating that of Henry Dudley, a plot in which Christopher Goodman and Bartlet Green were directly involved (Foxe, vii, 732–3, 734–5; *Ven. Cal.* 1555–6, pp. 269–70, 278). The moment chosen for this outbreak of 'audacious licentiousness' was the death of Gardiner on 12 November (*Ven. Cal.* 1555–6, p. 251). No one can piece together the facts regarding van der Erve's press, the regular train of messengers from Emden to England and the activities in the eastern counties of men such as Trudgeover, well known to have been agents of the exiles (*ibid.* p. 578), without coming to the conclusion that the pamphlet warfare was highly organized and most cleverly directed. There follows the very natural query: 'Why was Sir John Cheke of all the 472 Englishmen on the Continent alone singled out for the distinction of being kidnapped?' He was only one of a score of pamphleteers, most of whom were far more virulent in their language than he. But if Cheke's was the brain that directed the whole campaign, then there was good reason for preferring him to be under lock and key in London than at large in Emden. True, Sir Peter Carew was also kidnapped with him. But of the capture

---

[1] See *Egidius van der Erve and his English Printed Books*, Bibliographical Society, 1931. For a list of these pamphlets by Knox, John Olde, William Turner, etc. see p. 341.   [2] For the story of Trudgeover see above, p. 35 and note 2.

it is quite clear that Cheke and not Carew was the man wanted. One of the 'chief members of the Privy Council' told Michiel that Carew was only 'arrested because being in the company of Cheke against whom alone the warrant was given...' (*ibid.* p. 475) and it was rumoured that Sir Peter would be able to 'adjust his affairs by payment of a fine' (*ibid.* pp. 526–7). While Cheke's arrest was based explicitly upon the charge 'of having compiled one of those books against the King and Queen, and the present state of affairs, which were privily circulated here' (*ibid.* p. 480), the particular pamphlet in question was said by Michiel to be called the 'Dialogue', a book 'full of seditious and scandalous things against the religion and government...', of which an edition of 'a thousand copies had been taken to the Lord Mayor...' in May 1555 (*ibid.* p. 70). To-day the authorship of this pamphlet[1] is not attributed to Cheke (cf. *S.T.C.* p. 112), nor does its matter in the form of question and answer on points of doctrine, dignified and temperate in style, strike the modern reader as being nearly so inflammatory as most of its kind—in other words, it offered too slight an excuse for such an unparalleled measure as that of kidnapping unless, as I have suggested, it was used merely as a pretext for crippling the whole campaign of propaganda by removing its head. 'The fruit of Dr Cheke's recantation', said Michiel, writing in November 1556, 'begins already to take effect, well nigh 30 persons who were in prison in danger of being burned, having lately by the grace of God and through the efficacy of his [Cheke's] language been converted' (*Ven. Cal.* 1556–7, p. 769). Did the 'efficacy' of Cheke's 'language' possibly serve to convert himself as well? As he sat in prison accused of sedition, did the memory come back to him of certain words of his used against the rebels of Devon only seven years before? Then, in his pamphlet on *The hurt of Sedition*, he had demanded indignantly, 'Yee rise for religion. What religion taught you that?' (Sig. A 4, ed. 1569). To which question he prefaced the complacent statement that '...for our-selves we haue great cause to thanke God, by whose religion..., we learne not only to feare him truly, but also to obey our King faithfully, and to serue in oure owne vocation like subiectes honestly' (Sig. A 2vo), for 'the magistrate is the ordinance of God, appointed by him with the sworde of punishment, to looke streightly to all euill doers' (Sig. A 3vo).

Padua, B iv b; B v b 3; Strasbourg, A viii a; Emden; *D.N.B.*

[1] Supposing it to have been *A Dialogue or Familiar Talke...* from the press of Michael Wood at Rouen (Brit. Mus. C 25, C 26) and dated 1554. But Michiel's description fits far more accurately *The Copye of a lettre, etc.* with its running title of 'An Admonicion to all Englishemen' which was written by John Bradforth (*q.v.*) in 1555.

84. CHESTON, George: *Weaver*. Of Essex.

An exile at Aarau who is said, in Hans Dür's list, to have been born in 'Chensfort', probably Chelmsford, in Essex. He may have been the son or brother of the William Cheston below. Usher in his *Presbyterian Movement* (p. xxviii) mentions a 'Cheston' as member of the London 'classis', and as several others of the Aarau colony were also in the movement, his man is probably either George or William.

Aarau, A 1 a & b.

85. CHESTON, William: *Weaver and spinner*. Of Suffolk. Wife.

According to Hans Dür, he was born in Suffolk, and lived at 'Hadelea', from which we may presume that he had been a member of Rowland Taylor's congregation. In Aarau he lived in the house of Joachim Schmutzingers, and since his wife is only mentioned in the later or 'official' list (below, p. 355) he may have married abroad.

Aarau, A 1 a & b.

86. CHICHESTER, Sir John: *Gent*. Of Yolston, Devon. d. 1569.

Son of Edward Chichester (d. 1522) and Lady Elizabeth, daughter of John Bourchier, first Earl of Bath. He married Gertrude, daughter of William Courtenay of Powderham (Vivian's *Devon*, p. 173). In 1546 he was involved with Thomas Wyndham (*q.v.*) in the capture of a Spanish ship at sea and summoned before the Council (*P.C.A.* 1542–7, pp. 382, 411, 412). In 1549 he played an important part in suppressing the insurrection against the new Prayer Book, and is accused by Strype of having exacted as a reward all the clappers of the bells that were then removed from the churches, 'And no question they made good benefit thereof' (*Mem.* II, i, 270–1). But from this rather extraordinary bit of graft the editor of Vowell's *Life of Sir Peter Carew* exonerates him, saying that 'the bells were never removed' and that Chichester's action was probably 'for the express purpose of keeping them in their places'. At Mary's accession he was dubbed a knight (*Mem.* III, ii, 182) and sat for Devon in the parliament of 1553[1] (Vivian, p. 173), but he must have come under suspicion of complicity in the Western Rising of 1554, for he found it prudent to withdraw from England in the train of the Earl of Bedford, in whose company he is found at Venice in 1555, and among those English-ment licensed to bear arms by the Signory (*Ven. Cal.* 1555–6, p. 145). When he returned to England is not known, but in 1556 he was arrested as an accomplice in the Dudley plot, and on

[1] Browne Willis (p. 34) says 1554, as does also *Return, Members of Parliament*, I, 385, with, however, the words 'no date given'.

29 April was sent to the Tower with his father-in-law, Sir William Courtenay, Sir Nicholas Arnold and two others (*Machyn*, p. 104), the arrest of 'those five gentlemen' coming 'much to the surprise and regret of everybody by reason of their quality' (*Ven. Cal.* 1555–6, p. 440). Chichester, however, lived to sit again as M.P. for Devon in the parliament of 1562,[1] and died on 30 September 1569 (Vivian, p. 173).

Venice.

87. CHIDLEY (CHUDLEIGH), GEORGE: *Lawyer*(?). Of Devon(?).

No precise identification can be made of this man, but he was probably of the important family of the Chudleighs of Ashton in Devon (Harl. Soc. VI, 59). He may have been the 'master Chidley' who, as a 'temporal counsellor', officiated at the trial of Gardiner (Foxe, VI, 266) in 1551, but who had also been one of the commissioners for enforcing the Act of the Six Articles in 1540. Again, he may be the George Chidley who, for some reason unknown, was given a licence to wear his cap in the King's presence (*Mem.* II, ii, 245); or the George Chidley of Devon, Fellow of Oriel, who was prebendary of Exeter in 1546 (Foster, I, 275); or the 'Mr Chidley, Lawyer' who is mentioned in the records of the Privy Council in 1552–3 and again in 1556. As George Chidley, the exile, appears abroad but once and that in 1554 at Frankfort, when he signed the congregation's invitation to John Knox (*T.* p. 20), the above date, 1556, does not stand in the way of identification, nor is it impossible that 'Mr Chidley, Lawyer' and Chidley 'temporal counsellor' are one and the same man.

Frankfort, B III a.

88. CHILLESTER, JAMES: *Gent.*(?). Of London(?). fl. 1571.

This man of doubtful status, who figures in Herbert's Ames (II, 971) as the translator from the Latin, and publisher of *A most Excellent Hystorie, Of the Institution and first beginning of Christian Princes, etc.* (1571), seems also to have spent a turbulent life as a counterfeiter and rebel. In association with a certain Richard Vincent (*q.v.*) he coined money in Oxfordshire for the financing of Dudley's conspiracy, but claimed, as if in extenuation, that 'he coined none for himself' (*For. Cal.* 1553–8, p. 283). He fled to France upon Sir Henry Bedingfield's arrival at Oxford 'to prosecute enquiries', but by November 1556 he was confessing his offence to Dr Wotton in the hope of pardon. Though there is no record of his obtaining it, he survived into the next reign and continued his seditious practices irrespective of the sovereign on the throne. In 1572 we

---

[1] Cf. Browne Willis, p. 71 and *Return, Members of Parliament*, I, 403.

find a 'Mr Chillester', whom we presume to be the same man, being examined 'on the interrogatories' and reported to Burleigh as 'a dangerous fellow' but one 'from whom much information may be gained if skilfully handled' (*Dom. Cal.* 1547–80, p. 439).

France, B v b 1 & 2.

89. CHRISPE (CRISPE, CRIPPS), RICHARD: *Gent.* Of Kent.

Arrived in Geneva in 1556 and on 5 November became a member of Knox's congregation. He was the son and heir of that John Crispe of Cleave or Clive Court, Thanet, whose younger brother was Sir Henry Crispe of Quex, called 'eques auratus', and sheriff of Kent in the last year of Henry VIII (*Arch. Cant.* XII, 414–18 and Berry, *Kent, etc.* p. 154). Later Richard Chrispe became Captain of the Light Horse in Kent during the year of the Armada (*Arch. Cant.* XII, 415–16, and XI, 389), but the date of his arrival in Geneva lays him open to the suspicion of conspiracy under Mary.

Geneva, A IV a.

90. CHRISTOPHER, [GEORGE]: *Barber.*

A 'Chrystopher' is mentioned by Brett among the Englishmen in the train of the Berties at Weinham in 1556 (Brett, p. 125) and he would appear to be the same person as the George Christofer 'late barbour to the Marques of Northampton' who on 14 September 1553 was summoned to appear before the Privy Council (*P.C.A.* 1552–4, p. 348). This summons was no doubt the signal for his flight, since there is no further mention of him in the Council's minutes.

Weinheim, B IV a.

91. CHUDLEIGH (CHIDLEY, etc.), CHRISTOPHER: *Gent.* Of Devon. d. 1570.

Probably Christopher, son of Sir Richard Chudleigh of Ashton, Devon, who at his father's death in 1558 was 'aged 30 years and more' (Vivian's *Devon*, p. 189). In April 1556 he is found as a fugitive in France, an associate of Henry Dudley, says Strype, yet one who bore 'a good affection to his country' (*Mem.* III, i, 566, 569). This is evidently said to excuse the fact that in November 1556 Chudleigh turned informer, revealing to Wotton all Dudley's plans against Calais (*For. Cal.* 1553–8, p. 275), though there is no indication that he thereby gained the pardon he was seeking. By 5 February 1559/60, however, he had returned to England, and on that date married Christina, daughter of William Stretchleigh (Vivian, pp. 189, 716). Then nothing further is heard of him until September 1570, when the Earl of Bedford asks Cecil for the wardship 'of the son and heir to Christopher Chudley if the latter should die' (*Dom. Cal.* 1547–80, p. 392), which he did on 1 October (Vivian, p. 189).

France, B v b 1 & 2.

92. COCKBURN, ALEXANDER: *Student*. Of Ormiston, Scotland. 1535–63.

Eldest son of the Lord of Ormiston and pupil of John Knox (Laing, I, 185–6), who, as Alexander Cogburnus, matriculated at the University of Basle in 1556 (f. 194). He died at the age of twenty-eight and the inscription on his tomb in the church at Ormiston was written by George Buchanan (Laing, VI, 672).

Basle, A II a.

93. COCKCROFT (COCKCRAFT), HENRY: *Deacon and gent.* Of York. Wife. d. *ca.* 1567.

Because of the singularity of the name, this is almost undoubtedly one of the Cockcrofts of Mairoyd near Halifax, Yorks., who for generations intermarried with the Sutcliffes and bear their arms (Harl. Soc. XXXVIII, 540–3). In 1547 Henry Cockcroft became a Fellow of Trinity College, Cambridge, received his M.A. in 1549 (Venn, I, 362), and in 1551 was ordained deacon at York by the bishop of Hull (*Mar. Reac.* p. 217). Then in April 1554, as one of the original group of 'Students', he arrived at Zurich, where he remained until sometime after October in that year (*O.L.* II, 752 and *T.* p. 16). But by November 1555 he had reached Frankfort, where his name appears among the 'students' in the Standesliste, and again on the tax-list of October 1556, when his property was assessed at 220 florins (Jung, p. 29). In 1557 he was living with his wife and three children in the house of William Master (*H.S.P.* IV, 88). But the Henry Cockcroft admitted Fellow of St John's College, Cambridge, in March 1558 must have been the exile's son (Venn, I, 362).

Zurich, A VIII a; Frankfort, III a 2, 3, 4 & b 1, 2; Geneva, IV a & b;
B II

COKE, MICHAEL. *See* Cooke.

94. COLE (COLES), ROBERT: *Student*. Of Biggleswade, Bedfordshire. 1524(?)–76/7.

Scholar of Eton, M.A. of King's College, Cambridge, 1550, and Fellow, 1545–51. A 'free-willer' (*Mem.* III, i, 413; ii, 334) and originally one of the 'sustainers' (*ibid.* i, 224). Later he served as a messenger of the exiles (*ibid.* ii, 63), but unlike his colleague, John Ledley, he must have remained abroad for long enough periods, since he is included in Bale's list of exiles (*Scriptores*, p. 742). Foxe calls him one of the principal teachers of heretical doctrine in London (Foxe, VIII, 384), who with Ledley (*q.v.*) and Punte (*q.v.*) did 'lie at the sign of the Bell in Gracechurch-street', and from there did 'resort much unto the King's Bench, unto the prisoners about matters of religion' (*ibid.*). Undoubtedly he was one of the most industrious of the purveyors of heretical books, and also acted as go-between for the hidden congregation in London and the fugitive congregations abroad (*ibid.*). At the accession of Elizabeth he became rector of St Mary-le-Bow (1559–76) and of All Hallows, Bread Street (1569–76) (Venn, I, 367). And as time passed he seems to have undergone a change of heart in matters of religion until Grindal could exhibit him to his recalcitrant clergy as a model of conformity (*Grindal*, p. 145).

n.p.; B II; Cooper.

95. COLE, THOMAS: *Dean of Sarum.* Of Lincolnshire. d. 1571.

M.A. King's College, Cambridge, 1550, and head master of Maidstone School in 1552. For a short time he was dean of Sarum (*T.* p. 59). By September 1554 he had become an exile at Frankfort (*T.* p. 20) and in the following February was a member of the committee appointed by the congregation to 'drawe forthe' that order 'meete for their state and time' (*T.* pp. 36–7), which later with a few modifications became the Order of Geneva (*ibid.* and Martin, p. 27). Although a consistent member of Whittingham's party and signatory to its letter of secession in August 1555 (*T.* p. 55), Cole did not leave Frankfort for Geneva with the others in September, but remained behind, perhaps as an observer for Whittingham (*T.* p. 59), and there is good reason to believe that it was he and not Whitehead (cf. p. vii of Petheram's Introd. to the 1846 reprint of the *Troubles*) who continued Whittingham's narrative after the latter's departure. On this supposition it would be Cole who was the author of 'The historie of that sturre and strife which was in the Englishe church at Franckford from the 13. daie off Ian. Anno Domini 1557. forwarde.' (*T.* pp. 62–182), in which the story of the Horne-Ashley quarrel and the consequent evolution of a church-democracy is recounted. Both Tanner (*Bibl. Brit.* p. 189), Strype (*Annals,* I, i, 492), and the *D.N.B.* have asserted that it was Thomas Cole who later went to Geneva to assist in the translation of the Bible, but this we believe with Cooper (I, 296) to be an error for William Cole (cf. Martin, p. 241). Though it is true that Thomas Cole's name appears in no Frankfort list after the autumn of 1555, yet neither does it appear at Geneva, either in the Livre des Anglois or in the Registre des

Habitants. Possibly he went to Strasbourg, though even there his name is not recorded in the city's archives. On his return to England he was made archdeacon of Essex and as such signed the petition for a discipline in 1562 (*Annals*, I, i, 488).

Frankfort, III a 2 & b 1; Strasbourg (?); B II; B III; *D.N.B.*

96. COLE, WILLIAM: *Student.* Of Grantham, Lincolnshire. 1527–1600.

Educated at Corpus Christi College, Oxford, of which he was made a Fellow in 1545 (Foster, I, 302). Since he also came from Lincolnshire the two Coles, William and Thomas, may have been brothers. William is first found among the 'Students of Zurich' in April 1554 (*O.L.* II, 752) and does not appear at Frankfort until the autumn of 1556, when he was rated in the tax-list of October as worth 100 florins (Jung, p. 29). From Frankfort he evidently migrated to Basle with John Foxe, for he appears in Bale's short list of those who were resident 'in nostro collegio' (*Scriptores*, p. 742) during the winter of 1556–7. But he soon left for Geneva, where on 5 June 1557 he was received into Knox's congregation and on the following 29 November became a 'resident' of the city (f. 226). There, too, he married Jane Agar, daughter of the 'Ales Agar of Colchester, widowe' who had recently become the wife of Thomas Spenser (*q.v.*). Martin includes *William* Cole among those who 'regularly assisted' in the translation of the Bible (Martin, p. 241). On his return to England he became the first married president of Corpus Christi College, Oxford (1568), being supported in his election by Robert Horne, then bishop of Winchester, and strenuously resisted by the Fellows. Horne, however, lived to regret his advocacy, for Cole, as president, says Anthony Wood, 'acted so fouly by defrauding the College, and bringing it into debt' that the bishop was obliged to take action. In an interview with Cole he concluded his reproofs with 'Well, well Mr President,...you and the college must part without any more ado...'. Whereupon Cole, fetching a deep sigh, said, 'What, my good Lord, must I then eat mice at Zurich again?' (Wood's *Annals*, II, 164–6).[1] The question, we are told, saved him his presidency, for Horne and Cole had been exiles together. In 1596 Cole became dean of Lincoln.

B I a & b; Zurich, A VIII a & c; Frankfort, A III a 3; Basle, B II; Geneva, A IV a & b; *D.N.B.*

[1] This is the reference given for this story in T. Fowler's *History of Corpus Christi* (pp. 74–5), but I have not been able to verify it.

97. COLLYN (COLLYNS, COLINS), John: *Chantry priest.*

When received into the English congregation at Geneva on 17 February 1558, John Collyn is described as 'being a very aged man' (Martin, p. 333). It is therefore not at all unlikely that he was the ejected chantry priest 'John Colyns, parson of Littleton in the diocese of Bristol' who received '£3 and odd money out of the Churchwardens of Wotton-under-Edge' in the name of a chantry yet did 'no service there as he ought to do'[1] (Baskerville, *E.H.R.* XLIV, 5). On 24 October 1558 he was received as a 'resident' of the city (f. 264), and probably died in Geneva.

Geneva, A IV a & b.

98. COLTON, Edward: *Yeoman*(?). Of Staffordshire(?).

Perhaps from Colton in Staffordshire (Harl. Soc. LXIII, 266), but beyond the fact that he was in Frankfort in the spring of 1557 and signed the 'new discipline' in April, we know no more of him. A George Colton, said to be of Sutton Coldfield, Warwickshire, settled in Connecticut just before 1646 (*New Eng. Reg.* XXXIII, 202).

Frankfort, B III b.

99. COOKE, Sir Anthony: *Gent.* Of Gidea Hall, Essex. Wife (?). 1504–76.

One of Edward VI's tutors, and married to Anne, the daughter of Sir William Fitzwilliam. Through the marriages of their four daughters, Mildred, 'a tiresome bluestocking', according to the Count de Feria, Anne, Elizabeth and Katherine, Sir Anthony became the father-in-law of Sir William Cecil, Sir Nicholas Bacon, Sir Thomas Hoby (*q.v.*), and Sir Henry Killigrew (*q.v.*). He had been among the protestant auditors at the disputations on the Sacrament held in 1551 at the houses of Sir William Cecil and Sir Richard Morison (*Cranmer*, p. 386), and for his suspected complicity in the affair of Lady Jane Grey, he was committed to the Tower on 27 July 1553 with Sir John Cheke (*Machyn*, p. 38), though, unlike Cheke, he had not signed the Letters Patent for the Limitation of the Crown (*Chron. Q. Jane*, p. 100). After their release the two men went abroad together, arriving in Strasbourg on 14 April 1554 (Protocols, vol. 32, ff. 131vo, 167), but Sir Anthony for some reason unknown (yet strongly surmised) remained in Strasbourg while Cheke and Sir Richard Morison went on their way towards Italy. It is supposed that Cooke stayed behind to

---

[1] From Browne Willis, (*Abbies*, II, 90), I find that a John Collins, chantry priest of Workley Chapel, co. Gloucester, was still being pensioned in 1553, receiving £2. 16s. This seems to strengthen the identification.

attend Peter Martyr's lectures: and very likely he did (*Cranmer*, p. 513). But there were other grave matters afoot that summer in Strasbourg for which Sir Anthony's advice and co-operation would have been needed. Certain political pamphlets were in preparation against the coming reconciliation between England and Rome, the imminence of which was bruited as early as April 1554. And of these a petition to parliament under the title of *The Confession of the Banished Ministers*, by far the most significant of all the pamphlets written abroad, was in process of compilation probably through July and August (see above, p. 28 and note 13 and biographies of Becon and Ponet). Early in September Sir Anthony Cooke resumed his journey to Italy, carrying with him a letter of introduction to Bullinger at Zurich from John Burcher at whose house he had been staying. It is dated 3 September (*O.L.* II, 686). Sir Thomas Hoby records Cooke's arrival at Padua 'shortlie after' his own on 23 August (Cam. Misc. x, 116–17), and on 1 October Sir Anthony made one of the pleasure party that set out with the Hobys for Mantua. The following winter he spent at Padua; but on 12 June 1555 he turned his face northwards again (*ibid.* p. 120) and on 7 September was petitioning the Strasbourg Council for civic rights (Protocols, vol. 33, f. 363) on the plea that he had been banished from England because of his religion (*ibid.*). Like Sir Richard Morison he asked only for temporary residence, since they both hoped that 'in a short time they would be restored to their estates' (*ibid.*). The Council, however, took nearly a month to consider this request and on 1 October decided to exact 'further guarantees' of the two Englishmen before admitting them to residence (*ibid.* f. 393vo). To what their caution was due we can only guess. That Sir Anthony Cooke was Cecil's agent while abroad cannot be proved, but that some such relation existed between the two men and Sir Nicholas Bacon is not only possible but highly probable. Through the year 1556 we catch hints in Brett's narrative of mysterious comings and goings at Sir Anthony Cooke's house at Strasbourg, and of dealings with the 'Archeheretik of Geneva' (Brett, pp. 130–1). But of this the correspondence between father-in-law and son-in-law naturally reveals nothing whatever in the few commonplace letters that have survived Cecil's admirable discretion (*Salisbury*, I, 138, 140, 141). In 1557 we know nothing of Cooke's activities beyond the fact that he had purchased of Maria Ponet her husband's library, only to find that a considerable part of it belonged to Peter Martyr (*O.L.* I, 118). It was in March of that year that he wrote to Cecil 'My being here is not pleasant, but necessary' (*Salisbury*, I, 140). But on 21 December 1558 he notified the Council through John Abell of his departure for England (Protocols, vol. 36, f. 634vo), which had actually taken place on the 20th (*Z.L.* I, 5). After thanking the city for its protection, he assures the magistrates that 'he has only taken personal belongings with him' (Protocols, vol. 36, f. 634vo), and his leave-taking had indeed been nearly as precipitate as a flight, since confirmation of the rumours of Mary's death had not reached Strasbourg until 19 December (*Z.L.* I, 3). 'Many persons', wrote Jewel to Peter Martyr, 'are of opinion that [Sir Anthony] Cook will be the Lord Chancellor' (*ibid.* p. 8); but Jewel himself, though he considers Cooke 'a worthy and pious man', thinks him 'hardly qualified for that office' (*ibid.*). Neither did Elizabeth. It is a commentary on his career in exile and his strenuous opposition to the Supremacy Bill in the House of Commons in February-March 1558/9, that Sir Anthony's merits were studiously ignored by the queen (cf. *Z.L.* I, 53). In fact it was not until June 1559 that he received any appointment whatever, and then only that of commissioner for the Visitation of Cambridge (*Parker*, I, 86).

Strasbourg, A VII a; Basle; Padua, B IV b; Strasbourg, A VII a; A VIII a & b;
D.N.B.

100. COOKE (COKE), MICHAEL.

It was at first believed that the name 'Coke' was here a mistake for 'Cope', and that this was Michael Cope, from Geneva; but as Michael Cope has proved to be a Frenchman (see below), and as I am assured that, in any case, he was not absent from Geneva during March-April 1555, the only time when Mighell Coke, as a signatory to the 'new discipline', is noticed at Frankfort, the identification has broken down. Nor has it been possible to find a Michael among the sons of Sir Anthony Cooke, nor among those of Sir John Cope (*q.v.*).

Frankfort, B III b.

101. COOKE, RICHARD: *Gent.* Of Essex. 1531-79.

Called by Brett merely 'Cooke's son' but probably Richard the eldest, since it was he who watched Brett out of the town of Strasbourg in July 1556 (Brett, p. 131). He may have returned to England before his father, though the latter's words, 'I marvel leave could not be given for my son Richard. Would to God his sickness improved! I have not had at all times most cause to be content with him, but now, I fear, I shall be loth to lack him!' are enigmatical and may refer to a petition made to the queen to permit his son's return (*Salisbury*, I, 140: 27 March 1557). In the first parliament of Elizabeth a Richard Cook, possibly Sir Anthony's son, sat for Preston, Lancs. (*Return of Members*, I, 400).

Strasbourg, B IV a.

102. COOK (COOCK), RICHARD: *Weaver*. Of Hadleigh, Suffolk. Wife.

A refugee at Aarau living with his wife in the house of Joachim Schmutzingers. Hans Dür's list adds the information that he was born in Suffolk and lived at 'Haddelea', where he had probably been a member of Rowland Taylor's congregation.

Aarau, I a & b.

103. COPE, J(OHN): *Gent.* Of Northamptonshire(?). d. 1557/8.

We know that he was a member of the English colony at Frankfort in September 1555 because Sir Thomas Hoby mentions having met there 'Mr J. Cope' (Cam. Misc. X, 123). But there is no other record of his presence abroad, nor is it easy to identify him, though we believe him to have been the second surviving son of William Cope of Hanwell, Oxon., Cofferer to Henry VIII, and so the brother of Sir Anthony Cope, High Sheriff of Oxford (d. 1551) (Harl. Soc. v, 60 and *Pedigrees from the Visitation of Oxford*, 1634, p. 29). This Sir John Cope, of Canons (or Cope's) Ashby, Northants., was sheriff of Northamptonshire *ca.* 1546 and M.P. under Edward VI (Baker's *Northamptonshire*, I, 748; II, 13). He died in January 1557/8 (*ibid.*). His son Erasmus was the father of Sir Edward Cope.

Frankfort, B IV b.

*COPE, MICHAEL ('alias Michel Cop'): *Pastor*. Of Geneva. 1501–66.

For some 300 years 'Michael Cope', author of 'A godly and learned Exposition vpon the Proverbs of Solomon' (*Exposition familière des proverbes de Salomon*, Geneva, 1556[1]) and *Exposition familière du livre de l'Ecclésiaste*, Geneva, 1557 has been held to be an Englishman upon the slender basis of Anthony Wood's notice of him as 'a zealous Calvinist at Geneva', but whether he was 'of the same family with that of Sir Anthony's...or was educated at Oxford I cannot yet tell' (*Ath. Oxon.* I, 192; Herbert's Ames, II, 929; and cf. Tanner, *Bibl. Brit.* p. 199). In the *D.N.B.* this conjecture has been turned into a statement of fact, and Michel Cope, who was in fact of Swiss-French origin, is described as a 'protestant author' who 'fled from England to escape persecution in the reign of Mary, and took refuge in Geneva, where he preached much in French'. He did indeed go to Geneva, and there did preach much in the French which was his native language, for Michael Cope, or more accurately Michel Cop, was the son of Guillaume Cop, a famous doctor of Basle who, migrating to France, became physician to Francis I. His other son Nicolas

[1] Wood (I, 192) was ignorant of the date of its first publication.

(if Nicolas and Michel are not one person)[1] was rector of the Sorbonne. But Michel, because of his protestantism, fled from France to Basle, and finally in 1545 came to Geneva, where he was chosen pastor in the same year. There, too, he married Ayma Waremberg; there in 1554 he was received as a bourgeois of the city; and there in 1566 he died (Th. Heyer, *L'Église de Genève*). Of his two publications already mentioned, the *Proverbs of Solomon* only was translated into English, by one 'Marcelline Outred',[2] who prefaced it with a dedication to Sir William Cecil (*Ath. Oxon.* I, 192; Herbert's Ames, II, 929; Tanner's *Bibl. Brit.* p. 199).

104. CORNEWALL (CORNWELL, CORNEWAYLE), ED-WARD or ROBERT(?): *Gent.* Of Essex.

There is disagreement between Machyn and the Baga de Secretis as to the first name of this Marian conspirator. Machyn says that an Edward Cornwell fled to France as an associate of Dudley (p. 103). The Baga de Secretis calls him Robert. Edward can probably be identified as the third son of 'John Cornewall of Haverell', Essex (Harl. Soc. XIII, 6), but Robert, though called in the Baga (p. 254) a 'gentleman of London', seems also to have been from Essex and at one time a loyal supporter of the queen (*Dom. Cal.* 1547–80, p. 59). The two may have been brothers, but the pedigree names no Robert as a son of John, though this omission is not, of course, conclusive. Nor does the only mention of Cornewall in France help to establish his identity, for he is referred to by Dr Wotton merely as 'Cornwall, of Essex' (*For. Cal.* 1553–8, p. 222). We believe, however, that, whether Robert or Edward, there was but one Cornewall in France and the presumption of accuracy regarding his first name probably lies with the Baga de Secretis.

France, B IV c; B v b 1 & c.

105. CORNWALLIS, HENRY: *Gent.* Of Suffolk.

This is a younger brother of the Sir Thomas Cornwallis of Brome in Suffolk (Harl. Soc. IV, 161) who was a staunch catholic, a member of Queen Mary's Privy Council, and the man chosen first to treat with Wyatt and then to be present at his trial. But his brother Henry may have been implicated in that conspiracy, for

---

[1] I owe the correction of this case of mistaken identity and the information regarding Michel Cop to the great kindness of M. Gustav Vaucher, deputy archivist of the Archives d'État at Geneva, who also tells me that Michel and Nicolas Cop have been thought by some to be the same person. Though absolute proof is lacking that both existed and that they were brothers, this is the belief of Doumergue (*Jean Calvin*, III, 577 ff.).

[2] Probably 'Marcellanus Outred, cl.' (Newcourt, II, 414).

he was found by Sir Thomas Hoby among the group of fugitive protestants at Padua in 1554 (Cam. Misc. x, 116). He must soon have made his peace, however, for in February 1555 we find him, with his brother Richard, ordered to apprehend a suspected person in Suffolk (*P.C.A.* 1554–6, p. 100).

Padua, B iv b.

106. COTES (COTE, COATES), WILLIAM: *Student*(?). Of Yorkshire(?).

Possibly the William Cote or Gate who was suspected of heresy in St Gile's, Cripplegate, in 1541 (Foxe, v, 445) and the father or grandfather of the William Cotes of Yorkshire (born *ca.* 1560) who matriculated as sizar of Clare Hall, Cambridge, in October 1579 (Venn, i, 360) and was the author (1585) of the *Short Questions between the Father and the Sonne* (Herbert's Ames, ii, 1099 and Cooper, ii, 22). William Cotes went to Geneva in 1558 and some time during April was received into the English congregation.

Geneva, A iv a.

107. COTTESFORD (COTTISFORDE), THOMAS: *Priest.* Of Winchester. d. 1555.

Educated at Oxford and Cambridge, but Venn (i, 402) seems to doubt the M.A. given him by Cooper (i, 140). Under Henry VIII he had been imprisoned in the Fleet for setting forth, in violation of the Six Articles, an epistle of Melanchthon (*ibid.*), but by 1553 he had been made rector of St Martin's, Ludgate (Newcourt, i, 415), and in July of that year prebendary of York (*Ath. Oxon.* i, 231), an office of which he was not deprived until 1555 (Venn). Yet he was among the first to flee to the Continent. Very probably the memory of his imprisonment was yet vivid, and he had also in mind that he had appeared against Gardiner at the latter's trial in 1551 (Foxe, vi, 136). Since he first appears abroad at Copenhagen (Tanner, *Bibl. Brit.* p. 202), he was doubtless among those who left England with John à Lasco in September 1553, and it was quite possibly with à Lasco that he arrived at Frankfort in 1555. There on 20 September he was one of the signers of Whitehead's letter of justification to Calvin (*O.L.* ii, 763), yet his name is not mentioned in any of the official lists nor in the *Troubles at Frankfort.* Also, Wood's statement that he was 'lastly at Geneva' is not confirmed by the records. His death, 'venerabilis senex', at Frankfort on 6 December 1555 (*Scriptores*, p. 722) must therefore have occurred soon after his arrival. He was the translator of the *Zwinglische Bekenntnis* of 1530 (Jung, pp. 46–7), which appeared in English at Geneva in April 1555, under the title of the *Confession of the Faith of Huldrik Zwinglius* (*Ath. Oxon.* i, 232).

B i a & b; Copenhagen; Frankfort, A viii a; *D.N.B.*

108. COURTENAY, Sir EDWARD. Of Ugbrooke, Devon. d. 1566.

Son and heir of Sir Peter Courtenay of Powderham (d. 1552), who as sheriff of Devon in 1549 had been very active in suppressing the Cornish insurrection. As 'Sir' Edward Courtenay (called Esq. in his epitaph) was with Sir Peter Carew, his uncle, at Caen in March 1554 (*For. Cal.* 1553–8, p. 66), it is more than likely that he had taken part in the Western Rising in January. But of this his epitaph, once placed on the north side of the altar at St Margaret's, Westminster, makes no mention, but claims that he had lived 'a Life agreeable to his Estate and Stock' and had 'ended the same like a faithful Christian, the 27 of November 1556' (E. Cleaveland, *Gen. Hist. of Family of Courtenay*, 1735, p. 291). Elsewhere Cleaveland says that he died in 1566, and Collins (*Peerage*, VI, 264) gives 1559 as the date of his death, but his burial is registered as of 29 November 1566 (Burke's *Memorials of St Margaret's*, p. 14), where he is said to have been of Ugbrooke, Devon, and to have married Florence, daughter of Thomas Moore of Taunton.

France (Caen), B v b 1.

109. COURTENAY, EDWARD, eighth Earl of Devon. d. 1556.

Of the 'royal Courtenays' and perhaps the one strictly 'banished' person among the Marian refugees. Released by Queen Mary after twelve years' imprisonment in the Tower, Courtenay was led to aspire first to her hand, then to that of the Princess Elizabeth. The rising in the West of 1554 chose him as its candidate for the throne, but being as unstable in politics as in religion, it was Courtenay who revealed the plot to Gardiner (Noailles, III, 31) though certainly involved in it himself (Tytler, II, 320). When released from a second imprisonment in the spring of 1555, he was sent into honourable exile with a small retinue and a credit of 3–4000 crowns granted by the queen (*For. Cal.* 1553–8, pp. 168, 256), but Courtenay was well aware that during his prolonged stay at Brussels he was virtually a prisoner under strict surveillance. He had arrived there on 17 May (*Ven. Cal.* 1555–6, no. 84, p. 73), but his desire to see the world which 'displeasant fortune had caused him hitherto to lack' was not indulged until 15 October, when he at last obtained leave to go to Italy (*ibid.* no. 248, p. 215). No doubt his detention had been for the purpose of discovering what were his exact relations with the French king, who had every desire to use him as a tool 'to foment discord and division in England' (*ibid.* 1556–7, no. 584, p. 1073); and during his enforced visit he went 'in great fear for his life' (*ibid.* 1555–6, no. 123, p. 99).

Why he was allowed to depart at this moment is not clear,[1] but in December 1555 he passed by way of Augsburg to Italy 'intending to go first to Mantua, then to Ferrara, and perhaps to Milan, before going to Venice' (*ibid.* no. 273, p. 243), where on his arrival a plot had been formed to murder him (*ibid.* no. 328, pp. 294–7). It was for this reason that the Signory permitted him to surround himself with a bodyguard of twenty-five armed men (*ibid.* p. 343). This was in February 1556. The following June, Henry Killigrew was sent by Sir Henry Dudley to urge Courtenay to join his conspiracy (*For. Cal.* p. 229: 19 June 1556; also pp. 238, 245). Whether Courtenay ever actually lent himself to Dudley's designs is not clear, but in Wotton's letters to Queen Mary he constantly repeats the rumour that 'the Earl of Devonshire will join them [the conspirators] very shortly'. Then in the autumn of 1556 we find him quietly enrolled as a student at the University of Padua, yet not without a last pathetic flourish of his royal claims, for he was registered as 'Curtinek nob. anglus ex regia Albae Rosae brittanorum familia' (Andrich, p. 131). And on 18 September he who 'expected to be King of England' was dead at Padua (*For. Cal.* 1553–8, p. 255). Peter Vannes, suspected of having had some hand in hastening them, sent a graphic account of Courtenay's last days to Queen Mary (*ibid.* p. 260), and of his burial, which was to be conducted 'with as much sparing and as much honour as can be done' (*ibid.* pp. 255–6). He also assured her that the Earl died a good catholic; and indeed Courtenay's sole claim to protestant sympathies would appear to have been the translation made while he was a prisoner in the Tower of an Italian tract in defence of the reformed doctrines (*D.N.B.*). His epitaph in Padua is quoted, though how accurately we cannot say, in Cleaveland's *Gen. Hist. of Family of Courtenay* (pt III, pp. 261–2).

Brussels, B v; Venice; Padua, A vi; *D.N.B.*

110. COURTENAY, JOHN: *Gent.* Of Devon.

Second son of Sir William Courtenay of Powderham by his second wife Mary, daughter of Sir John Gainsford of Surrey (Vowell, p. 35), who later married Sir Anthony Kingston (Cleaveland, *op. cit.* pp. 291, 293). He was therefore an uncle of Sir Edward Courtenay (above) and, like him, one of the followers of Sir Peter Carew in Normandy in 1554 (*For. Cal.* p. 66). He had already served with distinction abroad under Lord Lisle and had been in the siege of Exeter when attacked by the rebels in 1549 (Rose-

---

[1] Unless it was connected with Charles V's purpose to abdicate (25 October 1555) and to marry the Archduke Ferdinand to the Princess Elizabeth (*Ven. Cal.* 1555–6, no. 248, p. 214).

Troup, pp. 151, 196, 376), and his stepfather, Kingston, was to become involved with Henry Dudley's plot in 1556 (Machyn, p. 98 and Rose-Troup, p. 313).

France (Caen), B v b 1.

111. COVERDALE, MILES ('alias Michael Anglus'): *Ex-religious and bishop*. Of Yorkshire. Wife. 1488–1568/9.

Student at Cambridge, and an Augustinian friar there under Robert Barnes. Probably abroad between 1528 and 1535 (see *D.N.B.*) while working on his English translation of the Bible published in 1535. From 1538 to 1540, Coverdale with Richard Grafton the printer (*q.v.*) was again abroad superintending at Paris the printing of the 'Great Bible' of 1539; and about 1540 he married Elizabeth Macheson, sister of the wife of John Macchabaeus, chaplain to the King of Denmark. Returning to England in 1548, he was appointed by letters patent to the see of Exeter, and consecrated bishop on 30 August 1551. On 28 September 1553 he was deprived (Le Neve, I, 377–8).

Although first summoned before Queen Mary's Council with Hooper of Gloucester on 22 August 1553 (*P.C.A.* 1552–4, p. 328), Coverdale was not committed to the Fleet with Hooper on 1 September, but merely remanded to await the 'Lordes pleasures' (*ibid.* p. 337). Indeed, in spite of Strype's assertion to the contrary (*Mem.* III, i, 77), in which he is not supported by Foxe (VI, 389, 393), Coverdale seems never to have been imprisoned. When on 8 May 1554 he subscribed to that last Edwardian summary of doctrine which was issued from the King's Bench and is known as the 'Eight Articles', it is evident that the document had to be sent to him for approval, for his is a separate signature appended with the statement that he agrees 'with these mine afflicted brethren being prisoners (with mine own hand)' (*ibid.* p. 553). Apparently unmolested,[1] then, he remained in England until the spring of 1555, when, upon the intervention of Christian III of Denmark (*ibid.* pp. 705–6), the Council granted him a passport on 19 February 1554/5, with permission to take with him to Denmark 'two of his servantes, his bagges and baggages, without any thier unlawfull lett or searche' (*P.C.A.* 1554–6, p. 97). The supposition that one of these servants was his wife is borne out by the records of the town of Aarau in Switzerland. But Coverdale stayed but a short while in Denmark, refusing there an offer of preferment in order to become preacher to the English congregation at Wesel which had gathered around the fugitive Duchess of Suffolk (*q.v.*). Yet even so he 'preached there no longe time' (*T.* p. 184). Whittingham

---

[1] Here it is true, Foxe speaks of Coverdale's 'captivity', but the meaning of the word is explained in the paragraph above where he says that the bishop 'at that time went under sureties'.

implies that he went directly from Wesel to Bergzabern 'to take the pastorall charge' in that town where he had been a schoolmaster between 1545–7 (*O.L.* I, 247), but from a letter of Coverdale's to Conrad Hubert, which proves to have been misdated[1] (Coverdale, *Remains*, pp. 527–8), we find him taking a journey to Frankfort in the company of John Abell the banker some time during the summer of 1555. The inference is that Cox had called him there to take part in the revision of the Prayer Book which was then in progress, for, in a marginal note to his narrative Whittingham informs us that 'Many off the lerned men were now come from all places' to share in the work (*T.* p. 45). It is hardly likely that so important a person as Coverdale should not have been one of them. From Frankfort then, in September when that work was finished, he would have gone on to Bergzabern in response to the call of the 'duke off bypont', and while there was instrumental in procuring for the Duchess of Suffolk a safer asylum than Wesel had become since the discovery in the spring of 1556 of the Dudley conspiracy in which that colony had almost undoubtedly been implicated (Ponet, *Treatise*, ed. 1556, Sig. I 7, and cf. above, pp. 50–51). In the spring of 1557 the whole congregation was obliged to find itself a new home. And when on 11 August the majority of the colony established itself at Aarau in the jurisdiction of Berne, Miles Coverdale, with his wife and two children, is found to have been among the company (Official List, see below, p. 354). The Frauenkloster in which they were domiciled still stands at the foot of the Stadtskirche of Aarau in which Coverdale must frequently have preached even though Thomas Lever was the official pastor of the English congregation. It was probably the remoteness and security of this little hill-town near Basle which had recommended it to Coverdale as a place suitable for study, possibly also for obscurity. Until now this Argovian episode of two years in his life has remained unknown. And he left it in the autumn of 1558 only for the purpose of collaborating at Geneva in the translation of the Bible (Martin, p. 241). There on 24 October he was received as a 'resident' of the city (f. 264). In the Livre des Anglois he is twice mentioned; once when he was elected a senior of Knox's congregation on 16 December 1558; and the other when he acted as 'witnesse' to the baptism of Knox's son, Eleezer, on 29 November. Not till 14 August 1559 did he take leave of Geneva to return to England (Martin, p. 242), and on 12 November he first preached in London at Paul's Cross (*Machyn*, p. 218). It has been supposed that he declined his former bishopric of Exeter because of his scruples in regard to vestments, but it is

---

[1] The date originally assigned to it is 20 September 1543; but the fact that Coverdale signs himself 'nuper Exon' places it in 1555.

far more likely that it was never offered to him, his official connection with the Genevan congregation of Knox making him *persona non grata* to Elizabeth (cf. Grindal, *Remains*, p. 284). In 1563 Cambridge honoured him with a D.D. and in the same year (1563/4) he was collated to the living of St Magnus, London Bridge, which three years later he resigned because of nonconformity. Thereafter he preached privately until his death in 1568.

Denmark; Wesel, B III; Bergzabern, B III; Aarau, I a & b; Geneva, IV a & b;
D.N.B.

112. COX, RICHARD, D.D.: *Priest and dean.* Of Whaddon, Buckinghamshire. 1500–81.

Originally of Eton and King's College, Cox alternated between Oxford and Cambridge, but received his D.D. from Cambridge in 1537. Tutor to Edward VI until 1550, Chancellor of Oxford till 1552, and Dean of Westminster 1549–53. Richard Cox was believed by his contemporaries to share responsibility with Ridley and Sir John Cheke for sanctioning the proclamation of Lady Jane Grey (Burcher to Bullinger, 16 August 1553, *O.L.* II, 684). He had been high in Cranmer's favour and was for ten years more intimately connected with Prayer Book history than any other Edwardian divine. He sat on the so-called Windsor Commission for the compilation of the Order of Communion (1548) and for the first Prayer Book (1549); he probably helped to draft the first English ordinal (1550) and the second Prayer Book (1552); while, during his exile abroad, he presided at Frankfort, in March 1555, over a self-constituted commission for further Prayer Book revision. After Elizabeth's accession he was appointed a member of Sir Thomas Smith's committee for the same purpose. And finally he was one of the protestant disputants at the Conference of Westminster (1559).

Between 1553 and 1559 his history is briefly as follows: committed to the Marshalsea on a charge of treason on 5 August 1553 (Foxe, VI, 537) he was released on 19 August but ordered to keep his house at Westminster (*P.C.A.* 1552–4, p. 427). On 6 May 1554 he and Edward Sandys made good their escape to the Continent (Foxe, VIII, 597). Landing at Antwerp, it may be assumed (though Foxe does not say so) that he went, in company with Sandys, Grindal and Sampson, first to Duisburg, and, after a two weeks' stay, on to Strasbourg, where the party may have arrived in June 1554. Yet there is no mention of Cox at any time in the Strasbourg protocols, nor does his name appear in the list of English refugees sent by the Strasbourg magistrates to the Duke of Württemberg on 28 December 1554 (Württ. Staatsarchiv). All that we certainly know is that he arrived at Frankfort on 13 March

1555 (*T*. p. 38) with enough followers to alter the balance of factions in the congregation and so to triumph over the anti-Prayer-Book party headed by Knox. It is impossible to believe, as Whittingham would have us believe, that this Coxian invasion was by pure accident. Cox had not only extraordinary prestige in all that concerned the Prayer Book, but also was of a domineering temper peculiarly well fitted to face Knox in controversy. Who sent him to Frankfort? Was it Ponet, ranking bishop abroad, and one who would have bitterly resented Knox's liturgical meddling? Of this there is no proof, but events moved too swiftly and surely to their anti-Knoxian climax not to suggest that Cox was acting under authority. Knox he browbeat in conference, and within two weeks had him expelled from Frankfort (26 March, *T*. p. 45). He then assembled the chief Edwardian divines in exile (*ibid.*, and marginal note; cf. also 'Coverdale', above), most conveniently present in the city, and with their aid completed on 28 March (*T*. pp. 46–7) a third revision of the Prayer Book which has probably survived in a manuscript found about 1871 among Thomas Sampson's papers (Hist. MSS. Comm. 1871,[1] Append. to 2nd Report, pp. 76–7) and now existing in the British Museum as Egerton MS. 2836. This I believe to be Cox's 'Liturgy of Frankfort' and not Knox's 'Liturgy of Compromise' drawn up on the preceding 6 February and in force at Cox's coming (*T*. p. 37), though I have the temerity to advance this view in opposition to that of Dr Lorimer, Dr Sprott (see H. J. Wotherspoon's *Second Prayer Book of Edward VI etc.* (Edinb. 1905), pp. 226–7) and the compiler of the Egerton *Catalogue* (p. 388, f. 1). For Sampson's transcript not only corresponds closely to Cox's own outline of his revised liturgy (*O.L.* II, 753–5) but also with Knox's account given in his 'Narrative' (Laing, IV, pp. 41–9) of the points at issue between himself and Cox.[2] Finally, we know from the signatures to Cox's letter, that Sampson was himself a member of that revising committee.

Upon the internal evidence supplied by the text of the liturgy itself, it seems probable that it did not reach its final form until the late autumn of 1555, when Cox took his departure from Frankfort. On or about 15 November he was still in Frankfort, for he is listed among the 'students' on the Standesliste and was then living on the Braidengasse (Jung, p. 47). But shortly afterwards (*T*. p. 59) he probably left for Zurich. It is characteristic of Cox that while in Frankfort (26 March) he had a lawsuit with an

[1] Published, 1874.

[2] As, for example, the question of the Litany, which Knox wished to reject and Cox to retain. It is present in this Liturgy of Frankfort.

English merchant at Antwerp, Thomas Aldersey, who owed him £80 (Jung, p. 47). In April 1557 he returned to Frankfort at the request of the magistrates to act as moderator in the quarrel between Horne and Ashley, but was not then living there (*T*. p. 99). At the time of Mary's death he was at Worms, and, by way of Cologne, was 'among the foremost' to return to England (*Z.L.* II, 41). Calvin, whose doctrinal jurisdiction in the matter of the English Prayer Book Cox had ignored, described him in 1556 as possessing 'ostentation; an immoderate fervour in meddling; and a proud and confident manner in his carriage and language' (Gorham, *Gleanings*, p. 353, note c). To this list of failings Calvin might have added 'avarice', otherwise (cf. Lord North to Cox, *Salisbury*, II, 121) his characterization is perfectly borne out by Cox's later history as bishop of Ely.

Strasbourg (?); Frankfort, A III a 2 & b 1; B I a & b; B III; *D.N.B.*

113. CRANMER, EDWARD (EDMUND): *Archdeacon*. Of Aslockton, Nottinghamshire. Wife. *ca.* 1557.

Brother to the archbishop. M.A. Cambridge, 1520. Archdeacon of Canterbury (1535) and prebendary of Canterbury (1550). Deprived in 1554 (Strype, *Cranmer*, pp. 471–2). One of the very few whose deprivation, for the cause of marriage alone, led to flight abroad. It seems not unlikely that he had been given the custody of the archbishop's son Thomas (below), which would doubtless have made flight seem to him imperative and would also account for the extreme secrecy observed in regard to his place of exile. Were it not for the witness of the Emden catalogue and of Bale's list we should doubt his presence on the Continent. Possibly he remained at Emden to fulfil the pious duty of publishing his brother's *Defensio*, and he is believed to have died in exile about 1557.

n.p.; B I a & b; B II; *D.N.B.*

114. CRANMER, THOMAS: *A minor*. Later of Kirkstall, Yorkshire. d. 1598.

Son of the archbishop by his second wife, and probably consigned, while abroad, to the care of his uncle, Edmund Cranmer (above). Upon Elizabeth's accession he was taken to Strasbourg and there left with John Abell to be delivered into Jewel's care for the return journey to England. 'In the youth's name', Jewel borrowed 'some crowns' from Abell for their travelling expenses (*Z.L.* I, 8; 26 January 1559). Oddly enough, the boy seems to have been one of the few whose continental experience caused a reaction against puritanism: his life was no credit to his father's memory (Pollard, *Cranmer*, p. 326 note).

n.p.; A IX b.

115. CRAWLEY, THOMAS, Esq.: *Gent.* Of Essex. d. 29 September 1559.

This is probably the Thomas Crawley of Wendon Lofts (Harl. Soc. XIII, 318, 346) who was a purchaser of chantry lands in Essex in the second year of Edward VI (*Mem.* II, ii, 404 and Morant's *Essex,* II, 604). His manor of Wendon Lofts he held of Henry, Earl of Sussex (Morant, II, 593). By the autumn of 1555 he appears as 'generosus' on the Standesliste at Frankfort, and in January 1557 his property was valued at 700 florins. He signed the 'new discipline' in April and by the dwelling-list of June is found to have had as inmates of his house Sigismund Broke, Thomas Wilson and James Peers (*H.S.P.* IV, 88). He was also one of those to whom Richard Chambers addressed his letter of justification (*T.* p. 182), and probably he is the Thomas Crawley who sat for Aylesbury, Bucks., in the first parliament of Elizabeth (Browne Willis, p. 62 and *Return of Members,* I, 400).

Frankfort, A III a 2, 3, 4 & b 1, 2; B III a & b.

116. CROFTON (CRAFTON, CROSTON), THOMAS: *Student*(?). Of Lancashire.

We are inclined to believe that the correct form of this man's name is that found in the Registre des Habitants at Geneva (f. 123)—'Croston'[1]—and that he may have been one of a family of Crostons of Bury, Lancs., who had representatives at Oxford in the sixteenth century and at Cambridge in the seventeenth (Foster and Venn). Judged from his propensity to wander, this Thomas Croston, or Crofton, was a 'student', found first at Strasbourg in November 1554 (*T.* p. 23) as 'Crafton'; then, in August 1555, at Frankfort, where he had become 'Crofton' and an adherent of Whittingham's party. With Whittingham he seceded to Geneva (*T.* p. 55), arriving there on 13 October 1555, and on 24 October he was received as a 'resident' of the city (f. 123).

Strasbourg, B III; Frankfort, B III; Geneva, IV a & b.

117. CROWLEY, ROBERT: *Author, printer, priest.* Of Gloucestershire. Wife. 1518(?)–88.

Fellow of Magdalen College, Oxford 1541–4, and called by Wood 'a very forward man for reformation' (*Ath. Oxon.* I, 542). In 1549 he set up a printing press in Ely Rents in Holborn (*ibid.* and Gordon Duff, p. 35), which he placed at the service of the new doctrines, and in his 'leisure times exercised the gift of preaching' (*Ath. Oxon.* I, 543). But in 1551 he was ordained both deacon

[1] The 'f', even in the Livre des Anglois, is not impossibly an 's' (cf. Bodleian MS. Facs. d. 49).

and priest, the record of his ordination calling him a 'stationer' living in the parish of St Andrew's, Holborn, but born at Tedbury, Gloucester (*Mar. Reac.* pp. 198, 200), thus correcting Bale's belief that he came from Northamptonshire (*Scriptores*, p. 728). Possibly his flight to the Continent was because of a wife that he had married; but it is more likely that his printing press and a probable connection with John Day (Bloxam, IV, 79, n. 1) made it seem to him prudent to leave London. He first appears at Frankfort in the autumn of 1555 among the 'students' of the Standesliste. In the tax-list of 1556 he is said to have 'usually had no property but debts' ('hat sonst nichts uber schulden', Jung, p. 29), which speaks eloquently of the conditions under which he and his wife and 'infant', together with twenty-five other inmates, must have been living in the house of Laurence Kent where they are found in June 1557 (*H.S.P.* IV, 89). In the previous March-April, Crowley had been a signatory of the 'new discipline' and on 30 September he put his name to Frankfort's uncompromising refusal to accept the mediation of Strasbourg in the quarrels which that discipline had occasioned (*T.* p. 174). Two years later, on 15 October 1559, he was in London again and preaching at Paul's Cross (*Machyn*, p. 215). Then in quick succession he was made archdeacon of Hereford (1559) and canon of St Paul's (1563), and almost as quickly found himself in conflict with Archbishop Parker over the wearing of surplices, which he called 'porters coats' (Parker, I, 434–5). But Crowley is chiefly remembered for the fact that in 1550 he 'first of all publish'd "The Visions of Pierce Plowman"' (*Ath. Oxon.* I, 544–5), though perhaps the publication was prompted more by his social than his poetic sympathies, for in 1548 he himself had written, 'with a bold freedom', *An informacion and petition against the oppressours of the pore commons of this Realme* (Herbert's Ames, II, 762; cf. *D.N.B.*).

B I a & b; Frankfort, A III a 2, 3, 4 & b 1, 2; *D.N.B.*

118. CUTTS, Sir JOHN: *Gent.* Of Cambridgeshire. d. 1555.

Of Horham Hall and Childersley, co. Cambridge, and married to Sibell, daughter of Sir John Hynde, also of Cambridge. In 1551 Sir John, being then sheriff of Cambridgeshire and Huntingdonshire (*Essex Arch. Trans.* vol. IV, O.S. pp. 30, 42), formed, with Sir Peter Carew, one of the train of the Marquis of Northampton on his embassy to France. Precisely what misdemeanour sent him as a refugee to Padua in the spring of 1554 we do not know, but on 13 and 19 January 1553/4 peremptory letters had been sent to him to appear at court, which he seems to have ignored (*P.C.A.* 1552–4, pp. 385–8). Between those dates he had probably fled.

At Padua the Hobys met him in August and with them he went to Mantua in October 1554 (Cam. Misc. x, 116, 120). But by 9 May 1555 Sir John had died in Venice (*For. Cal.* 1553–8, p. 170).

Padua, B iv b; Venice, B iv b.

119. DALE (DALLE), JOHN: *Gent. and haberdasher.* Of London.

A member of the Dudley conspiracy, who fled to France and was proclaimed a traitor on 4 April 1556 (Machyn, p. 103). He was probably the John Dale, 'Citizen and haberdasher of London', who was the second son of 'Matthew Dale of Bristowe, gent.' (Harl. Soc. i, 55), since in his indictment he is designated as 'late of London, Gentleman' (Baga, p. 254).

France, B iv c; B v c.

120. DANIEL, JOHN: *Weaver*(?). Wife.

An Englishman received as a 'resident' of Geneva on 14 October 1557, and designated in the register, 'tisserant' (f. 197). On the following 20 November he, with his wife and sons, became a member of the English congregation.

Geneva, A iv a & b.

121. DANNETT (DAUNET, DOYNET), THOMAS: *Gent.* Of Leicestershire. fl. 1550.

A cousin[1] and intimate friend of Sir William Cecil, who was 'out with Suffolk' in 1554 (Baga, p. 245) and in his indictment is called 'late of Brodegate' (or Bradgate), a seat of the Greys in Leicestershire (Nichols, iii, ii, 666–7). Apparently he had matriculated at St John's College, Cambridge, in 1548, but Venn (ii, 8) has mistaken him for the *brother* of Sir Gerrard Dannett, whereas he was Sir Gerrard's second *son*, Thomas, who married Anne, daughter of Sir Matthew Browne of Surrey (Harl Soc. ii, 64). His elder brother, Sir John Dannett, had been appointed, in 1539, Groom of the Privy Chamber to Anne of Cleves (*Chron. Calais*, p. 176), and in 1550/1 Thomas Dannett was associated with Sir William Pickering in the latter's embassy to France (*For. Cal.* 1547–53, pp. 76, 77). A gift to him in 1552 of lands formerly belonging to Protector Somerset would indicate that he was a member of Northumberland's party (*P.C.A.* 1552–4, p. 60).

For his participation in Suffolk's second rising, he was imprisoned in the Tower with Sir Edward Rogers (*q.v.*) on 24 February 1553/4 (*Chron. Q. Jane*, pp. 65, 71, note d). But released a month later, he fled with Sir William Pickering to France (cf. *P.C.A.*

[1] As the reference 'to his cousin Dannett' in the *For. Cal.* (1561–2, no. 570, p. 344) is ambiguous, the meaning has been verified at the P.R.O., the actual words being: '...I am in good hope that my coosyn Dannett shall be his revocquor home....'

1554–6, p. 37; 11 June 1554). There they joined the rebels who, though 'at first much rejoiced' by their coming, soon began to suspect their good faith (*For. Cal.* 1553–8, p. 79), and Dr Wotton recommended both to Queen Mary's mercy (*ibid.*) as men not willing to 'do anything which might turn to her Majesty's prejudice...'. Apparently Dannett as well as Pickering was pardoned, for he was in the latter's 'company' in Brussels on 9 May 1558, when Pickering invited Gresham to pay the money due for Mr Dannet's 'diet' (*ibid.* p. 375). At Elizabeth's accession Cecil attempted to further his cousin's fortunes by recommending him as a successor to the English ambassador, Throckmorton, in Paris in 1561 (*For. Cal.* 1561–2, pp. 344, 363, 389); but, whether because of Dannett's illness, or because of Elizabeth's disfavour, Throckmorton's urgent appeal to Cecil 'to take the ball at a bound, and toss Mr Dannett hither as soon as possible' (*ibid.* p. 418) was never acted upon. The sole honour accorded him was to be sent with Sir Thomas Smith in 1563 to demand the return of Calais (Strype, *Smith*, p. 69 note). Even 'his zeal for religion' profited him nothing and his identity seems gradually to merge into that of his son Thomas Dannett (*q.v.*).

France, B v b 1; Brussels, B v b 1.

122. DANNETT (DANETT), Thomas: *Gent. but a minor.* d. 1601.

Son of the above, and pupil of his father's intimate friend John Aylmer (*q.v.*), to whose care young Dannett was consigned during Mary's reign. He is the 'Onesimus' of Aylmer's letters (Aylmer, p. 7) and in the latter's company probably visited not only Strasbourg, Zurich and Basle, but Italy. It was no doubt as the fruit of this early Italian experience that in 1593 Dannett dedicated to Cecil an 'Epitome' of the history of Guicciardini (Herbert's Ames, II, 1196), and in 1596 a first essay at translation and continuation of the Chronicle of Philippe de Commines which he completed and re-issued in 1600 (*ibid.* p. 1197) and 1601 (*D.N.B.*). But he seems never to have taken any part in public affairs (cf. Aylmer, p. 12), for the references to 'Dannett' in the *Domestic and Foreign Calendars*, contrary to the suggestion of the *D.N.B.*, are to the father and not to the son.

Strasbourg (?); Zurich (?); Frankfort (?); Italy (?); *D.N.B.*

123. DAVAGE (DAVIDGE?), William: (?).

On 21 December 1557 this man signed the 'new discipline' at Frankfort. A John Davidge, possibly his son, received his M.A. from Oxford in 1569 (Foster); was made rector of Holton, Somerset in 1571; and, after preferment to two other livings, died in 1607.

Frankfort, B III b.

124. DAVIDSON, JOHN: *Student.* A Scot(?).

This person was registered on Monday, 24 October 1558 (f. 264), as a 'resident' of Geneva, and described as of the 'royaulme Dangleterre'. Yet it is not unlikely that he was the 'John Davidson, Principal of the College of Glasgow' who wrote an answer to Abbot Kennedy's *Compendius Tractive*, which was published at Edinburgh in 1560 (Laing, VI, 154). At Geneva, Davidson was not enrolled as a member of Knox's congregation. Geneva, A IV b.

125. DAVIES (DAVIDS, DAVID), RICHARD: *Priest.* Of Wales. Wife. d. 1581.

B.D. Oxon. 1536. Vicar of Burnham, 1550 (Foster, I, 382). Just possibly he is also the secular priest 'Dus Richūs Davys', vicar of Northales [Covehithe] since 1551, deprived in the archdeaconry of Suffolk in 1555 (Baskerville, *E.H.R.* 1933, p. 58). In any case he retired with his wife to Frankfort, where in the autumn of that year he is found listed among the 'students'. In January 1557 his name appears on the tax-list with the legend 'Prädikant, hat sonst kein narung' (Jung, p. 30). And in June we find him living in a house near the 'Prediger closter' with John Machet (*q.v.*) and his wife, John Machet having also been deprived in the diocese of Norwich in the same year. In January 1557 Davies was one of those specially appealed to by John Hales to aid in quieting the stir and strife in the Frankfort church (*T.* p. 65), but he seems never to have signed the 'new discipline', and his signature to the 'objections' to that discipline shows that he belonged to the small conservative group who throughout remained faithful to Horne (*T.* p. 168). On his return to England he was made bishop, first of St Asaph, then of St David's in 1561. Perhaps it is the fact that he translated both the Bible and Prayer Book into Welsh which has given rise to the belief that he had spent part at least of his period of exile at Geneva as an assistant in the work upon the Genevan Bible, but there is no documentary evidence to show that he was ever there. Frankfort, A III a 2, 3, 4 & b 1, 2; *D.N.B.*

126. DAWES (DOWES), JOHN: *Artisan.* Of Tonbridge, Kent.

Though not listed as a member of Knox's congregation, his marriage to Marie Malet of Dieppe is recorded in the Livre des Anglois, as having taken place on 10 April 1558 (Martin, p. 337). The year before, on 14 October, he had been received as a 'resident' of Geneva (f. 197) and his trade given as that of 'bonnetier'.

Geneva, A IV a & b.

127. DAY, JOHN: *Printer.* Of Dunwich, Suffolk and London. 1522–84.

Though no documentary evidence has been forthcoming to prove that John Day fled to the Continent under Mary, it is yet highly probable that from the winter of 1555 to 4 May 1557, when his name appears among the original charter members of the Stationers' Company (Arber, *Registers*, I, p. xxviii), Day was abroad: possibly he was at Antwerp; he may even have gone to Strasbourg. In 1552 Day had been given a licence to print the works of John Ponet, bishop of Winchester (*Mem.* II, ii, 114), and in 1553 the English version of Ponet's Catechism issued from Day's press. It is now made probable, both upon internal and external evidence, that a little-known pamphlet, entitled *The Confession of the Banished Ministers*,[1] was also, in great part, written by Ponet at Strasbourg in the summer of 1554 and published by John Day in London that autumn under the alias of Nicholas Dorcastor. For the probable identification of this unknown Dorcastor with John Day, I am deeply indebted to Col. F. S. Isaac, who has since put his surmise in print (*English Printers' Types of the Sixteenth Century* (1936), p. 47). Foxe probably supplies us with the date of the pamphlet's appearance in London, for he states (VI, 561) that about 5 October (i.e. on the eve of the opening of parliament) certain heretical books issued from the press and that within a fortnight most of the printers responsible for them had been caught and imprisoned. Among those apprehended was John Day, whose arrest on 16 October for the printing of 'noythy bokes' is recorded by Machyn (p. 72). He was imprisoned in the Tower, where at the same time was John Rogers, and it is important to note that after this date no books were ever published by 'Nicholas Dorcastor' nor any by John Day until after 1557. Now between Day and Rogers in the Tower a significant conversation is recorded (Foxe, VI, 610), which seems to have been held on the eve of Day's escape to the Continent, and which was later inserted in Foxe's narrative by Day himself, Foxe's future publisher. It is 'notoriously to be marked', he says, 'that he [Rogers] spake, being then in prison, to the printer of this present book, who then also was laid up for like cause of religion: "Thou", said he, "shalt live to see the alteration of this religion,...; and therefore have me commended to my brethren, as well in exile as others,...."' There then follows an exhortation by Rogers to create abroad such an organization of the refugee congregations as may eventually succeed in 'displacing the papists' by 'putting good ministers into

[1] See also 'Ponet', 'Becon' and 'Sampson', Census; and above, p. 28 and note 13.

churches'. Thus Day would seem to have been commissioned by Rogers, probably just before the latter's martyrdom on 4 February 1555, to carry to the exiled congregations his recommendations for a closer union. The mission very possibly took Day to Strasbourg where John Ponet already was and also Thomas Gibson (*q.v.*), whose pupil Day is thought to have been (*D.N.B.*). There is even a strong hint in the report of Rogers' conversation that he, with Hooper's approval, had actually worked out a scheme for obtaining greater unity abroad under a system of regional superintendents (cf. Foxe and *Annals*, I, i, 203). Can Day's arrival at Strasbourg in February 1555 have been the signal for Cox's departure for Frankfort in the following March and the gathering there of an ecclesiastical commission representing the best scholarship among the exiled divines (*T.* p. 45, marginal note)? My question can never probably be answered categorically, yet it is obvious that at the meetings of this commission some system involving superintendents did come up for discussion, and very possibly that one which Rogers had recently outlined to Day. It was rejected.

Antwerp (?); Strasbourg (?); *D.N.B.*

128. DENNY (DENIE), ANTHONY: *Gent.* Of Cheshunt, Hertfordshire. d. 1562.

Second son of Sir Anthony Denny (1501–49), Privy Councillor and favourite of Henry VIII, and a zealous protestant. He matriculated from Pembroke College, Cambridge, in 1551 (Venn, I, 32). In August 1554 he was found by Sir Thomas Hoby among the English refugees at Padua (Cam. Misc. X, 116) and, like them, had probably been involved in Wyatt's rebellion. In the winter of 1555–6 he, with his brothers, was a student at the University of Basle (below, p. 357), but, unlike his brother Henry, was never enrolled in the University of Padua. Upon his return to England, he was admitted to the Middle Temple on 14 November 1557 (Hopwood, *Middle Temple Records*, I, 114).

Padua, B IV b; Basle, A II a.

129. DENNY, CHARLES: *Gent.* Of Cheshunt, Hertfordshire.

Third son of Sir Anthony Denny, and also a student at Basle in 1555–6, but not at Padua, though he was with his brothers in that city in the summer of 1554. Foster (I, 395) records the presence of a Charles Denny at Merton College, Oxford, 'in and before 1564'.

Padua, B IV b; Basle, A II a.

130. DENNY, HENRY: *Gent.* Of Waltham Cross, Hertfordshire.
1540–74.

Eldest son and heir of Sir Anthony Denny, who had obtained
from Henry VIII some of the lands of the dissolved nunnery of
Waltham. By his wife Honour, daughter of Lord Grey of Wilton
(*Life of Lord Grey of Wilton*, Cam. Soc. XL, 58), Henry was the
father of Sir Edward Denny, Earl of Norwich. From his mother,
Joan, a daughter of Sir Philip Champernown of Devon, he had
also inherited a strong bias towards protestantism, and, with his
brothers, had evidently been involved in one of the risings of
1554. He was among the English refugees at Padua in August.
In 1555–6 the three Dennys with their cousin Sir Francis Walsingham (*q.v.*) and Cuthbert Hugh (*q.v.*), the son of their tutor, were
students at Basle in the rectorate of John Huber (below, p. 357),
who, in his account book, acknowledges the gift of III lib. 'a
nobilibus Anglis' (see Sources, A II e), given, perhaps, in lieu of
the usual matriculation fee which they did not pay. In 1558–9
Henry, alone of his brothers, went to study at the University of
Padua, where he was elected Consiliarius of the English students
(Andrich, pp. 32, 131). In November 1562 he was admitted to
the Inner Temple (*Members*, p. 48). And throughout Bullinger's
life, Henry Denny remained not only his friend and correspondent,
but also, apparently, his visitor (*Z.L.* I, 230).

Padua, A VI; B IV b; Basle, A II a.

131. DIXSON, GAWIN (GAYUS, JARVIS): *Gent.* Of Kent.

Probably the same person as Gayus Dixon, son of Nicholas Dixon
of Northfrith, Kent (Harl. Soc. LXXIV, 45), and nephew of the
Humphrey Dixon (Berry, *Kent, etc.* p. 392) who was summoned
for some unknown offence before the Privy Council on 21 April
1554 (*P.C.A.* 1554–6, p. 13). Gawin (or Jarvis, as Berry has it)
may well have been involved in the Dudley conspiracy, for he does
not appear at Frankfort until 1557 (and then only once), when he
signs the 'new discipline' in April. Further than that we only
know of him that he received a grant of arms as 'Gayus Dixon'
in the seventh year of Elizabeth (Harl. Soc. LXXIV, 45).

Frankfort, B III b.

132. DIXSON (DYXSONN), THOMAS: *Gent.* Of Kent.

This is probably Thomas, third son of Humphrey Dixon (above),
and therefore cousin to Gawin (above). He makes his only
appearance abroad in the Steuerliste at Frankfort on 15 October
1556, where his property is valued at 500 florins (Jung, p. 29).
This date, and the brief sojourn of the two Dixons at Frankfort,

strengthens the possibility that they had both been associates of Dudley, as does also the fact that Humphrey Dixon, the father, held his manor of Hilden (near Tonbridge, Kent, and once the property of the Vanes) by knight service of the Duke of Northumberland (Hasted, II, 334).

Frankfort, A III a 3.

133. DODMAN, JOHN: *Student*. Of Norwich.

Born in Norwich, but described at the time of his ordination as deacon in May 1552 as coming from Hadleigh in Suffolk (*Mar. Reac.* p. 203). We may therefore suppose him to have been a disciple of Rowland Taylor. He did not receive priest's orders before his exile, and in 1556–7 is found a student at the University of Basle (below, p. 357). On his return to England he, with 'Mr Pulleyn' (*q.v.*), was summoned before the Lords in April 1559 for preaching at Colchester without a licence in defiance of the proclamation of the previous December, forbidding this (*P.C.A.* 1558–70, pp. 87–8 and *Annals*, I, i, 63). Later he was preferred by Grindal to the livings of Bentley and East Mersea (Newcourt, II, 50, 414).

Basle, A II a; B II.

134. DONNELL (DONEL), THOMAS, B.D. d. 1571–2.

M.A. Oxon. 1544–5; incorporated at Cambridge in 1546, receiving his B.D. in 1549. He was prebendary of Lichfield in 1551 and vicar of Toppesfield, Essex, but was deprived of the latter before 15 March 1554 (Venn). The first mention of him abroad is at Frankfort, where he signed the 'new discipline' in December 1557, though he may at the time have been resident at Strasbourg. On his reappearance in Frankfort on 10 March 1559 he was probably on his way back to England, though he is said by Venn to have been reinstated in his living at Toppesfield in 1558. In 1559 he was given the living of Birdbrook, Essex, and the following year received from Grindal a commission for the consistory of Stortford (*Grindal*, p. 52).

Frankfort, B III b; B I; B II; Cooper.

135. DONNINGE (DONYNGE, DUNNING), ANTHONY: *Gent.*(?). Of Sussex(?).

Very possibly this is a younger son of Ralph Donynges, 'Customer' of Rye (Harl. Soc. LIII, 67; Berry, *Kent, etc.* p. 260). If so, it was his brother John Donning who on 5 November 1565 received a confirmation of his arms (Harl. Soc. LIII and Exhibit no. 717 in the Heraldic Exhibition at Birmingham, 1936). Except that Anthony was a signatory of the 'new discipline' at Frankfort in

1557, there is no other mention of him abroad. The John Donnynge who took part in Stafford's expedition and was executed at Whitby in 1557, Strype calls a Scot (*Mem.* III, ii, 519 and *ibid.* 68).

Frankfort, B III b.

136. DRANSFELD (DRANFFIELD), ROGER: *Gent.* Of Yorkshire (?).

Enrolled a member of Knox's congregation on 8 May 1557, and registered as a 'resident' of Geneva on 14 October of the same year (f. 196). The family of Dransfeld, with the name spelled as in the Livre des Anglois, was apparently of Yorkshire (cf. 'Chrystofer Dransfeld of Stubbes Waldynge', Harl. Soc. XVI, 101–2), but there is no mention of a 'Roger' in the Visitation of 1563. Possibly he was a younger son of that William Dransfeld whose daughter, Agnes, married John Wentworth and had a grandson Roger from whom descended Lord Wentworth (*ibid.* p. 340).

Geneva, A IV a & b.

137. DRURY, Mr (WILLIAM?): *Gent.* Of Hedgerley, Buckinghamshire. 1527–79.

I believe the 'one Drury' who was at Rouen on 24 March 1554 and the 'Mr Drury' whom Sir Thomas Hoby met at Padua in August 1554 were one and the same person, and identical with the William Drury who was employed on the Scottish border in 1559 and was knighted in 1570. According to Captain Crayer's report to Wotton on the 'one Drury' who was at Rouen, he was there 'tarrying the coming of the Vidâme [de Chartres] to go with him to Scotland...' (*For. Cal.* 1553–8, p. 67). And it is said of the William Drury of Hedgerley, Bucks. (who was the third son of Sir Robert Drury), that his protestant principles and connection with the Earl of Bedford had made him *persona non grata* to Queen Mary, for which reason he had 'prudently retired from court during her reign' (*D.N.B.*). In 1554 this William Drury would have been twenty-seven—an appropriate age for adventurous 'opposition'—and the title 'Mr' used by Sir Thomas Hoby of the Drury at Padua is that by which the William Drury, Cecil's agent in Scotland, is always addressed (*For. Cal.* 1558–9, p. 175; *ibid.* 1559–60, p. 85), and *he* is the William Drury of Hedgerley, Bucks.

Rouen, B v b 1; Padua, B IV b; *D.N.B.*

*DRURY, ROGER.

Not an 'exile' but a thief who, with Francis Kelewaye (Keilway), had lately stolen the Lady Knyvette's plate at Sutton, Surrey, and fled from justice to France (*P.C.A.* 1552–4, p. 372 and *For. Cal.* 1553–8, p. 41). He is not, we believe, the Drury at Rouen.

138. DUDLEY, Sir HENRY.

The identity of the chief actor in the Dudley conspiracy of 1556 may now be fixed as that of the second son[1] of the half-witted John Sutton de Dudley, 'Lord Quondam', by his wife, Cecily, daughter of Thomas Grey, Marquis of Dorset (Grazebrook, *Staff. Hist. Colls.* IX (1888), p. 99 and note 1). He was therefore the brother of Edmund (or Edward) Sutton, fourth Baron Dudley, who was Lieutenant of Hampnes (or Hammes) in 1556–8 (*For. Cal.* 1553–8, p. 276; cf. *Ven. Cal.* 1556–7, pp. 834–5), and also fourth cousin of John, Duke of Northumberland. Dr Wotton, writing to Queen Mary in November 1556, reports that 'One of her Majesty's subjects has recently been asked by a gentleman of the King's chamber, whether Dudley's [Sir Henry's] brother was not Captain of Hampnes?' and being answered in the affirmative, 'Why then', quoth the Frenchman, 'he may do the French King's pleasure' (*ibid.*). Scheyfve reports to the Emperor on 24 June 1553 that 'Henry Dudley, Northumberland's cousin', was to be lieutenant to Sir Thomas Cheyne, Admiral of the Narrow Seas (*Span. Cal.* p. 67), and this relationship to Dudley is confirmed by Renard (*ibid.* pp. 123–4). Dudley's young manhood was spent as Captain of the Guard at Boulogne (*For. Cal.* 1547–53, pp. 4, 92, 95) and he was early a familiar at the French court, where Mason commended him for behaving himself 'very honestly'—an equivocal compliment, since he seems to have been acting as a spy upon the Vidâme de Chartres (Montmorency) and to have been communicating to Mason 'all that he could learn by haunting' the Vidâme's company (*ibid.* p. 95 and *P.C.A.* 1550–2, p. 203). Strype has called Henry Dudley Northumberland's 'creature', and as he seems to have inherited his father's incapacity in money matters, Northumberland, who had possessed himself of the father's estates, probably controlled the son through the latter's debts, which were perennial (*P.C.A.* 1550–2, pp. 87 and 92; Grazebrook, p. 99 and note). But Dudley was made Captain of the Guard at Guisnes (*P.C.A.* 1550–2, p. 279) in May 1551, and in October of that year knighted by Northumberland. In 1552 he and his 'Garde' were for some time stationed at Portsmouth (*ibid.* 1552–4, p. 47) to supervise its fortification, and in 1553 he was also made lieutenant to the Admiral of the Narrow Seas (*Span. Cal.* 1553, p. 67). At this point it is extremely enlightening to find that Henry Dudley's later plot against Calais was not originally of his devising, but of Northumberland's. For, at the death of Edward VI, Dudley had been immediately sent as Northumberland's agent to the

---

[1] Not, as has been surmised by Nichols, the son of Andrew Dudley, brother to Northumberland (*Chron. Q. Jane*, p. 175, note).

French king for the surrender of Calais, Guisnes and Ireland in return for Henry II's support of Northumberland's designs upon the throne (*Span. Cal.* 1553, p. 208). But upon his return from this mission, Dudley was arrested at Guisnes by the Deputy-Governor of Calais (*ibid.* pp. 123–4) and on 6 August was brought to the Tower (*Mem.* III, i, 30), where by 16 August he had 'confessed without torture' (*Span. Cal.* 1553, p. 172) the circumstances of his mission. By 19 October he had been released (*ibid.* p. 307) and seems also to have been marked out for favour by the queen, who in 1554 restored to his brother Edmund Sutton the Dudley estates (Grazebrook, p. 104). It was proposed to make Henry a captain of one of the queen's ships, but upon the flight in that year of his 'cousins' the Staffords, he was dismissed (Tyler, Abstracts, P.R.O., Renard to the Emperor, 7 April 1554). Without a patron and now heavily in debt Dudley, having nothing to lose, attempted to make capital of his earlier relations with the French court, and his intimate knowledge of Calais and Portsmouth. The outlines of the plot hatched by him in the spring of 1556 are already clear. With Christopher Assheton and others (P.R.O., S.P. 11, vol. VIII, 23–4, etc.) he meant to rob the exchequer and either depose or kill Mary, placing on the throne Elizabeth married to Courtenay, Earl of Devon. But in March the plot was discovered,[1] and by 4 April Dudley and his chief confederates were fugitives in France (Machyn, p. 103). According to the editor of the *Verney Papers* (Cam. Soc. 1556, pp. 62–3) Dudley's purpose abroad was not only to betray Calais to the French, but to organize the English refugees then abroad 'in a hostile manner, to land them, together with such assistance as could be obtained from other countries, in the Isle of Wight...or at Portsmouth...' in order to 'drive out these Spaniards', or 'die for it'. But Mr Bruce, the editor, concludes that 'there is no proof or probability that any of the principal exiles were ever consulted on the subject', a conclusion in which we believe him to have been quite mistaken. In fact it is this particular connection between rebels in France and refugees in Germany which makes of the Dudley conspiracy one of the most far-reaching events of the Tudor period. The story of it may be followed in the Baga de Secretis (4th Rep. Deputy Keeper of Records, App. II, pp. 250–6 and in the *For. Cal.* 1553–8, see Index). But the inter-relation of the treacherous Sutton-Dudley interest, either by marriage or through identity of political purpose with the members of the English colonies along the Rhine, is one of the persistent phenomena which a study of the period of exile and

[1] The plot was betrayed to King Philip by Sir Peter Carew, who had been a confederate, but because of it, none the less, Calais was lost to England (*Ven. Cal.* 1555–6, no. 482, p. 447).

its personnel reveals. After Elizabeth's accession Henry Dudley remained in France at least for a time, still intriguing, still in debt (*For. Cal.* 1558–9, pp. 305, 328, 330; and Grazebrook, p. 99, n. 1). Adlard asserts that he married the daughter of Christopher Assheton (Sutton-Dudley, Ped. A), but for this Grazebrook finds no confirmation (p. 99, n. 2), and from a Council minute of February 1554/5 it would appear that at that date[1] Henry Dudley's wife was the daughter of Lord Audley. This might well account for the latter's[2] presence abroad as an exile (*P.C.A.* 1554–6, p. 101 and above, p. 75). Thomas Dudley (1576–1653), Governor of Massachusetts, was the great-grandson of Lord Quondam's brother, Thomas Sutton de Dudley.

France, B iv c; B v b 1.

139. DUNCE (DAUNCE), HENRY: *Artisan*. Of London.

A bricklayer of Whitechapel who in King Henry's reign 'used to preche the gospelle in his gardene every holydaye' (*Narr. of Ref.* p. 171). Forced to recant he 'bare a fagott at Paules Crosse for heresye' (Wriothesley, i, 82–3, 93). He is registered in the Livre des Anglois among those who were dwellers at Geneva before 13 October 1555, but he is not recorded among the 'residents'.

Geneva, A iv a.

140. DUWICK, JOHN: *Gent*. Of Berkshire(?).

Possibly a son or brother of Thomas Duwick (below). He became a 'resident' of Geneva on Thursday, 14 October 1557 (f. 197), and is designated as 'gentleman'. He was not a member of Knox's congregation.

Geneva, A iv b.

141. DUWICK (HUICK, HUYCK), THOMAS, D.C.L. Of Berkshire(?). Wife. d. 1575.

Of Merton College, Oxford, and probably brother of Robert Huick, physician to Henry VIII and Elizabeth. He received his D.C.L. in July 1554, but had been canon of St David's in 1551 (Foster, ii, 780) and rector of Buckland Denham, Somerset, in 1551–4. He fled to Geneva with his wife apparently in 1557. Though he was not enrolled as a member of Knox's congregation, the baptism of a daughter 'Marie' to whom John Bodley stood 'witness' is recorded in the Livre des Anglois on 19 December 1558. On his return to England, Grindal made him his vicar-general (*Grindal*, p. 52); and in April 1559 Dr Huicke 'a civilian'

---

[1] Yet in January 1556/7 Wotton told Petre that Dudley was in search of a wife in Normandy (*For. Cal.* p. 284).

[2] If, that is, Lord Audley and the John Audley (*q.v.*) of Aarau are the same person.

was one of the commissioners appointed 'to ride aboute the realme for th' establishinge of true religion' (Wriothesley, II, 145). Between 1561 and 1574 he was chancellor of the diocese of London (Foster).

Geneva, A IV a, pt II.

142. EAST, RICHARD: *Tailor*.

On 20 November 1557 Richard East was enrolled as a member of the English congregation at Geneva, and on the previous 14 October he had been received a 'resident' of the city and registered as 'couturier' (f. 196).

Geneva, A IV a & b.

143. EDMUNDS [ROBERT?]: *Preacher*.

This man is listed without Christian name in the Emden catalogue of exiles, but it is impossible that he should have been, as Strype asserts he was, the John Edmunds, Master of Peterhouse, who kept a wife privately, for that John Edmunds died in 1544 (Venn, II, 86). But he may have been the 'Edmondes', of no first name, who matriculated from Christ's College in that year (1544) and was 'perhaps scholar of Trinity' in 1548—whether son of John or not is not known—and we believe him to have been the Robert Edmunds who became rector of Fyfield, Essex, in 1560 (Newcourt, II, 262, 414) and who was one of the twenty-seven ministers of Essex who protested to the Privy Council against enforced subscription to Whitgift's articles in the Visitation of 1584 (Davids, p. 78). According to Usher, he was also the 'Edmons —' who became identified with the Classical Movement, and was a member of the London meeting of 1572 (Usher, p. xxxix; and Bancroft, *Dangerous Positions*, p. 5).

n.p.

144. ELYOT, MAGNUS: *Gent.* Of 'Stortford', Hertfordshire.

A most interesting person, for in the opinion of Mr H. F. Waters (*Gleanings*, II, 894) the family of Elyot to which this Magnus belonged was the same which later gave John Eliot, the famous 'Apostle to the Indians', to Massachusetts (*ibid.* pp. 907 ff.). Magnus was the son of 'George Ellyot of Stertford (*sic*), Herts.' whose brother was 'John Eliott of London mercer'. Dying in 1554, George Ellyot left his 'household stuff and plate' to be 'divided equally between Magnus, George and Kateryn Sparoke' his children (*ibid.* p. 894). And to Magnus he also left his lands in Essex and Hertfordshire to be delivered to him when his son should have reached the 'lawful age of twenty one years' (*ibid.* p. 895). As the will was made in January 1548 it would seem as if Magnus, when he made his single appearance at Frankfort in

April 1557 and signed the 'new discipline', was either still a minor or had only just attained his majority, and was therefore another doubtful voice[1] among those who consented to that document.

Frankfort, B iii b.

145. ESCOT, JOHN: *Merchant.* Of London(?). Wife.

The name may be Estcourt, which is found in the Visitation of London in the late sixteenth century (Harl. Soc. xv, 260), but a Christopher *Escot* was made one of a royal commission for the Visitation of the north in 1559 (*Annals*, I, i, 245). John Escot, listed on the Standesliste at Frankfort in 1555 as a merchant, belonged to the party of Whittingham and signed the letter of secession on 27 August 1555 (*T.* p. 55), but he nevertheless remained in Frankfort, where he was then living with his wife and daughter in the 'Kornmarck' (Jung, p. 48) in the house of Henry Parry (*ibid.* p. 49). The tax-list of October 1556 shows him to have been a rich man with property valued at 2250 florins (*ibid.* p. 29). Curiously enough he supported Horne in his quarrel with Thomas Ashley, and on that account refused to accept any office in the congregation (*T.* p. 99) or to sign the 'new discipline', rather subscribing his name to the objections to that democratic document (*T.* p. 169). After June 1557, when he carried a letter from Richard Chambers at Strasbourg to John Bale at Basle (*T.* p. 184), we hear no more of John Escot.

Frankfort, A iii a 2, 3, 4 & b 1, 2.

146. EUSTACE, JOHN: *Gent.* Of Middlesex(?).

As one of the young men in the train of Francis, Duke of Bedford, he was licensed to bear arms by the Signory of Venice on 1 August 1555 (*Ven. Cal.* 1555–6, p. 145). He may have belonged to Irish Eustaces (see James Eustace, *D.N.B.*), but it is more likely that he was of the humbler Eustaces of Highgate, Middlesex, who intermarried with the Hartes (Harl. Soc. LXV, 36).

Venice, B v b 3.

147. EVANS, JOHN: *Clerk.*

A John Evans, chaplain to Bishop Ferrar, of St David's, was instituted by the bishop to the vicarage of Pen Brynn (Foxe, VII, 11), but through the machinations of Ferrar's enemies, the king's candidate was appointed in Evans's place, whereupon Evans, a man 'estemed and trusted' by the bishop 'above other' but 'really a secrete enemie', brought suit against him for the loss of his parsonage (*Mem.* III, ii, 359–60). As two other members of

[1] See also, 'Richard Nagors', 'Thomas Serbis', 'Peter Sade', 'Richard Mason', etc., Census.

this cabal against Ferrar, such as Thomas Johns (*q.v.*) and William Chambers (*q.v.*), took refuge at Geneva, it seems very possible that the John Evans [Euens] who became a 'resident' of Geneva on 24 October 1558 (f. 264) was the bishop's former chaplain. He never, it would seem, became a member of Knox's congregation.

Geneva, A iv b.

148. FAWCONER (FAWKENER, FAULCONER), John: *Deacon.* Of Rutland(?). d. 1560.

An excellent example of the frequent laxity of the period in regard to orders. In 1535 he supplicated a B.A. at Oxford (O.H.S. i, 183). In 1545 he was vicar of Stanford-in-the-Vale, Berks. (Foster, ii, 487); and in 1548, rector of Barford, Wilts., before ever receiving ordination. In fact he was not even ordained deacon until November 1550 (*Mar. Reac.* p. 212 and note) and not priest before his flight. It was, then, with good reason that he made 'free and spontaneous resignation' of his living in 1554 (*ibid.* p. 108) and in that same year fled to Strasbourg, where in December he profited by the Duke of Württemberg's bounty to the amount of ten florins and signed his name to the exiles' letter of thanks (Württ. Staatsarchiv). By the autumn of 1556 he had removed to Frankfort, where his property was valued in October at the not inconsiderable sum of 500 florins. In the Horne-Ashley quarrel he was appointed one of the committee of eight arbiters in the dispute (*T.* p. 76), but he was probably not of those 'addicted to the pastor', for he signed the 'new discipline' in March-April. The dwelling-list of June shows that he was an inmate of the house of Thomas Wattes in 1557. He died at some time before 22 May 1560 (*Z.L.* i, 79), probably soon after his return to England.

Strasbourg, A vii c; Frankfort, A iii a 3, 4 & b 2; B ii.

149. FERRAR, John: *Priest.* d. 1556.

He arrived in Geneva in 1556 and was received into Knox's congregation some time before 12 July of that year. It is probable that he was the John Ferror, deprived in 1555 of his living at Stuston, Suffolk, which he had held since 1550 (Baskerville, *E.H.R.* 1933, p. 62). If his deprivation was for marriage, his wife does not seem to have gone with him to Geneva. Nor is it known whether he was restored to his living in 1559 though he did not die till 1566.

Geneva, A iv a.

150. FIELDE (FILLS(?)), Robert. Wife.

All that we certainly know of this Robert Fielde is that he and his wife Rose became members of Knox's congregation on 26 November 1557; and that on 29 November he was registered as a 'resident' of Geneva. But Martin suggests (p. 278 and note 2) that he was probably the 'Robert Fills' who is said by Strype to have been 'an exile at Geneva' (*Annals*, I, i, 552) and who, in 1562, had published in London, by Rowland Hall, a pamphlet on *The lawes and statutes of Geneva*...(cf. Martin, pp. 280, 320). This he dedicated to Lord Robert Dudley. Was he also, perhaps, the father of that John Field who became head of the London 'Classis' and co-author of the *Admonition to Parliament* in 1572 (Usher, p. xl)?

Geneva, A IV a & b.

151. FINCH (FYNCH), JOHN: *Priest*. Of 'Gynge at Stowe' (Buckinghamshire?).

This is probably the John Finch of Billericay who was ordained deacon by Ridley on 23 June 1550; and priest in London in 1552 (*Mar. Reac.* pp. 186, 204). He had not apparently been a student at either Oxford or Cambridge, but in the reign of Henry VIII had gone to Germany, where he was intimate in the house of Martin Bucer (*O.L.* II, 605–7). Very possibly he had fled from persecution under the act of the Six Articles, for an earlier John Finch of Colchester had been a Lollard, arraigned for heresy in 1428–31 (Foxe, III, 588, 598). In 1555 John Finch the former exile re-appears in Germany, where he is found at Frankfort living in the house of Robert Horne. His name appears among the 'students' on the Standesliste; and in the tax-list of 1556 he is reported as without property. But he is never mentioned in the *Troubles at Frankfort* and we may infer that he was a man of humble birth and no influence: 'I write to you and yours', he says to Conrad Humpard, 'but not to everyone, lest they should expose me to ridicule for this unpolished letter' (*O.L.* II, 607). If he lived to return to England he received no preferment.

Frankfort, A III a 2, 3, 4 & b 1, 2.

152. FISHER (FISCHER), (?): *Priest*(?).

Mentioned with his brother in the Emden catalogue as the 'duo Fischeri'. One of them is almost certainly the Fisher, parson of Amersham, Bucks., who on 22 August 1553 was brought before the Privy Council to answer for a seditious sermon (*P.C.A.* 1552–4, pp. 321, 328). Foxe mentions him (VI, 392–3) but does not give his first name, and it has so far been impossible to discover his place of exile. It is interesting to find that Amersham had, in 1511, been the headquarters of the Lollards (Urwick, p. 303).

n.p.; B I.

153. FISHER (FISCHER), (?): *Priest*(?).

Brother, we suppose, of the parson of Amersham. It may be worth noticing that a John Fischer, secular priest, but unbeneficed, appears on the deprivation list of Norwich in 1555 (Baskerville, *E.H.R.* 1933, p. 53).

n.p.; B I.

154. FITZWILLIAM (or FITZWILLIAMS), BRIAN: *Gent*. Of London and Yorkshire. d. 1586(?).

Grandson of Sir William Fitzwilliam, sheriff of London; brother of Sir William Fitzwilliam 'the sustainer' (later Lord Deputy of Ireland); and nephew to Sir Antony Cooke, the husband of his aunt, Anne Fitzwilliam (Bridges, *Northamptonshire*, II, 505–6; Harl. Soc. XVI, 126). A typical intriguer of the Tudor period. Implicated in Wyatt's rebellion (Baga, pp. 241–2), he escaped to France, where in July Wotton reports him as one of the leaders of the rebels (*For. Cal.* 1553–8, p. 108). On 12 July 1555 he sues Wotton for pardon 'for the heinous offences he has committed' (*ibid.* p. 178), but the suit was evidently refused, for in 1556–7 he had become 'one of T. Stafford's companions' (*ibid.* p. 283) and in the latter's feud with his brother-in-law, Sir Robert Stafford, fought Sir Robert one new year's afternoon 'on the bridge of Notre Dame' (*ibid.*). But he did not venture his neck in Stafford's rebellion. In 1559 Elizabeth welcomed his return to England by promptly (28 March) committing him to the Fleet with a letter to the Warden 'to kepe him in saffe custodye' (*P.C.A.* 1558–70, p. 75). Later with no very great success the government tried to make his relatives responsible for him (*ibid.* pp. 267, 274), and in 1574 we find him holding a captaincy in the Irish wars, but, characteristically, in debt to the town of Chester for a loan of £150 (*Dom. Cal.* 1547–80, p. 486). After 1586 he disappears from the Tudor scene.

France.

155. FITZWILLIAM, HUGH: *Gent*. Of Yorkshire.

He appears from the Visitation of Yorkshire (Harl. Soc. XVI, 125–6) to have been the fourth son of John Fitzwilliam of 'Hadysley', who was 'put young to my lord Fitzwilliam, Earle of Southampton', and to have been in Italy 'in the tyme of Quene Mary, as may appere by her lycence' dated the second year [1554] of her reign, 11 October. He is perhaps the 'Mr Phitzwilliam' who arrived in Paris in August 1559 from Italy, where he had been a student (*For. Cal.* 1558–9, pp. 434, 436).

Italy.

156. FITZWILLIAMS (FITZWILLIAM), Thomas: *Gent.* Of Northamptonshire. d. 1562.

A friend of Sir Thomas Hoby, who finds him among the English refugees at Padua in August 1554 (Cam. Misc. x, 116). They had met once before in Italy at the house of Edmund Harvel in 1548, when Harvel was English 'ambassador resident' at Venice (*ibid.* p. 8) and had gathered round him a distinguished group of young English protestants (F. C. Church, *Italian Reformers*, p. 150). In July 1555 Fitzwilliam was again at Venice in the train of the Earl of Bedford, and was then licensed by the Signory to bear arms (*Ven. Cal.* 1555–6, p. 145). But his identity is uncertain; though probably he was the Thomas Fitzwilliam, 'alias Fisher', natural son of the Earl of Southampton, whose death Machyn records at 'master Kyndylmarche('s) howse' in London on 18 June 1562 (*Machyn*, pp. 286, 391), and not the son of Sir William Fitzwilliam, sheriff of London, by his second wife Mildred Sackvile.

Padua, B iv b; Venice, B v b 3.

*FLORIO, Michael Angelo.

On Monday 30 July 1554, Michael Angelo Florio, father of John Florio, the translator of Montaigne, petitioned for burgher rights at Strasbourg (Protocols, vol. 32, f. 269vo). In December of the same year he received from the Duke of Württemberg's fund the large share of 20 florins, probably because he had 'weib und kind' (Württ. Staatsarchiv). The child was no doubt his son John. Florio, late pastor of the Italian congregation in London, was associated with the English colony at Strasbourg.

157. FOLGEHAM (FOLJAMBE), Nicholas: *Gent.* Of Derbyshire(?).

This man, who was received into the English congregation at Geneva on 5 November 1556, was probably an illegitimate member of the family of the Foljambes of Derbyshire who intermarried with the Fitzwilliams of Yorkshire (*Geneal.* n.s. XII, 255). Very possibly he was a son of that Godfrey Foljambe (1512–59) who married Margaret, daughter of Thomas Fitzwilliam of Aldwark (Harl. Soc. XVI, 128), but died leaving no legitimate offspring (*ibid.* L, 362).

Geneva, A iv a.

158. FOXE, John: *Martyrologist, Deacon.* Of Boston, Lincolnshire. Wife. 1516–87.

Foxe's life is too well-known to need re-telling except at certain points which have been somewhat too lightly dealt with. Educated at Brasenose and Magdalen Colleges, Foxe voluntarily resigned

(Foster says he was 'expelled' from) his Magdalen Fellowship in 1545 (Macray, II, 76), the year in which he became vicar of Stewkley, and in 1546/7 married Agnes Randall, then living in the service of the Lucys (*D.N.B.*). But as Macray notes (II, 77–8; cf. *Mar. Reac.* p. 187): 'It is curious that (...) a John Fox was vicar of Stewkley in 1545, deprived 1554, and restored 1559, who resigned in 1583 or 1588. But our Fellow was only ordained deacon June 24, 1550, and priest Jan. 25, 1559/60.' The dates leave little doubt that this was John Foxe the martyrologist, and the fact of his insufficiency of orders (not noted in Sir Sidney Lee's articles in the *D.N.B.*) probably provides the real reason for his deprivation in 1554: his fault was not merely that of marriage. At the time of his ordination, however, he was teaching in the household of the Duchess of Suffolk (*Mar. Reac.* p. 187), and was thus very early associated with that sharp-tongued disturber of Gardiner's peace. But his flight to the Continent was doubtless precipitated by the Latin protest which he issued 'in the name of the protestant exiles', and addressed to Mary's second parliament in April 1554, against a re-enactment of the Six Articles (*Cranmer*, II, 937–9). This, the initial protestant effort to influence the religious policy of parliament, was not only seditious by its nature, but contained an offensive reference to Gardiner in which the chancellor was likened (by implication) to certain animals which are 'born to create trouble and destruction' (*Cranmer*, ed. E.H.S. III, 100). After which Gardiner may very properly have intimated that it was time Foxe went abroad (cf. the legend given above, p. 11, n. 5). Foxe and his wife were certainly permitted to escape and in July 1554 reached Strasbourg in safety. There on 31 August a first draft of the *Acts and Monuments* was dedicated to the Duke of Württemberg and may have prompted the contribution made by him in December to the English exiles' support (*D.N.B.*). But by then Foxe had gone to Frankfort (*T.* p. 26), where he remained until he seceded with Whittingham in September 1555 (*T.* p. 55). Basle, however, and not Geneva, was his destination and the city of his adoption until his return to England in October 1559. There, probably in the Clarakloster (see frontispiece), he finished the *Book of Martyrs*; and there two daughters were born to him, one Christiana, baptized in the church of St Theodor on 22 September 1555 (Egerton MS. 1927, f. 116); and the other, Dorcas, on 8 September 1558 (*ibid.* f. 127). During the winter of 1556–7 he was a student at the University of Basle, where he paid 'nihil propter exilium' (below, p. 357); and among the MSS. in the University Library an unpublished[1] letter of his to the rector,

---

[1] Or so we believe.

Boniface Amerbach, is preserved (MS. Ki. Ar. 18 a, f. 181). It may very likely have been Foxe, chosen for what Strype calls his 'excellent pathetic style', who drafted the original appeal of 'the poor exiled Englishmen' for asylum in the city (below, pp. 358-9), and there he published his pamphlet on Philpot's martyrdom of which 'no copy is now known' (*Cranmer*, ed. E.H.S. III, 174 and *D.N.B.*). Oporinus the printer, with whom Foxe earned his living while at Basle as 'corrector of the press', first printed in 1557 Foxe's protest to the lords spiritual and temporal of England against the martyrdom of Ridley, Latimer and Cranmer (*Cranmer*, III, pp. 513-16), and in 1559 he also published the first Latin edition of the *Acts and Monuments*, which John Day was to issue in English in 1562-3. On his return to England Foxe was ordained priest on 25 January 1559/60 (Macray, II, 77), but apart from his restoration to his former living of Stewkley (*ibid.*) he received no preferment until October 1572, when Pilkington made him a prebendary of Durham, an office which Foxe resigned within the year because of his scruples against the surplice. But to the close association between Foxe[1] and John Day may in very large part be attributed the eventual triumph of the reformation in England.

Frankfort, B III a; Basle, A II c & d; *D.N.B.*

159. FRACHT (FROGGETT?), THOMAS: '*Engellender*' and '*Edelman*'. Of Lancashire(?). Wife.

The nearest English equivalent of this Germanized name 'Fracht' would seem to be 'Froggett'. But beyond suggesting that he may possibly have belonged to the Froggets of Mayfield, Staffs. (Harl. Soc. XXXVIII, 446; LXIII, 41), a family of lesser gentry, he cannot be identified. All that we know of this Thomas Fracht is that he was an associate at Strasbourg of the John Carus who was extradited, and that between June and October 1556 he, too, was giving trouble to the Strasbourg authorities and became amenable to the laws only upon threat of sharing the fate of Carus (below, pp. 368-9).

Strasbourg, A VII a.

160. FRANCK (FRANK), WALTER: *Gent.* Of Essex(?).

Possibly a member of the family of the Franks of Hatfield Regis, Essex, some of whom were J.P.'s for the county (Harl. Soc. XIII, 399). In the reigns of Henry VIII and Edward VI a John Franck

---

[1] It was not the martyrologist, however, who was made a freeman of the Stationers' Company on 5 March 1554/5 (Arber, *Registers*, I, 33 and cf. Sir Sidney Lee's article on Foxe, *D.N.B.* p. 583), but a John Foxe who was a stationer in London and died in 1570/71 (Gordon Duff, *English Book Trade*, p. 47).

was connected with transport between Boulogne and Dover (*P.C.A.* 1542–7, pp. 241, 471; 1547–50, p. 484). But I can find no mention of the Walter Franck who, as a refugee, makes his appearance but once, when he signed the 'new discipline' at Frankfort in March-April 1557.

Frankfort, B III b.

161. FRENSHAM (FRENCHAM), EDWARD: *Student*(?). Of Kent(?). d. 1559.

An Edward Frencham, who may be the exile, matriculated from St Catharine's College, Cambridge, in 1552 (Venn, II, 179). As a refugee he appears in none of the official lists, but is first mentioned by Christopher Goodman in a letter to Peter Martyr, dated 20 August 1558 (*O.L.* II, 771). Frensham was then at Zurich, and from that time on his name frequently appears in the exiles' correspondence as an object of slightly sceptical solicitude, for he was evidently looked upon as a bit of a hypochondriac. Jewel, referring to him in a letter from London in April 1559, says that he would have included Frensham in his salutations did he not suppose that he was 'now at the bath, or on a journey; for at this season of the year, when one hears the cuckoo, he is rarely at home' (*Z.L.* I, 22). Foxe is more kindly, urging Bullinger to afford the sick man any assistance in his power (*ibid.* p. 26) and writing himself to Frensham a comforting letter (*ibid.* pp. 37–8). But before November 1559 he was dead, and his will had become a matter of considerable importance both in England and Scotland (*ibid.* p. 58). He cannot be traced; but because the name is not a common one, it is just possible that he was a natural son of the Clement Frensham of Great Chart, Kent, who died in 1544 without legitimate heirs (Rawl. C. 728, f. 95 b[1] and Hasted, III, 250). If so, this might explain the agitation about Frensham's will, for the family in Kent seems to have become extinct in that generation.

Zürich, A VIII a.

162. FULLER, WILLIAM: *Gent.* Of London. Wife.

Married Joice (Jane or Jocosa), daughter of John Butler (*q.v.*) by his wife Margery (or Margaret), daughter of John Sutton de Dudley of Aston-in-the-Wall, uncle of John Sutton, Lord Quondam (Harl. Soc. v, 141). William Fuller was thus a member of the Dudley faction, and it is not surprising to find that his arrival in Geneva was in the significant year and month of July 1556. Martin says that he 'avait aidé la future reine Elisabeth dans les difficultés que lui suscitait la jalousie de sa sœur Marie' (Martin,

---

[1] Rawlinson MSS. Bodleian Library.

pp. 60–1). Fuller lived in considerable state in Geneva with three servants (see below) who were admitted with him to Knox's congregation on 12 July. The following year, on 7 January, he became a 'resident' of the city (f. 180) and in 1556 was made a senior of the congregation; in 1557, a deacon (Martin, pp. 334–5). On 15 December 1558 he was one of the signatories to Geneva's appeal for a crusade against ceremonies (*T.* p. 188). Whether or not he was the William Fuller who in 1570 was 'Auditor of the possessions of the late Duke of Somerset' has not been determined.

Geneva, A IV a & b.

163. FYENEUX, WILLIAM: *Gent.* Of Herne, Kent. d. 1557.

Son of John Fyneux, Lord Chief Justice of England, by his wife Elizabeth, daughter of Sir John Paston (Harl. Soc. LXXV, 128 and Brett, p. 116, n. 4). He was among those who had gone beyond seas without licence to whom John Brett carried letters under the privy seal in 1556, but on Brett's arrival in Venice on 16 August he learned that 'Maister Feneux was departed from Padua towardes Englande the thirde day of Auguste laste paste in company of Goodolphyn the lorde of Bedfordes manne...' (Brett, p. 129). He died in England in 1557, having evidently conformed (Foss's *Judges*, v, 165–6).

Padua, B IV a.

164. GAWTON, RICHARD: *Tailor.*

Received into Knox's congregation on 12 July 1556 as a servant of Sir William Fuller, and on 14 October 1557 admitted a 'resident' of Geneva with the designation 'couturier' (f. 197).

Geneva, A IV a & b.

165. GIBBONS (GIBBINS, GUIBINS), RICHARD: *Weaver.*

Received into the English Church on 5 June 1557 and as a 'resident' of Geneva on 14 October 1557, when he is called 'tisserant' (f. 197).

Geneva, A IV a & b.

166. GYBSON, THOMAS: *Physician.* Of Morpeth, Northumberland. d. 1562.

Owing to a false assumption on the part of J. S. Burn in his transcript of the Livre des Anglois (p. 11), a William Gibson (see below) has been mistaken for Thomas Gybson, printer, physician and gospeller. In consequence of this mistake it has been the accepted belief that *Thomas* Gibson spent the years of his exile in Geneva (Cooper, I, 553; *D.N.B.*; and F. S. Isaac, *English Printers' Types* (1936), pp. 17–18). A more careful reading of the Livre des

Anglois would have revealed the error that the protocols of Strasbourg have now finally corrected, for it was at Strasbourg that 'Thomas Gipson, Artzet' took refuge under Mary, and there that he established an enviable reputation as a physician, although his first appearance in the council minutes (on 16 February 1555) is as a retailer of medicines at illegally high prices (below, pp. 364–5). Wood (I, 331) believed Gybson to have been educated at Oxford. Foster neither accepts nor rejects this belief: Cooper claims him also for Cambridge (I, 217) and gives him the degree of M.B. in 1511; Venn admits his presence there, but gives him neither degree nor college; the Strasbourg protocols describe him 'as a physician though without training'. Already, however, the report of his skill had gone abroad in Germany, for on 11 September 1555 (below, p. 366) the ban that had been placed by the authorities upon his practice of medicine was temporarily lifted that he might treat a dropsical woman, coming from Innenheim 'on account of the English doctor' (ibid.). The next year Gybson petitioned the Council for permission to practise generally, claiming that he could cure both dropsy and lunacy [Unsinnigkeit](!). But he particularly begged that he might compound his drugs at home since he wished to keep his methods secret (below, p. 367).

This request was granted and henceforward he grew in the town's esteem until in 1558 the authorities were loath to let him leave even for the sake of travelling in the interests of his profession. Permission was indeed granted, but only on condition that he did not settle for good elsewhere (below, pp. 371–2). At this time he seems to have thought of going back to England to 'sell his estates' with a view to settling permanently abroad, but Mary's death brought different counsels and he was in London again in 1559, where he was granted a licence to practise (Cooper, I, 217). In Strasbourg, Gybson would seem to have been without a wife. Whether or not the sinister reference in Wriothesley (I, 76) to the 'Mrs Alen' who 'by the instigation of the devill cutt her throote with a knife', having been 'sometime wife to Mr Peerson...and afore him one Gibsons wife, a surgeon', refers to our Gibson's earlier marital relations, must be left to conjecture. (For his work as printer and author see the article in the *Dictionary of National Biography* and Gordon Duff's *English Book Trade*, p. 55.)

Strasbourg, A vii a; *D.N.B.*

167. GIBSON, WILLIAM: *Dyer.* Wife. d. 1558.

This is the man who has been mistaken for Gibson the physician (see above). When received with his wife and daughter into Knox's congregation on 20 November 1557 his Christian name is not given and Burn (p. 11) assumed it to be 'Thomas'. In the second part of the Livre des Anglois, however, the notice of his death (on 16 August 1558) proves him to have been 'William' Gibson (Martin, p. 338), a fact confirmed by the entry in the Registre des Habitants (f. 196), which states that William Gibson 'teinturier' was received as a 'resident' of Geneva on 14 October 1557.

Geneva, A iv a & b.

168. GILBY, ANTHONY: *Student.* Of Lincolnshire. Wife. *ca.* 1510–85.

M.A. Christ's College, Cambridge, 1535. Though he is said (*D.N.B.*) to have 'entered the ministry', this statement is ambiguous, as is also Gilby's own information that he was 'one of the Preachers of Goddes Worde' in Leicestershire (Preface to Knox's *Admonition to the Professors, etc.* 1554). Very possibly he had never been ordained priest. Nichols (*Leicestershire*, III, pt 2, pp. 619, 639) mentions his vicariate of 1560 but no earlier one. At Mary's accession Gilby fled to Frankfort, where in January–February 1555 he was associated with Knox, Whittingham, Foxe and Thomas Cole in drawing up that order 'meete for their state and time' which eventually became the Order of Geneva (*T.* pp. 36–7). Subsequently it was Master Gilby who with 'a godly grieff' tried to restrain the violence of the quarrel provoked by the new liturgy. In March he headed an appeal made to Glauburg the magistrate against the doings of Richard Cox, but this availing nothing, he fled to Geneva with his wife and son Goddred. There he is registered in the Livre des Anglois on 13 October 1555, and on the 24th he became a 'resident' of Geneva (f. 123). How it also happens that in the same autumn he was enrolled as a student at the University of Basle, is not clear. He did not matriculate (below, p. 357). Probably he never went, for on 1 November 1555, when 'the Church was erected', he was appointed with Christopher Goodman to preach and minister the sacraments in the absence of John Knox (Martin, p. 39). In the three following years he was chosen one of the 'seniors' of the congregation and according to Martin played with Whittingham the premier rôle in the translation of the Genevan Bible (Martin, p. 241 and *Annals*, I, i, 343). Since he was at one with Knox and Goodman in their justification of civil disobedience, he probably owed his preferment to the living of Ashby-de-la-Zouche on his return to England entirely to the patronage of the Earl of Huntingdon (*D.N.B.*) and from that vantage point became one of the most determined opposers of the Anglican Settlement and probably co-author of the so-called

First Admonition to Parliament in 1572 (Bancroft, *Survey of the Pretended Holy Discipline* (London, 1593), p. 54).

Frankfort, B III; Geneva, A IV a & b; Basle, A II a; D.N.B.

169. GILL, MICHAEL: *Gent.* Of Hertfordshire(?).

Given in the Genevan Register (f. 196) as a 'gentleman' and probably one of the fourteen children of George Gill, Esq., of Widdial, Herts. (Chauncey, *Hertfordshire*, p. 111 b). He was among the first English refugees to Frankfort, where on 2 August he signed Whittingham's invitation to the other English communities to join with them to form one community (*T.* p. 13). On 24 September he also signed the congregation's invitation to John Knox (*ibid.* p. 20), and he was still at Frankfort on 3 December (*ibid.* p. 26) and a member of Whittingham's party in the Prayer Book controversy. Soon after Knox's expulsion on 26 March 1555 (*ibid.* p. 45) Gill must have followed him to Geneva, for he was not among the secessionists of 27 August (*ibid.* p. 55) and he is in the list of those who reached Geneva before 13 October. On 14 October 1557 he became a 'resident' of the city (f. 196). Further than that we know nothing of him.

Frankfort, B III a; Geneva, A IV a & b.

170. GODOLPHIN (GOODOLPHIN, GUDOLPHYN), WILLIAM: *Gent.* Of Cornwall.

In Brett's 'Narrative' (p. 129) he is called 'the lorde of Bedfordes manne', and is probably the William Godolphin who was in the train of Francis, Earl of Bedford, at Venice in 1555 and permitted by the Signory to bear arms (*Ven. Cal.* 1555–6, p. 145). Which of the many Williams of that name he was, is hard to determine, for unfortunately Sir William the elder (d. 1570) called both his eldest and his third son William, the latter being distinguished by the epithet 'of Windsor' (Harl. Soc. IX, 81). Very likely it was this younger son who went abroad and, with the earl, passed through Padua on 12 June 1555, on his way to Venice (Cam. Misc. X, 120). But on 3 August, Brett reports (p. 129) that he had returned to England with 'Maister Feneux' (*q.v.*).

Padua, B IV a; Venice, B v b 3.

171. GOODMAN (GUDMAN), CHRISTOPHER, B.D. (1547). Of Chester. 1520(?)–1603.

M.A. of Brasenose College, Oxford, 1544; Lady Margaret Professor of Divinity, 1548–54 (Foster, I, 582 and Foxe, VII, 738). Goodman's defence of tyrannicide in his pamphlet on *How superior powers oght to be obeyd* (Geneva, 1558) would seem to have been, like most of the protestant pamphlets of the day, an apologia rather than a philosophical treatise. Before Goodman preached tyrannicide he had tried to practise it. Parsons's accusation in his *Three Conversions* (Maitland, *Essays*, p. 80 and *Ath. Oxon.* I, 721) that he had been implicated in the conspiracy of William Thomas[1] to kill the queen (Baga, p. 248) seems to be corroborated by Foxe himself in his account of Bartlet Green's examination (VII, 732–4, 738). Green and Goodman had been friends at Oxford and it was because of their intercepted correspondence that Green was arrested in 1555. The charge against Green was treason and not heresy, and in that treason Goodman appears to have been a continuing accomplice. To his inquiries as to the progress of their enterprise, Bartlet Green's significant reply was 'The queen is not *yet*[2] dead' (*ibid.* p. 733), and though the tell-tale 'yet' does not establish the guilt of either of them it leaves in the mind so strong a presumption of guilt that certain of Goodman's biographers have seen fit to omit the 'yet', quoting rather Foxe's indirect statement (p. 732) than Green's own words as they are given on the next page. As late as 25 March (1554) Goodman was in London, for on that date he and Green met 'in the chamber of John Pulline' to receive their Easter communion. He may not have left England until May when William Thomas, between the 9th and 17th, was on trial for 'compassing the Queen's death' (Baga, p. 248). And he is first found abroad at Strasbourg, where during that summer the leaders of the protestant 'opposition' forgathered. On 23 November he was one of the signatories of Strasbourg's admonitory letter to Frankfort in the Prayer Book quarrels (*T.* p. 23) and he was still living there in the house of Peter Martyr on 29 December, when he received ten florins from the Duke of Württemberg's bounty and signed the exiles' letter of thanks (Württ. Staatsarchiv and *O.L.* I, 347). But by March 1555 he himself had gone to Frankfort (*T.* p. 47), where he played such a part in the strife which rent the congregation that he later acknowledged that he 'had much to regret in that Frankfort controversy' (*O.L.* II, 768–71). Finally he followed Knox to Geneva, arriving there with Whittingham on 13 October. On 24 October he was received as a 'resident' of the city (f. 123) and on 1 June 1558 he was admitted as a 'citizen' (*O.L.* II, 768, n. 1). Meanwhile he was chosen on 1 November 1555 to officiate with Gilby as minister of the English congregation in Knox's absence (Martin, p. 334) and would thus, like Francis Hotman, appear to have received his degree at Basle in absentia (cf. *Ital. Reform.* p. 322), for he is found inscribed in the matriculation list of that

[1] For this conspiracy see Adair's essay in *Tudor Studies* (1924).
[2] Author's italics.

university for the winter of 1554–5 and to have paid his fee of VI sol (f. 191vo; see below, p. 357). As to the part he played in the translation of the Geneva Bible, Martin thinks that his collaboration was only intermittent (Martin, p. 241). In 1558 the publication of his *Superior Powers*, with Whittingham's preface to it, made this 'furious hot spirit' (*Ath. Oxon.* I, 721) the most hated man in England after Knox. He was therefore obliged to remain in Geneva until August 1559, officiating, it is supposed, as pastor of the much depleted English congregation (Martin, p. 259). Then he managed to get back to Scotland as escort to Knox's wife (*D.N.B.*); but it was not until 1565 that he ventured into England and became chaplain to Sir Henry Sidney (*Annals*, I, i, 187). Thereafter his career as one of the leaders of the puritan party is too well known to be repeated. But those who would gain insight into the mental processes of the exiles, who are curious to know what thoughts passed current among them, would do well to re-read Goodman's four famous questions put to Bullinger and Calvin in the spring of 1554 (*O.L.* II, 745–7). Studied in the light of the new material that I have gathered for these biographies it becomes evident, especially in the last two questions, that they were posed not as mere abstract propositions, but as the fruit of actual experience and the prickings of conscience.

Briefly paraphrased the questions are these:

1. Is a king, who is a minor, a lawful magistrate to be obeyed as of divine right?

2. Can a woman rule by divine right and transfer that right to her husband?

3. Must obedience be given to idolatrous magistrates or may those in positions of military trust lawfully resist such magistrates? (i.e. may they betray their trusts? cf. Thomas Carell and Edmund Beauper).

4. Are the godly justified in rebellion if it is that of a 'religious nobility' against 'an idolatrous sovereign'?

B I; B II; Strasbourg, A VII c; Frankfort, B III a; Geneva, A IV a & b; Basle, A II a; *D.N.B.*

172. GOSLING, WILLIAM: *Merchant*. Of London.

When John Brett arrived at Weinheim on 10 July 1556 (Brett, p. 122), in his pursuit of the Duchess of Suffolk, he found among her English retainers one named 'Goslinge' (*ibid.* p. 125) who is probably that Gosling whom Foxe calls a 'merchant of London', and who had sheltered the duchess at his house near Leigh, Kent, when she was fleeing to the continent (Foxe, VIII, 572).

Wesel (?); Weinheim, B IV a.

173. GOWER, THOMAS, Esq.: *Marshal and Surveyor of Berwick.*
Of Yorkshire. fl. 1543–77.

Thomas Gower, the son of Sir Edward Gower of Stettinham,
Yorks. (Harl. Soc. XVI, 144–5, 166), was a man heavily burdened
with debt (*P.C.A.* 1552–4, p. 57) who figures frequently in the
Privy Council minutes in the reign of Edward VI. He was then
Surveyor of Berwick (*ibid.*), but seems to have fallen into disfavour
with Northumberland (*ibid.* pp. 105, 127) and to have lost his
office in October 1552 (*ibid.* p. 136). Under Mary he fell into
further trouble; and on 20 August 1554, for words 'tending to
sedicion' was 'committed to the Fleete' (*ibid.* 1554–6, p. 64). On
17 September, however, he was discharged upon 'penitent behaviour' and 'willed to repaire home into the Northe Countrey'
(*ibid.* p. 73), but his debts (*ibid.* p. 240) would seem to have made
him desperate. In 1556 he was suspected of complicity in the
Dudley plot and fled to the Continent, where almost immediately
he turned informer against his accomplices. 'Gower is destitute',
wrote Wotton in July, 'and unless helped by the Queen knows not
what to do' (*For. Cal.* 1553–8, p. 238). Clemency was evidently
shown him for services rendered, for in January 1557 he was
appointed 'Master of thordinance' in the North (*P.C.A.* 1556–8,
pp. 242, 380), in which office he continued under Elizabeth. His
later career is fully treated in *D.N.B.*, which, however, makes no
mention of his connection with the Dudley conspiracy.

France, B v b 1; *D.N.B.*

174. GRASON (GRASSANUS, GRESHAM), RICHARD: *Priest.*
Of Westmorland.

From the record of his ordination as deacon in June 1550 we know
that Grason was born at Kirkby Thore, Westmorland (*Mar. Reac.*
p. 186) and already held the living of Chesterford Magna to which
he had been instituted the previous March (*ibid.* n. 3). In September
1550 he was made priest (*Mem.* II, i, 403) and, says Dr Frere
(p. 107), in December 1554 was definitely deprived for being
married. He went abroad, where in 1556–7, as 'Dominus Richardus
Grassanus' of London, he is found as a student at the University
of Basle (below, p. 357).

Basle, A II a.

175. GRAIE (GREY, GRAYE), JOHN: *Gent.* Of Braintree,
Essex. d. 1569 (?).

If the John Graie who first makes his appearance at Frankfort on
24 September 1554 (*T.* p. 20) could be certainly identified as Lord
John Grey of Pyrgo, who with Cecil in December–January 1558 was

one of the four members[1] of the secret committee of the Privy
Council for the alteration of religion (*Annals*, I, i, 74), the discovery
would be as important as any made during these researches into
the history of the Marian Exiles. Unfortunately, two stubborn
facts militate against the presumption, and with these I will deal
first. Holinshed says (ed. 1808, IV, 64) and also Foxe (VI, 561) that
Lord John was not released from the Tower until 30 October 1554.
Obviously then he could not have been in Frankfort in September
of the same year.

Again, when John Graie, the exile, was admitted to citizenship
at Frankfort in April 1555, he called himself of 'Brayndtry', which
we take to be Braintree in Essex, a manor belonging to Lord Rich
(Morant's *Essex*, II, 394–5), with which, so far as I can discover,
the Greys had no connection. Finally, though of less importance
because the grant may have been in pity for 'the lady Mary his
wife', Nichols says that Lord Grey received considerable grants
of land from the queen not only in 1555 (which would make no
difficulty as will be seen later) but in 1554, when we wish to prove
him in disgrace (Nichols, *Leicestershire*, III, 674). These facts, if
correct, are not easy to reconcile with a theory of Lord John
Grey's flight to the Continent.

But, on the other hand, what follows supports that belief
with considerable weight: Lord John had been imprisoned with
his brother Henry, Duke of Suffolk, on 10 February 1554
as an accomplice in the latter's second rising (*Chron. Q. Jane*,
pp. 53–4). On 11 June he was condemned as a traitor (*ibid.*
p. 77), but through 'the painfull trauell and diligent sute' of his
wife, who was a sister of that good catholic, Viscount Montague,
he was pardoned, and, as has been said, released on 30 October
(Holinshed, IV, 56, 64). And thereafter, says the *D.N.B.*, he 'lived
obscurely under Mary'. This sentence would cover a withdrawal
to the Continent, and, under the circumstances, to place himself
beyond the Channel would seem to have been the most sensible
thing for Lord John to do.

Now at Frankfort, where on 24 September a John Graie signed
the congregation's invitation to Knox, there appears also as a
signatory to the same letter a 'John Wood'; and it happens that
a John Wood, whether this man or another, was in 1564 a 'steward
of Lord John Grey of Pyrgo' (*Dom. Cal.* 1547–80, p. 235). Moreover, these two men appear together and disappear together from
Whittingham's narrative. And among the archives of Zurich is

[1] '...the matter being imparted to no man but the Marquesse of Northampton, the Earle of Bedford, John Grey of Pyrgo and Cecyl' (Camden,
Annals, ed. 1630, p. 16).

preserved a letter from Calvin to Lord Grey which may explain the disappearance. It is dated 13 November 1554 (*O.L.* II, 715–17) and in it, after commiserating Lord John upon 'the misfortunes of his house', Calvin exhorts him to 'carry on the warfare of the cross even unto the end' (p. 716). He then closes with an appeal for aid on behalf of a certain Antony Chevalier, once a teacher of the Princess Elizabeth, but at that moment a refugee and professor of Hebrew at Strasbourg (*ibid.* n. 1). If this letter was sent to Lord Grey in England, why is it now preserved at Zurich? And certainly it would have been a most tactless, not to say dangerous, appeal to make in writing to a known protestant who had just narrowly escaped being drawn and quartered. The inference can only be that Lord John was then somewhere abroad, and, as he did not sign the next letter of the Frankfort congregation on 3 December (*T.* p. 26), it is very possible that he had gone from there to Zurich —that Mecca of the English gospellers. He may even have spent the winter at Zurich, for it is not until 18 April 1555 that as 'J. Gray de Brayndtry' (Jung, p. 50) he bought burgher rights at Frankfort and paid his tax for them of '1 florin 4 albus'. This fact proclaims 'J. Gray' to have been a man of consequence; but then, again, he disappears. And this second disappearance coincides admirably with his recorded return to favour at court, for among the gifts received by Queen Mary on New Year's day, 1556–7, were 'six handkerchiefs wrought with gold and silver' from 'the Lord John Grey', who as a return present received from her 'a gilt cruse 12¾ oz.' (Nichols, *Leicestershire*, III, 674).

The name of John Graie or Graye is heard of no more at Frankfort until the important date 3 January 1559, when with Henry Carowe (*q.v.*), whom we believe to have been Lord Hunsdon, he signed Frankfort's refusal to join Geneva in her proposed anti-ceremonial crusade. Very significantly this letter displays a foreknowledge of the coming meeting in London of Sir Thomas Smith's committee for Prayer Book revision, a knowledge that could hardly have been possessed by anyone of the group but John Graye, if he was Lord Grey of Pyrgo. It is also signed by James Pilkington (*q.v.*), who was one of the four exiled divines chosen to sit upon that committee (*T.* p. 190). There can be little doubt, then, that at least this John Graye of 1559 was Lord John Grey of Pyrgo (in Essex). Was he also, or was he not, the John Graie at Frankfort in 1554?

Frankfort, B III a; Zurich, A VIII a; *D.N.B.*

176. GRINDAL, EDMUND, B.D. (1549): *Priest*(?). Of Hensingham, Cumberland. 1519(?)–83.
Of Magdalene, Christ's and Pembroke Colleges, Cambridge· Ordained deacon in 1544. Canon of Westminster, 1552–4 (Venn,

II, 270). It was evidently Grindal's early training in theological controversy and matters liturgical that determined the use made of him during the Frankfort-Strasbourg quarrels over Prayer Book revision in 1554–5. He had been selected by Ridley to argue on the protestant side in the disputations on the Sacrament held at Cambridge in 1549 (Foxe, VI, 322–7 and *Cranmer*, ed. E.H.S. II, 168–72), and he again took part in those held at the houses of Sir William Cecil and Sir Richard Morison in 1551. The next year, as king's chaplain (1551), he was one of the committee of divines to whom the 42 articles were referred for criticism (*P.C.A.* 1552–4, p. 148). Thinking it the wiser course in the 'ticklish unsteddy time' that followed Mary's accession he withdrew to Strasbourg, probably arriving there in the spring of 1554 with Sir John Cheke (*q.v.*), and Sir Richard Morison (*q.v.*; cf. Protocols below, p. 362 and *Grindal*, p. 12). That autumn he was despatched by John Ponet, then ranking ecclesiastic abroad, to compose the Prayer Book quarrels raging at Frankfort. Grindal's first diplomatic visit was made with Richard Chambers on 28 November (*T.* p. 22). By 13 December he had returned to Strasbourg (*T.* p. 27), having effected nothing, but bringing with him a report of the situation so disturbing that Ponet determined, on the strength of it, to choose an agent better qualified in temper to deal with John Knox. Richard Cox was therefore sent in the following March[1] (1555), with Grindal probably in his company (*T.* p. 38). He was certainly a member of Cox's commission for Prayer Book revision which reported on 28 March (*T.* pp. 46–7), for he was one of those who signed Cox's letter of explanation to Calvin on 5 April (*O.L.* II, 753–5). And on 6 May he was either still or again at Frankfort, for on that date he reported to Ridley that the church was now 'well quieted by the prudence of Master Coxe and other which met here for that purpose' (Grindal, *Remains*, p. 238). In 1556, however, he was back in Strasbourg, from which city his correspondence to John Foxe is dated until 18 June 1557 (*ibid.* pp. 219–26). Then comes a break. His letters are not resumed until the following 28 November (*ibid.* pp. 228–30), and it is possibly during that summer that he went to Wasselheim and Speyer to learn German in order 'that his voice might be heard in the German Churches' (*ibid.* p. iii, n. 5), since he then despaired of a return to England. Just a year later he was dating his last letter from Strasbourg 'in haste 19 Decemb. 1558' (*ibid.* pp. 237–8). He was therefore among the earliest of the exiles to return to England, and was appropriately chosen one of the four exiles to sit on Sir Thomas Smith's committee for the revision of the Prayer Book. Abroad he had

[1] Cf. the account of John Day, above, for other reasons.

been perhaps the chief collector of material for Foxe in the preparation of his *Book of Martyrs* (*Grindal*, pp. 19, 25, 30) and at home again 'our painful countryman', as bishop of London, was the most zealous in presenting his companions in exile for ordination, so much so that he brought down upon himself a reprimand from Archbishop Parker for having 'ordained severall artificers who had behaved thselves (*sic*) not to ye credit of ye gospell', and was forbidden 'any more to ordain artificers' (Harl. MS. 6955, f. 116). In 1570 he became archbishop of York; in 1576, archbishop of Canterbury, from which office, between 1577 and 1582, he was suspended.

Strasbourg, A vii a; Frankfort, B iii a; Wasselheim; Speyer; *D.N.B.*

177. HADDON, JAMES: *Dean*(?) *of Exeter.* Of Buckinghamshire. d. 1556.

Brother of the more famous Walter Haddon, President of Magdalen College, Oxford. He received his M.A. from Cambridge in 1544, was one of the original Fellows of Trinity, and in 1552 was made canon of Westminster. Into the moot question of his deanship of Exeter we shall not enter (cf. *D.N.B.* and *Cranmer*, ed. E.H.S. III, 70, n. b; also the omission of his name by Le Neve), but his chaplaincy to the Duke of Suffolk, and his position of tutor to Lady Jane Grey, played an important part in his activities as an exile. Shortly after 23 May 1554 he left London as 'a voluntary exile', bearing a letter from Bishop Hooper to Bullinger (*O.L.* I, 103), and about 9 July arrived with it at Strasbourg (*ibid.* p. 291).

His own correspondence with Bullinger, begun in 1551 when he was still one of the Duke of Suffolk's household at Bradgate in Leicestershire, was continued unbroken until 12 (or 15?) March 1556, a date which probably marks Haddon's death at Strasbourg from the plague (*O.L.* I, 279–302). These letters are illuminating; not only for their references to the progress of the reformation in England, but for the light they throw on the dubious domestic ethics of the Duke of Suffolk and Haddon's own disingenuousness in promoting the cause of the exiles abroad at the expense of those left to suffer the consequences of his acts in England. As his case seems to be a typical example of the peculiarly callous policy pursued in the matter of propaganda, we shall give our own reading of his letters to Bullinger in regard to the publication of the last papers of Lady Jane Grey. These papers by some agency had come into the hands of John Banks (*q.v.*), whose father was a printer in London. Banks wrote to Bullinger from London in March 1554 suggesting their publication abroad (*ibid.* pp. 303–5). But Bullinger, to his credit, did his best to dissuade Banks from the enterprise, arguing that the effect of publication would be 'injurious to many individuals' (*ibid.* p. 306). This letter Banks showed to Haddon. And Haddon in a long postscript to a letter written to Bullinger on 31 August (*ibid.* pp. 292–4) makes the usual excuse that Banks had written without his knowledge, and only refers obliquely to Bullinger's warning that publication would do harm to the English reformers at home. Bullinger's 'prudence' he commends purely from the personal standpoint—that such an act would 'occasion the greatest danger to' himself, James Haddon. Then he makes a noble gesture: 'If', he says, 'it were evident that all the statements were certainly true and proved, and that their publication would tend to the glory of God', then he, Haddon, would prepare himself 'to meet the danger' (*ibid.* p. 293). What that danger was, he being then safe abroad, is not specified, but he concludes: 'Were the statement published, it would probably do more harm to the truth, and to our cause, than it would do them good; to say nothing of the certain risk and peril which would hang over others.' And with amazing effrontery he adds: 'It will now be sufficient for me to have pointed out to your prudence, what you have already perceived of yourself, that is, that these things should not be published,...under any circumstances whatever,...' (*ibid.* p. 294). And what happened? The papers of Lady Jane Grey were all published, that summer. Not only that; they were also given to Michael Angelo Florio, then in Strasbourg, for his *Life of Lady Jane Grey*,[1] as well as to Foxe at Basle for his *Acts and Monuments*. But, we repeat, all of the papers, including her controversy with Harding, her last controversy with Feckenham, her letter to her sister Lady Catherine Grey, and her statement made on the scaffold—the most inflammatory of campaign documents—were first published that year of 1554 and in all probability at Strasbourg (A. Maunsell, ed. 1595, p. 66 and cf. Strype's *Aylmer*, p. 7). That Haddon was responsible for their appearance is not proven, but is highly likely. And thereafter little more is known of him. When asked in October to become pastor of the Frankfort congregation 'he desired for divers considerations to be excused' (*T.* p. 16). Perhaps Lady Jane's papers were then in the press. But he was present there at the time of the revision of the Prayer Book in March-April 1555 (*O.L.* I, 299). After which his letters to Bullinger continue until 15 March 1556, then cease, and his silence is probably evidence of his death. Both he and Ponet were very possibly victims of the plague.

B II; Frankfort, A VIII a; Strasbourg, A VIII a; *D.N.B.*

---

[1] See 'John Banks', above.

178. HALES, CHRISTOPHER: *Gent.* Of Kent and Warwickshire. Wife.

This Christopher Hales has frequently been confused with his great-uncle, another Christopher Hales, who was attorney-general to Henry VIII. Christopher Hales, the exile, was a younger brother of John Hales (*q.v.*) of Coventry (Brett, p. 120 and *O.L.* I, 189) and married to Mary Lucy (Harl. Soc. XII, 288), whose sister, spoken of as 'Elisabeth Lucia', lived with them at Frankfort (*H.S.P.* IV, 88). His genuine devotion to the reformed doctrines was probably the result of his education at St John's College, Cambridge, of which he was made a Fellow in 1539, and from which he received his M.A. two years later (Venn, II, 283). 'In my time, ten years since', he wrote to Bullinger in 1550, 'twenty crowns were a sufficient allowance' for the year's expenses; and he deprecates a growing extravagance at the university which in 'these latter days' necessitated a minimum of 'thirty French crowns' (*O.L.* I, 190). In 1548 his early religious bias was confirmed by a trip abroad with Sir Thomas Hoby, which included a visit to Strasbourg. And there in June he forgathered with men who became lifelong friends, and all but one of whom were to be fellow-exiles a few years later—John Butler, John Abell, John Burcher and Richard Hilles (Cam. Misc. X, 6; *O.L.* II, 661). It may also have been on this journey that he formed the intimacy with Bullinger and Rudolf Gualter that led to a correspondence with them on Hales's return to England (*O.L.* I, 184–96). From an amusing account he sends Gualter of a very near misadventure they all had at Calais on their return journey, it is evident that he knew no word of French nor cared to (*ibid.* p. 184). Whereas his lively Germanic sympathies are obvious in a commission he gives for five portraits to be painted 'on wood, not canvas' of Bullinger, Gualter himself, and three other divines of Zurich, 'holding books in their hands' and each having a copy of verses written underneath. These were to be executed by 'your Apelles'. Were they ever finished? and, if so, where are they now? And who may the Zurich 'Apelles' have been? Strictly within the confines of his protestantism Hales was also an author himself and a patron of letters. Froschauer the printer he generously befriended when the latter came to England in 1550–1 (*O.L.* II, 723–5). And had the MS. not been lost with his luggage during the disastrous crossing of the Channel already spoken of, Hales would have brought to Hooper a present of Bullinger's commentary on Isaiah (*O.L.* I, 83, 189). His own book of prayers, with its arresting title *The Reward of the mercifull* (Maunsell, ed. 1595, p. 56), seems to have perished. But that, and his devoted love for his brother, by whose side he is always found (*O.L.* I, 185, 189; Brett, pp. 119–20), would mark him as one of the gentler spirits of a ruthless decade—an attractive, if shadowy figure. While in exile he and his brother lived together at Frankfort in apparent comfort, served by '2 maids', and having property between them assessed in October 1556[1] at the considerable sum of 5500 florins (Jung, pp. 29, 51). As we should expect to find him, he was one of that group 'desirous off the peace off the churche' (T. p. 64) to whom John Hales earnestly appealed in January 1557 'to quiete this styrre'. None the less he subscribed in April to the 'new discipline', and after his return to England was actively concerned in secretly printing at Coventry some of the Martin Marprelate Tracts (Wm Pierce, Histor. Introd. to the Marprelate Tracts, p. 180). Eventually his son, John, fell heir to Hales's Place, the principal house of the elder John Hales at Coventry (Ath. Oxon. I, 405–6), to which in 1589 the Marprelate Press was removed from Fawsley.

Frankfort, A III a 3, 4 & b 2; B III a & b.

179. HALES, John: Gent. Of Kent and Warwickshire. d. 1571.

A younger son of Thomas Hales of Halden, Kent (Ath. Oxon. I, 404–6), brother of Christopher Hales (above), and Clerk of the Hanaper to Henry VIII and Edward VI (cf. Leadam, R.H.S. Trans. n.s. XI, 116 n. 6, and Bulletin, Inst. of Historical Research, I, no. 2, pp. 63–4). 'Clubfoot Hales', as Wood calls him, was not a university man nor one of scholarly tastes like his brother. As early as 1549 he began a career of agitation as one of the king's commissioners against unlawful enclosures; and, arousing the hatred of his class, was accused of encouraging the commonalty in sedition (Mem. II, i, 268). He would, they said, 'have liberty, liberty: and now it was come to a licentious liberty...' (ibid.). Under Northumberland he served a term of imprisonment (1550), probably as a supporter of Somerset (O.L. I, 185) and, on his release, prudently went abroad (ibid. p. 189). There, in some capacity unknown, he attached himself to Sir Richard Morison, then English resident at Brussels.[2] But Morison was unappreciative of his presence. He complained to Cecil that Master Hales plied him with precepts (For. Cal. 1547–53, p. 66). And there is more than a hint in Morison's restiveness, under 'the cauteries of the physician', that Hales had been sent to keep watch over that volatile agent, as well as to investigate agricultural conditions in Germany (ibid. pp. 95, 97). Germany, then, was a land already

---

[1] The first mention of him at Frankfort.

[2] F. S. Thomas (Historical Notes, I, 347) says that in 1552, Morison was made English resident at Brussels. Exactly what his position was in 1550 is not clear.

familiar to him when Mary came to the throne, and an attempt on the queen's part to deprive him of his office on 29 April 1554 (*P.C.A.* 1554–6, p. 16) was very possibly the occasion of his withdrawal to Frankfort, where he would be 'beyond the reach of legal process'. It is possible that in 1552–3 he had been Sir William Cecil's private secretary (F. S. Thomas, *Historical Notes*, I, 355). Besides this, Hales was a large holder of abbey lands in Warwickshire. There is every reason then for his 'hotte wordes and meanes used' to John Brett when that unlucky envoy of Queen Mary tried to deliver to him the queen's warrant (or letters) on 8 July 1556; also for his insistence that she 'had no power to sende proces into those parties' (Brett, pp. 119–20). Hales had been in Frankfort at least as early as September 1555 (Cam. Misc. x, 123). On that July day of 1556, he and his brother 'gyrte theyre Swordes aboute them and gotte them to the Consules howse' in haste, where 'the saide John Hales made a greate complaynte howe the Quenes Maiesty contrary to the liberties and lawes of those Countreys hadde sente to vexe hym and others that...were commed thyther to flye persecucion in Englande...'. The consul, however, was not to be intimidated. He stoutly refused to serve an injunction upon Brett 'for all the prayers or complayntes' of 'the saide Hales and his Compaignons' (Brett, pp. 120–1) and Brett escaped with his life.

In October 1556 the assessment (Jung, p. 29) of Hales's taxable property at 5000 florins[1] shows how large a portion of his wealth he had carried out of England. The confiscation of his property in 1557 (*D.N.B.*) was thus less crippling than it might have been. It was John Hales who, in March 1556/7, announced to Cecil the death of Sir Richard Morison, and besought aid for his 'very poor widow' (*Salisbury*, I, 140). In the strife at Frankfort following the Horne-Ashley quarrel he tried to play the part of peacemaker, though with no very conspicuous success (*T.* p. 65), and, like his brother, he signed the 'new discipline' in March-April 1557. Before 3 January 1558/9 he had returned to England, but not to acquiescence in the Elizabethan régime. With the connivance of Cecil and Bacon he became the pamphleteer of the Suffolk claim to the throne in the person of Lady Catherine Grey. In 1564 he justified the legitimacy of her secret marriage with Lord Hertford, and for his temerity was sent to the Tower, while his pamphlet on the 'Right of Succession to the Crown of England' (now Harl. MS. 1555, not 550 as given in *D.N.B.*) remained unpublished until

---

[1] For the contemporary value of the gulden in English money, see above, p. 19, n. 2. It would seem from what information I can find that the florin and the gulden were then of about the same value.

1723. Though Cecil's influence soon contrived his release from prison, Hales was under bond for four years thereafter not to quit his house without the queen's licence (*Dom. Cal.* 1547–80, p. 306). He died in 1571 without issue, leaving his property to his nephew John, son of Christopher.

Frankfort, A III a 3, 4 & b 2; B III a & b; B IV a & b; *D.N.B.*

180. HALL, ROWLAND: *Printer.* d. 1563.

The printer at Geneva of the English translation of the Bible, on the title-page of which his name is inscribed (Martin, p. 66). With William Williams he had set up his press in December 1558 (Reg. du Cons. vol. 61, ff. 87vo, 88vo; cf. Martin, p. 70). Gordon Duff (*English Book Trade*, pp. 64–5) says that he was an original member of the Stationers' Company, though his name does not appear in the charter. Sometime in 1556 he became a member of Knox's congregation and on 14 October 1557 (f. 196) he was received as a 'resident' of Geneva. The funds for the enterprise were largely supplied by John Bodley (*q.v.* and Martin, p. 240, n. 1). By 1561, Hall was re-established in London (*ibid.* p. 70), but died two years later (Gordon Duff, p. 65).

Geneva, A IV a & b.

181. HAMBY (HANSBY, HANBY), JOHN: (?) *Gent.* Of Brocklesby, Lincolnshire.

He was probably the son and heir of Edward Hamby (by his wife Eleanor Booth), who on 29 June 1559 died seised of the manor of Great Lymber and Auford, Lincs. (Harl. Soc. LI, 447). On 30 September 1559 John Hamby, his heir, is said to have been about '26 years and more' (*ibid.*), so that he is almost undoubtedly the 'John Hambeus' who was a student at the University of Padua in the winter of 1557/8 (Andrich, p. 131) and served as Consiliarius of the English (*ibid.* p. 32). But it was John Hamby (Hanby), his uncle, who in 1570 (*P.C.A.* 1558–70, p. 33 and *Dom. Cal.* 1547–80, p. 396) was Auditor of the Treasury, an office which tended to become hereditary in the family, for we find an Allen Hamby who died in 1607 holding the same office (Venn, II, 292). William Hamby, a younger brother of John the exile (Harl. Soc. LI, 447), was a scholar of St John's College, Cambridge, in 1561, and later rector of Brocklesby (Venn, II, 293).

Padua, A VI.

182. HAMILTON (HAMMILTOUN), JOHN (or JAMES?): (?) *Servant of Knox.*

Though this man appears in Bales's list as 'John', he may very possibly be the 'James' Hamilton who was 'Mr Knoxis servand'

(Laing, VI, 628) and with Knox at Geneva, where he was enrolled
a member of the congregation on 12 July 1556 as 'James', without
a surname.   Geneva, A IV a.

183. HAMMOND (HAMMON), WILLIAM: *Gent.* Of 'Acres',
      Kent.

Probably the William, son of Alexander Hamon, who in the
second year of Elizabeth received a patent to bear arms (Harl.
Soc. LXXIV, 58), and the same Mr Hammond of Somerset's party,
who on 16 October 1551 had been committed to the Tower
(*Machyn*, p. 10). The Hammonds were important land-holders in
Kent (Hasted, III, 346). William 'Hammon' made his appearance
at Frankfort as early as 29 July 1554, when he signed the Liturgia
Sacra of the French Church as one of the Seniors of the affiliated
English congregation (*Liturgia Sacra*, ed. 1554, p. 92). On
2 August he was also one of the signatories of Whittingham's
invitation to the other English colonies to unite with them at
Frankfort (*T.* p. 13), and on 23 August (or 13, cf. Jung, pp. 24, 51)
he was received as a burgher of Frankfort (*ibid.* p. 24), paying
2 florins 'Bürgergeld', and registering as 'W. Hamon Anglus
Cantuariensis'. His last appearance abroad was on 24 September,
when he was one of those who signed the invitation to John Knox
to become pastor of the congregation (*T.* p. 20). It is probable
that he returned home, for his name appears on no other list,
either at Frankfort or elsewhere.   Frankfort, A III a 1; B III a.

184. HAMOND, WILLIAM(?): *Gent.* Of Kent.

We believe this man, who appears in Machyn (p. 103) merely
as 'Hamond', to have been William, third son of the William
Hammon of Kent above. On 4 April 1556 he was proclaimed a
traitor among the other members of Henry Dudley's conspiracy
who fled to the Continent (*ibid.*). Though in the Baga de Secretis
he does not appear in the indictment, this identification of him is
based upon a Privy Council minute for 4 January 1555/6 (*P.C.A.*
1554–6, p. 216), which records that on that day 'William Hamond'
and 'Edmonde Harrys' (*q.v.*) made their personal appearance.
This suggests that he may have fled earlier than 4 April, and since
there is no evidence that he was ever with Dudley in France, he
may have joined his father in Germany.   n.p.; B IV c.

185. HANCOCK, THOMAS: *Preacher.* Of Twineham, Hampshire.
      Wife.

Probably an unordained preacher—one of those countenanced and
licensed by Cranmer in the first year of Edward VI (*Cranmer,*

ed. E.H.S. II, 83). In the reign of Henry VIII his 'mouth had been stopped by a strict inhibition' (*ibid.*) and he was suspended 'a celebratione divinorum' by Dr Raynold, commissary of Dr Steward, then chancellor to Bishop Gardiner (*ibid.* 84). At Mary's accession, however, he was minister of Poole in Dorset (*Mem.* III, i, 110), and his exemption from the queen's pardon was wholly attributed to a sermon of his in which he had said of Gardiner 'He hath been a Saul, God make him a Paul' (*ibid.* p. 112). Warned by William Thomas, a Clerk of the Council, that he was in danger (cf. Adair, p. 147), Hancock fled to Rouen, where according to his own time-table he spent two years (*Narr. of Ref.* p. 84). After six months more, divided between Paris and Orleans (*ibid.*), he came to Geneva, where on 5 November 1556 he with his wife and son, Gedion, were registered as members of Knox's congregation. Bale calls Hancock 'oxoniensis'. Foster (II, 643) records his having received his B.A. on 24 January 1532/3, but assigns him to no college. In view of his previous history it is interesting to find that when received as a 'resident' of Geneva on 14 October 1557 (f. 196) it is as a 'savant', not as a 'minister', that he describes himself. In Geneva he says that he remained 'thre yere and sumwhalt more', during which time a daughter 'Sara' was born to him to whom Anthony Gilby stood godfather (Martin, p. 336). His return to England, according to his own reckoning, must have taken place early in 1559, and he seems to have settled in London. Very possibly he is the Thomas Hancock of Aldersgate who is listed among the members of the Plumbers Hall congregation (C. Burrage, *Early English Dissenters*, II, 10), and the date of his Oxford degree would make it quite possible that he was the Thomas Hancock who was vicar of Amport in 1578 (*Dom. Cal.* 1547–80, p. 605). This suggestion, however, must be taken as pure conjecture.

Rouen; Orleans; Paris; Geneva, A IV a & b.

186. HARLESTONE, ROBERT: *Yeoman.* Of Mattishall (or Matsal), Norfolk.

Of the many Harlestones, we believe this Robert to have been the brother-in-law of Archbishop Parker who in 1547 had married Margaret, daughter of Robert Harlestone of Norfolk (Parker, I, 46 and II, 29, 31). Her brother, Simon Harlestone, in orders, and living at Mendlesham in Suffolk, was driven from the town with his family, Foxe tells us (VIII, 147), for heresy. Though he is said to have been 'eminent both for his piety and sufferings in Queen Mary's days' this Simon does not appear to have left England, but he had a younger brother, Robert, and it is he whom we should identify as the Robert Harlestone who made his appearance at Aarau in the year 1557, and is named in Hans Dür's list. On the town's official list, however (presumably of 1559), he does not appear. And the omission is probably explained by the presence at the University of Basle, in the winter of 1557-8, of a 'Rupertus Harlesdonus, Anglus' (below, p. 357), who seems to have matriculated, since he paid his VI sol. His identification as the brother of Margaret Parker is based on Strype's statement that 'Mrs Parker's brother or kinsman' stood bond for certain provisions under Margaret Parker's will. And that 'an indenture tripartite was made...between Robert Harleston of Mattishal [Matsal], in the county of Norfolk, Yeoman.... Which witnessed, that whereas Robert Harleston, for and in performance of the will and requests of Margaret Parker, daughter of Robert Harleston, late of Mattishal aforesaid, etc.' (*Parker*, II, 29). Her father, Robert, then, was dead. Presumably the living Robert Harlestone was his son and her brother. But the fact of his having gone first to Aarau, a colony so largely recruited from fugitives from Calais, points also to a possible relationship with the John Harlestone to whom on 13 June 1553(?) Edward VI had granted the Lieutenancy of the castle of Ruysbank for life (Baga, p. 259). The trial of this John Harlestone for the surrender of Calais took place on 22 December 1559 (*ibid.* p. 262).

Aarau, A I a; Basle, A II a.

187. HARRINGTON, PERCIVAL: *Student and preacher*(?).

Mentioned among the exiled divines on Bale's list this Percival Harrington was one of the signatories of the 'new discipline' at Frankfort in the spring of 1557. Doubtless he stood in some degree of relationship to Robert Harrington 'the sustainer' (below), but what it was I have been unable to discover.

B II; Frankfort, B III b.

188. HARRINGTON, ROBERT: *Gent.* Of Lincolnshire(?). Wife.

The identification of this Robert Harrington, as the third[1] son of Sir John Harrington of Exton, Rutland (Harl. Soc. LI, 461), and a cousin by marriage of Sir William Cecil (*Misc. Gen. and Her.* n.s. III, 286–7), however tempting, yet breaks down upon the point of the identity of Robert Harrington's wife. The wife of the exile is specifically named as Lucy[2] (*Mem.* III, i, 224 and cf. Foxe, VI,

---

[1] Called 'second son' in the *Misc. Gen. and Her.* n.s. III, 289, note.
[2] Lucy Sydney, daughter of Sir William, and sister of Sir Henry Sydney, was the wife of Sir James Harrington, elder brother of the Robert Harrington of Lincolnshire.

633–4); that of Robert Harrington of Witham-on-the-Hill, Lincs., was Alice Boys, who did not die till 1565 (Harl. Soc. LI, 461); while from what follows it will be found that Mistress Lucy Harrington died abroad. Robert Harrington of Frankfort, then, must go unidentified as to pedigree, yet about the man himself we possess considerable information.

He and his wife, for example, head the list of the committee of 'sustainers' (*Mem.* III, i, 224); and we know that both of them were devoted friends of Laurence Saunders the martyr, who, in his last letters before his death, bequeathed to Mistress Lucy 'the care and charge of [his] said poor wife;... to be unto her a mother and a mistress...' (Foxe, VI, 633). This was in 1555. By 15 November 1555 Robert Harrington, 'generosus', had found refuge in Frankfort, and in the autumn of 1556 was rated as worth 40 florins (Jung, p. 29). Though his name does not appear on the list of those who purchased burgher rights, Jung says (p. 52) that he did actually become a burgher, and on 10 June 1557 he appears on the dwelling-list as living with his 'wife, one child and a maid' (*H.S.P.* IV, 88) in the same house with Nicholas Carvell (*q.v.*) and Thomas Horton. As Nicholas Carvell was penniless and Horton boasted no wealth but books (Jung, p. 29), Harrington was probably supporting both of them; while we believe the 'maid' to have been the wife of Laurence Saunders. For on 18 June 1556 comes a curious and pathetic sequel to Saunders's last legacy of his wife to the care of Lucy Harrington as 'mother and mistress'. On that date Robert Harrington's wife is found to be no longer Lucy, but Joanna, 'honesta Joanna Harritoni', once wife to Laurence Saunders, but now true wife to Robert Harrington, citizen (Jung, p. 51). Bereavement and re-marriage frequently trod fast upon each other's heels in that matter-of-fact age, and Harrington would seem literally to have obeyed Philpot's behest to bring his wife, his godly yoke-fellow, 'for an usury to the Lord' (Foxe, VII, 699), but Harrington's child was now left motherless in a foreign land, and if faith was to be kept with Saunders, Harrington had no choice but to marry his widow, who could not otherwise have continued to live 'honestly' in his household. A good deal of poignant human history may lie within the narrow scope of a Latin entry in a sixteenth-century 'Gewaltsbuch' (Jung, p. 51). In the contest over the 'discipline', he was an ally of Horne and never subscribed to it (*T.* p. 169).

No more is known of this Robert Harrington unless, as is not unlikely, he was the one of that name ordained deacon by Grindal in January 1559/60 (*Grindal*, pp. 54–5).

Frankfort, A III a 2, 3, 4 & b 1, 2; B III a.

189. HARRIS (HARRIES, HARIES), Edmond: *Gent.* Of Essex.

Probably the fifth son of William Harris of Southminster, sheriff of Essex, by his third wife Anne Rutter (Harl. Soc. xiii, 59). This William Harris, who died on 26 September 1556 (*Machyn*, p. 115), was a man 'notabulle ryche both in landes [abbey lands?] and fermes' (*ibid.*). And as his second wife he had married Joanna Cooke, an aunt of Sir Anthony Cooke (Harl. Soc. xiii, 59). Thus the Edmond Harris who appears at Frankfort in April 1557 as a signatory of the 'new discipline', and again in the September following as one who subscribed to the letter rejecting Strasbourg's intervention in the quarrel ensuing upon that discipline's adoption, was a near connection of Sir Anthony. Unfortunately for identification, William Harris had two sons by his third wife, one, Edward (sixth(?) son), and one, Edmond (fifth son), either one of whom might have been the exile, since in the sixteenth century the two names appear to have been interchangeable. Choice, however, inclines to the fifth son, because on 4 January 1555/6 an 'Edmunde Harrys of Buntingforde'[1] was commanded to make his appearance before the Privy Council with the William Hammond (*q.v.*) who in the following April was proclaimed a traitor (*P.C.A.* 1554–6, p. 216). It is also possible that he was the 'oone Harrys' whose 'secret apprehension' was demanded in December 1556 (*ibid.* 1556–8, p. 37). His escape from England at this date would tally with his appearance at Frankfort in April 1557, and the words 'obiit sine prole' attached to his name in the Harris pedigree suggest that he may have died abroad unmarried. One of the descendants of Sir William Harris by his wife Joanna Cooke was the Sir Cranmer Harris whose mother, Anne, was the daughter of Robert Cranmer, great-nephew to the archbishop (*Cranmer*, ed. E.H.S. iii, 331 and Harl. Soc. xiii, 60, 213).

Frankfort, B iii b.

190. HARRISON, Richard: *Student.* d. 1595(?).

Nothing is known certainly though much may be conjectured about this man who became a member of Knox's congregation on 5 November 1556. Burn believes (*Parish Reg.* p. 278, n. 7), though without giving his authority, that Harrison was the 'honest spy' employed by Knox to carry to Cecil Knox's request for permission to pass through England in 1559. But it is quite possible that he was also identical with that 'Robert' Harrison who later became the close friend and collaborator of John Browne, the 'Separatist'. This 'Robert', observes Cooper, was 'uniformly' called 'Richard' Harrison by 'our older writers' (*Ath. Cantab.* ii, 177–8). And

[1] Hertfordshire.

though H. M. Dexter in his history of 'Congregationalism' throws no light on Harrison's early history, there is nothing in the lives of the two men to preclude their identity. We gather that the 'honest spy' was a young man. It was not unusual for those who left England at a time when they would normally have been at the university to finish their education on their return. Therefore 'Robert' Harrison's matriculation from St John's College, Cambridge, in 1564 (Venn, II, 317) would have been equally in order for 'Richard' the exile. Again, 'Robert's' objection to the use of the Prayer Book at his marriage was quite in character for 'Richard', late member of Knox's congregation. In fact 'Robert' Harrison's nonconformity both preceded his association with Robert Browne and survived it, for he is believed to have remained at Middleburg in Holland after Browne's return to England, and to have died there about 1595—a date very possible for the demise of 'Richard' Harrison of Geneva. Further search into the matter might throw some interesting light on the origins of Congregationalism.

Geneva, A IV a.

191. HARTE (HART), ROGER: *Deacon*. Of Stepney (Stebunhethe), Middlesex. Wife. d. 1559(?).

Miscalled 'Robert' by Strype (*Mem.* II, i, 403), this man was ordained deacon, as Rogerus Harte, by Ridley on 10 August 1550 (*Mar. Reac.* p. 189). Strype would seem to imply that he was afterwards ordained priest at the same time as Thomas Lever, but Dr Frere makes no mention of his having received other orders. Hart's first place of refuge abroad was Emden (Strype's *Whitgift*, I, 132),[1] where he served for a time as minister, but by March 1555 he was at Frankfort and of the party opposed to Cox (*T.* p. 58). Later in the year he seceded with Whittingham and his group, but he went to Aarau and not to Geneva. At Aarau in 1557 he was living with his wife and grown son in the house of Laurentz Wyerman, an old preacher (Hans Dür), but because of a long illness he eventually went to Basle where he died (Hans Dür), probably not long after January 1559, for his name still appears in the official list (cf. below, p. 355) compiled at Aarau about that date.

Emden, B I a & b; Frankfort, B III; Aarau, A I a & b; Basle.

192. HARVEL (HAREWELL, HAVELL), RICHARD: *Student and gent*. Of Besford, Worcestershire.

Eldest son of Edmond Harewell of Besford (Harl. Soc. XXVII, 72) and brother of Edmond, 'alias Sigismund', Harvel, Knight of the Bath (*ibid.*), and English envoy to Venice under Henry VIII and

---

[1] If this 'one Hart' of no Christian name is Roger Hart.

Edward VI, though he never seems to have attained to the full status of ambassador (*Ven. Cal.* 1534–54, p. 147; p. 292, N.B.). His house in Venice was a favourite resort of travelling Englishmen (Cam. Misc. x, 8) and also, says Church (*Ital. Reform.* p. 150), 'a refuge for evangelicals far and wide', among whom his brother Richard was probably one. That the latter was in exile under Mary we know from a letter of Lever's to Bullinger (Geneva, 17 January [1555], *O.L.* I, 158), in which Harvel is spoken of as 'a pious and worthy man' who 'having left England...for the sake of religion and learning' was then on his way to Zurich to meet Bullinger. In 1558, a Richard 'Havell', almost certainly the same man, was again at Geneva, where he was received as a 'resident' on 24 October (f. 264), though his name does not appear in the Livre des Anglois.

Geneva, A IV b; Zurich, A VIII a.

193. HARVEY, NICHOLAS: (?)*Gent.* Of Brockley, Somerset.

This man, who had arrived at Geneva before 13 October 1555, we believe to have been, not the nameless Harvey who was suspended from the ministry in 1576 (*Annals*, II, ii, 61), but the Nicholas Harvey of Somerset who purchased the manor of Brockley from Richard Pyke and was grandfather of the Nicholas Harvey, student of Brasenose and of the Middle Temple (1591), who was living in 1623 (Harl. Soc. XI, 47 and Foster, II, 667). Sir Thomas Hoby, on Friday, 18 August 1553, mentions a 'Mr Harvie' who was then with them in Brussels and may be the same man. William Thomas, Clerk of the Council, and later a conspirator, was also of the company (Cam. Misc. x, 96).

Geneva, A IV a.

194. HAWKES, PETER: *Cobbler.*

Was registered as a member of Knox's congregation on 7 June 1557 and received as a 'resident' of Geneva on the following 14 October (f. 197), when he was described as 'cordonnier'.

Geneva, A IV a & b.

195. HETON (EATON, ETTON), GUY (GUIDO), B.D.: *Ex-religious.* Wife. d. 1577.

This man appears from Foster (*Alum. Oxon.* II, 467), who calls him 'Guy Etton', to have been an ex-Franciscan who received his B.D. from Oxford in January 1534/5, and was archdeacon of Gloucester and chaplain of Bishop Hooper (see Baskerville, *E.H.R.* XLIV, 2–3) until the accession of Mary when, deprived for marriage, he withdrew to the Continent. He left London about 29 May 1554, as the bearer of a letter to Bullinger from Hooper, who speaks of him as 'my friend Guido, my most faithful associate in the labours of the Gospel' (*O.L.* I, 103). He probably arrived at Strasbourg just before 9 July, in the group with Haddon (*q.v.*) and Banks (*q.v.*), and in November, as Guido Eaten, was one of those who signed Strasbourg's admonition to Frankfort (*T.* p. 23). His name is also found in the official list, preserved at Stuttgart (Facsimile, Bodleian MS. German C. 10), of those English exiles who benefited by the Duke of Württemberg's gift of 200 gulden. Because, as it says, Heton 'had a wife and was poor', he received 18 gulden, the second largest share in the apportionment, and his signature as 'Guido Heton' is appended to the exiles' letter of thanks (*ibid.*).[1] After his return to England Heton again became archdeacon of Gloucester, and gave his weight to the Calvinistic party in the church, signing the petition of 1562 for a discipline (*Annals*, I, i, 512).

Strasbourg, A VII c; B III a.

196. HETON, THOMAS: *Gent. and merchant.* Of London. Wife. Still living, 1583.

Of the Lancashire family of the Hetons of Heton Hall (Chetham Soc. no. 81, p. 129) and in some degree a cousin of Thomas Lever whose mother was a Heton (*ibid.* p. 9). With his brother, George, he was one of the committee of 'sustainers' in 1554, and after his retirement to Strasbourg he kept his house always open to his distressed countrymen. There his first official appearance was on 4 April 1554, when he petitioned the Council for burgher rights with special exemption from the oath (below, p. 362); the only other mention of him in the protocols is on 5 December 1558, when he thanks the magistrates for their hospitality through the 'four years' of exile (*ibid.* p. 372). But on 29 September 1557 he had signed Strasbourg's letter of reconciliation to Frankfort (*T.* p. 174), and from the Zurich letters (I, p. 9) we find that he was still in Strasbourg on 26 January 1558/9. On his return to England, Heton as 'governor of the merchants' (*G.* p. 127) became one of the promoters of a scheme for making Emden a rival port to Antwerp by transferring there a body of English merchants. And in this curious financial-religious project (1563) Utenhovius, introduced to the merchants by Bishop Grindal, was involved as the agent of Anne of Oldenburg, in whose territory Emden lay. Perhaps its ultimate failure was quite as much responsible for Heton's financial straits in 1573 as his earlier generosity to the exiles though that is undeniable. Thomas Sampson was obliged to intercede for him with Cecil, asking that he might be allowed to transport some

---

[1] Facsimile in the Bodleian, press mark, 'Autographs I' R. Pal. fol. 180.

thousands of English cloth 'without paying of custom' (*Annals*, II, i, 397–8). But it is plain that in 1583 he had not recovered, for Grindal in his will (1583) remits unto his 'loving friend, Mr Thomas Eaton', the 'fifty pounds which he oweth unto me' (*G.* p. 604).

Strasbourg, A VII a; B III a.

197. HILLES (HILL, HYLLS), JOHN: *Student*.

Though Richard Hilles the merchant had a son John (Harl. Soc. I, 50) it is not very likely that he was in Frankfort in 1557. The exile was probably the 'John Hylls' who matriculated from Jesus College, Cambridge, in 1549 (Venn, II, 371). His first appearance at Frankfort is on the tax-list of January 1557, where he is said to have had 'usually nothing' in the way of property (Jung, p. 30). In June of that year he was living in the house of William Master (*H.S.P.* IV, 88); and on his return to England was very probably the John Hill whom Grindal ordained priest in March 1561 (*G.* p. 74) and who, in 1562, as 'Johan. Hylls' signed the Articles as 'proc. cleri. Oxon.' (*Annals*, I, i, 490).

Frankfort, A III a 3, 4 & b 2.

198. HILLIARD, NICHOLAS: *Painter*(?). Of Exeter(?). 1537–1619.

Though there is nothing to prove, neither is there anything to disprove, the identification of this man who became a member of Knox's congregation in May 1557 with Nicholas Hilliard the Elizabethan painter of miniatures, who was a younger son of Richard Hilliard of Exeter (*D.N.B.*). A Peter Hilliard, possibly his brother, was apparently either a fugitive or a 'masterless servant' at Calais, as early as 6 March 1554/5 (*For. Cal.* 1553–8, p. 158), and both may have taken part in the Western Rising of the previous year. If born in 1537 (cf. *D.N.B.*), Nicholas would then have been seventeen, a ripe age for sedition, and twenty on his arrival in Geneva, if, that is, the two Nicholas Hilliards were one person.

Geneva, A IV a.

199. HILTON, JOHN: *Student and ex-religious*. Of Norfolk. 1587(?).

Very possibly the John Hylton who had been a Franciscan of Northampton (8th Rep. Dep. Keeper of Records, App. II, p. 34). He first appears at Frankfort on 27 August 1555, when he signed Whittingham's letter of secession (*T.* p. 55). On the following 13 October he became a member of the English congregation at Geneva and on the 24th was received as a 'resident' of the city (f. 123). He may easily be the nameless Hilton who became chaplain to the Earl of Sussex, but whom Parkhurst refused to admit to the living of Diss in Norfolk for lack of a university degree (*Annals*, II, i, 327). According to Cooper, however, a 'John' Hilton did become rector of Diss in 1572 (Cooper, I, 509). Possibly he was the father of a John Hilton, B.A., of St John's College, Cambridge, in 1575, who denied the divinity of Christ (*ibid.* and Venn, II, 375) and was forced to recant.

Frankfort, B III a; Geneva, A IV a & b.

200. HINDESON (HYNDISON), BERNARD: *Labourer.*

Erroneously transcribed as 'Hurdeson' in Burn (p. 10). He was received into the English congregation on 7 June 1557 and as a 'resident' of Geneva on the following 14 October, when he is registered as 'laboureur' (f. 197).

Geneva, A IV a & b.

201. HOBBES, JOHN: *Servant.*

In the service of Henry Parry (*q.v.*) at Frankfort (*H.S.P.* IV, 88 and Jung, p. 52) and probably the son or brother of Leonard Hobbes (below).

Frankfort, A III a 4 & b 2.

202. HOBBES, LEONARD: *Servant.* Wife.

Also in the household of Henry Parry with his wife Joanna (*ibid.*). Neither John nor Leonard signed the 'discipline'.

Frankfort, A III a 4 & b 2.

203. HOBY, Sir PHILIP: *Gent.* Of Bisham Abbey, Berkshire. 1505-58.

Son of William Hoby of Leominster, Hereford, by his first wife Catherine Foster (Cam. Misc. x, Pedigree opp. p. xvi). A holder of abbey lands of which his manor of Bisham was part. Under Henry VIII, he had been sent on diplomatic missions, and under Edward was appointed ambassador resident in Flanders in May 1553. But at the accession of Mary his credentials were revoked (25 August 1553, *For. Cal.* 1553-8, p. 8) and he returned home, though he does not seem to have been held in disfavour until the spring of 1554. Then he fell under the royal displeasure with the Earl of Bedford. They had both been commissioned to conduct the 'Prince of Spaine' into England, 'but that determination', says Sir Thomas Hoby, 'was no more spoken of after Sir Thomas Wiatt was onse uppe in Kent...' (Cam. Misc. x, 97). Evidently he was regarded with suspicion of complicity and so found it prudent to withdraw to the Continent. Sir Thomas continues in his diary: 'My brother, disapointed (*sic*) of this his journey into Spaine... by long sute bothe unto the Quene's Majesty and the Counsell, obtayned license to go visitt the baynes of beyond the sees, for the better recoverie of a certaine old disease of his...' (*ibid.* p. 103).

This account of his departure from England puts the matter in rather a different light from that given in the *D.N.B.*, which oddly enough makes no reference to Sir Thomas Hoby's journal. There it is stated that Sir Philip, having regained the royal favour, was again sent to Brussels on a diplomatic mission (IX, 949). To Brussels he certainly went; and there, on 4 July, he delivered to the Lady Regent the queen's 'letters of credence' (Cam. Misc. x, 104). But that these were little more than letters of introduction and implied no ambassadorial mission would seem to be proved by the Hobys' departure for Italy four days afterwards (*ibid.*). Evidently it was Queen Mary's policy, where possible, to cover with an air of legitimacy the wanderings of political suspects, lest their presence abroad should indicate the degree of unrest at home. So Courtenay was to be treated, and so, with the prestige of official courtesies exchanged, the Hobys continued their journey to Padua, where they arrived on 23 August (*ibid.* p. 116). There they were welcomed by a group of Englishmen, fugitives guilty of actual treason, whose names would have been lost but for the faithful record of Sir Thomas Hoby. Several of them, including Sir John Cheke, joined the pleasure trip to Mantua which the Hobys indulged in in that autumn (*ibid.* pp. 117–19). But the winter of 1554–5 was spent at Padua itself, and in great intimacy with Sir John Cheke if not actually in the same house with him (*For. Cal.* 1553–8, pp. 173–4). In July they began to make their way northward, stopping at Frankfort in September (Cam. Misc. x, 120, 123), where Sir Thomas noted the presence of English 'men and womenn to the number of on (*sic*) hundrethe'; then on to Brussels again, where Sir Philip, before returning to England, evidently felt it wise to get an assurance of safety from King Philip, who promised that 'he might firmly rely on his [the king's] favour' (*Ven. Cal.* 1555–6, p. 258). This precaution recalls that of Sir Peter Carew (*q.v.*) in like case; while the action of Philip confirms the Venetian ambassador's assertion that he tried to curry favour with important Englishmen who might in the future prove of use to him. Whether or not Sir Philip's effort to get in touch with Edward Courtenay at this time had in it any political significance we cannot say, but his wish for the safety of the Earl of Devon's 'person' shows how well known was the latter's fear of foul play (*ibid.* p. 254).

The Hobys left for England on 7 January (*ibid.* p. 308), and three years later, on 29 May 1558,[1] Sir Philip, the friend of Titian and Aretino (*ibid.* p. 253, note), was dead.

Padua, B IV b; B v b 3; *D.N.B.*

[1] The *D.N.B.* gives 31 May, but Sir Thomas Hoby, who was with his brother at the time, gives 29 May (Cam. Misc. x, 127).

204. HOBY, THOMAS: *Gent.* Of Berkshire. 1530–66.

Half-brother to Sir Philip Hoby, and like him a cultivated gentleman of the Renaissance, 'wel lernd and languaged'—the translator
of *Il Cortegiano*. He was also, says his epitaph, of so comely a
shape, that it 'made ruful his end', that is, his early death in Paris.
The journal kept of his travels (Cam. Misc. x, 3–130) from the
year 1547 when he first went into Germany with John Abell (*q.v.*),
through 1555 when he travelled with Sir Philip to Italy and back,
has provided not only an invaluable source for the names of
English exiles of Padua and Frankfort, but also an authentic
calendar of their confused comings and goings. After Thomas
Hoby's return to England Sir William Cecil paid a visit to Bisham
Abbey in Lent 1557, bringing with him Lady Cecil's sister,
Elizabeth Cooke, daughter of Sir Anthony. And on returning to
London in May of the year following, Sir Thomas 'communed
with Mrs Elizabeth Cook in the way of mariage' to such good
purpose that their wedding took place five weeks later. In the
spring of 1566, Queen Elizabeth knighted him, then sent him to
France as her ambassador. But on 13 July he died in Paris,
leaving his 'woful wief' (then expecting a child) 'opprest with
heapes of grief'. She brought him back to Bisham Church for
burial, and there raised a magnificent monument to the two
brothers which happily still exists, and from the epitaph of which
I have quoted freely. The child when born was given the name of
Thomas Posthumous Hoby, and lived to grow up a Puritan of
more uncompromising stamp than his father.

Padua, B IV b; *D.N.B.*

205. HODGSTON, ROBERT: (?) *Gent. or physician.* Of London.

The identification here is by no means certain, there being two
possible candidates for the honour. The Robert Hodgston who
signed the 'new discipline' at Frankfort in December 1557 may
have been either the Robert Hodshon, Fellow of Merton, who took
his M.A. in 1535 and his 'B.Med.' in 1544 (Foster) and in the
register of Merton College is called 'medicus et uxoratus' (O.H.S.
IV, 257); or the Robert Hodgson or Hogeson, Esq., of London
who is listed among those assessed for the levies in 1574 (*Dom.
Cal.* 1547–80, p. 475) and who may have been a younger son of
Thomas Hodgeson of Yorkshire and his wife Agnes, daughter of
Robert Cooke of Essex (Harl. Soc. I, 46).

Frankfort, B III a.

206. HOLIDAY, ADAM: *Student.* Of Northumberland. d. 1590(?).

Under the name of Adam 'Hallidutz' he matriculated at the
University of Basle in 1555 (below, p. 357). In 1556 he went to

Geneva, where he became a member of the English congregation on 5 November of that year, and a 'resident' on 14 October 1557, when he registered himself as 'estudiant' (f. 196). On his return to England he was ordained deacon by Grindal in January 1559/60 (*Grindal*, p. 53), was given a B.D. by Cambridge in 1572, and between 1560 and 1590 was rector of Bishop Wearmouth and a prebendary of Durham (Venn, II, 392).

Basle, A II a; Geneva, A IV a & b.

207. HOLLINGHAM, JOHN: *Gent.*(?). Wife.

So far this man cannot be traced in England. His name appears at neither university. But he was among the earliest arrivals at Frankfort (3 December 1554, *T.* p. 26) and with Whittingham seceded from Frankfort in September 1555 (*T.* p. 55), arriving at Geneva on 13 October with 'Elene his wife and Daniel his sonne'. On 24 October he was received as a 'resident' of the city (f. 123) but without designation as to class.

Frankfort, B III a; Geneva, A IV a & b.

208. HOOPER, DANIEL: *Student.*

The son of Bishop Hooper, and a minor. His mother, Anne Hooper (Anne de Tserclas;[1] cf. *O.L.* I, 108), reached Frankfort as early as 20 April 1554, but her son, who had been left behind in England, did not join her until the following 10 November (*O.L.* I, 113–14). After his mother's death, which occurred a year later (7 December 1555; cf. Jung, p. 52), Daniel went to live with Edward Oldsworth (*q.v.*) who, with Valerand Pullain, his mother's relative by marriage and Daniel's godfather, had been appointed his guardian.

Frankfort, A VIII a.

209. HOPKINS, RICHARD, Esq.: *Draper.* Of Coventry. Wife.

Sheriff of Coventry and mayor in 1554 (Rolleson and Reader, *Mayors, Bailiffs and Sheriffs of Coventry*, p. 3). On 27 January of that year he was committed to the Fleet on a charge of 'evyll relygion' (*P.C.A.* 1554–6, p. 94), but there can be little doubt, from the fact that Coventry was closely involved in Suffolk's second rising in January, that Hopkin's misdemeanour was complicity, actual or suspected, in that abortive insurrection (*Chron. Q. Jane*, pp. 113, 123–4). 'After great intercession' he was restored to liberty, whereupon, says Strype, he fled to Germany with 'his wife and eight children' (*Mem.* III, i, 227). By the records of Aarau

---

[1] But born de Tilly according to Jung (p. 52), which would suggest that she was a widow when Hooper married her.

we know that he settled in Basle, where he became 'a reliever of others' of his fellow-exiles. And that he was a man of substance would seem to be proved by the 'costly monument' which in 1830 still stood in the Drapers' or Lady Chapel of St Michael's, Coventry, to the memory of 'Richard Hopkins, Esq. and Mary his wife' (Smith, *History of Warwickshire*, p. 212).[1] A Nicholas Hopkins, very possibly a son of Richard, was mayor of the city in 1562 (Rolleson and Reader, *op. cit.* p. 3).   Basle, A 1 a & b.

210. HOPKINS, Thomas. Of Warwickshire. d. 1558(?).

One of the eight children of Richard Hopkins (above). He is mentioned in Hans Dür's list as a 'resident' of Aarau, and a son of Richard Hopkins of 'Basle'. In the official list he is named among those who had died (below, p. 356).   Aarau, A 1 a & b.

211. HORNE, Robert, B.D.: *Dean of Durham*. Of Cumberland. Wife. 1519(?)–80.

Son of John Horne of Cleator, Cumberland. Fellow of St John's College, Cambridge (1536) and B.D. in 1546 (Venn). In 1550 he became rector of All Hallows, Bread Street, and chaplain to Edward VI, while the year following he was made dean of Durham, though much against the will of the chapter. In fact it required the special intervention of Cecil to ensure his being received and treated well (Cat. of Lansdowne MS. 981, no. 117, f. 194). Northumberland, who had thought to use him, finding himself in error, complained of Horne as 'this pevishe Dean' (S.P. Dom. Edw. VI, vol. xv, no. 62). Upon Mary's accession he was promptly summoned before the Privy Council on 15 September 1553, upon an unstated charge (*P.C.A.* 1552–4, p. 349). When he failed to appear, a second summons followed on 7 October (*ibid.* p. 355). But between these two dates Horne seems to have made good his escape to the Continent, probably leaving in John à Lasco's company, for he claimed afterward that he had received but one of the Council's letters and that 'on the road'. Burnet says that after he had reached safety he published an 'apology' for leaving England which admits that 'there were some crimes against the state objected to him' (Burnet, *History of the Reformation*, II, 403–4). And this admission, together with his precipitate flight, would imply that he had shared in the compromising activities of Archbishop Holgate.

Once abroad, having passed by Strasbourg to see Peter Martyr, Horne made his way to Zurich, where he arrived on 5 April 1554

---

[1] Whether still standing or not, I cannot ascertain.

(*Diarium*, p. 46 and *O.L.* II, 751–2), and where he stayed until called by Cox to Frankfort to assist in the revision of the English liturgy in the spring of 1555. There in Frankfort on 5 April he was one of the signatories to Cox's summary of that revision, sent to Calvin (*O.L.* II, 755), but he did not subscribe to Whitehead's letter of further justification sent in the following September (*ibid*. p. 763). He had, however, remained in Frankfort, where in the autumn he was chosen reader of Hebrew in the 'university' newly constituted by the exiles (*T*. p. 60). In November (?) his name appears on the Standesliste, and in October of the following year on the Steuerliste, where his taxable property is rated at 100 florins. By this time he was already pastor of the English congregation, having succeeded Whitehead in that office on 1 March 1556 (*T*. p. 62). But even among his brethren in exile Horne's reputation did not pass unchallenged: before entering upon his duties he felt it necessary that his name be 'cleared off certaine suspitions which some had bruted to the discredit off his ministerie' (*ibid*.). It is not unlikely that these suspicions concerned his administration, jointly with Richard Chambers, of the exiles' common purse, and that they were eventually the cause of the obscure but momentous quarrel between Horne and Thomas Ashley (*q.v.*) which broke out at supper on the night of 13 January 1557 (*T*. p. 62). If so, then the dissensions in the congregation to which this personal quarrel gave rise originated in a dispute over the allocation of public moneys—a cause both characteristic of Englishmen and prophetic. For it followed quickly upon this dispute, and by significant steps taken in rapid succession between 29 January and 2 February, that a religious congregation composed of fugitive Englishmen declared itself a body politic whose decrees had the force of law, binding alike upon congregation and pastor: 'the churche', declared the congregation of Frankfort, was 'aboue the pastor and not the pastor aboue the churche...' (*T*. p. 77). And thus in the space of seventeen days a democratic revolution had been effected and the first Bible Commonwealth been born. Whatever links with a Germanic past may lie behind it, the immediate prototype of the New England *town meeting*, composed of church members, came into existence by majority vote among Englishmen exiled in Germany, on Sunday, 30 January 1557 (*T*. pp. 70–2, 77). Thereupon Horne resigned, refusing to concur in 'the vaine shadowe onelie off authoritie' that was left him. And his resignation precipitated a struggle over the enactment of a 'new discipline' which was in reality an attempt, not over-scrupulous in method, to embody the results of the revolution in fundamental law. Throughout this 'hot stirre' Horne conducted himself with a lack of dignity bordering on the ludicrous and was eventually superseded in office.

But when the 'discipline' was finally adopted about 1 April he is found living in the same house with John Binks the merchant and three others, and there he remained until after 10 June (*H.S.P.* IV, 88). Then, as secretly and expeditiously as he had left England, he and Chambers left Frankfort for Strasbourg 'earely in a morninge' and without 'leaue takinge off the congregation', leaving behind them 'an accoumpt, which by cuttinge owte the leaues, and newe written, semethe not to be nowe at the last as it was at the firste...' (*T.* p. 178). What followed in Horne's life abroad is obscure. According to the Matrikel of the University of Basle he was a student there through the winter of 1558–9, paying his VI sol for matriculation (below, p. 357). But just before the death of Mary he and Chambers both appear at Geneva, having just completed a financial visitation of the English colonies (*T.* p. 186). How such double rôles were played remains the secret of the English exiles.

Early in 1559 Horne was back in England, where he was restored to his deanery of Durham. Also in March 1559 he was one of the protestant disputants at the Conference of Westminster; and in 1561 was elevated to the see of Winchester. It is a fact curiously in keeping with his earlier history that after his death in 1580 his goods were seized for debts to the Crown (*D.N.B.*).

> Zurich, VIII a, b, c; Frankfort, III a 2, 3, 4 & b 1, 2; B III; Strasbourg; Aarau and Geneva, B III b; Basle, A II a; *D.N.B.*

212. HORNEBY, NICHOLAS: *Student.*

Fellow of Peterhouse, Cambridge, 1531–43 (Venn, II, 407). He retreated to Frankfort, where in 1555 he is listed among the 'students' in the Standesliste. Thereafter he disappears. He may have been a brother or relative of the Robert Horneby below.

> Frankfort, A III a 1 & b 1.

213. HORNEBY, ROBERT: *Gent.*

Groom of the Chamber to the Princess Elizabeth while she was at Woodstock (Foxe, VIII, 580; cf. *Mem.* III, i, 343). On 29 April 1555 Horneby was 'convented before the Lords for his eronyouse opynions' and though 'muche travayled with' was found obstinate and committed to the Marshalsea (*P.C.A.* 1554–6, p. 119). Subsequently he was released upon the intervention of Dr Martin (*Mem.* III, i, 130–1), but he may afterwards have been involved in the Dudley conspiracy, or suspected of complicity in it, for it is not until June 1557 that he is found as a refugee at Frankfort, where he was living in the inn with John Geoffrey (*H.S.P.* IV, 89).

> Frankfort, A III a 4 & b 2.

214. HORSEY, Edward: *Gent.* Of Dorset and Somerset(?).
    d. 1582.

Son of Jasper Horsey of Exton (Somerset?). In 1551 he had been
one of the gentlemen in the train of the Marquis of Northampton
on his embassy to France (Cam. Misc. x, 66–7), but on 4 April
1556 he is named by Machyn (p. 103) among 'serten gentyllmen,
the whyche [fled] over the see, as trayturs'. He and his brother
both joined the disaffected under Dudley in France, and with
Dudley interviewed the French king at Amboise about 12 April
(*For. Cal.* 1553–8, p. 222). The following January Wotton reported
that the 'elder Horsey' was, he believed, married in Normandy
(*ibid.* p. 284), and he may then have made his peace with the queen
and returned to England for no more is heard of him abroad.
Under Elizabeth he was made governor of the Isle of Wight—an
easy base for his piratical operations against Spain (*Dom. Cal.*
1547–80, p. 324)—and there in 1580 he and Cornelius Stevenson
(*q.v.*), once of Knox's church in Geneva and probably a German
or Fleming, set up works for the making of saltpetre (*ibid.* p. 658).
He had previously been entrusted with several diplomatic missions,
to France in 1573 (*For. Cal.* 1572–4, nos. 1067–9) and more than
once to the Netherlands; and the *D.N.B.* speaks of him as a
confidant of Leicester. His epitaph was, and may be still, in the
church at Newport in the Isle of Wight (Kempe's Loseley MSS.
pp. 491–2), where the editor says that he died in 1582[1] (cf.
D.N.B.'s '1583').   France, B iv b & c; B v b 1, 2 & c; *D.N.B.*

215. HORSEY, Francis: *Gent.* Of Dorset and Somerset(?).

Younger brother of Edward Horsey, and like him not only involved
in the Dudley conspiracy, but also a fugitive in France, where he,
too, had gone in 1551 with the Marquis of Northampton (Cam.
Misc. x, 67). Though I have found no record of his activities under
Elizabeth, he probably shared in his brother's half-legitimate, half-
piratical attacks upon Spain.   France, as above.

216. HORTON, Thomas: *Deacon and student.* Of Derbyshire.
    d. 1564.

Probably the second son of John Horton of Catton, Derbyshire
(Venn, ii, 411). A scholar from Eton admitted at King's College
in 1537, when he was seventeen (*ibid.*). He received his M.A. from
Pembroke College, Cambridge, in 1549; and on 10 August 1550
was ordained deacon by Ridley (*Mar. Reac.* p. 189). He is not
found living abroad until 1556, when he appears at Frankfort in

---

[1] As does also *Misc. Gen. and Her.* 2nd ser. ii, 43.

the tax-list of October as 'studiosus' who 'hat sonst nichts dann bucher' (Jung, p. 29). But he had previously been one of the most active of the exiles' messengers, having 'used oftentimes to travel between Germany and England' for their 'behoof and sustenance' (Foxe, VIII, 576). Perhaps after 1556 he found this occupation too dangerous; yet it is interesting to find him in June 1557 as an inmate of the house of Robert Harrington (*q.v.*) who, as one of the original committee of 'sustainers', may have directed his journeyings back and forth. On his return to England, Horton was ordained priest by Grindal on 31 March–1 April 1560 (*Grindal*, p. 58; cf. *Mar. Reac.* p. 189, n. 1). In that same year he was made a prebendary of Durham (Le Neve, III, 316) and rector of St Magnus, London (Venn). Was he possibly the ancestor of Thomas Horton, regicide?

Frankfort, A III a 3, 4 & b 2.

*HOTSON, William.

An agent of anti-Spanish propaganda who in the spring of 1554 was operating in Dantzig, where he had had published by a local printer, who knew no English, a libel against Queen Mary and Philip, of which one hundred copies were strewn in the London streets. Dantzig had afterwards to apologize to the English government for the failure in supervision which permitted the attack to be issued and circulated. It is doubtful, however, whether Hotson should be numbered among the exiles, for he is not heard of elsewhere abroad, and his true base of operations was probably in England (*For. Cal.* 1553–8, nos. 238–9, p. 105).

217. HOUGHTON, John: *Servant.*

As 'servant' to Francis Withers, Houghton was received as a member of the English congregation at Geneva, on 5 November 1556.

Geneva, A IV a.

218. HUGH (HUGHES, HEWYS), Cuthbert: *Student.* Of Yorkshire.

Probably the son of William Hugh or Hughes, a divine of Yorkshire who was educated at Oxford (1543) and became chaplain to Lady Denny, to whom he dedicated the second part of his *Troubled man's medicine* (*Ath. Oxon.* I, 182; Herbert's Ames, I, 579 and II, 876; Bale, *Scriptores*, Cent. IX, p. 755). His son, Cuthbert Hugh, may have been the 'comes Hugo' mentioned by Bullinger as arriving at Zurich with Thomas Lever on 10 March 1554 (*Diarium*, p. 46). That winter, as 'Cutbertus Hugonijus, Eboracensis', he is found as a student at the University of Basle (below, p. 357), where his presence was perhaps responsible for the arrival of the three sons of Sir Anthony Denny at the university in the following winter.

Basle, A ɪɪ a.

219. HUMPHREY (UMPHREY, etc.), LAURENCE: *Student.* Of Buckinghamshire. 1527(?)–88/9.

Born at Newport Pagnell, Bucks.; a demy at Magdalen College, Oxford, in 1546, and Fellow from 1548 to 1556. The circumstances of Humphrey's life from 1553 onward, however, are so confused and contradictory that it will require more research to arrive at the truth than has been possible for this biographical note. About 1552 he is said by Bloxam to have taken Holy Orders (*Demies*, ɪv, 105), but his name does not appear either as deacon or priest in the list of those ordained under Edward VI (*Mar. Reac.* pp. 181–218). And although, as H. A. Wilson says (*Magd.* p. 102), Humphrey 'manages' to suggest that he was himself one of the Fellows expelled from Magdalen in the Visitation of Gardiner (1553) it is obvious from the college records that this is not true, for he was one of the twenty Fellows present at the mass de Spiritu Sancto celebrated at the election of Haddon's successor in the presidency on 31 October, and himself took part in the election (*ibid.*). But it is said by Bloxam (*op. cit.* ɪv, 104) that on 27 September Humphrey had been granted leave of absence to study abroad subject to official consent, a consent which he would seem to have obtained, since it was renewed on 24 December 1554 and again on 15 June 1555. Money was also allowed him to defray the cost of his studies, though with the proviso that he should not frequent 'those places that are suspected to be heretical' (*ibid.* p. 105). How the authorities, since they were obviously in communication with him, could fail to know that Humphrey had already frequented both Zurich and Basle, is one of the unsolved puzzles of the Marian Exile. In fact, at some date after 31 October 1553 (see above) he left England and by way of Strasbourg made straight for Zurich where he arrived with Horne's party of students on 5 April 1554 (*Diarium*, p. 46 and *O.L.* ɪɪ, 751). He was still there on 13 October, if we may trust the evidence of his signature to the letter of that date written by the 'Students of Zurich' to Frankfort (*T.* p. 16). And since he apparently never went to Frankfort (cf. Jung's list) he presumably remained at Zurich until the autumn of 1555, when he entered himself as a student at the University of Basle (Matrikel, below, p. 357). Thus the Matrikel itself refutes the general belief (cf. *D.N.B.*) that Humphrey went to Basle before he went to Zurich. Even after his year of study there was over, he would seem to have stayed on with Froben the printer (Tanner, p. 421) and may possibly at the same time have earned his livelihood and helped John Foxe with his *Book of Martyrs*. Some time during his years abroad he married, but where, or when, or whom, has not yet been discovered (Wilson, *Magd.* p. 116). The next known date in his life is that of 28 April (not the 23rd as given by Burn and *D.N.B.*) 1558, when he appeared at Geneva with Robert Blackman and was admitted into the English congregation. But Martin does not connect his name with the Geneva Bible, and Humphrey returned to Basle, where he was still living on 23 June 1559 (*Z.L.* II, 20). On his return to England he was appointed Regius Professor of Divinity at Oxford in 1560 and a year later became President of Magdalen. There, according to Wood (*Ath. Oxon.* I, 559), he 'did...stock his college with a generation of nonconformists' and in 1565 proved so intransigent in his opposition to vestments, that he found it advisable to retire for a time to the house of that Mistress Warcup (below, p. 198) who had once sheltered Jewell (Parker, I, 368).

Zurich, A VIII a, b, c; Basle, A II a; Geneva, A IV a; *D.N.B.*

220. HUNTINGDON (HUNTINGTON), JOHN: *Student and preacher*. Of Somerset(?). Wife. d. 1582(?).

Educated at Oxford but took no degree. Wood calls him 'a tolerable poet' (*Ath. Oxon.* I, 241); and Bale 'meus in Christo filius' (*Scriptores*, p. 742), since he believed that it was his own reply to Huntington's *Genealogy of Heretics* (1540) which converted the latter to protestantism. In 1547 Huntington was preaching at Boulogne apparently in support of the Reformation (*D.N.B.*), and on 20 November 1553 he was arraigned before the Privy Council as 'a seditiouse preacher remayning nowe about Lynne and Walsingham' (*P.C.A.* 1552–4, p. 369) who had 'made a rayling ryme against Doctour Stokes and the Blissed Sacrament'. However, on his promise to amend 'aswell in doctryne as lyving', he was dismissed on 3 December (*ibid.* p. 375). A year later (23 November 1554) he is found as a refugee at Strasbourg (*T.* p. 23) and in the list of needy English students sent that autumn to the Duke of Württemberg, he is described as 'ein predikant' with a wife and children, on whose behalf he received 20 gulden, the largest donation made out of the Duke's fund for their relief (Württ. Staatsarchiv). By 30 August 1559 he was back in England, where at the funeral of Edmund Allen (*q.v.*) 'dyd pryche for hym master Hyntyngtun the prycher—the wyche' says Machyn in disgust 'he had a wyf and viij chylderyn' (p. 208). In 1560 Huntington was made a canon of Exeter, and during his lifetime held five livings in Devon and Somerset, four of them simultaneously.

B II; Strasbourg, B III a; A VII c; *D.N.B.*

221. HUTTON, ROBERT: *Deacon and student.* Of Yorkshire. d. 1568.

It is upon Wood's authority that Hutton, translator of the *Summ of Divinity* (1548), is included among the exiles (*Ath. Oxon.* I, 364). He was sizar of William Turner (*q.v.*) when the latter was a Fellow of Pembroke College, Cambridge, but does not appear to have taken any degree (Venn, II, 443). On 2 July 1553 he was ordained deacon at York Minster (*Mar. Reac.* p. 218), and it is not unlikely that he was the same person as the Robert Hutton, described as 'chambre keper' to Sir Thomas Benger, who was apprehended with the latter on 28 April 1557 and committed to the Fleet (*P.C.A.* 1556–8, pp. 81, 82). If the two Huttons are one, then it would mean that he did not go abroad before 1557, when he seems to have attached himself again to William Turner, who was probably then living at Emden. At Elizabeth's accession Hutton returned to England and from 1560 to 1568 was rector of Little Braxted in Essex, and of Wickham Episcopi (Venn). Upon his death in 1568 he was buried in the church of St Mary-le-Bow (Venn).

Emden (?); *D.N.B.*

222. IRELAND, WILLIAM: *Student and ex-religious.* d. 1570–71.

Very possibly a former Benedictine of Ramsey Abbey, co. Huntingdon, who in 1553 was still receiving a pension (Browne Willis, *Abbies*, I, 156 and II, 67). In 1547 he was a Fellow of St John's College, Cambridge, where he was educated under Roger Ascham, who afterwards remained his friend. Cooper (*Ath. Cant.* I, 291–2) does not state that he went into exile under Mary, but he is found listed among the 'students' at Frankfort in 1555. Where he went after that is not known, though he must have left Frankfort before 16 October 1556, when the English residents were again listed for purposes of taxation (Jung, pp. 29–30). On his return to England he became rector of Chelmsford in Essex (20 February 1560–61; cf. Newcourt, I, 800 and II, 129).

Frankfort, A III a 2 & b 1.

223. ISAAC, EDWARD: *Gent.* Of 'Wel' and Patricksbourn, Kent. Wife.

A purchaser of chantry lands in seven counties (*Mem.* II, i, 368), whose wife was probably Margaret, daughter of Sir Thomas Wrothe (Harl. Soc. XIII, 330, 331). He was early associated with the Reformation and an intimate friend of Latimer, with whom in 1532 he went to Newgate to visit a man condemned for heresy (*Mem.* III, i, 372–3). He was also, according to Foxe, the patron of Edwin Sandys (*q.v.*), whose departure from England Isaac assisted, and to whom he entrusted his eldest son. Indeed, Sandys, at Strasbourg, would seem to have lived upon Isaac's bounty (Foxe, VIII, 597–8), but Isaac himself went as a fugitive to Frankfort and it was at Frankfort, Foxe says, that this son died (*ibid.*). He was certainly not living in his father's house on 10 June 1557, when the dwelling-list was compiled, for at that time Isaac had with him but three daughters.

The first mention of his name in the *Troubles* is in connection with the Horne-Ashley quarrel of 1557, when Isaac was a senior of the congregation and a supporter of Horne; but he had been living continuously in Frankfort from the early days of the colony and was evidently from the first one of the leaders of the Prayer Book party. Knox accuses Isaac of being the chief informer against him before the magistrates in March 1555 (Laing, IV, 46 and note 1). In the autumn of that year his name appears on the Standesliste among the 'generosi' and he is said then to have been 'dwelling by the bridge' (Jung, p. 54). In 1556 he was one of the gentlemen to whom letters were specially but ineffectually directed by the queen through the agency of John Brett (Brett, p. 116); and in December 1557 his rateable property was valued by the city at 5050 florins, showing that he was one of the richest Englishmen at Frankfort (Jung, p. 30). He refused in April 1557 to become a signatory of the 'new discipline' to which he had been steadily opposed (*T.* p. 168), but he remained in Frankfort until after 3 January 1558/9 when, as 'Edmond' Isaac, he subscribed to Frankfort's refusal to join Geneva in her proposed crusade against ceremonies (*T.* p. 190). After his return to England Isaac played but a small part in public affairs, though in the Bishops' Visitations of 1564 he is commended as 'a favourer [i.e. of the Gospel] and of goode truste' (Cam. Misc. IX, 63). He became sheriff of Kent in 1568/9 (Hasted, I, p. xci). Jung makes 'Edward' and 'Edmond' Isaac two separate persons, but they were undoubtedly, I think, one man, the names Edmond and Edward being then interchangeable.

Frankfort, A III a 2, 3, 4 & b 1, 2; B III a.

224. JACKSON, WILLIAM: *Student*(?). Wife.

Perhaps this is the William Jackson who was Fellow of St John's College, Cambridge, in 1532, and received his M.A. in 1533. He is said by Venn to have been of the diocese of Coventry and Lichfield. With 'Parnel his wife' and four children, he arrived in Geneva in 1555, and on 13 October was received into the English congregation. One of his sons, also a 'William', may well have been the one of that name who matriculated from St John's in 1567 (Venn). The father, on 24 October, became a 'resident' of Geneva (f. 123), but in 1557 may have gone on a journey, or sent his wife to Frankfort for some reason unknown, for in June of that year there is found dwelling in the same house with John Kelke and Laurence Kent a Mistress Jackson, wife of 'Jacson absentis' (*H.S.P.* IV, 89).

Geneva, A IV a & b.

225. JAMES, ARTHUR: *Servant.*

A 'servant' of Sir William Stafford who arrived with him in Geneva, at some date before 13 October 1555.

Geneva, A IV a.

JANSON, JOHN. *See* Johnson.

226. JEFFREY (GEOFRIE, GEFFRAI), JOHN: *Gent. and student.* Of Sussex. d. 1618(?).

This is probably the eldest son of Thomas Gefferey of Ripe in Sussex. If so, he was also first cousin to Sir John Jeffrey, Chief Baron of the Exchequer under Elizabeth (Harl. Soc. LIII, 46, 56). A John Jefferay, whom we presume to be the same man, matriculated from Michaelhouse, Cambridge, in 1546 and in 1552 became a Fellow of Trinity College (Venn, II, 465). He was probably one of the group of students chosen for education abroad, and the first appearance of his name occurs at Frankfort on 24 September, when he signed (as 'Geofrie') that congregation's invitation to John Knox (*T.* p. 20). By the following November, however, he had gone to Strasbourg, where on the 23rd he subscribed to the colony's letter of remonstrance to Frankfort (*T.* p. 23). And at Strasbourg he seems to have remained until the spring of 1557, when he was back in Frankfort as a signatory of the 'new discipline'. He was still there on 10 June, when, in company with Robert Horneby (*q.v.*), he is found living at the inn (*H.S.P.* IV, 89 and Jung, p. 49). After his return to England he was ordained priest at Norwich in 1561 (Venn). But it is not unlikely, since the dates make it possible, that he was also the John Jeffrey 'who had just previously' (1560) been made 'deacon-prebend' for Hurstbourn and Burbage in the diocese of Salisbury, and is described in a return for that year as 'diaconus non conjugatus, doctus, residens in Aula Regia praedicat licentiatus' (W. H. Jones, *Fasti Sarisberiensis*, p. 396). In 1566 he became rector of Berwick, Sussex, a living which he held until 1618, probably the year of his death (Venn).

Frankfort, A III a 4 & b 2; B III a & b; Strasbourg, B III a.

227. JEFFREYS, THOMAS: *Student.* Of Yorkshire.

M.A. from Clare Hall, Cambridge, in 1553 (Venn, II, 466). Abroad he lived at Strasbourg and there as 'Thomas Geffer' he received, in December 1554, a grant of 10 florins from the fund donated by the Duke of Württemberg (Württ. Staatsarchiv). His signature 'Thomas Jefferies' is attached to the letter of thanks written by John Ponet and sent to the duke (*ibid.*, and see Bodleian, 'Autographs', I, R. Pal. f. 180). In 1559 Grindal ordained him deacon and in 1561 he received from St John's College, Cambridge, the degree of B.D. Though Venn gives as his first cure that of Ashprington, Devon, in 1577, it is probable that he is the Thomas Geffreis who was rector of the little church of St Swithun, Hinton Parva, Wilts. in 1564 (cf. list of rectors in the church).

Strasbourg, A VII c.

228. JEWELL, JOHN, M.A.: *Priest.* Of Bude, Devon. 1522–71.

Fellow of Corpus Christi College, Oxford, 1542–3 and a pupil and friend of John Parkhurst (*q.v.*). Though the record of his ordination has been lost with that of his opponent in controversy, Thomas Harding, it seems to be accepted by Dr Frere that he did receive Edwardine orders (*Mar. Reac.* p. 119). About 1551 he was made archdeacon of Chichester and in that year rector of Sunningwell, Berks. (Foster). In April 1554 he acted as notary to Cranmer and Ridley in their disputation at Oxford (*Cranmer*, p. 483). But in the autumn of that year, like Barlow and Scory, he not only recanted but signed articles of recantation (*Mem.* III, i, 241 and *Cranmer*, p. 519). Soon afterwards, however, he fled from Oxford, and on his way to London was harboured by Mistress Anne Warcup, mother of Cuthbert Warcup (*q.v.*), the perpetual and ready friend of distressed gospellers (*Mem.* III, i, 227). While in London, according to Laurence Humphrey (*Vita Juelli*, pp. 82–3), he lodged with a merchant named Francis Goldsmith, and was given funds for his journey by Sir Nicholas Throckmorton (*ibid.*). It is believed that before he left Oxford Jewell had held some communication with Cranmer, then in prison there, and that he was the bearer of the archbishop's last letter to Peter Martyr at Strasbourg (Jewell's *Works*, IV, p. xii and *O.L.* I, 29). Hastings Robinson assigns this letter to the year 1555, and if his ascription is correct, then Jewell must have left London for the Continent perhaps late in January (1555) and gone directly to Strasbourg. Either Richard Cox had been in Jewell's company 'owte off Englande' (*T.* p. 38) or the two met in Strasbourg and were despatched together to Frankfort, where they arrived on 13 March (*ibid.*). But Frankfort gave Jewell no welcome. He was referred to indignantly as 'A stranger craftely brought in to preache, who had bothe byn at masse and also subscribed to blasphemous Articles' (*T.* p. 48). And although, on the advice of his friend

Richard Chambers, he made a public apology for his recantation, John Knox, as publicly, preached against him (*ibid.*), rousing the congregation's distrust to such a pitch that Jewell soon accepted Peter Martyr's invitation to become 'vice master', as Fuller calls it, in the latter's 'petty college in his house at Strasbourg' (Fuller, *History*, IV, bk VII, p. 230). On Peter Martyr's withdrawal to Zurich in July 1556 (cf. below, pp. 367–8) Jewell went with him, and from there it is said (*D.N.B.*) that he went to Padua on a visit, perhaps to study, but he is not listed among the students at the university during those years (cf. Andrich). The news of Queen Mary's death found him again at Zurich, whence he set out for England about 21 January, reaching Strasbourg five days later (*Z.L.* I, 6–7). In all, the journey to London took him fifty-seven days, and he arrived in England only on or just before 20 March (*ibid.* and p. 9), just in time to play his part as one of the disputants on the protestant side in the Conference of Westminster. On 21 January 1560 he was consecrated bishop of Salisbury (Le Neve, II, 606).

Strasbourg (?); Frankfort, B III a; Zurich, A VIII b; *D.N.B.*

229. JOHNS, THOMAS: *Gent.* Of Pembrokeshire(?).

A man difficult to identify who was received as a 'resident' of Geneva on 14 October 1557 (f. 196), and as a member of Knox's congregation on the following 20 November. We are inclined to think that he may be the Sir Thomas Johns of Stenton and Hermans Town in Pembrokeshire (Dwnn's *Pedigrees of Wales*, p. 98) who was made a member of King Edward's Council for the Marches of Wales in 1551 (*Mem.* II, ii, 161–2) and whose name frequently appears in connection with the charges made against Bishop Ferrar for maladministration of his diocese (Foxe, VII, 11, 12, 18–19). From Ferrar's own story (as related by Foxe) it is not clear whether Johns was the bishop's friend or adversary, but the fact that he arrived at Geneva at the same time as William Chambers (*q.v.*), who was probably Ferrar's 'servant' and enemy (*ibid.* p. 5), would tend to support the above identification and place Johns in the group of the bishop's opponents.

Geneva, A IV a & b.

230. JOHNSON, JOHN (John 'Janson'): *Merchant*(?). Of Glapthorne, Northamptonshire and London.

This person appears abroad but once, at Frankfort, when on 18 June 1556 he brought suit against the wife of Robert Harrington, widow of the martyr Laurence Saunders (Jung, pp. 54, 52). He then registered as of 'Glapthorne', which is in Northamptonshire. In spite of his unusually common name it seems possible to identify him as the John Johnson (evidently a London merchant) who in March 1553 was in debt to Sir William Cecil 'for the wools he had of Cecil's father' (*Salisbury*, I, 113), and in April was declared a bankrupt who owed John Utenhovius, of the Stranger's Church in London, the sum of £400 (*P.C.A.* 1552–4, p. 250).

Frankfort (see Jung's list of exiles).

231. JOHNSON, WILLIAM: *Priest*(?). Of Worcester(?). d. 1581.

Here identification is again somewhat hazardous, but we think it very likely that this man who arrived in Geneva on 5 January 1558 and was received into Knox's congregation on 2 June was the William Johnson, secular priest and unbeneficed, who was deprived in the diocese of Norwich in 1555 (Baskerville, *E.H.R.* 1933, p. 53). Again, a William Johnson of Worcester (quite possibly the same man) was educated at Cambridge and afterwards 'became Master of a Grammar School at Kilkenny in or before 1552' (Venn, II, 482). At Elizabeth's accession in 1559 he was made dean of Kilkenny (*ibid.*), and his record would suggest that he was also the Johnson who was Sir Thomas Smith's nominee (August 1573) for the headship of the free school of Aylsham in Norfolk to which Robert Harrison, associate of Robert Browne, was finally preferred.

Geneva, A IV a.

232. JONES, GALFRI (GEOFFREY): B.Civ.L., *Priest*. Of Wales. d. 1559/60.

This man, listed in the Emden catalogue of exiles, affords an interesting example of the policy of the Marian government in regard to married priests. In 1536–7 Jones received his B.Civ.L. from Cambridge, and eventually became rector of St Mary Woolchurch, London, from which, evidently on the score of marriage, he was deprived in 1554 (Venn, II, 485). He must however have done penance, for in the same year Bonner instituted him to the parish of St Swithin. Yet there, without record either of death or resignation, Jones is replaced in the living by a George Barton who retained it until his own deprivation in 1561 (Newcourt, I, 460, 543). Galfri Jones had simply disappeared, presumably to Emden, where his learning may have been requisitioned for the editing of Cranmer's *Defensio*. Though in 1559 he returned to England, he died on 23 January, 1559/60 and was buried at St Mary Woolchurch.

Emden(?), B I a & b.

233. JONES, GRIFFIN (GRIFFETH): *Merchant*(?). Of Bristol(?).

It might be supposed that this person listed by Bale (*Scriptores*, p. 742) was the same as the preceding, were it not that there was actually a 'Griffin' Jones, who was a citizen of Bristol and had the advowson in 1554 of the living of Tickenham in Somerset (Harl. MS. 6967: Register of Deprivations, diocese of Bath and Wells).[1] But more than this fact I have not been able to discover about him, nor any indication of his whereabouts abroad.

n.p.; B II.

234. JONES (JOHNS), THOMAS: *Gent.* (?). Of Cardiganshire (?). 1530–1620 (?).

It is just possible that this 'Thomas Jhones', who became a member of Knox's congregation in Geneva on 8 May 1557, was the Welsh bard and genealogist, Thomas Johns of Fountain Gate near Tregaron (Dwnn's *Welsh Pedigrees*, p. 45, n. 5 and *D.N.B.*), who considered himself to be a relative of Sir William Cecil. It is recorded that this Thomas Johns 'alias Cattye' stood in need of a pardon at the accession of Elizabeth, for his 'omnia escapia et cautiones'—a pardon which he obtained under the great seal on 1 January 1559–60 (*Notes and Queries*, 1st ser. II, 12), possibly through the influence of his 'cousin' Cecil.

Geneva, A IV a; *D.N.B.*

235. JOSEPH, JOHN, D.D.: *Ex-religious.* Of Kent. d. abroad (?).

Formerly Warden of the Grey Friars of Worcester (Baskerville, *Monks*, p. 238, note). He received his D.D. from Oxford in 1542 (Foster, II, 834) and in 1546 became rector of St Mary le Bow (*ibid.*). In the following year he was appointed by Cranmer one of the six preachers of Canterbury (*Cranmer*, p. 229). With Sir John Cheke and Richard Chambers he had been a witness at the trial of Gardiner in 1549 (Foxe, V, 770); and in 1550, the year that he was made a canon of Canterbury, he preached against the observance of Lent to Gardiner's great indignation (Foxe, VI, 32). Dixon calls him a 'fanatic' (IV, 146), and his deprivation as a married priest on 7 March 1554 is, apart from his marriage, not to be wondered at. Nor is his flight to the Continent, where his place of exile remains unknown. As he plays no part in the reign of Elizabeth, it is very possible that he died abroad.

n.p.; B I a & b; B II.

236. JOYNER, ROBERT: *Student and gent.* (?). Of Oxfordshire (?).

His only recorded appearance abroad was at Frankfort in December 1557, when he subscribed to the 'new discipline' with several members of the Strasbourg colony. In March–April 1560 a Robert Joyner, very probably the same man, received his ordination as deacon and priest at the hands of Grindal and at the same time as Richard Langhorne (*q.v.*) (*Grindal*, pp. 58–9). Quite possibly Joyner was a member of the Oxfordshire family of 'Joyner, alias

---

[1] This register of Bishop Bourne's has been printed in Dixon, IV, 152, note.

Lyde' which lived at Dorchester, and in which 'Robert' was a common name (Wood's *Life and Times*, O.H.S. III, 259 and Harl. Soc. v, 129). If so he would have been connected by marriage with the Skipwiths and so with Sir Peter Carew (see above).

Frankfort, B III b.

237. JUGGE, [RICHARD?]: *Printer*(?).

This man is listed among the 'preachers' on the Emden list, but without a Christian name. In the index to the Ecclesiastical History Society's edition of Strype's *Cranmer* he is identified as Richard Jugge the printer. But though the identification is very plausible, there is no direct evidence to support it. Richard Jugge the printer had been educated at Eton and King's College and was an original member of the Stationers' Company, named in their charter granted in May 1557 (Arber, I, p. xxviii). He may have taken it upon himself to 'prophesy' as well as to print, or the refugee may have been his son. In any case the whereabouts of Jugge 'abroad' are unknown, though it is quite possible that he was at Emden, where he may have assisted Egidius van der Erve in the preparation of the Emden edition of Cranmer's *Defensio* published in 1557 (cf. Colonel F. S. Isaac's Monograph, Bibliog. Soc. 1931, pp. 340, 351).

B I a & b; Emden (?).

238. KELKE, JOHN: *Merchant*(?). Of Bristol(?). Wife.

He cannot be identified as a relative of Roger Kelke below, but may possibly have been connected with the Thomas Kelke of Bristol who on 10 November 1555 was a prisoner in the Tower (*P.C.A.* 1554–6, p. 191) and discharged in the following December (*ibid.* pp. 205, 208). John Kelke first appears abroad at Frankfort on 27 August 1555, as a member of Whittingham's party (*T.* p. 55). But like Laurence Kent the merchant, who shared Kelke's house, he did not follow Whittingham to Geneva, though he must have absented himself from Frankfort temporarily since his name does not appear in the Standesliste. In 1557 he reappears at Frankfort in the tax-list of January, where his property is rated at 130 florins (Jung, p. 30), and in June he is found living with his wife and one maid in the over-crowded house that harboured twenty-two persons (*H.S.P.* IV, 89). With Kent he was a signatory of the 'new discipline'.

Frankfort, A III a 3, 4 & b 2; B III a.

**239. KELKE (KELBE, RELKUS), ROGER: *Student and gent.*
Of Lincolnshire. 1524–76.**

He was the fourth son of Christopher Kelke of Barnetby, Lincs. and Great Kelke, Yorks. (Harl. Soc. L, pt 2, pp. 556, 557), and therefore uncle of the Christopher Kelke who married Elizabeth, daughter of Sir Robert Carr of Sleaford and widow of William Fairfax. In 1545 Kelke was made a Fellow of St John's College, Cambridge (Venn, III, 3), receiving his M.A. there in 1547. It is therefore fair to suppose that he was one of the group of students who followed Thomas Lever, Master of St John's, to the Continent. He was not, however, one of the first company which arrived at Zurich with Robert Horne. Kelke made his first appearance there on 13 October (not 23rd as in *D.N.B.*) 1554, when he signed (as Roger Kelbe) the 'Students' equivocal answer to Whittingham's invitation to migrate to Frankfort (*T*. p. 16). From Zurich he went to Basle in the winter of 1555–6, where his name appears in the Matrikel of the university as Rogerus Kelkus, Anglus (below, p. 358), though without being followed by the 'vi sol' that indicates matriculation (*T*. p. 194). After his return to England Grindal ordained him priest in January 1559–60 (*Grindal*, p. 54), and in the same year he and 'one Makebray' (John Makebray? (*q.v.*)) were elected by the corporation of Ipswich as preachers and ministers of that town (Cooper, I, 342). Though Kelke survived Makebray in office, he was accused in 1562 of being a 'liar' and 'a preacher of noe trewe doctrine' (*ibid.*). Evidently he was a rigid nonconformist and as Master of Magdalene College, Cambridge, in 1565, went so far as to attempt, through Cecil, to stop the queen's proclamation for enjoining habits (*ibid.*). He was twice chosen vice-chancellor of the University.

Zurich, B III a; Basle, A II a; *D.N.B.*

240. KELLY, JOHN: '*Servant*'.

As 'page' to Sir John Borthwick (*q.v.*) he was received into Knox's congregation at Geneva with his master in 1556, at some date before 12 July.

Geneva, A IV a.

241. KELLY, WALTER: *Student*. Of Devon and Calais. Wife.

A member of the colony of Aarau, where he lived in the house of Hans Francken (cf. below, p. 356). No doubt he had been earlier at Wesel, for Hans Dür records that, though born in Devon, he had lived at Calais. He was one of those who, on 5 October 1557, signed Thomas Lever's letter of thanks to Bullinger for the latter's gift of money (*O.L.* I, 169–70). On his return to England he, as Walter 'Kelle', was ordained deacon by Grindal in April 1560 (*Grindal*, p. 59).

Wesel (?); Aarau, A I a & b.

242. KENT, LAURENCE: *Merchant*. Of Linford, Buckinghamshire. Wife.

Kent was one of the early arrivals at Frankfort, where his signature is found appended to that congregation's letter to Strasbourg, dated 3 December 1554 (*T*. p. 26). On 18 April 1555 he became a burgher of the city, registered as 'L. Kendt de Linfordt' and assessed 2 florins 8 albus Bürgergeld (Jung, pp. 24, 44). He was evidently a member of Whittingham's party since he signed their letter of secession on 27 August 1555 (*T*. p. 55), but he did not leave for Geneva until three years later. His name is found among the 'merchants' of the Standesliste that autumn and it must have been about the same time that his insistence on the baptism of a child of his according to the Genevan rite caused the 'seas' of dissension 'againe to swell' in that irascible congregation (*T*. p. 61). Kent would appear to have had his way, however, for John Makebray (*q.v.*) stood godfather to the child. In 1556, his taxable property was assessed at 300 florins (Jung, p. 29)—a modest sum for the support of the wife and six children who lived with him (and thirteen others) in John Kelke's house in the 'Kornmarck' (*H.S.P.* IV, 89 and Jung, p. 44). In the Horne-Ashley quarrel he is one of those to whom John Hales directly appealed with doubtful success for help in quieting the stir (*T*. p. 65). Kent signed the 'new discipline' in April, is found in the dwelling-list of June, but in the following spring went to Geneva, where with his wife and two children, William and Elene, he was received into the English congregation on 28 April 1558.

Frankfort, A III a 1, 2, 3, 4 & b 1, 2; Geneva, A IV a.

243. KETHE, WILLIAM: *Student and preacher.* Scot(?). Wife. d. 1608(?).

Author of the metrical version of the 100th psalm, known as 'Old Hundred'—'All people that on earth do dwell'. Though he is believed to have been born in Scotland he is described in the Registre des Habitants of Geneva as a 'native of Exeter' (f. 180). His first appearance abroad was at Frankfort in December 1554 (*T*. p. 26), and in August 1555 he signed the farewell letter of the disaffected followers of Whittingham. But as he did not go immediately to Geneva, he may have stopped for a time with John Foxe at Basle. Not until 5 November 1556 was he received with his wife into Knox's congregation, and he did not become a 'resident' of Geneva until the following 7 January (f. 180). It was in the late summer of that year (1557) that he and John Bodley 'travelled with' the exiled congregation of Wesel in search of the new home which was finally established at Aarau (*T*. p. 185). At Geneva he assisted in the translation of the Bible, but he also entered the political field when he prefaced Goodman's pamphlet on *Superior Powers* by a set of verses entitled *William Kethe to the Reader* (Maitland, *Essays*, pp. 88–90). The fall of Calais brought him even more hotly into the arena of politics with a metrical diatribe against Spain as bitter as the pamphlets of John Bradforth (*q.v.*). It seems that when Philip made his offer of aid in the recapture of Calais, a company of Londoners had been recruited for service over-seas which, according to Strype, included many gospellers (*Mem.* III, ii, 104). Goodman and Kethe suspected (and perhaps with reason) that they were being drawn forth 'out of their country' to 'please Jezebel'. Kethe protested with less of poetry than of righteous indignation that 'For England thus sold for Spaniards to dwell, Ye may not by right possess that ye sell' (*ibid.* p. 105).

After the death of Mary, Kethe was the bearer of Geneva's overtures of peace to the other English colonies (*T.* p. 186) and was in Strasbourg on 3 January 1559 and in Aarau on 16 January (*ibid.* pp. 190, 191). Though his letter of departure from Geneva is dated 30 May 1560, he lingered on there until 1561, possibly to see his metrical version of the psalms through the press (Neil Livingstone's preface to the reprint of the Psalms, 1635 ed. of the Scottish Psalter, p. 66, n. 80 and cf. Maitland, *Essays*, pp. 82–3), possibly also because of the hostility of Queen Elizabeth, whom he had provoked 'to issue out' certain 'angry declarations of her mind' (*Mem.* III, i, 132). Was there anything of the policy of her sister behind the fact that Kethe was appointed in 1563 preacher to the English army at Havre and again in 1569 to the forces sent to the north in the rebellion of that year? (*D.N.B.*).

Frankfort, B III a; Geneva, A IV a & b; B III a; *D.N.B.*

244. KILLIGREW, HENRY: *Gent.* Of Cornwall. d. 1603.

Younger brother of Peter Killigrew (*q.v.*) and fourth son of John Killigrew of Arwenack, Cornwall, Captain of Pendennis Castle (*Archaeologia*, XVIII, 99; Vivian's *Cornwall*, p. 268, and *P.C.A.* 19 April 1554, p. 12). In 1565 Henry married Catherine, fourth daughter of Sir Anthony Cooke. He was probably educated at Cambridge, was both musician and painter (Venn and Cooper, II, 348–9), and later became a benefactor of Emmanuel College, yet he was one of a family of pirates. In 1553 he was M.P. for Launceston; in the spring of 1554 he took part in the Western Rebellion and helped Sir Peter Carew to escape to France (*D.N.B.*), though he himself did not apparently become a fugitive until 1556, when he appears as one of Henry Dudley's accomplices at Paris (*For. Cal.* 1553–8, p. 238). At Whitsuntide the rebels sent him to Italy to enlist the support of Courtenay, Earl of Devon, then at Ferrara (*ibid.* p. 229). But the high hopes of Courtenay's co-operation were not fulfilled, and by July the rebels' base of activities had been removed from Paris to Rouen (*ibid*. p. 238), whence they were soon after making suit for pardon (*ibid*. p. 278) to Queen Mary. The family piracies, however, did not incline the queen to clemency in Henry's favour, though he himself seems not to have played any active part in them. So he was still in France at the battle of St Quentin in 1557 (*Memoirs of Sir James Melville*, p. 43, ed. 1735) and did not venture home until the accession of Elizabeth, whom he afterwards served as an able diplomatist (*D.N.B.*).

France, B v b 1, 3; *D.N.B.*

245. KILLIGREW, PETER: *Gent*. Of Cornwall.

The second son of John Killigrew of Arwenack (see above), and 'an old pirate, whose name and exploits are most notorious, and he is therefore in great repute and favour with the French' (*Ven. Cal*. 1555–6, p. 536). His piracies off the coast of Ireland, which had already given trouble to the government in the reign of Edward (*P.C.A*. 1552–4, p. 245), had now by 1554 become patriotic efforts against Spain. In March, Captain Crayer told Lord Grey that 'three ships of Englishmen' were 'already gone to the sea with Killegrew' (*For. Cal*. 1553–8, p. 66). In April, Wotton reported that 'The Killigrews with the Sacre have returned to Brest Haven again, and prepare to return to the sea' (*ibid*. p. 74); in October 1556, that this ship, which he now calls the 'Sacrette', had been a gift made directly by the King of France to the Killigrews (*ibid*. p. 261) and that with it and four or five barks, Killigrew had 'taken good prizes, trusting yet to take more, and in case the worst fall, the gains thereof will be able to find them [the rebels] all this next winter in some island' (*ibid*. p. 229). But the worst fell. In July 1556 the queen's ships captured six out of ten 'English pirate vessels' and brought them into Plymouth Harbour. One of the rebel captains, possibly the elder Assheton (*q.v.*), made his escape to Ireland in a small boat, but was there 'killed by the natives' (*Ven. Cal*. 1555–6, p. 536), while Peter Killigrew 'with six or eight of his chief comrades' was 'removed from Portsmouth(?) to the Tower' (*ibid*. p. 571). His father's efforts to buy him off failed (*ibid*.) and Peter under torture was forced to reveal the rebels' plans for an invasion of England (*Dom. Cal*. 1547–80, nos. 24–6, p. 86).

France, B v b 1, 3.

246. KILLIGREW, THOMAS: *Gent*. Of Cornwall.

The third son of John Killigrew, and fellow-pirate with his brother Peter. In October 1554 he was already in France, where he had become involved in some obscure process at Havre which caused his arrest (*For. Cal*. 1553–8, p. 123). We do not know the outcome of it, but he would seem to have been released, for thereafter it is probably Thomas who is linked with Peter under the title of 'the Killigrews'. Since Peter is the one known to have been captured in July 1556, Thomas was probably the 'one Killigrew' who escaped in the engagement at Plymouth (see above). What his ultimate fate was is not known, but he may have been one of the 'robars of the see' hanged at Wapping 'at the low-water marke' on 31 July (*Machyn*, p. 111).

France, B v b 1.

247. KINGE, ROBERT: (?) *Bishop of Oxford and ex-religious*. Of Oxfordshire. d. 1557(?).

Among the Doctors of Theology listed as exiles in the Emden catalogue is a 'Rober. Kinge'. But among contemporary doctors of theology I can find but one Robert King, and that the Cistercian monk who received his D.D. from Oxford in 1518/19 (O.H.S. I, 47) and who became successively abbot of Thame (1530), abbot of Osney and first bishop of Oxford in 1542. According to the *D.N.B.* he was made abbot of Osney under instructions from Thomas Cromwell, with whose family King was connected, and he was able to retain his bishopric through the reigns of Henry, Edward and Mary, dying on 4 December 1557. This argues, on the part of the bishop's religious views, considerable latitude; on the part of his character, not a little pliancy. Yet his reputation is that of a bigot and a persecutor of heretics. On what evidence does this reputation rest? Wood preserves two legends: one, that 'posterity' commended King 'for his mildness' because he 'did not care to have anything to do with such that were then called heretics'; the other, that he was a 'persecutor of protestants in qu. Mary's reign' (*Ath. Oxon.* II, 775). The only fact adduced by Wood in support of the second view is, that when suffragan to the bishop of Lincoln, King 'most fiercely inveighed against such as used the New Testament' (*ibid.* p. 774)—not so serious a charge after all, since a man who remained in favour through three changes of religion must needs have coloured his sermons according to the opinion prevailing in high places. And for this sin of accommodation he was amply punished under Edward by having to endure Richard Cox as his dean. Foxe should provide more incriminating evidence than this; but in the *Acts and Monuments* there are but two references in all to any 'Robert King'—one to the 'persecuting Bishops that died before Queen Mary', among whom King, called 'Bishop of Thame', is included (Foxe, VIII, 636); the other to Robert King, 'a cruel persecutor', who was not the bishop at all, but 'a deviser of interludes' who had 'lost one of his ears for his seditious talk' under Edward. Being present at the death of Rowland Taylor this man gave him some gunpowder as an act of mercy, not of cruelty (*ibid.* VI, 699). Upon such evidence as this rests Bishop King's anti-protestant reputation—this, and one other fact, that he presided at the trial and condemnation of Cranmer. But it is on this latter circumstance that an identification of Dr Robert King, of Oxford, with Dr Robert King, of the Emden list, may plausibly rest. As bishop of the diocese in which Cranmer's trial was held, King had no choice but to preside. Cranmer suffered in March 1556; the Emden list was of 1557. It is prefaced to an edition of Cranmer's *Defensio...Catholicae Sacramentae* reissued on the Continent in justification of the archbishop's doctrinal position. It is not at all beyond belief that remorse for his share in Cranmer's death moved King in his old age to throw in his lot at last with the heretics and to place his learning as a doctor of divinity at the service of the *Defensio's* editors, as an act of reparation. Here is no assertion of fact, merely the presentation of an interesting possibility. But if Robert King the exile was not Robert King the bishop, we have found no clue to his identity. Bishop King's tomb still stands in his cathedral; and eighty years after his death his great-great-grand-nephews placed above it a memorial window with a portrait of him and a picture of Osney Abbey in the background.

B I a & b; Emden (?).

248. KINGSMILL, Henry: *Gent.* Of Hampshire.

Probably the fifth[1] son of Sir John Kingsmill of Whitchurch and Sidmanton who was sheriff of Hampshire in 1543 (Harl. Soc. LXIV, 3 and *Notes and Queries*, 3rd ser. I, 376) and whose family claimed royal descent (*Geneal.* n.s. XII, 77). When, as Henry Kingismel, his son first appears abroad at Venice in July–August 1555, he was probably in the train of the Earl of Bedford, whose followers were permitted by the Signory of Venice to bear arms (*Ven. Cal.* 1555–6, p. 145). But he must soon after have left Venice for Padua, where Sir Thomas Hoby found a Mr Kingsmell on 23 August (Cam. Misc. X, 116). No other mention of him, however, occurs abroad and, as he is said to have died without issue, he may not have survived his foreign adventure. In 1555 he can have been little more than a boy, for his eldest brother William, who married Bridget Raleigh, was but thirty in 1556 (cf. *Notes and Queries*). Another brother, Richard (second son), was M.P. for Calne, Wilts. in the first parliament of Elizabeth (Bayne, *E.H.R.* XXIII, 663), while still another, the better known Andrew (*D.N.B.*), was a puritan divine who spent his last years in Geneva and Lausanne (Brook's *Puritans*, I, 419).

Venice, B v b 3; Padua, B IV b.

[1] So in *Notes and Queries*, *op. cit.*, but called fourth son in Harl. Soc. LXIV.

249. KIRK, HUGH: *Student and gent.* Of Derbyshire(?).

Possibly a younger son of Arnold Kirke of Whitehough, Derbyshire (Derbyshire Arch. Soc. II, 26). He was a demy and Fellow of Magdalen College, Oxford (1548–52) and in 1552 received his M.A. (Foster and Bloxam, IV, 103). Humphrey claims that he was expelled by Gardiner at the latter's Visitation in October 1553 (*Vita Juelli*, p. 73), but Kirk was one of those who had obtained leave of absence from the college before that visitation took place (Wilson, *Magd.* p. 101). Of his exile we know nothing but the fact, on the authority of Humphrey, that he did go to the Continent, and with Luke Purefoy. Very possibly he became one of the wandering scholars held in contempt by Goodman because they dwelt 'in papistical places' and joined themselves 'to no religious assembly of English'...'for their better safety, if they should return into England...' (*Mem.* III, i, 243–4). Though he did not receive orders under Edward (cf. Frere's list) he became rector of Hawkesbury, Gloucester, in 1559, and held other livings afterwards (Foster and Bloxham).   Italy (?).

250. KIRKHAM, JAMES. *Gent.* Of Blagdon, Devon.

The second son of Thomas Kirkham by Margaret, daughter of Richard Ferrers of Finniton (Vowell, p. 180, n. 3). An accomplice in the Western Rising he escaped with Sir Peter Carew to France in 1554 (*ibid.* App. E, no. 12), embarking at Weymouth on 25 January in one of the Killigrews' vessels. What became of him we do not know. His name is not mentioned abroad, nor, so far as we have found, afterwards.   France.

251. KNELL, THOMAS: *Preacher.*

On 14 October 1557 Knell was enrolled as a 'resident' of Geneva (f. 197) with the designation 'jadis ministre'. But there is no record of any such person either at Oxford or at Cambridge, nor does his name appear in the Emden list of exiles or in Bale's. Strype, however, gives the name 'Knel' as an alias of Jane Bocher, burned for Arianism by Cranmer (*Index*), and it is just possible that Thomas Knell was a relative of hers. If so it would account for the omission of his name from the official lists of fugitives, as in the case of Robert Sharp (*q.v.*) of the 'family of love'. Yet Knell was, eventually, received into Knox's congregation (26 November 1557), and some time after his return to England was made rector of Wareham, Dorset, in 1569 (*D.N.B.*). This living he resigned in 1573 to become chaplain to the first Earl of Essex in Ireland, and held his position until the earl died there, perhaps owing to the ignorant ministrations of Knell himself, who acted as one of the earl's physicians (*Annals*, II, ii, 83). He appears in the *D.N.B.* as the author of several pamphlets and 'a verse writer', but the account of him makes no mention of his sojourn in Geneva as a Marian exile.

Geneva, A IV a & b; *D.N.B.*

252. KNOLLES, JAMES: *Carpenter*.

Called in the Registre des Habitants (f. 196) the 'son of Thomas Knolles', and 'charpentier', James Knolles was admitted into Knox's congregation on 5 November 1556, and on 14 October 1557 became a 'resident' of Geneva.

Geneva, A IV a & b.

253. KNOLLES, THOMAS ('the eldest'): *Ex-religious.*[1] Of Oxfordshire. Wife.

A Benedictine of the Abbey of Eynsham, Oxon., who with his wife and with 'Michael and Nicholas', probably his sons, was received into the congregation at Geneva on 8 May 1557. From these dates it would seem that he and not the 'younger' Knols (below) was the father of James the carpenter, for both were received as residents of Geneva on the same day, 14 October 1557 (f. 196).

Geneva, A IV a & b.

254. KNOLLES (KNOLS, KNOLLE), THOMAS: *Ex-religious.*[2] Of Devon. Wife.

Formerly a Premonstratensian of the monastery of the Holy Saviour at Torr in Devon. He and his wife 'Johan' arrived in Geneva with Whittingham's party on 13 October 1555, and though my reasons for thinking so may seem obscure, I believe that he was also the Thomas Knols (Jung, p. 45) who appears in the Frankfort Steuerliste of October 1556 as having 'usually nothing' in the way of property. As Thomas Knolle he also signed the 'new discipline' in April 1557. Further than that we know nothing of him.

Geneva, A IV a; Frankfort, A III a 3; B III b.

255. KNOLLYS, Sir FRANCIS. *Gent.* Of Rotherfield Greys, Oxfordshire. Wife. 1514(?)–96.

According to Wood, Francis Knollys, only son of Robert Knollys of Rotherfield Greys in Oxfordshire, 'did receive for a time his grammatical and dialectial education at this university, particularly as it seems, in Magd. Coll.' (*Ath. Oxon.* I, 653), and he married Catherine Carey, daughter of William Carey and Mary Boleyn,

---

[1] Cf. 8th Rep. Deputy Keeper of Records, App. II, p. 21.
[2] *Ibid.* p. 45.

sister of Queen Anne. His wife was thus first cousin to the Princess Elizabeth, and sister of the Henry Carey (*q.v.*) who, in 1559, was created Lord Hunsdon. Sir Francis had long been identified with the protestant party at court and in parliament. In 1551 he was one of those present at the discussions on the Sacrament, held at the houses of Sir William Cecil and Sir Richard Morison (*Cranmer*, p. 386). And upon the accession of Mary he seems to have been the first important member of the protestant opposition to leave for the Continent. His departure in September was secret, so much so, that evidence for it rests, or has rested, solely upon a letter of farewell written by Elizabeth to Lady Knollys, signed 'Cor rotto' and endorsed as of 1553 (Lansdowne MSS. 94, Art. 10, printed in M. A. Wood's *Letters of Illustrious Ladies*, III, 279–80). But a letter of Calvin to Viret, to be quoted in a moment, may not only confirm the fact, but disclose the object of his journey, which was to have greater significance for the future of England than has ever been attached to it. Assuming then that Sir Francis and his family did leave England in the autumn of 1553, it may be supposed that they joined themselves either to John à Lasco's congregation that sailed from Gravesend on 15 September, or even more probably to the Glastonbury Weavers who left Dover on the 16th (*P.C.A.* 1552–4, p. 349). Yet not as fugitives; Mrs Green's (née Wood's) assertion that they 'were compelled to fly from the Marian persecution' is an obvious absurdity in view of the date of that 'flight'. Even Lady Knollys's close relationship to Elizabeth would have been insufficient reason for a withdrawal abroad before Mary's reign was two months old and while her policy was still marked by unusual clemency rather than rigour. Yet the very fact of close relationship to the 'protestant' claimant to the throne would have been an undoubted asset to one chosen by the protestant party to be their official emissary to Calvin. And such, I believe, Sir Francis was: an envoy sent by Sir William Cecil to Calvin at Geneva, and to Calvin's disciple, Viret, at Lausanne, with the object of obtaining permission for the establishment of a colony of English religious emigrants within their borders. His mission would thus have been the first fruits of those 'plottings' within the protestant party reported by the Spanish ambassador to the Emperor on 9 September 1553 (*Span. Cal.* 1553, p. 217). Apparently Sir Francis with his son Henry reached Geneva about 20 November, for on that date Calvin wrote to Viret introducing two English gentlemen who had recently been his guests. 'The elder' of them, he said, 'the father of the young man, is a person of good birth, and was wealthy in his own country. The son merits higher praise for piety and holy zeal; for, under the reign of King Edward, seeing that the Church suffered from want of pastors, he undertook voluntarily the labours of that office. Add to this, that they, with a generous liberality, assisted with their entire property our French brethren, who, on account of the Gospel, had crossed over to England' (*Letters of Calvin*, ed. Constable, II, 421–2). Now there is no other English family, known to have been abroad at this early date, to which this description of Calvin's would apply. The first groups of exiles did not leave England till later in January or early in February 1554 (see above, pp. 3, 8–10), by which time the reports of Sir Francis Knollys on the places abroad available for settlement could have been received and digested by Cecil. And my theory of the true nature of Sir Francis's journey to the Continent is further strengthened by the fact that in June 1555 he was back in England again, quietly fulfilling his official duties as Constable of Walling-ford Castle (*P.C.A.* 1554–6, p. 145). Nor is his presence abroad mentioned again until the winter of 1556–7, when he[1] was enrolled as a student at the University of Basle (Matrikel, f. 195, see below, p. 358). If he had been either at Frankfort or at Strasbourg in the summer of 1556, the fact would certainly have been recorded by John Brett, and his actual arrival at Frankfort must be placed between April and June 1557—for although he did not sign the 'new discipline' until 21 December 1557 yet he was living at Frankfort in John Weller's house, with his wife, five children and a maid on 10 June of that year (*H.S.P.* IV, 88). I have found no evidence as yet to prove Sir Sidney Lee's statement (*D.N.B.*, based on *Grindal*, p. 112 and Burnet, III, 500) that he afterwards removed to Strasbourg, though he evidently visited that city at the request of certain of the Frankfort congregation in an attempt at recon-ciliation between the two colonies (*T.* pp. 170–4).[2] Nor do I believe that the warrant issued to him on 5 November 1558 for lead out of the stores of Wallingford Castle for the repair of Windsor (a statement which seems to rest only on Cooper, II, 209, for I can find no record of the warrant in the *P.C.A.*) indicates, as does the earlier minute, that he was actually in England at the time of Mary's death (cf. Cooper, II, 209), for had he been, it is most unlikely that his admission to the Privy Council would have been delayed (as it was) until 14 January 1558/9 (*P.C.A.* 1558–70, p. 43), when he was also admitted Vice-Chamberlain of the queen's household. Whereas that very date, 14 January, marks the return of the second body of exiles to London, among whom were

[1] This cannot have been his son, Francis, who according to Fuller (*Worthies*, II, 227) did not die until 1648 when he was ninety-nine, and so would have been but a child of seven or eight in 1556.

[2] Though I admit that this enigmatical account given in the *Troubles* might bear such an interpretation.

Sir Anthony Cooke and Sir Thomas Wrothe, who had left Strasbourg on 20 December 1558 (*Z.L.* i, 5). In the first parliament of Elizabeth, Sir Francis sat as member for Arundel, but his subsequent career belongs to Elizabethan history. The magnificent monument raised to him and his wife in the Knollys Chapel at Rotherfield Greys by his son William, later Earl of Banbury, is still in existence, flanked by the kneeling effigies of Sir Francis's seven sons and seven daughters, five of whom may have shared his exile.

Geneva (?); Basle, A ii a; Frankfort, A iii a 4 & b 2; B iii a & b; *D.N.B.*

256. KNOLLYS, Henry: *Gent.* Of Oxfordshire. d. 1583.

It was probably Henry the brother, and not Henry the son, of Sir Francis Knollys, who was a fellow-member of the committee of mediation between Frankfort and Strasbourg in September 1557 (*T.* p. 174); who signed the 'new discipline' in the following December, and who, remaining in Frankfort until 3 January 1558/9, also signed that congregation's refusal to join Geneva in her anti-ceremonial crusade (*T.* p. 190). Under Elizabeth he was sent on a diplomatic mission to Germany in 1562; was member for Reading in the parliament of 1563; and acted as temporary warden to the Queen of Scots (*Salisbury*, i, 400), and to the Duke of Norfolk in the Tower in 1569 (*ibid.* i, 443).

Frankfort, B iii a & b; *D.N.B.* (under 'Sir Francis Knollys').

257. KNOLLYS, Henry: *Gent.* Of Kingsbury, Warwickshire.

Eldest son of Sir Francis Knollys, and married to Margaret, daughter of Sir Ambrose Cave. He was old enough in 1553 to have been the son praised by Calvin for his 'piety and holy zeal', who accompanied his father on the latter's mission to Geneva (see above, pp. 210–11), since in 1560 Robert, Sir Francis's fourth son, was of an age to be appointed keeper of Sion House (*D.N.B.*), and in 1561 Henry himself was recommended by Grindal for the provostship of Eton (*Parker*, i, 209). Hence it is not very likely that he was one of the '5 children' who were with Lady Knollys at Frankfort in June 1557. His experience of exile may easily have been confined to that one winter of 1553–4, after which, returning to England with his father, he probably pursued his education at Magdalen College, Oxford, though his name does not appear on the registers (cf. Foster). In the parliament of 1562–3 he sat for the borough of Shoreham, Sussex (*Returns of Members*, i, 406).

Geneva (?); Lausanne (?).

258. KNOT, Thomas: *Student*(?). Of Dorset(?).

Possibly a member of the Dorset family of Knott (Foster).
A Thomas Knott received his M.A. from Oxford in 1553 (*ibid.*)
and a man of the same surname, his Christian name not given,
was in 1580 a 'servant' of Sir Francis Knollys (*Dom. Cal.* 1547–80,
p. 664). As the only appearance of this Thomas 'Knot' abroad
was at Frankfort on 21 December 1557, when in Sir Francis
Knollys's company he signed the 'new discipline', it is not
improbable that he was, even then, a member of Sir Francis's
household.
Frankfort, B III b.

259. KNOX, John: *Preacher*. A Scot. Wife. 1505–72.

As nothing new has been discovered to add to the already volu-
minous literature regarding Knox's life in exile, it will be unnecessary
even to summarize his complicated itinerary, which is already
accurately given in the *D.N.B.* As to the merits and demerits of
the contest with Cox at Frankfort, Whittingham's account in the
Troubles at Frankfort should be supplemented by Knox's own
'Narrative' (Laing, IV, 41–9). It is a curious fact stated by Jung
(p. 5) that though Knox's case was debated before the magistrates,
and his decree of banishment pronounced by them on a charge of
treason against the Emperor, no word of that bitter quarrel is to
be found preserved in the Frankfort archives. In the judgment of
his fellow-exiles, it was the unremitting flow of Knox's incendiary
pamphlets from abroad, that 'added much oil to the flame of
persecution in England' (*O.L.* II, 761) and eventually earned him
the hatred of three queens. But it must be remembered that his
English accusers also wrote pamphlets nearly as virulent as his and
were therefore no less responsible than he for those flames.

B I a & b; B II; Dieppe; Geneva; Frankfort, B III; Geneva, A IV a; *D.N.B.*

Patrick, Knox's 'puple', since he is given no surname, must have
been little more than a child. He is therefore not 'numbered' in
the list of exiles, but, like Thomas Bodley, is counted among the
children.

260. LAKIN (LACON), Thomas: *Student and gent.* Of Thimbleby, Lincolnshire. d. 1575.

Probably the second son of Richard Lacon, and great-grandson
of Sir William Lacon, of Essex, 'one of the Iustices of the Kinges
benche' (Harl. Soc. XIII, 68). He received his M.A. from St John's
College, Cambridge, in 1551 (Baker, I, 285 and Venn, III, 35) and,
it may be presumed, was one of those who followed Thomas Lever,
master of the college, into exile. By 23 November 1554 he had

reached Strasbourg (*T.* p. 23), and in December of that year was one of those who profited by the bounty of the Duke of Württemberg, receiving 12 florins as his share of the latter's donation (Württ. Staatsarchiv). Bale reckons him among the 'preachers', but there is no record of Lacon's ordination before his flight abroad (cf. *Mar. Reac.* pp. 181–219), although in 1560 he was made rector of Bolton Percy, Yorks. and prebendary of York in 1564 (Le Neve, III, 226). A William and John Lakin were among the earliest founders of Groton, Massachusetts, in 1655 (*New Eng. Reg.*, see Index).

B II; Strasbourg, A VII c; B III a.

261. LANGE, PETER: '*Servant*'.

Servant to Sir William Fuller, and received with him into the Genevan congregation on 12 July 1556. The next year he became a 'resident' of Geneva on 14 October (f. 197), registering as 'serviteur'.

Geneva, A IV a & b.

262. LANGELEY, THOMAS: *Labourer*.

Since he called himself 'laboureur' when he was admitted to 'residence' in Geneva on 14 October 1557, he cannot be, as suggested in the *D.N.B.*, the Thomas Langley, once chaplain to Cranmer (*Cranmer*, p. 256) and publisher of an English version of Polydore Vergil's *De Inventoribus Rerum* (*D.N.B.*), who became a canon of Winchester in that same year, 1557. Thomas Langeley of Geneva had been received into the English congregation in 1556.

Geneva, A IV a & b.

263. LANGHORN (LANGHERN, LOCHERN), RICHARD: *Merchant*(?). Of Worcestershire and Calais. Wife. d. 1570(?).

Evidently this was a man of some substance, quite possibly a merchant, who became a burgher of Frankfort on 24 May 1555, paying 1 florin 3 s. 5 d. Bürgergeld (Jung, pp. 24, 54). He played no part in the congregation's quarrels, and perhaps seeking peace, withdrew to Aarau with his wife, seven children, and a maid (Hans Dür). There he appears as a signatory of Lever's letter to Bullinger, dated 5 October 1557 (*O.L.* I, 170), and also on both the official list and Hans Dür's, which latter confirms the Frankfort record of his birth in Worcestershire and residence at Calais (Jung, p. 54). While at Aarau he lived in the house of Heinrich Bär, a weaver (below, p. 355). Langhorn was also one of the signatories on 16 January 1559 of Aarau's unqualified acceptance of Geneva's invitation to an anti-ceremonial crusade (*T.* p. 191).

He returned to England some time in 1559 and in March and April 1560 received ordination as deacon and priest at the hands of the indefatigable Grindal (*Grindal*, pp. 58, 59). He would seem then to have become vicar of Edmonton, Middlesex, and to have died in 1570 (Newcourt, I, 599).

Frankfort, A III a 1; Aarau, A I a & b; A VIII a.

264. LANT (LAND), WILLIAM: *Gent.* Of the North.

This is probably the William Lant mentioned vaguely in the Visitation of London (Harl. Soc. XVII, 50) as himself coming 'out of the North', whose son, John, became a citizen of Exeter. Wotton first mentions him in November 1556, when Lant comes to him in the rôle of an informer against Dudley, introduced to Wotton by the London merchant, Hugh Offley (*For. Cal.* 1553–8, p. 276). After playing Wotton false several times, the Secretary concluded 'this naughty fellow' to be 'a very false liar' (*ibid.* p. 284), and refused to give much credence to Lant's story of a widespread plot against Queen Mary which 'he himself and another Englishman' had 'in hand' (*ibid.* p. 285). Nevertheless, quoting 'the Old Testament' to him earnestly, Wotton exhorted Lant against the sin of rebellion even if 'he were of another belief than was received in England' (*ibid.*); while to Queen Mary he makes the astute suggestion that the man had probably been 'suborned by the French King' to persuade her rather to take heed to herself at home than to aid 'King Philip in the war' (*ibid.* p. 286). We hear no more of Lant.

France, B v b 1.

265. LARGE, EDWARD: *Ex-religious.* Of Worcester.

A Franciscan of Worcester under the wardenship of John Joseph. In 1523 he had been ordained sub-deacon and thereafter 'was destined to get into constant trouble for the violence of his opinions' (Baskerville, *Monks* (1937), p. 238 note). He became 'assistant priest' [?] in the country parish of Hampton Bishop (or Lucy); then rector of Cherington, Warwickshire, in 1537; and vicar of Chipping Norton, Oxon., in 1549, a living which he resigned in 1551.[1] Some time before 1557 he went abroad according to the 'Catalogus' of Emden and Bale's list, but his place of exile is unknown.

n.p.; B I a & b; B II.

266. LAURENCE, Edmund: *Yeoman*(?) *and preacher.* Of Suffolk.

Probably the 'Ed. Laurence' who matriculated pensioner from Michael House, Cambridge, in 1544 (Venn, III, 53), and almost certainly the imprisoned preacher who was one of the signatories

---

[1] This information was kindly supplied to me by Mr Baskerville himself.

to the declaration of doctrine made from the King's Bench prison on 8 May 1554 (Foxe, VI, 553). With Thomas Mountain (*q.v.*) an Edmund Lawrence had been examined on a charge of publishing pamphlets against Philip and Mary (*Narr. of Ref.* pp. 187–8). It is therefore extremely likely that he was the same 'Edmond' Laurence who was committed for further examination, 'to sure and secrete warde in oone of the Counters' on 8 November 1556 (*P.C.A.* 1556–8, p. 16), and who in the following December, as 'Edmundus Laurence, de Brampton in comitatu Suffolk, fermour', was held for the sum of £100 owing to the queen (*ibid.* p. 32). On 23 January 1556/7 he made his appearance as commanded before the Privy Council, but as he failed to answer a second summons, it is probable that he had fled to Basle, where Bale in 1557 mentions him among the small group of Englishmen who were living there.

But he must have returned to England upon Elizabeth's accession, for he is almost certainly the 'one Laurence, a preacher, incumbent of some parish in Suffolk' whom the bishop of Norwich suspended in 1579 'by virtue of certain letters from her majesty' wherein the bishop 'was straitly charged to suffer none but such only to preach as were allowed of into the ministry...' (*Annals*, II, ii, 267, 383). An appeal to reinstate him failed.

Basle, B II.

*LEDLEY, a free-willer and messenger of the gospellers, but not permanently abroad.

267. LELANDE, HARRY: *Student*(?). Of Lancashire(?).

Very possibly either a relative or illegitimate son of John Leland the Antiquary (1506–52?) who in 1530 had been rector of Peppeling, Calais, though an absentee. Leland held protestant opinions. This 'Harrye Leylandt', for whom no other connections have been found, first appeared in Geneva in 1557, when on 14 October he was received as a 'resident' (f. 197) and on the following 26 November became a member of the English congregation.

Geneva, A IV a & b.

268. LETLER (LITTLER), RICHARD: *Gent.* Of Lincolnshire. Wife.

Probably the Richard Litler of Tathwell, Lincs., who married Edith, daughter of Sir Thomas Mussenden, Knt. (*Geneal.* IV, 192), and had a son Thomas Litler living in 1562. With his wife and one child, a daughter, 'Letler' arrived in Frankfort in the early spring of 1557 and was a signatory of the 'new discipline' in March-April. In June as 'Littler' he and his family were inmates of the household of Thomas Saunders (Sandes).

Frankfort, A III a 4; B III b.

269. LEVER, JOHN: *Student*. Of Little Lever, Lancashire.
      d. 1574(?).

Sixth son of John Lever, of Little Lever, Lancs. (Chetham Soc.
no. 81, p. 9), and younger brother of Thomas Lever (*q.v.*). This
relationship, doubtful before (cf. Venn), is now established by
Hans Dür's list in the records of Aarau (*Argovia*, XI, p. lxiii). He
received his M.A. from Cambridge in 1553, and either followed
or accompanied his brother, Thomas, to Germany, where, however,
no record of him exists before November (?) 1555, when his name
appears as a student on the Standesliste at Frankfort. Yet since
he is not found on either of the tax-lists in 1556–7, nor as a
subscriber to the 'new discipline' of March–April 1557, he must
have become in the interim before his arrival at Aarau one of the
wandering scholars, despised of Goodman (*Mem.* III, i, 243–4).
In the autumn of 1557 he arrived with his brother at Aarau, where
for 'forty weeks' he lived in the house of Hans Dür himself. On
his return to England he was made head master of Tonbridge
School from 1559 to 1574 (Venn), and the latter date may mark
the year of his death.

B I a & b; B II; Frankfort, A III a 2 & b 1; Aarau, A I a & b.

270. LEVER, RALPH: *Student*. Of Little Lever, Lancashire.
      d. 1585.

The fifth son of John Lever (Chetham Soc. no. 81, p. 9) and
brother of Thomas. He also was of St John's College, Cambridge,
of which he became a Fellow in 1549, and from which he received
his M.A. in 1551. And he, too, went abroad in Mary's reign,
being the third of the 'tre Leveri' mentioned in the Emden list.
But his whereabouts on the Continent are unknown, unless he was
at Zurich. In the list of Englishmen recorded in Bullinger's
Diarium (p. 46) is a 'Leverus' without Christian name, and as
Thomas Lever had by that time gone to Geneva, this may have
been either Ralph or John. It has, hitherto, been supposed that
Ralph was the brother who went with Thomas to Aarau, but
Hans Dür's list has now proved conclusively that it was not Ralph
but John. Ralph, then, must have been a wandering scholar. On
his return to England he became rector of Washington, Durham
(1560); reader or tutor to Walter Devereux, first Earl of Essex;
chaplain to Bishop Pilkington; and prebendary of Durham from
1567 to 1585. On the death of his brother Thomas, Ralph succeeded
him in the mastership of Sherburne Hospital.

B I a & b; B II; Zurich, A VIII c (?); *D.N.B.*

271. LEVER, Thomas, B.D.: *Priest.* Of Bolton,[1] Lancashire.
1521–77.

He was the second son of John Lever by his wife Elenor, daughter
of Richard Heyton (Eaton, Heton), which would suggest a relationship between Thomas Lever and Thomas Heton (*q.v.*), the
merchant-'sustainer' (Chetham Soc. no. 81, p. 9). Educated like
his brothers at St John's College, Cambridge, he was ordained
priest on 10 August 1550 (*Mar. Reac.* pp. 187, 190), and took his
B.D. in 1552. From 1551 to 1553 Lever was master of his college.
He had early identified himself with the extreme protestant party
at court, having preached before the king from 1549 to 1550, and
in May 1551 acted as chaplain to the Marquis of Northampton,
on the latter's embassy to France (Cam. Misc. x, 67). Consequently
at King Edward's death he espoused the cause of Lady Jane and
openly confirmed his support of Northumberland by supping with
him at Cambridge, on the night of 15 July 1553 (*D.N.B.*). His
flight to the Continent upon Mary's accession was thus inevitable,
but it must also have been premeditated, for he took with him into
voluntary exile a group of students 'partly from Oxford, and
partly from Cambridge', who arrived at Strasbourg, presumably
under his leadership, on or before 24 February 1554 (*O.L.* ii, 514).
Then from Strasbourg Lever went ahead to prepare accommodation
for them at Zurich, where he himself arrived on 10 March (*Diarium*,
p. 46 and cf. Vetter, *Relations*, pp. 53–4) with 'comite suo Hugone',
whom we take to be Cuthbert Hugh (*q.v.*) of Magdalen College,
Oxford. Having made his arrangements he left Zurich for Geneva,
where he arrived on 7 April (*O.L.* i, 153), just two days after the
thirteen 'Students of Zurich' reached their destination under the
leadership of Horne and Chambers (*Diarium*, p. 46). In a letter
to Bullinger of 23 April 1554, Lever casually refers to them as
'some Englishmen' who, he hears, 'have come to you at Zurich,
together with that very godly man, Richard Chambers...' (*O.L.*
i, 155), as if he himself were dissociated from them. Yet here
arises one of the many difficulties in connection with Lever's
chronology. According to his own letter of 11 April 1554 (*O.L.*
i, 153–5) he was then at Geneva, but when the 'Students', just
arrived at Zurich on 5 April, wrote to the authorities asking for
asylum, Thomas Lever was one of the signatories[2] to the letter
(*O.L.* ii, 752). He has given his own itinerary from Zurich to

---

[1] Cf. the record of his ordination (*Mar. Reac.* pp. 187–8). His brother
Richard married Catherine Bolton, of Little Bolton, Lancs. (Chetham Soc.
op. cit.).
[2] So far I have not seen the original of this letter at Zurich. It would be
interesting to see if the signature was in Lever's own handwriting.

Geneva by way of Lentzburg, Berne and Lausanne, which occupied at least five days. He must then have left Zurich about 2 April (*O.L.* I, 153). Why then the *D.N.B.*, mentioning this same itinerary, should say that he did not arrive at Geneva until 13 October 1554, is not easy to understand; yet on the other hand it is quite as difficult to explain why Lever, who remained at Geneva apparently without a break from 7 April 1554 to 17 January 1555 (*O.L.* I, 153–9), should have been able on that same date, 13 October, to be one of the signatories of another letter written by the 'Students of Zurich' this time to Frankfort (*T.* p. 16). Either he must have made a short journey to confer with his fellows on Frankfort's recent invitation to them, or somebody else must have signed for him. It was not until after 17 January that he left Geneva to take up pastoral duties at Frankfort and to become a thorn in the flesh of John Knox. His first letter from there, dated 12 February 1555 (*O.L.* I, 159), makes no mention of the hot contention in the congregation between the Prayer Book and anti-Prayer Book factions which his coming had merely aggravated. Knox had just very properly refused to adopt the order which was later to become that of Geneva, without the consent of the other colonies (*T.* p. 27), but he had also refused to administer the Sacraments according to the book of England. The state of deadlock thus created Lever proposed to break by introducing a new order of his own making. But his complacent invention, being summarily rejected by the congregation as not 'fit for a right reformed churche' (*T.* p. 28), made him a bitter enemy of Knox. It was at this point that Knox and Whittingham sought the intervention of Calvin (*T.* pp. 28–34); it may have been Lever who at this same time suggested at Strasbourg the coming of Richard Cox. It was certainly Lever whom Knox accused of bringing in John Jewel to preach 'who had been at Masse in England' ('Narrative', Laing, IV, 42–3); and it was by the 'subtle undermining of Mr Lever', said Knox, that 'the whole Church was broken' (*ibid.*). Whitehead was Cox's forerunner in opposition. Cox himself arrived on 13 March. On the 26th Knox was banished (*T.* p. 38) and on 5 April Lever was one of the signatories of Cox's explanatory letter to Calvin in which he summarized and justified his recent revision of the Prayer Book. Shortly afterwards Lever would seem to have returned to Geneva. He is listed among those members of the congregation who had arrived before 13 October[1] and it was not until December (probably) that he received his call to Wesel. By 4 January 1556 he was passing through Strasbourg

[1] This could hardly, I think, refer to his early sojourn when there was no English Church at all in Geneva.

on his way to take up his new pastorate (*O.L.* I, 160) in succession to Coverdale, and in Wesel he remained until the spring of 1557, when the English congregation was invited by the magistrates to leave the town (see above, pp. 50–51). Then it was that Lever, shepherding his flock to a new asylum at Aarau, became the prototype of those New England ministers, the Thomas Hookers and John Davenports of the future (Channing, *History of the United States*, I, 398–9), who were the organizers of a new type of colonization upon Lever's model. His next two letters (*O.L.* I, 162–4) are, I believe, misdated by Hastings Robinson. They belong to 1557, not to 1556, for they recount the difficulties experienced by the fugitive colony in finding a new home. But by 11 August 1557 the municipality of Berne had given them permission to settle at Aarau (*O.L.* I, 166–7, n. 1); and there for the next eighteen months Lever preached to his little congregation in the Stadtskirche, living quietly with his brother the while in the house of Hans Dür. He was still at Aarau on 16 January 1559, when he signed the congregation's acceptance of Geneva's proposal to embark on an anti-ceremonial crusade (*T*. p. 191). And on his return to England he made himself unpopular with Elizabeth by his opposition to the supremacy and by his nonconformity. But he was made rector of Coventry in 1559 and in January 1562/3 received the mastership of Sherburne Hospital, which he held to his death. Of his prebend of Durham he was deprived in 1567.

Zurich, A VIII a & c; Geneva, A IV a; Frankfort, B III a; Wesel, A VIII a; Aarau, A I a & b; *D.N.B.*

272. LEWIS(?), MICHAEL: *Student*. Of Barton(?).

Registered as a student at the University of Basle, under the name of 'Michael Levus ex Barthen, Anglus', on 17 November 1557. I have found no clue to his identity.   Basle, A II a.

273. LINSEY (LINDSAY), DAVID: *Student and preacher*. A Scot. 1531(?)–1613.

Received into Knox's church on 15 September 1558, and as a 'resident' of Geneva on 24 October 1558 (f. 264), with the designation 'du royaulme d'Ecosse'. He was probably the same David Lindsay, son of Robert Lindsay of Kirkton, and brother of David, ninth Earl of Crawford, who was later chaplain to James VI, leader of the Kirk of Scotland and bishop of Ross in 1600 (*D.N.B.*). In December 1566 he was one of the Superintendents of the Kirk who, as 'Dd. Lyndesay', signed a letter of admonition to the 'Bishopps and Pastors off Englande' which is incorporated in the *Troubles at Frankfort* (pp. 212–15).   Geneva, A IV a & b; *D.N.B.*

274. LUCK, JOHN: *Gent.* Of Sussex(?).

Describing himself as 'ex Territonia' (which we have interpreted as Terring or West Tarring in Sussex) John Luck became a citizen of Frankfort on 7 March 1555, and paid his Bürgergeld of 22 s. (Jung, pp. 24, 55). This was his first and last appearance at Frankfort and abroad. Probably he belonged to the family of Luck, living at Mayfield and Rotherfield in Sussex, in which a 'John' appears in nearly every generation (Berry, *Kent, etc.* p. 187 and Harl. Soc. LIII, 155). To which generation of Lucks this particular 'John' belonged, no genealogy and no other source of information regarding Sussex has given any clue.

Frankfort, A III a 1.

275. LUDDINGTON (LYDDINGTON), RICHARD: *Student.* Of London(?). Wife.

Very possibly this is the Luddington or Lodyngton, of no Christian name, who matriculated from St John's College, Cambridge, in 1544, and was 'perhaps' successively a scholar of Trinity College, in 1548, and of Christ's College in 1552–3 (Venn, III, 100). It is also possible that he was a son of that Nicholas Luddington, citizen of London whose sister married Sir Thomas Chamberlain (Harl. Soc. I, 46). In 1558 a William Luddington of London, grocer, was arraigned before the Privy Council for resisting the custom's officers and five days later had 'a good lesson geven' to him (*P.C.A.* 1556–8, pp. 393, 398). What relation, if any, this man was to the Richard Luddington who makes his first appearance at Frankfort on the Standesliste of 1555, we shall not attempt to say. He was there placed among the 'students'. Then he disappears, perhaps avoiding the tax assessments of October and January 1556–7 by temporary absence, but in March-April 1557 he re-appears as a subscriber to the 'new discipline', and on 10 June was living, with his wife and two children, in the same house with David Whitehead. After this no more is heard of him.

Frankfort, A III a 2, 4 & b 1, 2.

276. LYNBROUGHE, RICHARD. (?).

I can find, as yet, no trace of this name in Tudor England. The man makes his only appearance abroad on 21 December 1557, as a subscriber to the 'new discipline'. Quite possibly he was a servant.

Frankfort (or Strasbourg ?), B III b.

277. MACHET (MATCHET), JOHN: *Priest.* Of Norfolk. Wife.

A secular priest deprived in 1555 of his living of Bergh-cum-Apton (Burg-Apton), which he had held since 1545 (Baskerville, *E.H.R.* 1933, p. 55). In the autumn of that year (1555) he reached Frankfort with his wife, and was listed among the 'students' in the Standesliste. The following autumn his name also appears in the Steuerliste with the legend 'hat sonst kein narung'. From the fact that he was not a subscriber to the 'new discipline' and had even put his name to certain 'objections' to it (*T.* p. 169) we may presume him to have been of Horne's party. In June 1557 he was still in Frankfort, living in the house of Richard Davies (*H.S.P.* IV, 89). It is probably John Matchett the exile, who became chaplain to Archbishop Parker in 1574 (*A.* II, i, 479), though it must be another John Matchett, doubtless his son, who matriculated from Corpus Christi College, Cambridge, in 1571 and was made rector of Gimingham, Norfolk, 1577 (Venn, III, 160 and Harl. Soc. LXXXVI, 1). Frankfort, A III a 2, 3, 4 & b 1, 2; B III a & b.

278. MACKBRAY (MAKEBRAY, MACKBRAIR), JOHN: *Exreligious and priest.* A Scot. d. 1584.

He is called by Spottiswoode (*Hist. Church of Scotland*, ed. 1847, p. 192) 'a gentleman of Galloway'. Laing says that he was certainly 'in priest's orders before retiring to the continent' and had been incorporated in St Salvator's College, St Andrews, in 1530 (Knox, I, 529–30). In 1550 a 'Mr, *alias* Sir John M'Brair, formerly Canon of Glenluce' escaped from the castle of Hamilton where he had been imprisoned for 'sundry great and odious crimes, Heresies etc....' (*ibid.*, quoting Pitcairn's *Criminal Trials*, I, 352), and possibly then made his way to England, for in 1552 he was vicar of St Leonard's, Shoreditch (Newcourt, I, 687). Machyn records that in August of that year at 'ser Anthony Wynckfeld's funeral "dyd pryche [the vicar] of Sordyche, a Skott..."' (*Machyn*, p. 24). But in 1554 he was deprived and was among the first of the fugitives to arrive at Frankfort. On 19 July he signed the Liturgia Sacra (*T.* p. 7 and *Liturgia Sacra*, ed. 1554, p. 92) as the first pastor of the English congregation. On 2 August he also signed Whittingham's invitation to the other English colonies to resort to Frankfort (*T.* p. 13). But Mackbray's pastorate had been given him only 'for a time', and by 24 September first place among the ministers seems to have been ceded to John Bale (*ibid.* p. 20). By 3 December Mackbray had been absorbed again into the congregation (*ibid.* p. 26). Though he had signed Frankfort's invitation to John Knox to assume the pastorate, Mackbray would seem not to have been

of Knox's party, for he remained in Frankfort after the secession
of September 1555, as one of the very few adherents of David
Whitehead. That autumn he stood godfather to the child of
Laurence Kent (*q.v.*), who would, however, have preferred to
dispense altogether with that concession to 'mennes traditions'
(*T.* p. 61); but shortly afterwards he must have left to become
pastor of some congregation in Lower Germany of which according
to Bale he wrote an account (Knox, I, 530). Upon Elizabeth's
accession he returned to England where on 3 September 1559 he
preached at Paul's Cross (*Grindal*, p. 38). In 1568 he became vicar
of St Nicholas, Newcastle (Knox, I, 530).

B I a & b; B II; Frankfort, B III a; Lower Germany.

279. MAISTER (MASTERS), WILLIAM: *Student.* Of Willington, Bedfordshire. Wife. 1532–89/90.

A scholar from Eton admitted at King's College in 1549. In 1557
he took his M.A. (Venn, III, 160 and Foster), and it is in the
January of that year that he makes his first appearance abroad
on the Frankfort tax-list, where his property is valued at 100 florins
(Jung, p. 30). Jung stars his name to indicate that it had not
appeared before in the city's records. In June he is found living
with his wife and two children in the same house with Henry
Cockcroft, John Bedell, etc. (*H.S.P.* IV, 88), and in the previous
March-April he had been a subscriber to the 'new discipline'.
On his return to England he received his LL.D. from Cambridge
in 1568, became vicar-general of the diocese of Norwich in 1569
and successively vicar of Shipton-under-Wychwood and Burford,
1571. I have discovered among the Petyt MSS. in the Library of
the Inner Temple (no. 538, vol. 47, f. 28) an original letter of
Masters's written to Sir Christopher Heydon in 1574, in regard to
the 'putting down of prophesy men'.

Frankfort, A III a 3, 4 & b 2; B III a.

280. MANSFEILDE (MANSFIELD), JOHN: *Gent.* (?) Of Malton, Yorkshire (?). d. 1601.

If, as I believe, this man, who became a 'resident' of Geneva on
29 November 1557 (f. 226) and was received on the following
2 December as a member of Knox's congregation, is the same
person as the John Mansfield who in 1592 is spoken of as 'deputy'
of the Earl of Huntingdon (*Dom. Cal.* 1591–4, p. 268), then he
forms one of the most direct and interesting links between the
Marian Exodus of 1554, and that to Massachusetts Bay in 1630.
By Thomas, Lord Burghley, in 1599, this latter Mansfield is not
only designated as 'Lord Huntingdon's gentleman' but also as

'Lord Essex's man' (*ibid.* 1598–1601, p. 333), and such a strong puritan connection would seem to support my suggested identification with the earlier 'John Mansfeilde' of Geneva. If so, then in February 1598 John Mansfield, late of Geneva and the 'gentleman' both of Huntingdon and Essex, had received 'the office of collector of the rents and revenues of the dissolved monastery of St Mary's York', and also of 'the surveyorship of the Queen's lands in the North riding of Yorkshire, as held by the late Sir William Fairfax' (*ibid.* p. 19). Now Cotton Mather in his *Magnalia* (ed. 1853, I, 305) calls the father of Mrs Elizabeth Wilson, of Massachusetts Bay Colony, 'Sir John Mansfield, master of the Minories and Queen's Surveyor'. And by the will of a John Mansfield, Esq., of Malton, Yorks., which was proved on 31 July 1601 (Waters, *Gleanings*, I, 594), we find that he had a daughter, Elizabeth, who married the Rev. John Wilson (son of Isabel Woodhall, a niece of Archbishop Grindal), who in 1630 went to New England in Winthrop's company and became the first minister of the First Church in Boston (*ibid.* I, 55). He also had a son John who at his father's death was still in his nonage. If Cotton Mather is correct in his statement regarding Mrs Elizabeth Wilson's father, then John Mansfield, the Earl of Huntingdon's man and Queen's Surveyor, was also John Mansfield of Malton, Yorks. His son, John, went later to New England, where he spoke of his father as having been 'a justice of the Peace' (Waters, *Gleanings*, I, 595). We know from the Calendars of State Papers that Thomas, Lord Burghley, when President of the Council of the North, appointed a John Mansfield as *Sheriff*, presumably of Yorkshire (*Dom. Cal.* 1598–1601, p. 333). The only other discrepancy in the identification would seem to be Cotton Mather's statement that Mistress Wilson's father had been a knight, whereas John Mansfield in his will is 'Esquire' only, and as such appears in the State Papers.

Frequently the Marian Exiles are found to have been very young men, barely of age. There is nothing then in the dates to prevent the John Mansfeilde of Geneva; the 'deputy' of the Earl of Huntingdon; the John Mansfield of Malton, Yorks.; and the father-in-law of the first minister of Winthrop's colony of Massachusetts Bay, having been one and the same man.

Geneva, A IV a & b.

281. **MARSTON (MASTON), JOHN:** *Gent.* Of Shropshire and Coventry. d. 1599.

This is one of the mistaken transcriptions of Burn, who gives the name as 'Matson', whereas in the original of the Livre des Anglois

(Bodleian MS. Facs. d. 49) it is 'Maston' and in the Registre des Habitants (f. 123) 'Marston'. He was one of those who arrived in Geneva with Whittingham on 13 October 1555 and on 24 October was received as a 'resident' of the city. I believe him to have been the second son (called third in the *Records of the Middle Temple*, I, 171) of Ralph Marston of Ascott and Heyton, Salop (though himself of Coventry), and the father of John Marston (1575?–1634), dramatist and divine (Harl. Soc. xxix, 351, and *ibid.* xiii, 245). Through his marriage with his second wife, Mary, daughter of Andrew Guarsi the Italian surgeon of London (Harl. Soc. xiii, 245 and *D.N.B.* xii, 1141), he became the stepson-in-law of the exile John Butler (*q.v.*) who had married Guarsi's widow, and whose sister, Joice, was the wife of William Fuller (*q.v.*), also of Geneva. In 1570 Marston became a Reader (Wood says 'counsellor') of the Middle Temple (*Records*, I, 171) and Wood also says (*Ath. Oxon.* I, 763) that in his day the two John Marstons, father and son, were buried in the Temple Church under a stone marked 'Oblivioni Sacrum'. Unfortunately this no longer exists, nor does there appear to be any record kept of it.

Geneva, A iv a & b.

282. MASON, RICHARD: '*Servant*'.

A servant of John Hales, and allowed to be one of the subscribers to the 'new discipline' in March-April 1557 (*H.S.P.* iv, 87 and Jung, pp. 34, 56).

Frankfort, B iii b.

283. MAUDE (MAUDES), [JOHN or RICHARD?]: *Preacher*(?). Of Yorkshire (?).

This exile to Geneva in 1557, who appears on 20 November 1557 in the Livre des Anglois as 'Mawdes' without a Christian name, but as 'Richard Maude, jadis ministre', when registered as a 'resident' on 14 October 1557 (f. 197), was very possibly a younger son of the family of Maude or Montalto of Yorkshire. Of this same family was Bernard Maude, 'alias Montalto', a servant to Archbishop Sandys (*A.* ii, ii, 165), who later on became an 'enigmatic' principal in the Babington plot (A. G. Smith, *Babington Plot* (1936), pp. 4, 114–15). Bale gives a 'John' Maude in his list of exiles (*Scriptores*, p. 742). Whether Richard and John Maude were the same person; whether either was a relative of Bernard Maude (or Mawde) cannot be established, but there was a John Mawde, fourth son of Mawde of Hollyng Hall, Yorks. (Harl. Soc. xvi, 200), whose dates would not conflict with Bale's John Maude; while an Edward Maude, who matriculated from St John's College, Cambridge, in 1564, became a 'Preacher of the Word' at Northowram, Halifax, in 1582–8 (Venn, iii, 163). That is, nonconformity would appear to have run in the family of Maude. It seems to me not unlikely that the 'Maudes' so carelessly inscribed at Geneva may have been even then, as a younger son, attached to the Sandys family, and was possibly the father or a near relative of the 'enigmatic' Bernard who at the time of his association with the Babington plot was young neither in age (Smith, *op. cit.* p. 4) nor in conspiracy, since he had already plotted against his master, Archbishop Sandys (*A.* III, i, 142, etc.).

B II; Geneva, A IV a, and possibly A IV b.

284. MAYDWELL (MEDWEL, MAYDVELL, MAYDNELL), JOHN: *Ex-religious and student.* A Scot.

This man, whose place of exile is unknown, but whose name appears both in the Emden catalogue and on Bale's list, was doubtless the 'Maister John Maydwell, comenly callyd the Scottysshe frere' (Wright, *Monasteries*, p. 68). In 1533 he was a candidate for the office of priest in a chantry attached to the Charterhouse in London, but, though he 'exhortyd' the monks 'to the best', they would have none of him because they 'harde tell' that 'he prechide agaynst the honoryng of images and of sayntes...'. In 1550 he was probably the Maydwell who preached at the funeral of Christopher Machyn (Machyn, p. 3) and he may also have been the John Medwel, 'scrivener's servant', who was forced to abjure his heresies in King Henry's days (Foxe, IV, 586 and v, 39). It is not known when he fled to the Continent, but his presence in the two lists shows that he was abroad in 1557.

n.p.; B I a & b; B II.

285. MAYHEWE (MAHEWE), ANTHONY: *Student.* Of Lincolnshire. d. 1559.

Fellow of Pembroke College, Cambridge, 1547 and M.A. 1549 (Venn, III, 168 and Cooper, I, 198). Probably a fugitive from Pole's Visitation of Lincolnshire in April 1556, for Mayhew had but lately arrived in Frankfort, when, in October 1556 (cf. Cooper's '1554'), his property was valued at 130 florins (Jung, p. 29). He was one of the twelve members of Horne's party who registered their objections to the 'new discipline' in the spring of 1557 (*T.* p. 168), and in June he is found as one of the inmates of Horne's house (*H.S.P.* IV, 89). During the winter of 1558–9 he went to Basle, where he is registered in the Matrikel as Antonius Mayhewe, Anglus (f. 201vo and below, p. 358), who paid his fee of 'VI sol' for matriculation. But as there is no record, either in the Livre des Anglois or in the Registre des Habitants, to show that he was ever in Geneva, it seems somewhat gratuitous of Cooper to have assigned him a 'chief hand' in the translation of the Geneva Bible. Martin mentions no such collaborator. It is also said by Cooper, though not by Venn, that Mayhew was reinstated in his fellowship on his return to England. He died on 19 October 1559.

Frankfort, A III a 3, 4 & b 2; B III a; Basle, A II a; Cooper.

286. MERES (MEERES, MIERS, MEYRES), ANTHONY, Esq.:
Gent. Of Auburn, Lincolnshire. d. 1587–8.

The second[1] son and heir of Sir John Meeres of Kirton, Lincs., whose first wife was Katherine, daughter of Sir Everard Digby (Harl. Soc. LI, 664). His brother, Lawrence (*ibid.* p. 665), was in 1557 a Justice of the Peace 'in the partes of Hollande in the countie of Lincoln...' (*P.C.A.* 1556–8, p. 77). But Anthony seems to have come early under Queen Mary's displeasure, for on 18 September 1555 the commissioners who were sent to sequester the lands of Katherine, Duchess Dowager of Suffolk, were instructed 'to do the like towching thee landes, goodes and catalles of one Merys within the same shire;...' (*ibid.* 1554–6, p. 180). In April 1556 Pole's Visitation of Lincoln marks 'Fuga' before the name of 'Anthonius Meeres in com. Lincoln. armiger' (Lambeth MSS. Register of Cardinal Pole, f. 17, or Strype, *Mem.* III, ii, no. 51, p. 390). The record states further that he had fled because he was cited for not receiving the Sacrament at Easter, but his offence must have been a far graver one than that, since nothing short of conspiracy could have warranted the sequestration of his lands and goods. Moreover, he was among those especially named as offenders in Brett's commission of 1556 (Brett, p. 116). But before 12 July 1556 Meres had reached safety at Geneva, where he became a member of Knox's congregation. He died in March 1587/8 at the age of seventy-six (Harl. Soc. LI, 664).

Geneva, A IV a.

287. MEVERAL, [SAMPSON?]: *Gent.* Of Staffordshire (?).

Probably of the family of the Meverels of Throwly, Staffs. (Harl. Soc. XVII, 98). In 1556 he had been one of the conspirators in Dudley's plot, and with Dudley fled to France and was declared a traitor on 4 April (*Machyn*, p. 103). On the Continent, however, there is no trace of him, but he may possibly be the Sampson Meverell of Derbyshire mentioned in the Privy Council minutes of 30 January 1564 (*P.C.A.* 1558–70, p. 190).

France (?).

288. MOON (MOHUN), WILLIAM: *Gent.* Of Cornwall.

As William 'Mono' he was a student at Padua during the winter of 1556–7 (Andrich, p. 131), and was probably of the family of

[1] Or third, as in *Geneal.* IV, 257.

the Mohuns of Hall, Cornwall, and very possibly the Sir William
Mohun, son of Sir Reginald, who married as his first wife the
daughter of John Horsey (Vivian's *Devon*, p. 566). In 1572 a
William Mohun was sheriff of Cornwall (*Dom. Cal.* 1547–80,
p. 451). The family had also intermarried with the Carews (Harl.
Soc. IX, 30) and with the Courtenays (Vivian, p. 566).

Padua, A VI.

289. MORISON, Sir RICHARD: *Gent.* Of Cassiobury (Cashiobury), Hertfordshire. Wife. d. 1556.

The second son of Thomas Morrison of Sandon, Herts. (Harl. Soc.
XXII, 77, 116, but cf. Venn, III, 216 and also Foster, III, 1037, who
make Thomas Morrison of Chardwell, Yorks.), and married to
Bridget, daughter of John, Lord Hussey, who afterwards took as
her third husband, Francis, second Earl of Bedford. Morison was
educated at Eton and received his B.A. at Oxford in 1528, after
which his career became one of those curious combinations of the
lay, the spiritual, and the scholarly, which were characteristic of
King Edward's reign. In 1534 he was a student at the University
of Padua, where he evidently went to study Greek, and in 1537
he was made a lay canon of Sarum. He early came under the
influence of Latimer, while from Thomas Cromwell, whose
secretary he was, he received several monastic grants. In 1547
he entered parliament as M.P. for Wareham (Foster).[1] As Gentleman of the Privy Chamber he was in intimate association with the
boy king, and from 1550 to 1553 went as his ambassador to the
Emperor with Roger Ascham as secretary. Of this experience
Ascham published an account in 1553 under the title of *A Report
of the Affaires of Germany*. Lodge says that Morison returned to
England before the death of Edward (*Illus.* I, 191–2, note); Cooper
doubts whether he ever returned at all, but the question seems to
be settled by Sir Thomas Hoby, who was with Morison in Brussels
from April to August 1553 (Cam. Misc. x, 94–6). Having in-
judiciously alluded to Guilford Dudley as 'king' in a letter to the
Council (*Chron. Q. Jane*, p. 108 and note), Morison received his
recall on 5 August 1553 (MS. Cotton Galba B. XII, p. 253). On
his way home, he and Sir Thomas Hoby were entertained at
Brussels on 24 August by the Queen of Hungary with 'such a
dinner as they have seen few the like in all their lives'[2] (*For. Cal.*
1553–8, p. 8 and Cam. Misc. x, 96), after which they arrived
together at Richmond on 3 September, where with childish pleasure

---

[1] But not confirmed by the *Return of Members*, I, 375–7.
[2] The letter descriptive of this dinner, written to the queen by Morison,
Sir Philip Hoby, etc., is printed in Tytler, II, 235–7.

they displayed to the queen 'their rewardes geven them by th' Emperour'. Sir Richard had received 'two chaynes of on (*sic*) thowsand crownes the peece' (Cam. Misc. x, 96). Perhaps these chains provided some of the funds for the building of Cashiobury, an enterprise which was unfortunately interrupted by Morison's withdrawal to the Continent. In February 1555 he was again established in Brussels, where Sir John Mason dined with him on the 13th (*For. Cal.* 1553–8, p. 154). Evidently Morison's hope, then, was to take service with the Emperor, but this failing, he retired to Strasbourg, where he must have arrived early in April, having been 'exposed', as he tells Calvin, 'to the greatest danger' (*O.L.* I, 147–8, dated 17 April 1555). His plan had been to go on to Zurich, but as that city had just been obliged to close its doors to any more foreigners after an influx of Italian refugees from Lugano, Sir Richard decided that 'his next best plan' was to accept a house and garden which had been 'voluntarily offered' to him at Strasbourg (*O.L.* I, 148). This was towards the end of August; and in Strasbourg he decided to spend his 'voluntary exile' (*ibid.* p. 149) until such time as their 'affairs should induce [them] to return to England' (*ibid.*). Accordingly on 7 September he and Sir Anthony Cooke, with Edwin Sandys, petitioned the city council for temporary residence (Protocols, vol. 33, f. 363, cf. below, p. 366). On 1 October this request was granted on condition that the Englishmen should pay not only the 'necessary imports like other burghers and agree not to take either lodgers or lodgings without permission' (*ibid.* f. 393vo), but even a further money guarantee in view of the fact that 'their means of sub-sistence was not yet settled' (*ibid.*). This amount we learn from a later protocol (vol. 34, f. 284vo, below, p. 368) was the very considerable sum of 20 gulden annually, whereas from 8 to 12 gulden was that usually exacted. Obviously the Imperial City was suspicious of those guests who had 'left their country on account of religion' (below, p. 366).

Lady Morison, during that winter, stood godmother to John Ponet's son, John (Archives of St Thomas, Series A, N. 245, f. 70). In the spring she was left a widow by her husband's death on 17 March 1556, possibly from the plague; but the town still exacted payment from her of the tax of 20 gulden, which she agreed to pay because 'it was customary in England' (vol. 34, f. 284vo: 27 June 1556). If John Parkhurst's epigram on Sir Richard Morison testifies to his learning, Morison's own punning humour earned him the nickname of the 'Merry Morison', and Michael Throckmorton bears generous witness to 'the loving instinct of his nature, for where other men get money', says Throckmorton, 'he gets men's hearts' (*L. and P.*, Henry VIII,

XII, pt I, p. 430). This is a rare tribute in that self-seeking age of Henry and of Edward.

Brussels, B IV b; Strasbourg, A VII a & b; VIII a; *D.N.B.*

290. MORLEY, JOHN: *Gent.* Of Sussex(?).

Though identification in this case is a matter of conjecture it seems not unlikely that this Englishman who was licensed to bear arms by the Signory of Venice in July-August 1555 (*Ven. Cal.* 1555–6, nos. 169, 171) was John Morley, third son of Thomas Morley of Glyn or Glynd in Sussex, whose father, another Thomas, had married Katherine, daughter of Thomas Pelham of Laughton (Harl. Soc. LIII, 48). In July 1558 this family showed its doubtful loyalty to Queen Mary, by failure to supply their quota of demi-lances to the Crown. And for this dereliction a Thomas Morley (father or son?) with Sir Nicholas Pelham, his cousin, were imprisoned in the Fleet, from which they were released only upon compliance (*P.C.A.* 1556–8, pp. 353, 358, etc.). A younger son of the house might well be found in the train of Francis, Earl of Bedford, at Venice in 1555.

Venice, B v b 3.

291. MORLEY, WILLIAM: *Student and gent.* Of Sussex.

Probably the William Morley who was a Fellow of Queens' College, Cambridge, 1548–50 (Venn, III, 214). The fact that he arrived at Geneva on 26 November 1557 in a group which included John Pelham strongly suggests that he, too, was of the Morleys of Glynd, Sussex. A William Morley who married Anne, daughter of Anthony Pelham (Harl. Soc. LIII, 48), is called in the Visitation of Sussex the eldest son of Thomas Morley (*ibid.*). He would thus have been the elder brother of John Morley (above), and is probably also the 'Guglielmus Marleus' who in 1555–6 was a student at Padua, and on 22 March substituted for Francis Walsingham as Consiliarius of the English students (Andrich, pp. 31, 131), an office in which he was succeeded by John Pelham (*q.v.*).

Padua, A VI; Geneva, A IV a.

292. MORWIN (MORWING, MORWYN, MORWENT), PETER: *Student.* Of Lincolnshire.

'A most cordial Protestant', says Fuller (*Worthies*, II, 21). In 1552 he had been made a perpetual Fellow of Magdalen College (*Ath. Oxon.* I, 454), but in December of that year six months' leave of absence was granted him that he might wait on Secretary Cecil 'promotionis suae causae' (Macray, II, 129). Humphrey (*Jewel*, p. 73) makes Morwin one of those expelled from the college by

Gardiner[1] in October 1553, but H. A. Wilson (*Magd.* p. 103) does not include his name among the nine 'actual Fellows removed at the Visitation', and Humphrey speaks of him as a 'voluntary exile to Germany' (*Jewel*, p. 73). Hitherto his place of exile has been unknown, but the Matrikel of the University of Basle shows Morwin (Petrus Morwingus) to have been a student there from 1554 to 1555 (f. 191 and below, p. 358) and he was evidently still at Basle on 10 May 1556 (cf. Grindal to Foxe, *Remains*, p. 221). Macray states that while in Germany Morwin translated the 'fictitious' Joseph Ben Gorion's *History of the Jews* at the entreaty of John Day (II, 129), the first edition of which, printed by Day for Richard Jugge, was dated 1558 (Magdalen Library). In 1559 Day published Morwin's translation from the Latin of Conrad Gesner's *Treasure of Evonymus* (*ibid.*). Fuller states that Morwin supported himself while abroad by preaching to the English exiles, which at Basle can hardly have been a lucrative employment (*Worthies*, II, 21).

On his return to England Grindal ordained him deacon on 25 January 1559/60 (*Grindal*, p. 54), and in that year he became both rector of Langwith, Derbyshire (cf. Foster), and chaplain to Bishop Bentham. At the Bishops' Visitation of 1564 (Cam. Misc. IX, 47) 'Petrus Morwing' is called the 'Rector de Langforde' and deemed 'miet to continue or to be called vnto office' (*ibid.* p. 46). In 1567 he was made a prebendary of Lichfield and was still alive in 1570, when he charged Laurence Nowell (*q.v.*), then dean of Lichfield, with the uttering of seditious speeches against the queen (*Dom. Cal.* 1547–80, p. 393).

Basle, A II a.

293. MOSGRAVE, Thomas: *Labourer.*

On Thursday, 14 October 1557, he was received as a 'resident' of Geneva with the designation 'laboureur' (f. 197), and on the following 20 November became a member of Knox's congregation. One wonders whether some of these humble folk at Geneva were not employed in the households of William Fuller, or Sir William Stafford.

Geneva, A IV a & b.

294. MOUNTAIN, Thomas: *Priest.* Of Kent (?). d. 1573.

According to his own statement Thomas was the son of Richard Mountain, a servant to Henry VIII and Edward VI (*Narr. of Ref.* p. 213). He was educated at Cambridge and from 1545 to 1553 was rector of Milton, Kent. On 29 December 1550 he was

---

[1] A 'Morwine' seems to have written some verses 'touching Winchester's epitaph' (*Narr. of Ref.* p. 85).

instituted by Cranmer to the rectorate of St Michael, Tower Royal, a London peculiar (Newcourt, I, 494), which, previous to its dissolution by Henry VIII, had been known as Whittington College (*ibid.*). On the death of Edward VI Mountain was closely associated with Northumberland, whom he accompanied to Cambridge when the duke went there to establish the title of 'Queen Jane' (*Narr. of Ref.* p. 180). This fact was of course well known to Gardiner when he had Mountain arrested on 8 October 1553 while the latter was celebrating communion according to the still legal Prayer Book of Edward VI. Though in this Mountain was acting within the law, Professor Muller (*Life of Gardiner*, p. 231) thinks that he had probably disregarded the injunction against unlicensed preaching, but it was obviously upon the count of treason that Gardiner summoned Mountain to appear before him on 11 October, 'for thes ij', Gardiner complained, 'be alwayes lynked together, treson and herysy, and thow haste lyke a shameles man offendyd in bothe...' (*Narr. of Ref.* p. 181). Mountain was then sent to the Marshalsea and was therefore, because of his imprisonment, unable to answer the citation before the Vicar General of 7 March 1554 which followed the queen's proclamation of 4 March against married priests. But he was examined in prison and there admitted that 'he had been a priest for ten years and had been six years married, and continued to live so up to his imprisonment at Michaelmas' (*Mar. Reac.* p. 66). Apparently he had already been deprived of his rectorate by the re-establishment of Whittington College (Newcourt, I, 494, note k). The initials 'T. M.' appended to the declaration of doctrine issued on 8 May by the bishops in prison (Foxe, VI, 553) are probably those of Thomas Mountain, and he was accused of possessing one of the seditious pamphlets from abroad, probably Knox's *Admonition to the Christians of Newcastle*, of which he was even said to be the author (*Narr. of Ref.* p. 187). For a time he was removed to the Tower, where he was examined by a special commission (*ibid.* pp. 188–9), then, probably to avoid the onus of condemning him, Gardiner had Mountain sent to stand his trial for treason at Cambridge (*ibid.* p. 190), where he was freed on bail. From Cambridge he went back to London, then to Colchester, that 'harboror of all herytykes, and ever was' (*ibid.* p. 212). Had he there any traffic with Trudge-over,[1] agent of the exiles, and disseminator of seditious literature? From his own words it is highly probable that he did (*ibid.* pp. 210–11). And he returned to London a prisoner (*ibid.*), but a prisoner who was apparently permitted to escape, for at Gravesend he took ship for Antwerp, where he taught in a school for eighteen

[1] Cf. above, p. 35, n. 2 and p. 50.

months, then went to Duisburg—the only Englishman known by name in that colony. There he remained until the death of Mary, when he became rector of St Pancras, Soper Lane (1559–61) and of St Faith (1560–73) (Venn, III, 223).

B I a & b; B II; Duisburg (*Narr. of Ref.*); *D.N.B.*

295. MULLINS (MOLYNS (*D.N.B.*), MOLLEYNS, etc.), JOHN: *Deacon.* Of Somerset. d. 1591.

Fellow of Magdalen College in 1541, and M.A. in 1545. On 29 March 1551 he was ordained deacon, but not priest, at Oxford (*Mar. Reac.* p. 213). Although Mullins was one of those who had sought and obtained leave of absence from his college before September 1553, yet Wilson names him among the nine actual Fellows removed from Magdalen by Gardiner at his Visitation in October (*Magd.* p. 101), all of whom, be it remembered, received a grant of money 'ex voluntate inquisitorum' (*ibid.* p. 103). Doubtless this sum helped him to retire to Zurich, where he arrived with Horne's party on 5 April 1554 (*Diarium*, p. 46, and *O.L.* II, 751) and where on 13 October he was one of the signatories of Zurich's refusal to join the English colony at Frankfort. Nevertheless he did remove to Frankfort in 1555, probably upon an invitation from the congregation to become reader in Greek in their newly improvised university (*T.* p. 60). In the autumn of that year his name appears among the 'students' of the Standesliste; and in the tax-list of October 1556 his property is rated at 30 florins (Jung, p. 29). On 10 June 1557 he is found living in the house of Thomas Wattes (*H.S.P.* IV, 88), but he never subscribed to the 'new discipline'. Later in England Mullins became an opponent of Whittingham, and Petheram believes (Preface to *Troubles*, p. iv) that it was his sermon 'not entirely favourable' to Whittingham's party, preached at Paul's Cross in October 1573 (the text of which is now lost), that was responsible for the publication of the *Troubles at Frankfort*, framed as a rejoinder to Mullins's criticisms. Curiously enough it is in Bonner's Register that we find the record of Mullins's collation to the prebend of Kentish Town, on 29 July 1559; and of his appointment to the archdeaconry of London on 13 December, upon the deprivation of John Harpesfield (Harl. MS. 6955, f. 116). But Bonner, though not deprived of his bishopric until 29 June, had actually ceased to be responsible for institutions after 6 May, and the Register expressly states that from that date, until 8 December, all institutions were by Commissioners (*Mar. Reac.* p. 126). On 5 May 1560 the new archdeacon preached 'a goodly sermon' before the Lord Mayor and Aldermen 'and grett audyense was ther' to hear him (*Machyn*, p. 234). Mullins, in fact, as chaplain to Queen Elizabeth, was on the side of conformity, and in 1570/1 a curious letter of Archbishop Parker shows that he was to be used officially to 'tell the precisians that her Highness' sword should be compelled to cut off this stubborn multitude [the Puritans], which daily groweth' (Parker, *Correspondence*, p. 377). Hence it is to Mullins's sermon at Paul's Cross that we owe Whittingham's history of the troubles at Frankfort which, with all its omissions and prevarications, is still the only comprehensive account we have of the Marian Exile. Mullins was rector of Bocking from 1577 to his death in 1591.

B II; Zurich, A VIII a & c; Frankfort, A III a 2, 3, 4 & b 1, 2; *D.N.B.*

296. NAGORS, RICHARD.

A subscriber to the 'new discipline' in April 1557, whose identity remains a puzzle. No English equivalent of his name has been discovered, and it seems not unlikely that he was a foreigner, perhaps a Fleming.   Frankfort, B III b.

297. NEVILL, Sir HENRY, Knt. Of Billingbear, Berkshire. d. 1593.

Grandson of George Nevill, Lord Abergavenny (d. 1492), ancestor of the family of Braybrooke and second son of Sir Edward Nevill, beheaded for treason in 1538 (Harl. Soc. LVII, 181 and D. Rowland, *Family of Nevill*, pp. 141–2). This Sir Henry, who was the first of his name to settle at Billingbear, married Elizabeth, daughter of Sir John Gresham, Alderman of London (*Chron. Q. Jane*, p. 100 and note), and their son, another Sir Henry, Queen Elizabeth's future ambassador to France, later took to wife Anne, daughter of Sir Henry Killigrew. Thus both in antecedents and in marriage connections the elder Sir Henry is characteristic of those gentlemen who went into exile under Mary. In 1550 he had become a Gentleman of the Privy Chamber to Edward VI; in 1551 he was knighted with Cecil and Cheke (*Machyn*, pp. 10, 322); and in November of that year went to France as a member of Lord Clinton's suite, of which company was also Sir William Stafford (*q.v.*) (*Mem.* II, i, 507). Earlier in the year he had received the manor of Margrave, in the alienation of the bishop of Winchester's lands (*ibid.* pp. 484–5). At the death of Edward VI both he and his father-in-law, John Gresham, were signatories to the Letters Patent for the Limitation of the Crown (*Chron. Q. Jane*, p. 100). Hence it is not surprising to find Sir Henry Nevill among the English fugitives at Padua in August 1554 (Cam. Misc. X, 116) and to discover him also among those specially named in John Brett's commission of 1556 (Brett, p. 115). By that time, however, he had returned to England (*ibid.* p. 129). In 1576 he was placed upon an ecclesiastical commission with Sir Anthony Cooke, which would rather indicate a puritan bias to his protestantism (*Grindal*, pp. 309–10); but his friendship with Sir Henry Sydney has left us a note of human affection rare in the annals of the exiles. Writing in 1578 to his son Robin, Sydney says of his friend, 'There can be no greater love, than of long time hath been, and yet is, between Sir Harry Nevyll and me: and so will continue till our lives end...' (D. Rowland, *op. cit.* p. 142). According to his monument in the church of St Lawrence at Waltham, Berks., he died on 13 January 1593 (*Misc. Gen. and Her.* n.s. I, 436).

Padua, B IV b.

298. NEWTON, THEODORE: *Student.* Of Gloucestershire(?). d. 1569.

M.A. of Christ Church, Oxford, in 1551/2 and rector of Badgworth, Somerset, in 1551, Theodore Newton has the distinction of being the sole exile among the sixty-nine clergy deprived in the diocese of Bath and Wells between 1554 and 1558 (Bourne's Register, printed Dixon, IV, 153). Nor was the cause of deprivation marriage, but an insufficiency of orders which, under Elizabeth, was also to stand in the way of his preferment. Although deprived on 1 October 1554, he did not arrive in Geneva until nearly a year later, when, on 5 November, he was received into Knox's congregation. There he seems to have remained until his return to England some time in 1559. Grindal ordained him deacon on 25 January 1559/60 (*Grindal*, p. 54), and he was proposed for a prebend of Canterbury but rejected on the score of his not being a priest (*Parker*, I, 144). He had at that time already 'departed the realm' again 'by the Queen's license' (*ibid.*), but by 1565, having presumably received priest's orders in the interim, he became rector of Ringwould, Kent, and in 1567 of St Dionis, Lime Street, London (Foster, III, 1066).

Geneva, A IV a.

299. NICOLLS (NICOLIS, NICHOLLS), PHILIP: *Student.* Of Devon. Wife.

Except for the discovery of the records of Aarau, it would not have been known that Philip Nichols, the protestant author and controversialist, had been an exile to the Continent under Mary. In 1557 he was living at Aarau with his wife in the house of Laurentz Wyerman; and Hans Dür tells us that he was born at 'Ilfarcum' in 'Dewonenser'. This statement supports the belief already held that he was probably the son of John Nichols, rector of Landewednack, Cornwall (cf. Foster, III, 1069 and *D.N.B.*), and also the father, both of the Philip Nicolls, who was later a canon of Exeter (Foster, III, 1070 and Venn, III, 255), and of Josias Nichols (1555?–1639, *D.N.B.*), the puritan parson of Eastwel, who eventually became a member of the classis of Kent (Usher, p. xxix).

The Philip Nichols of Aarau had in 1547 gained some repute from his controversy with Richard Crispyn, a canon of Exeter, who denied that the 'Scripture was the Touch Stone or Trial of all other Doctrines...'. Nichols's defence of this thesis appeared in a pamphlet published by John Day in that same year (Herbert's Ames, I, 617), and dedicated by Nichols to 'his singular good maister, Sir Peter Carewe', who had instigated the printing of it. Nichols then was a protégé of Sir Peter and had probably been a member of the colony of Wesel before his appearance at Aarau. The fact of his exile also makes it probable that he was the same and not 'another Philip Nichols' (cf. *D.N.B.*) who in 1562 received the living of Kineton in the diocese of Wells on the presentation of Sir Francis Knollys.

Among the Sloane MSS. (no. 301) in the British Museum is a 17th century copy of the *Relation of the Third Voyage of Sir Francis Drake*, which asserts on its title-page that it was compiled by 'Philip Nicholls, Preacher', and that Sir Francis himself had corrected the text for publication. Drake's original dedication of it to Elizabeth is dated 1592 (cf. Hakluyt Soc. 2nd ser., No. 71, Pt. II). Whether, then, Nicholls the compiler, was the Marian exile, later of Kineton, or his son, the canon, is left in doubt.

Wesel (?); Aarau, A I a & b; cf. *D.N.B.*

300. NOWELL, ALEXANDER: *Priest and gent.* Of Whalley, Lancashire. 1507(?)–1602.

The author of the Prayer Book catechism is too well known to require any extended biography. He was the eldest son of John Nowell of Read Hall, Whalley, Lancs., and a Fellow of Brasenose College, in 1536 (*O.H.S.* I, 183; given in error as 1526 in *D.N.B.*). In 1543 he was appointed to the headmastership of Westminster School, a post which he held until his exile in 1555. The fact that in 1551 he had also been made a canon of Westminster, disqualified him as a member for Looe, Cornwall, in the first parliament of Mary (Churton's *Life*, p. 18). What necessity drove him abroad we do not know. Fuller would have us believe that while Nowell was quietly 'catching of Fishes' by the Thames, Bonner was inexpertly busy 'catching of Nowell', whom he designed 'to the Shambles', from which fate he was saved by 'Mr Francis Bowyer, then Merchant, afterwards Sheriffe of London' (*Worthies*, ed. 1811, I, 547), who conveyed him beyond seas. Foster asserts that he went to both Geneva and Basle; Strype, that he was also at Strasbourg. Both of these statements may be true, but there are no foreign records to corroborate them, and it is probable that he made Frankfort his headquarters. There, the first official reference to him is made in the tax-list of October 1556, where his property

is rated at 200 florins (Jung, p. 29) and Jung indicates him as
having but lately arrived. He is first mentioned in the *Troubles* on
26 January 1557, when he was one of those to whom John Hales
addressed an earnest plea for peace in the Horne-Ashley quarrel
(*T.* p. 65). On the memorable 2nd of February following, it was
Nowell who acted as 'the mouthe for the rest' (i.e. the minority)
when the new decrees and ordinances were presented to Horne, the
pastor, and the elders (*T.* p. 72). Yet he subscribed to the 'new
discipline' in April. What appears to be a second subscription of
his in the following December may be that of his brother Laurence,
or Laurence may have been the signatory in April and Alexander
in December, which would seem more in accord with Alexander's
earlier opposition. But however that may be, it was Alexander who
on 10 June 1557 was living with Thomas Wattes in the house that
the latter had recently bought from Whitehead (below, p. 327),
and he was also one of the last to leave Frankfort, for on 3 January
1559 he signed that congregation's refusal to join Geneva in her
anti-ceremonial crusade (*T.* p. 190). Thus his apparently continuous
residence in Frankfort makes it unlikely that Alexander was the
'one Mr Noel' who in December 1558 was acting as tutor to
'Mr Harrington's sons' at Padua (*For. Cal.* 1558–9, p. 22). By
28 May 1559 it seems probable that Alexander was back in
London, and I believe that it was he[1] who on that date sent an
account to John Abell, still at Strasbourg, of the forced enthusiasm
with which the new Prayer Book was received by the London
populace. 'The Lord Keeper and the whole Council being present',
he writes, 'the preacher proclaimed the restoring of the book of
King Edward, whereat the Lords and the people made (or at least
pretended) a wonderful rejoicing. Never a Bishop or Canon of
Paul's was present thereat' (*ibid.* p. 287). The following year he,
himself, was dean of St Paul's, but Parker's recommendation of
him for the provostship of Eton was rejected by the queen on the
score of Nowell's being 'a married minister'. Living to be ninety-
five, Nowell was one of the links between the Marian Exile and the
new age of the Stuarts.

B i a & b; B ii; Strasbourg and Basle (?); Frankfort, A iii a 3, 4 & b 2;
D.N.B.

301. NOWELL, Laurence: *Deacon.* Of Whalley, Lancashire.
d. 1576.

Younger brother of Alexander Nowell. Of Brasenose College,
Oxford, 1536, and Christ's College, Cambridge, (?)1538. M.A.
Oxford, 1544 (Foster and Venn). In 1546 he was made master of

---

[1] This is a conclusion reached after a careful consideration of dates and of
internal evidence, see below under Laurence Nowell.

Sutton Coldfield School and in 1550 was ordained deacon by Ridley (*Mar. Reac.* p. 191). But he did not proceed to priest's orders, for which neglect he was deprived of his living of Drayton Bassett on 5 June 1555 (*ibid.* pp. 59, 108–9). Cooper says that for some time he was concealed in the house of Sir John Perrot at Carew Castle, Pembrokeshire, but subsequently joined his brother in Germany (I, 357–8). Unless however one of the two Alexander Nowells who signed the 'discipline' at Frankfort is in reality Laurence, there is no evidence that he was ever there. In fact his whereabouts on the Continent are officially unknown, but we believe it to have been Laurence and not Alexander who was the 'one Mr Noel'[1] that was in France with Thomas Randolph, and afterwards 'instructor to Mr Harrington's sons, both there and in Padua...' (*For. Cal.* 1558–9, p. 22). Randolph goes on to say that at Padua he also professed 'the mathematicals openly' and was 'well entertained to his great honour' (*ibid.*). This was in December 1558, and doubtless the Mr Harrington referred to was the Robert Harrington, exile at Frankfort. If Laurence Nowell was in France and Italy, while abroad, the silence of the German records about him would be explained. On his return to England he was made dean of Lichfield in 1560 (Le Neve, I, 562–3) and showed his Calvinist sympathies by signing the petition for a discipline in 1562, but it is for his devoted work as an antiquary that Laurence Nowell deserves to be remembered. And to him Mr Robin Flower in an address to the British Academy delivered in 1935 has accorded the honour of the *Discovery of England in Tudor Times* (*Procs. Brit. Acad.* vol. XXI).

[1] A curious doubt seems to have entered into the mind of the editor of the *Foreign Calendar* for 1558–9 as to whether this was indeed Mr Nowell (Alexander as he assumes) and not rather Edmund Allen, to whom he also attributes the possible authorship of the letter of Alexander Nowell in regard to the Prayer Book, just quoted above. He bases his doubt upon the device of the wafer with which the letter was sealed and on which Churton thought he read an 'E.A.' and, as he also says, '(I think) a N. on the opposite margin' (note *For. Cal.* 1558–9, p. 288), but upon internal evidence the writer of that letter was almost certainly Alexander Nowell, for he speaks of having been 'at his new benefice in Kent...this last week' (*ibid.* p. 288). Now in 1560 Nowell was made rector of Saltwood, Kent (Foster, III, 1081), while Edmund Allen on 28 May 1559, the date of the writing of the above letter, was in Germany, for not till June is he found travelling towards England in the company of Christopher Mundt (*vide* Allen's letter to Cecil of 27 June 1559, dated from Augusta, *For. Cal.* 1558–9, no. 881). And in the postscript to this letter Allen refers to himself as the bishop elect of Rochester, an office which he was not, however, destined to fill. Why, again, Randolph should have *meant* 'Allen' when he *said* 'Noel', and Nowell had been personally known to him in Paris, is not easy to understand.

302. OFFLEY, HUGH: *Merchant*. Of London. d. 1594.

He was the seventh son of William Offley, sheriff of Chester in 1517, and Hugh was born at Chester (*Geneal.* n.s. XIX, 217 and XX, 78). In London he was a freeman of the Company of Leather-sellers, several times alderman, and Sheriff of London in the year of the Armada (Beaven, *Aldermen of London*, I, 36 and II, 43, 174). His eldest brother, Thomas Offley, sheriff in the year 1553–4, was the one to whom Lord Guilford Dudley was delivered to be beheaded (Offley MS., *Geneal.* n.s. XIX, 4); and in 1556 he was Lord Mayor of London. Thomas was therefore in a position to be of great use to his younger brother, when Hugh, having become involved in the Dudley conspiracy, fled to France in that year (*Mem.* III, i, 566). For as Thomas Offley had 'saved many who should have died' after Wyatt's rebellion he very probably exerted himself to get Hugh safely out of the kingdom. It was then, no doubt, that Hugh met those members of 'the Nobillity of France' with whom he later 'was in great Favour' (*Geneal.* n.s. XIX, 87), but he soon exchanged the rôle of conspirator for that of informer. He it was who introduced William Lant (*q.v.*) to Wotton (*For. Cal.* 1553–8, p. 276) with his fantastic tales of rebellions hatched against the queen, and it was so, we may suppose, that Offley purchased a pardon, for in November 1557 he was back in London again and in communication with the Privy Council 'towching the taking of diverse Frenche shippes by Englishemen' (*P.C.A.* 1556–8, p. 208). The Offley MS., already quoted, makes no mention of these early peccadilloes of Hugh, nor of his later connection with the Babington plot, in which, as the great-uncle of Gilbert Gifford (A. G. Smith, *Babington Plot* (1936), pp. 163, 167–8, etc.), he acted as the latter's intermediary for letters and funds (*Dom. Cal.* 1547–80, pp. 342, 418, 456, 458). But a more reputable side of Offley's career was his association with John Bodley in the development of the wool trade (*ibid.* p. 402) and his own efforts towards the improvement of London's water supply: as 'a Founder of the great Conduitt in the Markett place' (*Geneal.* n.s. XIX, 88) Offley should be remembered. Also, as a builder of beautiful houses, an associate of nobles, a merchant adventurer and a lavish dispenser of charities (*ibid.* p. 87), his career is typical of Tudor merchant princes. If he dabbled now and again in conspiracy, he would seem to have had no particular end in view beyond the appease-ment of his Tudor restlessness. He was buried in St Andrew Undershaft.

France, B v b 1 & 2.

303. OLDE (OLD), John, D.D.(?): *Priest*(?). Of Staffordshire.
Wife. d. 1557(?).

Strype calls John Olde a 'teacher of youth as well as of the gospel'
(*Mem*. II, i, 47); Bale describes him as 'insigniter eruditus' in
things sacred and profane (*Scriptores*, no. LXII, p. 721). He was
probably educated at Cambridge (Venn), but I can find no authority
other than Strype's for his 'D.D.' The Duchess of Somerset, whose
protégé he was, presented him to the living of Cubbington, Warwickshire (1545), at the suit of Hugh Latimer; and at the time of Mary's
accession he was also a canon of Lichfield, of which dignity he was
then deprived. Shortly after Thomas Becon's recantation in 1542
(*Mem*. I, i, 56) he took refuge in John Olde's house[1] in Staffordshire
which already sheltered Robert Wisdom, and it was then that
Becon speaks of him as 'a man old in name, notwithstanding
young in years', who to them was 'as Jason...to Paul and Silas'
(*Jewel of Joy*, Becon, *Works*, III, 422). When his friends Becon and
Wisdom left for Germany, Olde followed them, 'somewhat', as he
confesses, 'before extreme trouble came'. And at Frankfort, where
he established himself, his name first appears in the tax-list of
15 January 1557, in which he is recorded to have had no property
(Jung, p. 30). But it is probable that before his arrival at Frankfort
he had been elsewhere on the Continent, possibly at Emden, for his
pamphlet on *The acquital or purgation of the moost catholyke
Prince Edwarde the VI*, with its colophon 'Waterford, 7 November
1555', is now identified by Col. Isaac as among those English books
printed at Emden by Egidius van der Erve (Bibliog. Soc. 1931,
p. 341; cf. *S.T.C*. no. 18797, where Zurich and Froschauer are
suggested). From 1557 on, however, Olde, with his wife, remained
at Frankfort. There in April he signed the 'new discipline' and
there on 10 June he was living in the house of Edward Oldsworth
(*H.S.P*. IV, 88). On 30 June he was one of those to whom Richard
Chambers addressed his letter of justification for his administration
of the common funds (*T*. pp. 182–3), but on the following
15 September he died (Bale's *Index*, p. xxi). Olde was the author
of several pamphlets, and in 1548 had been one of the translators
of the *Paraphrases of Erasmus*.

B I a & b; B II; Frankfort, A III a 3, 4 & b 2; *D.N.B*.

---

[1] The article in the *D.N.B*. would seem to suggest that this episode took
place in the reign of Mary, but since the *Jewel of Joy*, in which Becon refers to
it, was published in 1553, the occasion must belong to Olde's earlier need for
shelter.

304. OLDSWORTH (ALDSWORTH, OLDISHORTHE), Edward (or Edmund): *Student and gent.* Of Tewkesbury, Gloucestershire.

Probably the son of Nicholas Oldesworth of Polten's Court, co. Gloucester (Harl. Soc. XXI, 256), and brother of Thomas Oldsworth (below). Evidently he was a friend of Bishop Hooper, for it was to Oldsworth's guardianship that the bishop's son, Daniel, was entrusted after the death of his mother (see above, p. 187). When he became a burgher of Frankfort on 15 March 1557 (Jung, p. 24), Oldsworth describes himself as of Tewkesbury ('Teusskisburig', see *ibid.* p. 57), but he had been in Frankfort since 1555, when he was registered as a student on the Standesliste. In October 1556 his taxable property was rated at 700 florins, and at some time during his exile he married a Helena Gravelet, whose name suggests that she was of French or Flemish origin[1] (Jung, p. 57). In March-April 1557 he signed the 'new discipline', in June he is found as a householder with five servants, and with him were also living John Olde and his wife, 'Egidia', wife of an absent John Maynard, and Daniel Hooper, Oldesworth's ward (*H.S.P.* IV, 88). Throughout the text of the *Troubles at Frankfort*, his name is never mentioned as a partisan in the strife—a rare distinction. After his return to England there is also silence in regard to him. We know only that he was still living in 1569, when his arms were confirmed to him (Harl. Soc. XXI, 256, note), and that his son Arnold became an associate to the bench of Lincoln's Inn in 1612 (Foster, III, 1088), and 'Clerke of the Hamper' to James I (Harl. Soc. XXI, 15).

Frankfort, A III a 1, 2, 3, 4 & b 1, 2; B III b.

305. OLDSWORTH, Thomas: *Student*(?) *and gent.* Of Gloucestershire (?).

He was probably a brother of Edward Oldsworth (above) but he appears abroad but once, when in March-April 1557 he signed the 'new discipline'. In 1572 a Thomas Oldesworth, quite possibly the same man, was prebendary of Liddington in Wiltshire, according to the list of incumbents preserved in the church.

Frankfort, B III b.

306. ORMESBY, Thomas(?): *Gent.* Of Lincolnshire. d. 1560(?).

Beyond the fact that the 'one Ormesby' mentioned by Nicholas Wotton in 1556 probably belonged to the family of Ormesby in Lincolnshire (Harl. Soc. LI, 739) there is not enough data to establish the exact identity of this rebel in Paris. It is possible that

---

[1] In the Visitation of Gloucester (p. 256) his wife's name is given as 'Tacye', daughter of Arthur Porter.

he was the Thomas Ormesby 'late serving in the Northe' who in 1551 had been appointed 'to serve the Kinge in Irelande' (*P.C.A.* 1550–2, pp. 263, 299). If so, he was the third son of John Ormsby of Louth and his wife Rose, daughter of William Woodford (*Lincs. Peds.* p. 739). To Wotton, he called himself 'a pensioner' and said that he had 'fled from England because he was sent for to come to the Court' (*For. Cal.* 1553–8, p. 229), but his association with Aston [Assheton], to whom he 'had sold a gown', proclaims him as an associate of Dudley, though Ormesby denied that he knew that either Assheton or Dudley 'had any conspiracy on hand' (*ibid.*). Wotton, who agreed to plead Ormesby's cause with the queen, seems to have done so with success, for Thomas Ormsby, son of John, lived to fight at Leith in 1560, and there was killed (Harl. Soc. LI, 739).

Boulogne, Paris, B v b 1.

307. ORPHINSTRANGE, [JOHN?]: *Student.*

A John Orphynstrange or Orphanstrange, who matriculated from St John's College, Cambridge, in 1544, received his B.A. and M.A. from Corpus Christi, Cambridge, in 1547 and 1549, while in 1546 he appears as a Fellow of Trinity in the Charter. So much is known of him to Cooper (II, 1) and to Venn (III, 283). But in 1552/3 a John Orphenstrange, whom we take to be the same person, was student and Consiliarius at the University of Padua, and in 1554 a 'Mr Orphinstrange' is found by Sir Thomas Hoby among the group of protestant gentlemen who gathered at Padua that autumn (Cam. Misc. X, 116). Were it not for this, his name would not have been included in the list of exiles, but he would seem to have felt safer abroad in the reign of Mary. By 1562 he had received an LL.D. and was attached to the archdeaconry of London (Cooper), a fact which tends to confirm the belief that his leanings were protestant.

Padua, A VI; B IV b; Cooper.

308. PARKER, ROGER (or ROBERT?): *Gent.* Of Essex. Wife.

Strype seems to know nothing of Robert (as he calls him) Parker, beyond the fact that he fled abroad with Anne his wife; Anne and Cecilie, his daughters; Wentworth and Peregrine, his sons. And from the son's name of 'Wentworth' he infers that Parker may have been some 'dependent of the lord of that name' (*Mem.* III, i, 225–6). It is, however, extremely easy from these very names of his children to identify the exile as Roger (not Robert) Parker of Kirby, Essex (son of Henry Parker of Frith Hall), who married Anne, daughter of Roger[1] Wentworth of Bocking, Essex, one of

---

[1] Called 'Bryen' Wentworth, son of Roger, in Visitation of Yorks. (Harl. Soc. XVI, 343).

the Wentworths of Yorkshire from whom descended Thomas Wentworth, Lord Stafford (Harl. Soc. XIII, 259). 'He seemed', says Strype, 'a person as of great piety, so of an inquisitive mind in the doctrines of religion', and he became the patron of Bartholomew Traheron, who in gratitude dedicated to Parker his lectures on Revelations (*Mem.* III, i, 226). Already Parker had been one of the committee of 'sustainers' who financed the migration, and he seems to have continued his kindly offices abroad both financially and as a mediator. Thus he stood between Traheron and one of the latter's critics (*ibid.* p. 544); and our only clue to his place of refuge abroad is his signature to Strasbourg's attempt on 29 September 1557 to reconcile the strife of factions at Frankfort (*T.* p. 174), though Strype evidently believed that Parker and his family actually lived at Frankfort.

Frankfort (?); Strasbourg, B III a.

309. PARKHURST, JOHN: *Priest.* Of Guildford, Surrey. Wife. 1512(?)–75.

According to Anthony Wood, Parkhurst was the only Fellow of Merton College (1529) who sought refuge abroad under Mary (O.H.S. IV, 48–9). While he was a tutor of Merton, Jewel had been his pupil and the two men remained intimate friends (*Annals*, II, i, 347). In 1547 Parkhurst was chaplain to Queen Catherine Parr. Later he filled the same office in the household of Katherine, Duchess of Suffolk, and just before the accession of Mary he had received the rich living of Cleeve in Gloucestershire. There he became a close friend of Bishop Hooper 'as well by disposition as by vicinity of residence' (*O.L.* I, 291). But early in 1554 he withdrew to the Continent, and the letter in which James Haddon introduces him to Bullinger provides the first known date for Parkhurst's appearance at Strasbourg—9 July 1554. I attach great importance to this date, for I believe that it was the news brought by Parkhurst direct from England—news of the approaching meeting of a parliament which gossip said[1] was to effect a reconciliation with Rome—that was responsible for the drawing up at Strasbourg of a pamphlet which bore the running title of the *Confession of the Banished Ministers* but which was, in effect, a first puritan *Admonition to Parliament* (above, p. 289; and cf. 'Ponet', *q.v.* and 'Becon', *q.v.*).

From Strasbourg Parkhurst went to Zurich carrying with him a letter from Hooper to Bullinger which was probably that written 'from prison' on 23 May 1554 (*O.L.* I, 103). As Haddon said by way of introduction, Parkhurst was able to give 'as much information about our friend Hooper as almost any one else' (*ibid.* p. 291).

[1] This was common rumour as early as April.

The exact date of his arrival we do not know, but it must have been some little time before October, and again I connect his appearance with certain activities among the exiles: in this case with an attempt on the part of the 'Students of Zurich' to exert over the other colonies, and especially over Frankfort, some measure of ecclesiastical control. Their effort towards a closer union, embodied in a letter dated 13 October 1554, of which Parkhurst was a signatory (*T.* p. 16), was especially directed against Whittingham's move in the same direction, and it set in motion that series of visitations of Frankfort from Strasbourg in the interests of Prayer Book conformity, which culminated in the discomfiture of Knox and Whittingham by Richard Cox (*T.* p. 40). While at Zurich, Parkhurst would appear to have made his home with Rudolph Gualter (*Z.L.* II, 10), and from a letter of Goodman's to Peter Martyr, dated 20 August 1558, we know that on the eve of Mary's death he was still living there with his wife (*O.L.* II, 771), said to have been Margaret, daughter of Thomas Garnish of Kenton, Suffolk (*D.N.B.*). The story of Parkhurst's future labour against 'papistical habits' (*Annals*, I, i, 264) and of his unsuccessful administration of his bishopric of Norwich, to which he was appointed in 1560, belongs to Elizabethan history.

B I a & b; B II; Zurich, A VIII a; B III a; *D.N.B.*

PARKYNS, HUMPHREY. *See* Perkyns.

PARPOINT, EDWARD. *See* Perpoint.

310. PARRY, HENRY: *Student and gent.* Of Herefordshire. Wife. d. 1571.

Since he is designated 'Herfordensis' in the Frankfort records, there can be little doubt that this was the son of William Parry of Wormbridge in Herefordshire (*Ath. Oxon.* II, 192), and also the Henry Parry who, in 1547, was collated to the chancellorship of Salisbury Cathedral (Le Neve, II, 651). But in 1553 he was deprived (W. H. Jones, *Fasti Eccles. Saris.* p. 340) and fled to Frankfort, where the first official notice of him is on 7 March 1555, when he became a burgher paying a tax of 2 fl. 9 s. 1. (Jung, p. 57). In the Prayer Book strife that spring, Parry was a lively partisan, and Knox accuses him of having been, with Edward Isaac, the chief informer against him before the magistrates ('Narrative', Laing, IV, 47). In the autumn his name is listed among the English 'students', and he is described as living 'on the Row [uff der zeil] in a garden' (Jung, p. 57). His taxable property is rated in 1556 at 200 florins, and he is found in June 1557 to have been one of the very few who could afford the luxury of a house to himself. With him lived his wife, his four children, and his two servants, Leonard (*q.v.*) and Joanna Hobbes (*H.S.P.* IV, 88). In 1559 Parry was restored to his chancellorship of Salisbury (Le Neve, II, 652), and in 1561 a son, Henry, was born to him (*Ath. Oxon.* II, 192) who later became bishop of Worcester (*D.N.B.*).

B II; Frankfort, A III a 1, 2, 3, 4 & b 1, 2; B III a & b.

311. PARRY, LEONARD: *Student*(?). Of Herefordshire(?).

His name appears abroad only among the signatories of the 'new discipline' at Frankfort. Though he was very likely Henry Parry's brother, there is no evidence to prove it.
Frankfort, B III b.

312. PEDDER, JOHN: *Priest*(?). Of Suffolk(?). 1520(?)–71.

M.A. from Peterhouse, 1542, and B.D. from Trinity College, 1551 (Venn, III, 334). This John Pedder can hardly be any other than the exile, yet there are facts difficult to explain in Venn's account of him. How, for example, could he have held the living of Redgrave, Suffolk, from 1551 to 1561, and been made a canon of Norwich in 1557, while at the same time he was a refugee for religion's sake in Germany? Yet of this last fact there is no doubt, unless there were two contemporary John Pedders. The exile went first to Strasbourg, probably as one of the group that followed Thomas Lever from Cambridge, and there on 23 November 1554 he signed that colony's admonition to Frankfort in the matter of Prayer Book conformity (*T.* p. 23). In December as 'ein predicant' he received 16 florins from the Duke of Württemberg's donation (Württ. Staatsarchiv). Later, however, he went to Frankfort, possibly in the train of Richard Cox, and appears among the 'students' in the Standesliste of that autumn of 1555. In the following year he is credited on the Frankfort tax-list with 40 florins' worth of property (Jung, p. 29) and in June 1557 is found living in the household of Erkenwald Rawlins (*H.S.P.* IV, 89). His religious opinions had steadily tended to the left, so that he was not only among the first subscribers to the 'new discipline' in the spring of 1557, but in September was also one of those who refused the way of reconciliation offered by Strasbourg in the quarrels that followed upon its adoption (*T.* p. 174). An intransigent puritan. On his return to England preferment did not come to him immediately (*Annals*, I, i, 229), but in 1560 he received the deanery of Worcester, and in the Bishops' Visitation of 1564 is commended as a 'Favorer' (Cam. Misc. IX, 5). He had voted in 1562 for the six articles altering rites and ceremonies, and had also petitioned for a discipline.

B I a & b; B II; Strasbourg, A VII c; B III a; Frankfort, A III a 2, 3, 4 & b 1, 2; B III b; *D.N.B.*

313. PEERS (PERSE, PEARSE, PERS), JAMES: *Student.* Of
Kent. Wife.

This is probably the James Pearse (Perse) who in 1540, as a
'chaplain', supplicated for a B.A. at Oxford and probably received
a benefice in Kent (Foster, III, 1133). A James Perse is listed
among the 'preachers' in the Emden catalogue, and also by Bale,
who calls him 'Peers'. At Frankfort, on 29 April 1555, a James
Pers, calling himself 'Cantuarensis', became a citizen, paying
'2 Taler' as Bürgergeld (Jung, pp. 24, 57), and in June 1557 James
Peers, with his wife, one son and three servants, was living in the
house of Thomas Crawley (*H.S.P.* IV, 88). Also he had signed the
'new discipline' in March-April, yet strangely enough his name is
neither on the Standesliste of 1555 nor on the tax-lists of 1556
and 1557. He may have absented himself from Frankfort at that
convenient time, and he certainly played no part in the Frankfort
quarrels. But can he have been involved in any way with a John
Peers, shipmaster of Southampton, who in March and April 1556
had been engaged in conveying Ashton and his company to
Newhaven (*Dom. Cal.* 1547–80, pp. 76, 79)?

B I a & b; B II; Frankfort, A III a 1, 4 & b 2; B III b.

314. PEKINS, JOHN, B.D.(?): *Priest.*

Student and Fellow of Exeter College, Oxford, and Rector of his
college from 1531 to 1534 (Foster, III, 1138). In 1543 he was made
a canon of Westminster (Le Neve, III, 354) and rector of Bradwell-
juxta-Mare, Essex, which he held from 1542 until his deprivation
some time before 1 May 1554 (Foster). Abroad his place of exile
has not been discovered, nor is anything known of him, apparently,
after the accession of Elizabeth. Possibly he died in exile.

n.p.; B I a & b; B II.

315. PELHAM (PELLAM), JOHN: *Gent.* Of Sandhurst and
Laughton, Sussex. 1537–80.

The eldest son and heir of Nicholas Pelham (d. 1560) and grandson
of Sir William Pelham of Sandhurst by his first wife Mary,
daughter of Sir Richard Carew. Thus John Pelham's grandmother
was a Carew, his mother a Sackvile, and his wife, Judith, a daughter
of Lord St John of Bletso (Harl. Soc. LIII, 20–1). Moreover his
family was one of those which, involved in conspiracy against
Mary, was later connected both with the death of Charles I and
with the history of Massachusetts Bay Colony. William Pelham,
John's uncle and the future Lord Justice of Ireland (d. 1587), was
indicted in Wyatt's rebellion in 1554 (Baga, p. 241) and imprisoned
(*P.C.A.* 1552–4, p. 401). But he contrived to escape and possibly

fled abroad,[1] though his name has not come to light among the exiles.

John Pelham's protestantism may have been early imbibed from Cambridge, where a John Pelham 'impubes' matriculated pensioner from Queens' College in 1549 (Venn, III, 336). In 1556 he was just nineteen (*Early Pelhams*, p. 218), and he may have been the Pelham who, having been apparently an associate of Dudley, escaped from ward before 28 June 1557 (*P.C.A.* 1556–8, pp. 110–11). In any case he is found as student and Consiliarius at the University of Padua during the winter of 1556–7. And from Padua he went to Geneva, where on 14 October 1557 he became a 'resident' (f. 197), and on the following 26 November was received into Knox's congregation with William Morley (*q.v.*), who was later to be one of the overseers of Sir Nicholas Pelham's will (*Early Pelhams*, p. 195). The fact of his early exile at Padua and Geneva seems not to have been known to John Pelham's biographer (*op. cit.*), nor that in 1564 he had not yet been received into the queen's favour, for in the Bishops' Visitation of 1564 (Cam. Misc. IX, 10) they deplore the fact that as one of the 'favourers of godly proceedings' he was not yet a Justice of the Peace. Not before 1569 (*ibid.* note a) was he chosen for that office, nor till 1573 was he knighted (*Early Pelhams*, p. 218). His monument, erected by his wife 'Dame Judith', still stands in Stanmer Church (*ibid.* facing p. 218). It was Penelope Pelham, daughter of John's second cousin, Herbert, who became the wife of Governor Bellingham of Massachusetts. It was her brother ('Herbert III') who in 1643 became the first treasurer of Harvard College (*ibid.* pp. 209, 217).

Padua, A VI; Geneva, A IV a & b.

316. PENTENY (PENNY?), JOHN: *Gent.*(?). Of Gressingham, Lancashire(?).

I can find no such name as this in Tudor England, but it is just possible that the surname 'Penny' is its contraction. If so, John Penteny may have been the John Penny of Gressingham, Lancs., whose son, Dr Thomas Penny of Trinity College, Cambridge (Venn, III, 342), was a refractory puritan whom Grindal describes in 1573 as 'a preacher, a layman and a physician' who should not 'be suffered to enjoy a good prebend at Paul's' (Grindal, *Remains*,

---

[1] By the pedigree in Harl. Soc. LII, 765, he had a son by his first wife, Eleanor, daughter of the Earl of Westmorland, suspiciously named Peregrine, but in that given in the *Early Pelhams* this child is made the son of his second wife. It was Sir William's grandson, Peregrine, who was M.P. for Hull in 1649 and signed the death-warrant of Charles I.

p. 348). John Penteny the exile appears abroad only as a subscriber to the 'new discipline' at Frankfort on 21 December 1557.

Frankfort, B III b.

317. PERKYNS (PARKYNS, alias 'Charite' or 'Cherite'), HUMPHREY, D.D.: *Ex-religious.*

A Benedictine monk who received his D.D. from Oxford in July 1538 (Foster, I, 266, under 'Cherite'). In 1540, as Humphrey Charite or Perkins, he was appointed to a prebend of Westminster (Le Neve, III, 355). But in 1553 he was deprived and, upon the evidence of Bale's list, fled to the Continent, where, however, his place of exile is unknown. In 1560, as an S.T.P., he was restored to his Westminster prebend by the queen's patent (Le Neve, III, 351) and in 1571 was made sub-dean (*Parker*, II, 52).

n.p.; B II.

318. PERPOINT (PARPOINT, PIERPONT), EDWARD: *Student*(?). Of Nottinghamshire.

Possibly Edward was the brother of Edmond Pierpont, a Fellow of Christ's, Cambridge, and Master of Jesus from 1551 to 1557, who mentions in his will a brother, Edward (Cooper, I, 162). Yet the fact that Edward does not appear as a refugee at Frankfort until 15 January 1557 makes it not impossible that he was himself the Master of Jesus, since Edward and Edmund are practically interchangeable names. Perhaps he was fleeing from Pole's Visitation of April 1556. In the tax-list he is said to have had no property, and the only other fact that we know about him abroad is that he subscribed to the 'new discipline' in March-April 1557. By June he had apparently left Frankfort since he is not noted in the dwelling-list. It may be mentioned that a Sir George Pierpont was knighted by Edward VI (*Mem.* II, ii, 328); and also that an Edmund Pierpont married a daughter of Sir William Fitzwilliam of Sprotborough (Harl. Soc. XIX, 28), but it has not so far been possible to establish any connection between these Pierponts or with Pierpont the exile.

Frankfort, A III a 3, 4.

319. PICKERING, WILLIAM: *Gent.* Of Yorkshire. 1516–75.

Educated at Cambridge and a pupil of Sir John Cheke. At Mary's accession he was ambassador to France, but refusing to obey the queen's order for his recall (12 August 1553) he threw in his lot with Sir Peter Carew and the rebels at Caen. On 7 April 1554 he was indicted with Sir Peter and Sir Nicholas Throckmorton for complicity in a plot hatched on the previous 26 November 'to deprive the queen of her crown and dignity' (Baga, p. 247). Soon wearying, however, of his rebel's trade he, with Sir William Cecil's 'cousin', Thomas Dannet (*q.v.*), turned informer on his late associates. And for this treachery he went in danger of his life until he made good his escape into Italy (*For. Cal.* 1553–8, pp. 79, 108). There and in Germany (*D.N.B.*) he travelled for a year. But finally in March 1555 he obtained a pardon with permission to return to England.

Caen; Paris; Italy, B v b & c; *D.N.B.*

320. PIGEON, JOHN: *Gent.* Of Huntingdonshire(?).

This is probably a son or brother of Edmond Pigeon, who in 1553 was Clerk of the Wardrobe to Edward VI (*Mem.* II, ii, 211) and the same John Pigeon who on 25 October 1558 received a grant, from Queen Mary, of the bailiwick of Hemingford Grey, in Huntingdonshire (*Dom. Cal.* 1547–80, p. 108). He was one of the group of refugees who arrived in Geneva before 13 October 1555, but he would seem to have returned to England and found favour with the queen before her death.

Geneva, A IV a.

321. PILKINGTON, JAMES, B.D.: *Priest*(?), *student and gent.* Of Lancashire. 1520(?)–76.

The third son of Richard Pilkington of Rivington, Lancs. Fellow of St John's College, Cambridge, 1539, and B.D. in 1551 (Venn, III, 364). The statement in the *D.N.B.* that he was president of his college in 1550 would seem to be an error for 1559 (cf. Venn). In 1547 he had received a licence to preach, together with Latimer, Cox, Horne, Sandys, Grindal and Knox (*Dom. Cal.* 1548–80, p. 5), and because of his known protestant sympathies he evidently deemed it prudent to withdraw to the Continent at Mary's accession. Then he formed one of the original group of the 'Students of Zurich' (*O.L.* II, 752) and at Zurich he apparently remained until the spring of 1556 when he went to Geneva (*O.L.* I, 134–6). His failure to indorse the 'Students'' refusal in October 1554 of Whittingham's invitation to Frankfort (*T.* p. 16) may have been due either to Pilkington's absence from the colony, or to a lack of sympathy with the rejoinder, for it is infinitely to his credit that he held himself studiously aloof from the contentions of the exiles. What Grindal extolled as his 'most exact judgment' (*Remains*, p. 234) was thus lacking to Cox for his revision of the Prayer Book at Frankfort in the spring of 1555 (cf. *O.L.* II, 754). About 7 April of the following year Pilkington was received with Robert Beaumont as a member of Knox's congregation at Geneva, but he remained there only until June, when for reasons of health he seems to have made a journey into the Cevennes (Letter to

Bullinger dated 27 June 1556, *O.L.* I, 136–7). In the autumn of 1556 he is found enrolled as a student in the University of Basle, where he paid his matriculation fee of VI sol (f. 195ᵛᵒ). There he appears to have been living as late as 28 December 1557, on which date Grindal recommended him to Foxe for an 'interchange' of 'counsels' (*Remains*, p. 234). His connection with Frankfort does not seem to have begun until 1558, when he may have been actually on his way to England. Dr Gee has raised the question whether James Pilkington, chosen as one of the four exiled clergy to sit upon Sir Thomas Smith's committee for Prayer Book revision, ever arrived home in time to take his seat upon it (*Elizabethan Prayer Book*, p. 68). And in this connection he cites the fact that on 3 January 1559 Pilkington was still in Frankfort. This is certainly true, for on that date he signed a very politic reply to Geneva (which he may also have composed) refusing that colony's invitation to enter upon an anti-ceremonial crusade (*T*. pp. 188–90). But the contents of this very letter and the signatures to it have not received the attention they deserve. The text reveals a distinct knowledge of the appointment of Sir Thomas Smith's committee; and it is also signed by two men who were, I believe, in closest connection with that committee—John Graye and Henry Carowe. John Graye (*q.v.*), as I have argued earlier, was probably Lord John Grey of Pyrgo, a member of that 'secret cabinet' (Camden, *Annals*, ed. 1630, p. 16) to which the committee of revision must have owed its existence (*Annals*, I, i, 74); and Henry Carowe was, we suspect, Henry Carey, the queen's cousin, created Lord Hunsdon for the support of the protestant cause in the House of Lords. Both men, as I conceive, had come to Frankfort to consider with Pilkington the advisability of putting forward the Liturgy of Frankfort as the basis of the coming revision, and to invite his participation in the work. And yet—if Jung is correct in his statement that Pilkington remained in Frankfort until the end of March as 'moderator' in a disputation on the Sacrament held in the French Church at the end of March (Jung, p. 58, Stadtsarchivs Reform-Akten I, f. 162 a), then the vexed question of Pilkington's presence on the Prayer Book committee is finally settled: he did not take his seat (but cf. Leonard Pilkington below). Machyn first records his being in London on 29 February 1559/60 (p. 226). In March 1561 he was consecrated bishop of Durham (Le Neve, III, 294).

B I a & b; Zurich, A VIII a; Geneva, A IV a; A VIII a; Cevennes, A VII a; Basle, A II a; Frankfort, B III a; *D.N.B.*

322. PILKINGTON, LEONARD: *Deacon and gent.* Of Lancashire.
1527(?)–99.

The fifth son of Richard Pilkington of Rivington and younger
brother of James. Fellow of St John's, Cambridge, and M.A. in
1547 (Venn, III, 365). He was ordained deacon by Ridley in May
1552 (*Mar. Reac.* pp. 201–2) but not priest until 1560 at Ely (Venn).
Though the *D.N.B.* asserts that he went to Frankfort during his
exile, I have found no evidence to corroborate the statement, unless
it was Leonard and not James who sat as 'moderator' in the
disputation on the Sacrament, noted above. It is said that he
married his first wife, Catherine, abroad (*D.N.B.* and Venn).

B I b; Frankfort (?); *D.N.B.*

323. PLAYSTO (PLESTO, PLAYSTOW): *Physician.* Of Suffolk.
Wife.

In Hans Dür's list of the English at Aarau this man is said to have
been a native of Suffolk who lived at 'Haddelea'. Probably, then,
he had been a member of Rowland Taylor's congregation at
Hadley. He is also called a physician, but apparently he had had
no university education and was, we suspect, of humble origin.
While at Aarau he and his wife lived at the Kloster just beneath the
Stadtskirche, which was also the home of Miles Coverdale.

Aarau, A I a & b.

324. PLOUGH, JOHN (alias 'Aratron'): *Student*(?). Of Nottinghamshire. d. 1562.

A son of Christopher Plough of the borough of Nottingham, and
a student of Oxford, where he supplicated a B.C.L. in 1543/4. He
became vicar of Sarratt, Herts., but in the reign of Mary fled to
Basle, where he indulged in controversy with William Kethe and
Robert Crowley on the one side (*Ath. Oxon.* I, 301–2), and on
the other with Miles Huggard 'the first trader or mechanic that
appeared in print for the catholic cause' (*ibid.*). Against Huggard
he wrote *An Apology for Protestants* (1558 or 1559), no copy of
which is now known to exist. And the only official record of his
presence abroad, beyond Bale's mention of him, is to be found
at Basle in the 'Rationes rectoratus' or Rector's account book,
where in 1558/9 Johannis Sphyracte, then head of the university,
notes 2 shillings received from 'Joannis Blougk Angli' for 'literis
testamonialibus', that is, for his passport to return to England
(St A. Univ. Arch. K. 8). In February 1559, Plough was preferred
by Grindal to the living of East Ham (Newcourt, II, 302).

Basle, B II; A II e; *D.N.B.*

PONCE, JOHN. *See* Poyntz.

325. PONET (POYNET, etc.), JOHN, B.D.: *Bishop*. Of Kent. Wife. 1514(?)–56.

Of John Ponet the man, there is little good to be said: he was quarrelsome, avaricious, unscrupulous and a coward. But of John Ponet the political pamphleteer, less has probably been said than he deserves. It is quite possible that the English bishop exercised more influence upon the trend of political thought in Europe from Hotman to Rousseau than has yet been admitted,[1] for though in the academic sense of the term he was a political theorist only by accident, yet as a political opportunist in print, his broadsides provided revolutionary ideas upon which other men were to build systems. Educated at Queens' College, Cambridge, under Sir Thomas Smith, Ponet received his B.D. in 1547 and about that time became chaplain to Cranmer. Bale calls him Cranmer's fidus Achates, who was 'of great authority' with the archbishop (*Scriptores*, p. 694): we should say rather, who 'dominated' him.

The first bishop to be consecrated under the new ordinal (*Cranmer*, ed. E.H.S. II, 131–2), Ponet passed rapidly from the see of Rochester in 1550 to that of Winchester in 1551. His matrimonial experiments we shall not dwell upon, except to say that at Croydon on 25 October 1551 Maria Hammond became his wife (*Collect. Topog. et Geneal.* IV, 91). In 1552 he was named by Northumberland as the author of the *Catechismus Brevis*, a summary of 'Christian Learning', designed for the use of school-masters (S.P. Dom. Edw. VI, vol. XV, no. 3 and *Liturgies of Edw. VI*, p. 486). And at the time of Mary's accession the opinions of Ponet and his theological referee, Peter Martyr Vermigli, seem to have carried more weight with the archbishop than those of any others in his immediate circle. Also the two men had a voice in the councils of the protestant faction at large. On 5 September 1553 Cranmer published throughout London a fateful declaration of his doctrinal position which was in effect a protestant declaration of war against the Marian government, and it has been conjectured, says Dr Jenkins, that the style of it shows 'so much more vehemence' than was usual with Cranmer that it was in reality not his but the 'production of Peter Martyr' (H. Jenkins, *Cranmer's Remains*, I, pp. cxi–cxii, note y). So much has also been hinted by Strype, but as against this view it should be remembered that Peter Martyr, on the explicit assertion of Terentianus, did not reach London

[1] Cf. J. W. Allen, *Political Thought in the Sixteenth Century* (1928), pp. 118–20.

from Oxford until *after* the declaration had been broadcast (*O.L.* I, 371); and also that there is a striking likeness between the preamble of that document and the opening apostrophe of a pamphlet called the *Confession of the Banished Ministers*,[1] which, published abroad in 1554, was in all probability the work of John Ponet. We have therefore a strong suspicion that the 'declaration', which left the government no alternative but to send Cranmer to prison, was not drafted by the archbishop of Canterbury but by the bishop of Winchester, his former chaplain.

Stow's story that Ponet took an active part in Wyatt's rebellion (*Annals*, ed. 1631, p. 620) seems now to be generally accepted, but Stow's conclusion, that after the bishop's desertion of his 'secret friends' for whom he offered to pray at a safe distance, he went directly (or such is the inference) to Germany, may be questioned. Apparently no notice has yet been taken of the initials 'J. P.' that are affixed to the declaration of doctrine issued by the bishops from prison on 8 May 1554 (Foxe, VI, 550–3). But unless they are John Ponet's whose are they? John Philpot's signature is already there; and concerning James Parkhurst there is no record either of seditious action or of imprisonment. That John Ponet, rebel, did not make good his escape, but got caught, is certainly not improbable—the very modesty of those initials being in itself suspicious—and if caught, neither is it improbable that he owed his eventual escape (or release) to the man of all others whom he hated most, Stephen Gardiner, his supplanter in the see of Winchester. Escape in May or June 1554 would have brought Ponet to Strasbourg about July, and there by August we actually find him offering himself as minister to the English congregation at Frankfort (*T.* p. 13). But his offer was not accepted. Ponet remained at Strasbourg, the highest ranking ecclesiastic in exile, and thereafter, as may be supposed, no friend to William Whittingham. It is during this August and September that I should place the compilation of the pamphlet already referred to as the *Confession of the Banished Ministers*. Sandys (*q.v.*), Becon (*q.v.*) and Sampson (*q.v.*), all three then in Strasbourg, may have had a hand in it, but the style of it is the style of Ponet. The very turns of phrase and temper of it are his. And, as it was designed to do, there is evidence that the pamphlet reached London about 5 October (Foxe, VI, 561), that is, just before the assembling on 12 November of the parliament which was to declare reunion with Rome. It was addressed directly to the Lords and Commons of England without mention of the queen (see title-page). Its obvious purpose was to influence coming legislation. Thus the *Confession*

---

[1] See above, pp. 28–9.

of the Banished Ministers may lay just claim to priority among puritan 'Admonitions' to Parliament, being the first attempt of a puritan party to direct the policy of the realm in accordance with its own religious views.

Yet another interest, still political but also more personal to Ponet himself, attaches to this pamphlet. Belief in his authorship of it is greatly strengthened by the fact that it provides what would be an essential first step in the evolution of his later argument against the current protestant doctrine of passive obedience—a line of thought dictated to him, we suspect, less by reason than by strong emotion. And Mr Champlin Burrage in his *Early English Dissenters* has found in it the earliest 'Clear presentment of the fundamental principle' of the Church Covenant upon which Congregationalism rests (I, 77–8). And from the idea of a covenant between God and his people for the keeping of God's law (*Confession*, Sig. D 7ᵛᵒ–D 8), it is but an easy step to the theory of a social compact between a king and his people for the defence of 'mennes iust ordinaunces' (*Politike Power*, ed. 1556, Sig. C 6), a compact to be broken by the king its steward only at his peril for 'common wealthes mai stande well ynough...', albeit ther be no kinges, but contrary wise without a common wealthe ther can be no king' (*ibid.* Sig. D 6).

Such official records as have survived of Ponet's life in Strasbourg are few but important. Some time in the autumn of 1554 a son was born to him, and on the second Sunday in Advent this son was baptized 'John'[1] in the church of St Thomas, Lady Morison and John Abell standing godparents to him (Bibl. de la Ville de Strasbourg, Archives of St Thomas, Series A, N. 245, f. 70). The following December a letter of thanks was sent by the English exiles then at Strasbourg to the Duke of Württemberg, in acknowledgment of his gift to them of 200 gulden (Württ. Staatsarchiv). The first signature to this, though not as a beneficiary, is that of 'Jo. Ponetus, Winton', showing that Ponet even in exile still maintained his claim to Winchester. I have now established the fact (as far as such can ever be established) that the letter itself was both composed and written by him.[2]

---

[1] Of his son I have found no other record than that of a letter of thanks addressed by him to Queen Elizabeth, and preserved at Corpus Christi College, Cambridge (Cat. MSS. C.C.C. I, no. 114, p. 260).

[2] As no example of Ponet's handwriting appears to survive in England, even at Winchester (according to the assurance both of Canon A. W. Goodman and of H. Chitty, Esq., Keeper of the College Archives), I sent to Zurich for photostatic copies of the letters of his, preserved in the Archives there. These were very kindly supplied by Professor Doktor Nabholz, and they have now been compared at the Public Record Office with the above letter from

But the following spring he seems to have concluded that the protestant cause in England was hopeless, for on 23 February 1555 he applied to the Strasbourg magistrates for full burgher rights (*Protocols*, vol. 33, ff. 70–1) and he also bought himself a house called 'zum Holderstock' in the Winemarket (*ibid.* vol. 34, f. 26ᵛᵒ). It was just a month later than this that the long liturgical contest between Strasbourg and Frankfort closed in the triumph of Richard Cox over Knox and Whittingham. Hostilities had opened the previous October with the despatch of David Whitehead to support the Prayer Book faction (*T.* p. 17). When Whitehead proved too weak an agent, Grindal and Chambers had been sent to reinforce him. And upon their failure, arrived the redoubtable Cox to achieve victory. There can be little doubt that John Ponet had been the chief director in that campaign. Unfortunately for him in the following September his newly acquired house burned to the ground and with it were destroyed 4000 crowns' worth of money and jewels—a considerable sum to be found in the possession of a hunted exile (*Protocols*, vol. 33, ff. 358–9, 411ᵛᵒ). It is difficult to avoid the conclusion that it was loot—either from Winchester itself, or from Gardiner's house in London which had been sacked during Wyatt's rebellion (Stow, *Annals*, ed. 1630, p. 619). 'The Lord God, I acknowledge,' wrote Ponet in pious resignation, 'has taken from me all that I had, which indeed was most ample'[1] (*O.L.* I, 116). According to an account of this same fire, given in the *Life of Sir Peter Carew* (Vowell, p. 62), it was Sir Peter himself who made a valiant effort, considering Ponet's 'distress and heaviness', to rescue this hoard from a cupboard in the unused room where it was kept. He failed. But the story goes to show that the two men were not only friends, but had probably been living together. It is therefore quite possible that, while together, Sir Peter had lent to Ponet that copy of Peter Martyr of Angleria's recently published *Decades of the New World* which now exists in the Bodleian Library with the name of Peter Carew scribbled in it, and the initials 'P. C.' printed by hand on the title-page (see 'Carew' above). There are also in this copy certain marginal notes which bear so strong a likeness to Ponet's own handwriting, that considering the circumstances of the two men's close association and the fact that Ponet not only quoted directly from the *Decades* in his *Treatise of Politike Power* (Sig. F 7ᵛᵒ) but also drew from it his knowledge of the 'Ethnikes' of the

Stuttgart, which I owe to the kindness of Herr Doktor Haering, Director of the Württemberg Archives. The report of experts is that the handwriting in the two cases is almost undoubtedly the same.

[1] On the strength of his losses, however, he asked for compensation from the city.

New World and his own deductions in regard to the existence of a 'law of nature' (Sig. A 2vo and Sig. C 7vo), it seems well within the bounds of possibility that the Bodleian copy (ed. 1555) was Sir Peter Carew's own and the actual volume in which Ponet found his inspiration. Was he the first to envisage a political philosophy based on the noble savage? Was Ponet, then, the original precursor of Rousseau? Certain provocative ideas were undoubtedly germinating in Ponet's mind, but it would be a mistake to consider his treatise an abstract thesis in political theory. Rather it was a campaign document, perfervid with the heat of personal experience and rancour. Peter Martyr's 'Ethnikes' were a controversial godsend to him, but Ponet's real purpose in writing the pamphlet was to give moral support to the conspiracy of Sir Henry Dudley to kill Queen Mary. Hence his justification of tyrannicide. Sir Peter Carew knew all the facts of that conspiracy, for it was he who had betrayed the plot to King Philip (see 'Carew' above), and if Sir Peter knew, then Ponet, his associate, can hardly have remained in ignorance. It is even highly probable that the one-time accomplice of Wyatt had been actually employed by the accomplices of Dudley to justify their proposed 'tyrannicide' by writing a political broadside in its defence. Such I conceive to have been the origin of the *Treatise of Politike Power*. Had Ponet also foreknowledge of Carew's betrayal of their friend Sir John Cheke? Certainly Ponet's story of the kidnapping was the first to reach the world in print—and an excellent bit of campaign material he made of it (Sig. I 6vo). The inclusion of the episode also serves to date the writing of the *Treatise*, upon which he must have been engaged at the moment. And here it should be remembered in connection with Ponet's advocacy of political assassination, that Francis Hotman was then in Strasbourg, and had been since October 1555 (*Ital. Reform.* pp. 321–2). As a friend of Peter Martyr, Hotman, author of the *Franco-gallia* and one of the future instigators of the conspiracy of Amboise,[1] could hardly have failed to know John Ponet, or to have read his pamphlet, which was passing through the press in August 1556. In fact the English bishop's work may have been much more than the mere 'prophecy' of future 'developments in France' that it has been called. Nor is the belief that for England 'it had little significance of any sort' borne out either by the facts above or by the facts of the future, though it is quite true that in *1559* his radicalism did not serve the political turn of Sir William Cecil and the party of Suffolk. But in *1639* and again in *1642*, ominous years, the *Treatise* was republished.

---

[1] Cf. Letter of Sturm, *Bibl. de l'école des Chartes*, 3rd series, vol. v, p. 365, ed. R. Dareste.

And upon England on the verge of civil war its influence was direct. No one who reads at Cambridge the University Library's copy of the edition of 1639, with its underscorings and marginal notes (Acton d. 48.305), can fail to be startled by the tragic immediacy of Ponet's arguments in support of a commonwealth at issue with its king.

It is true, of course, that his ideas were not new: but whose are? It may also be true that they were those 'potentially everywhere' in the mid-sixteenth century: yet the same might be said of Rousseau's in the eighteenth. If originality may ever be predicated of thought, then surely it is the man who first gives vivid expression to subconscious desires, and currency to them in print at the inflammable moment, who may best lay claim to it. Such was John Ponet, the first to provide theoretical countenance for the political ambitions unleashed by the minority of Edward VI. When, four years later, Frenchmen were confronted with the same situation—the problems arising out of a king's minority—they found Ponet's theories ready to their need and were to give them perpetuity.

He himself died at Strasbourg (probably from the plague, for he was then but forty-two) on 2 August 1556, and was buried there (*Scriptores*, p. 695). But as to his burial-place not even a legend survives.

Strasbourg, VII a, b, c.

326. PORREGE (PORRAGE, PORRIDGE), WILLIAM: *Student.* Of Sandwich, Kent(?).

In 1574 a Richard Porridge was Jurate of the town of Sandwich (Harl. Soc. LXXV, 59, 144). Possibly he was the son or brother of the William Porrege who, with Thomas Sprat, was one of the regular messengers employed by the exiles (Foxe, VIII, 576). Unlike the others, however, the headquarters of Porrege were apparently at Calais, not in England (*ibid.*); and it was while on a journey from Calais to Sandwich that he had the miraculous escape from death which Foxe relates with relish (*ibid.* pp. 576–8). In January 1559/60 Porrege was ordained priest by Grindal, for whose ordinands and in this connection, Strype feels bound to apologize, saying that some of them 'were no scholars, or of any University, but men of sober conversation, and that could read English well' (*Grindal*, p. 54).

Calais.

327. PORTER (POTTER), RICHARD: *Gent.* Of Sussex(?).

As the surnames Porter and Potter seem in the sixteenth century to have been interchangeable (cf. the Harl. Soc. Visitations of Kent and Sussex, and also Foster, III, 1186) it is probable that the

Richard 'Potter' who came to Geneva in Whittingham's company on 13 October 1555, and who, on the following 24 October was received as a 'resident' of Geneva (f. 123) is one and the same person with the Richard 'Porter' who signed the 'new discipline' at Frankfort in March-April 1557. In all probability he was the son and heir of John Porter of Beigham (Bayham) Abbey, Sussex, and the father of John Porter of Lamberhurst in Kent (Harl. Soc. LIII, 169 and *ibid.* XLII, 155). His second son, Richard, was very possibly the scholar of Trinity College, Oxford, in 1571, who is noted by Foster.

Geneva, A IV a & b; Frankfort, B III b.

POTTER, RICHARD. *See* Porter, above.

328. POWNALL (POWNOL, POTONAL), ROBERT: *Student.* Of Dorset. Wife. 1520–71.

From Hans Dür's list at Aarau we learn that Robert 'Potonal'— a spelling probably reminiscent of Pownall's sojourn at Calais— was born in Dorset, thus correcting the statement in the *D.N.B.* that his birthplace was in Somerset (and cf. Strype's *Grindal*, p. 59). From Calais, where he had lived (Hans Dür), he migrated first to Wesel and thence to Aarau by way of Geneva (*T.* p. 185) with his wife and three children (Official list, cf. below, p. 355), one of whom died at Aarau (*ibid.*). There Pownall was one of the ministers of the church under Thomas Lever (*T.* p. 191) and as such signed a letter of graceful acknowledgement to Bullinger for his kindness in having dedicated to them some recent work of his (*O.L.* I, 170). He was also one of those who approved, on 16 January 1559, Geneva's invitation to embark on a ceremonial crusade (*T.* p. 191). He employed his time abroad as a pamphleteer on his own account and also as a translator of French controversial pamphlets. That he had lived at Calais supports the identification with Robert Pownall of the 'R. P.' who wrote an *Admonition to the Towne of Callays*, published in 1557.[1] On his return to England he was ordained by Grindal on 1 May 1560, but whether as priest or deacon, Strype does not say (*Grindal*, p. 59). We doubt very much, however, Strype's identification of Robert Pownall with one Robert Pownde (*Annals*, I, i, 490, 491), since there was a Robert Pound of Berkshire, whom Foster (III, 1189) gives as a Fellow of New College in 1532–3 and who, dying in 1581, might easily have been the Pound in question.

Calais, A I a; Wesel, B III; Geneva, B III; Aarau, A I a & b.

[1] The only copy known is in the British Museum.

329. POYNTZ (PONCE, POINES, POYNYNGES[1]), GABRIEL: Student and gent. Of Essex. 1538–1607/8.

A 'Gabriel Poines Anglus' was registered as a student at the University of Basle during the winter of 1554–5 (f. 191; below, p. 358). There can be little doubt that he was Gabriel Poyntes (or Poyntz), son and heir of Thomas Poyntes of North Ockenden, Essex. The family was one which had intermarried with the Isaacs of Buckinghamshire and with the Chekes, but Thomas Poyntz, being a 'Grocer of London', had connections with Antwerp, and while 'occupying the seate of marchaundise in the Partes beyond the seas' had there married Anna van Calva (Harl. Soc. xxi, 133; Sir J. Maclean, Family of Poyntz, I, 35 and Foxe, v, App. p. 813). In Antwerp his children were born, including Gabriel the eldest and a daughter Susanna, who later married Sir Richard Saltonstall, Lord Mayor of London, and brother of Samuel, ancestor of the New England family of Saltonstall (ibid. and Harl. Soc. xxi, 133 and xxii, 90). Whatever leanings Thomas already had towards the new doctrines must have been confirmed at Antwerp by his association with Tyndale, for it was at Poyntz's house that Tyndale lodged for over a year and there that he was arrested (Foxe, v, 121, 123). Later Poyntz returned to London, where in 1541 his son Gabriel, then three years old, was naturalized by Act of Parliament (Maclean, I, 35). He was thus a boy of only sixteen while a student at Basle. Twice in later years he was sheriff of Essex (1577 and 1589) and in 1604 was knighted (Maclean, pp. 38–9). His wife was Audrey, a daughter of Peter Cuttes (Harl. Soc. xxi, 133 and xiii, 69, 92).

Basle, A ii a.

330. POYNTZ (PONCE), JOHN: Gent. Of Gloucestershire.

Burn, in his History of Parish Registers (p. 275, n. 4), has tried to identify the John Ponce who arrived at Geneva with William Whittingham on 13 October 1555 with John Ponet, bishop of Winchester. Martin first threw doubt on this identification (p. 54); and now by means of the Strasbourg council minutes Ponet's whereabouts in 1555 may be so accounted for as to make it practically impossible for him to have been at Geneva in the autumn of that year (see 'Ponet' above). Far more likely is it, that this is John Poyntz, fourth son (or fifth, cf. Maclean, p. 75) of Sir Nicholas Poyntz of Iron Acton, Glos. (Harl. Soc. xiii, 270). Sir Nicholas (d. 1556) had been a time-serving adherent to Lady Jane Grey who supported Mary in Wyatt's rebellion (Chron. Q. Jane, p. 44). His son, however, may not have done so—hence his

[1] It may have been in Antwerp that the English name of Poynings was translated into Poyntz.

appearance in Geneva. But except that he was named (or a son 'John' was named) in Sir Nicholas's will (Maclean, pp. 75, 96) nothing more seems to be known of him.

Geneva, A IV a.

331. PRETIE (PRETIO, PRETTY, PRATY), JOHN: (?) *Gent.* Of Hertfordshire(?). Wife.

Owing to the variety of forms in which his name appears, this man defies exact identification. He may have been John Prat, John Price, or John Pretty. He first appears at Zurich on 13 October 1554, where as John Pretio [Price?] he signed the letter of the 'Students of Zurich' to Frankfort (*T*. p. 16). Under the name of 'Praty' [Prate? Prat?] John Bale includes him in his list of exiles (p. 742). As John Prettie he is found at Geneva among those Englishmen who had arrived there before 13 October 1555. Hans Dür, with whom Pretie lived for thirty weeks when he arrived at Aarau in 1557, describes him as an 'edelman' (which may mean no more than 'gentleman'), spells his name 'Pretie' (cf. *O.L.* I, 170) and says that he was born in a village called 'Grawenest' near the town of Bedford in 'Härforddenser' [Gravenhurst, Beds.?]. Yet even with this specific information it has been so far impossible to find the man in either of those counties, though a family named 'Pretty' existed in Suffolk (Metcalfe, *Visit. Suffolk*, p. 159). But Strype knows no John Pretty, though he does know a John Price, Fellow of Catharine Hall, Cambridge, who was ordained priest by Grindal in December 1559. This might seem to be the exile; but Strype also knows a John Prat, archdeacon of St Davids, of whom he says definitely that he had been an exile for religion and a great friend of Foxe (*Annals*, I, i, 491–2). Unfortunately John Prat, the archdeacon, was a west countryman of Brasenose College, Oxford, who received his B.A. in 1557, the year John Pretie came to Aarau and who, according to Foster, never left England (III, 1198). Venn knows a John Pratt of the proper county, Hertfordshire, who matriculated from St John's College, Cambridge in 1564 (III, 391), and though he records nothing of his ancestry, the man might very easily be the exile's son, for John Pretie had a wife and one child with him at Aarau. Were it not for Venn's John Pratt, I should have concluded that John Pretie and John Praty were two distinct persons, but lean finally towards the belief that they were one and the same. According to the Privy Council Acts a John Pretye got into trouble in 1555 (*P.C.A.* 1554–6, pp. 141, 144, 166), but to add to the confusion, this year was too late to explain the presence of John Pretie (Pretio) at Zurich in 1554.

B II; Zurich, B III a; Geneva, A IV a; Aarau, A a & b; A VIII a.

332. PROCTOR (PROCTOUR), RICHARD: *Merchant.* Of London.

A son-in-law of the merchant, Richard Springham, whose daughter, Mary, Proctor married (Harl. Soc. XLI, 1307). When in April 1558, however, he became a member of Knox's congregation, he had then no wife with him. On 24 October he was admitted to 'residence' in Geneva (f. 264). We strongly suspect that the 'John Proctor alias Williamson' executed at Tyburn for his part in Stafford's insurrection of 1557 (*Mem.* III, ii, 68, 518; *Machyn*, p. 136) was Richard's brother, and that Richard's presence in Geneva, in 1558, was due to John's execution in London in 1557.

Geneva, A IV a & b.

333. PROUDE, RICHARD: *Student and gent.* Of Kent.

In the official list of Aarau this man is described as an 'edelman' living in the house of Mauritz Meggers. Hans Dür adds that he was born in Canterbury and lived at Feversham, Kent. No Richard is mentioned in the pedigree of the Kentish family of Proude, but we presume him to have been a younger son or brother of that William Proude whose wife was a sister of Edmund Crispe (cf. Harl. Soc. XLII, 35). On 31 March 1560 he was ordained priest by Grindal (*Grindal*, p. 58) and subsequently became the puritan parson of Burton upon Dunmore, Bucks. (*Annals*, I, ii, 148), who in 1579 took occasion to rate Lord Burghley 'with a freedom not very decent' for his failure to go into exile under Mary and for his 'going along with this present queen', Elizabeth (*Annals*, II, ii, 290–1).

Aarau, A I a & b.

334. PULLAIN (PULLEIN, PULLEYNE) JOHN ('alias John Smith'), B.D.: *Priest.* Of Yorkshire. Wife. 1517–65.

Of New College and Christ Church, Oxford. In November 1550 he was ordained deacon; and priest in 1551 (*Mar. Reac.* pp. 212, 214). In 1552 he was made rector of St Peter's, Cornhill (Harl. MS. 6955, f. 108), but was deprived in April 1554/5 (*ibid.* f. 113). But he remained some time in London before going abroad, for at 'two Easter-tides', as reported in Bartlet Green's confession of November 1555, he celebrated communion, first with Christopher Goodman, then with Michael Reniger (*q.v.*), at his own house, in the parish of St Michael's, Cornhill (Foxe, VII, 738). But he was also much in Colchester (*ibid.* VIII, 384), where he not only 'preached privately to the brethren' (*Annals*, I, i, 492) but took an active part, we strongly suspect, in disseminating the seditious literature for which Colchester was the chief distributing centre. Not till 1557 was he denounced to Bonner; then taking flight for Geneva he arrived there with his wife and daughter Faith, about 5 June, when all three were received into Knox's congregation. On his way he had passed through Basle, where he was arrested for lack of a passport which he should have obtained at Strasbourg (Protocols, vol. 35, f. 205). On 14 October 1557 he was admitted as a 'resident' of Geneva, being described as 'jadis ministre en Angleterre' (*ibid.* f. 196). Since Martin gives no support to the statement that Pullain had joined friends in Geneva as early as 1554, his chaplaincy to the Duchess of Suffolk, of which Foxe speaks, must have been before his flight to Germany (Foxe, VIII, 384 and *D.N.B.*). It is on the evidence of a certain witness, Stephen Morris, that Foxe reports Pullain's frequent journeys abroad to consult with the duchess between the time of his deprivation and that of his appearance at Geneva (*ibid.*). There can be little doubt that he was an agent in the pamphlet war. Martin also corroborates the assertion that Pullain was one of the collaborators on the Geneva Bible (p. 75), and adds that his translations of psalms 148 and 149 were made while at Geneva. He was one of the last exiles to leave there. On 15 December 1558 he signed Geneva's proposal to Frankfort and Aarau to embark on an anti-ceremonial crusade (*T.* p. 188), a fact which, in itself, would have made him *persona non grata* to Elizabeth on his return to England. But Pullain also promptly put himself in opposition to the queen's religious policy by disobeying the proclamation against preaching, for which on 17 April 1559 he was apprehended with John Dodman (*q.v.*) near Colchester (*P.C.A.* 1558–70, p. 88). By the following December, however, Grindal had succeeded in obtaining for him the arch-deaconry of Colchester (*Grindal*, pp. 87, 103), and, as archdeacon, Pullain signed the articles altering ceremonies, and also petitioned for a discipline in 1562. Weinheim (?); Geneva, A IV a & b; *D.N.B.*

*PULLEYN, WILLIAM.

An error of Strype's, I believe, for John Pullain, cf. *Mem.* III, ii, 64.

335. PUNTE, WILLIAM: *Messenger.*

Called by Strype a 'leading heretic' of Colchester (*Annals*, I, i, 378) and like John Pullain engaged in the war of propaganda. He was denounced to Bonner by Tye, the bishop's commissary, as 'a great writer of devilish and erroneous books'[1] (Foxe, VIII, 384), but were he not included by John Bale in his list of exiles, we should not have supposed that Punte lived for any length of time abroad,

[1] Cf. *S.T.C.* no. 20499: 'A new dialoge called the endightment agaynste mother Messe' [Init. W.P.].

though his devilish books were printed there for dissemination in England. He it was who provided Foxe with certain material for his *Book of Martyrs* of such doubtful authenticity that it was challenged even in Elizabeth's reign (*Annals*, I, i, 378-9). He was also the author of a tract against the Anabaptists (Foxe, VIII, 384 and *Mem.* III, ii, 64), but the scene of his activities on the Continent is unknown, unless he was at Basle with Foxe. B II; Basle (?).

336. PUREFOY, LUKE: *Student and gent.* Of Buckinghamshire.

He was the second son of Nicholas Purefoy of Shalstone, Bucks., by his third wife, Katherine Brayfield, the daughter of a yeoman (Harl. Soc. LXXV, 107-8). In 1548 he was a demy at Magdalen College (Bloxam, IV, 135) and from 1551 to 1554 a probationary Fellow. Strype asserts (*Mem.* III, i, 82) that he was one of those expelled at Gardiner's Visitation in October 1553, probably in this following a vague statement of Laurence Humphrey (Bloxam, IV, 103). But H. A. Wilson, in his account of Magdalen, does not include Purefoy in the list; and, both on Macray's (II, 130) and on Bloxham's statement (IV, 135), he would seem to have remained at Magdalen until 1554. Though it is known that he then went abroad, there has been found but one possible reference to connect him with Germany. This occurs in a letter written by Sir Richard Morison to Bullinger on 17 April 1555, and would suggest that Purefoy (if it indeed refers to him) had but lately arrived from England. 'As to what is going on at home', writes Morison, 'since everyone knows it, I suppose that you cannot be ignorant. This *our friend Luke*[1] will easily tell you all that I know' (*O.L.* I, 148). 'Luke' was then obviously on his way from Strasbourg to Zurich, and may have been going down into Italy. There is no later mention of him so far found, and Foster has even omitted Purefoy's name from his catalogue of Oxford alumni. But H. F. Waters, in his *Genealogical Gleanings in England* (II, 1087-8), has traced an interesting relationship between the Purefoys of Buckinghamshire and Thomas Dudley, governor of Massachusetts Bay colony. Strasbourg (?); Zurich (?); Italy (?).

337. PURFOOT, NICHOLAS: *Printer*(?). Of London(?).

Though there is no direct evidence to support the identification, it is not unlikely that this Nicholas Purfoot was a younger son of the London printer and stationer Thomas Purfoot, whose shop was in St Paul's Churchyard (Herbert's Ames, II, 993). Arber unhesitatingly calls Nicholas 'the London printer' (Introd. to 1907 edition of the *Troubles at Frankfort*, p. xi), but all that is

[1] Author's italics.

actually known of the man is that he was at Strasbourg in December 1554, when he received 10 florins from the Duke of Württemberg's donation to the exiles, and appended his signature 'Nicolas Purfyt' to their letter of thanks (Württ. Staatsarchiv); and that from Strasbourg he went to Frankfort. At Frankfort he was a member of Whittingham's party, for he signed the letter of secession in August 1555 (*T*. p. 55). But where he went from there we do not know. Quite possibly he returned to England, for Thomas Purfoot began printing again in 1557. Can Nicholas have been one of the apprentices who fomented the riot at Paul's Cross on 13 August 1553 (*Machyn*, p. 41; *Mem*. III, i, 32 and Steele, I, no. 427)?

Strasbourg, A VII c; Frankfort, B III a.

338. RAILTON, GREGORY: *Gent.* Of London. d. 1561.

He had been a Clerk of the Signet to Edward VI (*Mem*. II, i, 130 and *Dom. Cal*. 1547–80, p. 64) and also Treasurer of the North previous to Richard Bunny (*P.C.A.* 1552–4, p. 150). In 1552 he obtained a patent 'to eat flesh with four in his company during his life' (*Dom. Cal*. 1547–80, p. 43) and thus accounted himself a protestant. On a plea of illness he fled from England in 1554, and from Basle (November 19) reminded Sir William Petre that he had sued 'for the Queen's license' to go abroad 'by counsel of three or four notable physicians' (*For. Cal*. 1553–8, p. 139). But Railton's disease would seem to have been of the same nature as Richard Bunny's (*q.v.*)—peculation of government moneys (*Dom. Cal*. Addenda, 1547–65, p. 402 and *ibid*. 1547–80, p. 42). From Basle he went to Frankfort, arriving there about 25 July 1555 (Jung, p. 58), and in the city's tax-list of the following October appears as 'G. Railthonn' with property to the value of 2000 florins (*ibid*. pp. 29, 58). In January 1557 John Hales appealed to him, among others, to quiet the stir that had arisen over the Horne-Ashley quarrel (*T*. p. 65). In March-April of that year Railton signed the 'new discipline' and in June is found living with his two sons and a maid in the house of Thomas Wattes (*q.v.*). That he had aligned himself with the radical party is shown by his subscription to that democratic clause in the 'new discipline' by which the tyranny of a single pastor was to be replaced by the government of 'two or moo equall ministers' as being closer to apostolic custom (*T*. p. 137). In September 1557 his name is found among the signatories of Whitehead's letter to Bullinger, thanking him for his 'godly studies', consecrated to the exiles (*O.L.* II, 763–4). But on Railton's return to England he seems not to have regained status.[1] As were several other exiles, he was employed by Cecil

[1] Cf. Wright's conclusion that 'Raylton' was 'a sort of private secretary or decypherer' (T. Wright, *Elizabeth*, I, 15, note).

during 1559 in the secret negotiations with the Earl of Arran
(*For. Cal.* 1558–9, p. 516); and from 1559 onwards he served on
the border in some nameless capacity that involved frequent
correspondence with John Knox (*ibid.* 1559–60, pp. 51, 344; see
also Index under 'Railton'). A Gregory Railton, gentleman,
probably the same man, died in 1561 (P.C.C., Index Library XVIII,
154).

Basle, B v a & b; Frankfort, A III a 3, 4 & b 2; B III a & b.

339. RANDALL (RANDOLPH, RANDOLL), EDWARD: *Gent.* Of Kent. d. 1566.

The son of Avery Randolph of Badilsmere, Kent, and brother of
Thomas Randolph (*q.v.*), Queen Elizabeth's agent in Scotland
(Hasted, III, 112). The family was connected with the Chrispes
(*q.v.*), through the marriage of Mary, sister of these two, with
William Chrispe, Lieutenant of Dover Castle (Harl Soc. LXXIV, 42).
Though Randolph's name does not appear among those indicted
in Wyatt's rebellion (cf. Baga), there can be little doubt, from the
fact of his flight, that he had been 'out' either with Wyatt or
Suffolk. By 17 April 1554 he was begging for pardon on the plea
that he had 'only fled to save his life' and that unless driven to it,
he would 'never serve other than Her Majesty' (*For. Cal.* 1553–8,
p. 72). Wotton interceded for him, and by 29 May (*ibid.* p. 88) the
queen had gone so far as to say that Randall was forgiven but
that he must 'remain abroad until he thoroughly learns whereunto
the end of the rebels' enterprises tends' (*ibid.*). From then until
9 October, when he received his full pardon, Randolph plied the
ugly trade of informer (*Dom. Cal.* 1547–80, p. 63). It was he who
told Wotton that the number of rebels in France was never more
than 150 (*For. Cal.* 1553–8, p. 108) and on 10 August (1554)
Wotton sent him back to England as a messenger, with a recommendation to the queen that 'no man (was) better skilled in
military matters' (*ibid.* p. 113). So by 1555 we find him reinstated,
and a 'Colonel of Infantry' whom Philip specially rewarded for
his good services (*Dom. Cal.* 1547–80, p. 65). Under Elizabeth he
was appointed High Marshal to the garrison at Newhaven (Havre)
in 1563, and in 1564 Lieutenant of Ordnance (*ibid.* pp. 224, 237).
He was finally killed in battle in Ireland about 1566 (Hatfield MSS.
I, 341).

France, B v b 1, 2; *D.N.B.*

340. RANDOLPH (RANDALL), THOMAS, B.C.L.: *Student and gent.* Of Kent. 1523–90.

Son of Avery Randolph of Badilsmere, Kent, and brother of
Edward Randall (above). His first wife, married in 1571, was Anne

Walsingham, sister of Sir Francis (*D.N.B.*). In 1545 he was a student of Christ Church, Oxford, received a B.C.L. in 1547/8 and from 1549 to 1553 was Principal of Broadgates Hall (Foster, III, 1232). At Mary's accession he fled to Paris, where in 1557, though living as a scholar, he appears to have been well informed of the movements of the rebels, yet at the same time on very amicable terms with Wotton (*For. Cal.* 1553–8, p. 299), to whom he passed on his information. He also forgathered in Paris with many Scots; and in his *Memoirs*, Sir James Melville speaks of 'the fraternity of Religion so well grounded' among them during that period in France (*Memoirs*, ed. 1735, p. 231)—an association that Randolph, when restored to the queen's grace, was, according to Melville, in a fair way to forget. It was also Randolph from whom Wotton received news of Thomas Stafford's sailing on Easter day for Scarborough (*For. Cal.* 1553–8, p. 299). How long he stayed on in Paris we do not know, but on 6 December 1558 we find him in Strasbourg. Possibly he was the messenger chosen to carry to the exiles the news of Queen Mary's death, for a letter of his to Throckmorton on that date throws a most interesting if somewhat enigmatic light upon their reaction to the news. 'Our countrymen', he says, 'have no will longer to make their abode here'; but then adds 'The Genevians repent their haste; they blew their triumph before their victory' (*For. Cal.* 1558–9, no. 68, p. 22). The reference here is almost certainly to the recent publication of Knox's *First Blast of the Trumpet*, but it may also reflect the disappointment already felt among the fugitives at the conservative attitude adopted by the Elizabethan government towards religion. There had been no calling home of the religious exiles in triumph. The small group that left Strasbourg for England on 19–20 December (cf. *Z.L.* I, 5), evidently under the leadership of Randolph himself, was largely political and adventurous. 'There will be with him', he writes in a postscript, 'Sir T. Wr[othe] Sir Anto. C[ook], and he wots not who more besides himself'. He 'Would be happy', he says, 'if he might receive a letter at Antwerp where they will be in the course of a month' (*ibid.*). It is noticeable that both Sandys and Randolph thought it well to mask the names of Sir Thomas Wrothe and Sir Anthony Cooke under initials. And that Randolph himself was not returning home in good odour is shown by the fact that in 1559, under the name of 'Barnabie', he was assigned the task of secretly conducting the Earl of Arran from France to Scotland. By this back door he entered upon his diplomatic career of confidential agent in Scotland, and of special ambassador on the Continent in later life.

Paris, B v b 1 & 2; Strasbourg, *D.N.B.*

341. RAWLINS, ERKENWALD (EDWARD): *Merchant.* Of London. Wife. d. 1559.

Though generally known by his nickname of Erkenwald, derived perhaps from the Shrine of St Erkenwald in London near which he may have lived, the real name of this merchant was Edward (Jung, p. 58). He and his wife were the 'godly couple' beloved of John Bradford, whose letter to them has been preserved by Foxe (VII, 212). He arrived at Frankfort with his wife and three children in the autumn of 1555, for his name appears among the merchants in the Standesliste. In January 1557 his property was rated in the Steuerliste at 200 florins and we know that in the following June he was living in a house that stood behind the church of the Barefoot Friars, which sheltered not only his own family, but also his brother's, and two others, John Peddar and Thomas Carell (*H.S.P.* IV, 89). Unlike his brother, he was not a subscriber to the 'new discipline'. Perhaps the strife it occasioned was the reason for his withdrawal to Geneva, where he became officially a 'resident' on 24 October 1558 (f. 264). He is noticed in the Livre des Anglois only to record his death on 29 April 1559 (Martin, p. 338). It is possible that the John Rawlins who was apprehended in July 1557, for 'bringing in certaine lewde, seditious bokes from Andwerpe', was a relative, perhaps a son of Erkenwald (*P.C.A.* 1556–8, pp. 124–5).

Frankfort, A III a 2, 3, 4 & b 1, 2; Geneva, A IV a & b.

342. RAWLINS (RAULINGES), WILLIAM: *Merchant.* Of London. Wife. d. 1571(?).

Brother of Edward Rawlins, and perhaps the William Rawlins, grocer, whose daughter, Amye, married Rafe Hill, a London haberdasher (Harl. Soc. I, 29). According to the will, dated 11 January 1571, of a William Rawlins,[1] citizen and gentleman of London, who may be the same man, the family came originally from Hereford, a fact which corresponds with private information in regard to the Rawlins family given by E. M. S. Parker in 1904, to Col. Rawlins of Great Houghton Hall, Northampton. The same informant adds that 'no less than ten persons of the name of Rawlins arrived here [U.S.A.] between the years 1630 and 1680...'. William Rawlins arrived in Frankfort with his brother and like him is found among the merchants in the Standesliste; but in 1557, though named in the tax-list of 15 January, he was then without taxable property. He and his wife shared the house but not the opinions of Erkenwald Rawlins, for William both signed the 'new

[1] Another William Rawlins, mercer, of London, died in 1581 (P.C.C., Index Library XVIII, p. 256).

discipline' in April and refused the form of reconciliation offered by Strasbourg in the following September (*T*. p. 174).

Frankfort, A iii a 2, 3, 4 & b 1, 2; B iii a & b.

343. RAYME (REYMES, RAME), THOMAS: *Gent*. Of Norfolk(?).

Mentioned only once abroad, when at Venice in July 1555 he was permitted with other Englishmen in the train of the Earl of Bedford to wear his sword (*Ven. Cal.* 1555–6, p. 145). Possibly he was Thomas, second son of Richard Reyme, or Reymes, of Hempton, Norfolk.

Venice, B v b 3.

RAYNOLD and RENOLD. *See* Reynolds.

344. RENIGER (REYNIGER, RUNNIGER, RHANGER), MICHAEL: *Student*. Of Hampshire. 1530–1609.

Student at Cambridge, but a demy of Magdalen College, Oxford, and Fellow from 1546 to 1553. Strype, following Wood, says that he was one of those expelled by Gardiner in October 1553, but the records of Magdalen show that Reniger with Henry Bull had already vacated his fellowship before 29 July 1553 (Wilson, *Magd.* p. 103 and note). Probably he left to assume the duties of his rectorate at Broughton, Hants., to which he had been preferred in 1552 (Foster). In evident reference to this living Robert Reneger, writing to Cecil on 21 August 1551, says that 'His brother [Michael] readeth a lecture of philosophy at Magdalen College, Oxford, for a half year and more, and for 12 months past has been bound to the study and dispentations of divinity. Now also he is burdened to be a minister, inasmuch as he has been two years Master of Arts, whereby he thinks he shall be obliged to give up his lectures' (*Salisbury*, I, 91, no. 366). Robert Reneger, Comptroller of the Port of Southampton (*P.C.A.* 1556–8, p. 10), was himself the patron of the living—a fact which may explain why Michael, though a refugee abroad, was able to retain it until 1557. But it is questionable whether he had ever been ordained priest. There is no record of his having received orders under Edward VI (cf. *Mar. Reac.* pp. 181–219) and generally speaking his youth would preclude the possibility of ordination under Henry VIII, as he was but twenty-four when he left England. Abroad he went first to Zurich, where in April 1554 he was one of the original group of 'Students' (*O.L.* II, 752 and *Diarium*, p. 46). But by the following November he was in Strasbourg, where he subscribed to that colony's admonitory letter to Frankfort dated the 23rd (*T*. p. 23) and in December was one of those who received a share, 12 florins, of the Duke of Württemberg's donation (Württ. Staatsarchiv).

Then he appears to have gone back to Zurich, for we have a begging letter of his to Bullinger, sent by a bearer although, as Reniger apologizes, 'our houses are so near as almost to be united' (*O.L.* I, 375). This was probably in 1556. Again out of funds, what Reniger wanted was a letter of introduction to the Duke of Württemberg's secretary in the hope that the latter might be moved to add to the amount of 20 florins that he, Reniger, received yearly from John Burcher (*ibid.* p. 376). What success his appeal had we do not know, nor do we know when he returned to England, though after 1560 his preferment was rapid. In 1561 he became chaplain to the queen (*Annals*, I, i, 406), who nevertheless failed to approve Grindal's recommendation of him for the provostship of Eton (*Parker*, I, 209). In 1562 he is found among those who voted for the six articles altering ceremonies and who also petitioned for a discipline.

B II; Zurich, A VIII a & c; B III b; Strasbourg, A VII c; B III b; *D.N.B.*

345. RENOLD (REIGNOLDES, REYNOLDS, etc.), HENRY: *Student.* Wife.

This is probably the Henry Reynolds or Raynold who was a Fellow of Exeter College, Oxford, from 1547 to 1551 (Foster, III, 1247). There is no record of his ordination under Edward VI (cf. *Mar. Reac.*) but in 1552 he was, it would seem, preferred to the living of Badingham in the archdeaconry of Suffolk, of which in 1554 he was deprived (Baskerville, *E.H.R.* 1933, p. 58). If this is the 'Henri Renold' of the Emden catalogue, he was evidently married, for he appeared at Frankfort with a wife; yet even without one his lack of priest's orders would have led to his deprivation. He is first named at Frankfort in the autumn of 1555 among the 'students' in the Standesliste. In 1556 his property was reckoned at 10 florins—a small enough sum one would think with which to provide the house in which he and his wife are found living alone in June 1557 (*H.S.P.* IV, 89). In March-April he had signed the 'new discipline'. If he returned to England at Elizabeth's accession he apparently received no preferment.

B I a & b; B II; Frankfort, A III a 2, 3, 4 & b 1, 2.

346. RENOLDES (RAYNOLDS, etc.), [JOHN], B.D.: *Ex-religious.* Of Gloucester.

As 'Renoldes', without a Christian name, is listed in the Emden catalogue of exiles, among the Doctors of Theology. No other clue is given to his identity. But of doctors of theology named Reynolds in King Edward's reign, there would appear to have been but two. Robert, who as commissary to Bishop Gardiner is not likely to have been the exile; and John, ex-prior of the Dominicans of Gloucester, who at the time of the suppression is styled a 'bachyler in dyvinitie' (Wright, *Monasteries*, p. 200). This is no doubt the same 'John Reynold' who received his B.D. from Oxford about 1526 (Foster, III, 1247) and of whom it is also said that he was a preacher at Exeter. At the time of the Prayer Book troubles in 1549, a Dr Raynolds was appointed to act with Miles Coverdale as army chaplain to Lord Russell in the West (*Mem.* II, i, 263 and Rose-Troup, p. 157). Coverdale's co-worker can hardly be other than Foster's John Reynold, B.D., ex-Dominican, who preached in Devon, and it seems reasonably safe to conclude that he also became Miles Coverdale's fellow-exile in Germany.

n.p.; B I a & b.

347. REYNOLDS, Roger: *Gent.* Of Essex. d. 1557.

Probably the Roger Reynolds who was of West Thorock, Essex (Harl. Soc. XIII, 108). In April 1556 he was indicted in the Dudley conspiracy and described as 'late of London, Gentleman' (Baga, p. 254). On 4 April he was proclaimed a traitor with those who had fled beyond the seas (*Machyn*, p. 103) and he doubtless joined Dudley in France. There, in 1557, he attached himself to Thomas Stafford, and with others of that pathetic expedition against Scarborough was executed at 'Hassyl', Yorks., in 1557.

France, B IV c; B V c.

348. RICHARDSON, Water (Walter): *Weaver.*

On 5 June 1557 Richardson became a member of Knox's congregation, and on 14 October of the same year was received as a 'resident' of Geneva and designated 'tisserand' (f. 197). Upon his return to England he was ordained by Grindal on 25 April 1560 (*Grindal*, p. 58).

Geneva, A IV a & b.

349. ROBSON, Anthony: *Brewer.* Of Essex. Wife.

An exile at Aarau; and according to Hans Dür, who calls him 'Rabson', he was a native of 'Chensfort' (Chelmsford, Essex) and a brewer (Byersüder) by occupation. With his wife and six children he lived in the house of Hans Trinklers, a bricklayer. Very possibly he was related to the Reynolde Robson who was apprehended in July 1555 as one of the chief conspirators 'in the intended rebellion in Sussex' (*P.C.A.* 1554–6, p. 159) and in the November following was sent to the Marshalsea for trial (*ibid.* p. 192).

Aarau, A I a & b.

350. RODKYN[?], WILLIAM. (?)

The name as written in the Registre des Habitants at Geneva is indecipherable. Whoever this person was, his country of origin is given as the 'royaume d'Angleterre' (f. 264) and he was received as a 'resident' of the city on 24 October 1558, but never as a member of Knox's congregation. Possibly he was a Scot; possibly also the name may be a corruption of Rodeknight, which appears in Warwickshire in the sixteenth century (cf. Venn, III, 477).

Geneva, A IV b.

351. ROGERS, DANIEL: *Student.* Of Germany and Warwickshire. 1538(?)–90.

Son of John Rogers, the martyr. He was born at Wittenberg in 1538 and naturalized in 1552. After his father's death he returned to Wittenberg to study with Melanchthon and, possibly while on his way, became a subscriber to the 'new discipline' of Frankfort on 21 December 1557. Whether he was then at Frankfort or at Strasbourg is doubtful. At Elizabeth's accession he returned to England and took his M.A. at Oxford in 1561. Later he was employed on diplomatic missions and in 1587 became Clerk of the Privy Council. He was an intimate friend of William Camden.

Frankfort or Strasbourg, B III b; Wittenberg; *D.N.B.*

352. ROGERS, EDWARD: *Gent.* Of Devon and Somerset. 1498(?)–1567(?).

He was made Privy Councillor and Vice-Chamberlain of Queen Elizabeth on 20 November 1558 (*P.C.A.* 1558–70, p. 3); under Mary, according to Strype, he was in exile. The son of George Rogers of Lopit, Devon, his grandmother was a Courtenay; his wife, Mary, the daughter of Sir John Lisle of the Isle of Wight (Harl. Soc. XI, 128). Like so many others of the protestant gentry he had had early connections with Calais, having been bailiff in 1534 of the Castle of Hammes in the Calais marches. Also, like most of them, he was a holder of abbey lands, and profited besides, both in lands and estate, by the fall of Protector Somerset (*P.C.A.* 1552–4, p. 208). In 1547 he had been knighted (*Mem.* II, ii, 328), and in 1549 was appointed, with Sir Thomas Wrothe, a Gentleman of the Privy Chamber (*P.C.A.* 1547–50, p. 345). With his fortunes thus bound to the Edwardian régime it is no surprise to find him involved in Wyatt's rising. And on Wyatt's own testimony against him, Rogers was sent to the Tower on 24 February 1554 (*Chron. Q. Jane*, p. 65 and note b; *P.C.A.* 1552–4, p. 400). With him were Sir Nicholas Arnold and Leonard Dannett, who was probably of the same family as the Thomas Dannett (*q.v.*) whom Cecil invariably speaks of as 'my cousin Dannett'. On 16 April 1554 Rogers was indicted for complicity in the Western Rising (Baga, pp. 246–7), but a year later, on 18 January 1554/5, he was not only released but even had a portion of his goods restored to him on 4 April 1555 (*P.C.A.* 1554–6, p. 111). Yet if he went abroad, as Strype says he did, it must have been at this time; but where he kept himself while in exile has not been discovered. In any case his stay was brief, for in February 1557 we find him back again in England and petitioning the Privy Council for the satisfaction of 'suche losses as he susteyned at the tyme of his apprehencion and committing to the Tower' (*P.C.A.* 1556–8, p. 270: 15 February 1557/8).

France (?); *D.N.B.*

353. ROGERS, RICHARD: *Student and gent.* Of Kent. 1532(?)–97.

The son of Ralph Rogers of Sutton Valence, a cousin of Sir Edward Rogers (Harl. Soc. LXXV, 25). His elder brother married a daughter of Sir Henry Isley (*ibid.*) while Richard himself became later the brother-in-law of Thomas Cranmer (*q.v.*), son of the archbishop. He is said to have been a B.A. of Oxford and an M.A. of Cambridge in 1552 (Foster and Venn, but not in the Oxford Register of Boase, O.H.S. I). His place of exile was Frankfort, where he is first mentioned in January 1557, when he would have been about twenty-four. On the tax-list of that month his name appears with the legend 'hat sonst nichts'. In the following June he was living with Richard Alvey and Daniel Whitehead in the house of Richard Luddington (*H.S.P.* IV, 89). But he was not a signatory of the 'new discipline', although in September 1557 he was one of those who rejected the attempted mediation of Strasbourg in the strife which that discipline occasioned (*T.* p. 174). On his return to England, Rogers received a B.D. from Christ's College, Cambridge, in 1562, and in 1559 was given the archdeaconry of St Asaph's. As a member of the puritan party in the Church he signed the petition for a discipline in 1562. In 1568 he became bishop suffragan of Dover and eventually dean of Canterbury.

Frankfort, A III a 3, 4 & b 2; B III a; *D.N.B.*

354. ROO (or ROE), GEORGE: *Weaver*(?). d. before 1557(?).

He is said by Strype (*Mem.* III, i, 233) to have been a member of the colony of Wesel, a statement which seems to be substantiated by the record at Aarau of an Alice Roo, described as 'ein gstandene manbarene dochter', and probably George Roo's 'grown-up' daughter (Hans Dür). She was a weaver who lived in Hans

Gysin's house, if the 'Elsa Boo' of the official list (cf. below, p. 355) is the same person as the Alice Roo of Hans Dür's. Her father, John Roo or Roe, the friend of John Rough (Foxe, VIII, 447), had probably died at Wesel.

Wesel (?), and Aarau, A I a & b.

355. **ROUGH, JOHN**: *Scottish priest and ex-religious.* Wife. d. 1557.

The only martyr among the exiles. The account of this 'considerable man', who had been a Black Friar at Stirling and 'twice at Rome', is given by Foxe (VIII, 443–9) and repeated by Strype (*Mem.* III, ii, 44–5). But their tale may bear an interpretation not given to it by either of them. Rough had been dispensed 'for his habit and order' to serve the Earl of Arran as secular chaplain (Foxe, VIII, 443), and while with him had imbibed protestant doctrines. But during the reign of Henry VIII he was in receipt of a yearly pension from the king for promoting his 'reputation and interest in those parts', that is, he was an agent in English pay. Somerset, in Edward's reign, continued the pension and sent Rough to preach in the border towns of Carlisle, Berwick and Newcastle, while the archbishop of York (Holbeach) gave him the living of Hull (Foxe, VIII, 444). Then under Mary, as might be expected, he fled, going from Hull to Norden in Friesland, where he supported himself by knitting. It was the need to buy yarn, as Strype avers, which in October 1557 sent him again to England, where 'it so fell out, that he became minister to the congregation of gospellers at London' (*Mem.* III, ii, 45). The moment chosen for his return corresponds very nearly, in point of time, with that of the seditious stir caused by the activities of 'Trudgeover' in East Anglia (*P.C.A.* 1556–8, see Index). Trudgeover was executed in August 1557 (*ibid.* p. 142); Rough was apprehended in December, and the accusation against him was that, in addition to maintaining the gospellers, he had been 'a conveyer of their seditious letters and books into this realm' (Foxe, VIII, 446). The conclusion can hardly be avoided that Rough had been called home to replace Trudgeover. He was taken at Islington on 12 December 'for the redyng of [a lecture, and] odur matters', says Machyn (p. 160). On the 15th the Council sent him to Bonner and on the 20th he was condemned for heresy to be burned at Smithfield (*ibid.* p. 161). His execution took place on the 22nd (Foxe, VIII, 443). John Rough, says Bale, was a friend of Knox.

Noorden in Friesland; *D.N.B.*

356. **RUGGE (RUGG), JOHN**: *Gent.* Of Norfolk (?). d. 1581 (?).

Blomefield says that a younger branch of the family of Rugg in Staffordshire 'of good degree and eminency' settled in Norfolk

(*Norfolk*, XI, 36; cf. Harl. Soc. XXXII, 91), and this may be a younger son of that house. In July 1555 he was at Venice, probably in the train of Francis, Earl of Bedford, for he was among the group of Englishmen then permitted by the Signory to bear arms (*Ven. Cal.* 1555–6, p. 145). From Venice he drifted to Rome, where, according to a letter of Sir Edward Carne to Philip and Mary dated 26 September 1556, Rugge and his friend Windham (*q.v.*) 'came to see Rome' (*For. Cal.* 1553–8, p. 260). Whether he is the same person as the John Rugge who, having 'studied civil law in upper Germany 6 years', supplicated a B.C.L. from Oxford in 1566 and in 1576 became a canon of Westminster (Foster, III, 1288) cannot be said with certainty, but the dates make it not unlikely. If he was of the Ruggs of Norfolk, his uncle, William, had been bishop of Norwich from 1536 to 1550 (Blomefield and *D.N.B.*).

Venice, Rome, B v b 1.

357. RUSSELL, FRANCIS, second Earl of Bedford. 1527–85.

He was educated at King's Hall, Cambridge, and married Margaret, sister of Sir John St John of Bletso. His protestantism was probably imbibed at Cambridge and he was early a friend of Edward Underhill (*Narr. of Ref.* p. 140). In 1551 he attended the conferences on the Sacrament held at the houses of Sir William Cecil and Sir Richard Morison; and, as did his father-in-law, he witnessed Edward's devise of the Crown upon Lady Jane Grey (*Chron. Q. Jane*, p. 99). He was therefore imprisoned in the Fleet on 31 July 1553 (*Machyn*, p. 38), though soon transferred to the custody of the sheriff of London (*Chron. Q. Jane*, p. 15), then William Garrett (*P.C.A.* 1552–4, pp. 305, 314). During his confinement John Bradford wrote him two exhortations to be true to his protestant faith (*Letters of Martyrs*, pp. 275–80). Though Miss Scott Thomson in her *Two Centuries of Family History* does not actually say that he was secretly engaged with Wyatt while openly fighting against him, she does admit that he kept 'in close touch with the reforming party', sending weekly presents of money to those in prison (pp. 204–5, and cf. *Narr. of Ref.* pp. 145–6), while Miss Stone declares that Lord Russell owned to having carried letters between Wyatt and Elizabeth (*Queen Mary*, p. 296). Nor does Miss Scott Thomson mention his connection with the conspiracy that centred around Courtenay in 1555, though it is obvious from the letters of the Venetian ambassador in London that strong suspicion attached to him (*Ven. Cal.* 1555–6, nos. 77, 79, 84). Doubtless, too, this suspicion accounts for Bedford's desire to travel in Italy in the spring of that year, and a passport was issued to him in the name of Philip and Mary which is dated 20 April

1555. In this the authorities were commanded to suffer the Earl 'quyettly to passe by you with the nomber of eyght men and eyght geldings and the som of two hundred pounds in mony and all other his bags, baggages, utensiles and other necessaries, withowte any your searche...' (Scott Thomson, *op. cit.* Facs. opp. p. 206; original at Woburn Abbey). The names of some of these eight men are probably to be found in the list of Englishmen permitted with the Earl of Bedford to bear arms at Venice in the following July (*Ven. Cal.* 1555–6, nos. 169, 171). The unwieldy train left Dover and arrived at Calais on 26 April, but if Bedford then thought himself free to travel, he must have been grievously disappointed. Virtually he was a prisoner. He had a letter 'spontaneously' given to him by King Philip which had to be presented to the Emperor at Brussels. And the Emperor, when he should be a little recovered, wished to speak with him. Useless for Bedford to protest that for his part he did 'not wish to speak to the Emperor'. Soon he was adding 'that it seemed to him as if he were kept prisoner here' (*ibid.* 10 May 1555, pp. 67, 69), a salutary impression that the Emperor was probably trying to convey. Then on 16 May, the day before Courtenay himself arrived at Brussels, Bedford was at last permitted to leave for Italy—a permission, said gossip, that 'will not be given so immediately to Courtenay' (*ibid.* no. 84, p. 73). The two men were to be sedulously kept apart. As an example of dexterous dealing with a noble too powerful to offend overtly, yet one who must be made to feel the degree of strength opposed to him, this episode has seemed to me worth relating.

By 12 June the Earl reached Padua, where he met Sir Thomas Hoby (Cam. Misc. x, 120). By 31 July he had arrived at Venice, and was there to receive so much 'liberality and courtesy' that it moved his mother and wife in England to send a large stag as a present to Michiel, who seems to have been not a little embarrassed by it (*Ven. Cal.* p. 184). From Venice, Bedford went on to Rome, then Naples, about which he wrote enthusiastically to Cecil from Ferrara on his return journey in March 1556 (*For. Cal.* 1553–8, p. 219). But the winter of 1556–7 he was to spend at Zurich. Gualter, later referring to this visit, reveals its purpose to have been that of a 'diligent inquiry into all things which [made] for the cause of the church and of religion...', since it was 'easy to be perceived that this cause was far more dear to [him] than all other things whatever' (*Z.L.* II, 9). In view of Bedford's later membership in the 'secret cabinet' of 1559 which was to prepare for a further reformation of the English Church (cf. 'Grey' above), this is a significant sentence.

Probably it was the spring of 1557 that saw him again in Venice. A letter to Bullinger in which he speaks of his recent visit to Zurich bears the date 26 April no more (*O.L.* i, 138); but another apparently unpublished letter discovered in the Zurich archives (Scott Thomson, *op. cit.* p. 209, n. 1) was written on 6 May 1557. Gualter's reference then, writing on 16 January 1559, to Bedford's visit of 'last year' (i.e. 1558) must be taken as merely a bit of carelessness[1] (*Z.L.* ii, 8). Certainly Bedford was in Calais on 26 July 1557, and at the moment 'in readiness to set forwards', probably to the English camp at St Quentin (*Salisbury*, i, 142), for from there he writes excitedly to Cecil of the victory (*ibid.* pp. 143, 144). Thereafter his activities on the Continent are of no importance to the history of the Exile. But the significance of his stay in Zurich in relation to the parliamentary struggle over the Anglican Settlement can hardly be over-emphasized.

Brussels, B v b 1; Padua, B iv b; Venice, Rome, etc.;
Zurich, A viii a & b ; *D.N.B.*

358. RYTH (RYETH, RITH), [RICHARD]: *Gent.* Of Hampshire (?).

'Ryth', without a Christian name, was proclaimed a traitor with Henry Dudley on 4 April 1556 (*Machyn*, p. 103). He is perhaps the *Richard* Ryth of Rotherwyke, co. Southampton, mentioned in the Visitation of Hampshire (Harl. Soc. LXIV, 37). Possibly he was a son or younger brother of Christopher Ryeth (or Ryth) who was of Twickenham and a Justice of the Peace in Middlesex (Harl. Soc. LXV, 28). No Ryth is mentioned among the English rebels abroad, but the extraordinary series of Biblical names chosen for the children of the family, among which are Theophilus, Ismaell and Solomon, would indicate that the bias of its opinions was strongly puritan.

n.p.; B iv c.

359. SADE, PETER: *Servant.*

A servant of John Hales at Frankfort who was permitted to sign the 'new discipline' in March-April 1557. His name would suggest that he was of humble origin.

Frankfort, B iii b.

360. SALKINS (SALKYNS), WILLIAM: *Merchant.* Of London.

Though called a 'servant' of Richard Hilles, Salkins was obviously an apprentice of good birth, who later married the daughter of a gentleman (Harl. Soc. i, 22). When Hilles saw fit to live in London and conform under Mary, Salkins remained at Antwerp and

---

[1] But was it carelessness? If Bradford had actually spent the winter of 1556 in Zurich, the death of Conrad Pellican, which occurred on 14 September 1556, would not have been news to him (*O.L.* i, 138) I am doubtful of the accuracy of this chronology.

Strasbourg, acting as his agent and lamenting his master's fall from grace. Two letters of Salkins's to Bullinger, written on 26 November and 29 December 1554, express the hope that Bullinger, 'who has so much influence' with Hilles, may succeed in turning him 'from the abomination of the mass' which at that moment was 'placing his soul in jeopardy' (*O.L.* I, 345). This appeal was written from the house of Peter Martyr, where Salkins was then living. His next letter, which announces his approaching departure for Antwerp, shows that Bullinger did indeed write to Hilles (*ibid.* p. 347) but without effect, and the latter's apostasy created a breach between the two men which was never really healed (cf. Correspondence in the *Zurich Letters*). Salkins, however, continued to serve his master throughout the period, travelling freely in the Rhineland and presumably even back and forth to London. His last appearance abroad during Mary's reign was at Frankfort in September 1558, in connection with a law-suit (Jung, p. 59). But after Elizabeth's accession he frequently served as a means of communication between the returned exiles and their German friends. The last mention of him that I have found appears in a letter of Grindal to Conrad Hubert, dated in June 1562 (*Z.L.* II, 74).

Antwerp; Strasbourg, A VIII a & b; Frankfort.

361. SAMFORD (SANDFORD), JOHN: *Merchant.* Of Gloucester.

A draper of Gloucester who was evidently a friend of Hooper and for whom the bishop in 1551 requests of Cecil a licence to eat flesh upon fish days (*Dom. Cal.* 1547–80, p. 32). He may have been the John Sandford of Stonehowse, co. Gloucester,[1] who was a younger son of the Shropshire family of Sandford (Harl. Soc. XXI, 142), but so far I have failed to establish any connection between him and the literary Sandfords of Somerset, James and John (see *D.N.B.*). It was probably his close relations with Hooper that made Samford feel it prudent to retire to Frankfort, where he first appears, on 24 September 1554, as one of the signatories to the invitation to John Knox (*T.* p. 20). On 3 December his name appears again as a signatory of the Frankfort-Strasbourg correspondence (*T.* p. 26). But it is not till the tax-list of October 1556 that he is revealed as one of the richest members of the Frankfort colony with taxable property amounting to 4940 florins (Jung, p. 29). In that list his name appears in the form 'J. Sandforth'. Thereafter he disappears. If he returned to England there is no trace of him in the State Papers.

Frankfort, A III a 3; B III a.

[1] Cf. also *Narr. of Ref.* p. 57, and notes b and c.

362. SAMPSON, THOMAS:[1] *Ex-religious*(?) *and dean of Chichester*.
Of Suffolk. Wife. 1517(?)–89.

Of Playford in Suffolk, and perpetual Fellow of Pembroke Hall,
Cambridge, in 1548 (Cooper doubts this statement, but cf. the
record of his ordination where he is called 'perp. socius dicti Coll.
nuncupati Pembrook Hall'). On 10 August 1550 he was ordained
deacon by Ridley, but he was certainly not priested before his
exile (*Mar. Reac.* p. 189). It may be well to distinguish him
immediately from Thomas Sampson, the priest who on 8 February
1556 did penance at Paul's Cross because 'he had ij wyffes'
(Machyn, p. 100) and whom Cooper has confused with him (cf.
Ath. Cant. II, 43, and *D.N.B.*). Not only was Thomas Sampson,
the dean, then demonstrably at Geneva, but there is also record
of a contemporary Thomas Sampson in the diocese of Norwich,
made rector of Swillande in 1545, and deprived of his living in
1554–5 (Baskerville, *E.H.R.* 1933, p. 59). This was probably the
man who did penance. Nor does Dr Frere's suggestion that
Strype was in error when he made Sampson a dean before his exile
(*Annals*, I, ii, 147) hold in view of the Council's letter to Cranmer,
dated 2 February 1552/3, in which the archbishop is urged to give
John Knox the living of All Hallows, Bread Street, now free 'by
the preferment of Thomas Sampson to the Deanery of Chichester'
(*P.C.A.* 1552–4, p. 212). But Sampson, having evidently taken
part in the riot at Paul's Cross on 13 August 1553, did not have
long to enjoy his dignity, for when Bradford, Becon and Veron
were committed to the Tower on the 16th (*ibid.* pp. 321, 322), Foxe
says that Sampson, who 'should have been committed', was sought
for in vain at Master Elsing's house in Fleet Street: he had already
fled (Foxe, VI, 538). It seems doubtful, however, whether he went
to the Continent before 1554. Foxe intimates that he was with
Sandys and Coxe when they left England on 6 May (*ibid.* VIII, 597),
but that after their arrival at Antwerp the party separated, Sampson
going to study under 'Emanuel, a man skilful in Hebrew' (*ibid.*
p. 598). Later he rejoined his friends at Strasbourg, but his
itinerary abroad fully confirms Bullinger's description of him to
Beza in 1567, in which Bullinger confesses that he had 'always
looked with suspicion upon the statements made by master
Sampson' who, though not 'amiss in other respects', was 'of an
exceedingly restless disposition. While he resided amongst us at
Zurich, and after he returned to England, he never ceased to be

---

[1] Can the Thomas Samson, once a Dominican of Cambridge (Rep. Dep.
Keeper of Records, p. 14), be Sampson, the exile? The Sampson who did
penance was a secular priest. Scory, *Bishop* of Chichester, had been a Dominican of the same house.

troublesome to master Peter Martyr of blessed memory', who 'often used to complain to me, that Sampson never wrote a letter without filling it with grievances: the man is never satisfied; he has always some doubt or other to busy himself with' (*Z.L.* II, 152). This revelation of Sampson's fussy dependence upon the opinion of Peter Martyr whom he adjures to assist him 'in his little studies' (*O.L.* I, 183), adds weight to an identification I have made on other grounds of the person to whom Peter Martyr addressed a letter, without place or date, but assigned by Gorham to the year 1554. The letter contains a critical analysis of a mysterious 'written Confession' which had just been sent to him 'sealed up with little twigs' (Gorham, *Gleanings*, pp. 333–5; and Anthonie Marten's translation of Martyr's *Commonplaces*, ed. 1583, 'Diuine Epistles', p. 107, col. 2). Now a 'letter sealed with twigs' could hardly have travelled by the ordinary post: it must have been carried by hand. Peter Martyr was in Strasbourg in 1554, and so also was Sampson, who from there addressed his letter 'to the trew professors of Christes Gospell inhabiting in the parisshe off All-hallowis, in Brebstrete [*sic*] in London'—that is to his former parishioners (*S.T.C.* no. 21,683). Thus the Confession might well have been sent by hand and the absence of place and date on Martyr's reply would thus be explained. Now upon internal evidence we also believe Sampson to have been the author of the preface to the *Confession of the Banished Ministers*, which was probably composed in Strasbourg during August-September of the same year (cf. 'Ponet' above). It may well have been this 'Confession', one unknown to Gorham (cf. *Gleanings*, p. 334, n. 1), which was sent by the self-distrustful Sampson to his oracle, Peter Martyr, for criticism. Sent, we venture to think, without the knowledge of John Ponet, its author-in-chief: hence the 'little twigs'. And it may be noted, in passing, that Peter Martyr wholly disapproved of its theology: he could not believe, he said, that written as it was it had been 'put forth by our party' (*ibid.*).

On 23 February 1555 Sampson was still in Strasbourg, whence he wrote to Calvin his version of the 'strong controversy' that had arisen in the Church of Frankfort (*O.L.* I, 170–2). But by April he was himself in Frankfort, called there after Knox's expulsion, to sit upon Cox's committee for the revision of the Prayer Book (*O.L.* II, 755); and in Frankfort he appears to have remained until 6 August, when he is again found in Strasbourg (*O.L.* I, 172). Thereafter his changes of place are bewildering. Before 12 July 1556 he was in Geneva, with Pilkington, Scory and Beaumont; but Martin thinks it unlikely, because of Sampson's short stay in Geneva, that he collaborated to any extent in the translation of the Bible (p. 242). Between August and October he was in Lausanne

(*O.L.* I, 176–80) and from Lausanne went possibly to Zurich, for during that winter his letters to Bullinger and Peter Martyr cease. In the spring of 1557, however, he was again at Strasbourg (*ibid.* p. 180), whence he made a short journey to Frankfort in April 1558 (*ibid.* p. 181) with the evident intention of going on from there to Zurich again. But the last letter of this series was written from Strasbourg in July 1558 (*ibid.* p. 182) and in it he first mentions the possession of a wife and child—'our Joanna'; but whether this wife was the niece of Bishop Latimer (*Annals*, I, ii, 147) or one married abroad, I cannot say. His last letter from Germany, written on 17 December 1558, the eve of his departure for England (*Z.L.* I, 2), indicates not only a searching of heart on his part regarding the morality of Church dignities, but a change that a good many other exiles were also experiencing in that matter. 'In case the queen', he asks Peter Martyr, 'should invite me to any ecclesiastical office, such, I mean, as the government of a church, can I accept such appointment with a safe conscience, seeing that these things appear to me a sufficient excuse for non-compliance?' (*ibid.* p. 1). Obviously a deanery or even a bishopric was in his mind, and it is to Sampson's credit that in 1560 he refused the bishopric of Norwich. His nonconformity in the matter of vestments also led to his deprivation of the deanery of Christ Church by special order of the queen, though 'Bishop Grindal prayed Sampson even with tears that he would but now and then, in the public meetings of the University, put on the square cap...' (*Parker*, I, 368). Hence it is not surprising to find that the man whom we believe to have been part author of a first 'admonition to parliament' in 1554, that is, the *Confession of the Banished Ministers*, should have been also (on the word of Archbishop Bancroft) one of the collaborators in a second *Admonition to Parliament* in 1572 (cf. Bancroft's *Survey of the pretended Holy Discipline*, p. 42). But we may close with a final word to Sampson's credit. It was he who interceded with the Council on behalf of Thomas Heton (*q.v.*), 'such a friend to him, as was alter ego', who had become impoverished in his old age, largely, it is said, because of his generosity abroad to his fellow-exiles (*Annals*, II, i, 397).

Strasbourg, B III a; A VIII a & b; Frankfort, A VIII a; Lausanne, A VIII a; Zurich; Strasbourg; *D.N.B.*

363. SAMUEL (SAMEVALL), WILLIAM: *Student and gent.* Of Cornwall(?). Wife. d. 1569(?).

In the article on William Samuel 'divine and poet' in the *D.N.B.* it is said that the man described himself 'in 1551' as servant of the Duke of Somerset, but from 1558 onwards as minister of Christ's

Church. The reason for the change may be attributed to the fact, unmentioned by this biographer, that in 1557 Samuel was an exile in Geneva, where on 7 January of that year he became a 'resident' of the city and, on 8 May following, a member of Knox's congregation. The ministry he speaks of, therefore, was probably after the order of Geneva. What relation he was, if any, to the Francis Samwel who in the second year of Edward VI purchased from the Crown lands in Dorset belonging to the Chantry of St Mary's (*Mem.* II, ii, 403) cannot be determined, but some connection is not unlikely, for we are inclined to believe that he was not of Northampton (*D.N.B.*) but himself the William Samuell, of Shevyock, Cornwall, whose wife was the daughter of Thomas Tremayne, and whose son, John, married in 1620 the daughter of Sir John Chichester (Harl. Soc. IX, 196). This latter fact would make Samuel the exile of the same generation as Chichester the exile (*q.v.*). It is also interesting to find that these Cornish Samuels intermarried with the Scorys (Harl. Soc. IX, 204).

B II; Geneva, A IV a & b.

364. SANDELL (SANDALL, SANDYL, SENDALL), RICHARD: *Merchant* (?). Of Norfolk (?).

Here it seems possible to identify the family, though not the individual. Richard Sandell makes his single appearance at Frankfort in December 1557, when he became a subscriber to the 'new discipline'. But the name is associated with Cambridge, where several Richard Sandells were students, and one, admitted in 1620, was son of Edmund Sandell, a gentleman of Lynn. There the family had some civic importance, for Blomefield records a nameless Sendyll as mayor of Lynn in 1587, and a Thomas Sandhill as mayor in 1601 (*Norfolk*, VIII, opp. p. 533). Richard the exile may well have been one of this family of gentleman merchants.

Frankfort, B III b.

365. SANDES (SAUNDERS), THOMAS: *Gent* (?). Of London (?). Wife.

As one of the subscribers to the 'new discipline' in March-April 1557, his name is given as 'Sandes', but in the tax-list of 15 October, where he is rated at 200 florins, he is called 'Sanders'. The 'r' was thus probably omitted through carelessness in the earlier case, for in the dwelling-list of June he is 'Saunders' (*H.S.P.* IV, 89 and Jung, p. 60). He was then living with his wife and little son (filiolo) in the same house with the families of Edward Boyes, Francis Wilford and Edward Caunt, making twenty-eight persons in all. Very probably he was the Thomas Saunders of Amersham, Bucks. and of Long Marston, Herts., who being related to the

Saunders family of Northamptonshire, was thus a cousin of Laurence Saunders, the martyr (Harl. Soc. XLIII, 18; *ibid.* XXII, 90).

Frankfort, A III a 3, 4 & b 2; B III a.

366. SANDYS, EDWIN, D.D. Of Lancashire. Wife. 1519(?)–88.

Probably born at Esthwaite Hall, Lancashire (for the date cf. Venn and *D.N.B.*), the sixth son of George Sandes, a J.P. and King's Receiver in the county, and Margaret, daughter of John Dixon of London (Harl. Soc. XL, 6). An elder brother, Christopher, married a Margaret Carus (cf. 'Carus' above). Sandys was educated at St John's College, Cambridge, and at Mary's accession was Vice-Chancellor of the University. But he was a partisan of Northumberland and an open adherent of Lady Jane Grey's claim to the throne, in support of which he preached such a sermon (commanded by Northumberland the night before) that it 'pulled many tears out of the eye of the biggest of them' (Foxe, VIII, 590). Only the proclamation of Mary as queen prevented the two Levers, Thomas and Ralph, who were 'ready booted', from carrying it to London for publication (*ibid.* p. 591). On 25 July 1553 Sandys was therefore committed to the Tower (*Machyn*, p. 37), from which he was transferred to the Marshalsea on 26 January 1554 (*Chron. Q. Jane*, p. 39). Sometime between that date and May, he was released, and Foxe has preserved a story of his escape to the Continent which may well be Sandys's own narrative (VIII, 590–8). In his party, which set sail on 6 May, were not only the son of Edward Isaac (*q.v.*) but also Cox, Grindal and Sampson (*ibid.* p. 598), who, after landing at Antwerp, went their several ways. Sandys made a fortnight's visit to Augsburg[1] before going to Strasbourg, where his presence is first recorded on 23 November (*T.* p. 23), but where he made no request for burgher rights until 7 September 1555 (Protocols, vol. 33, f. 363). Then his petition seems to have been denied, for his name does not appear in the list kept of the city's burghers, and the ground of the Council's refusal was very possibly Sandys's public record of opposition to Queen Mary at Cambridge. But at least the right to 'residence' must have been accorded, for at Strasbourg Sandys's wife and child joined him, only to die, both of them within the year. Whether he married his second wife, Cicely Wilford, abroad or after his return to England, I have not so far discovered, but she was the sister of his fellow-exile, Thomas Wilford (*q.v.*) of Kent. In 1558 he followed Peter Martyr from Strasbourg to Zurich, where he was still living at the time of Queen Mary's death. His journey back to England was by way of Strasbourg, where he stayed long

[1] So in the text, but probably Duisburg as suggested, p. 598, n. 1.

enough to preach a sermon (Foxe, VIII, 598). Then on 21 December, immediately following the departure of Sir Anthony Cooke and Sir Thomas Wrothe, he set out again for London, which he reached on the very day of Elizabeth's coronation, 13 January (Foxe, *ibid.* and *Z.L.* I, 3–6).

So far we have followed what we suspect to be Sandys's own narrative. But in his itinerary there are important omissions. For example, he fails to speak of a visit made to Frankfort in the spring of 1555 when, as a member of Cox's committee for the revision of the Prayer Book (*O.L.* II, 755), he was one of those responsible for the resulting Liturgy of Frankfort (see 'Cox' above). Presumably it was this experience of his which led to his appointment to Sir Thomas Smith's Prayer Book committee in January 1559, when he was one of the four exiles on that board. In its stormy sessions during late January and early February, Sandys's quarrelsome temper and 'Germanical nature', acting in support of the arrogance of Cox, must have added almost insupportably to the 'grief and distress' of Parker as moderator (*Parker*, I, 156 and *Correspondence of Parker*, pp. 57–9). One fact alone remains to be recorded of Sandys's foreign sojourn. He did not, like others at Strasbourg, subscribe to the 'new discipline' of Frankfort, but did attempt with Sir Francis Knollys to reconcile the factions which that discipline created (*T.* p. 174).

In view of the close association of his notable son, Sir Edwin Sandys, with the early fortunes of the colony of Virginia and with those exiles from Leyden who eventually settled at Plymouth in Massachusetts, it is particularly interesting to find an early association existing between the families of Sandys and Washington in Lancashire before the Washingtons emigrated. In 1577, Sandys the exile became archbishop of York, and while archbishop, he founded at Hawkshead, Lancs., a grammar school which has preserved his Bible. In this is the record of the baptisms of his great-grandchildren, to whom either Sir John or Lady Washington frequently stood godparents. Also Robert, the archbishop's grandson, married Alice Washington, sister of Laurence Washington of Sulgrave (Waters, *Gleanings*, I, 494).

B I a & b; B II; Augsburg; Strasbourg, A III a; B III a; Frankfort, A VIII a; Zurich; *D.N.B.*

367. SAULE, ARTHUR: *Student.* Of Gloucestershire. d. 1585.

Fellow of Magdalen College, Oxford, from 1546 to 1553 and M.A. in 1549. He was one of the extreme party in the college who had sought and obtained leave of absence from it before September 1553 (Wilson's *Magd.* p. 101), but was probably among the nine actually expelled at Gardiner's visitation in October since he received a special grant of money 'ex voluntate inquisitorum' (*ibid*. p. 103). He then retreated to Strasbourg where, in 1554, he was one of the signatories of that colony's refusal to remove itself to Frankfort (*T*. p. 23). In December of that year he received his share of the Duke of Württemberg's bounty to the amount of 10 florins[1] (Württ. Staatsarchiv) and he was still in Strasbourg at the time of Brett's visitation in the summer of 1556. In fact Saule is one of the only two religious exiles whom Brett mentions in his report, and that because Saule tried to suborn Brett's servant in order to procure easier access to Brett's person—for what intent we dare not say (Brett, p. 129). On 23 June 1556, Saule was registered as a student 'of the diocese of Bristol' at the University of Heidelberg (Matrikel, p. 7), which may mean that he was attached to the household of the Duchess of Suffolk at Weinheim nearby. On his return to England he allied himself with the puritan party and signed for a discipline in 1562. In 1559/60 he was made a canon of Salisbury, and in 1565 of Gloucester.

B ɪɪ; Strasbourg, A ᴠɪɪ c; B ɪɪɪ a; B ɪᴠ a; Heidelberg, A ᴠ; *D.N.B.*

368. SCORY, JOHN, B.D.: *Ex-religious*(?) *and bishop of Chichester.* Of Norfolk. d. 1585.

A friar in the Dominicans' house at Cambridge,[2] who had preached at the execution of Joan Bocher (*Mem*. ɪɪ, i, 335). He was also one of the six preachers of Canterbury and chaplain both to Ridley (*ibid*. p. 402) and to Cranmer (*Mem*. ɪɪ, ii, 171), who appointed Scory, when bishop of Rochester, to the commission for the reform of ecclesiastical laws (*Cranmer*, p. 388). At Mary's accession he was deprived of his bishopric, but with Barlow of Bath and Wells he recanted (*Mem*. ɪɪɪ, i, 241) and was actually absolved under Bonner's seal on 14 July 1554. Yet it was Scory who on the previous 5 September had, without Cranmer's permission, placarded copies of the archbishop's declaration against the Mass in the streets of London (Foxe, ᴠɪɪɪ, 38). His haste in doing so was, we believe, due to premeditated policy and not to mere excess of zeal. Cranmer, the vacillating, was to be committed to opposition before he had had time for second thoughts, and upon Scory and Ponet (*q.v.*) must therefore lie the odium of Cranmer's immediate imprisonment and eventual martyrdom. After that violent declaration, the greater part of which was composed in all likelihood by Ponet himself (see above), the Marian government had no other alternative than to commit the archbishop to ward. Ponet and Scory fled the coming storm; Cranmer remained.

[1] His signature, attached to the exiles' letter of thanks, is now preserved at Stuttgart. A facsimile will be found at the Bodleian, 'Autographs', ɪ, R. Pal. f. 180.

[2] 8th Report, Deputy Keeper, Public Records, App. ɪɪ, p. 14.

On 2 August 1554 Scory was already at Emden, where he was in charge of the 'not very frequent' English congregation. His offer, at Grindal's instigation, to become minister of the church at Frankfort was, like Ponet's, rejected (*T*. p. 13). His recent recantation had not been forgotten. In 1555 the press of Egidius van der Erve published his *Epistle wrytten vnto all the faythfull that be in pryson in Englande* (*S.T.C.* no. 21854, and cf. F. S. Isaac, p. 341), which was a manifesto of complacent pity for those unfortunates, issued from his own safe retreat at Emden. Nevertheless he felt obliged in it to defend the 'self-banished', and also his own temporary defection to the papist side. He then seems to have drifted with many of his congregation to Wesel.(*Mem*. III, i, 233); and from Wesel in 1556 went to Geneva, where he appears some time before 12 July in company with Pilkington, Beaumont and Sampson. But his stay there was short. Martin gives him no share in the translation of the Bible and his services may have proved unacceptable. It seems possible that from Geneva he returned to Emden to resume his duties as superintendent of the English church there and also perhaps to aid in the publication of the Emden edition of Cranmer's *Defensio* (cf. F. S. Isaac, pp. 340, 351). His first public appearance in England after Elizabeth's accession was on the first Sunday in Lent, 1558/9, when he preached before the queen (*Machyn*, p. 189). At Easter he was chosen one of the disputants on the protestant side at the Conference of Westminster. On the 23rd of the following June he was preferred to the see of Hereford (*Machyn*, p. 201).

Emden, B III a; Wesel; Geneva, A III a; D.N.B.

369. SEBURNE (SEABORNE) (alias 'Plumer'), CHRISTOPHER: *Gent*. Of Hereford. fl. 1569.

This was undoubtedly the son and heir of John Seborne of Sutton, co. Hereford (Weaver, *Visitation of Hereford*, p. 64). His grandfather, Richard, had married Elizabeth Elton, whose mother was a Carew. The family of Seborne alias Plumer[1] seems to have been one of some importance on the Welsh Marches both in Gloucestershire and Herefordshire, for a Richard Seborne, under Philip and Mary, was charged with the peace of the border (*P.C.A.* 1554–6, p. 145 and *ibid*. 1556–8, p. 175). Christopher arrived at Geneva with the party of Whittingham on 13 October 1555, and on the 24th of that month (his name being wrongly deciphered as 'Staburn' in Ferrer Mitchell's notes now in Geneva) he was received as a 'resident' of the city (f. 123). In December he became also a

---

[1] In 1567 a Robert Seaborne alias Plumer sold a tenement to a Christopher Aylway who in 1562 had married 'Anne Hooper' (Harl. Soc. xxi, 229 note, 231 note).

deacon of the English congregation (Martin, p. 334). If he was then married, his wife, Mary, daughter of John Arundel of Chidiock (cf. Weaver, *op. cit.*), was not with him. Probably Seborne had been involved in the rising of the West in 1554. A house built in the sixteenth century and still known as Seaborne's Farm is standing to-day at Brockhampton by Ross in Herefordshire (Royal Comm. for Hist. Mon. II, no. 5, p. 36).

Geneva, A IV a & b.

370. SEFOLD (SEAFOLD), GEORGE: *Student*(?).

This name seems to be unknown to Foxe, to Strype, to Venn, to Foster, to the Privy Council minutes, to the Domestic and Foreign Calendars, and to any genealogical guide. He was a student at the University of Basle during the winter of 1557-8, where he was registered under the name of Georgius Sefoldus Anglus (see below, p. 358) and credited with his matriculation fee of VI sol—the only contribution he has apparently made to history.

Basle, A II a.

371. SELYE (SEELEY, SEELE, SILLY), RALPH: *Gent*(?). Of Cornwall(?).

Probably one of the Cornish family of Seeley which derived its name from a Johan de Seilly, Sire de Sully in Berry (Planche's Roll of Arms, *Geneal.* n.s. VIII, 211). In 1550 a John Sely was paid by the government 'for water carriages...to the fortifications of Alderney' (*P.C.A.* 1550-2, p. 27) and on the same day the Chancellor of Augmentations was instructed to draw up a new lease for a parcel of the lands of Barking for Nicholas Sellye, gent., 'one of the Ewerie', in respect of his long service. These gentlemen were possibly in some degree relatives of Ralph, but so far I have found no pedigree of the family. Ralph Selye's sole appearance abroad was at Frankfort (or Strasbourg), when on 21 December he signed the 'new discipline'. Curiously enough a Richard Selye was in 1576 a *papist* 'fugitive beyond sea' and in 1580 a harbourer of Campion (*Annals*, II, ii, 360, 596).

Frankfort, B III b.

372. SERBIS, THOMAS.

No English name such as this and no plausible English equivalent has been discovered, though I have invoked the aid of the British Museum. He is recorded abroad once only, as a signatory to the 'new discipline' at Frankfort in April. I am beginning to think that the men in that list who make no other appearance abroad may have been young pensioners or servants attached to the household of the Duchess of Suffolk at Weinheim. Richard Bertie was certainly present in Frankfort once (*T.* pp. 101, 102, 141, 185) and possibly more than once in 1557.

Frankfort, B III b.

373. SHARP, ROBERT: *Preacher*(?). Of Cambridgeshire(?).

The presence of this man abroad is known only through my recent discovery at Stuttgart of the list of exiles who received a share of the Duke of Württemberg's donation (Württ. Staatsarchiv). But he is known to Strype as a member of a nonconforming group called the Family of Love which was held in high disfavour by the exiles. It must be for this reason that his name is never mentioned by them, nor is it found attached to any document but that of the letter of thanks sent to the duke for his contribution: an interesting example of religious ostracism even in common calamity. Sharp had either been, or was soon to be, parson of Strethall in Essex[1] (*Parker*, II, 340, 381–5), where in 1573 he was reported to be one of the two recalcitrant preachers in the diocese of Norwich who refused to wear the surplice (*ibid.* p. 340) and who was accused of marrying persons in the fields 'after a new way of his own' (*ibid.* p. 381). This sect came under the particular displeasure of Sir Francis Knollys, who may well have known Sharp at Strasbourg; and in September 1581, being 'zealous in his opposition to heresy', Sir Francis begged Burghley to redress such 'anabaptisticall sectaries' as the members of the Family of Love 'who do serve the turn of the papists' (Wright, *Queen Elizabeth*, II, 152–4).

Strasbourg, A VII c.

374. SIMSON (SYMSON), DAVID: *Ex-religious and priest.* A Scot.

This exile of Bale's list and the Emden catalogue is, almost undoubtedly, the David Symson who was a Dominican priest of Newcastle (8th Rep. Dep. Keeper of Records, App. III, p. 32). He may also have been a relative of the Andrew Simson who was Master of Perth Grammar School from 1550 to 1560 (*D.N.B.*), and he is very likely the 'Scotchman named Simpson' who fled with John à Lasco in 1553, and was a member of the party of Micronius in the dispute held with Westphal at Hamburg on 4 March 1554 (Pocock, *E.H.R.* X, 435).

B I a & b; B II; Hamburg.

375. SINGLETON (SHINGLETON), HUGH: *Printer and book-binder.* Of London. d. 1593.

A son of John Singleton or Shingleton, alias Lee, citizen of London (H. J. Byrom, *Library*, XIV (1934), 122). The controversy

---

[1] A list of the vicars of the parish, to be found in the church of St Edmund, at Hauxton, Cambridgeshire, shows that a Robert Sharp was installed on 29 March 1561, but later deprived. In 1573 his son, Robert, was made vicar.

over Hugh Singleton's whereabouts between 1553 and 1557 has now been settled conclusively by the discovery abroad of official records of his presence as an exile both at Strasbourg and at Basle during the reign of Mary. The council minutes of Strasbourg attest that on Saturday, 21 August 1557, Singleton was not only then in the city but that he had already been there for some time, having on two previous occasions been granted permits for residence (Protocols, vol. 35, f. 326ᵛᵒ; cf. below, p. 370). At that moment he was asking, not for the 'Grossbürgerrecht', which he says he cannot afford, but for the 'Kleinbürgerrecht', and the right to pursue his trade of book-binder. His request was refused (*ibid.* and f. 334), possibly because of guild jealousy, possibly also because something was known of his previous record in London as a printer of seditious pamphlets (cf. *P.C.A.* 1552–3, p. 269). In any case he went to Basle, where on 11 June 1558 he was received as a citizen (Öffnungsbuch, VIII, f. 179; cf. below, p. 361) and also permitted on the 'Sunday before St John's Day' to become a member of a printers' guild, known as the Saffron Guild (Eintrittsrodel, II, 1553–1600; cf. below, p. 361). On 5 September 1559 Singleton petitioned for a year's extension of his burgher rights and permission to return to England (*ibid.*). So much is official fact. But there is nothing in this to contravene another fact upon the evidence of which, however, Mr Byrom suggests that Singleton was not abroad in 1557, but in London (Byrom, pp. 127–8). This was the debt he owed to Mr Seres, a record of which appears in the Stationers' Register for 19 July 1557–9 July 1558 (Arber, *Registers*, I, fol. 29 b or p. i, 90). But obviously this debt was one contracted at some time previous to May 1557, on which date Singleton had already made part payment. The balance of the sum was thus still owing during a period which exactly corresponds to the time when, by the records of Strasbourg and Basle, he is found to have been abroad. Nor for the same practical reason is his name among those of the 'Chartermen' at the time of the incorporation in 1557 of the Stationers' Company (Arber, I, pp. xxxiii–xxxiv; cf. Byrom, p. 128). Unfortunately these new facts do not yet solve the problem of where and when Singleton published the pamphlets which bear his rebus and the colophon 'Rome before the Castle of St Angelo'. My own belief that Singleton was imprisoned with John Day (*q.v.*) on 16 October 1554, and that with Day he fled to the Continent probably in the spring of 1555, still awaits proof. Of his supposed relations with Knox we know nothing, but that he must have had personal intercourse with John Bale at Basle in 1558 can hardly now be doubted (cf. Byrom, p. 128).

Strasbourg, A VII a; Basle, A II b.

376. SMYTH, HARRY: *Merchant.* Of Leicestershire.

Though it may seem presumptuous to claim to have identified a 'Henry Smith', we believe, nevertheless, that the 'Henry Smith, gentleman' who was admitted to 'residence' at Geneva on 14 October 1557 (f. 196), and the 'Harrye Smyth' who became a member of Knox's congregation on 26 November 1557, were one and the same person as the 'master Smyth marchand' who was committed to the Tower with John Throckmorton on 18 March 1555/6, and on 21 November following was condemned at the Guildhall 'to perpetual presun' (*Machyn*, pp. 102, 118). This Henry Smith, merchant of London, had in April 1551 been given a licence to bring foreign glassmakers into the realm (*Mem.* II, ii, 250). In June of that year he appears as a creditor of the Crown for wheat delivered for Ireland (*P.C.A.* 1550–2, p. 287). Very possibly he was a member of the Leicestershire family of Smith alias Harris, and son of Ambrose Smith, a London draper (Harl. Soc. I, 33, and II, 66–7), whose affiliations were strongly protestant. If so, then Henry Smith the exile had himself married the sister of Sir William Skipwith, Sir Peter Carew's father-in-law, while his uncle, Erasmus Smith, was the husband of Margaret, sister of Sir William Cecil, and the father of another Henry Smith, a puritan divine, who was known by the epithet of the 'silver-tongued' (*D.N.B.*). After the accession of Elizabeth I can find only one reference to Henry Smith the merchant, and that in connection with an import of wines in 1568 (*Dom. Cal.* Addend. 1566–79, p. 54).

Geneva, A IV a & b.

377. SOCCUS, WILLIAM: *Student.*

Of this Englishman, who was a student at Padua in 1558–9 and Consiliarius of the English students, no trace can be found whatever nor even an English equivalent for his name.

Padua, A VI.

378. SOOTHOUS (SOUTHOUSE), CHRISTOPHER: *Student.* Of London. d. 1591(?).

Matriculated from Trinity Hall, Cambridge, in 1552 (Venn, IV, 124). He is first mentioned at Frankfort on 27 August 1555, when he signed the letter of secession of Whittingham's party (*T.* p. 55). He did not, however, follow Whittingham to Geneva, but probably went directly to Basle, where on 10 December 1557 he entered the university, paying his matriculation fee of VI sol (below, p. 358). Venn thinks it possible that Southouse, the student of Cambridge, became in 1560 a prebendary of Lincoln who in 1579 was deprived for not paying his tenths. Also a Christopher Southouse appears with John Mansfield (*q.v.*) in 1582 on behalf of the Earl of Huntingdon when an investigation was made into the latter's 'conduct' in the working of certain mines (*Dom. Cal.* Addend. 1580–1625, p. 65). His association with Mansfield would suggest that this was Christopher Southouse, the former exile.

Frankfort, B III a; Basle, A II a.

379. SORBY (SOWERBY, SOERSBY, etc.), THOMAS: *Student.* Of Lincolnshire(?).

Probably of humble origin, possibly of Lincolnshire, where a Roger Sorsby, Fellow of Peterhouse, was ordained priest in 1544 (Venn, IV, 122). He first appears at Frankfort on 24 September 1554, when he signed the congregation's invitation to John Knox (*T.* p. 20). In the autumn of 1555 he stood friend to Whitehead in the quarrel that ensued upon the latter's resignation of his pastorate (*T.* pp. 60–1). In November of that year he is listed among the 'students' on the Standesliste (Jung, p. 26) and in the tax-list of the following autumn he is described as 'usually having nothing' in the way of property. Contrary to Jung's statement (p. 60) his name does not appear among the subscribers to the 'new discipline' in the spring of 1557, but he was in Frankfort in June, sharing the house of John Escot. The addition of 'civis' to his name in that list is, according to Jung, an error (*ibid.*); he never became a burgher. On 17 September 1557 he was one of the signatories to a letter of thanks written to Bullinger, in return for a gift of books or money (*O.L.* II, 764), and on 30 September he was among those who refused Strasbourg's offer of mediation in the quarrel arising out of the 'new discipline' (*T.* p. 174). He was also one to whom Richard Chambers wrote in defence of his administration of the public funds (*T.* p. 182). Evidently he was a man of some consequence among the exiles. On his return to England he subscribed to the articles of 1562 'proc. cleri. Cicestrensis' (*Annals*, I, i, 488) and also voted both for the alteration of ceremonies and the adoption of a discipline.

B II; Frankfort, A III a 2, 3, 4 & b 2; B III a; A VIII a.

*SOUTHWELL, —.

Wotton, writing to Petre on 17 April 1554, announces that 'Sir Robert Southwell's son is at Orleans. Trusts to find the means to send to him shortly' (*For. Cal.* 1553–8, p. 72), but the reference is too ambiguous to include this son of a catholic father among the exiles.

380. SPENSER (SPENCER), Thomas: *Student.* Of Wiltshire.
1525(?)–71.

A demy of Magdalen College in 1540; M.A. of Christ Church in
1547, and proctor in 1552–3 (Foster, iv, 1398 and Venn, iv, 134).
He was one of the first group of students to arrive at Zurich in
April 1554 (*O.L.* ii, 752 and *Diarium*, p. 46). But on 5 November
1556 he became a member of Knox's congregation at Geneva and
on 14 October 1557 was received as a 'resident' of the city (f. 196).
Possibly he had been called in to do yeoman service on the Geneva
Bible, although Martin does not name him among the collaborators.
In 1557 he there married Ales Agar, a widow of Colchester (Martin,
p. 337), while he himself is described as of 'Wroghton', Wilts.
Grindal ordained him deacon on 14 January 1559/60 (*Grindal*,
p. 53), and in 1560 he became archdeacon of Chichester and rector
of Hadleigh in Suffolk, Rowland Taylor's former parish (Foster),
where Spencer is buried. His epitaph contains the line 'At fourty-
seven years age God gave mee rest' (Macray, ii, 89). He had been
of the puritan party, both voting against ceremonies and petitioning
for a discipline in 1562. Some works of the German reformers he
bequeathed to the library of Magdalen, which still possesses them.

B ii; Zurich, A viii c; Geneva, A iv a & b.

381. SPRAT, Thomas: *A tanner.* Of Kent.

He had been a servant to one Brent, a justice of Sandwich, but
'forsaking his master for religion' sake' he went to Calais, which
then became the headquarters from which he made frequent
journeys back to England, acting with his associate, William
Porrege (*q.v.*), as one of the regular messengers of the exiles. The
lively story of their escape from Sprat's former master, on one of
these visits, is told by Foxe (viii, 576–8).

Calais.

382. SPRINGHAM, Richard: *Merchant.* Of London. Wife.

The story of these English merchant-bankers of the mid-sixteenth
century forms an interesting chapter of Tudor history yet to be
written. The impression they leave on the mind is a pleasant,
human one that invites sympathy and a closer acquaintance.
Richard Springham, a trader in English cloth, was one of the
original committee of ways and means organized by the protestant
party in 1553–4 to supply the needs of the exiles overseas. His
protestant affiliations are revealed as early as 1551, when he acted
as executor to Lady Locke, widow of Sir William Locke[1] (*Machyn*,
pp. 12, 323) and probably the mother-in-law of Knox's friend

[1] For an account of Sir William Locke, mercer and alderman of London,
d. 1550, see A. B. Beaven's *Aldermen of London*, ii, 31.

Anna Locke, later an exile at Geneva. Whether he himself went to Zurich as early as June 1554 for a banker's conference with Richard Chambers, John Abell and Thomas Heton is questionable, though Strype certainly implies this (*Mem.* III, i, 233). His first authentic appearance abroad was not till the winter of 1556–7, when he became a student at the University of Basle (below, p. 358). In August 1557 he petitioned for burgher rights at Strasbourg, claiming that he had fled from England with his wife and child 'because of the war and on account of religion' (Protocols, vol. 35, ff. 296–296vo; cf. below, p. 370). But he especially stipulates that such citizenship shall not entail the loss of his rights in England and Brabant, and to this the council must have agreed for he was granted six years' residence. The only fact that we know about his life in Strasbourg is that on 29 September 1557 he was one of the subscribers to the colony's vain effort to ensure peace at Frankfort (*T*. p. 174), but he continued to live there until the spring of 1559, when Alexander Nowell reported to John Abell (on 28 May) that 'On Wednesday last came home Mr Spryngham and his wife, with his company' (*For. Cal.* 1558–9, p. 287). Later in the same year he is found associated with the merchant Michael Loke [Locke] in an effort to establish silk manufacture in England (*Dom. Cal.* 1547–80, p. 147).

Zurich (?); Strasbourg, A VIII a; B v b 1.

383. STAFFORD, Sir ROBERT: *Gent.* Of Northamptonshire.

In spite of current belief that Robert Stafford was the brother of Thomas Stafford (*q.v.*) and so nephew to Cardinal Pole and brother to Lady Dorothy Stafford of Geneva (see *Ven. Cal.* 1534–54, Index; *For. Cal.* 1553–8, pp. 69, 79 and Martin, pp. 57–8), this is an error, indicated by the context of the references to him in the State Papers, and actually proved by the Stafford Pedigree in J. Campbell's *Stafford Peerage* (1818), Table I. In that he is shown to have been the third son of Sir Humphrey Stafford of Blatherwick, younger brother of Sir William Stafford the exile at Geneva, and so only brother-in-law to Lady Dorothy, Sir William's wife. Before his flight to France with Thomas Stafford in March 1554 (*For. Cal.* 1553–8, p. 69 and *Ven. Cal.* 1534–54, p. 481), Robert had been a turbulent adventurer in Italy. Sir Thomas Hoby met him in Siena in the autumn of 1549 and shortly afterwards in Rome (Cam. Misc. x, 19, 24). In November 1550 his gratuitous rudeness to Peter Vannes, the English ambassador at Venice, called down upon Stafford's head a severe reproof from the Council of Ten (*Ven. Cal.* 1534–54, no. 687, p. 331). When a refugee in Paris in 1556, his melodramatic and incessant quarrels with Thomas Stafford elicited from Wotton the sarcasm, 'If ever there were a tragico-comedia played, surely these men played it' (*For. Cal.* 1553–8, p. 264). Eventually Sir Robert fell out even with his friend Henry Dudley (*ibid.* p. 282), and he seems to have been the one person whose temper could prevail against the will of Calvin. Calvin, after the death of Sir William Stafford in May 1556, claimed the custody of Lady Dorothy's son, John Stafford, to whom he had stood godfather, and forbade her to take the child away from Geneva. Lady Dorothy appealed to her brother-in-law, Robert, who promptly threatened to invoke the aid of the French king against Geneva if his sister-in-law were not allowed to go with his nephew where she pleased (Martin, p. 57). And Calvin eventually yielded to this seemingly empty menace on Stafford's part, which was, however, pointed with a sneer that may have struck home (see p. 14, n. 7, above). In April 1557 Robert was still in France with Dudley 'and other of that sort' (Wotton to Queen Mary, *For. Cal.* p. 299) and in fact did not return to England until February 1559. Then being evidently in doubt about the kind of reception he might receive from Elizabeth, he appealed to Cecil for a personal interview with him (*Dom. Cal.* 1547–80, p. 121). This Cecil would seem to have refused, for a month later Stafford is still pleading 'to the Queen's mercy' (*ibid.* p. 124) and it was evidently not until 1566 that he was fully restored to favour and could thank Cecil 'for benefits conferred' (*ibid.* p. 270).

Rouen; Paris, B iv b; B v b 1, 2, 3.

384. STAFFORD, Thomas: *Gent.* Of Staffordshire. 1531(?)–57.

Thomas Stafford, nephew to Cardinal Pole, was of royal descent on both sides and posed as a claimant to the English throne. At Mary's accession he was in Poland winning golden opinions from its king, Sigismund Augustus, who begged the queen to restore Stafford to his dukedom of Buckingham (*For. Cal.* 1553–8, pp. 15–16). It is obvious, from the presence of three of the Stafford family abroad in the last years of Edward VI, that their claims had made them feared by Northumberland (*For. Cal.* 1547–53, pp. 70, 71, 119, 121). Like Sir Robert, Thomas Stafford found it wise to travel in Italy until Mary's accession (*Ven. Cal.* 1534–54, p. 376). Then he returned to England, evidently full of hope that this would mean the restoration of the Staffords to their title and estates. The disappointment of this hope turned him traitor. On 16 February 1553/4 he was apprehended as an accomplice, either of Wyat or of Suffolk (*P.C.A.* 1552–4, p. 393), and on the 20th was lodged in the Fleet with John Rogers (*ibid.* p. 395). From prison he escaped 'with his brother-in-law' (*Ven. Cal.* 1534–54, p. 481) to France, where he had the audacity to present himself to Pole at Fontainebleau, who promptly expelled him the house (*ibid.* p. 489). Possibly Pole's rebuke to 'malcontents as impassioned as his nephew himself. . . ' (*ibid.*) sent Stafford back to England, where he seems actually to have been in the queen's service for a time (*ibid.* p. 495). Certainly the *Foreign Calendar* makes no mention of Stafford abroad again until October 1556, while on 23 July 1555 the Privy Council addressed a letter of instructions to 'Thomas Stafford', as if he were in England fulfilling his ordinary functions as country gentleman (*P.C.A.* 1554–6, p. 163). It was Dudley's conspiracy which seems to have involved him a second time in treason and sent him again to France, a fugitive. There in January 1556/7 he defiantly assumed 'the full arms of England on his seal, without any difference' (*For. Cal.* 1553–8, p. 283) and from then on developed his mad scheme of invading England. Dudley, 'laughing merrily', had dubbed him the 'King of Scarborough' before he sailed (*ibid.* p. 306) and between 14 April and 8 May 1557 the tragi-comedy of invasion played itself out (*ibid.* p. 294). He actually did take Scarborough Castle, but his sounding proclamation of himself as king brought him no adherents (*Mem.* iii, ii, 515 and *Ven. Cal.* 1556–7, p. 1026, Surian to Doge, 29 April). On 28 April he and his handful of English, French and Scottish followers were apprehended, and on 28 May Stafford himself was beheaded (*Machyn*, p. 137). Yet his 'lewde traiterous doinges', fruitless as they were for himself, did contribute to England's declaration of war against the France that had abetted them (*Ven. Cal.* 1556–7, p. 1150).

France, B v b 1.

385. STAFFORD, Sir WILLIAM: *Gent.* Of Chebsey, Staffordshire. Wife. d. 1556.

Another exile of royal descent, being of the 'Bagot' line of the Staffords and second son of Sir Humphrey Stafford of Blatherwick, Northants. (Stafford Pedigree, Table I). Sir William's first wife was Mary Boleyn, sister of Queen Anne and, by her first marriage, mother of Catherine Carey, Lady Knollys. He was thus uncle by marriage of the Princess Elizabeth and stepfather-in-law of Sir Francis Knollys, his fellow-exile. In 1545 he married, as his second wife, Lady Dorothy Stafford (*Gent. Mag.* xxvi, 32–3), sister of Thomas Stafford (above) and daughter of Henry, Baron Stafford, and Ursula Pole, granddaughter of George, Duke of Clarence. At a time of disputed succession the Staffords were dangerously near the throne. Knighted in 1545, Sir William in 1548 was made standard-bearer of the band of Gentlemen Pensioners formed by Henry VIII in 1539 of men of noble blood (*Narr. of Ref.* pp. 320–2). In the Stafford Pedigree he is also given the rank of Privy Councillor, and was one of those chosen in 1551 to accompany Lord Clinton in his special embassy to France (*Mem.* II, i, 359). After Queen Mary's accession and the troubles of 1554, Sir William and his patriarchal household, including not only his wife and two children (one of them the future ambassador, Edward) but also Jane Stafford alias Williams, his sister;[1] Mistress Sandes alias Foster, his cousin; and four servants, left England without licence probably early in 1555 (*P.C.A.* 1554–6, p. 257). Martin says (p. 55) that he went first to Paris, but of this statement we have found no confirmation. He must have arrived at Geneva in March, for on 29 March 1555 he was received there as a 'resident' (f. 104) and known as Lord Rochford, taking the title of Rochford, in Essex, acquired from his first wife (Martin, p. 55). Martin also says that he embroiled himself in the politics of Geneva, for which reason he was set upon and nearly killed when returning to the city after the uprising of May 1555 (quoting Gautier, *Hist. de Genève*, III, 619–20). Shortly afterwards, as 'excellent personnage, homme de bien et de cognoissance', he was permitted to wear a sword (Martin, p. 56). As soon as the English congregation was organized on 1 November 1555, Sir William and his household became members, and his son John, to whom Calvin stood godfather, was the first child to be baptized in it on 4 January 1556 (*ibid.* p. 335). Then on the following 5 May Stafford died. John Brett, in whose commission he was named, learned of Sir William's death while he himself was in Italy (Brett, p. 114), but in England, on 15 May, the Privy Council being ignorant of it was ordering that 'no payment of money by exchange or otherwise' was to reach Stafford abroad (*P.C.A.* 1554–6, p. 271). I have already alluded (see 'Robert Stafford' above) to the quarrel that ensued in Geneva over the custody of John Stafford, Calvin's godson (cf. also Martin, pp. 56–8), which resulted in Lady Dorothy's withdrawal to Basle. On 3 November 1557 she was received there as a burgher of the city (Öffnungsbuch, f. 177, see below, p. 360) and there she remained until 14 January 1559 (*ibid.*) living, we suspect, in the 'hüslein'—the 'little house' attached at right angles to the Clarakloster where dwelt the other members of the English colony (see frontispiece). A memorial tablet to Lady Dorothy, with an inscription, still hangs in St Margaret's, Westminster, on the west wall.

Paris (?); Geneva, A IV a & b.

[1] Soon to marry in Geneva the Italian preacher, Count Maximilian Celsus (Martin, p. 337).

386. STANLEY, Thomas: *Gent*(?).

Since this cannot be Thomas Stanley, bishop of Sodor and Man, who was deprived in 1545 but restored to his bishopric under Mary in 1556, we suggest that he may be the Thomas Stanley who in 1552 had been made Comptroller of the Mint in the Tower (*Mem.* II, ii, 62). It is by no means unlikely that he used his position to aid Sir Henry Dudley in his plot to rob the Exchequer, since Stanley arrived at Geneva on 5 November 1556, and in the company of several seditious gentlemen of eminence (cf. Martin, pp. 332–3). Under Elizabeth a 'Thomas Stanley' appears again as 'under treasurer of our mint in the Tower' (*Dom. Cal.* Addenda, 1547–65, pp. 515–16). We should suppose that this was the same man.

Geneva, A IV a.

387. STAUNTON (STANTON), John: *Chantry priest and gent.* Of Nottinghamshire.

We take this man to be the 'Sr. John Stanton a preest' who was second son of Thomas Stanton of Nottinghamshire (Harl. Soc. IV, 180–1) and, according to Foster (IV, 1411), chantry priest in the cathedral of Hereford in 1542 and rector of Morley in Derbyshire in 1553. If so, he was probably the uncle of another exile, William Staunton (below). What we certainly know of him is, that he was in Frankfort as early as 29 July 1554, when he was one of the five Englishmen to sign the *Liturgia Sacra* (ed. 1554, p. 92); that on 24 September he subscribed to the calling of John Knox as pastor and was also among those of Knox's faction who on 3 December asserted, in a letter to Strasbourg, their conformity to the Prayer Book only 'so farre as gods worde dothe assure it and the state off this countrie permit' (*T.* p. 26), and that in September 1555 he seceded with Whittingham to Geneva (*T.* p. 55). There he first appeared on 13 October and on the 24th was granted the right to 'residence' (f. 123). In December 1555 he was chosen one of the deacons of the congregation and re-elected to the same office in the following year (Martin, p. 334). But also during the winter of 1555–6, in that mysterious fashion known to so many exiles, he was a student at the University of Basle, though there is no record that he paid his matriculation fee (f. 194).

B II; Frankfort, B III a; Geneva, A IV a & b; Basle, A II a.

388. STAUNTON (STANTON), Captain William: *Yeoman.*

Possibly this was the second son of Anthony Stanton, of Nottinghamshire, and his wife Cicely Nevill (Harl. Soc. IV, 180–1). If so, he was the nephew of John Staunton (above). Implicated in Wyatt's rebellion, in which he had 'commanded companies' (*Ven.*

Cal. 1555–6, pp. 440, 454), he fled to France, where with Brian Fitzwilliam he became organizer and leader of the rebels (*For. Cal.* 1553–8, p. 108). Soon, however, Wotton was pleading for his pardon (*ibid.* pp. 72, 79), which the queen tentatively granted on 29 May 1554 (*ibid.* p. 88). On 10 August Wotton was able to report that Staunton's 'band of rebels' was dissolved (*ibid.* p. 113). But Staunton's repentance and good behaviour were short-lived. In 1556 he was involved with Henry Dudley and was seized by the Warden of the Cinque Ports in March (*Dom. Cal.* 1547–80, p. 78 and *P.C.A.* 1554–6, p. 257). In his confession made on 10 April he asserted that Dudley had lived in his, Staunton's, house in London while hatching the conspiracy (*Dom. Cal.* 1547–80, p. 79), which makes it possible that he was the man referred to by Michiel as 'Stadan' and described by him as a former servant of Courtenay, and 'step-son of one of the wealthiest aldermen in London'. He had 'the reputation', said Michiel, 'of being a very meddlesome busybody, and not devoid of ability' (*Ven. Cal.* 1555–6, no. 448, p. 398). On 12 May he was indicted at the Guildhall (*Machyn*, p. 105) and on the 19th he was hanged at Tyburn (Baga, pp. 253–4; *Ven. Cal.* no. 489, p. 454 and Machyn, p. 106).

France, B v b 1, 2 & c.

*STEPHINSON (STIVENS), Cornelius: *Merchant.* Wife.

This Stephinson, certainly a foreigner and probably a German or Fleming, appeared in Geneva in 1558 and there on 10 October was living with his wife, Margery. Though he is not named in the Livre des Anglois as a member of Knox's congregation, there is a record in the second part of the death of his two children 'borne at a byrthe'. He is there called Cornelius 'Stivens', but as Cornelius 'Stephinson' he was received as a 'resident' of Geneva on 24 October (f. 264) and it is therefore probable that he was the same person as the Cornelius Stevenson who had taken part in the anti-predestinarian controversy which arose in January 1555 among the prisoners for religion in the King's Bench (John Trewe's Narrative, pp. 69–70, in R. Laurence's *Authentic Documents, etc.* 1819). But there is nothing in that to preclude the possibility of his having been also Stevenson 'the pyrat' who in 1556 had his headquarters in Ireland and was probably serving under the Horseys (*P.C.A.* 1554–6, p. 317; cf. *For. Cal.* 1553–8, p. 231), for after Elizabeth's accession a Cornelius Stevenson is found associated with the Horseys in a scheme for the manufacture of salt petre in the New Forest (*Annals*, ii, ii, 313–15) which had Lord Burghley's approval.

Geneva, A iv a & b.

389. STERN, JOHN: *Apothecary.* Of Cambridgeshire(?).

A John Stern, 'apoticaire', was received as a 'resident' of Geneva on 14 October 1557 (f. 196) among a group of Englishmen, but he was not a member of the English congregation. A John Sterne of Cambridgeshire, possibly the same man, matriculated from Christ's College, Cambridge, in 1554 (Venn, IV, 159).

Geneva, A IV b.

390. STEWARD (STUARD), THOMAS: *Student.* Of Norfolk.

M.A. of Cambridge (?1513–14), and brother of Robert Steward, first dean of Ely, 1541–57 (Venn, IV, 162 and 161). In September 1554 he was at Frankfort and one of those who supported the congregation's invitation to John Knox (*T.* p. 20). But on 23 November he is found at Strasbourg as a signatory of that colony's letter of admonition to Frankfort for its liturgical waywardness. Late in December he was still there, and was among the beneficiaries of the Duke of Württemberg's bounty. In the city's official list of these he is called 'Magister Stuwart', who received 10 florins. Sometime in 1555, however, he went back to Frankfort, where he allied himself with Whittingham's minority and signed the letter of secession on 27 August (*T.* p. 55). He next appears in Geneva, there to be received as a member of Knox's congregation on 5 November 1556 and a 'resident' of the city on 14 October 1557 (f. 197). Yet notwithstanding this, he appears to have left Geneva for Basle that same winter to become a student in the university, where he matriculated on 15 May 1558 (below, p. 358). And at Basle he stood godfather to Gerson the posthumous son of John Bartholomew (*q.v.*), who was baptized in the church of St Alban on 3 January 1559 (Kirch. Archiv, x, 8, 1, p. 125). This must have been just before Steward's return to England, where Cooper believes (I, 263) that he was made canon of Ely in 1560. Venn, however, assigns this office to a younger Thomas Steward of Corpus Christi, who died in 1568 (IV, 162).

B II; Frankfort, B III a; Strasbourg, A VII c; B III a; Geneva, A IV a & b; Basle, A II a & d; Cooper.

391. STOWELL (STAWELL), [WILLIAM]: *Gent.* Of Somerset. d. 1557.

An associate of Thomas Stafford, whom Henry Dudley mockingly called Stafford's 'Lord Treasurer' (*For. Cal.* 1553–8, p. 306). He 'must needs have good success', said Dudley, 'who uses the advice of such councillors' (*ibid.*). In the list of those taken prisoner with Stafford at Scarborough is a 'Willyam "Scowell", gent.' (*Mem.* III, ii, 518), evidently an error for the Stowell who was afterwards lodged in the Tower and who in his indictment is called William Stowell of Bagborough, Somerset (Baga, p. 258). Hence it is probable that he belonged to the very ancient family of the Stowell's of Somerset, and was a younger son of the Sir John Stowell (temp. Henry VIII) who married Dorothy, daughter of Sir Edmund Carew (Harl. Soc. xi, 107), for West Bagborough was one of the manors of which Sir John Stowell the younger (temp. James I) died seised (ibid. and Collinson's Somerset, iii, 250–1 note). William Stowell was executed in 1557.

France, B v b 1 & c.

392. STUBBES, JOHN: *Artisan.* Wife(?).

Were this man not designated as 'couturier' in the Registre des Habitants which records (f. 159) his admission to 'residence' in Geneva in November 1556, we should have tentatively identified him as the famous John Stubbs, author in 1579 of the *Discoverie of a gaping gulf*, for which pamphlet written against Elizabeth's marriage with Anjou he lost his hand. But that Stubbs was a gentleman of Norfolk who matriculated at Trinity College, Cambridge, in November 1555, and though from the dates it is not impossible that the two men were identical, it is hardly likely that the gentleman zealot of the 70's had received his calvinistic bent as the humble tailor John 'Steubz' received as a member of John Knox's congregation at Geneva in 1556. On 25 August 1558 John Stubbes had a son baptized Zachary, to whom John Bodley stood godfather (Martin, p. 336). As no wife is mentioned on his arrival it is possible that he married abroad, though there is no record of it. Nor is there any record, so far as I know, that Stubbs the pamphleteer had a son Zachary.

Geneva, A iv a & b.

393. SUTTON, EDMUND: *Gent.*

As every effort has failed to identify this person either as a member of the family of Sutton de Dudley, or otherwise, we must be content to give just those particulars concerning him which are found in the records of his exile. Evidently he was a person of substance and importance, for on 7 March 1555 he became a citizen of Frankfort, an honour that only the rich could pay for. Moreover, he was then described as 'generosus' and 'oriundus in oppido Suttona' (Jung, pp. 24, 61), and it seems possible that he may have been of the family of Richard Sutton of Sutton, Cheshire, who in the Bishops' Visitation of 1564 was named as favourable to religion (Cam. Misc. ix, 75). No *Edmund* Sutton, however, appears in that family's pedigree (Harl. Soc. xviii, 220). He was one of the original company of four gentlemen who arrived at Frankfort with Whittingham on 27 June 1554 (*T.* p. 5). In

September of that year he endorsed the invitation to John Knox, which he signed as one of the three ministers (or deacons?) of the congregation (*T.* p. 20). On 3 December he was also a signatory of Frankfort's truculent reply to Strasbourg's plea for Prayer Book conformity (*T.* p. 26), yet he did not follow Whittingham to Geneva. Sir Thomas Hoby found him still at Frankfort when he paid his visit there in September 1555 (Cam. Misc. x, 123) and Sutton's name appears among those of the gentlemen on the Standesliste in November(?). In October 1556 his taxable property was rated at 700 florins (Jung, p. 29). In January 1557 John Hales addressed to Sutton, among others, his plea for help to quiet the stir that had arisen over the Horne-Ashley quarrel (*T.* p. 65), and it was Sutton who reviewed the later quarrel of Frankfort with Horne and Chambers, in an able letter in which he also made a strong appeal for funds for the congregation's poor (*T.* pp. 174–82). His association with John Hales would seem to have been close. Not only was he an inmate of Hales's house (*H.S.P.* iv, 88) but he is also dubbed by Brett, when he left his letters upon John Hales in July 1556, as 'one Sutton his Compaignon' (Brett, p. 120). In the spring of 1557 he signed the 'new discipline'. If he returned to England under Elizabeth, there appears to be no record of him, and it seems possible that he may have died abroad.

Frankfort, A iii a 1, 2, 3, 4 & b 1, 2; B iii a & b; B iv a & b.

394. SWIFT, JASPER: *Gent.* Of Yorkshire. Alive in 1589.

A younger brother of Robert Swift (below) and probably, like him, born at Rotheram, Yorks. (Harl. Soc. xvii, 273). By 1568 he is found in London, a Sergeant of the Admiralty and married to Catherine Holme, daughter of a London merchant (Harl. Soc. i, 34 and *Dom. Cal.* 1581–90, p. 486). But as a young man he had had a short experience of exile at Frankfort, where on 24 September 1554 he acquiesced in the congregation's invitation to John Knox (*T.* p. 20). As this, however, is his single appearance abroad, he must have returned to England shortly afterwards. In 1588 he was actively engaged in conditioning the fleet to meet the Armada (*Dom. Cal.* 1581–90, p. 486) and in 1589 the Privy Council gave him four days to provide vessels enough for the transportation of 900 men to Dieppe (*ibid.* p. 619). In this 'busyness' of his there is quite a suggestion of Pepys, his successor at the Admiralty. Another Jasper, his son, who matriculated at Christ Church, Oxford, in 1590/91, became a canon of Exeter, and archdeacon of Cornwall in 1616 (Foster, iv, 1447 and Harl. Soc. i, 34).

Frankfort, B iii a.

395. SWIFT, ROBERT: *Student and gent.* Of Yorkshire. d. 1599.

Born at Rotheram, Yorks., about 1534 and an older brother of Jasper Swift (above, but called 'John' in Harl. Soc. XVII, 273). He was a B.A. and Fellow of St John's College, Cambridge (1553), and probably one of those students who followed Thomas Lever to the Continent, for it was Lever's daughter Anne whom he eventually married (*D.N.B.*). He received an LL.B. from Louvain, and returning to England was ordained deacon at Durham on 5 October 1563 (Venn, IV, 192). He had already, in 1561, been made Chancellor of Durham, an office which he held till 1577. Dean Swift is said to have been a descendant of this family.

Louvain; *D.N.B.*

396. TAILOR, JAMES: *Student.* Of Lancashire.

Probably the James Tailor who matriculated from St Catharine's College, Cambridge, in 1544 and received his M.A. in 1553 (Venn, IV, 205). In 1557 he arrived at Geneva, where on 14 October he was received as a 'resident' (f. 196) and on the following 20 November became a member of Knox's congregation.

B II; Geneva, A IV a & b.

397. TAMWORTH (TAUMWORTH), [JOHN?]: *Gent.* Of Lincolnshire. d. 1569(?).

This 'Mr Taumworth', who was one of the English exiles whom Sir Thomas Hoby met in Padua in August 1554, may have been either the 'John' Tamworth who died in 1569, or his cousin 'Christopher' who died in 1571 (Harl. Soc. LII, 948). But if John, as we are inclined to think, then he was very likely the John Tamworth, relative of Cranmer, to whom William Thomas, unfortunate Clerk of the Privy Council, dedicated his *Italian Grammar* (Adair, *Tudor Studies*, p. 139). Through his marriage in 1562 with Christian, daughter of William Walsingham of Kent, he was to become the brother-in-law of Sir Francis Walsingham and of Sir Walter Mildmay (Adair, and Harl. Soc. LII, 948). In 1563 he may have been M.P. for Boston,[1] and in 1566 received an M.A. from Oxford (Foster, IV, 1455). As he also held the office of Privy Councillor and Gentleman of the Chamber to Elizabeth, he was doubtless the 'one Tamworth, who had obtained so much favour' from the queen that she had granted him, oddly enough, 'the next avoidance of a prebend' at Canterbury, which would have put him in succession to John Bale (*Parker*, I, 285). Whether the versatile gentleman was likewise the 'Mr Tamworth' who in 1565 was invited to become a member of a company formed for the draining

[1] Foster says he was, but cf. *Return of Members*, I, 404 and note, also Browne Willis, p. 73.

of mines, a scheme which had the patronage of Sir William Cecil and the Earls of Pembroke and Leicester, is uncertain (cf. *Dom. Cal.* 1547–80, p. 255).

Padua, B IV b.

398. TAVERNER, JOHN: *Gent.* Of Essex. d. 1606.

Probably this was the John Taverner of Upminster (Harl. Soc. XIII, 499) who became Surveyor-General of the Woods to Elizabeth. He was nephew to Richard Taverner of Wood Eaton, Oxon., who had been Clerk of the Signet to both Henry VIII and Edward VI (*ibid.* XXII, 96) and was also a gospeller. In 1552 Richard, though not in orders, had been granted a licence to preach (Foster, IV, 1458). John, his nephew, at the time he was in Frankfort, can have been little more than a boy. His single appearance there was as signatory on 17 September 1557 to Whitehead's letter of thanks to Bullinger for some contribution the latter had just made to the colony (*O.L.* II, 764). According to the *D.N.B.* there are many letters of John Taverner's, on forestry, preserved among the Lansdowne MSS.

Frankfort, A VIII a; *D.N.B.*

399. TEMPLE, WILLIAM: *Gent. and student.* Of Dorset.

Probably William, fourth son of John Temple of Stow, Bucks., and his wife Susanna, heir of the Spencers (Harl. Soc. II, 168). If so, then he was a younger brother of Thomas Temple, ancestor of Peter Temple, the regicide.

William Temple of Stower Provost, Dorset, was educated at Eton and King's College, where in 1553 he received his M.A. Venn says that he was 'an excellent mathematician and travelled beyond the sea' (IV, 213). His surmise that Temple had been a student at Basle is now confirmed by the Matrikel of the university, which records in the winter of 1555–6 the admission 'Guglielmus Templeus, Anglus' (f. 193; cf. below, p. 358). But the absence of the usual 'VI sol' after his name would suggest that he never matriculated.

Basle, A II a.

400. TETERSALL, RICHARD: *Weaver and yeoman.* Of Lancashire. Wife. 1494(?)–1587.

An exile at Aarau, who lived with his wife in the house of Hans Gysins (cf. below, p. 355). Since he was a Lancashire weaver (Hans Dür), and presumably abroad either for the cause of religion or sedition, it seems not unlikely that he was a son or relative of 'another called Tartarsall' who being 'a cloath man' and also from 'the north country' was 'hanged and headed' in the reign of Henry VIII for raising 'a new conspiracy or insurrection' in Lancashire about 1541 (Wriothesley, I, 124). The combination of names immediately suggesting Richard, founder of the famous 'Tattersalls' of London, it is most interesting to find that he too came from Lancashire, and that his birthplace, Hurstwood, was one with which 'his family had long been connected' (*D.N.B.*). Now the 'oldest possession' of these Tattersalls of Hurstwood was a farm called the 'bottom o' th' fold' which in 1598 belonged to a Janet Tattersall, widow of Richard Tattersall of Ridge, who may well have been Tetersall, the exile, and she, Janet, the wife who was with him in the house of Hans Gysins. For this Tattersall of Ridge was both the son and the grandson of a Richard Tattersall, and it is highly significant that in Tattersall's *Memoirs of Hurstwood* (p. 127), though the date of the grandfather's death is known (1524), and that of his grandson as 'a very old man', in 1587, nothing is said either of the life or death of the father, who would have been the Richard 'hanged and headed' under Henry VIII. Another fact which lends support to my identification is that in 1571 John, youngest son of Richard Tattersall of Ridge, was a 'poore Scholler of Brasnose in Oxforde' whose money to continue his studies came to him from a fund established by Roger Nowell (*ibid.* pp. 127–8). Janet Tattersall, the wife, seems to have been a Barcroft of Barcroft Hall. To-day the name Tattersall still flourishes in the north country, for I find that a Mr George Tattersall is now (1936) a cotton merchant in Manchester (cf. *Manchester Directory*, 1936).

Aarau, A 1 a & b.

401. THOMSON, EDMUND: *Priest.* Of London.

Born in the parish of St Michael's, Cornhill, and a citizen of London (*Mar. Reac.* p. 187), Thomson was a Fellow of University College, Oxford, who supplicated a B.D. in 1546. In June 1550 he was ordained deacon by Ridley at the same time as John Foxe and priested the following November, when he is said to have been of the Hospital in Southwark (*ibid.* p. 191). He fled to Frankfort under Mary, but was one of the late arrivals, his name appearing for the first time on the tax-list of 15 January 1557, when he is said to have had no taxable property (Jung, p. 30). Beyond this we know nothing of his life abroad except that he signed the 'new discipline' in March–April 1557, and in June was living in the house of Richard Beesley (*H.S.P.* IV, 89). But on his return to England he has the unique distinction of being the only exile to have been instituted to a living by Bishop Bonner: on 31 March 1558/9 he became vicar of South Mimms, Middlesex (Newcourt, I, 728). But in 1570 he was forced to resign, and in 1592 was imprisoned not merely as a puritan but also as a separatist (*Annals*, IV, 129). Very possibly he was the 'Thompson' mentioned in a letter to Ambrose Cave in 1576, who had translated the New Testament, with Beza's notes, from the French (*Dom. Cal.* 1547–80, p. 524). Such a work is, however, unknown either to Anthony à Wood or to Ames, and was probably never published.

Frankfort, A iii a 3, 4 & b 2; B iii b.

402. THROCKMORTON (THROGMERTON), JOHN: *Gent.* Of Warwickshire. d. 1556.

Son of Sir Thomas Throckmorton of Coughton and great-nephew of Sir Nicholas Throckmorton (see note, p. 349). By an error in the index of the *Foreign Calendar*, 1553–8, he has been identified as Sir Nicholas; hence John's presence as a rebel in France during 1554 has not been indicated. But at the time (14 July 1554) when Wotton was writing to know 'her Majesty's pleasure concerning Throckmorton, who... continues his suit still to be received to mercy...' (*For. Cal.* p. 96), Nicholas Throckmorton was in prison in London (see below). John, then, who in 1556 was to become leader in England of the Dudley conspiracy, had already served an earlier apprenticeship as a rebel in France, having probably been implicated in Wyatt's rebellion. Though not yet twenty-eight years old when he was executed for treason at Tyburn on 28 April 1556 (*Machyn*, p. 104 and *Ven. Cal.* 1555–6, p. 422) he had nevertheless, on the word of the Venetian ambassador, 'been a long while in Italy and at Venice' (*ibid.*). If so, it would mean that, failing mercy in 1554, he had followed the usual path of exiled Englishmen across the Alps. But it is possible that here Michiel was confusing John Throckmorton's record with that of a George Throckmorton, who in 1551–2 had spent some time in Venice (*Ven. Cal.* 1534–54, p. 370 and *For. Cal.* 1547–53, p. 110), for I have found no mention of a Throckmorton in Italy during Mary's reign. So much for John Throckmorton's record as an exile.

But in connection with him it may be well to give a calendar of the events of the Dudley conspiracy so frequently referred to in the text. The facts are mainly drawn from the Baga de Secretis, pp. 252–6.

1. 25 January 1555/6. First movement in conspiracy.

2. 28 January 1555/6. Agreement made between Throckmorton, Dudley and Assheton (Aston) to counterfeit sufficient English coin to pay their forces (see 'Caltham' above, p. 103 and *Ven. Cal.* 1555–6, no. 466, p. 423).

3. 30 January 1555/6. The services of Thomas White enlisted, who provided a copy of Henry VIII's will to prove Mary's usurpation.

4. 6 March 1555/6. Robbery planned of the Receipt of the Exchequer where more than £50,000 was then deposited. On this day the vessel was hired to transport the treasure (to be taken through William Rossey's garden to the Thames) in a crayer to France.

5. 10 March 1555/6. Meeting of the conspirators at the Mansion house near Southampton, belonging to Richard Uvedale (Vuedall), then governor of Yarmouth Castle. It was there agreed to introduce into England 'a great force of armed men from amongst the rebels... beyond the seas'.

6. 12 March 1555/6. Rendezvous at Chelsham Court, Surrey, where Uvedale promised that if landed in the Isle of Wight, this force would meet no resistance.

7. 16 March 1555/6. Oath of the conspirators taken on the Bible.

But the plot was discovered and on 31 March 1556 John Throckmorton's examination began. He stoutly denied that any oath of secrecy had been taken, or that he had ever said that 'the Queen took down King Philip's picture, and kicked it out of the Privy Chamber' (*Dom. Cal.* 1547–80, p. 78).

On 21 April he was indicted, and convicted, as Michiel says, 'on the evidence of the conspirators themselves' (*Ven. Cal.* p. 422), though for his part he had implicated no one and persisted in denying all the charges brought against him (*ibid.*).

France, B v b 1 & c.

403. THROCKMORTON, Sir NICHOLAS: *Gent.* Of Warwickshire. 1515–71.

The career of Sir Nicholas Throckmorton, Elizabethan diplomatist, is too well known to bear repetition. Fourth son of Sir George Throckmorton and great uncle of John (above) he married Anne, daughter of Sir Nicholas Carew (Harl. Soc. XII, 89). His early years were not only spent much abroad, but also in and out of conspiracy. It is asserted that he was at first loyal to Queen Mary (*Legend of Sir Nicholas Throckmorton,*[1] verses 111–14; but cf. *Chron. Q. Jane,* p. 180 and p. 12). Yet for complicity in Wyatt's rebellion he was sent to the Tower on 20 February 1554 (*ibid.* p. 63). It is also said that at his trial at the Guildhall on 17 April his acquittal was due to popular pressure (*ibid.* p. 75 and *D.N.B.*), but he was kept in the Tower until 18 January 1555 (*P.C.A.* 1554–6, p. 90). Obviously then he could not have been a refugee in France during the summer of 1554, as alleged in the *Foreign Calendar* (cf.

[1] Edited by John Gough Nichols for the Roxburghe Club.

'John' above). But after the failure of Dudley's plot in 1556, he did flee, landing, as we learn from Wotton, at St Malo in the last week of June (*For. Cal.* 1553–8, p. 241). 'The fagot I didd feare' is the excuse given for his flight (*Legend*, v. 125), yet Wotton felt it necessary to warn him 'by no means to have any communication with the rebels' or he 'would so damage his business, that Wotton would never thereafter have anything to do with it' (*For. Cal. ibid.*). Perhaps Sir Nicholas heeded the warning, perhaps he did not. He remained however in France 'full two yeares and more' (*Legend*, v. 126), presumably not venturing home again until the very close of Mary's reign or the beginning of Elizabeth's. It is curious that Sir Sidney Lee, in his article on Throckmorton in the *D.N.B.*, makes no mention of this foreign episode; nor does Strype.

France, B v b 1; *D.N.B.*

404. THYNNE [WILLIAM]: *Canon and gent.* Of Shropshire. d. 1584.

A single reference to the presence in France 'of a brother of Sir John Thynne' is made by Wotton to the Council on 23 December 1553 (*For. Cal.* 1553–8, p. 41). The 'brother' had just been mistaken by Wotton's messenger, on the road to Rouen, for one Francis 'Kellwaye', a notorious burglar who had recently (25 November) 'toke awaye the Lady Knyvettes plate' (*P.C.A.* 1552–4, p. 372). He was followed to Paris where his identity as a Thynne was established, though his first name is not given. According to the pedigree of the family of Thynne in Hoare's *Modern Wiltshire* (Heytesbury, p. 60), Sir John (d. 1580) had but one brother, and that was William, a canon of Wells. The Thynnes, who had been adherents of Somerset (*Mem.* II, ii, p. 260 and Le Neve, I, 202), suffered persecution in consequence under Northumberland, who had imprisoned Sir John (*P.C.A.* 1552–4, pp. 78, 82, 84, 86). Why then the canon was a fugitive in 1553— whether from Queen Mary (cf. *ibid.* p. 417) or earlier from Northumberland—is not clear, but the affiliations of the family were strongly protestant.

France, B v b 1.

405. TODCHAMBER [TOD, alias 'Chamber'?], THOMAS: *Student*(?). Of Lincolnshire(?). d. 1580(?).

As no such English surname as this can be discovered, we suggest that it may represent a contraction of Tod alias Chamber (or Chambers). His only appearance abroad was as a signatory to the 'new discipline' in December 1557, and, as in the case of Thomas Serbis (above, p. 287), it seems quite possible that he was attached in some capacity to the household of the Duchess of Suffolk. He may be the Thomas Todd who matriculated from Trinity College, Cambridge, in 1566 and was ordained deacon and priest at Lincoln in 1573/4 (Venn, IV, 246). If so, he died in 1580. A Gregory Tod had been chaplain to Cranmer in 1547 (*Cranmer*, p. 251).

Frankfort, B III a.

406. TRAHERON (TRAHERREN, TRAHERNE), BARTHOLOMEW, B.D.: *Ex-religious and student.* Of Cornwall. 1510–58 (?).

A Franciscan friar. He studied at Oxford in 1527 but obtained his B.D. at Cambridge in 1532/3. Twice before Mary's accession he had been abroad: in 1537 sitting at the feet of Bullinger and dwelling with 'Praepositus' at Zurich; in 1538 studying at Strasbourg (Vetter, *Eng. Flücht.* p. 8); and again in 1546 living at Geneva under Calvin, whose disciple he became (*O.L.* I, 317–18, 325). Between these two visits to Germany he had returned to England to become servant to Cromwell, whose fall was responsible for his second withdrawal, at first into retirement, then to the Continent (*ibid.* p. 226). Traheron was one of those strange half-clerical, half-lay persons who, during the English reformation, passed through many varieties of religious and political experience. In 1532, though not in orders, he was dean of Chichester. Between 1547 and 1552 he was M.P. for Barnstable, chosen probably in order to secure his influence in the debates on the Eucharist (*ibid.* pp. 322–3). On Cheke's recommendation he succeeded Roger Ascham as King's Librarian in 1549, and Cranmer placed him, as a civilian, on the commission for ecclesiastical laws. During 1549–50 he became, like so many of his fellows-to-be of the Marian Exile, tutor to the young Duke of Suffolk, and in this position he acted as the patron of young protestant foreigners who came to study in England. Of these, John ab Ulmis received the office of tutor to Lady Jane Grey through Traheron's influence (*ibid.* p. 321 and Vetter, *op. cit.* p. 8). Possibly owing to the opposition he had experienced from the chapter at Chichester, he resigned his office of dean in September 1552 to become a canon of Windsor. And it is in this same month that he wrote despondently to Bullinger of 'the wickedness of those who profess the gospel', which 'is wonderfully on the increase' (*O.L.* I, 324)—doubtless a reference, as were also Knox's laments in the same vein, to Northumberland.

Then, at Mary's accession, he resigned his appointments and for a third time went abroad. But though still only forty-five he seems to have been broken in health, and consequently unable to take 'the diuinitie lecture in hande' which was offered to him in the newly improvised English university at Frankfort (*T*. p. 60). He had already taken part in the hot controversies aroused by Whittingham's secession (*T*. p. 57) and was signatory to Whitehead's letter to Calvin of 20 September 1555, written in defence of the congregation's action (*O.L.* II, 763), but evidently the atmosphere of Frankfort was not conducive to composition, and on the evidence of his pamphlets he retired to Wesel, where he is supposed to have died in 1558. Vetter speaks of the early influence upon him of Richard Tracy who, on the death of Traheron's parents, had become his foster-father (Vetter, *Eng. Flücht.* p. 8).

Frankfort, B III a; *D.N.B.*

407. TREMAYNE, ANDREW: *Gent.* Of Devon. d. 1563.

Son of Thomas Tremayne of Collacombe in Devon, by his wife Philippa, daughter of Roger Greenfield (Grenville). The family of Tremayne was also closely connected with that of the Drakes and the Raleighs (Vivian, *Devon*, p. 293). Andrew and Nicholas Tremayne (below) were twin brothers who seem to have lived and died inseparable. On the night of 25 January 1554, Andrew set sail for France from Weymouth with Sir Peter Carew, John Courtenay (*q.v.*), James Kirkham (*q.v.*) and one of the Killigrews (Vowell, p. 180 and note). But after depositing Sir Peter in France he would seem to have returned to the channel and there been joined by his brother, for in February both were caught and both imprisoned, Andrew in the Marshalsea, Nicholas in the Gate House, on a charge of piracy (*P.C.A.* 1554–6, p. 99). Nothing further is known of Andrew until 1563, when both he and Nicholas met their deaths at the siege of Newhaven (*Dom. Cal.* 1547–80, p. 225 and Vowell, p. 180, n. 1).

France, B v b 1.

408. TREMAYNE, EDMUND: *Gent.* Of Devon. d. 1582.

The second son of Thomas Tremayne of Collacombe and married to Ulalia, daughter of Sir John St Leger (Vivian, *Devon*, p. 731). His mother's sister Amy having married John Drake, Edmund Tremayne was thus a first cousin of Sir Francis Drake (Vivian, p. 293) in the older generation, and is said to have regarded him as his own son (*Geneal.* I, 328). In the autumn of 1553 Tremayne entered the service of Edward Courtenay, Earl of Devon, and being concerned in Wyatt's rebellion was sent to the Tower (*P.C.A.* 1554–6, p. 45). There, according to Foxe's story, he refused, even under torture, to implicate the Princess Elizabeth (Foxe, VIII, 619). And this constancy of his was later rewarded by Elizabeth, when queen, with the post of Clerk of the Privy Council (*Geneal.* I, 329).

On 18 January 1554 he was released from prison upon payment of a fine (*P.C.A.* 1554–6, p. 90) and in 1555 evidently went abroad in the Earl of Devon's train, for he was with Courtenay later in Venice. There, however, Tremayne left him, but Courtenay's ambiguous words to Mason, 'I am sorry for Tremayne's foolish departure, albeit satisfied and content therewith as he shall well perceive...' (2 May 1556, *Dom. Cal.* 1547–80, p. 82), must be interpreted in a different sense from that given to them in the *D.N.B.*, where they are taken to refer to Tremayne's departure from England to *enter* Courtenay's service. On the contrary, Tremayne was just then *leaving* his service and going from Venice to Paris, where 'the elder Tremaine' (i.e. Edmund) is found on 13 July 1556, two months before the death of Courtenay. Courtenay's regret probably concerned Tremayne's purpose to join his brother, Nicholas, and the other rebels at Rouen (*For. Cal.* 1553–8, p. 238). Richard at that time seems to have been at Strasbourg. In the following April, 1557, 'the Tremains' were in Paris again, consorting with Christopher Assheton and the two Staffords. Wotton believed that some enterprise against England was then brewing (*ibid.* p. 294), but if this was the expedition to Scarborough, neither Tremayne proved so foolhardy as to follow Thomas Stafford's lead. Nor, so far as the Calendars are concerned, has any support been found for the guess (cf. *D.N.B.*) that after Courtenay's death Edmund entered the service of the Earl of Bedford, though he may have done so later. As we have seen he was in Paris in April 1557 and his name does not appear in the list of those, supposedly the earl's gentlemen, who were with Bedford at Venice in July-August 1555 (cf. *Ven. Cal.* 1555–6, p. 145). His later career in Ireland and England belongs to Elizabethan history; but a suggestion made by H. H. Drake, writing on the 'Arms of Sir Francis Drake' in the *Genealogist* (I, 328–31), connects the age of adventure with the Marian Exile and so is worth recording. It is his belief that the favour first shown by Elizabeth to Francis Drake, then 'a ruined man', was due to her gratitude to Edward Tremaine, who loved Drake as his own son.

Venice, B v b 2; France, B v b 1, 2; *D.N.B.*

409. TREMAYNE, Nicholas: *Captain and gent.* Of Devon.
    d. 1563.

Still another son of Thomas Tremayne of Collacombe. His arrest and imprisonment with his brother Andrew in 1554 has already been recorded (above), but whereas Andrew seems not to have been directly implicated in Dudley's plot, both Richard and Nicholas were, and 'fled over the see as trayturs' (*Machyn*, p. 103) on 3 February 1556 (Baga, p. 254). One of them had been lodging in London to arrange the details of the plot (*Dom. Cal.* 1547–80, p. 81). Both brothers evidently went together to Paris, there to be joined by Edmund from Italy, but Richard seems to have left later in the year for Strasbourg, whereas Nicholas remained in France. After Elizabeth's accession he served in France first as a messenger (*For. Cal.* 1560–1, nos. 16, p. 7, 232, p. 143, etc.), then as a soldier, with Andrew, and there both were killed at Newhaven towards the end of May 1563 (*Dom. Cal.* 1547–80, p. 225).

France, B IV c; B v b 1.

410. TREMAYNE, RICHARD: *Student*. d. 1584.

Fourth son of Thomas Tremayne of Collacombe and married in 1569 to Johanna, daughter of Sir Peter Courtenay. In 1553 he was made a Fellow of Exeter College (Foster, IV, 1506), but at Mary's accession he fled to Louvain with his pupil, the son of Sir Nicholas Arnold (*Dom. Cal.* 1547–80, p. 72 and *Exeter Coll. Reg.* ed. Boase, pp. lxxix, 67). Thence he probably returned early in 1556, to act as agent for Sir Nicholas in Henry Dudley's conspiracy. Though indicted with his brother for their share in it, he and Nicholas Tremayne made good their escape to France (*Machyn*, p. 103), where they were joined by Edmund (above). But whereas Nicholas remained, Richard seems to have gone to Strasbourg. And there in July was probably the 'one Tremayne' sent with Arthur Saule[1] to suborn John Brett 'contrary to [his] duty and allegiaunce' to accept some lucrative position in exile rather than report to the queen what 'had happenyd' to him abroad at the hands of the rebels (Brett, pp. 128–9). Brett refused; Richard eventually went back to France, where he still was when Elizabeth came to the throne. Then, as so often in the case of those with the taint of treason upon them, Elizabeth employed him in the business of secretly conducting the Earl of Arran from Geneva to England. 'No man', Throckmorton wrote to her in July 1559, was 'so fit for a guide through Germany as the said Tremayne, he having the High Dutch tongue very well' (*For. Cal.* 1558–9, pp. 387, 415). Having properly acquitted himself of his task, Tremayne returned to England. There in January 1559/60, Grindal ordained him deacon (*Grindal*, p. 54) and in 1566/7 Oxford gave him his D.D. Besides the treasurership of Exeter Cathedral, which was his from 1560 to his death, he held simultaneously three livings in Cornwall and Devon (Foster). But his relations with his bishop, William Alley, were somewhat stormy, for Dr Tremayne, a strong puritan, gave a licence to catechise and expound the Scripture to a young

---

[1] For the intimate connections between the families of the Saules and the Tremaynes see *Genealogist*, I, 328.

man 'not entered into the ministry', and the doctrines of this young man so 'offended the ears' of simple Cornishmen that they tended to let in a flood of 'mischiefs'. Also Dr Tremayne was given to nepotism (*Annals*, II, ii, 33–5) and altogether caused so much anxiety to poor William Alley that the latter resigned (1576).

Louvain, B v b 2; France, B IV c; B v b 1; B v c; Strasbourg, B IV a; *D.N.B.*

411. TRULO (TREWLOVE?), ANTHONY: *Gent.* Of Essex(?).

One probably in the train of the Earl of Bedford, for in July–August 1555 he was granted the right to bear arms by the Signory of Venice (*Ven. Cal.* 1555–6, p. 145). In 1578 Bishop Aylmer appealed to Cecil on behalf of a William Trewlove, who had been dispossessed of the property of his grandfather, Thomas Cawston of Essex. This is but a suggestion in regard to Anthony 'Trulo's' identity (*Dom. Cal.* 1547–80, p. 598).

Venice, B v b 2.

412. TRYTSON (TOYLSON), THOMAS: *Gent.*

Both forms of this man's name are used in the grant to bear arms, given to him by the Signory of Venice (see 'Trulo' above). He, too, was probably in Bedford's train, but he cannot be identified.

Venice, B v b 3.

413. TURNER, JOHN, B.D.: *Priest.*

Turner, an M.A. of Magdalen College (Macray, II, 50), received his B.D. from Oxford in March 1535/6 (Foster, IV, 1520), and in 1540 was instituted by Cranmer to the living of St Leonard's, Eastcheap (Newcourt, I, 391). Cited for marriage on 7 March 1553/4 among the nine others under the jurisdiction of Canterbury, Turner was deprived, made confession and did penance (*Cranmer*, pp. 468–70), but was apparently not restored to his living. By 29 September 1557 he had made his way to Strasbourg, where he signed one of the letters in the dispute over the discipline (*T*. p. 174). This is his only appearance abroad. We wonder very much whether John Turner had not possibly been guilty of sedition as well as matrimony in 1554, for in 1579 a John Turner, priest, is found 'making contemptuous speeches' against Queen Elizabeth, while taking forcible possession of Bramblety Chapel and lands for Lord Buckhurst (*Dom. Cal.* 1547–80, p. 624). It was usual under Mary, where the priest's sole fault had been matrimony, to restore him to some other living after confession and penance.

Strasbourg, B III a.

414. TURNER, RICHARD ('of Windsor'), B.D.: *Chantry priest.* Of Staffordshire. d. 1565(?).

As it seems a nearly hopeless matter to disentangle the facts regarding the lives of the two Richard Turners, who had the misfortune for posterity to graduate B.A. from Oxford within six years of each other, I shall confine myself to an account of the exile Richard's life abroad, and for all controversial points refer the reader to Macray's biography of him in the Magdalen Register (II, 50–4). Macray accepts Wood's statement (*Ath. Oxon.* I, 277) that he was born in Staffordshire, and Knox, who came into conflict with him at Frankfort, would have endorsed Wood's characterization of him as 'a forward and conceited person'. Foster (IV, 1521) says that in 1535/6 he had been elected to a perpetual chantry in the king's college of Windsor, and it was from this that he drew his designation 'of Windsor', though he was also made a canon of Windsor in 1551. His early tumultuous espousal of the doctrines of the Reformation had brought him into conflict with authority in Kent three times before the accession of Mary. Ralph Morice, Cranmer's secretary, who had appointed him to the living of Chatham, defended him when attacked in 1544 (*P.C.A.* 1552–4, p. 107 and Foxe, VIII, 31–4). Cranmer himself had made him one of the six preachers of Canterbury, four of whom later became exiles and one a martyr (*Cranmer*, p. 229). No doubt it was his early experience of the danger of nonconformity that sent him abroad under Mary. But when arrived in Frankfort, he is found as an adherent of Cox and conformity, ready to visit upon John Knox the full penalties of resistance to authority which he had just escaped himself. It was to Turner's information, lodged by him with the Frankfort magistrates, that Knox owed his banishment in March 1555 (Laing's *Knox*, IV, 47). Turner himself was still in Frankfort in September, for then Sir Thomas Hoby met him there (Cam. Misc. X, 123), but not long afterwards he went with John Bale to Basle (*Mem.* III, i, 232), where he preached to the exiles on the Epistle to the Hebrews. These sermons he prepared for the press in 1558, but for some reason never published them (Wood, *Ath. Oxon.* I, 277). Foxe, who was in Basle at the time, says that Turner died there (*ibid.*); and Laing gives the date of his death as about 12 October 1558, when his living of Hillingdon fell vacant (*Knox*, IV, 47, n. 3). But according to Foster (IV, 1521) the living of Hillingdon belonged to the other Richard Turner, and both Macray and the *D.N.B.* assume that it was Turner of Windsor who returned from exile, preached at Paul's Cross on 10 September 1559 (*Machyn*, p. 210; cf. also pp. 214, 279) and was restored to the vicarage of Dartford (Macray, II, 53–4).

B I a & b; Frankfort, B III a; Basle (Foxe); *D.N.B.*

415. TURNER, Robert: *Student* (?).

Though Macray (ii, 54) thinks that Foxe may have mistaken Robert for Richard Turner when he records the latter's death at Basle (cf. above), there is nothing but Macray's suggestion to connect Robert Turner with Basle at all. Even his presence abroad as an exile is only vouched for by the inclusion of his name in the Emden catalogue. We know neither who he was nor where he went—unless he was of the Emden congregation.

n.p.; B 1 a & b.

416. TURNER, William (alias 'William Wraughton'): *Dean and physician.* Of Northumberland. d. 1568.

A native of Morpeth, Northumberland (*Scriptores*, Cent. 8, p. 697) and of humble birth, but one who had been chaplain and physician to the Duke of Somerset. He studied at Cambridge, where he was intimate with Latimer and Ridley, and soon his radical views brought him into conflict with the government. Though ordained deacon at Lincoln in 1536, he did not take priest's orders till 1550. Meanwhile, 'following', as Wood says, 'his old trade of preaching without a call' he was imprisoned (*c.* 1542) and his books ordered to be burned (*Ath. Oxon.* i, 361 and Wriothesley, i, 169). Then, being banished, he went abroad (1546), where he completed his education in Italy, at Zurich and also at Basle. On his return to England under Edward, Turner made unsuccessful efforts to obtain a post either at Magdalen or Oriel, and complaining that 'The Papists will live their time in the College benefices' he appealed directly to Cecil (*Dom. Cal.* 1547–80, p. 31), who finally secured for him the deanery of Wells though Turner was still but a deacon. But his attempt to take possession met with severe opposition. He complained to Cecil (*ibid.* p. 33) that the canons annoyed him and favoured Goodman (who succeeded under Mary): hence it may have been that he finally proceeded to the priesthood on 21 December 1550 (*Mar. Reac.* p. 207). At some time during this period Turner was responsible for the fateful introduction of John à Lasco both to Somerset and to the king (Schickler, i, 10). Then, upon Mary's accession, he 'vacated' his deanery 'by flight' in September 1553, prudently remembering the opposition he had met with in taking possession of it (*Mar. Reac.* p. 108 and cf. *P.C.A.* 1552–4, p. 341). It is very likely that he took ship with John à Lasco on 13–15 September, but on the Continent he was a wandering scholar, doing valuable work in collecting plants in Friesland and the Rhine country and having experimental gardens at Cologne and Weissenburg (*D.N.B.*). In the bewildering list of the places that knew him during his exile—Bonn, Strasbourg,

Speyer, Worms, Frankfort, Chur and Basle—it is difficult to see when he found time to become physician to the 'Erle of Emden' (*ibid.*), yet it was almost certainly in that period that Turner wrote his *New booke of spirituall physik* (*S.T.C.* no. 24361) and *The huntyng of the Romyshe vuolfe* (*ibid.* no. 24356). Both of these pamphlets are assigned by Colonel Isaac (*op. cit.* pp. 341, 343) to the press of Egidius van der Erve at Emden. If the colophons may be believed, the latter was published in 1554, the former in 1555.

On his return to England he was reinstated in his deanery of Wells, but was suspended for nonconformity in 1564 and died in 1568. Towns in Germany and Switzerland; Emden; *D.N.B.*

*TURNOUR, Captain EDWARD: *Gent.* 'Late of London.'

Though said to have gone beyond seas with Dudley (Baga, p. 254), Turnour appears to have been captured before he reached the coast (*Ven. Cal.* 1555–6, p. 484, no. 514, dated 16 June; and *ibid.* p. 496, no. 525, of 23 June) and was afterwards tried and condemned (Wriothesley, II, 135) but not executed (see *P.C.A.* 1556–8, p. 74: 12 April 1557; and *Dom. Cal.* 1547–80, p. 116: 11 December 1558).

417. TURPIN, JOHN: *Gent.* Of Calais and Leicestershire.

Probably the son of Richard Turpin 'of Caleys, and Bowrges [burgess] there' (*Chron. Calais*, p. 1), supposed author of the *Chronicle of Calais* (cf. Nichols's Preface, p. xiii). Originally the family came from Northumberland, but as John, grandfather of Richard, married a Leicestershire heiress the main line may be called of Leicestershire (*ibid.* and p. xvi, note). William Turpin, son and heir of that marriage (d. 1523), with his fifth son Richard, migrated to Calais as a soldier under Henry VIII (Fuller, *Worthies*, I, 570–1). And there, according to Bale, Richard wrote the first book of *Sui temporis Chronikon*, and died in 1541 (*Scriptores*, pt II, p. 103). It was this man's two sons, John and Thomas, who as members of the protestant minority in Calais migrated from there to Wesel in 1554(?), and from Wesel to Weinheim in 1556. There, in July, John Brett met 'two englisshmen surnamed Turpyn' who were attached to the household of the Duchess of Suffolk (Brett, p. 125). Later, however, probably on the Bertie's departure for Poland, the brothers separated, John going to Frankfort, where he signed the 'discipline' in April 1557. Thereafter, no more is heard of him, but a George Turpin, of the same family, was knighted in 1565, and a cousin, another Richard Turpin, was present at the surrender of Calais in 1558 (Nichols's *Leicestershire*, IV, pt I, p. 225, n. 3).

Wesel (?); Weinheim, B IV a; Frankfort, B III b.

418. TURPIN, THOMAS: *Gent.* Of Calais. Wife.

Of Thomas Turpin we have more specific knowledge than of his brother, John, for he eventually went with the congregation of Wesel to Aarau. It is from Hans Dür's list, in fact, that we know that the Turpins came from Calais; also, that Thomas had a wife and two children, one of whom, another 'Thomas', died at Aarau. The family lived in the rear of Sebastian zum Schwärtz's house (cf. Official List, below, p. 355), and Turpin was one of the important members of the colony who on 5 October 1557 signed the letter to Bullinger announcing their safe arrival (*O.L.* I, 170). He was also one who agreed to Geneva's proposals for an anti-ceremonial crusade (*T.* p. 191: 16 January 1559). It was thus as a puritan that he was ordained deacon by Grindal on 30 November 1560, and priest by Pilkington in London on 9 March 1561 (*Grindal*, pp. 73–4).

Wesel (?); Weinheim, B IV a; Aarau, A I a & b; A VIII a.

419. 'U'... (or 'N'...), JAMES: *Servant or artisan*(?).

Whether 'U' as in Burn, or 'N' as in Martin, makes little difference; the man cannot, of course, be identified, but an examination of the MS. entry shows Martin to be the more correct. The man became a member of Knox's congregation on 5 June 1557, and from the carelessness shown in regard to his name he was probably a servant or an artisan.

Geneva, A IV a.

420. UNSWORTH (UNSWORTZ), RICHARD: *Weaver.* Of Lancashire.

A member of the Aarau colony who was a weaver (Hans Dür), born in Lancashire and 'poor'. He lived in the house of Hans Gysins (Official List).

Wesel (?); Aarau, A I a & b.

421. UPCHER (UPCHAIER, etc.), THOMAS: *Weaver.* Of Essex. Wife.

In June 1557 Thomas Upcher, a weaver of Bocking in Essex, was settled at Frankfort with his wife and two children in the house of Laurence Kent (*H.S.P.* IV, 89). Bocking had long been a place of sectaries (Davids, p. 22), among whom in 1551 such contention arose as to the necessity of kneeling at prayers, that they were apprehended and brought before the Council. In 1555 an Upchear, very likely Thomas the exile, is found among the prisoners of religion in the King's Bench who took part in a dispute over predestination, so hot a dispute that the two parties to it refused to be reconciled (Trewe's Narrative, p. 57). Some of them, however, were 'delivered out of prison' and among these Upcher, who thus had ample time to reach Frankfort by 1557. We gather that he was a man of some substance and that possibly he had originally gone to Wesel, for during that summer he was made one of the committee under Thomas Lever who went to Geneva to 'haue the aduice off that churche what was best to be done touching the erection off a new churche'—that at Aarau (*T*. p. 185). Thereafter he with his family moved to the new colony where, like Unsworth above, he lived in the house of Hans Gysins, and where his two sons, John and George, both died. On 25 April 1560, Upcher was ordained deacon by Grindal (*Grindal*, p. 58), whose zeal thus to supply the empty churches brought down upon himself an order from Parker 'to forbear ordaining any more artificers, and others that had been of secular occupations, that were unlearned;...' (*ibid*. pp. 59, 60). But Thomas Upcher became successively rector of Fordham and of St Leonard's, Colchester, which latter he resigned in 1582, having like others of the Aarau colony joined the Classical Movement (Usher, p. xlvii).

Wesel (?); Frankfort, A III a 4 & b 2; B III; Aarau, A I a & b.

422. VATES, JOHN: *Servant* (?).

This name, like that of several others of the subscribers to the 'new discipline', cannot be identified. Like 'Nagors' (*q.v.*) he appears on no other of the Frankfort lists and nowhere else abroad. He may, as I have already suggested in other such cases, have been a servant in the employ of the Berties or of some other English family. But it looks as if the radical party at Frankfort had been none too scrupulous in obtaining, for the discipline, those forty-one voices which were 'the greateste parte off our churche by a great deale' (*T*. p. 101).

Frankfort, B III b.

423. VENTRIS (VENTRICE), JOHN: *Servant* (?). Of Cambridge (?).

Probably the John Ventrice, footman of Edward VI, on whose behalf a warrant was issued to Sir Ralph Sadler in 1550, for 'two yards and a half of crimson velvet' to make him a new 'running coat' (*Mem*. II, ii, 282). His name does not appear among the members of Knox's congregation at Geneva, but he was admitted to 'residence' there on 24 October 1558. A Thomas Ventris, alderman of Cambridge and very possibly father or brother of John, sat for Cambridge in the parliament of 1559, and in 1564 figured in a dispute between the town and university (*P.C.A.* 1558–70, pp. 153, 161).

Geneva, A IV b.

424. VINCENT, RICHARD: *Gent.* Of Lancashire(?) or Yorkshire(?). d. 1593(?).

An accomplice of James Chillester (*q.v.*) in the counterfeiting of English coin to finance the Dudley plot. He fled with Chillester to France, where on 15 November 1556 they both sued for pardon through the good offices of Wotton (*For. Cal.* 1553–8, p. 275). Vincent cannot be surely identified, but he may have been the Richard Vincent of Suedon [Sudden, Lancs.?] who frequently figures in the Privy Council minutes in connection with the confiscated lands of the bishopric of Durham (*P.C.A.* 1550–2, pp. 182, 185, 455) and who, in July 1552, was appointed for the survey of church goods 'within that diocese' (*ibid.* 1552–4, pp. 106, 191). But no pedigree of any Vincents can be found in the Visitation of Lancashire (Chetham Soc. nos. 81, 82), while a Richard Vincent, who died in the appropriate year 1593 and was buried at Conisborough, appears in Dugdale's Visitation of Yorkshire (*Geneal.* n.s. XVI, 59).

France, B v b 1.

425. VIVIAN, RICHARD: *Merchant apprentice.* Of Devon.

In the Livre des Anglois, Vivian is called a 'servant' of John Bodley, with whom he was admitted to membership in Knox's congregation on 8 May 1557. But on 14 October 1557, when he was received as a 'resident' of Geneva (f. 197), he is called 'marchant', so that, like John Boggens (*q.v.*), he was no doubt one of Bodley's apprentices.

Probably he was a grandson of the Richard Vyvian of Trelowarren who was sheriff of Cornwall in the reign of Henry VII (Vivian's *Devon*, p. 748).

Geneva, A IV a & b.

426. WALLIS (VALLIS), JOHN: *Baker.*

On Thursday, 14 October 1557, the same day on which Richard Vivian was admitted to 'residence', we find also this John Wallis, of whom we know nothing more than that he was an Englishman and a 'bolinguer' (f. 196). Possibly he, too, was of John Bodley's household.

Geneva, A IV b.

427. WALKER, THOMAS: *Deacon and student.* Of co. Northampton. Wife.

One of this name matriculated sizar from Jesus College, Cambridge, in 1549 (Venn, IV, 318). He was very probably the Thomas

Walker of Castle Ashby, Northants., who, when ordained deacon
by Ridley in 1551, had 'for a year and more' been teaching school
at Cransley in the same county (*Mar. Reac.* p. 200). But he was
not priested, and having also married a wife, he retired to Frankfort, where he first appears in the autumn of 1555, among the
'students'. In March-April 1557 he subscribed to the 'new
discipline', and in June of the same year is found living with his
wife and child in his own house. This indication of means consorts
oddly with the fact that he had been a sizar at Cambridge and that
his name appears on neither of the Frankfort tax-lists (cf. Jung,
pp. 29-30). On his return to England he became an 'eminent
minister' of Ipswich (*Annals*, I, i, 379), but in 1571 he, with
Goodman, Lever, etc., was arraigned before the ecclesiastical
commission on a charge of nonconformity (*Grindal*, p. 252), while
previous to this even the efforts of Archbishop Parker had been
unable to procure him a prebendal stall at Norwich (*Parker*,
I, 496-7).   Frankfort, A III a 2, 4 & b 2; B III b.

428. WALSINGHAM, Francis: *Gent.* Of Kent. 1530(?)-90.

Son of William Walsingham, a lawyer of Chislehurst, Kent, and
of London, who married Joyce, daughter of Sir Edmund Denny
of Cheshunt, Herts. Francis's younger sister Mary was the wife
of Sir Walter Mildmay, one of the leaders of the protestant party
at Elizabeth's accession, while the inter-relationships of the
Walsinghams with the protestant, not to say anti-monarchical,
families of the Wentworths and the Boyes (*q.v.*) show the trend of
the family mind. Francis went to Cambridge, where he matriculated from King's College in 1548, but where he seems to have
taken no degree though he remained at the university till 1550
(Venn, IV, 326 and *D.N.B.*). In 1552 he was a student at Gray's
Inn and upon the accession of Mary went abroad to continue his
studies. Dr Conyers Read, Walsingham's biographer, questions
whether this withdrawal was wholly for the sake of his religion as
his epitaph in St Paul's asserted (Cooper, II, 89), for his stepfather,
Sir John Carey, had been Mary's custodian at Hunsdon, Herts.,
just before Edward's death, while many of his relatives, all of
them of the party of Northumberland, had also been involved in
Wyatt's rebellion (Read, I, 22). I should question it also, since he
went abroad with his three cousins, the Dennys, sons of Sir
Anthony Denny, friend of Sir John Cheke and husband of Joan,
daughter of Sir Philip Champernoun of Devon, one of the most
ardent adherents of the Reformation in the West. All four were
entered as students at the University of Basle in the autumn of

1555; but the absence of the 'VI sol' after their names in the Matrikel (f. 193; cf. below, p. 358) would indicate that they did not matriculate, and would also explain Walsingham's registration at the University of Padua that same winter. Leaving his cousins at Basle (Rector's Account Book, 4 September 1556) he went down into Italy some time in the autumn, for on 29 December 1555 he was chosen Consiliarius of the English Nation in the Faculty of Civil Law (Andrich, pp. 31, 131; cf. also Read, I, p. 22). From that time onwards, however, his whereabouts on the Continent are unknown. He probably sampled other universities, though apparently not that of Heidelberg (cf. G. Toepke, ed. of the Matrikel), but upon Elizabeth's accession he came back to England and was returned M.P. for Banbury in the parliament of 1559. As he was not yet thirty he may be included among those 'beardless boys' to whom the alteration of religion had been entrusted. His long training abroad had given him better qualifications for his later career as head of Elizabeth's secret service. But a recent rendering of his activities in the Babington plot (A. Gordon Smith, *Babington Plot*, 1936) has thrown a strange light upon the intricate methods resorted to by Mr Secretary Walsingham and his intelligence department, not so much in the unravelling, but in the actual fabrication, of plots against the throne in Elizabeth's struggle with Mary Stuart.

Basle, A II a; Padua, A VI; *D.N.B.*

429. WALTON, WILLIAM: *Ex-religious and student.* Of Somerset(?) and Gloucester.

We believe that this William Walton, who fled to Frankfort in 1554, who signed the invitation to John Knox on 24 September (*T.* p. 20) and Frankfort's reply to Strasbourg on 3 December (*T.* p. 26), and who, in August 1555, seceded with Whittingham (*T.* p. 55), was 'Fryer Wyllyam Walton', an ex-Dominican of Gloucester[1] (Wright, *Monasteries*, p. 200). He may well have been the eldest son of Thomas Walton, gentleman of Somerset (Harl. Soc. I, 57), and was perhaps the father of a William Walton who, in 1561, matriculated sizar from Pembroke College, Cambridge, and who is believed to have been ordained priest at Ely in 1567 (Venn, IV, 328). The elder Walton, though endorsing Whittingham's letter of secession, yet failed to follow him to Geneva. Nor has his name been found at Basle. Quite possibly, being an old man, he died abroad.

Frankfort, B III a.

[1] Cf. also the William Walton, who with Thomas Parker received a yearly pension of £5. 6s. 8d. for the auditorship of the monastery of St Peter (*Trans. Bristol and Gloucestershire Arch. Soc.* XLIX, 110).

430. WARBERTON, Thomas: *Weaver.* Of Lancashire. Wife(?).

A 'poor' weaver of Lancashire, living while at Aarau in the house of Hans Gysins. Since the Official List mentions a wife (below, p. 355) and Hans Dür does not, he must have married while at Aarau.
Wesel (?); Aarau, A I a & b.

431. WARCOPE (WARCUP), Cuthbert: *Gent.* Of Oxfordshire. Wife.

Eldest son and heir of Michael Warcup, Esq., of English, near Nettlebed, Oxon. (Visitation, Oxfordshire, 1634, p. 29). His mother, Anne, daughter of Thomas English, was the Mistress Anne Warcup who befriended first John Jewel in his flight from Oxford in 1554 (*Mem.* III, i, 227) and later Laurence Humphrey when sequestered for nonconformity in 1565 (*Parker*, I, 368). From her, Cuthbert Warcup must have received his strong protestant bias, but what we believe to have been his active participation in the Dudley plot no doubt confirmed it. Chillester (*q.v.*) and Vincent (*q.v.*), it may be remembered, carried on their counterfeiting operations in Oxfordshire and buried their tools there. Suspicion points to Warcup as having connived in that work, which would provide ample reason for his flight to Frankfort in the autumn of 1556 with his wife, ten children and six servants (*H.S.P.* IV, 88). The first appearance of his name there is on the tax-list of 15 January 1557, when his taxable property was valued at 3650 florins.[1] But it is specifically stated that he was not obliged to pay taxes on the full amount since he had been in Frankfort only two months. This fixes the time of his arrival as in November 1556 (Jung, p. 30). In the colony he played a rôle of importance on the conservative side. John Hales appealed to him on 26 January to aid in preserving the peace of the community (*T.* p. 65). When the struggle came over the 'new discipline', which Warcup did not sign, he is found to have been a supporter of Horne and Chambers (*T.* pp. 76, 169). Besides his own ample family he sheltered under his roof Mistress Jane Wilkinson, one of the original committee of 'sustainers', and also Elizabeth, the wife of Anthony Browne 'absentis'. Who she was is not clear. Of Warcup's ten children we know the names of only five (Harl. Soc. v, 163). Leonard, the second son, became heir to the elder branch of the Warcups in Yorkshire, while Ralph (or Rodolph), eleven years old in 1556, is said by Anthony à Wood to have been 'the most compleat esquire of his time' (*Ath. Oxon.* I, 754). He was

---

[1] It is not clear whether this represented the whole or only the half of his taxable property.

a student of Christ Church in 1563 (Foster, IV, 1568), and later became J.P. and knight of the shire for Oxfordshire.

Frankfort, A III a 3, 4 & b 2; B III a.

432. WATER (WARTER, WATERS), THOMAS: *Priest.* Of London. d. 1567(?).

Born in London and ordained deacon by Ridley in 1550 and priest in 1551 (*Mar. Reac.* pp. 186, 194). At the time of his ordination as deacon he was curate of St Bride's in Fleet Street, but became vicar of Rodmersham, Kent, on 19 May 1553, though Dr Frere surmises that he resigned this living soon after (*ibid.* pp. 186–7, n. 5). But his first appearance abroad was not until 1557, when his property was assessed at Frankfort in January at 110 florins (Jung, p. 30). He thus belongs to the second migration of 1556. In March-April he signed the 'new discipline' and on 10 June was living in the household of Richard Beesley (*H.S.P.* IV, 89). In July 1561, Grindal instituted him to the living of Baddow, in Essex, which he held till 1567 (Newcourt, II, 25), which possibly marks the date of his death.

Frankfort, A III a 3, 4 & b 2; B III b.

433. WATSON, JOHN: *'Servant'* and gent.(?). A Scot(?). d. 1557(?).

Though called a 'servant' of Sir William Fuller, he was probably a gentleman attached in Tudor fashion to Sir William's household and present with him in Geneva before 13 October 1555. He may well have been the John Watson (junior) who matriculated from Corpus Christi College, Cambridge, at Easter, 1550 (Venn, IV, 348). It is more doubtful that he was the 'John Watsone, Scot' who was taken with Thomas Stafford at Scarborough in 1557 and executed (*Mem.* III, ii, 68, 518), yet the death of Sir William Stafford in May 1556 may have set him adrift like Courtenay's gentlemen, who at his death were left 'masterless' and 'moneyless' (*For. Cal.* 1553–8, p. 256).

Geneva, A IV a; France (?).

434. WATSON, ROBERT: *Student.* Of Norfolk.

Born in the city of Norwich and afterwards steward of Archbishop Cranmer (*Scriptores*, IX, 729, and *Cranmer*, p. 610). Strype calls him 'a great civilian' and Bale declares him to have been 'learned in the Scriptures'. Watson himself, in his pamphlet called *Aetiologia* (Brit. Mus. 1371, a. 7), gives an account of his imprisonment of 'one year and almost 4 mos.' for 'the sake of the gospel'. This work, written in November 1555 (*Aetiologia*, p. 6), was published according to the title-page in 1556, and probably abroad, though the place of printing is not named. It is dedicated to all sincere Christians and especially to 'his brother Englishmen dispersed over the world' (*ibid.* p. 2). But the obvious quibble in regard to the doctrine of the Sacrament by which he obtained his release from prison does more credit to the humanity of his friend John Barret, ex-Carmelite, than to the moral courage of Watson. Where he took refuge abroad we do not know.

n.p.; B i a & b; B ii.

---

435. WATTES, Thomas: *Student.* Of Yorkshire. d. 1577.

Born in Yorkshire (Jung, p. 63), he received his B.A. from Christ's College, Cambridge, in 1552–3 (Venn, iv, 352). He was evidently a man of some importance,[1] for he purchased the 'Grossbürgerrecht' at Frankfort on 12 October 1556, paying 2 fl. 18 s. 'Bürgergeld' (Jung, pp. 24, 63). On 16 October his property was assessed at 380 florins (*ibid.* p. 29) and on the same day he bought from Whitehead the garden property which the latter felt obliged to sell after his wife's death (see below). The house was probably intended to serve as a community house, not for Wattes's private use alone, for in June 1557, Gregory Railton, John Fauconer, Alexander Nowell and John Mullins are all found living in it with him (*H.S.P.* iv, 88), and Railton held a mortgage on it (Jung, p. 63). Except that he was a citizen of Frankfort and figured in this transaction, we know no more of Wattes's life abroad than that he signed the 'new discipline' in March-April. But on his return to England his name frequently appears. Cambridge gave him his M.A. in 1560; and Grindal ordained him both deacon and priest in the January of 1559/60 (*Grindal,* p. 55). In the following year two of those who had lived together in Frankfort, Wattes and Mullins, became Grindal's chaplains (*Parker,* i, 209). And in August 1570, Dr Story, who had just been kidnapped in Antwerp, was lodged in Wattes's London house, during the time that, with no small irony, the Lollards' Tower 'of which the locks and bolts of the doors' had been 'broken off at the death of Queen Mary, and never since repaired' was 'got ready for his [Story's] reception' (*Dom. Cal.* 1547–80, pp. 390, 391). As archdeacon of Middlesex, Wattes signed the articles altering rites and ceremonies, but apparently not the petition for a discipline (*Annals,* i, i, 504 and 512). Venn records the fact that he was a benefactor of Pembroke College, Cambridge.

B ii; Frankfort, A iii a 1, 3, 4 & b 2; B iii b.

---

[1] He may have been the son of 'the kyng's grocer mr. Wattes' (*Narr. of Ref.* p. 28).

436. WELLER, JOHN: *Merchant*. Of London. Wife.

Weller appeared in Frankfort in 1555 with his wife, five sons and four servants, and on 7 March became a burgher of the city, paying the very high tax of 22 s. and registering as 'J. Weller, Londinis' (Jung, pp. 24, 63). In the autumn he is found among the 'merchants' in the Standesliste, but since his name appears in neither of the tax-lists (*ibid.* pp. 29, 30) he must have prudently withdrawn from the city during the winter of 1556–7. By 10 June 1557, however, he was back again, and received into his house Sir Francis Knollys with his wife, five children and a maid (*H.S.P.* IV, 88). Perhaps because of absence Weller had not subscribed to the 'new discipline', nor did he take any part in the strife at Frankfort.

Frankfort, A III a 1, 2, 4 & b 1, 2.

437. WHETNALL (WHETENHALL), GEORGE: *Gent.* Of Kent. d. 1573.

Though the family seems to have come originally from Wetenhall Manor in Cheshire, George Whetenhall was the son of William Whetenhall of East Peckham, Kent, and sheriff of the county under Henry VIII (Hasted, I, p. xc). He married Alice, daughter of Thomas Berkley of Hampshire, whose wife, Elizabeth Neville, was the daughter of Lord Abergavenny (Harl. Soc. LXXV, 116 and Thomas Becon, *Works*, p. 191 note). If, as seems possible, he was also the Whetenhall, of no first name, who in 1544 matriculated Fellow Commoner from Queens' College (Venn, IV, 382), this would have made him a young contemporary of the early protestant movement at Cambridge, and George Whetenhall's friendship with Thomas Becon adds support to the identification. About 1542, Becon dedicated to him his *Nosegay* (*Works*, pp. 191–229; cf. *S.T.C.* no. 1742), probably begun when Becon was vicar of Brenzett in Kent. The two Whetnalls, father and son, both very likely involved with Wyatt, made their appearance together at Frankfort in December 1554. On the 3rd they put their names to the letter of high stomach sent by that colony to Strasbourg in the course of the Prayer Book controversy (*T.* p. 26); but since they played no subsequent part in the 'troubles', it is fair to presume that they returned to England, for George Whetenhall, at least, did not die until 16 December 1573 (*Works*, p. 191 note).

Frankfort, B III a.

438. WHETNALL (WETNALL), ROGER: *Gent.* Of Cheshire.

Though Mr Leadam suggests that this man, who was specially named in Brett's commission of 1556, was of Besthorp, Norfolk (*R.H.S. Trans.* n.s. XI, 116, n. 5; cf. Blomefield, I, 497), I am more inclined to think that he was the Roger Whetnall, younger son of William Whetnall of Nantwich, Cheshire—Cheshire being the early seat of the Wetenhall family—who was half-brother of Thomas Whetnall (1566) of Nantwich (Harl. Soc. xviii, 244–6). The anxiety of the Marian government to get hold of him in 1556 implies that he had played a part in the Dudley conspiracy, yet nothing to implicate him has yet come to light. His place of refuge on the Continent is unknown.

n.p.; B iv a.

439. WHETNALL, Thomas: *Gent.* Of Kent.

Son of George Whetnall of East Peckham (above) and present with his father as a refugee at Frankfort in 1554. Later he married Dorothy, daughter of John Vane of Tonbridge.

Frankfort, B iii a.

440. WHITCHURCH (WHYTCHURCH), Edward: *Grocer and printer.* Of London. d. 1561.

Famous as a partner with Richard Grafton in the publication and dissemination of the early editions of the Bible in English, and also printer of the first Prayer Book of Edward VI. Being excepted from the pardon issued at Queen Mary's coronation (*Cranmer*, p. 446), it is supposed that he went abroad where, after 1556, he married Cranmer's widow, the niece of Osiander of Nüremberg (cf. Pollard's *Cranmer*, Geneal. Table). Possibly then it was to Nüremberg that Whitchurch fled, for no trace of him has been found in the English colonies of the Rhine valley. Under Elizabeth he again set up his press in London, but died on 1 December 1561.

n.p.; *D.N.B.*

441. WHITEHEAD, David: *Priest*(?). Of Cornwall. Wife. 1492(?)–1571.

A few facts discovered abroad in regard to David Whitehead may be added to the account of him given by Professor Pollard in the *D.N.B.*, and one correction made touching his county of origin. Following Wood (*Ath. Oxon.* i, 396) he is there called a native of Hampshire, but Whitehead himself, when made a burgher of Frankfort on 20 May 1556, gave his name as 'D. Whitedus, Cornubiensis ex Anglia'. Nevertheless, he may have been, as Wood says, 'of the same family with those of Tuderley in Hampshire' (*ibid.*), for no Whiteheads are mentioned in Cornwall either by Vivian or in the Harleian Society's visitations. Wood also believes that this 'most heavenly professor of divinity of his time' had been a student at Oxford, either of Brasenose or of All Souls, and chaplain to Anne Boleyn, to whom he owed his advancement.

Though this latter statement is not proven (cf. *D.N.B.*), there is no doubt that he was tutor to Charles Brandon, the young Duke of Suffolk who died in 1551. Whitehead took part in the conference on the Sacrament, held at Sir William Cecil's house in November of that year, but apart from being Cranmer's candidate for the vacant archbishopric of Armagh, a post which Whitehead refused, he seems to have had no preferment (cf. Foster) previous to his departure from England with John à Lasco on 13–15 September 1553. The story of the wanderings of à Lasco's company, from Denmark where they first landed and were called 'martyrs of the devil', to Wismar, Lübeck, Hamburg and finally to Emden, where they were permitted to settle and organize a church, is a confused tale of arrivals, theological disputes and forced departures due to Lutheran animosity (*Narratio* of Utenhovius; *O.L.* II, 512–13; *E.H.R.* X, 433–5; V. Krasinski, *Reformation in Poland*, I, 264–8). But on 24 October 1554 Whitehead at last reached Frankfort, and there, Knox having not yet arrived, 'he tooke the charge for a time' at the congregation's request (*T.* p. 17). Whitehead was no friend to Whittingham; and there is something suspicious about his timely arrival on 24 October at the height of the liturgical controversy between Frankfort and Strasbourg, and only ten days before the appearance of Richard Chambers on his embassy from Zurich (*T.* p. 17). It looks very much as if he had been sent as an advance agent in the combined effort of Strasbourg and Zurich to supplant Whittingham's influence at Frankfort and raise up a formidable opposition to John Knox. Whitehead certainly aggravated the strife and, noticeably, was given no share later in the preparation of the compromise liturgy adopted by the congregation of 6 February 1555 (*T.* p. 37). His failure led, we believe, to a second embassy of Chambers, this time accompanied by Edmund Grindal, on 28 November (*T.* p. 22); and eventually to the intervention of Richard Cox in March 1555 (*T.* p. 38). At what time Whitehead was made official pastor of the reorganized church is not clear, but probably it was just after 28 March, when the revised liturgy was adopted (*T.* pp. 46–7), though on 5 April his name appears second to that of Cox in the letter of explanation sent to Calvin (*O.L.* II, 755). On 20 September, however, when a spirited defence was made against Calvin's charge of idolatry, Whitehead was certainly pastor and probably also author of the letter (*ibid.* pp. 755–63). It was then that Sir Thomas Hoby met him at Frankfort (Cam. Misc. X, 123). But there follows a period of confusion. As Thomas Cole maliciously observed, Whitehead resigned the pastorate because 'he woulde escape the labour off the [divinity] lecture' in the newly organized university (*T.* p. 60); but, if so, he had resumed it again before 6 January 1556, when

Horne was elected to the office in his place (*T.* p. 62). When his name was given in the Standesliste in the autumn of 1555, Whitehead, with his wife and two children, was living in a house on the Schnurgasse (Jung, p. 63). On 20 May 1556 he became a burgher of Frankfort, and, as if the better to support his new dignity, on the 23rd he bought from the widow of the magistrate, Adolph von Glauburg, a new house with a garden and a courtyard on the corner of the Breiten Gasse beyond the Wall (*ibid.*). For this he paid 500 gulden, though in the October following his taxable property is rated at only 240 florins (*ibid.* p. 29); and it is interesting to find that he is described in the transaction as 'der hailigen Geschrift Baccalaureen', which may be an equivalent of D.D. (cf. Wood, I, 396). Then something happened, which we believe to be the death of Anna his wife, and Whitehead sells his house to Thomas Wattes (*q.v.*). Though it is true that the transfer is made not only in his name but also in hers, it is found that on 10 June 1557 Whitehead was without a wife, and living with his two children in the household of Alvey, Luddington and Rogers (*H.S.P.* IV, 89). Previously he had signed the 'new discipline', and at Frankfort he probably remained until his return to England, for he is there throughout the summer of 1557 (*T.* pp. 174, 182). In 1559 he was made a member of the committee for Prayer Book revision which met in the house of Sir Thomas Smith, and later represented the protestant side at the Conference of Westminster (*Annals*, I, i, 128–9). So much we know; but 'whether he had any spiritualities of note conferr'd on him is yet doubtful' (Wood, I, 396). More doubtful still is the legend that he was offered the archbishopric of Canterbury (cf. *Parker*, I, 71). In 1561 Cecil did actually offer him a living (probably the mastership of the Savoy Hospital), which Whitehead refused (*Dom. Cal.* 1547–80, p. 185), and in 1564 he was sequestered for nonconformity. Elizabeth's remark to him, 'I like thee better because thou livest unmarried' (Wood), was, if true, certainly made in ignorance of the wife he had had in Frankfort, and still more in ignorance of the young widow he was to marry at eighty when near his death (*Z.L.* I, 242).

Copenhagen; Emden; Frankfort, A III a 1, 2, 3, 4 & b 1, 2; B III a & b; B IV b; *D.N.B.*

442. WHITTINGHAM, WILLIAM: *Student and gent.* Of Chester. 1524(?)–79.

The exact relation borne by Whittingham to the Marian Exile is still an enigma. Was he sent to Frankfort by direction of the protestant administrative committee in London? or was he from the beginning an unruly spirit in his own party, a nonconformist to nonconformity? The riddle has found no answer abroad. The story of the liturgical struggle between Frankfort and Strasbourg can be reconstructed only from hints, and the conclusion reached, whatever it is, must be followed by a point of interrogation. At the accession of Mary, William Whittingham, son of William Whittingham of Chester, was already a much-educated, much-travelled man, and also, that rare thing among contemporary Englishmen, a linguist. He spoke both French and German. His years at Brasenose (1540–5) and at Christ Church (1547), Oxford,[1] had been supplemented by study at the Universities of Orleans and Lyons which qualified him to act on occasion as interpreter to Sir John Mason, then English ambassador to France. In 1552 he also went to Germany and Geneva, whence he returned to England in 1553(?) a cosmopolitan and a convinced Calvinist of about twenty-nine. By age, by foreign experience and by training, then, he must have appeared an admirable instrument for the protestant adventure overseas which was under discussion in London during August and September 1553. To Sir John Mason, father-in-law of Sir John Cheke, but now member of Queen Mary's Council, Whittingham was already well known; and it was through an appeal to Mason that he obtained for Peter Martyr an honourable passport from England to the Continent with 'permission to remove all his goods' (*O.L.* I, 370, 372). In reality there had been little difficulty in getting this permit. The government seems to have been entirely ready to speed an uncomfortable guest,[2] but Whittingham's part in the affair reveals the fact that he stood high in the counsels of his party. Cranmer had been earnestly wishing for Peter Martyr's coming (*ibid.* pp. 370–1), but why a complaisant Council should have permitted him while in London actually to stay with the archbishop, who even then was under the shadow of indictment for treason, must remain a mystery. It was upon his arrival that Peter Martyr gave his approval to Cranmer's declaration against the Mass already promulgated on 5 September. And it was then, as I believe, during the earnest discussions taking place on protestant policy, what Renard called the 'plottings, discontent and secret communings' of 'the hardened followers of that sect' (*Span. Cal.* 1553, p. 217, dated 9 September), that an exodus to the Continent was agreed upon and Peter Martyr chosen as one of the earliest advocates of the cause of English protestants abroad. Whittingham had been instrumental in getting him to London for the discussion. Events followed fast upon it. John

---

[1] Also Fellow of All Souls, 1545? (cf. *Ath. Oxon.* I, 396).

[2] The whole story of Peter Martyr's 'imprisonment' at Oxford as told by Terentianus to John ab Ulmis (*O.L.* I, 369–72) needs, we believe, re-interpretation. Peter Martyr was hated there, and his six weeks' confinement to his own house was probably in the interests of his own personal safety.

à Lasco and his two shiploads of followers, among whom were
many English, left England on the 13th–15th; Valeran Pullain and
his Glastonbury weavers on the 16th (*P.C.A.* 1552–4, p. 349);
Peter Martyr about the 19th (*O.L.* ii, 372); all were allowed to
pass freely. And in one or the other of these groups was Sir
Francis Knollys (*q.v.*). The date of Whittingham's own departure
is unknown, but it is obvious that he kept in close communication
with Valeran Pullain at Frankfort, and that his arrival there on
27 June 1554, with three other English gentlemen and their
servants, was entirely expected. The casualness of Whittingham's
narrative shows this (*T.* pp. 5–7). It is also clear that provision
had already been made by the Frankfort magistrates for their
reception. But beyond this, nothing of his personal responsibility
towards the colony may be gathered from his evasive, intricate
account of the 'troubles' of the Frankfort congregation. How far
he was acting as an agent for Cecil and the party at home, how
far he was acting on his own ambitious initiative when he proposed
on 2 August a unification of all the English colonies abroad at
Frankfort (*T.* pp. 8–13) must remain a matter of doubt. The whole
question is complicated by the rapid doctrinal drift away from the
Prayer Book that manifested itself immediately in a colony where
no bishop, no man of ecclesiastical authority, was present. My
own reading of the situation, at the moment, is that the bitter
quarrel that ensued between Strasbourg and Frankfort was due to
an attempt by Bishop Ponet to exert episcopal coercion, but that
his action was induced by a double motive: sense of responsibility
as ranking ecclesiastic, personal pique against Whittingham who
had refused his services as pastor. Whittingham was a layman; the
whole tendency of the Frankfort colony was towards the establishment of a Bible Commonwealth in which there would be no place
for bishops. And by every sign Ponet meant again to be bishop
of Winchester. Political antagonism also underlay the struggle.
To Frankfort, speaking generally, had come the elements among
the exiles, hostile to Northumberland: Knox, for example. While
in Strasbourg were gathered the remnants of the duke's party who
were to be the supporters, under Elizabeth, of the Suffolk claim to
the throne. There were the members of William Cecil's own circle,
Sir Anthony Cooke, Sir Thomas Wrothe, Sir John Cheke and
many others, as these biographies will show, who were closely
connected with him either by sympathy or by marriage. If
Frankfort aimed at democratic unity, Strasbourg was looking to
aristocratic hegemony among the English colonies, preparatory to
a struggle against the royal prerogative. Independency at Frankfort, whiggery at Strasbourg, found each a fertile soil for growth
in the freedom of exile. But in this conflict Whittingham was

worsted. If he had indeed left England as an accredited agent of Cecil, we believe that his independence of temper lost him favour. Whitehead is evidently referring to Whittingham and Knox when he speaks in a letter to Calvin of 'the clamours of individuals, possessing no weight whatever. . .' (*O.L.* II, 757, of date 20 September 1555). In September 1555, therefore, Whittingham took his way from Frankfort to Geneva. There on 24 October he became a 'resident' of the city (f. 123) and in due time was received as a bourgeois (Martin, pp. 44, 331). In December he was elected a senior of the congregation (*ibid.* p. 334), and on 15 November 1556 he married Katherine Jaquemayne of Orleans, whom he may have met when he was there as a student at the university.[1] Not till December 1558 was he chosen deacon of the congregation (*ibid.* p. 335), and, according to the Livre des Anglois, he was never made a 'minister' even at Geneva (cf. *ibid.* pp. 50–1). But his literary work there was considerable and his metrical versions of fifteen psalms, 'médiocrement poétique', were added to the Sternhold and Hopkins collection (*ibid.* pp. 111, 113; Maitland, *Essays*, p. 83, n. 10). Martin even concedes to him the initiative in the work of translating the Bible and assigns to him and to Anthony Gilby the chief direction of it. He remained in Geneva until the work was finished, but on 30 May 1560 left for home (Reg. du Con. vol. 56, f. 44vo, quoted Martin, p. 261, n. 2). In his later career he may have come to regret the preface he had written to Christopher Goodman's pamphlet on 'Superior Powers', published in 1558. In the eyes of Elizabeth it gave him no title to favour, and his subsequent life as dean of Durham (1563), a promotion which he owed to Robert and Ambrose Dudley, was filled with echoes of his Genevan experience. Finally, in the Visitation of 1578 he was obliged to confess that he was 'no minister, according to the. . . ordinances of this realme' and that he had also been 'a furtherer to the setting forthe of the wicked book against the lawfull regiment of women' (Cam. Misc. VI, Whittingham, Append. II, p. 47). In the midst of the proceedings against him he died on 10 June 1579. Of his two children born at Geneva, Zachary in 1557 and Susanna in 1558, both died young, Susanna at Geneva in 1560 (Martin, pp. 336, 338).

B I a & b; B II; Frankfort, B III; Geneva, A IV a & b; D.N.B.

[1] For the whole vexed question of his marriage see E. Doumergue's *Calvin*, III, App. 5, pp. 666–75; Martin, p. 337; Mrs M. A. E. Green's edition of the MS. Life of Whittingham, Cam. Misc. VI, p. 2, n. 4.

443. WIBURNE (WYBORNE, VUIBURNE), PERCIVAL: *Student and gent.* Of Kent. 1534(?)–1606.

Probably a younger brother of John Wyborne of Hakewell, Kent (Harl. Soc. LXXV, 50), and Fellow of St John's College, Cambridge, in 1552 (Venn, IV, 481). He withdrew to Geneva towards the close of Mary's reign, arriving there on 8 May 1557, when he must have been about twenty-three years old. On 14 October following he became a 'resident' of the city (f. 196) and probably remained there until the return of the colony early in 1559. He then received his M.A. from St John's, and in January–March 1560 was ordained deacon by Grindal and priest by Richard Davies of St Asaph (*Grindal*, pp. 54, 58). In the same year he was made a canon of Rochester, then of Norwich, and in 1561, canon of Westminster. But his very strong puritan leanings which led him to support the articles against rites and ceremonies, and to petition for a discipline (*Annals*, I, i, 504, 512), resulted in his sequestration in 1564, though his preaching in public was connived at (*Parker*, I, 483) and he was allowed to retain his prebends. Why then he was obliged 'to take to husbandry' (*Grindal*, pp. 145–6) it is difficult to see, and it is certain that he used this period of semi-disgrace to make a journey of complaint to Zurich. This was in 1566 (*Z.L.* I, 187), when for Bullinger's instruction he wrote his *State of the Church of England*[1] (*ibid.* II, 358–62). Neither Beza nor Bullinger welcomed his appearance. 'Some of them' (i.e. the English objectors), said Beza, 'are rather hard to please' (*ibid.* p. 128), and Wiburne complained that Bullinger had snubbed him and resorted to a diplomatic illness rather than listen to his grievances (*ibid.* I, 187–91, and cf. Gualter to Parkhurst,[2] *ibid.* II, 140–2). Also this visit of his raised a storm among the bishops (*ibid.* p. 178) and in 1571 he was again cited for nonconformity. In 1573 he was suspected of having had a share in the composition of the *Admonition to Parliament*; while of his sympathy with the Classical Movement there seems to be no doubt (Usher, p. xlviii), nor that he had a tongue in controversy, for he is believed to be the 'P. W.' who in 1581 wrote *A checke or reproofe of M. Howlets vntimely screeching* (*S.T.C.* no. 25586). In 1590 he appears to have been chaplain to Lady Bacon, who rejoiced in his 'comfortable company' (Urwick, p. 331).

B II; Geneva, A IV a & b.

[1] In the archives of Zurich.

[2] This letter, says Hastings Robinson, was printed in the *Admonition to Parliament* (*Z.L.* II, 140, note). It also called down upon Gualter an admonishment from Cox (*Z.L.* I, 234–8).

444. WILFORD (WILSFORD), FRANCIS: *Gent.* Of Kent. Wife.

The family of Wilford, originally from Devon, had come to London and made money in the city (*Machyn*, pp. 3, 314 note). This Francis appears to have been the second son of Thomas Wilford of Hartridge, Kent, by his first wife Elizabeth Colepeper of Bedgeberry. His (Thomas's) second wife was Rose, daughter of William Whetenhall (Harl. Soc. LXXV, 117–18; for the family of Whetenhall, see above). Francis Wilford, who is styled 'of Nonington', Kent, married Alice, a daughter of William Sympson who had been vice-marshall of Calais under Lord Lisle (*ibid.* p. 118 and *Chron. Calais*, p. 138, etc.). He is not mentioned at Frankfort, his only place of exile, until 10 June 1557, when, with his wife, four children and four servants, he was lodged in the house of Thomas Sandes (or Saunders) together with the families of Edward Boyes (*q.v.*) and Edward Caunt (*q.v.*), making in all twenty-eight souls (Jung, p. 34 and *H.S.P.* IV, 89). The children in exile with him were probably his eldest son James (cf. Harl. Soc. XIII, 128 and *ibid.* LXXV, 118); Francis, who appears to have matriculated from St John's College, Cambridge, in 1571 (Venn, IV, 408); Henry; Jasper, who perhaps died abroad; and a daughter, who from her name, Peregrine, was evidently born abroad. So far as the records go, Francis, the father, did no more in Frankfort during the struggle over the 'new discipline' than endorse objections to it on 29 September 1557 (*T.* p. 174), then finally sign it on 21 December. But on 3 January 1559, being still in Frankfort, he put his hand to the colony's refusal to follow Geneva in her anti-ceremonial crusade (*T.* p. 190). He did not leave there until 10 March, when the Frankfort council finally handed over the balance due on the English letters of credit (Jung, p. 7, no. 4 and p. 65). In all this there is little to indicate the family's affiliations, but from the will of Francis's elder brother, Sir James Wilford 'the defender of Haddington' (*D.N.B.*), we learn of his warm friendship for Sir Philip Hoby, to whom he left a suit of engraved white armour; and for Sir Thomas Wyatt the younger, who was made an overseer of the will (*Geneal.* IV, 5). At Sir James's funeral in November 1550 Miles Coverdale had preached (*Machyn*, p. 3). Such family associations are hints to show why the Wilfords had to retire to the Continent under Mary.   Frankfort, A III a 4 & b 2; B III a & b.

445. WILFORD, JOHN: *Merchant.* Of London. Wife.

This John Wilford was probably the second son of John Wilford of Enfield, alderman of London, younger brother of Thomas Wilford of Hartridge, and uncle of Francis Wilford above (Harl.

Soc. LXV, 35 and cf. *ibid.* L, 15 and XIII, 127). If so, then John Wilford the exile was, or was to be, father-in-law of Sir Thomas Smith, secretary to King Edward and chairman of the committee for Prayer Book revision in 1559 (*ibid.* XIII, 101). Three children were with him when he arrived in Frankfort in 1556 (Jung, p. 65) and of these one was Philippa, Sir Thomas Smith's second wife. The tax-list of 16 October values his property at 1000 florins, making him one of the richest men in the English colony, one who could therefore afford to live in his own house with his wife, one maid and the children aforesaid (*H.S.P.* IV, 88). John, his eldest son, was to matriculate from Pembroke College, Cambridge, in 1571 (Venn, IV, 409); Gerson, who from his name was born abroad, was to be a student at Cambridge in 1575 (*ibid.*). But except that Richard Chambers addressed to Wilford, among other English gentlemen, a justification for his (Chambers's) administration of the English poor fund, he seems to have done nothing at Frankfort but sign the 'new discipline' in March-April.

Frankfort, A III 3, 4 & b 2; B III a & b.

446. WILFORD, Thomas: *Gent.* Of Kent. 1530(?)–1604(?).

Half-brother of Francis Wilford above, being the son of Thomas Wilford of Hartridge, by his second wife Rose, daughter of William Whetenhall of Peckham (Harl. Soc. XIII, 127–8). His own sister Cecily became in 1558/9 the second wife of Edwin Sandys (*q.v.*). If Thomas was born as is believed in 1530, he was but twenty-seven when he signed the 'new discipline' at Frankfort in December 1557, and, like many others among the signatories, this act marked his first and last appearance in the colony. But we suspect that he may have been engaged elsewhere, for early in 1559 a nameless Wilford is found associated with Henry Strangwish the pirate, both suspected of having a casual 'mind to go as adventurers and to take an island of the King of Spain's' (*For. Cal.* 1558–9, pp. 228, 233). Nor is it impossible that he was the Thomas Wylford 'cast for deth' in 1562 on a charge of counterfeiting. Unfortunately his career, as given in the *D.N.B.*, does not open till 1585, when he had reached respectability and the command of a company at Ostend. Thereafter he was to see much service both in the Netherlands and in France, and eventually was to become superintendent of the admiralty works in Dover Harbour and governor of Camber Castle. His wife, Mary, was the daughter of Edward Poynings and, according to Prof. Pollard, it was his son, not Francis's, who married Elizabeth, eldest daughter of Sir Edwin Sandys.

Frankfort, B III b.

447. WILKINSON, ROWLAND. *Gent.*(?). Of Essex(?). d. 1557.

Was this a younger son of Mistress Jane Wilkinson, friend of Cranmer, wife of John Wilkinson of Goldhangar, co. Essex, and great-great-granddaughter of Ralph, first Lord Lumley (Harl. Soc. I, 57)? We know nothing of him except that as 'ein iunger gsel' who had no wife, no child and no relatives, he died at Aarau about 1557 (Hans Dür). On the Official List (below) he is noted only as dead. And Jane Wilkinson was also dead by July 1557—that is before the English colony at Aarau had been established—leaving at Frankfort a daughter of whom nothing more is heard. There is no mention of any son of hers, and my identification has little to support it, but Mistress Wilkinson herself deserves a word. She was a woman of wealth, one of the original committee of 'sustainers', and so prominently connected by sympathy with the reformers that Cranmer had urged her to flee to the Continent as early as September 1553 (*Cranmer*, pp. 449, 916). She delayed however till the summer of 1556, when, without licence, she withdrew from England to Frankfort, taking with her property to the amount of 6100 florins—the largest sum accredited to any of the Frankfort exiles (Jung, p. 30). In Brett's commission of 1556, her name was specially mentioned, but when he delivered the queen's letter to her that summer (Brett, p. 119) she pleaded that it was only 'her indisposycion and sekenes was cause of her comming oute of England to see if she coulde recover her healthe at the Bathes in those Countreys...' (*ibid.*). If not the only motive for her flight, this was at least a genuine one, for she was to die within the year (*T.* p. 178). By her will she left 'liberall relief' to the poor among the English exiles; and in the letters to her from her friends among the martyrs, a memory of loyal devotion to their cause (see Coverdale's *Letters of the Martyrs*).

Aarau, A I a & b.

448. WILLIAMS, CHARLES: *Merchant*(?). Of Bristol.

When Williams was admitted to membership in the English congregation at Geneva on 13 August 1559, it is recorded of him that he was 'borne in Bristow' and that he had 'made his confession of his fayth' before he was received. This last, being the only notice of its kind in the Livre des Anglois, leads to conjecture. He may have been a young man just come to maturity; yet he had been old enough on the previous 24 October to be made a 'resident' of Geneva (f. 264). Martin speaks of his late admission to the church as 'surprising' and suggests that he had come to study in the new university (p. 260). Perhaps he had, but the mention of Bristol may mean that there were other reasons for his presence in Geneva. In August 1554, a *Richard* Williams of Bristol had been sent for by the Privy Council (*P.C.A.* 1554–6, p. 59). The reason for his summons may be indicated by a second entry in the Council Minutes for 11 December 1557 (*ibid.* 1556–8, p. 214), when the mayor of Bristol is thanked for his apprehension of one *Thomas Williams*, whom he is to examine in order to discover 'the hole neste of those malefactours' (illicit traders, apparently) and then do justice upon them. Thus the name of Williams of Bristol was not at that time in good odour with the government. This may explain why two men of the name, and both of Bristol, had sought safety at Geneva.

Geneva, A IV a & b.

449. WILLIAMS, WALTER: *Merchant.* Of Bristol. d. before 1598.

Probably a relative of Charles Williams above, though in what degree we dare not say. He arrived at Geneva apparently alone in the spring of 1556 and before 12 July had been admitted into the English congregation. Who he was may be guessed from the will of Thomas Aldworth, alderman and merchant of Bristol, whose executor was a 'Thomas Aldworth als Darbridg', husband of 'Marie the daughter of Walter Williams, draper of this city of Bristol deceased,...'. The will is dated 22 November 1598 (Waters, *Gleanings*, I, 632).

Geneva, A IV a.

450. WILLIAMS, WILLIAM: *Gent.* Of Dorset (?). Wife.

This important member of the colonies of Frankfort and of Geneva was probably the son and heir of Sir John Williams of Herringstone, Dorset, and his wife Eleanor, daughter of Henry Vuedall, also of Dorset (Harl. Soc. xx, 98). He himself married Anna, daughter of William Disney and widow of Thomas Brune (cf. John Brune, his cousin, above, and *ibid.* xx, 22). Strype's identification of him as the William Williams presented by Bonner with the living of All Hallows in the Wall in July 1556 (*Mem.* III, i, 591 and Newcourt, I, 257) is manifestly impossible, since Williams the exile was then in Frankfort. There is far more likelihood of his having been William Williams, assay master of the Mint in Dublin (*Mem.* II, i, 600 and *P.C.A.* 1552–4, p. 74) and friend of John Bale. In 1553 Bale had been concealed in Williams's house in Dublin, and his flight from Ireland facilitated by him (Cooper, I, 226). Mary's accession probably deprived him of his office, since, if he is the William Williams of Dorset, his family connections were strongly protestant. Hence he may very well be the man who arrived in Frankfort with Whittingham on 27 June 1554, and the first Englishman to become a Frankfort burgher. On 5 July he paid his 'Bürgergeld' of 2 crowns (Jung, pp. 24, 65), and throughout the period of Whittingham's ascendancy in the colony Williams never wavered in his support of the radical party. On 2 August 1554 he endorsed Whittingham's effort to unite the English congregations at Frankfort (*T.* p. 13); on 27 August 1555 he signed Whittingham's letter of secession. Together the two men went to Geneva, as together they had come to Frankfort. With Jane his wife (Jana or Anna? cf. Harl. Soc. xx, 22) Williams was admitted to the English congregation on 13 October and on 24 October became a 'resident'. Later on, like Whittingham, he was also received as a bourgeois of the city (cf. Preamble, Livre des Anglois). It was Williams who in December 1558 collaborated with John Bodley in setting up a press for the printing of the Geneva Bible (Martin, p. 70); and from 16 December 1555, until his departure for England he was annually chosen a senior of the congregation. On 30 May 1560, Whittingham and he left Geneva together, their association having been unbroken throughout the period of exile. In view of his earlier supposed connection with the Mint, we rather suspect that it was Williams the exile who in 1565 associated himself with William Humfrey, Paymaster of the Mint, in the promotion of mining works (*Dom. Cal.* 1547–80, pp. 258–9); while one other reference to him in 1571 would suggest that he was himself still connected with the Mint in some official capacity (*ibid.* p. 428). Such early industrial experiments, as for example those of the Horseys (*q.v.*) and Cornelius Stephenson (*q.v.*), indicate in what direction other than religion the thoughts of the refugees had been turning during their exile.

Frankfort, A iii a 1; B iii a; Geneva, A iv a & b.

451. WILLOCK (WOLLOCK, etc.), JOHN: *Ex-religious*. A Scot. Of Ayrshire. d. 1585.

An ex-Franciscan or Dominican,[1] who as a reformer has been called 'next to Knox in initiative' (*D.N.B.*). He came to England about 1539 (*Wodrow Soc. Misc.* I, 262) and in 1541 was imprisoned in the Fleet for preaching against confession (Foxe, v, 443, 448).[2] In August 1549, John ab Ulmis, then in London, speaks of having had supper with John Wullock 'who is well skilled in Greek and Latin,...' (*O.L.* II, 393). By that time he had become chaplain to Henry, Duke of Suffolk, who had given him the living of Loughborough (Laing, vi, 572, n. 1), and he was then scheming to obtain from Bullinger a dedication of some of the latter's works to 'our patron the marquis' (*O.L.* II, 393). To this, Bullinger agreed and also made 'affectionate mention' in his preface of Willock himself

---

[1] Bishop Lesley, a contemporary authority, says Dominican (*Wodrow Soc. Misc.* I, 262).

[2] Called 'Wilcock' by Foxe.

who thanks him effusively in May 1552. Apparently Willock had but just returned from the Scottish border, where Suffolk, 'his highness' as Willock calls him, had been in camp (*O.L.* I, 314–16). And in view of this close connection between the two men, it is not surprising to find that Willock's flight abroad was due to his indictment for complicity in Suffolk's second rising. His identity in this case is fixed by the designation of him as 'late of Lough-borough in the said county [Leicester], clerk' (Baga, p. 245). But he managed to escape to Emden, where he began to practise as a physician, and whence he twice (in 1555 and 1556) made diplomatic journeys to the Queen Regent of Scotland on behalf of the Duchess of Friesland (Laing, I, 245 and n. 2). In 1557 he returned to Emden, but in the following year settled in Scotland where he was several times Moderator of the General Assembly and made Superintendent of Glasgow and the West (*ibid.* II, 87). This latter position he continued to hold even after his return in 1562 (*D.N.B.*) to his parish of Loughborough, where he died in 1585 (Nichols, *Leicestershire*, III, pt II, p. 892).

B I a & b; B II; B v c; Emden (Laing's *Knox*, Index); *D.N.B.*

452. WILLYES (WILLIS), PETER: *Merchant and apothecary.* Of Devon. Wife.

On 20 March 1553/4 'Petrus Willys, de Totnes in comitatu Devon, marchaunte potecary' appeared before the Privy Council charged with a debt of £50 to the queen (*P.C.A.* 1552–4, p. 410). The wording of the minute suggests that if the debt were paid before the 'All Haloutyde next commyng' Willis would have satisfactorily compounded for his offence—probably some share in the Western Rising. But the fine was evidently not paid, for early in 1556 'Peter Willyes' is found in exile at Geneva. On 14 October 1557 he was admitted to 'residence' there with the status of 'merchant' (f. 196) and on 16 December 1558 was chosen a deacon of the congregation (Martin, p. 335). He would seem to have been a dependant of the Tremaynes, for in 1565 Edward Tremayne was recommending 'his countryman', Willes, to Sir Nicholas Throck-morton 'for anything you commit to him', but also warning Throckmorton that if he refrained from 'showing the merchant favour' he would 'drive him from bringing wines, or else to entering them in Cornwall' outside of Throckmorton's grant and so to his loss (*Dom. Cal.* Addenda, 1547–65, p. 562). From 'potecary' to wine merchant was but a short and logical step.

Geneva, A IV a & b.

453. WILLOUGHBY (WILLOBIE, etc.), Thomas: *Priest and gent.* Of Lincolnshire. Wife. d. 1585.

Foster records two students at Oxford of the name of Thomas Willoughby who were practically contemporaries, while Boase (O.H.S. I, 180) knows but one, and that one was 'dispensed' in February 1535/6, because he was 'going to take Holy Orders'. Accordingly he was licensed on 3 May 1539. If there was but one Thomas Willoughby, he obtained his B.D. from Cambridge, and in 1550 was made a canon of Canterbury (Venn, IV, 423). Both Cooper (I, 514) and Venn agree that he was deprived in 1553, so that Strype must be in error when he names the canon deprived in that year for marriage as 'William' (*Cranmer*, p. 471). None of his biographers seems to have been aware that Willoughby became a refugee at Frankfort. His name appears on the Standesliste of 1555, as 'Th. Wilobaeus studens', and in 1556 he was taxed on property worth 20 florins (Jung, p. 29). He signed the 'new discipline' in the spring of 1557, and in June was dwelling alone in Frankfort with his wife and little son. But he played no part in the contentions of Frankfort and on his return to England was both reinstated as canon of Canterbury and made chaplain to Queen Elizabeth and to Archbishop Parker. In 1574 he became dean of Rochester. The Visitation of Kent in 1619 gives the name of his wife as 'Alice', daughter of 'Thomas Whod' of Hadleigh in Suffolk, and says of Willoughby himself that he came of an ancient family in Lincolnshire (Harl. Soc. XLII, 8).

Frankfort, A III a 2, 3, 4 & b 1, 2.

454. WILSON, Thomas: *Student.* Of Kendal, Westmorland. d. 1586.

There were two Thomas Wilsons abroad in the reign of Mary. This one, the student, received his M.A. from St John's College, Cambridge, in 1549, and was a Fellow of the college from 1548 to 1553. Probably he was one of the group that followed Thomas Lever into exile, but he went to Frankfort, where he was listed as a 'student' in 1555 and in 1556 was said to have no property but his books (Jung, p. 29). In February 1557 he was chosen one of the arbiters in the Horne-Ashley dispute (*T.* p. 76). He signed the 'new discipline' that spring, as he was to sign the petition for a discipline in 1562. And while in Frankfort he was an inmate of the house of Thomas Crawley (*H.S.P.* IV, 88). Grindal ordained him deacon on his return to England (January 1559/60: *Grindal*, p. 54) and the following year he was made a canon of Worcester. From 1571 to 1586 he filled the office of dean and is buried in Worcester Cathedral.

Frankfort, A III a 2, 3, 4 & b 1, 2; B III a & b.

455. WILSON, Thomas: *Lawyer and statesman.* Of Lincolnshire.
    1525(?)–81.

A more interesting Thomas Wilson was the son of Thomas Wilson
of Strubby, Lincs., author of the *Arte of Rhetorique* and later
(1577) secretary of state to Queen Elizabeth (*P.C.A.* 1577–8, p. 85).
Educated at Eton and King's College, he was an intimate in the
circle of Roger Ascham and Sir John Cheke, and was also one of
the many tutors chosen by Katherine, Duchess of Suffolk, for her
two sons, Henry and Charles Brandon. Wilson, a staunch adherent
of the Dudleys, fled to the Continent on Northumberland's fall and
is said by the *D.N.B.* to have been in Padua with Sir John Cheke
in 1555, though Sir Thomas Hoby makes no mention of him in
his journal, and he was not registered as a student at the university
(cf. Cam. Misc. x and Andrich). Strype thinks, however (that he
may have been tutor to the Earl of Devon), and it was he who
pronounced the funeral oration over Courtenay in 1556 in
St Anthony's Church (*Mem.* III, i, 551 and ii, no. 57, p. 420).
From Padua he went to Rome, where he acted as Chetwood's
solicitor in the famous case of Chetwood and Agnes Woodhull
which has its unique place among the clauses of the Act of
Supremacy[1] (*For. Cal.* 1553–8, p. 345). There, too, Wilson carried
on certain secret negotiations with the pope behind the back of
Sir Edward Carne, the ambassador, which are supposed to have
concerned a plot against Cardinal Pole (*ibid.* pp. 380, 384, 389).
For this Wilson was recalled to England in March 1558 (*Dom.
Cal.* 1547–80, p. 100), but he ignored the summons. And perhaps
it was at the queen's instigation that he was afterwards imprisoned
in Rome as a heretic and nearly lost his life (*Arte of Rhetorique,*
ed. 1562, Sig. A 4vo). Challoner, writing to Cecil on 31 August
1559, 'trusts poor Wylson is one of the number' that escaped when
a mob stormed the Court of the Inquisition on the death of
Paul IV (*For. Cal.* 1558–9, p. 514). 'In thende by Gods grace',
says Wilson himself, 'I was wonderfullie deliuered, through plain
force of the worthie Romaines... (*Rhetorique,* Sig. A 5). From
Rome he went to Ferrara, where he obtained his LL.D., and
finally in 1560 returned to England.

B II; Padua; Rome, B v b 1, 3; Ferrara; *D.N.B.*

456. WISDOM (WYSDOME), Robert, B.D.: *Priest.* Of
    Oxfordshire(?). d. 1568.

One of those who had undergone persecution under Henry VIII.
Perhaps he was of Burford, Oxon. (*D.N.B.*), but whether educated
at Oxford or Cambridge is doubtful. Venn claims that his B.D.

[1] It is Proviso II (and cf. *Annals,* I, i, 52), *Statutes of the Realm,* IV, pt 1, 355.

was certainly from Cambridge (IV, 441). In 1540 he was committed to the Lollards' Tower for disobedience to the Act of the Six Articles (*Mem.* I, i, 570). In 1543, the year when Foxe says that he was parish priest of St Margaret's, Lothbury, and Wriothesley curate of St Mary's, Aldermansbury (Foxe, v, 448; cf. *Mem.* I, i, 567), he was forced with Thomas Becon to recant at Paul's Cross (Wriothesley, I, 142). He then withdrew with Becon to the north, where both were sheltered by John Olde (*q.v.*) in Staffordshire (see 'Becon'). Under Edward VI, his fortunes improving, he was made vicar of Settrington, Yorks., but when deprived in 1555(?) he retired to Frankfort. There in the autumn of that year he was listed among the 'students' and said to be living 'unter den kremmern' (Jung, p. 66). Upon what authority he is stated to have been an opponent of Knox and Whittingham I do not know (cf. *D.N.B.* and Jung), for Knox in his own Narrative nowhere mentions him (*Works*, IV, 41–9), nor does his name appear in the *Troubles at Frankfort*. If he had been of the Prayer Book party one would expect to find him a signatory of Cox's letter to Calvin of 5 April 1555 and of Whitehead's of 20 September, but he is in neither list (*O.L.* II, 755, 763). In fact it is very doubtful whether he was in Frankfort at all before November 1555, when he is first mentioned, and he must have left again within the year, for he does not appear in the tax-lists of 1556–7, and was not a subscriber to the 'new discipline'. The only other trace of him abroad is found at Strasbourg on 7 February 1558, when in the none too reputable company of Thomas Baxter (*q.v.*) he petitioned for civic rights (Protocols, vol. 36, f. 65vo, and below, p. 371). Then he disappears until 1559, when his name is found in a list of those to be preferred (*Annals*, I, i, 229), and in 1560 he was made arch-deacon of Ely (Le Neve, I, 352). Though he *claimed* his former parish of Settrington (*Annals*, I, i, 246), he seems to have received instead the livings of Haddenham and Wilburton, Cambs. As archdeacon of Ely he supported the articles against ceremonies in 1562. In 1568 he died.

B I a & b; B II; Frankfort, A III a 2; Strasbourg, A VII a; *D.N.B.*

457. WITHERS, FRANCIS: *Merchant and gent.* Of London. Wife.

On 7 January 1557, when Francis Withers[1] was received as a 'resident' of Geneva, he describes himself as 'of London'. Probably then he was the son of John Wither, of the Merchant Taylors' Company, believed by Venn to have been the father of

[1] In the transcript of the Livre des Anglois already spoken of (above, p. 24, note), printed at Geneva with a preface by Dr Ferrier Mitchell, is found a 'François Worchere', which name I take to be a misreading of 'Withers'.

Henry Withers, whom we know to have been Francis's brother (Clode, *Mems.* p. 560). This John Wither, or Withers, was one of the four members of the Merchant Taylors' Company summoned with the Lord Mayor to Greenwich on 8 July 1553 to approve the alteration of the succession in favour of Lady Jane Grey and he thus became signatory to the King's Letters Patent (*Chron. Q. Jane*, p. 100 and Clode, *Early Hist.* II, 107, 119). This fact would provide a sufficient motive for the retirement of no less than four of the family to Geneva, where they all became members of the English congregation on 5 November 1556. With Francis Withers were also admitted 'his wife, John Houghton, his servant and Ales Broughton, his maide'. On 16 December he was elected a deacon of the congregation and held the office continuously through 1558. Whether the 'wife' mentioned was Christian, daughter of Thomas Marbury, haberdasher of London, we cannot say, but such a person did marry *a* Francis Withers (Harl. Soc. I, 51). No information has come to light regarding the exile's later career in England, if, indeed, he lived to return. Geneva, A IV a & b.

458. WITHERS, HENRY: *Gent.* Of London. d. 1609.

Specifically named in the Livre des Anglois, when received on 5 November 1556 into the congregation, as a brother of Francis Withers, but, evidently, as is shown by the date of his death, a young boy while at Geneva. Venn believes him to have been then a student at Calvin's university, which is of course possible (IV, 444). On his return to England he matriculated from St John's College, Cambridge, in 1560 and received his M.A. from Trinity College in 1568. Then he migrated to Oxford for his B.D., and to Wittenberg for his D.D. (in 1592), having meanwhile been made vicar of Kensington, Middlesex (1572–1608). Geneva, A IV a.

459. WITHERS, STEPHEN: *Gent.* Of London.

A still younger brother of Francis and 'Harrye' Withers who was received into Knox's congregation on the same date as they. He, too, was probably a student at the university, for Strype mentions a Stephen Withers, doubtless the same man, who in 1561 made a translation of Calvin's *Treatise of Relics* from the French (*Annals*, I, i, 384) which was printed by Rowland Hall (*q.v.*) (Herbert's Ames, II, 802). Geneva, A IV a.

460. WITHERS, WILLIAM: *Merchant*(?). Of London.

Though not mentioned in the Livre des Anglois, he was received as a 'resident' of Geneva on 24 October 1558 (f. 264) and said to be of the 'royaulme d'Angleterre'. A William Withen, which name seems to have been interchangeable with that of Withers, was of Southend in the parish of Eltham, Kent, and was apparently a first cousin of Francis Withers or Withen (Harl. Soc. XLII, 188). But the identification is very uncertain.

Geneva, A IV b.

461. WOOD, HENRY: *Ex-religious and student.* Of Kent. Wife.

In Hans Dür's list at Aarau there appears a 'Heinricus Wud' who had lived in 'Dower', but was then lodging with his wife and three children in the house of Melchior Zenders (cf. Official List, p. 355 below). The mention of his place of origin as Dover makes it highly probable that he was the Henry Wood, once of the 'Monastery[1] of La Maison Dieu' (Masendewe) or St Mary's Hospital, Dover, of which John Thompson was Master (*Arch. Cant.* VII, 280, n. 2). In December 1534 this house had acknowledged the king's supremacy; in December 1536 it was surrendered to the king (8th Rep. Dep. Keeper of Records, App. II, p. 19) by the Master and the three brothers of whom Henry Wood was one. In Cardinal Pole's Book of Pensions, of date 24 February 1556, it is found that Wood had received at the dissolution a pension of 'vj li. xiij s. iiij d. per annum', which was still being paid him at the time of Pole's inquiry (*Arch. Cant.* II, 60). Perhaps the existence of his wife and children led to the withdrawal of Wood's pension, but, for whatever reason, he is found a refugee at Frankfort in June 1557, dwelling in the house of William Master (*H.S.P.* IV, 88). At that time he was alone, and he remained in Frankfort through 21 December 1557, when he signed the 'new discipline'. Then he must have sent for his family and with them gone to Aarau in August 1557. It would seem not unlikely that he was a younger son of the family of the Woods of Sandwich. One of his children, Eleazar, died at Aarau.

Frankfort, A III a 4 & b 2; B III b; Aarau, A I a & b.

462. WOOD, JOHN.

The appearance together of the two names John Graie and John Wood as signatories at Frankfort of the congregation's invitation to John Knox in September 1554 (*T.* p. 20) makes a strong presumption in favour of the identification of that John Graie (*q.v.*) as Lord John Grey, later of Pyrgo, and of the John Wood, as his steward, who on 23 January 1564 was to give his receipt for Lady Hertford (Lady Catherine Grey), 'her son, and servants', when she was placed in the keeping of her uncle after 'her enlargement from the Tower' (*Dom. Cal.* 1547–80, p. 235). John Wood's name

---

[1] A hospital founded for the entertainment of travellers and served by Augustinians (*Dugdale*, VI, pt. 2, Prefatory note and pp. 655–8).

appears at no other time at Frankfort and nowhere else abroad; neither does that of John Graie until after Elizabeth's accession, when on 3 January 1559 he reappears at Frankfort with a Henry Carowe whom we believe to be the queen's cousin Henry Carey, Lord Hunsdon. We shall not hazard any identification of the man's status or county, but it is not impossible that he was the John Wood who was Sir Thomas Smith's nephew and executor (Strype, *Smith*, pp. 151, 155, 158).

Frankfort, B III a.

463. WOOD, THOMAS: *Merchant*. Of London. Wife.

Since this Thomas Wood signed himself as 'of London' when received as a 'resident' of Geneva on 24 October 1555 (f. 123), it is fair to presume that he was the Thomas Wood, mercer of London and 'servant to Henry Locke', who was summoned before the Council on 12 November 1553 to answer for his 'lewde reportes towching that the late King shulde be yet on live (*sic*)...' (*P.C.A.* 1552–4, pp. 363–4). For this offence he was fined £100 and ordered to appear 'at the Starre Chamber on Frydaye next' (*ibid.* p. 367). Wood, however, failed to appear, and we must suppose had fled from England leaving his sureties, Edmond Coles, mercer, and Geffrey Newton, grocer, to pay the forfeit (*ibid.* p. 364). As he arrived at Frankfort with William Whittingham on 27 June 1554, the date of his flight between 17 November and 'Frydaye next' 1553 may supply the date for Whittingham's own departure from London, for the two men remained in close connection throughout the full period of exile. Also Wood is described as a 'servant' of Henry Locke who was an English merchant stationed at Antwerp. Hence it is quite possible that Locke harboured the two Englishmen through that winter and that from Antwerp they negotiated with the Frankfort magistrates, through Valeran Pullain, for their reception at Frankfort in the spring.

Throughout their stay there, Wood faithfully supported Whittingham's policy. He endorsed the latter's invitation of 2 August to the other English colonies to unite with them (*T*. pp. 8–13); he subscribed to the invitation to Knox (*T*. p. 20); he signed Frankfort's refusal to conform to the Prayer Book (*T*. p. 26); he was one of the eighteen who announced their intention to secede from the colony (*T*. p. 55); and, still with Whittingham, he arrived at Geneva on 13 October 1555. With him then were his wife, Anne, and his daughter, Debora. His reception as a 'resident' of Geneva has already been mentioned, and in 1557 he was chosen a senior of Knox's congregation. In September 1559 Knox, in a letter to Anna, Henry Locke's widow, mentions Wood's name in connection with the journey of Knox's wife to Scotland (Laing, VI, 78–9).

Antwerp (?); Frankfort, B III a; Geneva, A IV a & b.

464. WOODDE, WILLIAM: *Gent.* Of Shropshire(?). d. 1598(?).

Though not mentioned by Jung as one of the English colony at Frankfort, William Woodd was certainly a member of it in July 1556, when John Brett presented his letter to Mistress Wilkinson in the presence 'of one Chambers, John Ade and William Woodde englisshmen' (Brett, p. 119). On the same day Woodd was also present when Brett left similar letters upon John Hales, who 'after many hotte wordes and meanes' tried to 'rydde [Brett] owte of his doores' (*ibid.* p. 120). But these are the only references I can find to any William Woodd abroad, and there is nothing but plausible dates, and the similarity of the spelling of the name, to support the suggestion that he was William Woodd of Shynewood, Salop, third son of Peter Woodd whose wife, Felicia, was a daughter of Henry Warham and Anne Harrington (Woodd, *Family of Woodd*, p. 36). This William Woodd was still living at Shynewood in 1593–8, but died without issue.

Frankfort, B IV a.

465. WROTHE, OLIVER: *Gent.* Of Middlesex.

Second son of Robert Wrothe of Durants in Enfield, Middlesex (*Arch. Cant.* XII, 315), and brother to Sir Thomas Wrothe (below). While Sir Thomas was an exile at Strasbourg, Oliver, who had evidently been implicated in the Dudley conspiracy, was at Paris. He tried to excuse his presence there in doubtful company, by explaining to Nicholas Wotton that he had 'by ignorance frequented the company of some in England who afterwards were committed to prison, and being a poor young man and fearful of getting into trouble' that he 'had fled hither, where he has lived quietly, saving sometimes he has been in company with such here as be offenders'. But he 'begs their Majesties'' pardon and asks for permission to return to his native country (*For. Cal.* 1553–8, p. 278). On 1 December 1556 Wotton wrote to Sir William Petre that 'the bearer' of his letter, Sir Thomas Wrothe's brother, was venturing to return home since Dudley and the rebels had sworn his death and had 'sent men to Paris to watch and kill him' (*ibid.* p. 279).

Paris, B v b 1.

466. WROTHE, Sir THOMAS: *Gent.* Of Middlesex. Wife. 1516–73.

Son and heir of Robert Wrothe of Durants in Enfield, co. Middlesex, Sir Thomas Wrothe, Chief Gentleman of the Bed-Chamber to Edward VI, married Mary, daughter of Lord Chancellor Rich (*Arch. Cant.* XII, 315). The fact that he had a son called Gerson who later had to be naturalized by act of parliament, shows that his wife was with him in exile. Both by interest and conviction,

Wrothe was heavily committed to the Edwardian Reformation. He had received from the king large grants of abbey lands in Middlesex and also in Essex (*Mem.* II, i, 387–9); he had been present at both conferences on the Sacrament in November and December 1551 (*Cranmer*, pp. 385–6); and one of the last acts of Edward's government was to appoint him Lieutenant of Middlesex (*P.C.A.* 1552–4, p. 277). Thus Northumberland was able to secure his support for the alteration of the succession (*Chron. Q. Jane*, p. 100) and in consequence Wrothe followed Robert Dudley to the Tower on 27 July 1553 (*Grey Friar's Chron.* p. 81). Exactly when he was released does not appear, but it was in time for him to be implicated so heavily in the Duke of Suffolk's second rising that Gardiner instructed Sir William Petre that he 'muste in any wise send for th' apprehension of Wroth, and this matier wyl cume out and towche fully' (*Chron. Q. Jane*, p. 184: 27 January 1553/4). Yet Sir Thomas was not apprehended, and managed to escape to the Continent with Sir John Cheke, who travelled with the queen's licence (*For. Cal.* 1553–8, p. 112). So far, however, I have found no confirmation for the statement that Wrothe too had been given a permit (cf. *D.N.B.*). In any case the two men arrived together in Padua on 10 July 1554 (*For. Cal.* p. 112), and there Sir Thomas Hoby met them on 23 August (Cam. Misc. x, 116). Two months later both Wrothe and Cheke went with the Hobys on their pleasure party to Mantua,[1] and in August 1555, still together, they left Padua because of the plague and joined the Hobys at Caldero on their journey northward (*ibid.* p. 120). By 28 August the party had reached Augsburg. Then somewhere on the route Wrothe and Cheke separated from the others and went to Strasbourg, where they remained, while the Hobys continued on to Frankfort (f. 123). Late in August of the next year (1556) came John Brett seeking Sir Thomas on the queen's business;[2] yet 'all that while colde [he] here no worde of Sir Thomas Wrothes being there nor that he bene sene in the saide Towne [Strasbourg] in xiiij dayes afore [his] comminge thither' (Brett, p. 130). But Brett once gone, Sir Thomas emerged from hiding and, perhaps for greater security, petitioned the magistrates for a permit of 'residence' (Protocols, vol. 35, f. 337), which in the following year he asked to have renewed on the ground that he could not yet return to England because of religion (*ibid.*). His request was granted on 1 September 1557, and on the

[1] Sir Thomas Hoby seems here to have been careless about his dates, for he says that they set out on 21 October but were back in Padua on 19 October of the same year (Cam. Misc. x, 117–19). For the second 'October' we should probably read 'November'.

[2] Had he been travelling with a licence he would not, presumably, have been mentioned in the commission, for Cheke was not.

29th he was one of those who signed an attempt at reconciliation between Strasbourg and Frankfort (*T.* p. 174), after which he does not emerge from obscurity until 19 October 1558, when he again asks for an extension of his right to residence. But the permit carried with it no civic rights, while it exacted a payment to the town of £8 for the year and a promise of obedience to the city's regulations (Protocols, vol. 36, f. 530vo). Two months from that day, 19 October, Sir Thomas Wrothe and Sir Anthony Cooke began their return journey to England (20 December, *Z.L.* I, 5). But any hopes which they may have entertained of public advancement under Elizabeth were not to be realized. 'Believe me', wrote Jewel to Peter Martyr a year later, 'believe me they are neither in the rank or position you suppose them to be, and in which all [our] Israel hoped they would be.' He further excused the failure of the two knights to write to their friends abroad by saying that 'they were really ashamed to write', and such was their chagrin that it seems actually to have brought on a severe attack of ague (*Z.L.* I, 53, 59). Once again it is evident that, to Elizabeth's mind, a traitor to one queen was like to be a traitor to another: Mary's enemies were not looked upon as her friends. And as member for Middlesex in the parliament of 1559 Sir Thomas Wrothe was prominent in the party opposed to the Supremacy Bill—to any extension that is of the royal prerogative. True to the family tradition his grandson, another Sir Thomas Wrothe, sat in the Long Parliament and moved the impeachment of Charles I.

Padua, B IV b; Strasbourg, A VII a; *D.N.B.*

467. WULMER (WOLMER, WILMER), ANTHONY: *Gent.* Of Lincolnshire.

In Hans Dür's list at Aarau, Anthony Wulmer is described as a 'half-noble' who had been obliged to become a servant because his property had been confiscated. His birthplace was said to be 'Schwinshet' in the county of 'Lingkon', and he was then living in the house of Melchior Zenders. 'Schwinshet' is obviously Swineshead in Lincolnshire, where the family of Wolmer is found to have lived. And this Anthony was the third son of Richard Wolmer (d. 1564) and in 1573 was parson of Bloxham, probably through the influence of his mother Isabel, daughter of Nicholas Upton. In 1564 she is called 'of Bloxham, widow' (Harl. Soc. LII, 1105).

Aarau, A I a & b.

468. WYNDHAM, SIGISMUND: *Gent.* Of Norfolk.

Student at Padua in the winter of 1555–6 and electionarius of the English students for 1556–7 (Andrich, pp. 31, 131). As the name

Sigismund seems to have been used at times as a foreign equivalent for Edmund (cf. 'Harvel' above) and one with a distinctly protestant flavour to it, we hazard the guess that this was Edmund Wyndham, younger brother (perhaps half-brother) of Thomas (below) and probably fourth son of Sir Edmund Wyndham of Felbrigge, Norfolk (Blomefield, VIII, 114). If so he would be the same Edmund who matriculated from St John's College, Cambridge, in 1564 and was admitted at Lincoln's Inn in November 1568 (Venn, IV, 436). Sir Thomas Hoby speaks of meeting a 'Mr Windham' in Padua in August 1554 (Cam. Misc. X, 116) who is more likely to have been Sigismund (Edmund) than his brother Thomas. In 1577, Edmund Wyndham was still alive (*Dom. Cal.* 1547–80, p. 575, where he is called the brother of Roger Wyndham, and Roger was the brother of Thomas; cf. Blomefield) and in 1579 was imprisoned for an affray with Lord Rich (*ibid.* p. 620).

Padua, A VI.

469. WYNDHAM, THOMAS: *Gent.* Of Norfolk. d. 1592(?).

Probably the third son of Sir Edmund Wyndham of Felbrigge, and so younger brother of Francis Wyndham, Justice of the Common Pleas, who married Elizabeth, daughter of Sir Nicholas Bacon, and died in 1592 (Blomefield, VIII, 114). He first appears abroad at Venice in 1555 in the train of the Earl of Bedford, and was one of those specially licensed by the Signory to bear arms (*Ven. Cal.* 1555–6, p. 145). Later he appears to have gone to Rome, where Sir Edward Carne reports to Queen Mary on 26 September 1556 the presence of three Englishmen, two of whom were 'young gentlemen of the names of Windham and Rugge (*q.v.*) who say they came to see Rome' (*For. Cal.* 1553–8, p. 260).

Venice, B v b 1; Rome, B v b 2.

470. YONGE, JAMES: *Tailor.* Wife.

In 1556 there came to Geneva, James Yonge and his wife, Anne, who were received into the English congregation before 12 July. When on 7 January 1557 he became a 'resident' of Geneva, he was designated 'couturier' (f. 180). It is possible that he was the James Young to whom Knox sent a message by Anna Locke on 15 October 1559 (*For. Cal.* 1559–60, p. 40). Mrs Locke, Thomas Cole and James Young were then at Frankfort, probably on their way home.

Geneva, A IV a & b.

*YOUNG, JOHN.

This name, like Michael Cope's (*q.v.*), is that of a misappropriated Englishman. Though two letters concerning the settlement of

English exiles at Aarau are quoted by Hastings Robinson as written by 'John Young' to Bullinger on 17 May and 5 August 1557 (*O.L.* I, 164, n. 1, 167, n. 2), I am told by Professor Nabholz, of the University of Zurich, that he was not 'John Young' at all, but 'Johannes Jung', a Swiss from Bischofszell in the Canton of Thurgau; that he was at first 'Custos' of the monastery of Petershausen, near Constance; then a protestant preacher in Constance, who, eventually driven from there, became pastor of St Peterskirche at Basle and died in 1562.

471. YOUNG (YONGE), THOMAS, LL.D.: *Priest.* Of Pembroke-
      shire. 1507–68.

Son of John Young of Hodgeston, Pembrokeshire, and both student and principal (1542–6) of Broadgates Hall, Oxford. In 1547 he became precentor of St David's, and was also commissary to Bishop Ferrar, with whom, like so many others of the bishop's household, Young had a violent quarrel (*Mem.* III, ii, no. XLVI). As one of the six protestant members of the first convocation under Mary (Dixon, IV, 75) he publicly avowed his principles and so may have felt it prudent to leave England, but no trace of him has been found abroad though Strype, in an ambiguous paragraph, places him either in Friesland or at Wesel (*Mem.* III, i, 233). On Young's return to England he was consecrated bishop of St David's in 1560 (Le Neve, I, 316) and looked for patronage to Robert Dudley (*Dom. Cal.* 1547–80, p. 151). In 1561 he was made archbishop of York in the room of Nicholas Heath (*ibid.* p. 161 and Le Neve, III, 114).

B I a & b; B II; Wesel (?); *D.N.B.*

472. YOUNG (JONG), WILLIAM: *Gent.* Of Sussex(?).

A William Jong (Young or Yonge?), called of 'Westwittrich', was admitted to burgher rights at Frankfort on 7 March 1555 (Jung, p. 24) and paid 2 fl. 5 s. 1 d. 'Bürgergeld' (*ibid.* p. 54). There is, however, no other mention of him at Frankfort nor anywhere else abroad: he must either have returned to England or died at Frankfort. At a guess Westwittrich may be a Germanized form of West Wittering in Sussex, and there a William Yong, son of a John Yong who had come out of Yorkshire, temp. Edward IV, died in 1553 (Harl. Soc. LIII, 185). The family is said to be the same as that of Thomas Young (above), later archbishop of York, and William married a Bowyer of Lethorne. All the circumstances suggest that it was either this William, who, disappearing abroad, might well be thought to have died in 1553, or a younger son of his named William, for the only recorded sons are John and Anthony. I rather lean to the first suggestion, for it is unlikely that a younger son would have become a burgher, and the date 1553 may easily be an error for 1555. Nicholas Yonge the musician, born at Lewes, was also of this family (*D.N.B.*).

Frankfort, A III a 1.

List of the followers of Sir Thomas Stafford at the taking of Scarborough Castle. Strype, *Mem.* III, ii, no. LXXII.

*Thomas Stafford, gent.
Mr Brissell, Frenchman
Rychard Saunders, gent. } Five prisoners in the Tower of London.
*Willyam Scowell, gent.
*John Proctor, gent.

John Browne	*Roger Raynoldes	Rogere Thomas
Owen Jones	John Momford, Scot	Robert Hangate, Scot
Henrye Gardyner	Thomas Spencher	John Wallyce
John Watsone, Scot	William Wilke	John Donnynge
John Graye, Scot	John Adames	Jaques Lartoys, Fren
Willyam Williamson	Willyam Palmer	John Thomas
Anthony Parriuall	Laurence Alsop	Thomas Jurdyne
Clement Tyled	*John Bradforde	John Creswell
John Wilborne	Thomas Wilkinson	Thomas Warre

Those with the * are to be found in the Census.

NOTE. Cf. above, p. 305. John Throckmorton the conspirator of 1556, usually spoken of as a 'kinsman' of Sir Nicholas, has never, I think, been exactly identified. Strype has confused him with the John Throckmorton, Master of Requests in 1557, who, though brother to Sir Nicholas (cf. Strype's Index; *P.C.A.* 1554–6, pp. 70, 188; Harl. Soc. XII, 88–9) was yet a faithful adherent of Queen Mary. Another John, great-grandson of Sir George Throckmorton of Coughton, is probably the man, in spite of the intervening generations. Both the Warwickshire (Harl. Soc. XII) and the Huntingdonshire pedigrees (Cam. Soc. 43, pp. 123–4) agree as to his descent but not as to his wife, yet it is by his wife, said by the latter to be the daughter of Thomas Wilford, that the conspirator's identity can probably be fixed. For in 1557, the year after Throckmorton's execution, three of the family of Wilford appear as exiles at Frankfort for no apparent reason (above pp. 332–3). One of them, a Thomas, was then twenty-seven. If he was John Throckmorton's brother-in-law, his presence at Frankfort would be fully explained. And it is also significant that in the Huntingdonshire pedigree, this John is said to have died before his father.

APPENDIX OF DOCUMENTS

I. ARCHIVES OF AARAU

Entries regarding the English Exiles at Aarau, taken from the town archives, and including the 'Official List' of the members of the colony.

Englische Flüchtlinge in Aarau
1557/1559.[1]

I. Engelländer.

Zewüssen, das uff den einliften Tage Augstens (1557) in unser Statt Arouw kommen sind Herre Thomas Leverus, ein Predicant, sampt ettlichen mer uß Engelland, so von wegen des heligen Euangeliums vertriben sind von der Künigin Mariae, weliche nach Absterben ires Bruders des cristenlichen Künigs Eduardi seligen angehept ze regieren und zu irem gemachel genommen Künig Philippum, des Keysers Caroli sone, uß Hispanien, weliche treffen= lichen wider das helig Euangelium tyrannisiert und das Babstumb aller dingen widerumb uffgericht und die Euangelischen durchächtet, veriagt und verbrönt etc. Und habend also ein offnen Fürdrung= briefe von u. g. Herren und Obern von Bern byhendig gezeygt, das ir Gnaden Wille sye, by uns und öbriger ir Landschaft inen Vnderschlouf zegeben. Hieruff begärende sy also umb Gottes und des heligen Euangeliums willen fründlich uffzenemmen, so wellend sy gar niemands beschwärlich sin.

Also habent mine herren die burgere inen zugelassen ungeuarlichen bis in die zechen oder einlif Eeen hinder uns zezüchen, doch mit Bescheydenheyt, wann es unsern gnedigen Herren von Bern, ouch einer Burgerschaft hie zu Arouw wolgeuellig, das man sy möge yeder Zyte widerumb hinwäg wysen, und hat man inen also gar keinen Inzug nit abgenommen, ouch sonst keinswägs beschwärt, sonders vergünstiget, wo sy Herbärg bekommen mögend, sich allda niderzelassen und umb ir Gelt inzekouffen wie andre Burger.

Also sind sy hie beliben ein Jar lang und widerumb in dem andren Jare bis uff den letsten Tag Decembris, in dem LVIII. Jare

[1] Edited by Dr W. Merz-Diebold, and first printed in the *Kirchliches Jahrbuch der reformierten Schweiz*, VI, 1900.

do iſt inen Botſchaft kommen, diſere Künigin Mariam vß Schicken
Gottes Thodes verſcheyden, vnd das an ire Statt ir Schwöſter
Eliſabeth Künigin worden, welche ouch dem Euangelio anhold vnd
ſy die Vertribnen in ir Land widerumb eruordert. Alſo ſind ſy in
dem Januario des LIX. Jares vaſt fründlich vnd mit hocher Dankbarkeyt nach vnd nach heimgezogen, Gott verlyche inen ein ſälige
Widervart. Sy habend ouch in miner Junkeren der Waldneren
Roßgarten zwüſchet den Rentzenthoren Thuch gemacht vnd gewäben
vnd daſſelbig in vnſerer Begrebnus vffgeſpannen.

Hienach volgend die Namen der Eerenlüthen, ſo vß Engelland by
vns geweſen.

Herre Thomas Leuerus ir Predicant vnd Johannes ſin Bruder
ſind zehus geweſen by Hans Thürren.

Her Michael Couerdal, ein Biſchof geweſen zu Excitorcens mit
ſiner Frouwen vnd zwöyen Kinden ſind in dem Cloſter zeherberg
geweſen etc.

Stand hienach alle eygentlichen im Januario des 59. Jares den 8.
tag ſchier im End dis Buchs.[1]

II. Angelländer.[2]

Es habend mine Herren die Bürger gutigklichen vergünſtiget den
Engelländeren by vns Winthyerszyten vnſere Kyrchen vnd gemeynen
Tempel Winthyerszyten vnd nebend denen Stünden, als wir vnſere
Predginen habend, ze geprüchen in aller Zücht vnd Erſamheit vnd
allda ire Predginen thun vnd die Sacramenten miniſtrieren.

III. Engelländer.[3]

Vff den letſten Tag Nouembris diſers 59. (!) Jares habend die
guten frommen Lüth vß Engelland verſtanden vnd vernommen,
das ire Vervolgeri Künigin Maria Thodes verſcheyden vnd Eliſa-
bethen, ire Schwöſter, an ire Statt Künigin worden, welche ſy

---

[1] Dieſe Eintragung, ſowie die, worauf verwieſen wird (vom Jahre 1559),
ſind von der Hand des Samuel Meyer, eines Sohnes des Stadtſchreibers
Gabriel Meyer, der folgende Abſatz dagegen vom Stadtſchreiber ſelbſt
geſchrieben.

[2] Eintragung ohne Datum; das folgende iſt Mittwüchen vor Galli 1557.

[3] Eintragung ohne Datum; das vorhergehende iſt Donſtags nach Hylary
(19. Jänner), das folgende Mittwuchen nach Letare (8. März) 1559.

allenthalben widerumb in ir Land berüffe vnd eruordre. Derohalben
find fy im Januario difers LIX. Jars von vns mit groſſer Dankbarkeyt
gefcheyden. Gott verlyche inen ein fröliche Widervart.
Vnd ſind alſo diß ir aller, ſo by vns gewonet,
Namen vnd Anzal.

Herre Thomas Leuerus, ir Predicant, vnd Johannes ſin Bruder,
ſind by Hans Thürren zehus gewäſen.

Her Michael Couerdall ein Biſchof geweſen zu Excerticens mit
ſiner Hußfrouwen vnd zwöyen Kinden, iſt im Kloſter gewäſen.

Rogerus Hart mit ſinem Wyb vnd einem Kinde, by Laurentzen
Wyerman, ein alter Predicant.

Robertus Powall mit ſinem Wyb vnd zwöyen Kinden, by
Mathis Thürren.

Richardus Laughernus mit ſinem Wyb, einer Jungkfrouwen vnd
ſüben Kinder, iſt by Heinrich Bär dem Wäber gewäſen.

Thomas Allin mit ſinem Wyb, einer Schwöſter vnd zwöyen
Kinden, in Mauritz Meggers dem nidren Huſe.

Thomas Turpinus, ein Edelman mit ſinem Wyb vnd zwöyen
Kinden, in Sebaſtian zum Schwärt Huſe dem hindren.

Johannes Pretie, ein Edelman mit ſinem Wyb, in Michel
Rudtſchis Hus.

Philippus Nicolis mit ſinem Wyb, in Laurentz Wyermans Hus.

Johannes Ancley, ein Edelman, mit ſinem Wyb vnd zwöyen
Kinden, in Jacoben Murer des Schumachers Huſe.

Anthonius Robſon der Byerſüder oder ir Schnyder mit ſinem
Wyb vnd ſechs Kinden, in Hans Trinklers des Zieglers obren Hus
in der Vorſtatt.

Gulihelmus Cheſton mit ſinem Wyb, Richardus Cooke mit ſinem
Wyb, Margaretha Dibney ein wydtwen mit zwöyen Kindern, vnd
Gulihelmus Betts mit ſinem Wyb, alle Wäber vnd Spinner vnd
in Joachim Schmutzingers dem niederen Huſe geſeſſen.

Thomas Öpſchere mit ſinem Wyb vnd einem Kind, Eliſabetha
Wardenn, Richardus Teterſaul mit ſinem Wyb, Elſa Boo, Richardus
Vnswortz vnd Thomas Warbertone mit ſinem Wyb, alle des
Thuchgewärbs vnd in Hans Gyſins Hus geſeſſen.

Heinricus Wood mit ſinem Wyb vnd zwöyen Kindern, Rogerus
Aſchton vnd Anthonius Wulmer, ein junger Edelman vnd doch ir
aller Diener, alle in Melchior Zenders Hus off dem Kilchhof
geſeſſen.

Edmondus Barcker mit sinem Wyb vnd einem Kind, in Jacob Nüsperlis Hus gesessen.

Gwaltherus Kelley mit sinem Wyb vnd zwöyen Kindern, in Hans Francken vndren Stüblin gewesen.

Margaretha Adams, ein alte Frouw vom Adel mit einer Tochter, in Michel Rudtschis Hus.

Rychardus Playsto mit sinem Wyb, ein Artzet in dem Closter.

Rychardus Proude, ein Edelman, in Mauritz Meggers dem nidern Hus.

Georgius Cheston der Tischmacher, in der Färwi ossen.

Der Kinden Namen, so hie worden sind.

Thomas Turpinus, ein Son Thomae Turpini.

Daniell Robson, ein Son Anthony Robson.

Susanna Laughern, ein Thochter Richardi Laughern.

Nathaniell Powall, ein Son Roberti Powall.

Johannes Ypchere, ein Son Thome Ypchier.

Johannes Audlee, ein Son Johannis Audlee.

Deren Namen, so allhie Thodes verscheyden.

Rowlandus Wilkeüson.

Georgius Ypchier, ein Son Thome Ypcheir.

Jhon Ypcheir, ouch desselbigen Son.

Eleasarus Wood, ein Son Heinrici Wood.

Eleasarus Powall, ein Son Roberti Powall.

Thomas Hopkens, ein Son Richardi Hopkens zu Basel wonende.

Thomas Turpinus, ein Son Thome Turpimi (!).

Der Rat zu Bern war von der menschenfreundlichen Aufnahme der Vertriebenen in Aarau sehr erbaut; er schrieb am 30. Brach=monat 1558 an Schultheiß und Rat zu Aarau, die englischen Ver=triebenen hätten ihrem Seckelmeister gerühmt, wie „vil guts ir inen bewysind vnd wie brüderlich ir ooch gegen inen erzöugind"; sie sollen so weiter fahren und der Anerkennung der Obrigkeit versichert sein.[1]

[1] Stadtarchiv Aarau: Akten Bd. 167, Missiven III, Nr. 67.

II. ARCHIVES OF BASLE

ENGLISHMEN AT THE UNIVERSITY OF BASLE, 1554-9

From the Matrikel, I, 1460–1568, ff. 191–201ᵛᵒ.[1] Basle, Universitätsbibliothek, Mscr. AN. II, 3, f. 191.

Amondesham, William	[Gulielmus Amundesam, Anglus] VI		1556
Audley, John	[Ioannes Audlaeus, Anglus] VI sol		1556
Bale, John	[Jo'es Baleus, Anglus, quondam Episcopus Ossoriensis in Hybernia]		1555
Banks, James	[Jacobus Bantus, Anglus]		1555
Bartholomew, John	[Ioannes Bartholomeus, Anglus] duos thaleros soluerunt[2]		1556
Bentham, Thomas	[Thomas Benthamus Anglus]		1555
Blake(?), John	[Ioannes blochus Anglus] Maius 12 VI		1558
Bradbridge, Augustine	[Augustinus Bradbrydge anglus VI Dioces. Cicestren̄]		1554
Bunny, Richard	[Richardus Bunnus Anglus] XV		1554
Cockburn, Alexander	[Alexander Cogburnus, Scotus]		1555
Denny, Anthony	[Anthonius Denneius ⎫ nobiles		1555
Denny, Charles	[Carolus Denneius ⎬ ex		1555
Denny, Henry	[Henricus Denneius ⎭ Anglia]		1555
Dodman, John	[Ioannes Dodmanus, Anglus] VI		1556
Foxe, John	[Ioannes Foxus, Anglus. exul. n.p. exil]		1556
Gilby, Anthony	[Anthonius Gylbaeus, Anglus]		1555
Goodman, Christopher	[Christophorus Goodmannus Anglus Cestrensis] VI		1554
Grason (Gresham), Richard	[D. Richardus Grassanus, Londinen, Anglus] VI		1556
Harlestone, Robert(?)	[Rupertus Herlesdonus Anglus] VI Octob. 8		1557
Holiday, Adam	[Adamus Hallidutz Anglus Northumbren̄] VI		1554
Horne, Robert	[Robertus Horn Anglus] VI		1558
Hugh, Cuthbert	[Cutbertus Hugonijus eboracensis] nihil		1554
Humphrey, Laurence	[Laurentius Homphredus, Anglus]		1555

[1] Of which facsimiles are now (1935) in the Bodleian Library.
[2] Sir Francis Knollys and Richard Springham shared in this payment.

Kelke, Roger	[Rogerus Relkus, Anglus]		1555
Knollys, Francis	[Franciscus Knolleus]		1556
	duos thaleros soluerunt[1]		
Lewis, Michael	[Michael Leuus ex Barthen An-	VI	1557
	glus] November 17		
Mayhewe, Anthony	[Antonius Mayhewe Anglus]	VI	1558
Morwin, Peter	[Petrus Morwingus Anglus]	VI	1554
Pilkington, James	[Iacobus Pilkinton, Anglus]	VI	1556
Poyntz, Gabriel	[Gabriel Poines Anglus]	XV	1554
Sefold, George	[Georgius Sefoldus Anglus] Oc-	VI	1557
	tober 15		
Stanton, John	[Johannes Stantonus, Anglus]	VI	1555
Steward, Thomas	[Thomas Stuardus Anglus]	VI	1558
	Maius 15		
Soothous,	[Christopherus Suthesus Anglus]	VI	1557
Christopher	December 10		
Springham,	[Richardus Springham, Anglus]		1556
Richard	duos thaleros soluerunt[1]		
Temple, William	[Guilielmus Templeus, Anglus]		1555
Walsingham,	[Franciscus Walsinghamus nobilis		1555
Francis	ex Anglia]		

PETITION OF THE EXILED ENGLISHMEN, APRIL 10th 1555

Basle, Staatsarchiv: Ratsbüchlein, 1553–64, Niederlassungsakten, L5, 1555 ff.
[In German: Unpublished.]

To the noble, worthy, righteous, prudent, honourable and wise lord burgomaster and councillors of the honourable city of Basle: dear lords and fathers. Your worships are well aware what strange reversals of fortune ever afflict the human race, but most especially those people who prove themselves god-fearing. So that he who but lately was in high position, prosperous and living in peace, is now brought low, suffers want, and is exposed to great persecution: And he who formerly could give others kindly encouragement, lodging and shelter, must now himself seek comfort, aid, and support from other members of God's community. As regards the condition of Englishmen during recent times, honourable and wise lords, as well as to-day under Spanish and popish tyranny, which is grievously oppressive both in temporal and spiritual government, your Worships know already (since you have shown great mercy towards us, and had pity on us, as we have often heard from many people). It is therefore unnecessary to describe it in full. Instead of piety there is superstition; godless people have supplanted the devout, and whosoever favours righteousness is exposed to danger.

[1] See note on p. 357.

Because the persecution has increased exceedingly and still continues, and because there is little room for those who will not submit to these conditions, many of our countrymen must of necessity leave their dear native land, and in God's name look further afield, where the Lord of Heaven, to Whom the earth with its fulness belongs, will show them a house and home. Consequently some must look for quarters for themselves and their dependents here, others elsewhere, because they can not all find lodging together in one town. Accordingly, your Worships, our need at the moment compels us to come humbly to you begging for shelter. Our wretched condition is excuse enough for presenting our situation in many words and with urgent entreaties, in the hope that we may obtain this from your Worships. As, however, we think that our present lamentable situation and manifold need are sufficiently evident, we will merely thank your Worships in God's name and in filial reverence, commending ourselves entirely to your kindness and mercy. May the faithful God, who alone knows what is good for each one, guide your hearts, so that you may act in this matter in whatever way may be most profitable for your Worships, the City, the Country, and the Church; and may He afford you fatherly protection in these dangerous times.

Your Worships' ever willing servants,
The poor, exiled Englishmen.
[Unsigned]

Endorsed:

Petition of the exiled Englishmen (in a later hand:) for protection, 10th April, in the year LV. (1555), presented and heard.

PASSPORT ISSUED TO THE ENGLISH EXILES AT AARAU[1]

Basle, Staatsarchiv: Kirchenakten, A. 3, f. 198 (Religionssachen).
[In Latin: Unpublished.]

We, the consul and senate of the Swiss town of Berne, confirm and make known by these presents: That when the bearers of these letters were expelled from their country by Queen Mary of England on account of the Religion of the Gospel, and were sent into exile, they came to us, begging us to allow them to take up their abode within our territory. This we did for the sake of duty and Christian love. And they dwelt in our town of Aarau for the space of a year.

---

[1] Cf. The Council of Basle to Queen Elizabeth, 11 February 1558/9, *For. Cal.* 1558–9, no. 319; and The Council and State of Berne to the Queen, 11 January 1558/9, *ibid.* no. 226.

Now, however, since by the favourable Will of God and the death of Queen Mary the Kingdom of England has come into the hands of the most serene lady Elizabeth, they have prepared themselves for the journey home, having been bidden by her to return to their own country. For this reason they have requested from us a permit to depart, certifying to the original grant of residence and also to their good conduct while they were living in our town of Aarau. This we cannot lawfully refuse them. For we have been truthfully informed by our subjects in the aforesaid town, that each and every one of them has lived, behaved, and conducted himself there as an honest and peaceful Christian. Therefore we earnestly entreat the magistrates, governors, and their officers, through whose territory they will pass, to be well disposed towards them, to treat them kindly, and to allow them to come and go freely. You will do us a favour in this matter, for which when occasion offers we shall requite you.

Given under our hand and our seal, on the 2nd day of the month of January, in the year 1559 after the birth of Christ Jesus, our Saviour.

[Unsigned]

ENGLISH EXILES RECEIVED AS BURGHERS AT BASLE

Basle, Staatsarchiv: Öffnungsbuch, VIII (1530–45), ff. 177–9

LADY DOROTHY STAFFORD.

On Wednesday, 3 November 1557, my lords received and accepted the noble lady Dorothy Stafford from England as a citizen. According to the decision of a worthy councillor, the gist and purport of the civil oath was read to her in French by the town-clerk in the presence of the highest 'Knecht'. Instead of swearing the oath, she undertook to observe it, by giving her hand, pledging herself, and making a promise. f. 177.

LADY DOROTHY STAFFORD.

On Saturday, 14 January 1559, Lady Stafford from England was, at her friendly request, given an open permit, since she wished to return to England; and her right of citizenship was extended for two years, regardless of her departure, so that if she were to return here in two years, the magistrate would recognise her again as a citizen; but under one condition: namely, that in the event of any misfortune befalling her in the meantime, one should render her no assistance, apart from what might be accomplished and achieved by letters of recommendation [?].

Ibid.

HUGH SINGLETON (Hugo Singlettion).

On Saturday, 11 June 1558, Hugo Singleton, the book-binder from England, was accepted as a citizen, and swore according to the usual custom. *Ibid.* f. 179.

HUGH SINGLETON.

On Monday, 5 September 1559, the right of citizenship was extended for a year on behalf of Hugo Singlettion (*sic*), as he wished to return to England. *Ibid.*

Register of admissions (Eintrittsrodel) to the Saffron-Guild (Safranzunft-Archiv, 25, p. 221).

HUGO SHYNGLITON from London, 1558. Admission to the Saffron-Guild.

Item. On the Sunday before St John's day at the solstice, the worthy Hugo Shyngiliton, the book-binder from London, in England, appeared before the chief alderman and six others, and begged my lords to be so kind as to allow him to join an honourable guild. Whereupon my lords granted him his petition, and allowed him to join an honourable guild. The decision was given, but at the same time he was charged the same amount as everyone else, and therefore paid 4 lb. 14 b[atzen?] to his guild, according to the regulations of the guild—under Herr Thomnann Sylberberg, Master at this time.

Basle, Staatsarchiv: St Clara R Corpus, 1557–8.

f. 17ᵛᵒ Rent of the Clarakloster, 1557.

The Englishmen at the St Clara Closter gave yearly as rent for the same, 24 lb.

III. ARCHIVES OF STRASBOURG

A CALENDAR OF THE 'PROTOCOLS OF THE COUNCIL AND 21' OF STRASBOURG, 1554–8

Vol. 32, 1554

f. 113 THOMAS HETTENUS *Wednesday, 4 April* 1554.

Thomas Hettenus [Heton] of London, England. He would like to purchase civic rights, but since it is forbidden in England to acquire citizenship elsewhere, this would entail the forfeiture of his English rights and involve him in grave consequences. He therefore begs to be accepted as a resident under the protection of my lords of the Council and swears in return fidelity to the town and gives pledge of good conduct.

His testimonials will be looked into and the matter given due consideration. Carle Mieg and Odratzheim.

f. 118ᵛᵒ THOMAS HETTENUS *Saturday, 7 April* 1554.

Enquiry by Herr Hans von Odertzheim[1] and Herr Carl Mieg into the character of Thomas Hettenus [Heton] who wishes to become a resident.

John Abel and Doctor Peter Martin[2] have given testimony to his respectability in London. His grounds for emigration were religious only. He seeks to be accepted as were Reichart Hillis[3] and Johann Burghart [Burcher] and agrees to pay dues (as the latter) to the bishop and £12 as a guarantee to the town.

f. 131ᵛᵒ JOHN ABEL *Saturday, 14 April* 1554.

John Abel of England reports that three English noblemen wish to go to Basle, but being ignorant of the route, are applying for two servants [to escort them].

Granted upon payment of the necessary fee.

f. 167 JOHN ABEL *Monday, 7 May* 1554.

John Abel, in the name and on behalf of three English knights, namely, Morisin, Johan Kick [Cheke] and Anthoni Kuck [Cooke], begs the services of two natives of Basle [to act as guides].

Granted.

---

[1] Odratzheim, Alsace.

[2] Probably Peter Martyr (Vermigli), late regius professor of divinity at Oxford.

[3] Cf. Hilles to Bullinger, from Strasbourg, 18 September 1541 (*O.L.* I, 218), and note that the price of such citizenship had risen considerably, from 10 florins to 12 pounds.

Vol. 32, 1554

f. 269vo MICHAEL ANGELUS [Florio?][1] *Monday, 30 July* 1554.

The following Monday the Council deliberated on the question of Michel Angelus who would like to become a citizen, but wishes to be exempt from the obligation of bearing arms (harnach),[2] and of 'presenting himself before the cathedral (vors münsterlauffen)'.[3] Agreed that he be exempt from bearing arms, and that he be treated like other priests.

f. 290vo BURGER WERDEN ENGELLENDER
Monday, 20 August 1554.

On the fifth instant, it was agreed that the magistrates who have to negotiate [illegible] with the Englishmen should proceed with · the matter expeditiously and, where they discover anyone acting contrary to regulations, report him for correction to the Ameister.[4] Herr Jacob Meier, alt ameister.

f. [?][5] FREMBDEN ENGELLENDER
Wednesday, 12 September 1554.

Herr Ameister reports that Mundt[6] has been to him to announce the arrival of an Englishman who came by boat, and who wishes to lodge with John Burckhart [Burcher] if the authorities will permit it. John Burckhart called on him immediately and himself supports the plea.

---

[1] This is the father of John Florio, translator of Montaigne. He had lately been minister of the Italian congregation in London. For his presence and business in Strasbourg see his *Apologia*, p. 78, quoted by Miss Yates in her *John Florio* (1934, p. 13). His identity is established by the list of exiles sent to the Duke of Württemberg (see below, p. 364), where his name appears in full, and also the fact that with him was 'ein kind', probably his son, John.

[2] 'Harnasch' or 'harnach', used in the sense of an obligation to bear arms in defence of the town, is derived from the French word 'harnaschier', meaning 'to don harness', i.e. armour.

[3] This was the muster-roll, incumbent on all members of guilds and all able-bodied men. They were to present themselves before the cathedral in case of alarm, for drill, and on all ceremonial occasions.

[4] The Ammeister was one of the six consuls who shared with six Stettmeisters the magistracy of Strasbourg. They were nominated by the plebeian senators and chosen from among the former senators. Cf. E. Müller, *Le Magistrat de la Ville de Strasbourg*.

[5] There is a mistake in the paging of the original, so that from f. 290vo to f. 311 the page numbers have been duplicated.

[6] This is evidently Christopher Mundt who, though a German by birth, acted as an English agent to Germany under Edward VI.

Vol. 32, 1554

f. [?] FREMBDEN ENGELLENDER

Wednesday, 12 September 1554.

Herr Mathis, minister, is deputed to look into the case of the Englishman, who came by ship and to discover what sort of person he is and the grounds for granting his request. On his report the latter is allowed to stay for six weeks.

f. 311 BERAUBTE ENGELLENDER

Monday, 17 September 1554.

Hemas and Andreas Natingen, brothers, of Kine[1] on the English-Flemish frontier are stranded, owing to their having been robbed, and having in consequence incurred debts which they cannot pay. They beg for an advance to assist them out of their difficulties.

They are granted a few gulden from the Poor Fund.

f. 349vo JOHAN ABEL, schirms verwandte

Saturday, 27 October 1554.

John Abel, an Englishman, requests once more that his grant of residence be renewed, in view of which he will undertake all civic responsibilities incurred by regular citizens and will pay rates, except that he begs to be exempted from the civic oath for which he would have to forfeit his rights in England.

Granted. This grant is subject to annual renewal.

Vol. 32, 1554–5

f. 410vo HERTZ: CHRISTOFF. V. WÜRTTEMBERG under die vertrieben Englend   2 *January* 1555.

Record of the gift of 200 gulden by Duke Christopher of Württemberg to be distributed among the English exiles. He asks for a report on their numbers and condition, which is sent, together with a letter of thanks.[2]

Vol. 33, 1555

f. 58vo ARTZET, THOMAS GIPSON

Saturday, 16 February 1555.

Enquiry into medical affairs by Hans Hamer and Carlo Mieg: The following irregularities were brought to light:

1. A woman took upon herself the dispensation of medicine, whereof some died and some were seriously incapacitated.

---

[1] This is probably Gujnes, near Calais. The surname 'Natingen' cannot so far be identified.

[2] Acting upon the hint offered by this 'minute', I sent for the list in question, which was discovered in the Württemberger Staatsarchiv, Stuttgart, through the kindness of the Director, Dr Haering.

Vol. 33, 1555

2. Thomas Gibson, practising as a physician, though without training, was retailing medicines of which he had laid in a stock, at illegally high prices.

This state of affairs was dealt with as follows:

1. The woman, being unable to give a satisfactory account of herself, was forbidden to dispense till vigorous enquiries had been pursued.

2. Thomas Gibson, since he had been permitted to practise by my Lord, was instructed in the regulations and swore to observe them in future.

ff. 70vo–71 JOHANNES PONETUS [John Ponet, bishop of
    Winchester]   *Saturday, 23 February* 1555.

Johannes Ponetus, doctor of theology, sometime bishop in England, begs to be accepted as a citizen. He offers to fulfil all the duties of a citizen; but he begs that he may be exempt from keeping guard, standing sentinel, and bearing arms.

Decision: that he be accepted as a citizen, and exempt from keeping guard, standing sentinel, and bearing arms. Herr Peter Sturm and Herr Carl Mieg tell him of the decision. They report immediately that he has been advised of it. He appeared again at once, and asked for the right of citizenship. He swore the civil oath, which was read to him in Latin, and administered by Herr Peter Sturm.

ff. 358–359 JOHANNES BONETUS [John Ponet]
                          4 *September* 1555.

John Ponetus appears, supported by John Burckhart, and pleads that he has sustained great losses and incurred penalties owing to the disastrous fire, which broke out without any guilt or negligence on his part. (This is proved by the fact that the fire began in a room which had been locked for four weeks.) He begs therefore to be absolved from blame or penalty. Secondly, since he has lost about 4000 crowns [kronen] in silver, jewels and cash, in the fire, he would be glad of help to get some sort of compensation.

Thirdly, he requests that if the landlords have been trying to lay the blame on him he wishes his name cleared.

The Stadtmeister Sturm expresses his deep sympathy. A committee of eleven has been set up to investigate, to whom Ponet is requested to communicate any suspicions or information of value.

The cost of this enquiry and all expenses will be paid, and they hope to arrive at some conclusion satisfactory to both landlord and tenant.

Vol. 33, 1555

ff. 363–363vo REICH. MORISINUS, ANTHONIUS KOPUS,
    EDIVINUS SAUNS [Morison, Cooke, and Sandys]
                                    Saturday, 7 September 1555.

Reichardus Morisinus, Anthonius Kopus, and Edivinus Sauns, a Doctor of Theology, all Englishmen, having been banished by the Queen of England because they will not accept the religion of the Papacy, have come to dwell here for some time. The first two desire only temporary residence because they have a hope that in a short time they will be restored to their estates. So they beg to be allowed their own 'fire and smoke' [dwelling?] and will pay whatever the costs may be. They also hope to deserve well of the state. But Edwin Sandys would like to remain permanently and become a burgher;[1] only, that as a Doctor of Theology he begs exemption from watch duty, service at fires, and the muster roll. He will not be the less ready to serve the state in case of war. All three gentlemen await an answer.

Decided: to grant their request if they will pay the necessary imposts like other burghers, be loyal to the state, agree not to take either lodgers or lodgings without permission, and pay stabling charges like other noblemen.

f. 369 THOMAS GIPSON   *Wednesday, 11 September* 1555.

Report of the town council.

Peter Bürtsch [says that:] he has a relative from Innenheim, who is suffering from dropsy and has come here on account of the English doctor. Since, however, he is forbidden to practise, he will not undertake her case. He therefore asks that he may be allowed to treat her.

Decision: that he should be allowed to practise.

f. 393vo MORISON and COOKE   *Monday, 1 October* 1555.

Herr Peter Sturm and Herr Frederic of Gottesheim report that Richardus Morisinus and Anthonius Kopus [Cooke], two Englishmen, have appeared before the Council and have asked to be received as citizens of the town of Strasbourg. The conditions upon which they may be received have been explained and they have agreed to them. Nevertheless, as the question of their means of subsistence is not yet settled since they left their country on account of religion, it is considered advisable to ask certain further guarantees of them.

The proposition has been approved.

---

[1] He does not appear, however, in the list of those received as burghers.

Vol. 33, 1555

f. 411vo PONETUS und BRUNS *Saturday, 12 October 1555.*

The committee on the fire have met to discuss what answer shall be given to Ponet and Diebolt Schwarz, and are hopeful of vindicating the parties concerned.

Vol. 34, 1556

f. 26vo JOHAN PONETUS *Wednesday, 22 February 1556.*

Herr Diebolt Schwartz, pastor of the church of St Aurelia, presents the following plea: The prebendaries of Old St Peter's let him a house (called 'zum Holderstock' and situated on the Weinmarkt) for as long as he or his wife should live, at an annual rent. When he was appointed to the pastorate of St Aurelia, he passed the premises on to John Ponet, formerly bishop of Winchester in England. The house was burnt down, whilst the prebendaries were still uncertain whether to ratify the transaction [the MS. is here very obscure], and they now request a statement of the whole affair, so that they can assess relative responsibilities.

ff. 29–29vo JOHAN PONETUS *Wednesday, 22 February 1556.*

Hans Braun, Hans Funffrock and the steward of Old St Peter's demand a copy of Diebolt Schwartz's plea. Diebolt Schwartz asks them to take into consideration his age and office and deal generously with him, and also acquit the bishop of responsibility.

Decided: to give to the prebendaries the desired copy, and to take such action that they will be able to give an answer in a week's time.

f. 109vo THOMAS GIPSON, Engellender
Wednesday, 18 March 1556.

Thomas Gibson of England, a doctor, begs that, since he is able to heal diseases, such as dropsy and lunacy, he be permitted to make up his prescriptions at home as he does not wish to make his methods public. He promises to buy his materials from the chemists and to observe the rules applying to them.

Granted.

f. 190 PETER MARTYR *Monday, 4 May 1556.*

The Burgomaster and Council of Zurich write that L. Cunradus Pellicanus, reader in Hebrew for them, has died and they wish someone to fill his place. They therefore ask my lords of the Council to open negotiations with Peter Martin [Martyr] to whom they promise an adequate salary.

Vol. 34, 1556

Decided: to find out through the 'Schulherren'[1] whether he is willing to go, or not. They will not retain him if he wishes to go, but otherwise would like to keep him.

ff. 284[vo] RICH. MORISINUS — Saturday, 27 June 1556.

Concerning Fredus [Fredericus] Torvellus, the servant of Richard Morison's widow, who reports to the Council that permission to reside [in Strasbourg] had been granted to Richart Morisini in return for 20 gulden to be paid to the town before the close of the year. Payment has been demanded in spite of Morison's subsequent death. The widow is willing to pay this, since it is customary in England for a dead man's taxes to be paid before the legacy is enjoyed. She begs for permission to reside herself and contribute in future according to her means.

The town is willing to accept the 20 gulden but will make every allowance for her straightened circumstances.

ff. 287–287[vo] ZURICH, PETER MARTYR — Monday, 29 June 1556.

Herr Peter Sturm and the other Schulherren report that, with regard to the request from Zurich, they have discussed the matter with Doctor Peter Martyr, and have made every effort to retain his services themselves. But he has pointed out that when he accepted the position here, he signed the Augsburg Confession—conveniently interpreted to accord with his Calvinism—but that since then he has been subjected to all manner of unpleasantness from the preachers, and has suffered from considerable interference with his lectures. He makes freedom from such interference his condition for remaining.

Decided: that the Council does not wish to oblige him to do anything against his will, and in either case will try to meet his desires. If he wishes to go it will be readily allowed and a letter of recommendation sent to Zurich.

f. 285[vo] THOMAS FRACHT:[2] Engellender — Saturday, 27 June 1556.

Thomas Frachtus of England—a nobleman—asked for rights of free citizenship—which were granted on the understanding that he should contribute something to the scholars at Wilhelmer.[3] But

---

[1] *Sic.* But probably the 'Schultheissen' or Bishop's bailiffs are meant. See below, p. 370.

[2] Possibly 'Frogget'(?), see Census.

[3] 'Wilhelmitaner', i.e. the students of the protestant faculty of theology.

Vol. 34, 1556

he immediately went off and gave nothing. When his comrade John Carus was arrested and sent back to England, he came to his senses and negotiated with the authorities. Residence was once more granted on condition that he give 10 gulden to the poor scholars, and should henceforth subject himself to the municipal laws.

ff. 286–286ᵛᵒ THOMAS FRACHT   *July*, 1556 [day of week omitted].

Thomas Fracht hands over the 10 gulden. [In margin: 'He says that he has no house but is boarding with Morison's widow.']

ff. 309–310ᵛᵒ JOHN BURCHARD   *Wednesday, 15 July* 1556.

John Burckhart has left the town suddenly under suspicion of having fled to avoid paying his debts which amount to a 1000 gulden. His creditors press for a warrant of arrest. This is refused on the intervention of Burckhart's agent and wife, who testify that his absence is only temporary and that he has plenty of assets.

f. 384ᵛᵒ   *Wednesday, 19 August* 1556.

The magistrates have at the instance of the Council considered the request of John Burcher, Englishman, for a passport, and have agreed to give him one for his coming journey.

ff. 464ᵛᵒ–465 THOMAS FRACHT   *July* 1556.

Thomas Fracht of England was allowed to reside temporarily but his permit has expired. His wife has just given birth to a child, and that, coupled with the coming of winter, makes it difficult to move now. He therefore applies for permission to remain for one or two years or at least till Easter.
Granted.

Vol. 35, 1557

f. 205 ENGELLENDER   *Monday, 31 May* 1557.

The Mayor and Corporation of Basle write that as John Polanum [Pullain], English, was travelling to Uffhien near Basle, the authorities at Eusisheim arrested him and asked for his passport. He had none. However they set him free but made it understood that they would not let any Englishman pass in future without a passport.

It is suggested that John Abel or some other Englishman be appointed to warn any of his countrymen, intending to travel that way.

Vol. 35, 1557

ff. 296–296ᵛᵒ ENGELENDER BEIWOHNUNG
Wednesday, 4 *August* 1557.

Reichart Springandt [Springham] left England with his wife and child because of the war and on account of religion and is willing to buy such civic rights as would not entail the forfeiture of his rights in England and Brabant. He promises to pay rates to the town and to take on civic duties.

There is also a testimonial of his high character to hand.

He carries on a trade in English cloth.

Granted six years' residence on those conditions.

ff. 326ᵛᵒ–327 HUGO SINGELTEN, England
Saturday, 21 *August* 1557.

Hugo Singleton of London, imprisoned in England on religious grounds, fled hither, and on two separate occasions has been granted permits for residence here for two months.

He cannot afford to buy the Grossbürgerrecht but wishes to be accepted as a Kleinbürger and to support himself by his trade of bookbinder.

Petition refused.

f. 334 HUGO SINGELTEN
Saturday, 28 *August* 1557.

Hugo Singleton of London, having been refused civic rights,[1] points out the difficulty of moving in the winter, and begs permission to stay till March.

Granted.

f. 337 THOMAS WROTHE
Wednesday, 1 *September* 1557.

Thomas Wrothe, an Englishman, was granted permission to reside one year, which has almost expired. As he cannot yet return

---

[1] Full rights of citizenship, or the 'Grossbürgerrecht', were open to those whose property exceeded '10 livres'. It conferred the right to vote, and imposed such civic duties as that of bearing arms (harnach), of the civic muster (vors münster lauffen), and of service at fires, all of which have already been noted in the protocols. For foreigners, possibly for all, this evidently entailed further an oath of allegiance to the city which did not permit the retention or acquisition of rights elsewhere (see below the case of Thomas Gibson). It was this unqualified oath that the English would not take. As the price of full citizenship was relatively high, the artisan class was excluded. But they might possess the 'kleinbürgerrecht' or right of 'residence', which conferred no political rights; but they could pass into the other class if their wealth increased. They were nominated by the bishop's bailiff, known as the 'Schultheis', and are frequently called on that account 'Schultheissenbürger'. See E. Muller, *Le Magistrat de la Ville de Strasbourg.*

Vol. 35, 1557

to England, on religious grounds, he requests an extension of his permit.

Granted for one year with possible further extension on re-application.

Vol. 36, 1558

ff. 65ᵛᵒ–66 THOMAS BACTS, ROBERT WISDOM
Monday, 7 February 1558.

Thomas Baxter of London, England, was driven from England four years ago because of his religion, and settled for a while at Frankfort and then came here in the service of Anthony Cooke. Now that his circumstances have changed he would like to be accorded full civic rights, consistent with his retaining his rights in England.

Adjourned for enquiry into his life and his reasons for leaving Frankfort.

ff. 124ᵛᵒ–125 THOMAS BACTS *Saturday, 12 March* 1558.

Particulars concerning Thomas Bacts [Baxter], his conduct and his reasons for leaving England, have been collected. These could only be obtained from Englishmen. One, who had once let him a house, declared him to be an honourable man. William Saltins [Salkins], Richard Hilles's servant, said that he had known Thomas Baxter in London, where he had an excellent reputation, and that he left there on no other grounds but those of religion. After leaving England he stayed for a while at Frankfort, which he quitted owing to some misunderstanding not revealed. He then came here and was servant for a time to Anthony Cork [Cooke], until he was forced to leave owing to unpleasant incidents caused by his wife.

He has no particular trade, but excellent testimonials as to his honesty are to hand.

Be it known that his plea is 'amicably refused and that he is bidden to go whithersoever it may please God to take him'.

ff. 235ᵛᵒ–236 THOMAS GIPSON vorbehalt des Burgrechten
Monday, 2 May 1558.

Thomas Gibson, Englishman, citizen here for some time, desires to continue his citizenship, but begs leave to reside elsewhere for a while in the interests of his profession, and even, if possible, to go back to England to sell his estates. He requests a certificate of citizenship.

Vol. 36, 1558

Leave is granted on the understanding that he must not settle for good elsewhere, nor give allegiance to any other master. He may retain his citizenship for which a certificate is granted.

f. 530ᵛᵒ THOMAS WROD   *Wednesday, 19 October* 1558.

Thomas Wrod [Wrothe] of England begs for leave to extend his residence without civic rights.

Granted to him for another year, provided he pays the town as before £8 for the year and obeys the municipal regulations.

ff. 621–621ᵛᵒ FREMBD. ENGLEND *Monday, 5 December* 1558.

Doctor Christopher Mont and Thomas Hettenus [Heton] wish to tender heartiest thanks to the magistrates on behalf of the Englishmen who have now lived here for four years and have been so graciously treated by them. Now that they see some prospect of returning to their own country, they invite the magistrates to meet them in common at Herr Umend's house.

This is acknowledged. Hospitality has been gladly given and would gladly be extended if necessary. They are wished much joy of their return. The invitation is politely refused on the grounds of pressure of business.

ff. 634ᵛᵒ–635 ANTHONIUS COCUS und JOHAN ABEL
Wednesday, 21 December 1558.

Johan Abel, resident, writes on behalf of Anthony Cooke, an Englishman, who settled here some years ago. Cooke begs to notify his departure and tenders thanks for the protection accorded him. He adds a guarantee, that he has only taken personal belongings with him. (The MS. is faulty.)

ABBREVIATIONS USED FOR THE BOOKS
REFERRED TO IN THE CENSUS

Adair   = E. R. Adair, *William Thomas: a forgotten clerk of the Privy Council.* In Tudor Studies, London, 1924.

Adlard   = G. Adlard, *The Sutton-Dudleys of England and the Dudleys of Massachusetts.* London, 1862.

Ames (see Herbert's Ames).

Andrich   = Register of the English Students, University of Padua, see 'Sources'.

Annals, or *A.*   = Strype, *Annals of the Reformation,* ed. Clar. Press. 1824.

Arber, *Registers* = E. Arber, *Registers of the Stationers' Company.*

Arch. Cant.   = *Archaeologia Cantiana.*

Ath. Oxon.   = Anthony à Wood, *Athenae Oxonienses,* ed. Bliss.

Baga   = Baga de Secretis, 4th Report, Deputy Keeper of the Public Records, Append. II, pp. 232–59.

Bale's *Index*   = *Index Britanniae Scriptorum,* ed. R. Lane Poole. 1902. (This is John Bale's autograph note book from the Selden MSS.)

Baskerville, 'Gloucester'   = Geoffrey Baskerville, 'Elections to Convocation in the Diocese of Gloucester under Bishop Hooper'. *E.H.R.* vol. XLIV, pp. 1–32.

Baskerville, *Monks*   = Geoffrey Baskerville, *English monks and the suppression of the monasteries.* London, 1937.

Baskerville, 'Norwich'   = Geoffrey Baskerville, 'Deprivation Lists in the diocese of Norwich'. *E.H.R.* vol. XLVIII. 1933.

Bayne, *E.H.R.* XXIII   = C. G. Bayne, 'The first House of Commons of Queen Elizabeth', pts I and II. *E.H.R.* vol. XXIII.

Beaven   = A. B. Beaven, *The Aldermen of the City of London.* 2 vols. 1913.

Berry, *Kent, etc.*   = Wm. Berry, *Genealogies of Kent, Surrey, Sussex.*

Bertie, *Five Generations*   = Lady Georgina Bertie, *Five Generations of a Loyal House.* London, 1845.

Blomefield   = F. Blomefield, *History of Norfolk.* 11 vols. and Index. 1805.

Bonnet   = J. Bonnet, *Lettres de Jean Calvin.* 2 vols. Paris, 1854.

Brett   = John Brett's 'Narrative of the Pursuit of the English under Mary', ed. I. S. Leadam. *R.H.S. Trans.* new series, vol. XI. 1897.

Brook's *Puritans*	= Benj. Brook, *The Lives of the Puritans*. 3 vols. London, 1813.
Browne Willis	= Browne Willis, *Notitia Parliamentaria*, 1750.
Browne Willis, *Abbies*	= Browne Willis, *History of the Mitred Abbies*. 2 vols. London, 1718.
Burn	= J. S. Burn, *Transcript of the Livre des Anglois*. 1833.
Burrage	= C. Burrage, *The Early English Dissenters*, 1550–1641. 2 vols. Cambridge, U.S.A., 1912.
Byrom	= H. J. Byrom, 'Edmund Spenser's First Printer, Hugh Singleton'. *The Library*, vol. xiv, no. 2, 1933.
Cam. Misc. ix	= *Original Letters from the bishops to the Privy Council*, 1564, ed. by M. Bateson.
Cam. Misc. x	= *Journal of Sir Thomas Hoby*, 1547–64.
Chron. Calais	= Richard Turpin, *Chronicle of Calais to* 1540. Camden Society, no. 35.
Chron. Q. Jane	= *Chronicle of Queen Jane and Queen Mary*. Camden Society, no. 48.
Clode, *Early Hist.*	= C. M. Clode, *Early History of the Merchant Taylors' Company*.
Clode, *Mems.*	= C. M. Clode, *Memorials of the Merchant Taylors' Company*. London, 1875.
Cooper	= C. H. Cooper, *Athenae Cantabrigienses*. 3 vols. 1858.
Coverdale, *Martyrs*	= Miles Coverdale, *Letters of the Martyrs*. London, 1564.
Coverdale, *Remains*	= Miles Coverdale, *Remains*, ed. Parker Society. London, 1846.
Cranmer or C.	= Strype's *Memorials of Archbishop Cranmer*. 2 vols. Clar. Press, 1840.
Cranmer, ed. E.H.S.	= Strype's *Memorials, etc.*, ed. Ecclesiastical History Society. 3 vols. 1854.
Cranmer, *Works*	= *Writings and Disputations relative to the Sacrament. Works* of Abp. Cranmer, vol. i, ed. Parker Society. 1844.
Cussans, *Herts.*	= J. E. Cussans, *History of Hertfordshire*. 3 vols. 1870–81.
Davids	= T. W. Davids, *Annals of evangelical nonconformity in Essex*. London, 1863.
D.N.B.	= *The Dictionary of National Biography*.
Dom. Cal. 1547–80	= *Calendar of State Papers, Domestic*, 1547–80.
Dom. Cal. Addend.	= *Calendar of State Papers, Domestic*, 1601–3, Addenda, 1547–65.

Duff's *Cent.*   = E. Gordon Duff, *A Century of the English Book Trade.* Bibliographical Society. London, 1905.

Emden Catalogue (see 'Sources').

Fasti, Eccles. Saris.   = W. H. Jones, *Fasti Ecclesiae Sarisberiensis.* 1879.

For. Cal.   = *Calendars of State Papers, Foreign,* for the reigns of Edward VI, Mary and Elizabeth.

Foster   = J. Foster, *Alumni Oxonienses.* 4 vols.

Fowler, *Corp. Christ.*   = T. Fowler, *History of Corpus Christi, Oxford.* 1898.

Foxe   = J. Foxe, *Acts and Monuments.* Pratt's revised edition of Townshend's, with Index. 8 vols. 1877.

Fuller, *Worthies* = Thomas Fuller, *The Worthies of England.* 2 vols. 1811.

Gardiner, *Letters*   = J. A. Muller, *The Letters of Stephen Gardiner.* Camb. Univ. Press, 1933.

Gorham, *Gleanings*   = G. C. Gorham, *Gleanings . . . during the Reformation in England,* 1553–58. London, 1857.

Grindal or *G.*   = Strype's *Life of Abp. Grindal.* Clar. Press, 1821.

Grindal, *Remains*   = Abp. Grindal, *Remains,* ed. by William Nicholson for the Parker Society. 1843.

Hans Dür   = Hans Dür's contemporary list of the English Exiles at Aarau, see 'Sources'.

Harl. Soc.   = The series of Herald's Visitations of the Counties published by the Harleian Society.

Hasted   = Edw. Hasted, *History of Kent.* 4 vols. 1778.

Herbert's Ames = Wm. Herbert's edition, Joseph Ames' *Typographical Antiquities.* 3 vols. London, 1785.

H.S.P. IV   = *Proceedings of the Huguenot Society,* vol. IV. London, 1894.

Humphrey's *Jewel*   = Laurence Humphrey's *Vita Juelli.* London, 1573.

Isaac, F. S.   = Col. F. S. Isaac, 'Egidius van der Erve'. *The Library,* 4th series, vol. XII, pp. 336–40.

Ital. Reform.   = F. C. Church, *The Italian Reformers,* 1534–64. New York, 1932.

Jung   = Rudolf Jung's *Englische Flüchtlings-Gemeinde* see 'Sources'.

Knox, Narr.   = Knox's Narrative of the proceedings of the English Congregation at Frankfort in March, 1555. From Calderwood's MS. History of the Kirk of Scotland. Published in Knox's *Works,* ed. Laing, vol. IV.

Laing	= *Works of John Knox*, ed. D. Laing. 6 vols. Edinburgh, 1846–64.
Le Neve	= *Fasti Ecclesiae Anglicanae*. 3 vols. Oxford, 1854.
Linc. Inn Reg.	= *Register of Admissions*, vol. I, 1420–1799.
Lodge, *Illus.*	= Edm. Lodge, *Illustrations of British History*. 3 vols. Ed. 1838.
Machyn	= *The diary of Henry Machyn*, 1550–63. Camden Society, no. 42.
Macray	= W. D. Macray (ed.), *Register of Magdalen College, Oxford*. New series, 8 vols. 1894–1915.
Maitland, *Essays*	= S. R. Maitland, *Essays*. 2nd ed. London, 1899.
Mar. Reac.	= Dr W. H. Frere, *The Marian Reaction in its relation to the English clergy*. London, 1896.
Martin	= C. Martin, *Les Protestants Anglais réfugiés à Genève...* 1555–60. Geneva, 1915.
Martyr's *Commonplaces*	= Peter Martyr Vermigli's *Commonplaces*, trans. Anthonie Marten. London, 1583.
Martyr's *Decades*	= Peter Martyr of Angleria's *Decades of the newe worlde or West India, etc.* English translation of Rycharde Eden. London, 1555.
Matrikel	= Matriculation lists of the University of Basle, see 'Sources'.
Maunsell	= Andrew Maunsell, *Cat. of English Printed Books*. London, 1595.
Mem.	= Strype's *Ecclesiastical Memorials*. 3 vols. Clar. Press, 1822.
Moryson, *Itin.*	= Fynes Moryson, *An Itinerary*. English translation. London, 1617.
Narr. of Ref.	= ed. J. G. Nichols. Camden Society, no. 77.
Newcourt	= R. Newcourt's *Repertorium Ecclesiasticum*. London, 1710.
New Eng. Reg.	= *New England historical and genealogical Register*, ed. by Rayne and Chapman. Boston, 1906–7.
O.H.S. I	= *Register of the University of Oxford*, 1449–1571, ed. C. W. Boase. Oxford Historical Society, vol. I. 1885.
O.L.	= *Original Letters of the Reformation*, ed. Hastings Robinson. 2 vols. London, 1846–7.
Parker	= Strype's *Life of Abp. Parker*. 2 vols. Clar. Press, 1821.
P.C.A.	= *Acts of the Privy Council*, ed. Dasent.

Pocock = N. Pocock, 'The Condition of morals and religious belief under Edward VI'. *E.H.R.* vol. x. 1905.

Ponet, *Treatise* = John Ponet's *Treatise of Politike Power.* Strasbourg, 1556.

Reg. Gray's Inn = *Register of Admissions, Gray's Inn*, 1521–1889, ed. J. Foster. London, 1889.

Reg. Inner = *Students admitted to the Inner Temple*, 1571– *Temple* 1625. London, 1869.

Reg. Middle = *Middle Temple Records*, ed. C. H. Hopwood. *Temple* London, 1904–5.

Rose-Troup = F. Rose-Troup, *The Western Rebellion of* 1549. London, 1913.

Return of = *Return of Members of the House of Commons, Members* 1213–1874, vol. xvii, pt i of *Accounts and Papers*, 1878.

Salisbury, i = Historical MSS. Commission, *Salisbury MSS.* vol. i.

Schickler = F. de Schickler, *Les Églises de refuge en Angleterre.* 3 vols. Strasbourg, 1892.

Scriptores = J. Bale, *Scriptorum Illustrium...Britanniae... Catalogus.* Basle, 1557–9.

S.T.C. = *Short Title Catalogue of English Books*, 1475– 1640. Pollard and Redgrave, London, 1926.

Staffs. Hist. = Staffordshire Historical Society Collections. Colls. No Index.

Steele, i = *Catalogue of Tudor and Stuart Proclamations.* Vol. i, ed. Robert Steele.

T. = *Troubles begonne at Frankfort*, ed. Petheram. 1846. (Reprint of Black Letter edition of 1575.)

Tanner = Thomas Tanner, *Bibliotheca Britannico- Hibernia.* London, 1748.

Trewe's Narr. = R. Laurence, *Authentic Documents relative to the Predestinarian Controversy...* [1555]. Oxford, 1819.

Tytler = P. F. Tytler, *The Reigns of Edward VI and Mary.* 2 vols. London, 1839.

Urwick = Wm. Urwick, *Nonconformity in Hertfordshire.* London, 1884.

Usher = R. G. Usher, *The Presbyterian Movement in the reign of Queen Elizabeth.* Camden Society, 3rd series, no. 8.

Venn = J. Venn, *Alumni Cantabrigienses.* Camb. Univ. Press, 1922.

Vetter, *Eng. Flücht.* = Th. Vetter, *Die Englische Flüchtlinge in Zürich, etc.* Zurich, 1893–4.

Vetter, *Relations* = *Relations between England and Zürich during the Reformation.* London, 1904.

Vocacyon = *The Vocacyon of John Bale*, ed. Hugh Singleton. 1553.

Vowell = J. Vowell (alias Hooker), *Life of Sir Peter Carew*, ed. J. Maclean. London, 1857.

Waters, *Gleanings* = H. F. Waters, *Genealogical Gleanings in England.* 2 vols. Boston, 1901.

Whittingham = *The Life and death of William Whittingham.* Bodleian MSS. Wood E 4 or Camden Miscellany, vi, ed. Mrs Everett Green.

Wilson, *Magd.* = H. A. Wilson, *Magdalen College.* London, 1899.

Wood's *Fasti* = Anthony à Wood, *Fasti Oxonienses*, ed. Bliss. 2 parts. London, 1815.

Wood, *Illust. Ladies* = M. A. E. Wood, *Letters of Royal and Illustrious Ladies.* 12th century–1558. London, 1846.

Wotherspoon = H. T. Wotherspoon, *The Second Prayer Book of Edward VI and the Liturgy of Compromise.* Edinburgh, 1905.

Wright, *Monasteries* = Thomas Wright, *Suppression of the Monasteries.* Camden Society, no. 26.

Wriothesley = *Wriothesley's Chronicle.* Camden Society. 2 vols. 1875 and 1877.

Yates, *Florio* = F. Yates, *John Florio.* Camb. Univ. Press, 1934.

Z.L. = *Zürich Letters*, ed. Hastings Robinson. 2 vols. 1842–5.

INDEX TO THE INTRODUCTION